# Reports of Cases in the Supreme Court of Appeals of Virginia, Volume 47

## Conway Robinson, Benjamin Watkins Leigh, Peachy Ridgway Grattan, James Muscoe Matthews, Martin Parks Burks, Virginia. Supreme Court Of Appeals

# REPORTS OF CASES

DECIDED IN THE

# SUPREME COURT OF APPEALS

AND IN THE

# GENERAL COURT

OF

# VIRGINIA:

BY PEACHY R. GRATTAN.

## VOL. VIII.

FROM JULY 1, 1851, TO JULY 1, 1852.

SECOND EDITION.

RICHMOND:
J. H. O'BANNON, SUP'T PUBLIC PRINTING.
1898.

Entered according to the Act of Congress, this twenty-second day of December, one thousand eight hundred and fifty-two, for the Commonwealth of Virginia, in the Clerk's Office of the District Court of the Eastern District of Virginia.

# PREFACE.

With this volume the report of the decisions of the Court of appeals under the constitution of 1829, and of the General court, are completed. The first court is succeeded by the Supreme court of appeals under the constitution of 1851. In this court is vested the criminal as well as the civil appellate jurisdiction; and the General court has been abolished. The General court was one of the earliest courts established in the province of Virginia, and was then held by the Governor and Council. It received its name of General court in 1661-2, and then had general jurisdiction of all causes, civil and criminal. After the revolution and the establishment of the Supreme court of appeals, the jurisdiction of the General court was confined to the appellate criminal jurisdiction, cases connected with the revenue, and to the taking probat of wills and granting administration upon intestates' estates, in which its jurisdiction was concurrent with the District and afterwards the Circuit, County and Corporation courts throughout the State. After an existence of one hundred and ninety years under the same name, it has at length been abolished; leaving to us only the memory of its faithful and pure administration of justice.

Until the constitution of 1851 went into operation, the judges of the Supreme court of appeals and of the General court held their offices for life; and the advocates of an independent judiciary looked forward with some apprehen-

sion to the working of that provision of the constitution of
1829 which authorized the General Assembly, by a concurrent vote of two thirds of both houses, to remove a judge.
It however was never acted on during the existence of that
constitution. By the constitution of 1851 the judges are
elected by the people; the judges of the Supreme court
of appeals for twelve years, and the judges of the Circuit
courts for eight years: And they are all re-eligible after
their term of service is expired.

Although there have been complaints of the delay of justice in Virginia, delays arising rather from the defects in
our judicial system than from any defect in the persons who
filled the office, the public mind has ever reposed with an
unquestioning confidence in the purity of its administration. And although an unfortunate suitor might well believe that human judgment is fallible, none ever questioned
the integrity of the decision. How much of this judicial
integrity and public confidence was due to the system, and
how much was due to the men who administered the justice of the country, or what influence the system exerted
upon the men, it were vain now to enquire. Certainly the
selections for these offices were generally most fortunate, if
not most sagacious and patriotic: And every Virginian
will recall, with an honest and honourable State pride, the
many names enrolled in the list of our judicial worthies,
who in all respects, as men, as citizens, as gentlemen, and
as judges, were the ornament and the pride of the country.

What will be the working of the present system, time,
the wisest of all things, must determine. Certainly no
apprehension can be felt of any immediate failure of those
qualities which have honoured the bench of justice, and
secured to it the public confidence. Integrity in a judge,

and purity in the administration of justice, is so thoroughly
a part of the moral sense of the public and the individual
man, that years must pass, under the influence of the worst
system that could be devised, before a judge in Virginia
can realize that it is not a necessity of his position that his
judicial conduct shall be above suspicion; and it will probably require a still longer period for the public mind to be
reconciled to entertain a doubt on that subject.  If, indeed,
the people shall realize the truth that every power is a
trust, the abuse of which, from the necessity of its nature,
carries with it its own punishment, and the proper discharge of which elevates whilst it prospers, then may we
well anticipate the happiest results from this experiment.
And although the wisdom of experience may excite fears,
we are to remember that we are not any other people; and
all our past history teaches that we are not to be measured
by their capacities.  What we can do we must learn from
ourselves; and the duty and the business of every man is,
not to excite doubts of success, or apprehensions of failure,
in a matter upon which the people have determined, but to
unite with all his heart in the effort to accomplish a successful result.  Believing that our past history affords many
evidences of the guardian providence of God over us as a
people, we go forward with an abiding confidence in the
same kind care in the future.

# JUDGES

## OF THE

# COURT OF APPEALS

### DURING THE TIME OF THESE REPORTS.

---

WILLIAM H. CABELL, President.

JOHN J. ALLEN.

BRISCOE G. BALDWIN.

WILLIAM DANIEL.

RICHARD C. L. MONCURE.

---

### ATTORNEY GENERALS.

SIDNEY S. BAXTER.

WILLIS P. BOCOCK. *

---

\* Elected under the constitution of 1851, and went into office on the 22d day of January, 1852.

# JUDGES

## OF THE

## GENERAL COURT

### DURING THE TIME OF THESE REPORTS.

---

RICHARD H. FIELD.

JOHN T. LOMAX.

WILLIAM LEIGH.

LUCAS P. THOMPSON.

BENJAMIN ESTILL.

PRINTED BY

WARE & DUKE,

RICHMOND.

BOUND BY

EVERETT WADDEY COMPANY,

RICHMOND.

# TABLE OF CASES REPORTED.

# TABLE OF CASES CITED.

# CASES

DECIDED IN THE

## SUPREME COURT OF APPEALS

OF

## VIRGINIA.

---

### 𝕷𝖊𝖜𝖎𝖘𝖇𝖚𝖗𝖌.

MINOR *v.* MINOR'S *adm'r.*

(Absent *Cabell,* P.)

**July 12th.**

1851.
July
Term.

1. In an action of *assumpsit* by an adm'r for a debt due his intestate in his lifetime, defendant cannot set off a debt due him for money paid as the surety of the intestate since his death.

2. The count in an action of *assumpsit* by an adm'r is for money had and received, and the bill of particulars merely states an account in which the defendant is debtor to the adm'r for money received, stating a sum certain. The count and the bill of particulars are not sufficient to admit proof of an admission by the defendant that he had received from a third person a certain sum belonging to the estate of the plaintiff's intestate.

This was an action of *assumpsit* brought in the Circuit court of Monongalia county by A. W. Tenant, adm'r of John Minor, against Samuel Minor. The declaration contained two counts for money had and received; the first for money had and received to the use

VOL. VIII.—1

1851.
July
Term.

Minor
v.
Minor's
adm'r.

of the plaintiff's intestate in his lifetime, the other for money had and received to the use of the plaintiff, as administrator of John Minor. The bill of particulars filed with the declaration was:

Samuel Minor,

   To John Minor, for money received,    $300

Samuel Minor,

   To plaintiff as adm'r, for money received,  $300

The defendant appeared and pleaded the general issue, and also a plea of set off to the first count, and the statute of limitations, on which issues were made up. He also offered a plea to the second count of the declaration, which is called the defendant's third plea, in which he alleged that the plaintiff, as the administrator of John Minor deceased, before and at the commencement of the action, was indebted to the defendant in the sum of 1500 dollars, for money by the defendant paid as the security of John Minor, since his death, which exceeded the damages complained of in the declaration, and out of which money the defendant was willing and offered to set off and allow to the plaintiff, as administrator as aforesaid, the full amount of the said damages. This plea the plaintiff moved the court to reject, which motion the court sustained, and the defendant excepted.

On the trial of the cause the plaintiff offered evidence tending to prove that the defendant admitted in March 1846, that he received from one Lancaster Minor, in the spring of that year, 250 dollars belonging to the estate of John Minor deceased, the plaintiff's intestate; to the introduction of which evidence the defendant objected, upon the ground that neither the declaration nor the bill of particulars filed therewith gave to the defendant sufficient notice of any such claim. But the court overruled the objection and admitted the evidence; and the defendant again excepted. There was a verdict and judgment for the plaintiff for 250 dollars, with interest from the 31st of March 1846; whereupon the defendant applied to this court for a *supersedeas*, which was allowed.

1851.
July
Term.

Minor
v.
Minor's
adm'r.

*A. F. Haymond*, for the appellant.
*Guy R. C. Allen*, for the appellee.

ALLEN, *J.* delivered the opinion of the court.

It seems to the court here, that the Circuit court did not err in rejecting the plea No. 3, tendered by the plaintiff in error, and set forth in the bill of exceptions taken to the decision of the court rejecting the same. But it further seems to the court here, that the court erred in overruling the objection of the plaintiff in error to the introduction of evidence offered by the defendant in error, as tending to prove the particular item or claim sought to be recovered, as set forth in the bill of exceptions taken by the plaintiff in error at the trial to the decision of the court admitting said testimony; this court being of opinion that neither the declaration or bill of particulars gave the plaintiff in error sufficient notice of any such claim or item. Reversed with costs, verdict set aside, and cause remanded for a new trial, upon which, under the pleadings as they now stand, and unless another bill of particulars be filed describing the claim or item with sufficient certainty, such evidence offered and objected to is not to be admitted.

## Lewisburg.

1851.
July
Term.

### HOGUE *v.* DAVIS *& als.*

(Absent *Cabell*, P. and *Baldwin*, J.)

#### July 14th.

Where several endorsers of negotiable paper have endorsed it
for the accommodation of the maker, they are responsible
in the order of their endorsements, unless there has been
an agreement among them to be jointly and equally
bound : And the burden of proving such an agreement is
upon the prior endorser who seeks the benefit of it.

This was a motion in the Circuit court of Monongalia county by James T. Davis, Waitman Davis and three
others, against Bushrod Q. Hogue, to recover from him
the amount which they had been compelled to pay as
subsequent endorsers upon a note made by Robert Davis to Bushrod Q. Hogue, and discounted at the bank
in Morgantown.   The note bore date July 29th, 1844,
and was for 2500 dollars, payable in ninety days, at the
Lancaster Bank, in the State of Pennsylvania, and was
endorsed by all the parties for the accommodation of
Robert Davis.   Before the note fell due Robert Davis
absconded.

The ground of defence was, that all the endorsers were
to be jointly and equally bound.   The only witnesses
who spoke to the making of the note were John Davis,
a brother of two of the plaintiffs, and Albert G. Davis,
a cousin.   According to their testimony Hogue boarded
with Robert Davis, and endorsed the note at Davis's
house, in the absence of the other endorsers; and Robert Davis then took the note to obtain other endorsers
upon it.   That he applied to his father, Thomas Davis,
to endorse it, who declined to do it, when Robert Davis
told him there was no danger, as both he and Hogue

1851.
July
Term.

Hogue
v.
Davis
& als.

would have to fail before said Thomas Davis could be liable. Albert G. Davis stated that Hogue informed him he had furnished Robert Davis money to buy cattle, and intended to do so as long as he wanted to do business, and that he was to have a share of the profits arising from the business. That this was before said Davis absconded, and after the witness had understood they had gotten money out of the bank at Morgantown.

It was proved that after the note was protested and returned to the bank at Morgantown several of the endorsers, including Hogue, came to the bank for the purpose of making arrangements for its payment. They first proposed to give a bond for the whole amount, and the bond was prepared and some of them signed it.

They arranged to borrow some four or five hundred dollars from a Mr. Hanway to aid them in the payment; and a note was prepared and taken away by them but was not returned; and they all left the bank without making arrangements to take up the original note. Shortly afterwards some of the sureties informed Mr. Hanway they had ascertained that the note was not of such a character as they had supposed; and that they would not be liable, as they believed, until the property of Bushrod Q. Hogue was exhausted; and that they declined taking the loan. On the same day they were at the bank, James T. Davis, one of the endorsers, had a conversation with the cashier of the bank, and that officer understood from him that although they might not be legally bound to pay any part of the note, yet they were joint endorsers with Hogue, or something to that effect, and did not intend to take any advantage of him; and that they considered themselves equally bound with Hogue, as the cashier understood him. It seems probable that neither Hogue or the endorsers knew the difference between the note payable as it was and a joint endorsement of it.

1851.
July
Term.

Hogue
v.
Davis
& als.

The Circuit court gave the plaintiffs a judgment against the defendant for 1179 dollars and 38 cents, with interest from October the 6th, 1846, until paid, that being the balance due upon the note, after applying thereto the proceeds of certain property of Robert Davis, which the plaintiffs had been compelled to pay. And thereupon Hogue applied to this court for a *supersedeas*, which was allowed.

*A. F. Haymond*, for the appellant.

*Grattan*, for the appellees, referred to *Chalmers* v. *McMurdo*, 5 Munf. 252; *Farmers Bank* v. *Vanmeter*, 4 Rand. 553; *Bank U. S.* v. *Beirne*, 1 Gratt. 234; *McDonald* v. *Magruder*, 3 Peters' R. 470.

BY THE COURT: The judgment is affirmed.

---

## Lewisburg.

1851.
July
Term.

### CALES v. MILLER & al.

(Absent *Cabell*, P.)

#### July 19th.

1. A party offering in evidence a deed purporting to be executed by a commissioner under the decree of a court, and conveying land, must offer with it so much of the record of the cause in which the decree was made as will shew the authority of the commissioner to convey the land described in the deed.

2. A deed executed in 1799, which shews upon its face that the parties to it resided out of the State of Virginia, was properly acknowledged before the mayor of a city in another State, and the certificate of the mayor, describing himself as such, and purporting to be under the seal of the city, was a sufficient authentication of the deed to authorize its admission to record.

3. In such a case the certificate of the acknowledgment of the deed by the grantor before the mayor of the city is sufficient evidence that the grantor, for the time being, resided

1851.
July
Term.

Cales
v.
Miller
& al.

in the said city, though the deed on its face described him as being a citizen of another State.

4. It seems that a residence, however temporary, is sufficient to authorize the acknowledgment of a deed there, by a non-resident of Virginia, under the act of 1792, ch. 90, § 5.

5. The caption of a deposition describing it as taken in a proceeding of forcible entry and detainer, is sufficiently accurate to authorize the reading of the deposition, though the proceeding is for an unlawful detainer.

6. A bond with condition to convey land of which the obligor had neither title or possession passes nothing. And a decree in a cause between the parties, for a conveyance of the land by a commissioner, and his conveyance, passes nothing; none of the parties ever having had either title or actual possession.

On the 29th day of February 1848 John Miller and Joel McPherson made complaint before a justice of the peace of the county of Greenbrier, that James Cales had unlawfully turned them out of possession of a certain cabin and tenement containing about forty acres, on the end of Chestnut mountain, part of a survey or tract of eleven hundred acres, in the county aforesaid; whereof they prayed restitution. A warrant was thereupon issued by the justice, directing the sheriff to summon a jury for the 18th of March, and to give notice to two justices at least, to attend at that time. This was done, and the cause was regularly continued from that time until June 1848, when it came on to be tried.

In the progress of the trial the plaintiffs introduced as evidence a deed from Jacob Maddy to John Miller, bearing date in the year 1846, by which, in consideration of 40 dollars, Maddy conveyed to Miller one moiety of a tract of eleven hundred acres of land, lying in the county of Greenbrier, on New river, above and below the falls of the river. The plaintiffs also offered in evidence two decrees, which purported to be decrees of the Circuit court of Greenbrier, the first made at its May term 1842, in a cause therein depending, in which Jacob Maddy and Richard Thomas were plaintiffs and

1851.
July
Term.

Cales
v.
Miller
& al.

Samuel Fox was defendant. This decree, after directing the defendant to pay to the plaintiffs certain sums
of money therein specified, being for the purchase money of the land thereinafter mentioned, provided that if
the money was not paid within ninety days a commissioner named should proceed to sell the tract of land
mentioned in the bill, &c.; and that he report his proceedings to the court. The second decree was made
at the May term 1843, and came on upon the papers
formerly read and the report of the commissioner appointed to sell the land. This report was confirmed,
and Thomas C. Burwell was appointed a commissioner
to convey the land to the purchasers.

The plaintiffs also offered in evidence a deed dated
the 26th of October 1843, executed by the commissioner, Thomas C. Burwell, to Jacob Maddy and Joel
McPherson, whereby, after reciting the foregoing decrees, he conveyed to them the land referred to in said decrees. To the introduction of these decrees and the deed
from Burwell, the defendant objected, upon the ground
that it was incumbent on the plaintiffs to shew by evidence that a suit existed authorizing such decrees and
deed: And for this purpose it was necessary that the
whole record should be produced to the court and jury.
But the court overruled the objection and admitted the
evidence; and the defendant excepted.

In the further progress of the cause the defendant
introduced in evidence a patent from the Commonwealth to David Morton, bearing date the 13th day of
March 1798, for the land in controversy; and he then
offered in evidence an office copy of a deed bearing
date the 1st of August 1799, purporting on its face to
be from David Morton, of the borough of Wilmington,
in the State of Delaware, to John Morton, of the city
of Philadelphia, in the State of Pennsylvania, by
which the tract of eleven hundred acres mentioned in
the aforesaid patent was conveyed to John Morton.

1851.
July
Term.

Cales
v.
Miller
& al.

Upon this deed was endorsed a certificate of Robert Wharton, who styled himself mayor of the city of Philadelphia, that the above named David Morton personally appeared before him and acknowledged the above written indenture to be his act and deed, and desired the same as such might be recorded according to the laws of the State of Virginia. This certificate purports to be under the seal of the city of Philadelphia, and bears date the 1st of August 1799; and upon this certificate the deed was admitted to record in the District court held at the Sweet Springs, on the 19th of May 1800. To the introduction of this copy of the deed as evidence, the plaintiffs objected, and the court sustained the objection, and excluded the evidence, on the ground that the original deed was not duly authenticated for record. And the defendant again excepted.

The defendant also offered in evidence the deposition of Benjamin Willard. On this deposition the plaintiffs' counsel had endorsed two exceptions. The first was, " because there is no warrant or action of *forcible entry*, &c., depending in Greenbrier County court, between the parties in the cause mentioned therein." The affidavit by the defendant which was the foundation of the motion for permission to take the deposition of the witness, the commission, and notice to the plaintiffs, spoke of the proceeding depending in the County court of Greenbrier, between the plaintiffs and defendant, as a writ of forcible entry and detainer. It was therefore, of course, that the justice who took the deposition described it as a deposition to be read as evidence on the trial of a writ of forcible entry and detainer. The court sustained the exception, and excluded the deposition; whereupon the defendant again excepted.

The jury found a verdict for the plaintiffs, which the defendant moved the court to set aside, on the ground that it was contrary to the evidence; but the court overruled the motion, and rendered a judgment for the

1851.
July
Term.

Cales
v.
Miller
& al.

plaintiffs; whereupon the defendant again excepted:
and the facts were stated on the record.

In addition to the evidence hereinbefore stated to
have been introduced on the trial, the plaintiffs introduced a patent from the Commonwealth to themselves,
for eleven hundred acres of land, including the land in
controversy, bearing date the 29th of February 1848.
They also proved that a certain Abraham Bragg occupied a portion of the tract of eleven hundred acres,
known as the "old bottom," for some ten years. That
he took possession of the old bottom about the year
1831, and resided there without claiming the land.
That he sold his improvements at the "old bottom" to
the plaintiff, Jacob Maddy, together with two hundred
acres of land for which he had the legal title; and
when he was about to give a title bond to Maddy the
latter requested him to make him a title bond for the
whole of the eleven hundred acre tract. That Abraham Bragg at first refused to do it, stating to Maddy
that he did not own the land, and had only sold his improvements on it, and that the land was claimed by
Joseph Willard; and that if he gave such title bond his
brother, Daniel Bragg, who lived on the mountain place
at the time, would be displeased; but Maddy said to
him, as he was going off it would make no difference.
Abraham Bragg then consented to give, and did give, a
title bond to Maddy for the eleven hundred acre tract.
That Maddy, at the time he traded with Abraham
Bragg, knew that Joseph Willard claimed the tract of
land embracing the improvements on the "old bottom."
That Maddy afterwards sold the tract of land he purchased of Abraham Bragg to Richard Thomas, and
passed to him Bragg's title bond. That Thomas sold
the same land to Samuel Fox, and passed to Fox the
same bond; and that Thomas only sold to Fox Bragg's
improvements at the "old bottom" and two hundred
acres aforesaid.

1851.
July
Term.

Cales
v.
Miller
& al.

The defendant, in addition to the patent to David Morton, which it was proved covered the same land embraced in the patent to the plaintiffs, proved that in the year 1815 or 1816 Jeremiah Meadows took possession of the land embraced in the grant to Morton, under and as the tenant and agent of Joseph Willard, who claimed said land; and Meadows agreed to hold the land for Willard and pay the taxes that might accrue thereon. That Meadows, as such tenant, held the land for two or three years, paying the taxes during that time, and residing thereon at the place called the "old bottom." That Meadows in 1820 or 1821 placed Daniel Bragg in possession of said tract of eleven hundred acres of land on a small improvement on another part of the same tract called the "mountain place"; Daniel Bragg agreeing to hold and occupy the land as tenant of Willard, and pay the taxes as they should accrue thereon, and give possession to Willard when it should be demanded. That Daniel Bragg cleared some forty or fifty acres on the mountain, and resided there until 1838 or 1839, paying the taxes, when, by an agreement between him and Thomas Bragg, he gave possession to the latter, who was to occupy the land in the same manner in which Daniel Bragg had occupied it. That Thomas Bragg held the possession until the fall of 1847, and then gave it up, and the defendant went into possession of the mountain place.

The defendant further proved that Abraham Bragg, at the time he took possession of the "old bottom," agreed to pay the taxes on the Willard tract, but failed to do so. And he also proved that the eleven hundred acre tract was entered upon the commissioner's books of Greenbrier county, in the name of Joseph Willard, in 1816, and continued thereon in his name to the time of the trial; and that the taxes on said land had all been paid.

1851.
July
Term.

Cales
v.
Miller
& al

The defendant applied to the Circuit court of Green-brier county for a *supersedeas* to the judgment, which was awarded; but when the cause came on to be heard in that court the judgment of the County court was affirmed. Whereupon the defendant applied to this court for a *supersedeas*, which was granted.

*Reynolds*, for the appellant.
*William Smith* and *Price*, for the appellees.

ALLEN, *J.* delivered the opinion of the court.

The court is of opinion, that as the decrees offered in evidence merely directed the commissioners thereby appointed to sell and convey the tract of 1100 acres referred to in the bill, such a general description of the land did not satisfactorily prove the authority of the commissioner, Thomas C. Burwell, to convey the particular tract of land in Greenbrier county described in his deed of the 26th October 1843, to Jacob Maddy and Joel McPherson; and it was incumbent on the parties claiming under such deed to have shewn, by the record of the suit referred to in the decrees and deed, what specific tract of land the commissioner was authorized to sell and convey.

The court is therefore of opinion that the County court erred in permitting said deed to be read in evidence, as set forth in the first bill of exceptions taken by the plaintiff in error, without the production of the record of the suit therein referred to, or so much thereof as would have shewn the particular tract of land the commissioner was empowered to sell and convey.

The court is further of opinion, that as it appears upon the face of the deed dated the 1st of August 1799, between David Morton, of the State of Delaware, of the one part, and John Morton, of the State of Pennsylvania, of the other part, and set forth in the 2d

1851.
July
Term.

Cales
v.
Miller
& al.

bill of exceptions filed by the plaintiff in error, that the parties to said deed resided without the jurisdiction of this State, the acknowledgment by the non-resident grantor before the mayor of the city of Philadelphia afforded sufficient evidence that said grantor, for the time being, dwelt in said city of Philadelphia, and said deed was duly authenticated for record; and the court is therefore of opinion the County court erred in rejecting a copy of said deed as evidence, because the same had not been properly authenticated for record.

The court is further of opinion that the said County court erred in excluding the deposition of Benjamin Willard, offered to be read as evidence by the plaintiff in error, as set forth in his third bill of exceptions, on the ground of a misdescription of the complaint in the notice, commission and caption of the deposition. The general description of the action, as contained in the act under which the proceeding was had, is " an act to explain and amend an act reducing into one the several acts concerning forcible entries and detainers "; and though the form of complaint was modified to suit the particular injury complained of, the description of the action was sufficient to give notice to the parties of the controversy in which the deposition was intended to be used. Whether the evidence would have been proper if not excluded for the cause aforesaid would have depended upon the fact that the plaintiff in error had in some way connected his possession with said Joseph Willard; for though it would not have been competent to prove a transmission of the title alleged to have been vested in David Morton, the patentee, to said Joseph Willard, by such parol evidence, the evidence, in connexion with other evidence tending to prove that said Joseph Willard had entered into said land by himself or his agents, held possession thereof by his tenants and agents, and had the same assessed in his own name and paid the taxes thereon, and also shewing the dura-

1851.
July
Term.

Cales
v.
Miller
& al.

tion of such possession so taken and held, would have been proper to shew the intent with which said Willard entered and held possession, whether as a claimant of the land as owner or as a mere intruder; and if as owner of the land, whether such possession so taken and held had not continued for a sufficient length of time to protect said Willard and those holding under him against any adverse claimant.

And the court is further of opinion, that upon the facts certified as proved upon the trial of the complaint, the County court erred in overruling the motion of the plaintiff in error to set aside the verdict and grant him a new trial, on the ground that the verdict was contrary to evidence. The defendants in error had not shewn either a possession or a right to the possession of the tenement in the complaint mentioned. If they claimed under the alleged contract and title bond of Abraham Bragg, it does not appear he was ever in possession of the tenement in question. On the contrary, it appears that at the time of such alleged sale by Abraham Bragg the tenement in question was in the actual occupation of Daniel Bragg as tenant of Joseph Willard, and that the defendants in error, or those under whom they claim, never had possession thereof. The deed executed to the said Maddy and McPherson by the commissioner of the court, Thomas C. Burwell, and the deed from Maddy to John Miller, one of the complainants, passed neither possession or right of possession, it not appearing that any of the parties connected therewith ever had title to the land conveyed; nor is any possession of any part of the land conveyed shewn to have been ever actually held by any of them, except Abraham Bragg, and his possession was as tenant of said Joseph Willard, and did not extend to or embrace the tenement in controversy.

If the defendants in error claimed under their patent of the 29th day of February 1848, the patent of itself

1851.
July
Term.

Cales
v.
Miller
& al.

vested them with no title or seisin, actual or constructive, the whole title thereto having passed out of the Commonwealth by the prior grant of the same land to the said David Morton; and there is no evidence proving any actual entry of the defendants in error, claiming under and by virtue of their junior grant. The plaintiff in error had entered into possession of the tenement in question prior to the date of the patent of the defendants in error, and held the same at the date thereof; their patent bearing even date with their complaint before the justice. His entry may have been unlawful as regarded Morton or Willard claiming under him, but could not have been so as to the defendants, claiming under a patent bearing date after such entry, and which of itself, in the absence of all proof of actual possession thereunder, conferred no title whatever, as the land had been previously granted to another.

It is therefore considered that the judgment of the Circuit court, affirming the judgment of the County court, is erroneous; and the same is reversed, with costs to the plaintiff in error. And this court proceeding to render such judgment as the Circuit court should have done, it is further considered that the judgment of the County court is erroneous; and the same is reversed, with costs to the plaintiff in error; and the verdict is set aside, and the cause is remanded to the County court for a new trial, upon which the County court will be instructed to govern itself by the principles above declared and adjudged.

## 𝕷𝖊𝖜𝖎𝖘𝖇𝖚𝖗𝖌.

### NEWBROUGH *v.* WALKER.

(Absent *Cabell*, P.)

July 19th.

In an action of covenant for the failure to deliver to the plaintiff possession of a mill which he had rented of the defendant, the plaintiff not having sustained any special damage, he is entitled to recover only the difference between the rent contracted to be paid and a fair rent for the property at the time when it should have been delivered. A conjectural estimate of the profits which may have been made is no legitimate basis upon which to fix the damages.

This was an action of covenant, brought in August 1846, in the Circuit court of Frederick county, by Robert S. Walker against Joshua Newbrough. The declaration set out a covenant by which Newbrough agreed to rent to Walker his mill, in the county of Frederick, for two years from the first of July 1846, for the rent of 300 dollars a year, payable every three months. And the plaintiff averred that the defendant had broken his covenant in this, that although the plaintiff was ready and willing and offered to comply with the same on his part, and had requested the defendant to permit him to take possession as tenant as aforesaid of the said Newbrough's mill in the said covenant mentioned, viz: on the first day of July, at the county aforesaid, the defendant positively refused; and forbid said plaintiff from so taking possession. And that said defendant, after the making of said agreement, and before giving possession of the premises, or any part thereof, to the plaintiff, viz: on the      day of July 1846, rented, demised and leased the said premises to a certain Benjamin Ford, and put said Ford in possession of the same;

1851.
July
Term.

New-
brough
v.
Walker.

whereby the plaintiff was prevented from entering upon and enjoying the said leased premises. Wherefore the plaintiff avers he sustained damage to the amount of 500 dollars.

The defendant appeared and demurred to the declaration; but the demurrer was overruled. He then filed two pleas, one a general, and the other a special plea of *non est factum;* on which the plaintiff took issue. Upon the trial the jury found a verdict for the plaintiff for 250 dollars damages; whereupon the defendant moved the court for a new trial, on the ground, first, that the verdict was contrary to the evidence; and second, that the damages were excessive. But the court overruled the motion, and rendered a judgment upon the verdict; and the defendant excepted. The material facts of the case are as follows:

The plaintiff was a young man with a family dependent on his labour. He had been employed previous to the first of July 1846, by a Mr. Hollingsworth, as his head miller; and his time with him expired on the 13th of July. The covenant was executed some days before the 1st of July. Whilst the scrivener was preparing it the plaintiff proposed to give security for the payment of the rent, but the defendant declined it. After it was signed by the parties the plaintiff again proposed to give security for the payment of the rent, to which the defendant then assented, and a clause was added to the covenant to be signed by the sureties, by which they bound themselves for the true performance of the contract by Walker; and he took the agreement to have it signed by the sureties; and when so signed it was to be left with the person who had prepared it, for safe keeping; and it was signed and delivered accordingly before the 1st of July.

It appears that the plaintiff went to take possession of the mill on the 1st of July; that he took with him

Vol. viii.—2

1851.
July
Term.

New-
brough
v.
Walker.

the agreement signed by the sureties, and also a copy of it which was not signed, and shewed them to the defendant, who said that the agreement was correct, and requested the plaintiff to get the copy signed by the sureties, or to leave the original with a Mr. Bowles.

It appears that on the second and third of July the plaintiff expressed himself doubtingly about taking the mill. On the 4th Ford applied to the defendant to rent it; but defendant declined to rent it to him, and sent a messenger to the plaintiff, informing him that Ford wanted to rent the mill, and that he must come and take possession of it. To this message the plaintiff replied that he would come over that day, and attend to it; but he failed to go. On the 6th of July Ford was again at the house of the defendant to rent the mill, when the defendant again sent a messenger to inform the plaintiff that there was a person there who wished to rent the mill, and that the plaintiff must come over and fix the papers and take possession of the mill, or he would rent it to Ford. The plaintiff not coming, it was on that evening rented to Ford for 275 dollars a year, on the same terms in other respects as it had been rented to the plaintiff. Some eight or ten days afterwards, Ford, hearing that the plaintiff was dissatisfied at not getting the mill, went to him and told him, that if he wanted it he could still have it on the same terms on which Ford had gotten it; but the plaintiff declined to take it.

It appeared further, that the plaintiff was continued in the service of his previous employer, upon the same terms as before; and that 300 dollars was a fair rent for the property; though one witness stated that he had offered the plaintiff 100 dollars for his lease, and another witness thought the plaintiff might have cleared three or four hundred dollars during the first year.

The defendant applied to this court for a *supersedeas* to the judgment, which was awarded.

*Cooke*, for the appellant.

There was no counsel for the appellee.

1851.
July
Term.

New-
brough
v.
Walker.

MONCURE, *J.* delivered the opinion of the court.

The court is of opinion that the Circuit court did not err in overruling the demurrer to the declaration ; but did err in overruling the motion for a new trial. On the facts proved and certified in the cause, the jury was warranted in finding a verdict for the plaintiff in the court below; but the damages awarded were excessive. The defendant in the court below seems to have acted in good faith, and his breach of contract for which the suit was brought seems to have been the result of misunderstanding on his part. He derived no benefit from such breach, but, on the contrary, rented out the property for twenty-five dollars less than the plaintiff was to have given him. It was not averred in the declaration or proved on the trial that the plaintiff sustained any special damage by reason of the defendant's breach of contract. The plaintiff did not lose his situation, but continued in the same business in which he was engaged when he entered into the contract. The tenant to whom the property was rented offered, a few days after the renting and before he had received or purchased any wheat, to let the plaintiff have it on the same terms on which said tenant had rented it ; but the plaintiff declined to accept the offer. Under these circumstances the plaintiff was entitled only to general damages, and the measure of such damages is the difference between the rent contracted to be paid and a fair rent for the property at the time when it should have been delivered to him. It was proved that 300 dollars, the rent stipulated in the lease to the plaintiff, was a fair rent for the property. On the other hand, it was proved by a witness that he offered the plaintiff one hundred dollars for his lease, which he refused to take. If upon this evidence the jury had found a verdict for

1851.
July
Term.

Now-
brough
v.
Walker.

one hundred dollars damages, this court would not have disturbed the verdict. But there is nothing in the case which warrants a verdict for greater damages than one hundred dollars. The evidence of a witness that during the first year of the lease the plaintiff could have cleared three or four hundred dollars was necessarily speculative and conjectural, and furnished no legitimate basis on which to estimate the damages. It is therefore considered by the court that the judgment of the Circuit court be reversed and annulled, with costs to the plaintiff in error; that the verdict of the jurors be set aside; and that the cause be remanded to the Circuit court for a new trial to be had therein.

## Lewisburg.

### LYLE v. OVERSEERS OF THE POOR OF OHIO COUNTY.

(Absent Cabell, P.)

**August 14th.**

The County court made an order that the putative father of a bastard child, the mother of which was a married woman who had been deserted by her husband, should pay to the overseers of the poor a certain sum annually for six years commencing from the birth of the child, if it should live so long. And this held to be proper.

This was a proceeding in the County court of Ohio county, by the overseers of the poor of that county against James Lyle, for the purpose of charging him with the support of a bastard child. It appeared from the evidence that the mother of the bastard child was a married woman. She had been married in March 1843, but her husband left her in the fall of that year

1851.
July
Term.

Lyle
v.
Overseers
of the Poor
of Ohio
county.

and had not returned. Since that time she had lived with her father; and the child was born in October 1847. It appeared that the mother was entitled to an interest worth about 200 dollars in a small tract of land. This proceeding was commenced on the 29th of April 1848. The case came on to be heard before the County court at the September term of that year, when the court made an order that the defendant Lyle be charged with the annual payment of 25 dollars to the overseers of the poor of the county, for the space of six years from the birth of said child, to wit: for six years from the 18th day of October 1847, if the child shall live so long. Lyle obtained a *supersedeas* to this judgment from the judge of the Circuit court of Ohio county, but when the case came on to be heard in that court the judgment of the County court was affirmed; whereupon he applied to this court for a *supersedeas*, which was awarded.

*Price*, for the appellant, and
*Jacob*, for the appellees, submitted the case.

BY THE COURT: The judgment is affirmed.

### Lewisburg.

1851.
July
Term.

BELL & al. v. CALHOUN.

(Absent *Cabell*, P.)

**August 16th.**

1. In December 1842 C assigned to B a bond on E, who was in doubtful circumstances, for 529 dollars and 6 cents, due on 26th October 1838, and subject to a credit of 15 dollars paid 1st October 1842; for which B gave him 494 dollars and 25 cents; and C at the same time executed a deed of trust on property with condition that if the bond with its interest was not paid in twelve months, the trustee should sell and pay the amount to B. This was usurious.

2. On a bill to enjoin a sale under the deed of trust, the plaintiff says he has proof and does not wish a discovery, but that the sale may be enjoined until the validity of the deed can be tried at law. Upon an issue directed by the court, the jury find the usury; and that the usurious premium is the difference between the sum advanced by B to C and the bond with interest to that time, subject to the credit for 15 dollars. HELD: That the proper relief is, not to perpetuate the injunction for the whole amount of the bond and its interest due, but only for the amount of the usurious premium.

In March 1844 George A. Calhoun applied to the judge of the Circuit court of Augusta county for an injunction to restrain a sale of slaves under a deed of trust. In his bill he alleged, in substance, that in December 1842 he ascertained that he would be compelled to raise a sum of money of over four hundred dollars by the first or second of January 1843. That he finally made an arrangement with Samuel H. Bell and William Crawford, whereby he assigned to them a bond which he held on John Edmondson for 529 dollars and 6 cents, due on the 26th of October 1838, subject to a credit of 15 dollars, paid the 1st of October 1842, for which he received the sum of 494 dollars and 25 cents; and he at the same time, in pursuance of the agreement between them, executed a deed of trust, a copy of which was exhibited with the bill, whereby he conveyed to Littleton Waddell four slaves, upon trust, that if within twelve months from that date the bond so assigned, with interest, should not be paid to said Bell and Crawford, then the trustee should sell the slaves at public auction for cash, and pay the whole amount of said bond to Bell and Crawford. He charged that this arrangement was not a sale of the bond, but a usurious agreement, whereby Bell and Crawford agreed to lend to the complainant 494 dollars 25 cents for twelve months, for which he was to pay the full amount of Edmondson's bond, amounting to about 693 dollars 43 cents, something over thirty-three *per cent.*

The bill as originally prepared, after making Waddell, Bell and Crawford parties, called upon them to answer the bill upon oath, and asked that they might be restrained from selling under the deed of trust; that the deed might be declared usurious and void; or, if not, that the plaintiff might at least be relieved from the payment of all over the sum with its interest which he had received. Afterwards, but before the bill was filed, a clause was added by which the complainant alleged that he could prove all the allegations of the bill going to establish the usury charged therein, and that he did not require a discovery of the usury from the defendants by their answers; and he asked for an injunction to restrain the sale of the trust property until the validity of the deed could be tried at law. The injunction was granted.

The defendants Bell and Crawford answered the bill. They alleged that Edmondson was insolvent at the time, and the bond referred to in the bill was secured by a deed of trust; but there were so many other debts secured by the same deed, having priority to this, that it was very doubtful whether it would be paid. That the agreement between the complainant and themselves was, that he should assign the bond to them at a discount of twenty-five *per cent.;* and secure them for the money they should advance to him by a deed of trust on negroes. That accordingly, on the same day, the defendant Waddell, at the instance and under the directions of the complainant, prepared the trust deed; and on the same day the bond was assigned to them, and they advanced to the complainant the sum of 494 dollars 25 cents.

They aver that their understanding of the contract at the time, and ever since, has been, that they had a right to the whole amount of the bond on Edmondson, if they could collect it of him. Of this, however, they had considerable doubt: and if they failed, then that they had a right to look to the trust deed executed by the complainant, as a security for the money actually advanced to him, with the legal interest accruing thereon. And they aver that they never have claimed or demanded under said deed of trust more than the said sum of 494 dollars 25 cents, with legal interest thereon.

The deed of trust recites that its object is to secure to Bell and Crawford the full payment of the bond assigned, with interest thereon; and it provides that if it is not paid in twelve months, the trustee shall, at the request of Bell and Crawford, or their assigns, sell for cash so much of the trust property as may be necessary to make the amount which may be then due upon said bond, which amount he shall pay over to those entitled.

At the June term 1844 the cause came on to be heard on a motion by the defendant to dissolve the injunction; whereupon the court overruled the motion, and ordered that an issue be made up between the parties and tried at the bar of that court, before a jury, to ascertain whether the assignment of the bond of Ed-

1851.
July
Term.

Bell & al.
v.
Calhoun.

mondson by the plaintiff to Bell and Crawford, and the deed of trust of the same date, were founded on a corrupt and usurious agreement or not; and if upon a usurious agreement, what was the amount of the usurious premium reserved on said contract. Upon the trial of this issue the jury found that the assignment of the bond and the deed of trust were founded in a usurious agreement; and that the usurious premium amounted to the difference between the sum of 494 dollars 25 cents and the sum of 529 dollars with interest thereon from the 8th of May 1838 to the 31st of December 1842, the date of the deed of trust, subject to a credit of 15 dollars, as of the 1st of October 1842.

The cause came on to be finally heard at the June term 1847, when the court approved the verdict of the jury; and being of opinion that the measure of relief consequent on the verdict, upon the authority of *Marks* v. *Morris*, was the annulment of the trust deed and assignment, and forfeiture by the defendants of the entire debt, perpetuated the injunction with costs. From this decree Bell and Crawford applied to this court for an appeal, which was allowed.

The cause was argued by *Fultz*, for the appellants, and *Michie*, for the appellee, but as the authorities are all cited in the case of the *Bank of Washington* v. *Arthur*, 3 Grattan 173, it cannot be necessary to refer to them here.

BALDWIN, *J.* delivered the opinion of the court.

The court is of opinion that there is no error in so much of the decree of the Circuit court as approves the verdict of the jury, ascertaining that the assignment and trust deed in the bill and proceedings mentioned were founded in a corrupt and usurious agreement and contract between the appellants and the appellee, and ascertaining the amount of usurious premium reserved on said agreement and contract; but that the said decree is erroneous in holding that the proper measure of relief consequent upon the verdict of the jury is the forfeiture by the appellants of the entire debt, and in wholly perpetuating the injunction which had been granted to the appellee to restrain proceedings under said trust deed; this court being of opinion that the proper measure of relief to the appellee is a credit for the amount of the usurious premium found by the verdict of the jury, against the principal money and interest secured by said assignment and trust deed, and a further credit against the same for the sum of 15 dollars mentioned in said verdict; and that the said assignment and trust deed ought to stand as securities for the balance of the principal money and interest thereby secured, and payment thereof enforced, if necessary, by a sale, under the direction of the court, of the property conveyed by said trust deed. It is therefore adjudged, ordered and decreed, that so much of the said decree as is above declared to be erroneous be reversed and annulled, and the residue thereof affirmed, with costs to appellants. And the cause is remanded to the Circuit court, to be proceeded in according to the principles above declared.

DECREE REVERSED.

## Lewisburg.

BOURLAND *v.* EIDSON.

1851.
July
Term.

(Absent *Cabell, P.*)

August 23d.

1. It is no defence in an action of slander, even in mitigation of damages, that previous to the speaking the slanderous words laid in the declaration, the plaintiff had used equally offensive and insulting words towards the defendant.

2. In an action of slander, under the plea of not guilty, the defendant may, in mitigation of damages, prove any facts as to the conduct of the plaintiff in relation to the transaction which was the occasion of the slanderous language complained of, which tend to excuse him for uttering the words, provided the facts do not prove or tend to prove the truth of the charge complained of, but in fact relieve the plaintiff from the imputation involved in it.

This was an action of slander in the Circuit court of Augusta county, brought by William Eidson against James Bourland. The declaration contained but one count, in which the slander alleged to have been uttered was stated to be, " that the plaintiff was a rogue, and had stolen from the defendant an order on Stofer, and that the plaintiff had sworn to a lie in court."

The defendant pleaded " not guilty." And on the trial of the cause he offered to prove, in mitigation of damages, that at and about the time of speaking the words set out in the declaration, the plaintiff and defendant were engaged in an angry and exciting controversy in the court in which this case was then on trial, and that they were both in the habit of using towards and concerning each other violent and abusive language; and that about that time, although not at the time when the words set out in the declaration were spoken, the plaintiff had used to and about the defendant language equally offensive and insulting as that set out in the declaration. But the court, being of opinion that such evidence was inadmissible for any purpose, refused to admit the evidence: And the defendant excepted.

In the further progress of the trial, the defendant, as to the words set out in the declaration, as imputing to the plaintiff a theft of an order on Stofer, offered evidence to prove the circumstances under which the plaintiff became possessed of the order on Stofer, and his whole conduct in relation thereto; and to shew that, although not justifying the speaking of the words as importing theft, these circumstances and the conduct of the plaintiff were in themselves highly improper, and such as were calculated justly to excite the defendant and arouse his suspicions. But the court being of opinion that such evidence was inadmissible under the plea of "not guilty," which was the only plea in the cause, refused to admit the evidence: And the defendant again excepted. This exception does not state that the plaintiff had introduced any evidence upon the charge of theft in stealing the order on Stofer, or indeed that he had introduced any evidence, unless as that may be inferred from what is hereinbefore stated.

The jury found a verdict in favour of Eidson for 900 dollars: upon which the court rendered a judgment. Whereupon Bourland applied to this court for a *supersedeas*, which was awarded.

*Hugh Sheffey* and *Michie*, for the appellant, insisted:

1st. That the evidence referred to in the first bill of exceptions should have been admitted, not for the purpose of offsetting one slander by another, but for the purpose of shewing the provocation under which the appellant spoke the words attributed to him. And they referred to *Watts* v. *Fraser*, 32 Eng. C. L. R. 544; *Judge* v. *Berkeley*, Id. 545, in note; *Tarpley* v. *Blaby*, Id. 555; *Fraser* v. *Berkeley*, Id. 658.

2d. That the evidence referred to in the second bill of exceptions should have been admitted. They said that if the bill of exceptions was improperly taken, the court for that reason would reverse the judgment and send the cause back for a new trial. *Brooke* v. *Young*, 3 Rand. 106; *Raines* v. *Philips' ex'or*, 1 Leigh 483; *Thompson* v. *Cummins*, 2 Id. 321. But that the court would construe the exceptions so as to get at the merits. *Trimyer* v. *Pollard*, 5 Gratt. 460.

They insisted further that whilst the defendant would not be allowed, under the plea of " not guilty," to prove the charge, yet that it was admissible to prove the circumstances which justly excited the suspicions of the defendant, together with other circumstances not then known to the defendant, which shewed that the plaintiff was not guilty of the offence imputed to him. And they referred to *Leicester* v. *Walter*, 2 Camp. R. 251; *East* v. *Chapman*, 12 Eng. C. L. R. 268; *Rigden* v. *Wolcott*, 6 Gill & John. 413; *Minesinger* v. *Kerr*, 9 Penn. R. 312; *Gilman* v. *Lowell*, 8 Wend. R. 573; *Updegrove* v. *Zimmerman*, 13 Penn. R. 619; *Alderman* v. *French*, 1 Pick R. 1; *Larned* v. *Buffinton*, 3 Mass. R. 546; *Van Ankin* v. *Westfall*, 14 John. R. 233; *Bradley* v. *Heath*, 12 Pick. R. 163; *Williams* v. *Miner*, 18 Conn. R. 464; Cook on Defam. 286; 53 Law Libr., citing *The King* v. *Halpin*, 17 Eng. C. L. R. 332; *Knobell* v. *Fuller*, Peake's Evi. 287, 288, Appendix 92; recognized in *Bailey* v. *Hyde*, 3 Conn. R. 463; in *Leicester* v. *Walter*, 2 Camp. R. 251; in *East* v. *Chapman*, 12 Eng. C. L. R. 268, and in *Buford* v. *McLuny*, 1 Nott & McC. 268; *Hart* v. *Reed*, 1 B. Munroe's R. 166; *Eagan* v. *Gantt*, 1 McMul. R. 468; *Cooper* v. *Barber*, 24 Wend. R. 105; *Petrie* v. *Rose*, 5 Watts & Serg. 364.

*Fultz*, for the appellee.

On the first point said the law did not authorize a set

off in slander; and referred to *McAlexander* v. *Harris*, 6 Munf. 465.

2d. He insisted, first, that it did not appear that the plaintiff had introduced any proof as to the charge of having stolen the order from Stofer, and therefore it did not appear that the evidence offered and rejected was relevant. *McDowell* v. *Burwell*, 4 Rand. 317; *Rowt's adm'x* v. *Kile's adm'r*, 1 Leigh 216; *Carpenter* v. *Utz*, 4 Gratt. 270.

3d. That the evidence offered was not admissible under the plea of not guilty. And he said the distinction was between the cases where the action was maintainable without proving special damage, and those where special damage must be proved in order to sustain the action. In the latter he admitted that any facts might be proved under the general issue which disproved the malice: And such he said were the cases of *Leicester* v. *Walter*, 2 Camp. R. 251; *Smith* v. *Spooner*, 3 Taunt. R. 246; *Watson* v. *Reynolds*, 22 Eng. C. L. R. 231; *Rowe* v. *Roach*, 1 Mau. & Sel. 304; *Wyatt* v. *Gore*, 3 Eng. C. L. R. 111; *Sims* v. *Kinder*, 11 Eng. C. L. R. 392. But that where the words were actionable without proof of special damage the rule was that such evidence was not admissible under the general issue. And he referred to *Vessey* v. *Pike*, 14 Eng. C. L. R. 420; *Dance* v. *Robson*, 22 Id. 311; *Waithman* v. *Weaver*, 16 Id. 412; *Van Ankin* v. *Westfall*, 14 John R. 233; *Shepard* v. *Merrill*, 13 John R. 475; *Wormouth* v. *Cramer*, 3 Wend. R. 395; *Henry* v. *Norwood*, 4 Watts R. 347; *Petrie* v. *Rose*, 5 Watts & Serg. 364; *Purple* v. *Horton*, 13 Wend. R. 9; *Cooper* v. *Barber*, 24 Wend. R. 105; *Eagan* v. *Gantt*, 1 McMul. R. 468; *McGee* v. *Lodusky*, 5 J. J. Marsh. R. 185; *Hart* v. *Reed*, 1 B. Munroe's R. 166; *Buford* v. *McLuney*, 1 Nott & McC. 268; *Cheatwood* v. *Mayo*, 5 Munf. 16; *McAlexander* v. *Harris*, 6 Id. 465; *Moseley* v. *Moss*, 6 Gratt. 584.

1851.
July
Term.

Bourland
v.
Eldson.

BALDWIN, *J.* I shall treat this case, in the first place, as if it were exclusively an action for slander at common law.

The case was tried upon the general issue, and the questions presented by the record are in reference to evidence offered by the defendant, and rejected by the court, in mitigation of damages.

The authorities in regard to the evidence proper under the general issue, in mitigation of damages, are numerous, and a good deal conflicting; and the difficulties which have embarrassed the courts seem to have arisen out of opposing considerations, entirely proper in themselves, but often hard to be reconciled: the propriety and justice, on the one hand, of submitting to the jury the ungarbled merits of the controversy, so as to enable them to give to the plaintiff the full damages he ought to recover, and no more; and on the other hand, the policy and necessity of excluding evidence irrelevant to the substance of the grievance, or to the issue joined between the parties.

It is obvious that the purposes of justice require us to look as far as practicable to the conduct and motives of both parties in connection with the subject matter of the grievance, in order to estimate fully and fairly the amount of damage sustained by the one, and of retribution which ought to be made by the other. If the plaintiff has been free from blame, and has been made the victim of the defendant's cool and deliberate malice, the case presented is widely different from one where the plaintiff has, by his own misconduct, occasioned or provoked the injurious imputation, or where the defendant, though subject to the legal inference of malice, from the criminality of the imputed act, and the falsehood of the charge, has been prompted in making it by a plain mistake, without his default, as to the nature of the plaintiff's conduct. And the soundness of any mere technical reasoning may be questioned which, against the plain dictates of common sense, would place cases so dissimilar in complexion upon the same footing as to the *quantum* of damages.

The elements of redress in the action for defamation are the wrong done to the plaintiff, and the malice or vicious intent of the defendant : these modify each other, and are modified by circumstances, so as to allow much scope for the judgment and discretion of the jury, upon a subject somewhat indefinite in its very nature, the amount of *pecuniary* compensation which ought to be paid for an injury of such a character. Whatever, therefore, tends to throw light upon the question ought, within fair and reasonable limits, to be brought, in some form or shape, to the consideration of the jury.

It is of course under the general issue that evidence must be offered which presents no bar to the action, but tends only to mitigate the damages. At one period, indeed, the idea seems to have prevailed to a considerable extent, that whenever the defendant's evidence answered the whole ground of the plaintiff's action, it was admissible under the general issue, and therefore (I presume) that as some occasions of speaking or publishing defamatory words divested them of the essential of legal malice, so proof of their truth took away the equally essential ingredient of their alleged falsehood. And so the truth of the defamatory words was so repeatedly admitted in evidence under the plea of not guilty as to become, in the opinion of the judges of England, a mischief in practice requiring correction. Accordingly, in the case of *Underwood* v. *Parks*, 2 Strange 1200, in which the defendant pleaded not guilty, and offered to prove the words to be true, in mitigation of damages, the chief justice refused to permit it, saying that at a meeting of all the judges, upon a case that arose in the Common Pleas, a large majority of them had determined not to allow it for the future, but that it should be pleaded, whereby the plaintiff might be prepared to

1851.
July
Term.

Bourland
v.
Eidson.

defend himself, as well as to prove the speaking of the words : That this was now a general rule amongst them all, which no judge would think himself at liberty to depart from; and that it extended to all sorts of words, and not barely to such as imported a charge of felony. The rule thus adopted has since been recognized both in England and in this country, is sustained by numerous authorities, and I believe has never been denied by any judicial decision.

But although the rule of *Underwood* v. *Parks* has been thus universally admitted, yet its spirit has, as I conceive, been often broken in upon by decisions and *dicta*, both in England and in this country. It has been repeatedly said and held that, under the general issue, evidence may be given in mitigation of damages, which stops short of a complete justification. Now this surely cannot be considered as an exception to or modification of the rule of *Underwood* v. *Parks*, but is in effect, though not so designed, a practical negation of it; for where is the line to be drawn between perfect and imperfect proof of the plaintiff's guilt; and upon what principle is light evidence to be preferred to that which is cogent and conclusive ? What is the admission of such evidence but an invitation to the jury to act upon suspicion instead of proof ? And indeed that aspect is given to the proposition by some of the authorities, which assert that circumstances of suspicion may be received in mitigation of damages. The rule which excludes proof of the truth of the words must of necessity exclude evidence tending to prove it, or the rule itself is rendered nugatory or merely mischievous. · And so is the preponderance of authority, both English and American. See the cases referred to in 3 Stephens' Nisi Prius 2255–6, 2253, 2519 ; 2 Stark. Ev. 877–8 ; 1 Stark. Sland. 413, n. ; 2 Id. 78 to 89—American editions of those works; *Root* v. *King*, 7 Cow. R. 613 ;

VOL. VIII.—3

*Gilman* v. *Lowell*, 8 Wend. R. 573, in which most of the cases are reviewed.

Indeed, nothing but an anxiety to get at the supposed merits of the case could have misled some judges into so obvious a deviation from the principle of *Underwood* v. *Parks;* and it is remarkable that others, while condemning and overruling such departure, have at the same time received other evidence of the same general nature, but still more objectionable. I allude to the admission of evidence to prove that the plaintiff laboured under a general suspicion of having been guilty of the charge, or of rumors imputing to him such criminal acts. It may be easily seen that the effect of such evidence, when a party comes into court for the purpose of establishing his innocence, and so putting down false rumors of his guilt, may be to crush him under the weight of those very rumors. And yet the current of English authority allows the introduction of such evidence, upon the supposition, it seems, that it goes to the character of the plaintiff, though it surely does not, in the legal acceptation of the term, if general character be meant. On the other hand, the weight of American authority, with better reason, it seems to me, excludes such evidence. See the cases *pro* and *con*, referred to in 2 Stark. Ev. 877; Phillips' Ev., vol. 3, p. 249, 250; 2 Stark. Sland. 96–7—American editions of those works.

It seems to me, therefore, that evidence is not admissible under the general issue, in mitigation of damages, which proves, or tends in any form or shape to prove, the truth of the words.

On the other hand, I cannot doubt that where the defamatory words point to a specified act of the plaintiff, and the evidence offered in mitigation of damages neither proves, nor tends to prove, or upon the whole negatives, the truth of the words, it is admissible where it serves to shew improper conduct of the plaintiff in re-

1851.
July
Term.

Bourland
v.
Eldson.

ference to the particular transaction, calculated to vex, harass, aggrieve or provoke the defendant.

In such cases, it is often important that the jury should have some information of the transaction to which the words refer, in order to understand correctly their true import and meaning, and the design with which they were spoken. The defendant may, through ignorance or excitement, misapprehend the plaintiff's conduct, or use inappropriate language and epithets in the expression of his indignation or resentment; and yet that conduct may have been wholly unwarranted, or extremely injurious or provoking. The aggravation of a fraud or a trespass into a felony, whether from ignorance or exasperation, surely stands upon a different footing, in regard to the *quantum* of damages, from a sheer fabrication. Thus if a party should obtain the money of another by a fraudulent contrivance, or dishonest breach of trust, or his property by open violence under a false claim of title, and the party injured, in speaking of the transaction, should designate it, in the former case as a theft, or in the latter as a robbery, a recovery of heavy damages in an action of slander would not be so much for actual defamation as for inaccurate phraseology. And if a plaintiff, without moral guilt, but to disport himself with the fears or feelings of the defendant, has misled or provoked him to the use of defamatory words, this should be made known to the jury, otherwise the plaintiff, to a greater or less extent, would recover damages for his own misbehaviour.

In the cases mentioned, the defendant could not protect himself from heavy damages under the plea of justification, inasmuch as the evidence would not prove or tend to prove the truth of the words; and yet, for that very reason, and because they were begotten, as it were, by the plaintiff's own misconduct, the evidence is proper, under the general issue, in mitigation of damages. Of this the plaintiff has no right to complain, for he suffers no injustice, nor is he taken by surprise, the particular transaction being pointed to by the words themselves, and the defendant not having declined any privilege of pleading the matter specially, inasmuch as such pleading was beyond his competency.

The admissibility of evidence such as above mentioned in mitigation of damages is warranted by the spirit of familiar doctrines. Thus the defendant may prove, as a complete defence under the general issue, that the publication of the defamatory words was procured by the contrivance of the plaintiff for the purposes of the action. 2 Stark. Ev. 876; *King* v. *Waring*, 5 Esp. Ca. 13. So in an action for a libel, the defendant may give in evidence a former publication of the plaintiff to which the libel was an answer, to explain the subject matter, occasion and intent of the defendant's publication, and in mitigation of damages. 2 Stark. Ev. 877; *Hitchcoss* v. *Lathrop*. And in 2 Stark. Sland. 95, n., it is mentioned with approbation that the counsel for the defendant in *Leicester* v. *Walter*, 2 Camp. R. 351, said, *arguendo*, that in a case before Le Blanc, J., at Worcester, that learned judge received evidence under the general issue of attempts of the plaintiff to commit the crime which the defendant had imputed to him. In *Gilman* v. *Lowell*, 8 Wend. R. 573, in an action for charging the plaintiff with false swearing in relation to the existence of a deed, the defendant was allowed to prove, in mitigation of damages, that after diligent search of the registry, before the speaking of the words, the deed could not, from a defect of the index, be found. And in *Grant* v. *Hover*, 6 Munf. 13, in an action for charging the plaintiff with perjury, the defendant was permitted to prove under the general issue what the plaintiff did swear to, though not its falsity.

In the case before us, the declaration, consisting of a single count, comprises two distinct allegations of defamation; one imputing to the plaintiff that he stole from the defendant an order on Stofer; the other that he had committed perjury in a court of justice. As to the former, the defendant on the trial, as appears from the second bill of exceptions, offered evidence to prove the circumstances under which the plaintiff became possessed of the order on Stofer, and his whole conduct in relation thereto, and to shew that although not justifying the speaking of the words in the declaration mentioned as imputing theft, those circumstances and the conduct of the plaintiff were in themselves highly improper, and such as were calculated justly to excite the defendant, and to arouse his suspicions. But the court being of opinion that such evidence was inadmissible under the plea of not guilty, which was the only plea in the cause, refused to admit the evidence. In this decision I think the Circuit court erred.

It seems to me that it was entirely competent for either party to give evidence of the existence, the custody, the contents, the nature, and the value of the order on Stofer, to explain the subject matter, occasion and intent of the speaking of the words. Without such evidence the jury could not but be very much in the dark in regard to the very subject of the defamation. There is nothing in the declaration, nor any part of the record, to shew by or in whose favour, or for what purpose, the order was drawn, or whether it could have been of any substantial benefit to either of the parties; and if the defendant could prove that the plaintiff obtained possession of the order without authority, though not *lucri causa*, to vex, harass, provoke or injure the defendant, and that the latter consequently, without deliberate malice, but from the exasperation or misapprehension of the occasion, spoke the words in question, these were matters perfectly proper for the consideration of the jury upon the question of damages.

The 1st bill of exceptions presents another question which occurred at the trial in relation to the exclusion of evidence offered by the defendant in mitigation of damages, as well it seems in reference to the imputation of perjury, as to that of theft. The defendant offered to prove, in mitigation of damages, that at and about the time of speaking the words in the declaration mentioned, the plaintiff and defendant were engaged in an angry and exciting controversy in the court, and that they were both in the habit of using towards and concerning each other violent and abusive language, and that about that time, although not at the time when the words charged in the declaration were spoken, the plaintiff had used to and about the defendant language equally offensive with that in the declaration mentioned. But the court, being of opinion that such evidence was inadmissible for any purpose, refused to permit evidence of slanderous, defamatory, or insulting words spoken by the plaintiff to, of, or concerning the defendant at other times or on different occasions from the times and occasions on which the words charged in the declaration were spoken. In this decision of the Circuit court, it seems to me, there was no error.

It is certain that mutual defamations cannot be made a matter of account and set off against each other, and a balance struck in favour of the most injured or least culpable of the parties: and such would be the effect of allowing evidence of reciprocal criminations unconnected except by a general spirit of hostility and revenge. The only principle upon which defamatory words spoken by the plaintiff can be proved in mitigation of damages is that he has thereby brought upon himself, at least to some extent, the grievance of which he complains. This cannot be conceded with any propriety or safety, unless where such provocation occurs, or is referred to, in the same conversation with the defamation by the defendant, or is communicated to him at that time. I need not consider whether there may not be exceptions to this restriction, there being no foundation for any in the present case.

1851.
July
Term.

Bourland
v.
Eldson.

It will be seen in this case, that the whole structure of the declaration indicates an action for defamation at common law, except that the words are charged to be insulting as well as slanderous; which word insulting would seem to have been introduced for the purpose of enabling the plaintiff to recover for an insult, under the 8th section of the act to suppress duelling, Supp. Rev. Code, p. 284, if his evidence should fail on the trial to make out a case of common law slander. This mode of declaring, in one and the same count of the declaration, for a common law defamation and an insult under the statute, is not allowable, (*Moseley* v. *Moss*, 6 Gratt. 534,) and therefore open to demurrer. But the defendant having failed to avail himself of the misjoinder by demurrer, a question might occur whether the plaintiff might not recover, for an insult, though he should fail to establish a common law defamation; and, if so, whether the defendant would not be at liberty to prove any mitigating circumstances which would be allowable in an action founded upon the statute. These, however, are questions which do not require consideration in this particular case; for in regard to the evidence stated in the 2d bill of exceptions, the same being admissible in an action for common law defamation, it would be at least equally so in an action founded upon the statute; and in regard to the evidence stated in the 1st bill of exceptions, the reasons for excluding it are equally strong, whether in an action for a slander or in an action for an insult.

ALLEN, *J.* The declaration charged the speaking and publishing of words actionable at common law; the issue was not guilty; and at the trial the defendant tendered two bills of exceptions to opinions of the court rejecting evidence offered by him in mitigation of damages. By the first bill of exceptions it appears that the defendant offered evidence to prove, in mitigation of

damages, that at and about the time of speaking the
words in the declaration mentioned, the parties were engaged in an angry and exciting controversy in court ;
that they were both in the habit of using towards and
concerning each other violent and abusive language ;
and that about the time, though not at the time, when
the words charged in the declaration were spoken, the
plaintiff had used to and about the defendant language
equally insulting and offensive with that in the declaration mentioned.  The court, deeming such evidence inadmissible for any purpose, excluded it from the jury.
Evidence of all that occurred at the time of speaking the words, being part of the *res gesta*, and tending
to explain the words spoken, and the intent of the party in making the charge, would be admissible ; but it
is not competent for the defendant to set off one slander against another, uttered by the plaintiff concerning
the defendant, at a different time.  And it was accordingly held by this court in the case of *McAlexander* v.
*Harris*, 6 Munf. 465, that such evidence was improper.
It, therefore, seems to me there was no error in rejecting
the evidence referred to in the first bill of exceptions.

The second bill of exceptions sets forth in substance
that the defendant, as to the charge imputing to the
plaintiff a theft of an order on Stofer, offered evidence
to prove the circumstances under which the plaintiff
became possessed of the order, and his whole conduct
in relation thereto, to shew that, although not justifying
the speaking of the words as importing theft, those circumstances, and the conduct of the plaintiff, were in
themselves highly improper, and such as were calculated justly to excite the defendant and to arouse his suspicions.  The court, deeming the evidence inadmissible
under the issue joined, rejected it.  The rule established
in the case of *Underwood* v. *Parks*, Strange 1200, requires of the defendant, if he intends to justify the
speaking of the words, that he should file a plea of jus-

1851.
July
Term.

Bourland
v.
Eldson.

tification, in order that the plaintiff may know what defence he is to meet. Whether it is competent for the defendant, in mitigation of damages, to introduce evidence proving the truth, or tending to prove the truth, of the words spoken, has been a controverted question both in England and our sister States. The cases are variant and conflicting, and cannot, perhaps, be reconciled. In this State the rule of *Underwood* v. *Parks* has been fully recognized and acted upon in the cases of *Cheatwood* v. *Mayo*, 5 Munf. 16, and *McAlexander* v. *Harris*, 6 Munf. 465. These decisions have never been questioned in this court since; but, on the contrary, the principles established by them, so far as respects words actionable at common law, were approved in the more recent case of *Moseley* v. *Moss*, 6 Gratt. 534. It becomes necessary, therefore, to ascertain what was the precise point established in each of those cases.

In the first case of *Cheatwood* v. *Mayo*, the defendant offered in mitigation of damages, and not by way of justification, to prove facts which, if they did not altogether, almost established the truth of the charge. He could not offer such evidence in bar of the action, because he had failed to file the plea of justification. But if permitted to introduce it in mitigation of damages, the same impression would be made on the minds of the jury, and the plaintiff could not know what defence he was to meet. The case therefore establishes that evidence falling short of a full justification, but tending to prove the truth of the words charged, and *leaving that impression on the minds of the jury*, is inadmissible, notwithstanding the declaration that it is offered in mitigation of damages, and not by way of justification. In the case of *McAlexander* v. *Harris*, the evidence was offered, not as amounting to actual proof of the plaintiff's guilt or a complete justification of the defendant, but as shewing a *probable ground of suspicion*, in mitigation of damages. The character of the evidence is not stated, but if it shewed a probable ground of suspicion, it must have been evidence of circumstances tending to prove the guilt, or proving a link in the chain of facts necessary to make out the guilt of the plaintiff; which, if it shewed probable ground of suspicion on the part of the defendant when speaking the words, was equally calculated to make and leave a similar impression on the minds of the jury if unexplained; and so the character of the plaintiff might be destroyed by a defence of which the pleadings gave him no notice.

Where, however, the defendant relies upon evidence not implying the truth of the charge, or evidence not tending to prove a fact which might constitute a link in the chain of facts establishing the guilt of the plaintiff, but, on the contrary, evidence which of itself disproves the truth of the words spoken, and shews the plaintiff's innocence of the charge imputed to him, such evidence, though it might shew improper conduct in the plaintiff, or a mistake on the part of the defendant, would, it seems to me, be proper evidence, under the plea of not guilty, to repel the presumption of malice, and in mitigation of damages, in every action for slander at common law. By such evidence the plaintiff cannot be surprised or injured, for it disproves the truth of the charge, and so relieves his character from the imputation complained of; and it is evidence which, though bearing materially on the question of malice, and so affecting the damages, the defendant could not rely on under the plea of justification, because it would disprove it. If the evidence in the case under consideration had been testimony to prove that the plaintiff, in a mischievous spirit, or to provoke or irritate the defendant, had possessed himself of the order in the presence of others, avowing his motives at the time, and that defendant, in ignorance of these facts, had spoken the words in the declaration mentioned, such evidence, or

1851.
July
Term.

Bourland
v.
Eldson.

evidence of a like character, might have had an important influence upon the jury in fixing the amount of damages. But it would neither prove, or tend to prove, the charge of guilt, or leave any suspicion of the truth of the charge on the mind of the jury, because it would shew that there was no felonious intent in the act of becoming possessed of the order: and though it would or might shew improper conduct on the part of the plaintiff, he should not be permitted to avail himself of his own misconduct, to the prejudice of the defendant, by excluding evidence bearing upon the presumption of malice, when such evidence shewed his innocence of the charge complained of. If, therefore, the bill of exceptions had set forth the purport of the evidence offered, so as to disclose whether it was of such a character, it would, under the restrictions aforesaid, have been admissible to repel the presumption of malice, and in mitigation of damages. But this is not shewn by the bill of exceptions. It sets forth that the defendant offered to prove the circumstances under which the plaintiff became possessed of the order, and to shew that those circumstances, though not justifying the speaking the words as importing theft, were improper, and calculated to arouse suspicion in the defendant. The evidence rejected might not have amounted to a justification; it could not be offered in justification, for that would have been in bar of the plaintiff's action, and there was no such plea; but the circumstances relied on might, as in the case of *Cheatwood* v. *Mayo*, have amounted almost to full proof of the words in the declaration mentioned, or, as in the case of *McAlexander* v. *Harris*, have left on the minds of the jury a suspicion of the plaintiff's guilt, in the absence of explanatory evidence shewing there was no just ground for such suspicion.

The bill of exceptions may have been designed to shew that the evidence offered, whilst it disproved the truth of the charge, merely tended to prove such improper conduct on the part of the plaintiff, and mistake in the defendant, as would have been proper evidence in mitigation of damages, according to the views before presented. But it would have been equally competent, according to the statement of the bill of exceptions, to have offered evidence similar to the proof offered in the cases of *Cheatwood* v. *Mayo* and *McAlexander* v. *Harris*, and there decided to be inadmissible.

The bill of exceptions is therefore, I think, too imperfect to enable this court to determine what was the precise question intended to be raised and decided ; and for this reason the judgment should be reversed.

DANIEL, *J.* concurred in the opinion of *Allen*, J.

MONCURE, *J.* concurred in reversing the judgment.

The judgment was as follows:

It appears from the first bill of exceptions, that at the trial " the defendant offered evidence to prove, in mitigation of damages, that at and about the time of speaking the words in the declaration mentioned, the plaintiff and defendant were engaged in an angry and exciting controversy in the court, and that they were both in the habit of using towards and concerning each other violent and abusive language, and that about that time, although not at the time when the words charged in the declaration were spoken, the plaintiff had used to and about the defendant language equally offensive and insulting with that in the declaration mentioned : But that the court, being of opinion that such evidence was inadmissible for any purpose, refused to permit evidence of slanderous, defamatory and insulting words spoken by the plaintiff to, of, or concerning the defendant, at other times or on different occasions from the times and occasions on which the words charged in the declara-

1851.
July
Term.

Bourland
v.
Eldson.

tion were spoken." In this decision of the Circuit court, it seems to this court there is no error.

It further appears from the second bill of exceptions, that at the trial "the defendant, as to the words in the declaration mentioned as imputing to the plaintiff a theft of an order on Stofer, offered evidence to prove the circumstances under which the plaintiff became possessed of the order on Stofer, and his whole conduct in relation thereto, and to shew that, although not justifying the speaking of the words in the declaration mentioned as importing theft, those circumstances and the conduct of the plaintiff were in themselves highly improper, and such as were calculated justly to excite the defendant and to arouse his suspicions: But that the court being of opinion that such evidence was inadmissible under the plea of not guilty, which was the only plea in the cause, refused to admit the evidence." And it seems to this court, that if this bill of exceptions is to be understood as importing that the evidence offered, as therein mentioned, neither proved nor tended to prove that the plaintiff was guilty of stealing the order on Stofer, but upon the whole relieved him before the jury from all imputation of such guilt, then that the Circuit court erred in rejecting said evidence. But if, on the contrary, the bill of exceptions is to be understood as importing that the evidence so offered did prove or tend to prove that the plaintiff was guilty of such theft, so as to leave him before the jury unrelieved from all imputation of that crime, then that said evidence was properly rejected by the court. And while some of the members of this court are of opinion that the bill of exceptions justly bears the former interpretation, others think that the evidence offered is not set forth with sufficient certainty to free it from the latter, and therefore that the bill of exceptions is too imperfect to enable us to determine what was the precise question intended to be presented, and that the judgment ought for that reason to be reversed.

It is therefore considered by the court, that the said judgment of the Circuit court be reversed and annulled, and the verdict of the jury set aside, with costs to the plaintiff in error.   And the cause is remanded to the Circuit court for a new trial to be had therein, which new trial is to be governed, so far as applicable, by the principles above declared.

---

### Lewisburg.

### MAYS v. SWOPE.

(Absent *Cabell*, P.)

**August 25th.**

Though the vendee of land has abandoned possession for a technical defect of title, yet upon a bill to enjoin the collection of the purchase money, if the vendor can make a good title at the time of the decree, the vendee is bound to take it.

This was a bill filed by Edwin Mays in the Circuit court of Greenbrier county, against Jonathan Swope, to enjoin a judgment for 300 dollars, with interest and costs, recovered by Swope against Mays in that court. The bill charged that this judgment was for part of the purchase money of a tract of land in the county of Monroe: That the complainant had discovered since the purchase of the land that Swope had no title to it, and complainant had therefore left the land of which he had taken possession under the contract.   The injunction was granted.

Swope answered, insisting he had a good title; but if it was defective, he could and would at any time, if the complainant had suggested the defect, have had it supplied.

There seemed to be no doubt that the land had belonged to Adam Swope, of Pennsylvania. That he, by his will, which was duly admitted to probat in that State, had authorized his executors to sell the land: and that the executors had, by deed bearing date the 5th of December 1825, conveyed it to Jonathan Swope, who had been in undisputed possession of the land until he sold it to B. Perkins in 1840; which contract was rescinded, and he then remained in undisturbed possession until he sold to the complainant in September 1847. The ground of objection seems to have been that the will had not been admitted to probat in this State, and the executors had not qualified as such here.

Whilst the cause was pending, the will was admitted to probat in the County court of Monroe, and Samuel A. Swope qualified as administrator with the will annexed; and he then, on the 17th of December 1849, conveyed the land to Jonathan Swope; and he and his wife, in April 1850, executed a deed by which they conveyed it to Mays; and the same was acknowledged before two justices of the peace so as to be ready for admission to record.

The cause came on to be heard in May 1850, when the court held, that as the defendant had, since the filing of the bill, procured a conveyance of the legal title to the land sold to the plaintiff, and had executed to him a deed therefor, the injunction should be dissolved, but without damages, and with costs to the plaintiff. From this decree Mays applied to this court for an appeal, which was allowed.

*Price*, for the appellant, insisted, that Swope had no title to the land when he sold, and until the purchase was abandoned by Mays, and therefore it was not a case in which he would be allowed time to perfect his title. He referred to *Garnett* v. *Macon*, 6 Call 308; 2 Story's Equ. Jur., § 776, note 1.

*Caperton*, for the appellee, insisted, that a court of equity will enforce the contract of purchase if the vendor can make a title at the decree. He referred to *Hepburn* v. *Dunlop*, 1 Wheat. R. 179; *Hepburn* v. *Auld*, 5 Cranch's R. 262; *Taylor* v. *Longworth*, 14 Peters 172; Sugd. on Vend., p. 430, 431.

By THE COURT: The decree is affirmed.

---

# Lewisburg.

## BEERY *v.* HOMAN'S *committee.*

(Absent *Cabell*, P.)

### August 26th.

1. R, the committee of a lunatic, was summoned to give counter security, as appeared by the order of the County court. The order then proceeds: "Whereupon the said R appeared in court and acknowledged notice of the motion, and with K and B gave the security as required by the above order, condition as the law directs, which bond was duly acknowledged by the parties thereto, and ordered to be certified." In fact the bond produced was not a bond for counter security, but was a new bond, and though B signed it, his name does not appear in either the penal part or the condition, but there is a blank in the penal part after the name of K. HELD:

　1st. That the bond, acknowledged and certified as this was, became a part of the record, and is to be taken and construed with the order, as shewing what was required by the court, and therefore it must be taken that the court required the committee to execute a new bond.

　2d. That it is the bond of B, though his name is not in either the penal part or the condition.

1861.
July
Term.

Beery
v.
Homan's
committee.

2. In a suit against several the bill is dismissed as to one; but before the case is decided as to the others, the plaintiff files a bill to review the decree, and the defendant answers. The case on the bill of review is not set for hearing, nor is the decree sought to be reviewed set aside, but the original cause is brought on to be heard without noticing the other case at all, and the court decrees against the defendant as to whom the bill had been dismissed. HELD: This is no cause for reversing a decree right upon the merits.

In May 1828 John Rader was appointed by the County court of Rockingham the committee of David Homan, a lunatic, and executed a bond with Richard Pickering and David Bowman as his sureties. At the June term of the County court in 1836, on the motion of David Bowman, an order was made that John Rader be summoned to appear at the next court to give said Bowman counter security. The entry of the order then proceeds: "Whereupon the said John Rader appeared in court, and acknowledged notice of the motion, and with Joseph Kratzer and Abraham Beery gave the security as required by the above order, condition as the law directs; which bond was duly acknowledged by the parties thereto, and ordered to be certified."

The bond executed by these parties, though it was signed and sealed by Beery, does not contain his name in either the penalty or condition; but there is a blank after the name of Kratzer, in the penalty. Moreover it is not a bond for counter security, but is in the form of a new bond of a committee.

Some time subsequent to 1836, probably in 1843, though the record does not state the time, Rader was removed from the office of committee of David Homan, and Abraham Lincoln was appointed in his place. And in 1844 Lincoln instituted a suit in the Circuit court of Rockingham county against Rader, Kratzer and Beery, for the purpose of recovering the lunatic's estate which went into the hands of Rader.

1851.
July
Term.

Beery
v.
Homan's
committee.

At the May term 1844 Beery appeared and demurred to the complainant's bill; and assigned for causes of demurrer:

1st. That the bond executed in 1836 was executed without the authority of the court to which it is made payable, and against the order of the court: it purporting to be a new bond, and not a bond of indemnity to David Bowman, which the court had ordered to be given.

2d. That the names of John Rader and Joseph Kratzer, two of the obligors on the bond, being inserted in the body of the bond, and the name of the defendant being nowhere inserted therein, it is not binding on him.

The court sustained the demurrer, and dismissed the bill as to the defendant Beery. And at the October term of the court Kratzer appeared and likewise demurred to the bill, assigning as ground of demurrer the first cause stated by Beery. This demurrer was overruled in May 1845; and the plaintiff was allowed to amend his bill and make Pickering and Bowman, the sureties to the first bond, parties defendants.

In May 1846 the plaintiff filed a bill of review to the decree of May 1844, dismissing the bill as to Beery; and in October 1847 Beery filed his answer, relying upon the same grounds of defence upon which he rested his demurrer.

In May 1848 the court directed a commissioner to state the accounts of the defendant Rader as committee of the lunatic. And these being returned, shewing the amount due from Rader to be 527 dollars 70 cents, with interest on 233 dollars 71 cents, a part thereof, from the 1st of July 1844 until paid, the cause was finally heard in May 1850, though the bill of review was not set for hearing, and there is no other indication that the case was heard on the bill of review, except that the cause was heard as to Beery, who was a defendant only in that case, along with the defendants in the original suit. Upon the hearing the court held that the bond executed in 1836 by Rader, Kratzer and Beery was a valid bond as to all of them, and that the execution of it released and discharged the sureties in the first bond. And it was therefore decreed that the plaintiff recover against these parties the sum of 527 dollars 70 cents, with interest according to the commissioner's report; and the bill was dismissed as to the defendants Pickering and Bowman's executor. From this decree Beery applied to this court for an appeal, which was allowed.

*Grattan*, for the appellant.
*Price*, for the appellee.

ALLEN, *J*. delivered the opinion of the court.

The court is of opinion, that to constitute a valid bond of the party, the intention to bind himself must appear on the face of the instrument; that the signature and seal form a part thereof, and furnish *prima facie* evidence that the person so signing and sealing the bond intended to make himself a party thereto, and to be bound by the stipulations thereof; although the name of the party so signing, sealing and delivering the bond may not be inserted in the penalty or recited in the condition. The case of *Bell* v. *Allen's adm'r*, 3 Munf. 118, does not actually decide that the bond there offered in evidence was not the bond of the security, because his name did not appear in the body of the instrument, but it was rejected, when offered in evidence, on the ground of an alleged variance between it and the bond described in the declaration. If, however, it is to be inferred that the case was decided upon the ground that the bond was invalid as to the surety for the cause aforesaid, the authority of the case is impaired by the decisions of this court in the cases of *Bartley* v. *Yates*, 2 Hen. &

1851.
July
Term.

Beery
v.
Homan's
committee.

1851.
July
Term.

Beery
v.
Roman's
committee.

Munf. 398; *Beale* v. *Wilson*, 4 Munf. 380; *Raynolds* v. *Gore*, 4 Leigh 276; and was in effect overruled in *Crawford* v. *Jarrett*, 2 Leigh 630. In that case the name of one of the sureties, Shrewsberry, did not appear in the body of the writing; and there was no blank left for the insertion of other names; which has sometimes been supposed to show an intention not to exclude other parties who have signed the instrument. Yet the said security was held bound upon proof that he executed the instrument with the intention of becoming a party thereto. In the case of a sealed instrument declared upon, proof of the execution thereof becomes necessary by the plea of *non est factum* at law (or the answer in chancery, if a case in equity), putting that fact in issue. The circumstance that the writing declared on in *Crawford* v. *Jarrett* was not under seal does not affect the principle involved in this question. The intention to become a party to, and be bound by the instrument, is the fact to be determined in either case. In this case the execution of the bond by the surety, Abraham Beery, was not denied by the answer, and therefore, in the opinion of the court, no further proof of its execution was necessary. The fact of execution, however, is conclusively established by the order of the County court, from which it appears that the principal, John Rader, appeared in court, and with Joseph Kratzer and Abraham Beery gave the security required; which bond was duly acknowledged by the parties thereto, and ordered to be certified.

The court is further of opinion, that as the order of the County court sets forth that the said John Rader appeared in court, and with the said Kratzer and Beery gave the security as required by the above order, and acknowledged a bond, which was ordered to be certified, the bond so acknowledged and certified constitutes a part of the record, and must be taken and construed with the order as shewing what was required by the

1851.
July
Term.

Beery
v.
Homan's
committee.

court. By the condition of the bond it appears that the said Rader was required to execute a new bond, and in pursuance thereof executed the bond in the bill and proceedings mentioned; and this distinguishes the present from the case of the *Greenesville Justices* v. *Williamson*, 12 Leigh 93. In that case the bond not being mentioned in the minute of the court to have been required, executed, or accepted, could not be regarded as part of the record; and so the order itself was the true and only record; and the new bond found in the office could not be looked to or considered for the purpose of ascertaining what was done by the court. The principal in this case was summoned to appear at the next succeeding court to give counter security; whereupon he appeared forthwith, and as the condition of the bond shews, being required to execute a new bond, thereupon executed the bond in question, which was received, acknowledged in court, and ordered to be certified. Whatever mode of relief the party may apply for, it is within the discretion of the court, under the act 1 Rev. Code, chap. 104, § 38, to require counter security or a new bond: and upon the execution of the new bond the securities to the former bond are discharged.

The court is further of opinion, that although it was irregular to proceed in the original cause until, by a decree on the bill of review, the decree sustaining the appellant's demurrer had been reversed and annulled, yet the irregularity is one more of form than substance. The answer of the appellant applied as well to the bill of review as to the original and amended bills, the cause was heard thereon, and the question of law presented by the bill of review was in effect adjudged by the final decree. The effect upon the rights of the parties is the same as if there had been first a formal order and decree on the bill of review, reversing and annulling the

1851.
July
Term.

Beery
v.
Homan's
committee.

former decree, and then a decree giving relief on the original and supplemental bills.

The court is therefore of opinion that there is no error in the decree, and it is adjudged and ordered that the same be affirmed, with damages and costs to the appellee.

---

### Lewisburg.

1851.
July
Term.

### LUSTER *v.* MIDDLECOFF *& als.*

(Absent *Cabell*, P. and *Moncure*, J.*)

August 26th.

1. The official bond of an executor contains in the penal part the names of the executor and several sureties, and there is no blank for the name of another; but it is signed and sealed by all those whose names are in the penal part, and also by another person. HELD: It is the bond of the person who executed it, though his name is not in the penal part.
2. A legatee being dead, a decree for the distribution of the estate should be in favour of his personal representative, and not of his distributee.

This was a bill filed in the Circuit court of Botetourt county by the legatees of John Middlecoff against Jacob Carper, the executor, and John Luster, Absalom C. Dempsey, and others, as his sureties, for the purpose of obtaining a settlement of the executorial account and a distribution of the estate. They charged that the executor was hopelessly insolvent; and they filed as exhibits with their bill certified copies of their testator's will and the executorial bond. The bond reads:

---

* The cause had been argued before his appointment.

1851.
July
Term.

Luster
v.
Middlecoff
& als.

Know all men by these presents, that we, Jacob Carper, Joseph K. Pitzer, John Luster and Matthew S. Robinson, are held and firmly bound," &c. This bond was executed by the parties before named, and also by Absalom C. Dempsey.

Dempsey appeared and demurred to the bill; and although no special cause of demurrer was stated, the attempt was to sustain it on the ground that Dempsey's name not having been inserted in the penal part of the bond or the condition it was not his bond. The Circuit court sustained the demurrer and dismissed the bill as to Dempsey.

The cause proceeded as to the other parties, and accounts were taken which shewed a considerable balance in the hands of the executor, which was apportioned among the legatees according to their interests; and there was a decree against the sureties in favor of the legatees for the sums ascertained to be due to them respectively. And thereupon Luster applied to this court for an appeal.

There were other questions in the cause which it is unnecessary to state.

*Lackland* and *Cooke*, for the appellant, insisted, that the bond was the bond of Dempsey, and therefore that the demurrer was improperly sustained. They referred to Bac. Abr., title Obligation, letter C; 2 Lomax Dig. 113; *Bartley* v. *Yates*, 2 Hen. & Munf. 398; *Beale* v. *Wilson*, 4 Munf. 380; *Crawford* v. *Jarrett*, 2 Leigh 630; *Holman* v. *Gilliam*, 6 Rand. 39; *Clark* v. *Blackstock*, 3 Eng. C. L. R. 159; Bailey on Bills 44; 1 Story's Equ. Jur. § 155, 162, 166, 168; Fonb. Equ. Book 1, ch 1, § 7; 1 Madd. ch. 49, 50; *Wiser* v. *Blackly*, 1 John. Ch. R. 607.

*F. T. Anderson*, for Dempsey, insisted, there was no evidence that he intended to bind himself; and

1851.
July
Term.

Luster
v.
Middlecoff
& als.

that the intention was necessary to bind him, and should appear on the face of the bond. *Catlin* v. *Ware,* 9 Mass. R. 218; 2 Lomax Dig. 206; Black. Com. Book 2, p. 298; 1 Tuck. Com. 234, 275; *Bell* v. *Allen's adm'r,* 3 Munf. 118. And he insisted that if Dempsey was not bound at law he was not bound in equity. *King* v. *Baldwin,* 2 John. Ch. R. 554; Buller, J., in *Straton* v. *Rastall,* 2 T. R. 367; *People* v. *Spraker,* 18 John. R. 390; *Moses* v. *Liblingarth,* 2 Rawle's R. 428; 2 Rob. Pr. 37: *Commonwealth* v. *Jackson's ex'or,* 1 Leigh 485; *Graves* v. *McNeil,* 1 Call 488; *Ward* v. *Webber,* 1 Wash. 279; *People* v. *Jansen,* 7 John. R. 331.

*J. T. Anderson* argued the case for Middlecoff's legatees, but they were not particularly interested in this question.

Baldwin, *J.* delivered the opinion of the court.

The court is of opinion, that upon the face of the bill of the plaintiff, and of the official bond of Jacob Carper, executor of John Middlecoff the elder, therewith exhibited, the defendant Dempsey must be regarded as one of the sureties in the said bond, he appearing to have executed the same, although his name is not therein mentioned as one of the obligors; and therefore that the Circuit court erred in sustaining the said Dempsey's demurrer and dismissing the bill as to him, instead of overruling said demurrer and requiring him to answer the bill, which error is to the prejudice of the appellant and of the appellees Pitzer and Robinson. And the court is further of opinion that there is no other error in the decree of the Circuit court, unless it be in decreeing in favour of the children and heirs of John Middlecoff the younger and the children and heirs of George Middlecoff, instead of their personal representatives; it being uncertain from the record whether the

1851.
July
Term.

Luster
v.
Middlecoff
& als.

said John Middlecoff the younger and George Middlecoff, sons and legatees of the said John Middlecoff the
elder, died before or after the death of their father ; and
unless it be in the omission of the decree to state that
the recovery in favour of Thomas J. and Harriet Middlecoff, infant children and heirs of the said John Middlecoff the younger, is by their guardian and next friend ;
in regard to which alleged errors no action of this court
need be had, inasmuch as for the error above declared, in
sustaining the demurrer of said Dempsey, the decree must
be reversed and the cause remanded to the Circuit court
for further proceedings to be there had, and any such
irregularities may be there corrected, after enquiry into
the facts bearing thereupon.   It is therefore adjudged,
ordered and decreed that so much of the said decree as
sustains the demurrer of the said Dempsey, and dismisses the bill of the plaintiffs as to him, be reversed and
annulled, with costs to the appellant against the appellees who were plaintiffs and said Dempsey.   And it is
further adjudged, ordered and decreed that the said demurrer be overruled, and that the said Dempsey do answer the bill of the plaintiffs; and that the reports of
the commissioner in regard to the matters of account
be recommitted, in order that the same may be reformed,
in respect to any responsibility which may appear on the
part of the said Dempsey or to any errors therein which
may be shewn by him.   And the cause is remanded to
the Circuit court to be proceeded in as above indicated.

### Lewisburg.

## MANN *v.* GWINN *& als.*

(Absent *Cabell,* P.)

August 26th.

In a proceeding of forcible entry and detainer, the court is constituted and then adjourns to a day certain. The court
failing to meet on the day to which it is adjourned, the
cause is not discontinued, but stands adjourned, by operation of law, to the next term of the County court.

This was a case of forcible entry and detainer in the
County court of Fayette, by William T. Mann against
Lockridge Gwinn and others. The warrant of the
justice directed the justices and the jury to be summoned to meet on the 14th of November 1849. Accordingly the justices met and constituted the court on
that day, and then, on the motion of the defendants,
the cause was continued until the 29th of March 1850,
to which day the court was adjourned.

The court did not meet on the 29th of March; but
at the regular term of the County court in June the
cause was tried, and there was a verdict and judgment
in favor of the plaintiff. The defendant then applied
to the Circuit court of Fayette county for a *supersedeas*
to the judgment, which was granted; and on the hearing of the cause in that court the judgment of the
County court was reversed, on the ground that the failure of the special court to meet on the 29th of March
operated as a discontinuance of the cause, and therefore
that the County court had no jurisdiction to try the case
at the June term of the court. Mann then applied to
this court for a *supersedeas,* which was awarded.

1831.
July
Term.

Mann
v.
Gwinn
& als.

*Price* and *Caperton*, for the appellant, and *Reynolds*, for the appellees, submitted the case.

ALLEN, *J.* delivered the opinion of the court.

The court is of opinion, that as by the act of 3d January 1834, p. 76, it is provided that whensoever the justices summoned to form a court for the trial of any case of forcible entry shall fail to meet, and no court be formed on the day appointed, such failure shall not operate a discontinuance of the cause, but the same shall stand continued until the next regular court of the county or corporation, whether monthly or quarterly; the act, by a fair construction, applies as well to a failure of the court to meet on the day to which it stood adjourned, as to a failure to meet on the day appointed in the warrant; and in either case the cause stands continued to the next County court, and no discontinuance is operated. It therefore seems to the court here that the judgment of the Circuit court reversing the judgment of the County court is erroneous; and the same is reversed, with costs to the plaintiff in error. And this court, proceeding to render such judgment as the Circuit court should have rendered, it is considered that the judgment of the County court be affirmed, with costs in the Circuit court expended.

## Lewisburg.

1851.
July
Term.

ALLEN *and* ERVINE *v.* MORGAN's *adm'r & als.*

(Absent *Cabell*, P. and *Daniel*, J.\*)

August 27th.

In a bill by a creditor against an administrator and his sureties, charging a *devastavit* by the administrator, and the liability of his sureties for it, though some of the sureties insist in their answer that under the circumstances one of the sureties is liable to the others, if they are liable to the plaintiff, though there is a decree for the plaintiff, and though it appears from the proofs that the *devastavit* was occasioned by a payment of a debt of inferior dignity to the surety sought to be charged, yet it is not a proper case for a decree between the co-defendants.

This was a bill filed in the Circuit court of Botetourt county by William Morgan against William A. Watson, administrator of Robert Tinsley, and his sureties in his official bond, among whom were Bernard Owen and the appellants, James S. Allen and Robert Ervine. The bill charged that the complainant had, in 1829, recovered a judgment against Robert Tinsley in his lifetime for 1055 dollars 96 cents, with interest from the 28th of January 1823, until paid. That Tinsley died in 1839. That a *scire facias* to revive the judgment against Watson, the administrator, was issued in April 1839, and served upon him. That the administrator had been guilty of a *devastavit* in paying away the assets of his intestate's estate. That Tinsley had in his lifetime executed a bond to the firm of Watson & Owens, of which firm the administrator was a partner, for the sum of 4721 dollars 57 cents; and they had,

_____

\*Judge *Daniel* had been counsel in other cases out of which this originated.

1851.
July
Term.

Allen and
Ervine
v.
Morgan's
adm'r
& als.

after Tinsley's death, assigned this bond to Bernard Owen, who brought suit upon it against the administrator; and that he, with the knowledge of the plaintiff's judgment, had confessed a judgment for the amount of the bond, with interest, for the purpose of giving the assignee of Watson & Owens a preference over the other creditors of the estate. That upon this judgment execution was immediately issued, and was levied on the slaves of the intestate in the hands of the administrator, which were sold to the amount of 2378 dollars 37 cents.

Watson answered, calling for proof of the plaintiff's judgment against Tinsley, and denying notice of it. But the *scire facias* to revive the judgment seems to have been served upon him before the confession of judgment to Owen. The defendant also set up other grounds of defence, which it is not necessary to notice.

Bernard Owen also answered, taking the same grounds of defence as Watson. The other sureties, Allen and Ervine, also answered, and insisted that if the plaintiff's judgment was entitled to priority over that of Owen, so that the application of the assets to the satisfaction of the latter was a *devastavit*, then that Owen should be held responsible personally to the creditors of Tinsley's estate, before resort was had to the other sureties; because said Owen was one of Watson's sureties, as administrator of Tinsley, and had no right to unite with him in the misapplication of the assets of the estate, and thereby to benefit himself by the injury of his co-sureties.

The accounts of the administrator were referred to a commissioner, who, excluding the payment to Owen's debt, reported a balance due to the estate of 2728 dollars 51 cents, with interest on 2617 dollars 31 cents, a part thereof, from the 31st of December 1840, until paid.

1851.
July
Term.

Allen and
Ervine
v.
Morgan's
adm'r
& als.

The cause came on to be heard in April 1846, when the court rendered a decree in favour of the plaintiff against the defendant Watson, and all his sureties. From this decree Allen and Ervine applied to this court for an appeal, which was allowed.

*Michie*, for the appellants, and *Boyd*, for the appellees, submitted the case upon notes. The questions were: 1st. Whether the court below should have decreed between the co-defendants, without a cross bill. And 2d. Whether, under any state of the pleadings, the other sureties of Watson were entitled to a decree over against Bernard Owen.

ALLEN, *J.* delivered the opinion of the court.

The court is of opinion that the only questions raised by the issue between the complainants and defendants in the court below were the *devastavit* charged to have been committed by the administrator of Robert Tinsley, and the joint liability of his sureties in his official bond therefor; and that upon the case as made out by the pleadings and proof between the said complainants and defendants, no decree could have been properly rendered as between the co-defendants. The court, therefore, without deciding upon the equities of the co-defendants, as amongst themselves, is of opinion, that as between the complainants and defendants in the court below, there is no error in the decree. It is therefore adjudged and ordered that the same be affirmed, with costs to the appellees.

## Lewisburg.

### RANKIN *v.* ROLER *& als.*

1851.
July
Term.

(Absent *Cabell,* P.)

#### August 29th.

An instrument, binding the parties thereto to pay a sum of money,
purports to be under their hand and seals; but it is signed
by one of the parties without a seal, and by the other parties with seals to their names. HELD: Upon demurrer,
that one action of debt may be brought against all the
parties.

This was an action of debt in the Circuit court of
Augusta county, brought upon the following paper:

$485. One day after date we promise and bind our-
selves, our heirs, &c., to pay to George Rankin or order
the sum of four hundred and eighty-five dollars, for
value received. As witness our hands and seals.

*Roler & Crawford.*

*Benjamin Weller,*      \*\*\*\*\*\*
                        \* Seal.\*
                        \*\*\*\*\*\*

*John W. Roler,*        \*\*\*\*\*\*
                        \* Seal.\*
                        \*\*\*\*\*\*

The action was in the name of George Rankin,
against all the other parties to the paper; and the declaration complained against Jacob C. Roler and John
Crawford, late partners under the firm of Roler & Crawford, Benjamin Weller and John W. Roler, and set out
the paper as a promissory note as to Roler & Crawford,
and as a writing obligatory as to Weller and John W.
Roler, and charged that all the parties had jointly promised and bound themselves to pay, &c.

The defendants appeared and pleaded payment; and
at another day they demurred to the declaration; the

1851.
July
Term.

Rankin
v.
Roler
& als.

plaintiff joined in the demurrer, and, upon the hearing of the case, the court rendered a judgment for the defendants, upon the demurrer. Whereupon the plaintiff applied to this court for a *supersedeas*, which was awarded.

*Fultz*, for the appellant, and
*Michie*, for the appellees, submitted the case.

DANIEL, *J.* If the plaintiff had in this case declared on the paper, of which *profert* is made, as the joint bond of Roler, Crawford, Weller and John W. Roler, I am not prepared to say that such a declaration might not have been good: For though there are but two scrolls to the paper, one of which is opposite to the name of Weller and the other opposite to the name of John W. Roler, and though the names of Roler and Crawford are signed as a firm, yet it might be that each of the last named parties signed the paper, and adopted one of the scrolls upon it as his seal; or that one of them executed the paper as the bond of each, being duly authorized by the other so to do. The plaintiff, however, does not so treat the transaction, and, most probably, because the facts of the case would not justify him in so treating it. He declares on the paper as the promissory note of Roler & Crawford, and the bond of Weller and John W. Roler; and the simple question presented is, whether upon such a paper a joint action of debt against all the parties will lie.

If such an action can be maintained, it must be because the undertaking of the parties is either joint and several or merely joint. That is not a joint and several undertaking the plaintiff in error concedes in his petition, and such a conclusion necessarily follows from the language of the paper, " We promise," &c. That it is not *one joint undertaking* is, I think, equally plain. The paper contains upon its face two instruments, and

1851.
July
Term.

Rankln
v.
Roler
& als.

its language is to be distributed and applied to each according to their respective characters.   Roler & Crawford by *their joint promissory note* promise to pay the debt ; and Weller and John W. Roler, by *their joint bond,* at the same time promise and bind themselves and their heirs to do the same thing.  The undertakings of the two sets of contractors are as distinct as if they had been evidenced by different papers.

Though the defendants in error have all agreed, at the same time, to pay the money, yet they have thought proper to sever in the use of the instruments selected to evidence that agreement.   Two have expressly reserved to themselves the right to enquire into the consideration of the agreement; whilst the other two have estopped themselves from so doing.   Roler & Crawford, upon the plea of "*nil debet,*" might have shewn that the paper was without consideration ; and, if so, they would have been discharged.   Now, one of the most familiar rules governing joint actions is, that the discharge of one of the defendants, upon a plea going to the original merits of the cause of action, operates a discharge of all ; and yet Weller and John W. Roler have by their contract estopped themselves from denying that there was a consideration, and have in effect stipulated that, though want of consideration should in any way appear, they would still stand bound.   To render judgment in such a supposed state of pleading, in favour of Roler & Crawford and against Weller and John W. Roler, would be to violate the rule, in respect to joint actions, just above mentioned ; whilst, on the other hand, to discharge the two latter would be to give them the benefit of a defence which, by giving a bond, they have voluntarily precluded themselves from making.   I cannot think that such a conflict between a well settled rule of pleading and an equally well established law of contract could arise in an action properly brought.

VOL. VIII.—5

1851.
July
Term.

Rankin
v
Roler
& als.

Again, Weller and John W. Roler have expressly covenanted to pay the debt; whilst Roler & Crawford
have at the same time assumed to do so. What is there
in the nature of the transaction to debar the plaintiff of
a right to sue the two former in covenant or the two
latter in *assumpsit?* Such a right seems to me to be
necessarily attached to the undertaking, and its establishment is wholly inconsistent with the idea of there being
but *one joint contract*, upon which there must be a
joint action against all the parties, if against any.

The question here is not one in respect to the joinder
of *actions*, but of *parties;* not whether an action of
debt on a bond and an action of debt on a note may
not be joined, but whether two parties who have undertaken to pay a debt, by bond, may be sued as joint
contractors with two others who have, at the same time,
undertaken to pay the same debt by promissory note;
not whether two distinct causes of action against the
same parties may not be blended in one suit, but whether
the two sets of parties have not united in a single cause
of action. The settlement of the former question does
not, therefore, tend in any degree to aid us in solving the
latter.

It seems to me, that whilst the defendants in error
have all contracted to pay the same debt, yet that the
respective rights and responsibilities of the parties, growing necessarily out of the different instruments by which
they have bound themselves, are of such a character
that they could not, in case of a controversy, be litiga-
ted and adjudged in one action without doing violence
to well established rules of pleading; and that the demurrer to the declaration on account of the improper
joinder of parties ought to have been, as it was, sustained by the court. I think, therefore, that the judgment ought to be affirmed.

MONCURE, *J.* delivered the opinion of the court.

The court is of opinion that the Circuit court erred

in sustaining the demurrer to the declaration. The
contract on which the suit was brought is a joint contract. The defendants contracted together, with the
plaintiff, for one and the same act, to wit, the payment
of the debt in the declaration mentioned; and it appears on the face of the contract that they intended to
become jointly liable. The fact that there is no seal
or scroll annexed to the signature of Roler & Crawford, and that there are scrolls annexed to the signatures of Benjamin Weller and John W. Roler, while
it makes the instrument a promissory note as to the
former, and a single bill obligatory as to the latter, does
not change the joint nature of the contract. Without
intending to decide in this case that several actions
might not be maintained upon the instrument, regard-
ing it in one action as the simple contract of Roler &
Crawford, and in another as the specialty of Benjamin
Weller and John W. Roler, the court is yet of opinion
that one action of debt may be maintained upon it
against all of the joint contractors; each of whom will
in such an action be entitled to make any defence which
he might make in a separate action. In this way the
intention of the parties is effectuated, multiplicity of
actions is avoided, and no injury or inconvenience is
occasioned to any person. Therefore it is considered
that the said judgment be reversed and annulled, and
that the plaintiff recover against the defendants his
costs by him expended in the prosecution of his writ
aforesaid here. And this court proceeding to give such
judgment as the said Circuit court ought to have given,
it is further considered that the demurrer to the declaration be overruled, and that a trial be had of the issue
in fact joined upon the plea of payment. And the
cause is remanded to the said Circuit court for further
proceedings to be had therein.

1851.
July
Term.

Rankin
v.
Roler
& als.

## Lewisburg.

### DUNCAN *v.* HELMS *& others.*

(Absent *Cabell*, P.)

**August 29th.**

A record to which neither the demandants or the tenant was a party is not even *prima facie* evidence against the tenant that the grantor in the deed to the demandant was heir at law of the grantee in the patent under which the demandant claimed title.

This was a writ of right in the Circuit court of Floyd county, brought by Madison B. Helms and others, who sued for John Belden, against Squire Duncan, to recover a tract of land of eight thousand acres. The tenant appeared and filed a plea, by which he defended his right to ninety acres of the land, and pleaded non-tenure as to the remainder. And the record states that the demandants filed their replication to the plea, and so the mise was joined; but the replication does not appear to have been in writing.

On the trial, the demandants claimed under a patent from the Commonwealth to Austin Nichols; and having introduced in evidence the copy of a record in a suit in equity in which John Belden was plaintiff and Daniel Nichols, alleged in that case to be the only heir at law of Austin Nichols deceased, and others, were defendants, the object of which suit was to obtain the naked legal title to a large tract of land, embracing the land in question, the equitable title having been previously conveyed, and in which there was a decree appointing a commissioner to convey the title to the plaintiff, the demandants moved the court to instruct the

1851.
July
Term.

Duncan
v.
Helms
& others.

jury that said record was *prima facie* evidence that the said Daniel Nichols was the heir at law of Austin Nichols, and that the legal title was in him; which instruction the court gave; and the tenant excepted.

There was a verdict and judgment for the demandants, and the tenant thereupon applied to this court for a *supersedeas*, which was allowed.

*The Attorney General* and *Staples*, for the appellant.
*J. B. J. Logan*, for the appellees.

DANIEL, *J.* delivered the opinion of the court.

The court is of opinion that it was not competent for the demandants on the trial to rely on the record of the suit in chancery between John Belden and Daniel Nichols and others, for the purpose of shewing that the said Daniel was the heir of Austin Nichols, and that the legal title to the land in controversy was in him; neither the demandants nor the tenant having been parties to said suit: And consequently, that the judge of the Circuit court erred in giving the instruction asked for by the demandants and excepted to by the tenant; and that for this error the judgment of the Circuit court ought to be reversed, the verdict set aside, and the cause remanded. Such being the opinion of the court, it becomes unnecessary to decide the other question presented in the petition, to wit, whether the issue on the first plea of the tenant was ever properly joined in the cause, and if not, whether the irregularity was cured by the verdict. The cause being remanded for a new trial on account of the erroneous instruction aforesaid, the judge of the Circuit court can, before such new trial is had, cause the alleged defect in the pleadings to be supplied by requiring the demandants to file the written replication required by the statute.

Judgment reversed with costs; verdict set aside, and

1851.
July
Term.

Duncan
v.
Helms
& others.

cause remanded for further pleadings and a new trial,
and with directions to the judge of the Circuit court
not to repeat, on such new trial, the instruction complained of, should it be again asked for by the demandants.

---

## Lewisburg.

### JENNINGS v. PALMER.

(Absent *Cabell, P.* and *Daniel, J.\**)

**August 30th.**

A surety holds a security for the repayment to him of the amount
of certain debts he has paid for his principal, and for his
indemnity as to another large debt for which he is surety.
He makes an arrangement with the creditor, whose debt
is yet unpaid, by which he pays a part of it; he assigns
with recourse to himself the debts he had paid for his
principal; and he also transfers the security held by him,
all of which is agreed to be taken in discharge of the debt
for which he is bound. It is obvious that at the time of
the transfer the surety is ignorant of the amount of the
security which he transfers; and when the fund is finally
ascertained, it proves to be much more than sufficient to
discharge the debts assigned with recourse to the surety,
and also the balance of the debt for which the surety had
been bound. HELD: That under the circumstances equity
will treat the assignment as a security for the benefit of
the creditor for the payment of the whole amount due on
his debt, but for nothing more.

By deed bearing date the 9th day of July 1838,
Thomas A. Fourquorean, an apothecary in the town of
Lynchburg, conveyed to David R. Edley his whole

---

*Judge *Daniel* had been counsel in a cause from which this case
originated.

stock of goods, and his interest in his mother's estate, for the purpose, as stated in the deed, of indemnifying Chancey Steen as his surety in a bond executed to James A. Meriweather, dated the same day with the deed, for the sum of 1753 dollars 85 cents, and payable six months after date, and as endorser of Fourquorean upon notes discounted at the banks in Lynchburg for 500 dollars more. This deed was duly admitted to record on the 12th of July.

On the     day of September 1838 Fourquorean executed another deed to Frederick Isbell, whereby he conveyed the same property in trust to pay, first, certain debts due and notes endorsed by P. & J. W. Dudley; second, a debt due to J. W. Dudley; thirdly, certain notes on which Robert Jennings was endorser, described in the deed as a note for 250 dollars, dated July 12th, 1838, payable sixty days after date, and endorsed by Robert Jennings and Joseph Marsh, another for 150 dollars, dated 5th of July 1838, on which Chancey Steen and Robert Jennings were endorsers, another for 300 dollars, dated the 31st of August 1838, endorsed by P. & J. W. Dudley and Robert Jennings, another for 150 dollars, dated July 5th, 1838, endorsed by Robert Jennings and Joseph Marsh, a like note for 150 dollars, dated 2d August 1838, with the same endorsers, and a note for 100 dollars, endorsed by Robert Jennings and held by Michael Hart, and also a bond due Reuben D. Palmer for 1460 dollars, on which Joseph Jennings and Tilden Reed were sureties; and fourth, to pay Marsh a debt due him of 689 dollars 7 cents. This deed was admitted to record on the 3d of September.

The trustee Isbell being about to sell the property conveyed in the deeds, Steen filed his bill in the Circuit court of Lynchburg to enjoin the sale, on the ground of his prior lien under the deed of the 9th of July 1838 to Edley. The injunction was granted, and in the progress of that cause the trust property was sold

and deposited in one of the savings banks in Lynchburg, subject to the order of the court.

Whilst this suit of Steen's was pending, and previous
to January 1844, Jennings had paid off the four notes
above mentioned on which he was the first or only endorser; and Palmer had instituted an action against
him in the Circuit court of Halifax county upon the
bond for 1460 dollars, mentioned in the deed of trust
to Isbell, on which Jennings and Reed were the sureties of Fourquorean; and Reed, as well as Fourquorean,
was insolvent.   On the 25th of January 1844 Palmer
and Robert Jennings, the latter acting by his brother,
William B. Jennings, entered into an agreement in
writing whereby Robert Jennings was to execute his
bond, with William B. Jennings as his surety, for 500
dollars, payable to Palmer on the 25th of January 1846,
with interest from the date of the agreement; to assign
to Palmer, with recourse to Jennings, the four notes of
Fourquorean which Jennings had paid, which were
then in the hands of his counsel in Lynchburg; and
also to assign to Palmer all his other interest in and to
all claims secured to him by the deed of trust executed by
Fourquorean to Isbell in 1838:  And Jennings further
bound himself to pay all the costs which had accrued
in the suit of Palmer against him upon the said bond,
except so much as had arisen from the employment of
more than one lawyer.   And in consideration of this arrangement Palmer agreed to stop the suit as soon as the
conditions were complied with; and that the arrangement, when complied with, should be in full of the bond
of Fourquorean on which Jennings and Reed were
sureties.   From this paper it appears the bond was executed on the 9th of March 1838, and that 60 dollars
had been paid upon it.

On the 27th of February 1844 Robert Jennings executed another paper, by which, in conformity with the
contract of the 25th of January, he assigned to Palm

the four notes aforesaid, with recourse to him, and he
also assigned to Palmer all his interest in the deed of trust to Isbell, which interest was first to be applied to
the payment of the said four notes, and the residue he assigned without recourse.

The case of *Steen* v. *Fourquorean & others* came on to be heard in November 1846, when the court held that the debt secured by the deed of the 9th day of July 1838 was usurious. A statement of the trust fund under the control of the court, and of the debts secured by the deed to Isbell, was then made, marked A A, from which it appeared that the fund to be divided among the beneficiaries in that deed amounted on the 12th November to                          $5749 41

The debts secured in the first and
    second class amounted at the
    same date to                          $1127 15
The amount of the four notes paid
    by Jennings,                             977 54
The amount of the bond due to
    Palmer,                                 2174 68
These were in the third class spe-
    cified in the deed.
The fourth class consisted of the
    debt due to Marsh,                      1011 91
And there was in addition the note
    endorsed by Steen and Jennings,
    as to the payment of which it
    was doubtful whether it was by
    Steen or Jennings,                       223 66
                             $5514 94

The court then made a decree, by which the bond claimed by Steen, and the deed of trust to secure it, were directed to be delivered up to be cancelled; and the trust fund was distributed among the beneficiaries in the deed to Isbell, according to and to the extent of their respective interests ; the decree being in favour of Palmer, as the assignee of Jennings, for the sum of 977 dollars 54 cents, the amount of the four notes paid by Jennings, and in favour of Jennings for 2174 dollars 68 cents, the amount of the bond of Palmer, and which Jennings had settled with him by the agreement of the 25th of January, and the assignment of the 27th of February 1844.

After the decree had been entered, the counsel for Palmer suggested that under the agreement and assignment aforesaid, Palmer was entitled to the decree for the sum of 2174 dollars 68 cents, and that if there was any doubt of Palmer's right, on the construction of these papers, that Jennings would state that such was the intention of the parties to the agreement ; and on his motion the court suspended the decree in favour of Jennings for thirty days, in order to give Palmer an opportunity to assert his claim, if any he had, in such mode as he might be advised to adopt.

In December 1846 Palmer filed his bill in the Circuit court of Lynchburg, against Jennings and the officer of the court who had the proceeds of the trust property in his hands, to enjoin the payment by the officer to Jennings of the sum of 2174 dollars 68 cents, as directed by the decree in the case of *Steen* v. *Fourquorean & als.* In his bill he stated the execution of the bond to him by Fourquorean, Reed and Jennings, and that the whole thereof, except 60 dollars, was due in 1843, at which time the two first named were insolvent ; his suit against Jennings, and the agreement and assignment of January and February 1844 ; the deeds of trust to Edley and Isbell, and the proceedings in the case of *Steen* v. *Fourquorean & others ;* and he charged that by the agreement and assignment he was entitled to the whole of Jennings' interest in the trust deed to Isbell ; that such was the intention of the parties to the said agreement and assignment, and, in pursuance

1851.
July
Term.

Jennings
v.
Palmer.

of such intention, Jennings, on the 25th of November 1846, gave to the plaintiff an order authorizing him to receive the money; but that notwithstanding said compromise and assignment Jennings had given notice to the officer not to pay over the money to the plaintiff, and demanded it for himself. The prayer of the bill was for an injunction, and for general relief. The injunction was granted. The order referred to in the bill, and which was exhibited with it, bore date the 25th November 1846, and recited that by the agreement of January 1844 it was Jennings's intention to convey to Reuben D. Palmer all his interest in and to everything coming to him under the deed of trust to Isbell, and then relinquished all the proceeds of said deed of trust in his favour, to said Palmer, and authorized the payment of the same for the benefit of Palmer.

Jennings in his answer denied that the agreement and assignment aforesaid was intended to transfer to Palmer so much of his interest in the trust fund as he was entitled to for having satisfied the bond to Palmer, and insisted that there was doubt at the time whether the two notes mentioned in the deed to Isbell on which Jennings was endorser, on one of them after the Dudleys, and on the other after Steen, had been paid by him, the payments made by him having been made by his agent and attorney in Lynchburg, who had collected monies due to him in that place; and that it was these debts to which the latter branch of the agreement referred; it being intended to give to Palmer the benefit of the payments if they had been made by Jennings, and only in that event. He went into a minute statement of the circumstances under which the paper dated the 25th of November 1846, and filed with the bill, was obtained from him. It is unnecessary for the purposes of this report to state the facts. The court below was of opinion that it was not obtained under such circumstances as vitiated it ; and this court thought it was entitled to no weight in deciding upon the rights of the parties.

When the cause came on to be heard, the court below perpetuated the injunction, and directed the officer in whose hands the trust fund was to pay to Palmer the sum of 2174 dollars 68 cents, with the accruing interest thereon. From this decree Jennings applied to one of the judges of this court for an appeal, which was allowed ; and by consent of parties, the case was sent to the court at Lewisburg.

The case was argued in writing by *Bouldin* and *Cooke*, for the appellant, and *Garland* and *Cabell*, for the appellee, and turned upon the true construction of the agreement of January, and assignment of February 1844. That question was considered as upon the terms of the writings themselves, and also in connection with the facts appearing in the record.

ALLEN, *J.* delivered the opinion of the court.

The court is of opinion, that by the literal terms of the agreement of the 25th January 1844, as carried into execution by the transfer of the 27th February 1844, it was the intention of the appellant to assign and transfer to the appellee Palmer all his interest secured by the deed of trust in the agreement referred to, embracing the amount paid by the appellant towards the discharge of the bond for which he was the security for the said Fourquorean for 1460 dollars ; yet said agreement and transfer were executed under such circumstances, as in a court of equity, to require it to be treated as a security for the benefit of the appellee for the payment of the whole amount due to him on his bond, and nothing more. It appears from the statement A A, referred to and made part of the decree in the case of Steen's administrator against said Fourquo-

1851.
July
Term.

Jennings
v.
Palmer.

rean and others, that the fund collected under said deed of trust, and under the control of the receiver, would have been sufficient on the 25th of January 1844, the date of the agreement aforesaid, to have discharged all the debts entitled to priority of satisfaction over said bond, and the balance left unpaid of said bond after crediting the same with the amount secured by said agreement, even if the validity of the prior deed of trust had been sustained. Of this fact it does not appear that either party was apprised : It certainly does not appear that the appellant, who resided at a distance from the scene of the transactions, knew any thing of the state of the fund, when to obtain a discharge he paid a large proportion of the bond, and agreed to transfer his interest in the deed, under which an amount was secured sufficient, under any aspect of the controversy, to discharge the balance due to the appellee on the bond ; nor is there any proof of knowledge of the true state of the facts on the part of the appellee. If known to him and concealed from the appellant it would have been a fraud ; but, in the absence of any proof of such knowledge, and from the fact that the appellant was required to transfer the notes or bonds in the agreement set out with recourse, it is the fair presumption that both parties were ignorant of the real state of facts, and the contract was entered into under a mutual mistake ; and it would be unjust, oppressive and inequitable to enforce it against the appellant according to the literal terms thereof ; and full justice is done to the appellee by holding it as a security for his benefit for the payment of the whole amount of his demand, with interest.

The court is further of opinion that the order of the 25th of November 1846 was obtained under circumstances which entitle it to no weight in deciding upon the right of the parties. The court is therefore of opinion that the decree of the Circuit court is erroneous, and it is adjudged, ordered and decreed that the same be reversed and annulled, and that the appellee pay to the appellant his costs by him expended in the prosecution of his appeal here. And the cause is remanded to the Circuit court with instructions to refer the same to a commissioner to ascertain the balance of principal and interest due to the appellee on the bond for 1460 dollars, after crediting the same with 60 dollars, the credit endorsed thereon; with 500 dollars, the amount of the bond given by the appellant and W. B. Jennings, his security, as of the 25th of January 1844, and with the sum of 977 dollars 54 cents on the 12th of November 1846, the sum decreed to be paid to the appellant for the use of the appellee by the decree of the 20th of November 1846 in the case of *Steen's adm'r v. Fourquorean & others.* For the balance due upon the bond after deducting said credits, together with the costs in the Chancery court, the appellee will be entitled to satisfaction out of the sum of 2174 dollars 68 cents, with the accruing interest thereon, mentioned in the decree appealed from, and the appellant will be entitled to the residue of said last mentioned sum, with the accruing interest thereon.

# Lewisburg.

## PRICE *v.* VIA's *heirs.*

(Absent *Cabell,* P.)

September 1st.

1. In an action on an award, if upon the face of the submission it does not clearly appear that the award does not cover the whole matter submitted, a demurrer to the declaration will not be sustained; but the defendant will be left to his plea of "no award"; to which the plaintiff may reply and shew that the award does cover the whole matter submitted.
2. So if the parties may have waived a decision on one branch of the matters submitted, and requested the arbitrators to decide.the other matters, though this is not stated in the declaration, a demurrer will not be sustained; but the plaintiff will be allowed to reply the facts to the plea of "no award."

This was an action of covenant brought by Barnett W. Price against James Via and others in the Circuit court of Patrick county, and removed from thence to the Circuit court of Montgomery. The declaration was upon a covenant by which the parties bound themselves, in the penalty of 600 dollars, to submit certain matters in dispute between them to the award of arbitrators, and to abide by their award.

The covenant was entered into in August 1841, and was, in substance, that whereas a controversy has arisen between the parties in relation to a certain tract of land claimed by the heirs of William Via deceased, they claiming the land, amounting to two hundred and ninety-one acres, under an entry and patent to John Ingram sen'r, deceased, and Price claiming under a large survey made by John Ward previous to the one made by Ingram, and the parties being then at law about their respective rights to said land, covenanted with each other

1851.
July
Term.

1851.
July
Term.

Price
v.
Via's
heirs.

to dismiss the suit and refer the matter to five disinterested men chosen by the parties, viz.: Thomas Penn, &c., &c.; and it is agreed that these men so chosen for the purpose shall meet on the land on a day appointed by the parties; and a surveyor shall run the land according to the papers which may be produced by the parties; and after the parties have produced their evidence, and the same has been heard by the arbitrators, they shall decide to whom the land belongs in law and equity; and their judgment shall be final between the parties. And the parties agree that the costs of the suit aforesaid, and of the arbitration, shall be paid by the losing party. And the parties further agree that whereas the patent the heirs of William Via claim under seems defective in respect to the proper courses to cover the two hundred and ninety-one acres claimed in the patent, and the said Price has laid a warrant on that part of the land which the patent seems not to cover, and contends against the said heirs of William Via for the right to said land, the parties jointly agree to leave the same matter to the aforesaid arbitrators to be decided by them, after having the same surveyed and hearing the evidence they may think proper to hear. And the parties bind themselves to abide by the award of the arbitrators, and that the expenses of the survey and the compensation to the arbitrators shall be paid by the losing party, who shall relinquish all right, title and interest in said lands, so far as to comply with the award of said arbitrators.

The arbitrators proceeded to hear the case and made an award, which is as follows, viz.:

We, the undersigned arbitrators, mutually chosen by Barnett W. Price, sen'r, on the one part, and the heirs of William Via deceased, on the other part, to settle all matters of difference between the parties in a certain writ of right depending in the Circuit court of Patrick county, in which the said Barnett W. Price is demand-

1851.
July
Term.

Price
v.
Via's
heirs.

ant and the said heirs are tenants, have, after hearing all the evidence adduced by both parties, agreed unanimously that the said B. W. Price has more right to recover the land demanded by him than the said heirs have to hold it; and that he therefore recover of them the land demanded by him in his said writ as he demands it, and his costs about his suit by him expended. Given under our hands and seals this the 14th of September 1841 : And the award was signed and sealed by the arbitrators.

The declaration set out the submission and award as above given, and laid the breach of the covenant first in the refusal to abide by the award as a final decision of the suit for said land, but that they had always since the rendering the award defended, and continued to defend, the said suit; to settle which the said covenants and award were made; second, in their failure to pay the costs of the suit, survey and award; and third, in their failure to relinquish all right, title and interest in the land aforesaid.

The defendants appeared and craved oyer of the covenant and award, and then demurred to the declaration; and stated as causes of demurrer, that the award set out in the declaration does not correspond to the submission contained in the covenant, but varies therefrom in this, that the said award is parcel only of the things submitted to arbitrament by the covenant aforesaid.

The plaintiff joined in the demurrer; and when the cause came on to be heard the court sustained the demurrer and gave a judgment for the defendants. Whereupon Price applied to this court for a *supersedeas*, which was awarded.

*Eskridge* and *John T. Anderson*, for the appellant. and *Staples*, for the appellee, submitted the case.

VOL. VIII.—6

1851.
July
Term.

Price
v.
Via's
heirs.

ALLEN, *J.* delivered the opinion of the court.

It seems to the court here, that upon the bond of submission taken by itself and without reference to the record of the suit referred to in the condition, it does not clearly appear that both the subjects referred to the arbitrators were not involved in and embraced by the controversy pending between said parties in court, and that the plaintiff in error was not asserting in said action a title to the whole of the said tract of land of 291 acres, partly in virtue of the Ward survey, and in part under the warrant referred to. If such were the fact the award covered the whole matter referred to the arbitrators: and whether such was the fact, or if not, and the latter branch of the submission was of an independent controversy not involved in the suit, whether the parties may not have waived a decision thereon, and requested the arbitrators to make their award on the subject in controversy in said suit alone, are matters which can only be shewn by proper pleadings in the cause, and which the plaintiff in error should have an opportunity of shewing by his replication to a plea of no award; and that it was not incumbent to set out such matters in his declaration; the award itself on its face purporting to be of the whole matter submitted. It is therefore considered that the judgment of the Circuit court is erroneous, and the same is reversed with costs. And this court, proceeding, &c., it seems to the court that the declaration and matters and things therein contained are sufficient for the plaintiff to have judgment. It is therefore considered that the demurrer to the declaration be overruled; and the cause is remanded to said Circuit court, with leave for the defendants to plead, and for further proceedings: Which is ordered to be certified.

DANIEL, *J.* dissented.

## Lewisburg.

### Higginbotham v. Cornwell.

1851.
July
Term.

(Absent *Cabell*, P.)

September 2d.

1. Husband during the coverture sells and conveys land with
   general warranty, but his wife does not join in the deed.
   By his will he gives his whole estate, real and personal, to
   his wife for her life, remainder to his children. Held:
   She is entitled to take under the will, and also to have her
   dower in the land sold.
2. That a provision for a wife in the will of her husband shall be
   held to be in lieu of her dower, the will must so declare in
   terms; or the conclusion from the provisions of the will
   ought to be as clear and satisfactory as if it was expressed.

This was a suit instituted in the Circuit court of
Monroe county on the 19th of January 1847, by Jane
Higginbotham against William Cornwell. In her bill
she charged that her late husband, Thomas Higginbotham, had, during their marriage, sold and conveyed
to Cornwell a tract of land in the county of Monroe.
That she had not united in the deed. That Thomas
Higginbotham died in 1846; and she was therefore entitled to dower in said land, which she prayed might be
assigned to her. With her bill she exhibited the deed
to Cornwell, which bore date on the 4th of November
1807.

In May 1847 Cornwell answered the bill, admitting
the sale and conveyance of the land to him; but he
alleged that Thomas Higginbotham had left a will,
which had been duly admitted to probat, by which he
bequeathed his whole estate, real and personal, to the
plaintiff for her life, and at her death to his son and
two daughters. That the plaintiff had accepted the

1851.
July
Term.

Higginbot-
ham
v.
Cornwell.

provision made for her by the will, as she had failed to
renounce that provision within a year from the testator's death: And he insisted that the provision made
for her by the will was in lieu of dower. And he exhibited a copy of the will, which was presented for
probat at the February term of the County court of
Monroe. The provision for the plaintiff is as stated in
the answer.

The cause came on to be heard in October 1847,
when the court dismissed the bill. Whereupon Mrs.
Higginbotham applied to this court for an appeal,
which was allowed.

*N. Harrison*, for the appellant.
*Lackland*, for the appellee.

BALDWIN, J. delivered the opinion of the court.

It appears in this case from the testator's will, that
after charging his estate, real and personal, with the
payment of his debts, he devised the same to his wife
for life, with remainder to his children. Upwards of
thirty years before the making of his will, he had sold
and conveyed, with general warranty, a tract of land to
the appellee, but his wife did not unite in the conveyance. The sale and conveyance to the appellee are in
no wise mentioned or alluded to in the will. Shortly
after the testator's death, this suit was brought by the
appellant to recover her dower in the land so sold and
conveyed to the appellee. And the defence made by
the answer is, that the widow is barred of the dower
claimed by the provision made for her in the will,
which was intended by the testator to be in lieu of
dower of all the lands which he at any time owned;
which provision it is averred she has accepted. The
will of the testator and his deed of conveyance to the
appellee are the whole evidence in the cause. And the
question presented by the record is, whether the widow

1851.
July
Term.
———
Higginbot-
ham
v.
Cornwell.

is entitled to recover the dower claimed, and also to retain the provision made for her by the will.    If she is,
then her acceptance or refusal of that provision is a
matter wholly immaterial.

The dower provided by law in behalf of a widow,
by which is secured to her one third of all the lands
of her husband of which he was at any time seized
during the coverture, is paramount to all conveyances,
incumbrances, contracts, debts or liabilities of the husband.    But as there is no obligation upon him to make
a greater provision for her than that which is conferred
by the law, it is competent for him, in the exercise of
his testamentary power in her behalf, to couple it with
the condition that it shall be a substitute for and stand in
lieu of her legal dower in the whole or any part of his
estate, and thus propose to become the purchaser of the
latter ; and then if she accepts the devise, she takes it
with the condition thereto attached, or if she rejects
the condition, she thereby rejects the devise itself; and
so she cannot have both the legal dower and the devise
which she accepts as its substitute.    And the devise in
her favour may thus be made conditional by its express
terms or by a clear and necessary implication of the
testator's intent to that effect, to be derived from the
will.    But as the exercise of a testator's testamentary
bounty in behalf of his wife, beyond or irrespective of
the provision made for her by law, is natural and frequent, it is not allowable to infer an intent on his part
to the contrary from other parts of the will, by conjecture or probability : the conclusion ought to be as satisfactory as if it were expressed.

This clear and necessary implication, which puts the
widow upon her election, is to be derived from provisions of the will which would be defeated or disturbed
by allowing her to claim in both characters of devisee
and dowress : for example, if a testator devises his estate, or a part of it, to his wife and others, to be equally

1851.
July
Term.

Higginbot-
ham
v.
Cornwell.

divided amongst them, the equality required would be
defeated if she were permitted to claim one third of
the property so devised as her dower, and also a third
of the remaining two thirds under the will.  But a
mere disappointment of the expectations of others under the will does not put the widow to her election: as
in the case of a devise by the testator to her of a specific part or portion of a farm, say a moiety, and of the
other moiety to his children.  In that case the widow
may take her moiety under the will and one third of
the other moiety under the law, though it may perhaps
have been his design that she should have but a moiety
of the whole: there being no plain and necessary implication that the children were not to take subject to
her right of dower.

In the present case, the purchaser from the testator
in his lifetime was in no wise an object of his testamentary care or bounty.  There is no devise to him of
the property he had purchased, nor any indemnity provided for him by the will against the assertion of the
widow's right of dower.  That right of dower was not
and could not have been even conveyed to him by the
husband, and it is only by force of the warranty, express
or implied, of the latter, that he could have any claim
against his estate for compensation, in the event of
eviction by the paramount claim of the widow.  Such
a liability of the husband's estate under his contract
stands upon the same footing as his debts and contracts
generally, and furnishes no implication of an intent on
the part of the husband to bar his widow's right of
dower by the provision made for her by his will.  A
testator is understood to speak of his real property as
of the date of his will, and of his personal property as
of the time of his death ; and how can we know in
this case that the testator had in his mind at the date
of his will real property which was no longer his, but
had been sold and conveyed by him many years before

1851.
July
Term.

Higginbot-
ham
v.
Cornwell.

to another; or if it was present to his thoughts, that
he recollected the failure of his wife to unite in the
deed to the purchaser; or if he did, how can we safely
infer an intent to deprive her of her lawful right in the
subject by a testamentary provision in her favour in regard to his remaining property?

Nor is there any incompatibility of a liability of the
husband's estate, by reason of the widow's eviction of
the purchaser, with the provisions of the will. The
devise to her, it is true, is of all the testator's real and
personal estate during her life; which is liable to be
diminished by a claim of the purchaser, if he should
choose to assert it, upon the covenant of warranty in
the deed. But there is no repugnancy in such diminu-
tion of the value of her interest in the estate under the
will, nor of that of the devisees in remainder, if that
were material, with the assertion of her right of dower
against the purchaser; and indeed it is entirely compatible as well with the charge upon it in the will in
behalf of creditors, as with that which is given them
by operation of law.

It cannot be that the claim of a purchaser from the
husband in his lifetime, founded merely upon the warranty of the latter, to compensation out of his estate,
in case of eviction by the widow, falls within any rule
of equity requiring her to elect between her right of
dower under the law and the provision made for her
in the testator's will: for in equity the rule of election
is also a rule of compensation, and not one of forfeiture.
It is applicable only to the case of a beneficiary under
the will, the provision in whose favour is defeated by
the enforcement of the claim against the will; and then
invariably the defeated devisee or legatee receives compensation out of the claim under the will, so far as it
may extend, or be requisite, of the claimant who de-
feats him; and if there be any surplus, the latter is entitled to receive it. Now how can such compensation

1851.
July
Term.

Higginbot-
ham
v.
Cornwell.

be made to a purchaser from the husband in his lifetime? He is not designated in the will, as is the case
with the defeated devisee or legatee; and can be no
more entitled to the compensation than any other purchaser from the husband. Suppose, then, the fund for
compensation be exhausted by the claim of such a purchaser, where is another purchaser of other land from
the husband to look for redress, and by what rule can
he be relieved, unless it be by a rule of forfeiture?

The court is therefore of opinion that the decree of
the Circuit court is erroneous in dismissing the appellant's bill, instead of sustaining and enforcing her claim
of dower, and extending to her such other and consequent relief as it may appear she is entitled to; therefore reversed with costs, bill reinstated, and cause remanded for further proceedings in conformity with the
foregoing opinion and decree.

---

## Lewisburg.

## CALHOUN v. PALMER.

(Absent *Cabell*, P.)

### September 4th.

A gives and conveys to his son B a lot of land, on which is a mill
    seat. B then applies to the County court for leave to build
    a mill and dam, and when the inquest meets on the land
    A attends, and when the jury propose to level the stream,
    to ascertain how high B may be permitted to build his
    dam, A tells them he had levelled it, and that B may be
    permitted to build a dam twelve feet high without flowing
    the water back on the land of any person but A; that
    such a dam will hurt no one but himself, and he does not
    believe it will hurt himself. The jury act upon his opin-
    ions and information, and allow B to build a dam twelve
    feet high, and report that it will inflict no damage on any
    person: and this inquisition is confirmed by the court, and
    leave is given to build the dam. B builds his dam ten feet
    high. Afterwards he raises the water about six inches by

putting boards on the top of the dam; and of this A complains, and B takes them off; and in the ten years B keeps the mill he does not attempt to raise the dam. A becoming embarrassed B determines to sell the property to relieve him; and A adds twenty acres to that owned by B, and they join in the conveyance of the whole to C. After C takes possession of the mill he ascertains that the inquisition authorized the dam to be built twelve feet high, and he elevates it 8 inches, which seriously injures the land of A which lies immediately above on the stream, where upon A sues C for the damages occasioned by the raising of the dam. HELD:

1st. That the inquest and judgment of the court is no bar to an action for damages sustained by A which were not actually foreseen and estimated by the inquest.

2d. That as C relied on the inquisition and judgment of the court authorizing the dam, as the ground of his defence, it is not competent for him to deny the ownership of the land by B at the time of said proceedings, or to assert the continued ownership of the land by A.

3d. That the right of A to recover damages for the injury arising from raising the dam by C is not defeated by the conduct of A at the time the inquest was taken.

4th. That the fact that B did not raise the dam in the first instance to the height authorized by the inquest did not have the effect of precluding him from raising it to the full height authorized by the inquest, provided by so doing he did not occasion injury to others.

5th. That A having united in the conveyance to C, he cannot recover damages against C for any injury done him by any reflow of the water to the extent the injury existed at the time of said conveyance.

This was an action of trespass on the case, brought by William Calhoun against Philip O. Palmer, in the Circuit court of Augusta county. The injury complained of was that the defendant, who owned a mill on the Middle river, immediately below the land of the plaintiff, had raised his dam, so that the land of the plaintiff was overflowed, and the health of his family injuriously affected.

On the trial of the case the plaintiff proved that the defendant purchased the mill and milldam mentioned in the declaration in 1844; at which time the dam did not exceed ten feet in height. That after his purchase he had raised the dam; but that it was not yet more than twelve feet in height. And he proved that his land had been seriously injured by the increased height of the dam. The defendant then offered in evidence a deed by which the plaintiff conveyed the land on which the mill and dam was situate, to his two sons, William B. and James W. Calhoun; and also a deed, in which the plaintiff and his said two sons and their wives united, to convey to the defendant the land conveyed to the sons, and about twenty acres more adjoining, taken from the land of the plaintiff. And the defendant then offered in evidence the record of the proceedings upon a writ of *ad quod damnum* in the County court of Augusta, upon the application of William B. and James W. Calhoun to have permission to erect a dam for a mill, it being the same which was the subject of controversy in this case, by which the jury authorized them to raise the dam twelve feet from the foundation, and found by their inquisition that it would not injure any person: and upon the return thereof the court had authorized them to build the mill and dam in accordance with the inquest of the jury. To the introduction of this record the plaintiff by his counsel objected, on the ground that as the record shewed that the damages which he had sustained had not been foreseen and estimated by the jury, that proceeding could not be a bar to the plaintiff's action. But the court overruled the objection, and admitted the evidence, not as constituting of itself a bar to the recovery of damages by the plaintiff, but as a link in the chain of evidence which the defendant's counsel alleged they were prepared to adduce, and by which they expected to establish that the plaintiff was personally present when the inquest was taken, was

fully apprised of said inquest and order of court, and
acquiesced in and assented to them; and that William
B. and James W. Calhoun had proceeded within one
year to erect their dam and mill, and had finished it
within three years; and that the defendant, after he
had purchased the property, finding that the dam was
not twelve feet high, had proceeded to raise it to a
height not exceeding twelve feet. To this opinion of
the court admitting the evidence, the plaintiff excepted.

The defendant then offered parol testimony to prove
that the plaintiff was present when the inquest was
taken, and assented to the action of the jury, and aided
them in their examinations: that he suggested twelve
feet as the height of the dam, and when they proposed
to ascertain, by actual levelling, how far the water would
be flowed back by the dam, he stated that he had himself levelled it, and that the dam would flow back the
water to a particular point, which he shewed to the
jury; and he said that it would not back the water on
the lands of any one but himself, and that nobody but
himself would be injured, and that he was satisfied he
would not be injured by it. To the introduction of
this evidence the plaintiff objected, but the court overruled his objection, and he excepted.

After all the evidence had been introduced, the plaintiff moved the court to instruct the jury as follows,
viz. :

1st. If the jury shall believe, from the evidence in
the cause, that the milldam in the declaration mentioned was established by an order of the County court of
Augusta, upon a writ of *ad quod damnum*, and an inquisition and verdict thereupon, had upon the petition
of William B. Calhoun and James W. Calhoun, who
were at the time the owners in fee simple of the mill
seat, and that the plaintiff William Calhoun was not
in any manner interested in the property, and was not
a party to the said proceedings, then the said writ, ver-

dict, and order of court cannot operate as a bar to this action, unless the damages now claimed by the plaintiff were actually foreseen and estimated by the jury upon the said inquest. And any acts or declarations of the plaintiff at the time of the inquest, indicating his assent to or approbation of the act of the jury, but constituting no part of the record and proceedings upon the said writ, could not operate as a bar to any subsequent action by him for damages sustained, unless such acts or declarations amounted to a contract with the said William B. and James W. Calhoun, founded upon a consideration, whereby the said plaintiff bound himself not to claim such damages: And in considering such acts and declarations of the plaintiff, the jury must take them all together as fixing the terms, conditions and limitations of such contract.

2d. And if the jury shall believe, from the evidence in the cause, that after the said writ, inquisition and order of court, and after the supposed contract so made by the acts and declarations of the plaintiff, the said William B. and James W. Calhoun went on to erect the said dam to a height short of the twelve feet allowed by the inquest, viz., to the height of ten feet, and shortly afterwards attempted to raise it still higher; that the plaintiff objected to such increase of elevation, on the ground that it would injure him to an extent not foreseen by the jury, or by any of the parties at the time of the inquest; and that the said William B. and James W. Calhoun, in consideration of such injury, agreed with the plaintiff that they would not further increase the elevation of said dam; and that in fact the said William B. and James W. Calhoun did not afterwards, during their ownership of the property, which was about ten years, attempt further to elevate said dam; and that the dam in its then condition was sold and conveyed to the defendant with the mill and its appurtenances: then the said William B. and James W. Cal-

houn had no right, at the time of the said sale and conveyance, to increase the height of said dam, so as to
damage the lands or other property of the plaintiff, and
could not convey such a right to any other person ; and
no such right could pass by a deed conveying the mill
with its appurtenances, nor could the plaintiff, by uniting in the deed and warranty, upon such conveyance,
grant any such right, without express words to that
effect.

These instructions the plaintiff by his counsel moved
the court, in the first place, to give as a whole, and that
being refused, he offered each of them separately ; and
the court having refused to give either, he excepted to
both opinions of the court.

The plaintiff by his counsel then moved the court
to instruct the jury as follows, viz.:

1st. If the jury shall believe, from the evidence in
the cause, that the milldam in the declaration mentioned was authorized in 1831 by an inquest and order of the County court of Augusta, regularly and legally made, authorizing it to be raised to the height of
twelve feet from the foundation ; that the parties applying therefor began to build the same within one year,
and finished it within three years after such leave of
the court obtained, so that it was in good condition for
the public use, but to a height much less than twelve
feet, say nine or ten feet ; that within a few years after
such leave obtained, the said parties applying for leave
undertook to raise the said dam five or six inches over
the height to which it was first finished, as aforesaid, but
yet under the height of twelve feet ; that the plaintiff
objected to said last mentioned raising, on the ground
that it would injure and damage his lands, and that
thereupon, and in consideration thereof, the said parties, being still the owners of said mill and dam, ceased
from their undertaking, and never again attempted to
raise said dam ; that said parties applying for leave held

and owned said mill and dam until the year 1844, when they, in conjunction with the plaintiff, sold and conveyed and warranted said mill and dam, with other lands, to the defendant, and that the defendant afterwards, viz., some twelve or eighteen months after his said purchase, and before this suit was brought, without any new writ of *ad quod damnum*, or leave of the court, proceeded to raise said dam, and did raise it higher, thereby causing damage to the plaintiff, over and above any damage resulting to the plaintiff from the dam as it originally stood, then the jury must find for the plaintiff.

2d. If the jury shall believe, from the evidence in the cause, that the plaintiff was present with the jury of inquest who acted in 1831, and rendered a verdict authorizing the erection of the dam in the declaration mentioned, which verdict was the foundation of the leave afterwards given by the court to build the dam ; that he aided and directed the jury in their action and examination on that occasion ; that he had previously levelled the water above said dam, and told the jury he had done so, and that he dispensed with such examination by them ; that he said to the jury that no one could be injured but himself, and that he did not believe he would be injured by raising said dam ; that he then and there consented that the jury should fix the height of the dam in their verdict at twelve feet ; that after said leave was granted, the parties applying therefor went on to begin, and finished the same within the time allowed by law, to the height of only nine or ten feet ; that afterwards they raised the dam some inches higher, being still owners thereof, whereupon the plaintiff remonstrated and forbade them ; that they at once yielded, abated the additional height, and continuing owners of said mill property and dam for many years afterwards, viz., until the year 1844, never afterwards attempted to raise the dam higher ; that the defendant purchased said mill property and dam in 1844, which, together with several acres of adjacent land of the plaintiff, was conveyed to the defendant by a joint deed from the parties who had applied for leave to build the dam and the plaintiff, with general warranty of title; and that the defendant, after the lapse of twelve or eighteen months from the date of his purchase, and before the institution of this suit, raised the said dam to an additional height of five or six inches, without any new leave of court granted, whereby the plaintiff suffered damage; then, from the foregoing state of facts, the jury are well warranted in inferring that any consent, if proven to have been given by the plaintiff at the time of the inquest, only extended to the raising of the dam to the height to which it was originally raised as aforesaid, and does not bar his right of action for damages for raising it to an additional height.

But the court refused to give either of the said instructions, and the plaintiff again excepted.

After the court had refused to give the instructions set out in the foregoing exceptions, the defendant moved the court to instruct the jury as follows, viz.:

If the jury believe, from the evidence in this cause, that the plaintiff advised and prompted the application by his sons, one (if not both) of whom was an infant at the time of the application for the writ of *ad quod damnum*, and other proceedings on the petition for the establishment of the mill and dam in the declaration mentioned; and that the plaintiff was present when the jury were acting in regard to the assessment of damages, and aided them, and suggested the height of the dam twelve feet, and when the jury were about to level the water, to see how far it would be dammed back on the land of plaintiff, the plaintiff then said he had himself levelled the water, and ascertained that it would flow it back to a particular point, which he then shewed to the jury, and said that it would not injure any one but him, and that he claimed no damages; and that by rea-

son thereof the jury found their verdict, awarding him
no damages, to which the plaintiff assented, such assent and agreement to said verdict is sustained by the
consideration of benefit to plaintiff's sons, who were
the objects of his bounty, and whose interests were intended to be promoted by the establishment of said mill
and dam, and will be sufficient to bar the plaintiff from
obtaining damages incurred by reason of the erection of
said dam : Which instruction the court gave, and the
plaintiff excepted.

The plaintiff then moved the court to give to the
jury the following instruction :

The writ of *ad quod damnum*, verdict, and order of
court, authorizing a milldam to be raised to a certain
height, named and designated in the verdict, only con-
fers the right upon the applicant and his assigns to
erect the dam to the height thus designated, subject to
the right of adjacent tenants to their action for all damages occasioned thereon, not actually foreseen and estimated by the jury of inquest; and such right to raise
the dam becomes appurtenant to the land on which
leave is given to raise it, subject to the said right of the
adjacent tenants.

If, therefore, such land is sold by the party acquiring
such right to erect a dam, with general warranty of the
title and appurtenances thereto, and the purchaser subsequently elevates the dam to a height within that authorized by the verdict and order of court giving leave,
so that damages not actually foreseen and estimated by
the jury of inquest are suffered by an adjacent tenant,
who sues for and recovers the same, the covenants of
such deed are not thereby broken, and no action thereupon accrues to such vendee against such vendor on
said covenants.   But the court refused to give the instruction ; but instead thereof instructed the jury, that
the jury of inquest having estimated and allowed no
damages to the plaintiff, upon the writ of *ad quod dam-*

*num,* their verdict presents no bar to the recovery of damages in this action, unless the plaintiff be precluded from their recovery upon other grounds.

If the jury shall be satisfied, from the evidence, that the plaintiff was the real owner of the land on which leave was asked to erect the mill, and the real applicant for the writ, and that his sons were only nominally the legal owners, and only nominal or ostensible applicants for the writ of *ad quod damnum ;* and that no damages were allowed by the jury of inquest, not only because none were claimed, but because, on the contrary, damages were disclaimed or waived, whether by parol, by writing, or by deed ; and that after the privilege to erect the dam and build the mill was established by the inquest or verdict of the jury and the judgment of the court thereupon, the plaintiff united in selling, conveying and warranting the premises with its appurtenances to the defendant, received the cash payment of the purchase money, and receipted for it in his own name, and took bonds for the deferred instalments payable to himself, the plaintiff, by reason of such ownership, and disclaimer or waiver of damages, and by reason of his sale and conveyance by deed with warranty to the defendant, is precluded from any recovery against the defendant for any damages resulting to himself from the dam of the height not exceeding twelve feet, that being the height ascertained by the verdict of the jury of inquest ; and any private understanding or agreement between the plaintiff and his sons, before their sale to the defendant, limiting or restricting their rights and privileges under the inquisition, of which the defendant had no notice at the time of the purchase, cannot impair or derogate from his right to a dam of the altitude fixed by the jury of inquest, however valid and obligatory such agreement or understanding may have been between the father and the sons before they united in selling and conveying to a purchaser without notice.

To the opinion of the court refusing the instruction asked, and giving the instruction given, the plaintiff again excepted.

After the court had refused the instruction asked by the plaintiff, and given its own instruction as mentioned in the last exception, the plaintiff's counsel moved the court to give the following instructions:

The fact that the plaintiff united in selling and conveying and warranting the mill, the dam and premises in the declaration mentioned, with the appurtenances, to the defendant, standing by itself, will not preclude him from recovering in this action. If the jury believe, from the evidence, that the plaintiff was not, at the time of the verdict or judgment by the County court, giving leave to erect the dam in the declaration mentioned, the real owner of the land on which said dam was to be erected, but that he had made a *bona fide* advancement thereof to his sons, William B. and James W. Calhoun; and that the plaintiff did not before the jury disclaim or waive damages, or that if he did, he received no consideration therefor; then, though the plaintiff afterwards united with his said sons in a conveyance to the defendant of said lands, with general warranty of title and appurtenances, he is not thereby barred of his right to bring this suit. But the court refused to give the said instructions, and the plaintiff again excepted.

The jury then found a verdict for the defendant, and there was a motion by the plaintiff for a new trial, which the court overruled, and gave a judgment on the verdict for the defendant; and the plaintiff again excepted, and applied to this court for a *supersedeas*, which was allowed.

From the facts stated in the exceptions, it appears that in October 1831 the plaintiff gave and conveyed to his two sons, William B. and James W. Calhoun, twenty acres of land, including the site of the mill and dam which was the subject of the suit. One of these sons was about eighteen or nineteen years old, and the other a few years older.   In November 1831 they applied to the County court of Augusta for leave to build a milldam across the Middle river; and a writ of *ad quod damnum* was directed.   When the jury of inquest met upon the premises, the sons being young, the plaintiff was present and managed the business, shewing the premises and making explanations to the jury; and he suggested twelve feet as the height of the dam.   It being proposed by some of the jury that they should level the water, the plaintiff stated that he had levelled it as for a nine foot dam, and that dam would not flow the water back off his own land; and he shewed the jury the point to which he said the water would flow back, which satisfied them.   Plaintiff said he thought no one would be injured; that if any one was injured it would be himself, and that he did not believe he would be injured.   The jury accordingly returned a verdict that the erection of the dam would injure no one.

1851.
July
Term.

Calhoun
v.
Palmer.

Soon after the County court made the order granting leave to erect the dam, William B. and James W. Calhoun went on to build the mill and dam, with means furnished them by their father; the dam being raised about nine or ten feet high.

In the first year of the operation of the mill, which was in 1834 or 1835, the sons desired to raise the dam a little higher, and made the experiment by placing boards on the top of it to the height of five or six inches.   This was done without consulting the plaintiff, but he soon discovered it, and complained that he was injured by the raising of the dam, and required them to pull it down; which was accordingly done.   And from that time until 1844, when the property was sold to the defendant, these parties made no attempt to raise the dam.

In the year 1844 the plaintiff was seriously embarrassed in his circumstances, and as his embarrassments arose in a great measure out of his expenditures in fitting up the mill property for his sons, they determined to sell it and apply the proceeds to his relief; and this, though the plaintiff at first refused it, he afterwards consented to accept; and the property, with twenty acres of the land of the plaintiff, was sold to the defendant, and it was conveyed to him by a deed, in which the plaintiff and his sons united, with a general warranty. Some twelve or eighteen months after his purchase the defendant ascertained that the order establishing the mill authorized the erection of the dam to the height of twelve feet; and he thereupon elevated it about eight inches, which occasioned serious damage to the plaintiff's land.

*Michie* and *Baldwin*, for the appellant, and *Stuart*, for the appellee, submitted the case.

BALDWIN, *J.* delivered the opinion of the court.

It seems to the court that by the express provision of the 9th section of the statute concerning mills, &c., 2 Rev. Code, p. 222, no inquest taken by virtue of that act, and no opinion or judgment of the court thereupon, is a bar to any action which could have been had or maintained if the said act had never been made, other than actions for such injuries as were actually foreseen and estimated upon such inquest: And therefore, and inasmuch as the inquest in the record set forth finds that no person will be injured by the erection of the dam therein mentioned, that the plaintiff in this action, who was no party to the proceedings in which said inquest was had, is not thereby barred from the recovery of such damages as he may have sustained by the reflow of the water upon his land, occasioned by such dam.

And it further seems to the court, that inasmuch as the said dam, and the mill to which it pertains, were established upon the application of William B. Calhoun and James W. Calhoun, as the owners of the land upon which the same are situate, and the defendant in this action asserts in his defence the regularity of the proceedings by which said mill and dam were established, and claims the protection thereof under the title derived by him from the said applicants, it is not competent for him to deny the ownership of the said land by the said applicants at the time of said proceedings, or to assert the continued ownership thereof by the plaintiff, from whose conveyance to said applicants they derived their title.

It further seems to the court, that the record of the proceedings by which said mill and dam were established cannot be aided or supplied by parol evidence of what passed before the jury at the time of their inquisition, for the purpose of shewing that the plaintiff assented to the establishment of said dam at the height fixed by the jury, and thereby renounced any claim which he might thereafter have for damages unforeseen and unestimated by the jury; and that although the plaintiff may have attended the inquisition of the jury, and given them information as to the height to which it would be proper the applicants should have leave to erect their dam, and expressed to them his opinion and belief, founded upon observation and actual levelling, that a dam twelve feet high would not back the water upon the lands of any person but himself, and that as to himself he was satisfied that he would not thereby be injured, still that such conduct and declarations of the plaintiff would only serve to shew that any injury thereafter actually occasioned him by said dam was not foreseen and estimated by himself any more than by the said jury; and that such conduct and declarations of the plaintiff cannot be treated as a contract with said applicants, giving them leave to erect such dam and thereby occasion injury to the plaintiff; for, as a contract, so far as it allowed them to erect a dam upon their own land, it would be idle and nugatory, and so far as it authorized them to injure the plaintiff by backing the water upon his land, it was voluntary, executory and personal to the said applicants, amounting at most to nothing more than a parol license to them, indeterminate in point of time, and revocable at the pleasure of the plaintiff.

And it further seems to the court, that if, as the evidence at the trial tended to prove, the said William B. and James W. Calhoun complied with the condition imposed by the statute, requiring such applicants to begin to build their mill and dam within one year, and finish the same within three years after the leave of the court obtained, so as to be in good condition for the public use, but that the height to which the dam was so finished by them was not greater than about nine or ten feet, yet that their so stopping short of the full height fixed by the inquest aforesaid did not have the effect of precluding them, or their assignees, from afterwards raising the said dam to the full height of twelve feet allowed by the inquest, provided by so doing they should not occasion injury to others.

And it further seems to the court, that if, as there was evidence at the trial tending to prove, after the mill was finished and in operation, and when the dam was at the height of about nine or ten feet, the said William B. and James W. Calhoun desired to raise the latter somewhat higher, and did so by placing boards on the top to the height of several inches, which was done without consulting the plaintiff, who, however, soon discovered it, and complained that he was injured by such elevation, and required them to pull it down, and they, being satisfied upon examination that the plaintiff was really thereby injured, consented, and took off the increased height, then that this was a revocation of any such parol license as above supposed.

And it further seems to the court, that if, as the evidence at the trial tended to prove, the said dam was erected and finished by the said William B. and James W. Calhoun, as above mentioned, only to the height of about nine or ten feet, at which height it was not complained of but acquiesced in by the plaintiff, until their sale and conveyance of the property on which it is situate, to the defendant, in the year 1844, and was standing at that height at the time of such sale and conveyance, then that inasmuch as the plaintiff united in said sale and conveyance, the said dam as of that height must be considered as passing to the defendant by the terms and true intent and meaning of the deed of conveyance, and the plaintiff cannot recover damages against the defendant for any injury done him by any reflow of the water to the extent to which it existed at the time of said sale and conveyance; this court expressing no opinion as to any injury from the reflow of the water not existing at that time; the declaration only claiming the damages occasioned by the defendant's raising the dam since his purchase.

And it further seems to the court, that the instructions and opinions of the Circuit court at the trial, so far as the same conflict with the principles above declared, are erroneous. It is therefore considered that the said judgment of the Circuit court be reversed and annulled, and the verdict of the jury set aside, with costs to the plaintiff in error; and the cause is remanded to the Circuit court for a new trial of the issue between the parties; which new trial is to be governed, so far as applicable, by the principles above declared.

## Lewisburg.

1851.
July
Term.

### KELLY *v.* LINKENHOGER.

(Absent *Cabell*, P.)

September 5th.

1. In a proceeding by foreign attachment, the home defendant
   denies that he has any effects of the absent debtor in his
   hands. He says that a tract of land which had belonged
   to the absent debtor had been purchased by himself and
   paid for: And he in fact held the receipt of the absent
   debtor for the amount of the purchase money. As, however, he did not pretend he had paid the amount in money,
   and as the accounts which he endeavoured to establish
   were not proved to the satisfaction of the commissioner
   and the court, the land was held liable.

2. In such case, upon an appeal from an interlocutory decree for
   the sale of the land, the appellate court will not reverse
   the decree because the court did not decree against the
   absent debtor or direct the giving the security as provided
   by law in behalf of absent defendants: The final decree
   may provide for these things.

This was a proceeding by foreign attachment in the
Circuit court of Botetourt county, by John Linkenhoger, who sued for the benefit of George W. Carper,
against George W. Kelly, as an absent debtor, and John
Q. A. Kelly, a home defendant. The plaintiff charged
that George W. Kelly owed him the sum of 100 dollars, due by bond executed the 28th January 1839, and
payable on the first of May 1842. That Kelly had removed from the Commonwealth and resided in Georgia.
That he was the owner of an interest in a tract of land
in the county of Botetourt and in two slaves, which
had been the property of his father; and that he had
conveyed his interest in said land and slaves to the defendant, John Q. A. Kelly, without consideration, and

for the purpose of enabling him to sell and convey it .for George W. Kelly.

1861. July Term.

Kelly v Linken- hoger.

.The home defendant answered, denying that he had anything in his hands belonging to George W. Kelly; and insisted that he had bought the land for 500 dollars, which was a full price, the land being sold subject to a debt due from the estate of John Kelly, the father, from whom the land was derived.

The court below directed a commissioner to enquire and report what was the consideration on which the land in the bill mentioned was conveyed by George W. Kelly to John Q. A. Kelly. In obedience to this order the commissioner reported that although the conveyance purported to be in consideration of 500 dollars, and there was a receipt of George W. Kelly to John Q. A. Kelly for that sum, yet that the services which the latter claimed to have rendered to the former, for which there was due this sum of 500 dollars, were sustained by evidence entirely too indefinite to be the foundation of a statement of an account between the parties; and he therefore reported that the conveyance was without consideration.

This report was excepted to by the defendant, on the ground that the commissioner had not stated the accounts between the parties; and it was insisted that the evidence was sufficient to enable the commissioner to make the statement.

The cause came on to be heard in April 1848, when the court overruled the exceptions to the commissioner's report, and held that the plaintiff was entitled to have satisfaction of his claim out of the land in the bill and proceedings mentioned. And it was decreed that, unless the defendants should, within sixty days from the expiration of the present term of the court, pay to the plaintiff the sum of 100 dollars, with interest thereon from the 1st of May 1842 till paid, and his costs, a commissioner named should, after advertising, &c., sell the

1851.
July
Term.

Kelly
v.
Linken-
hoger.

said tract of land at public auction on the premises on a credit of six, twelve and eighteen months, in equal instalments, for the residue, after requiring so much of the purchase money to be paid in hand as might be necessary to defray the expenses and charges of sale. From this decree John Q. A. Kelly applied to this court for an appeal, which was allowed.

*F. T. Anderson*, for the appellant, and
*Boyd*, for the appellee, submitted the case.

BALDWIN, *J.* delivered the opinion of the court.

The court is of opinion that the appellant has in his hands, of the purchase money of the land in the proceedings mentioned, more than enough to satisfy the debt and interest thereon, due from the absent defendant George W. Kelly to the appellee Linkenhoger; and therefore that the decree of the Circuit court is right upon the merits; and that the said decree being only interlocutory, it will be time enough, upon the final hearing of the cause, to decree against said absent defendant and to direct in his behalf the security provided by law in behalf of absent defendants. It is therefore adjudged, ordered and decreed that the said decree of the Circuit court be affirmed, with costs to the appellee Linkenhoger.

𝔏𝔢𝔴𝔦𝔰𝔟𝔲𝔯𝔤.

ADAMS *v.* MARTIN.

(Absent *Cabell*, P.)

September 5th.

1. Upon the trial of a writ of unlawful detainer, defendant sets
up title in himself.  Plaintiff may prove that the defendant
entered on the premises under a parol lease from himself;
though the lease proved was to continue more than one
year.
2. The defendant claiming title under a deed made to himself
and another as joint tenants, that other person is not a
competent witness for him to sustain his right of possession.

This was a proceeding by writ of unlawful detainer
in the County court of Lee, in which William Adams
was plaintiff and Wilkerson Martin was defendant.  On
the trial the defendant claimed to hold the land in controversy under a deed from David H. Campbell, administrator with the will annexed of Arthur Campbell, to
himself and Joseph P. Bishop, bearing date the 28th
November 1844.  The plaintiff alleged that there existed a verbal contract between the plaintiff as landlord
and the defendant as tenant of the land in controversy,
commencing in the year 1840; and to prove the same,
introduced a witness who stated that the defendant had
informed him that he had come in possession of the
land in controversy upon an oral contract with the
plaintiff, that the defendant should proceed to improve
the land and premises, and that he was to enjoy the
use and occupation thereof until he should be thus paid
for all the improvements he should make.  And the
defendant contending that from the statements made by
the witness it appeared that the time of the continuance
of the alleged lease was indefinite, and from its charac-

ter not to be performed as an agreement or terminate as
a lease within the period of one year from the alleged commencement thereof, he by his counsel objected to the introduction of oral testimony to prove
such lease, on the ground that it was in violation of the
statute of frauds and perjuries.  But the court overruled the objection and admitted the evidence :  And
the defendant excepted.

In the further progress of the cause the defendant
offered to introduce Joseph P. Bishop as a witness, but
the plaintiff objected to his introduction, upon the
ground that the witness was interested in the result of
the suit ; the land having been conveyed by Campbell
to the defendant and the witness jointly, under which
conveyance they claimed title, and which was relied
upon and given in evidence on the trial by the defendant.   The court sustained the objection and excluded
the witness : And the defendant again excepted.

There was a verdict and judgment for the plaintiff;
and Martin thereupon obtained a *supersedeas* to the
judgment from the Circuit court of Lee county :  And
when the cause came on to be heard in that court, the
judgment was reversed for the refusal of the County
court to admit Joseph P. Bishop as a witness.   From
this judgment Adams applied to this court for a *supersedeas*, which was allowed.

*J. W. Sheffey*, for the appellant, and
*S. Logan*, for the appellee, submitted the case.

ALLEN, *J.* delivered the opinion of the court.

Inasmuch as it appears from the 2d bill of exceptions taken by the defendant in error to the decision of
the County court excluding Joseph P. Bishop as a witness, on the ground of incompetency, that said Bishop
was a joint tenant with said defendant of the premises,
the possession whereof was the subject in controversy,

that the defendant had relied upon the deed which constituted said joint tenancy with said Bishop in his defence, it seems to the court here that said Bishop was directly interested in the result of the suit, being seized with his co-joint tenant *per my et per tout*, the possession of the defendant was his possession, and his evidence tending to maintain such possession in the said defendant was evidence tending to establish a fact enuring to his own benefit; and that he was properly excluded as an incompetent witness.

And it further seems to the court, that the County court did not err in overruling the objection of the defendant in error to the testimony set out in his first bill of exceptions, inasmuch as although the contract the evidence tended to prove may have been void under the statute of frauds, it was still competent for the plaintiff to shew that the defendant had entered under an agreement to rent the premises, and stood in the relation of tenant to the plaintiff; and whether such tenancy was to endure for a year or a longer period, could not affect the question depending on the relation the parties bore to each other when the defendant entered upon the premises.

It is therefore considered by the court that the judgment of the Circuit court, reversing the judgment of the County court, is erroneous; and the same is reversed, with costs to the plaintiff in error. And this court proceeding to render such judgment as said Circuit court should have done, it is further considered that the judgment of the County court be affirmed, and that the plaintiff in error recover of the defendant in error his costs by him about his defence in the Circuit court expended.

BALDWIN, *J.* dissented.

He said he thought the judgment of the Circuit court was wrong in holding that Bishop was an incompetent witness, whatever might be the rule in regard to other actions. That by express provision of the statute regulating writs of unlawful detainer, a judgment in such a proceeding concluded nothing in regard to the title or the right of possession, the effect being only when for the plaintiff to give him the mere possession, and when for the defendant to leave him in the possession; but in no wise affecting the title or right of possession in any higher action between the same parties. That the judgment, if for the plaintiff, would give him no action against the defendant or the witness for *mesne* profits, and if for the defendant, no protection to him or the witness in respect to future profits; and that in this case a judgment for the defendant would be no evidence between him and the witness as to the title or right of possession, nor give any possession to the witness if he should be kept out by the defendant.

---

## Lewisburg.

### Bell *v.* Crawford.

(Absent *Cabell*, P.)

September 6th.

1. In *assumpsit* defendant pleads *non assumpsit*, and with it files affidavit of set-off, and the set-off, which is a note. Though there is no plea of set-off or bill of particulars, the evidence in relation to the set-off is properly admitted.

2. A promise which will remove the bar of the statute of limitations must be a promise to pay a debt: And a promise to settle with the claimant is not sufficient.

3. If a part payment will take a case out of the statute, it must be a payment upon the specific debt, and not a payment upon account.

This was an action of *assumpsit*, brought in July 1845, in the Circuit court of Augusta county, by James Bell against John Crawford. There was no question about the debt claimed by the plaintiff from the defendant; but the contest arose upon a set-off relied upon by the defendant, and which was objected to by the plaintiff as being barred by the statute of limitations. The question whether it was barred depended upon whether there was a sufficient promise in writing to pay the debt, or a sufficient part payment, to take the case out of the statute. The facts of the case are sufficiently stated in the opinion of Judge *Moncure;* and the statement of facts is so mingled with his views of the law that they cannot be separated. There having been a verdict and judgment for the defendant, the plaintiff applied to this court for a *supersedeas*, which was awarded.

*Michie* and *Fultz*, for the appellant, insisted:

1st. That if part payment would take a case out of the statute under our act of 1838, it must be a payment in part of the very debt, and not a payment generally on account. And for this they referred to *Tippetts* v. *Hearne*, 4 Tyrw. R. 775; *S. C.*, 1 Cromp. Mees. & Ros. 252; Joynes on Lim. 124, 126; *Waugh* v. *Cope*, 6 Mees. & Welsb. 824; *Beirn* v. *Bolton*, 52 Eng. C. L. R. 476.

2d. That a promise to settle, or the acknowledgment that there will be something due upon a settlement of accounts, though in writing, will not take a case out of the statute. And for this proposition they referred to *Wetzell* v. *Bussard*, 11 Wheat. R. 309; *Bell* v. *Morrison*, 1 Peters' R. 351; *Ayletts* v. *Robinson*, 9 Leigh 45; *Sutton* v. *Burrus*, Id. 381; *Linsell* v. *Bonsor*, 29 Eng. C. L. R. 319; Angel on Lim. 300; Joynes on Lim. 278–285; *Buckett* v. *Church*, 38 Eng. C. L. R. 83.

*[margin: 1851. July Term.]*

*[margin: Bell v. Crawford.]*

*Fultz* further insisted :

3d. That a part payment did not remove the bar of the statute. That the English statute did not exclude from its operation mutual accounts and accounts stated. *Jones* v. *Ryder*, 4 Mees. & Welsb. 32 ; *Mills* v. *Fowkes*, 35 Eng. C. L. R. 175 ; *Waller* v. *Lacy*, 39 Id. 349 ; *Cottam* v. *Partridge*, 43 Id. 146 ; Angel on Lim. 302. That the English statute had received this construction when the act of 1838 was passed, adopting the Tenterden act, but omitting the proviso ; and according to a well settled principle we adopt the construction with the statute. And now by the Code of 1850 no doubt is left on the question.

*Baldwin* and *Hugh W. Sheffey*, for the appellee, insisted :

1st. That a part payment takes a case out of the statute ; and they referred to the English decisions on the *insimul computasset* count, as analogous in principle. These were *Smith* v. *Forty*, 19 Eng. C. L. R. 305 ; *Ashby* v. *James*, 11 Mees. & Welsb. 542 ; *Worthington* v. *Grimsditch*, 53 Eng. C. L. R. 479.

2d. That though the part payment must be upon a specific debt ; and though the proof of the acknowledgment of the payment must be in writing, yet the writing need not state the amount of the debt, or refer in terms to it. And they referred to *Beirn* v. *Bolton*, 52 Eng. C. L. R. 476 ; *Buckett* v. *Church*, 38 Eng. C. L. R. 83 ; *Gardner* v. *McMahon*, 43 Id. 867 ; *Frost* v. *Bengough*, 8 Id. 317 ; *Pierce* v. *Brewster*, 22 Id. 452 ; *Waller* v. *Lacy*, 39 Id. 349 ; *Hooper* v. *Stevens*, 32 Id. 504 ; *Ilsley* v. *Jewett*, 2 Metc. R. 168.

3d. That the statute does not change the nature of the acknowledgment which will take a case out of the statute ; but requires it to be in writing. This was clearly intended by the provision which declared that the acknowledgment should draw down the original consideration ; and thus established the Mansfield doctrine in opposition to the doctrine broached in *Butcher* v. *Hixton*, 4 Leigh 519, and *Farmer's Bank* v. *Clarke*, Id. 603. And they insisted that the acknowledgment of the debt proved in this case was clearly sufficient. They referred to *Lechmere* v. *Fletcher*, referred to in Joynes on Lim. 273 ; *Hartley* v. *Wharton*, 39 Eng. C. L. R. 276 ; *Waller* v. *Lacy*, Id. 349 ; *Hooper* v. *Stevens*, 32 Id. 504 ; *Ilsley* v. *Jewett*, 2 Metc. R. 168.

MONCURE, *J.* In April 1844 the appellee Crawford bought of the appellant Bell a parcel of horses, at the price of 725 dollars, promising to pay the money "punctually at six months," and to give security for its payment. On the 18th of July 1845 Bell brought an action of *assumpsit* against Crawford, in the Circuit court of Augusta, to recover the money. On the 15th of November 1845 the defendant plead *non assumpsit ;* and at the same time filed an affidavit, stating that he had a defence consisting of a set-off, to an amount greater than the whole amount of the plaintiff's demand, which in the opinion of his counsel constituted a good legal defence to the action ; and also filed, as the set-off referred to in the affidavit, a note of the defendant to B. Davis, dated the 24th of December 1839, for 1700 dollars, payable by draft, one half on the 1st of April, and the other on the 1st of May next after the date. This set-off was the only defence relied on by the defendant ; though no notice seems to have been taken of it upon the record. It was resisted by the plaintiff, on the ground that it had been paid, and also that it was barred by the act of limitations. The defendant insisted that it was taken out of the operation of the act, by an acknowledgment or promise in writing, and also by part payment. The case was tried at November term 1848, when a verdict and judgment were rendered for the defendant. Exceptions were taken by the plaintiff to various opinions given by the court upon the trial, and to the opinion of the court overruling his motion for a new trial; and these opinions are now to be reviewed by this court. I will notice them, or such of them at least as I deem it necessary to notice, in the order in which they are presented on the record.

1. The plaintiff moved the court to exclude from the jury all evidence introduced by the defendant to prove his set-off, upon the ground that he had not filed with his plea an account of the set-offs, as the statute directs.

The court overruled this motion; and I think rightly overruled it. The defendant, substantially, if not literally, complied with the directions of the statute by filing with his plea the note in writing which was the subject of his set-off. The statute does not require the set-off to be noticed on the order book. It requires an account to be filed " stating distinctly the nature of the set-off and the several items thereof. The object of this requisition is to give the plaintiff full notice of the character of the set-off. If the set-off consist of a single item, as of a promissory note, the best notice which can be given of the character thereof is to file the note with the plea. No description of the note which could be given in an account could be more plain and particular than the note itself. The record shows that the plaintiff had full notice of the character of the set-off, and that he was not taken by surprise on the trial. He did not object that an account had not been filed until after all the evidence and arguments had been fully heard, and to have allowed the objection then would have been to have taken the defendant by surprise.

2. The plaintiff moved the court to exclude from the jury all the evidence introduced by the defendant in

support of the set-off, on the ground that it was barred by the statute of limitations, and that said evidence in law was not sufficient to remove the bar.

The cause of action on the set-off accrued on the first days of April and May 1840, and the suit having been instituted on the 18th of July 1845, it was conceded that the set-off was barred unless it could be taken out of the operation of the statute. The defendant insisted that it was taken out, on the ground, either of a new acknowledgment or promise in writing, or of a part payment, made within five years before the institution of the suit. The new acknowledgment or promise relied on by the defendant consisted of a letter from the plaintiff to him in these words:

" *Mr. John Crawford.*

I give you above 6 drafts for $300 each, payable at 40, 50, 60, 70, 80 and 90 (days), which I hope will suit you. It is the shortest time I could draw to be ready to pay; when you come back we can settle. Take care of this, and it will shew what you have received.

*James Bell.*"

The part payment relied on consisted of the drafts mentioned in said letter, which were proved to have been drawn on and paid by Jacob Shook, of the city of Richmond. The letter has no date. But it appearing that the draft at 40 days was paid on the 19th December 1840, the fair presumption is that the letter was written forty days before, or on the 9th November 1840; which was within five years before the institution of the suit, but not the filing of the set-off.

Conceding, for the present at least, that the time of the institution of the suit, and not of the filing of the set-off, is the period to which the limitation of the set-off is properly referrible, and also that a part payment will take a debt out of the operation of the statute; let us proceed to enquire whether there was such an acknowledgment or promise in writing, or such a part payment, in this case, as will take the set-off out of the operation of the statute? To avoid confusion I will consider the questions separately.

First. As to the acknowledgment or promise in writing. Shortly after the passage of the act of 9 Geo. iv., ch. 14, called "Lord Tenterden's act," it was stated by its author, Lord Tenterden, that the object of the act was the prevention of fraud and perjury in proving an acknowledgment, or a new promise, by rendering it necessary to procure that in writing for which words were previously sufficient. *Dickenson* v. *Hatfield*, 24 Eng. C. L. R. 204. And it was said by Tindal, chief justice of the common pleas, that the statute did not intend to make any alteration in the legal construction to be put upon acknowledgments or promises made by the defendants, but only to require a different mode of proof. To enquire, therefore, whether, in a given case, the written document amounts to a written acknowledgment or promise, is no other enquiry than whether the same words, if proved, before the statute, to have been spoken by the defendant, would have had a similar operation and effect. *Haydon* v. *Williams*, 20 Eng. C. L. R. 86. Our act of 3d of April 1838 was copied, with some alterations, from Lord Tenterden's act; and having been passed after the above cited cases were decided, should, I think, receive the same construction which in those cases was put upon the English act. In deciding, therefore, whether the letter from Bell to Crawford, before mentioned, is a sufficient acknowledgment or promise to take the set-off out of the operation of the statute of limitations, it is necessary to enquire whether the words of the letter, if proved, before the act of April 1838, to have been spoken by Bell, would have had a similar effect.

The operative words of the letter are, " when you come back we can *settle*." And the question is, whether, by the words " we can settle," the plaintiff promised to pay to the defendant a particular debt, or made a direct, unqualified admission of a present, subsisting debt from which a promise to pay would naturally and irresistibly be implied; or merely promised to settle accounts with the defendant for the purpose of ascertaining and paying what might be due to him.

If the former be the true construction of the words used, I admit that the set-off is thereby taken out of the operation of the statute of limitations. It was not necessary that the amount of the debt should have been specified in the letter. The particular debt to which the letter refers may be identified by extrinsic evidence; and has been so identified to be the amount of the set-off, if the words aforesaid imply a promise to pay a debt, and not to settle an account.

But if by the words in question the plaintiff merely promised to settle accounts with the defendant for the purpose of ascertaining and paying what might be due to him, I am clearly of opinion that the set-off is not thereby taken out of the operation of the statute.

In the case of *Bell* v. *Morrison*, 1 Peters R. 351, it was proved that one of the defendants expressed his willingness " to settle with the plaintiff," but the books and papers were in the hands of another of the defendants; said " he was anxious that the plaintiff's account should be settled "; that he knew the defendants were owing him; that he was " getting old and wished to have the business settled "; and proposed to give the plaintiff 7000 dollars, in satisfaction of the claim; and letters of several of the defendants, containing admissions of a like nature, were exhibited and proved on the trial. The Supreme court decided that this evidence was insufficient to take the case out of the statute of limitations; and Story, Justice, in delivering the opinion of the court, comments at length on the wisdom and policy of the statute; and makes several observations which are so appropriate to the present case that I hope I may be excused for quoting some of them. On page 360 he says : " If we proceed one step further, and admit that loose and general expressions from which a probable or possible inference may be deduced of the acknowledgment of a debt by a court or jury ; that, as the language of some cases has been, any acknowledgment, however slight, or any statement not amounting to a denial of the debt; that any admission of the existence of an unsettled account, without any specification of amount or balance, and however indeterminate and casual, are yet sufficient to take the case out of the statute of limitations, and to let in evidence *aliunde* to establish any debt, however large and at whatever distance of time, it is easy to perceive that the wholesome objects of the statute must be in a great measure defeated, and the statute virtually repealed." Again, on page 366, he says : " The evidence is clear of the admission of an unsettled account as well from the letters of Butler as the conversation of Morrison. The latter acknowledged that the partnership was owing the plaintiff, but as he had not the books he could not settle with him. If this evidence stood alone it would be too loose to entitle the plaintiff to recover anything. The language might be equally true whether the debt were one dollar or ten thousand dollars. It is indispensable for the plaintiff to go farther, and to establish by independent evidence the extent of the balance due him, before there can arise any promise to pay it as a subsisting debt. The acknowledgment of the party, then, does not constitute the sole ground of the new implied promise; but it requires other intrinsic aid, before it can possess legal certainty. Now if this be so, does it not let in the whole mischief intended to be guarded against by the statute ? Does it not enable the party to bring forward stale demands, after a lapse of time when the proper evidence of the real state of the transaction cannot be produced? Does it not tend to encourage perjury, by removing the bar upon slight acknowledgments of an indeterminate nature? Can an admission that something is due, or some balance owing, be justly construed into a promise to pay any debt or balance which the party may assert or prove before a jury?" &c.

*Bell* v. *Morrison* has, ever since its decision in 1828, been regarded in the United States as a leading case on the statute of limitations; and as Angell truly says in his work on Limitations, p. 245, upon the authority of the language of the court by Mr. Justice Story in that case, the State courts in many instances have relied with emphatic confidence. Of none of them is that remark more true than of the courts of Virginia. In this State the doctrine settled in that case has been recognized, and carried to its fullest extent, as the two cases next cited will shew.

In *Ayletts* v. *Robinson*, 9 Leigh 45, the action was *assumpsit* on an account for carpenter's work amounting to 320 dollars, commencing in March 1823 and ending in June 1825. The debtor died in 1831. The suit was brought in 1833, against his executor. The defence relied on was the statute of limitations. To take the case out of the statute, the plaintiff proved in 1829 he applied to the debtor to settle the account; and the debtor said, " I am too unwell to do business now; *when I am better I will settle your account.*" The court decided that the evidence was insufficient to take the case out of the operation of the statute. Parker, J. cited with approbation the modern cases which decided that a " promise or acknowledgment, to take the case out of the statute, must be an express promise, or such an acknowledgment of a *balance* then due, unaccompanied by reservations or conditions, as that a jury ought

1851.
July
Term.

Bell
v.
Crawford.

to infer from it a promise to pay." "It is plain," he said, " that the declarations of the testator in the case now before us were made in reference to an *unsettled demand*, and therefore very unsatisfactory evidence of the *quantum* of damages." If the promise to be inferred from these declarations " is to be taken," he further said, " as a promise to pay any balance that may be found due on a future settlement between the parties, then that settlement ought to be averred, and that a certain balance was found thereupon to be due." See his opinion in full, and also the opinions of Brockenbrough and Brooke in same case.

In *Sutton* v. *Burruss*, 9 Leigh 381, the action was *assumpsit* on an open account. Plea, the statute of limitations. Proof, that within five years the defendant acknowledged the items of the plaintiff's account to be just, but said that he had some offsets; and that at a subsequent time the defendant promised the plaintiff that he would settle all their accounts and differences fairly, and would not avail himself of the act of limitations. It was held that this proof was not sufficient to justify the jury in finding for the plaintiff. Parker, J., after shewing that the proof was insufficient to sustain the count of *insimul computasset*, said: " I am inclined indeed to think that under no form of pleading could the acknowledgments and promises proved in this case, coupled with a claim of offsets to an indefinite amount, have had the effect of taking the case out of the statute of limitations. I had occasion to advert to the modern decisions on this subject in the recent case of *Ayletts* v. *Robinson*, and I heartily approve their spirit. If an acknowledgment is relied on, it ought to be a direct and unqualified admission of a present subsisting debt, from which a promise to pay would naturally and irresistibly be implied. When the amount is left open and is to depend on proof *aliunde*, the wholesome objects of the statute in affording security against

stale demands would be defeated," &c.  Cabell, J., who
did not sit in the case of *Ayletts* v. *Robinson*, after citing with approbation a portion of Story's opinion in *Bell*
v. *Morrison*, said : " If this principle be correct, (and I
believe it to be incontrovertibly so,) no promise which
is founded merely on the consideration of the old debt,
and which still leaves the party exposed to the inconveniences which the statute was intended to remedy,
ought to revive the old debt, and take the case out of
the statute."  And after stating the facts of the case,
he further said : " The utmost that ever a jury could
infer from all this is a promise to pay an unascertained
balance.  That balance might be one cent only ; or it
might be within one cent of the original amount of the
plaintiff's demand.  What it really was depended on
testimony *aliunde*.  This promise, then, certainly left
the defendant exposed to all the inconveniences arising
from the loss of testimony in relation to his offsets ;
and we cannot therefore give effect to it, without frustrating the great object of the statute," &c.  Tucker,
P., who had dissented from the opinion of the court in
*Ayletts* v. *Robinson*, said he felt bound to follow the
decision in that case, and did not see how the acknowledgment in the case of *Sutton* v. *Burruss* could be considered as taking the demand out of the operation of
the statute.

I have stated these two cases so much at length because they seem to me to be directly in point, and to
have settled the law of Virginia upon the subject.  The
statute of April 1838 was passed about the time they
were decided ; and was dictated by the same policy of
giving effect to the statute of limitations and the intention thereof, and of avoiding the frauds and perjuries which had arisen in regard to parol promises and
acknowledgments.  I think there is nothing in the proviso to that statute, " that every such written promise
or acknowledgment shall be held and taken to be a

drawing down of the original debt or contract to the date of the said promise or acknowledgment," which can have the effect of reviving the doctrine of what were called in the argument " the Mansfield cases," or of taking any case out of the statute of limitations which would not have been taken out by the same promise or acknowledgment if made before the act of 1838 was passed. Such a construction of the proviso would be opposed to the obvious intention of the legislature, and, as has been properly said, would " contribute as much to thwart the policy of the statute of limitations as the rest of the act will to advance it." Joynes 225, 226. That proviso was, I think, produced by the opinions expressed by several of the judges in *Butcher* v. *Hixton*, 4 Leigh 519, and *The Farmers Bank* v. *Clarke*, Id. 603, that the new promise does not bring down the old cause of action, but creates a new one, on which the action must be brought; and that in an action of debt on a promissory note, the case will not be taken out of the statute by proof of a new promise, unless there be a general *indebitatus* count in the declaration. And I think the object of the proviso was, and its proper construction is, to authorize, if not require, the suit to be brought on the original cause of action, wherever, and only wherever, the new promise or acknowledgment would have been sufficient, if the proviso had not been adopted, to have taken the case out of the statute of limitations. So that in an action of debt on a promissory note, counting only on the note itself, proof of a new promise in writing would, under the proviso, take the case out of the operation of the statute. So also, in any action of debt in *assumpsit* on a simple contract, counting on the original cause of action, proof of a new promise in writing, and of the performance of any conditions annexed thereto, would, under the proviso, take the cause out of the operation of the statute. In fine, the operation of the proviso, according to my construc-

1831.
July
Term.

Bell
v.
Crawford.

tion of it, is to authorize a recovery only to the same extent and against the same parties in a suit upon the original cause of action, as in a suit upon the new promise. This construction gets rid of a technical difficulty, is consistent with the words and intention of the act of April 1838, and does not thwart the policy of the statute of limitations.

I think, therefore, it may be fairly concluded that in Virginia a promise in writing to settle an account, however plain and positive such promise may be, is not sufficient to take the account out of the operation of the statute. And now let us see whether the written promise in this case was to settle an account or pay a debt. I think it was clearly the former. The proper meaning of the operative word in this case, "*settle*," is, " to go into a settlement, to adjust, to fix or determine a balance, which may be on the one side or the other." But it is certainly a word of somewhat equivocal import, and may, by the context or the surrounding circumstances, be explained to mean "*pay*." In each of the cases of *Bell* v. *Morrison*, *Ayletts* v. *Robinson*, and *Sutton* v. *Burruss*, the word " settle " was the operative word used, and the question arose whether it was used in its ordinary acceptation or was intended to imply a promise to pay, and in each of them it was construed in the former sense. In *Ayletts* v. *Robinson*, Parker, J. said: " I do not mean to say that a promise to *settle* an account may not, under some circumstances, be equivalent to a promise to pay, so as to take a case out of the statute of limitations. It depends upon the nature of the application and the terms of the answer; as evincing a mere intent to adjust the account and see where the balance lies, or an acknowledgment of a stated balance, which to settle means to pay. Thus if one, upon an account being presented to him, says, 'It is right, and I will settle it at a future day,' there could be no doubt about his meaning, and a

jury would infer a promise. But in the present case,"
&c. Is the proper meaning of this word " *settle* " varied in this case either by the context or the surrounding circumstances?

It is not varied by the context. The words of the
letter are not, " your account is right, and I will settle
it "; nor even, " I will settle your account." But the
words are, " when you come back *we can settle.*"
This form of expression, " we can settle," plainly implies an accounting together, and not a promise of payment by one to another. These words, whether taken
alone or in connection with the context, can hardly be
said to be of equivocal import, so as to admit of extrinsic evidence to explain them.

But let us look to the extrinsic evidence in the case,
and see if it will shew that the words were used in any
other than their ordinary and proper sense of " accounting together."

Two witnesses were relied on by the defendant to
furnish means of explaining the sense in which the
words were used, and of shewing that the plaintiff
thereby intended to promise payment of the former's
set-off. The first was Jacob C. Roler, who proved that
in November 1840, at the defendant's request, he presented to the plaintiff an account amounting to 2504
dollars 7 cents, consisting of four different items, of
which the note now claimed as a set-off was one; at
the foot of which account was an order signed by the
defendant, requesting the plaintiff to draw on Mr. Shook
at sight for 2504 dollars, and hand over the draft to the
witness. That the plaintiff examined the account and
order, but told witness he did not know what he could
do till he heard from his agent Shook, in Richmond;
that he was going to Staunton that day and expected a
letter from Shook; and if he heard from him, would
send to defendant, or witness for him, drafts for as much
as it would be safe for him to draw on Shook for. That

he raised no objection to said account, and did not deny
that he owed the amount, although he did not say that
it was right.    That a day or two thereafter witness received from the plaintiff a letter, enclosing the letter in
question from the plaintiff to the defendant, and the six
drafts for 300 dollars each, therein referred to; and that
witness handed the said letter in question, and the said
account and order, to the defendant, in whose custody
he supposes them to have since remained.    I think
there is nothing in this evidence which can have the effect of explaining the words of the letter so as to make
them imply a promise of payment.    The mere failure
to dispute an account, or to claim offsets against it, is
slight evidence of an acknowledgment; and instead
of having the effect of varying the ordinary meaning
of words used by the supposed debtor in a letter to the
creditor concerning the debt, written about the time of
the presentation of the account, could itself be explained away by such letter, if the natural and ordinary import of the words of the letter excluded the idea of
such an acknowledgment.    The account was not left in
the plaintiff's hands.    A day or two after it was
presented to him, probably the next day, he wrote the
letter in question, and enclosed that and the six drafts
on Shook, to the witness for the defendant.    That letter affords written and positive evidence of a promise,
not to pay, but to settle an account; and repels the parol
and negative evidence of a promise to pay, which might
be implied from a mere failure to dispute the account.
So much for the evidence of Roler.    The other witness
was George W. Hulvey, who proved that in the fall of
1840 the defendant received from the plaintiff six drafts
for 300 dollars each, and, not being satisfied with the
amount, sent witness to see the plaintiff, with a statement
in writing, intended to shew how much more he desired
to have.    That he shewed the statement to the plaintiff,
who, upon examining it, remarked that he could not do

anything more at that time, as he had no more money in Mr. Shook's hands; and that he wanted to have a settlement with Mr. Crawford, by which time he would probably have more money in Shook's hands. And that he, the witness, thought he left the statement in the plaintiff's hands. If there were any doubt as to the meaning of the words "we can settle" in the letter, I think it would be completely removed by the evidence of Hulvey, who proved that the plaintiff said "he wanted to have a settlement with the defendant"; that he wanted such settlement to precede any further payment: and therefore that he could not have intended by the words "we can settle," used in the letter, to promise to pay the entire balance of the defendant's account after crediting the amount of the six drafts.

The other facts proved in the case, instead of shewing that the plaintiff intended in his letter to promise to pay the entire balance of the account after crediting the drafts, I think, strongly tend to shew not only that the plaintiff never intended to promise to pay such balance, or to admit that he owed it, but even that the defendant considered his accounts with the plaintiff unsettled, and the balance due upon them, if any, uncertain. The note of the defendant to the plaintiff, on which the suit was brought, tends strongly to that conclusion. That note is dated April 4th, 1844, and by it the defendant promised to pay to the plaintiff 725 dollars, the purchase money of the horses, *punctually at six months.* It was proved by a witness that the defendant agreed. if he bought the horses *to give security for the purchase money and pay it punctually when due.* It was proved by another witness that the note for 725 dollars was assigned to him by the plaintiff in part payment for cattle. That some time thereafter, and before the note became payable, he enquired of the defendant about it, who told the witness that the claim was right and would be paid when due; that there were unsettled mat-

ters between the plaintiff and defendant, and that he did
not think there was much coming either way on that
account; and witness understood from defendant that
that account would not prevent him from paying the
725 dollars when due. That when the note became
due the witness called on defendant for payment, who
refused to pay the note, alleging that there were unsettled accounts between the defendant and plaintiff; that
he had an offset against the claim, and did not consider
that he owed the plaintiff anything. It did not appear
from any evidence in the cause that after the interview
between the witness Hulvey and the plaintiff, before referred to, there was ever any settlement of accounts between the plaintiff and defendant; or, until after the
purchase of the horses in 1844, any demand by the latter of the former for such a settlement, much less for
the payment of a specific debt, or an ascertained balance of an account. It was proved by a witness that
the deputy sheriffs of Augusta, of whom the defendant
was one, were in the habit, during the year 1838 and
previous years, of letting the plaintiff, who was largely
engaged in the cattle business, have as much money as
they could spare, with the understanding that he would
have funds ready for them to pay in the revenue. That
prior to 1838 there had been no disappointment; but
that in December of that year his drafts on Shook were
not paid. Among those drafts was one in favour of the
defendant for 2490 dollars, which was introduced as evidence by the defendant, and is copied in the record. It
is dated November 22, 1838, and the 2490 dollars is
therein expressed to be " the sum he had paid for me,
and I am bound to pay him in Richmond, that sum, so
much of the revenue of Augusta." It was proved by
a witness that on the 3d of January 1839 the plaintiff paid into the auditor's office 2298 dollars 81 cents,
being that part of the revenue from Augusta for 1838
which was due by the defendant. No evidence was of-

fered to shew the particulars of the sum of 2490 dollars mentioned in the draft. It was contended by the counsel for the appellant that at least one of the items of the account presented to the plaintiff by the witness Roler, to wit, the bond of plaintiff to defendant for 368 dollars 50 cents, was settled in that draft. The bond is copied in the record, is dated the 12th of August 1838, and the amount is therein expressed to be money borrowed of the defendant, " to be returned in time to pay the revenue of this year." The account aforesaid consisted of four items, two of which had accrued before the date of the draft for 2490 dollars, and were supposed, in the argument of the appellant's counsel, to have been settled therein. The other two consisted of the note to Davis for 1700 dollars, dated 24th December 1839, payable in April and May 1840, and being the set-off now claimed by the defendant, and a bond of 71 dollars, dated 15th November 1839. The appellant's counsel contended that the six drafts of 300 dollars each were paid on account of the two last mentioned items. Davis proved that he assigned the note which is the set-off in this case to the defendant. That when he assigned it he thought it would be punctually paid, and so told the defendant. That sometime after it was due, the defendant informed him that the plaintiff had not paid it, and requested him to urge the plaintiff to do so ; saying nothing of any other claim he had against the plaintiff. That witness did urge the plaintiff to pay it, and plaintiff afterwards informed the witness that he had given the defendant drafts to pay the note. That witness told defendant what plaintiff said, and defendant replied that plaintiff had let him have some drafts, but that he had applied, or intended to apply them in part to pay some other debts which plaintiff owed him.

Upon the whole I think that whether we look to the letter itself, or to the declarations and conduct of both of the parties and the other extrinsic evidence in the case, we can come to no other conclusion than that the plaintiff did not intend by his letter enclosing the six drafts to promise to pay the balance of the account or to acknowledge it as a subsisting debt. It was argued by the counsel for the appellee that there were but four items of the account, and that the plaintiff had never disputed either of them. He did not dispute them because they were doubtless originally just. If he had expressly admitted them to be originally just, that would not have been sufficient. In *Clementson* v. *Williams*, 8 Cranch's R. 72, Chief Justice Marshall said: "It is not sufficient to take the case out of the act, that the claim should be proved or be acknowledged to have been originally just; the acknowledgment must go to the fact that it is still due." In *Sutton* v. *Burruss*, 9 Leigh 381, the defendant acknowledged the items of the plaintiff's account to be just; *but said at the same time that he had some offsets.* This was held by a unanimous court not to be sufficient even to put the defendant on the proof of his offsets. Judge Cabell said: "This promise, then, certainly left the defendant exposed to all the inconveniences arising from the loss of testimony in relation to his offsets; and we cannot therefore give effect to it, without frustrating the great object of the statute." These four items may have been, and doubtless were, very proper items of an account between the parties; but they may not have been all the items that would have been proper in such an account. There may have been payments and set-offs. There was a palpable error on the face of the account which might have been detected almost at a single glance. The plaintiff was charged with one year's interest too much on 1700 dollars. That this error was not detected shews that the plaintiff had no idea of assuming to pay the balance of the account; and paid

VOL. VIII.—9

no attention to it except to see that he owed as much as 1800 dollars, which he paid by the drafts on Shook.

There was, then, no such acknowledgment or promise in writing as will take the set-off out of the operation of the statute.

Secondly. Has there been such a part payment of the set-off as will take it out of the statute?

I will have very little to say in answer to this question, as most of what I have said in answer to the preceding applies with at least as much force to that now under consideration. A part payment can have no effect in taking a case out of the statute, except so far as it implies an acknowledgment of a debt, and promise to pay it. If a part payment be made of a particular debt, as of a promissory note, it affords strong evidence of an acknowledgment of the balance as a subsisting debt. But the mere fact of payment is insufficient. It must be shewn that the payment was made in part discharge of a larger debt, and of the particular debt sued for. Joynes, p. 124; *Tippetts* v. *Hearne*, 4 Tyrw. R. 772. "The part payment," as Mr. Joynes correctly says, "being only evidence of a promise to pay, gives a new action only for so much as the party thereby admits himself to be liable for." "Thus when a defendant pays money into court he does not thereby lose the benefit of the statute, as to the residue of the plaintiff's demand, because the only effect of the payment into court is to admit the defendant's liability for the sum so paid." See the cases cited by Joynes, p. 130. A payment made on account may or may not amount to an acknowledgment of the balance of the account. "If the part payment is made under circumstances which shew that the debtor did not intend to recognize his liability, or admit his willingness to pay the balance, it will not avail the creditor against a plea of the statute." Joynes, p. 128; *Linsell* v. *Bonsor*, 29 Eng. C. L. R. 319. We must therefore always look

1851.
July
Term.

Bell
v.
Crawford.

not only to the fact of the payment, but to all the surrounding and attending circumstances, to see whether a
payment on an account implies an intention to acknowledge the balance of the account and promise to pay it.
What the debtor says at the instant of making the payment is the best evidence of his intention, and usually
sufficient to explain it. In this case the payment was
accompanied by a letter, which affords the best possible
evidence of the character of the payment and the intention of the plaintiff in regard to the balance of the
account. What the meaning of that letter is in this
respect, whether construed alone or in reference to all
the surrounding circumstances, has already been considered. And the questions whether a promise to pay the
balance of the account is implied by the letter, as an
acknowledgment or promise in writing under the act of
April 1838, and whether such promise is implied by
part payment, arising out of the drafts enclosed in that
letter, are in effect one and the same question, and must
receive the same answer. Having already answered
the former in the negative, I therefore answer the latter
in the same way.

Then did the Circuit court err in refusing to exclude
from the jury all evidence introduced by the defendant
in support of the set-off, on the ground that it was
barred by the statute of limitations, and that said evidence in law was not sufficient to remove the bar? I
think it did; and that this conclusion necessarily follows from what I have already said. If the evidence,
taken (and I have taken it) to be all true, shews neither
such an acknowledgment or promise in writing, or such
a part payment as can take the set-off out of the operation of the statute, then the set-off must of necessity
fall, and with it the evidence offered in its support. If
the court had been moved to instruct the jury that
even if they believed the whole of the said evidence, it
was not sufficient to justify them in finding that the set-

off was not barred by the statute of limitations, it would have been the same in form with the motion in the case of *Sutton* v. *Burruss*, 9 Leigh 381; for overruling which the judgment of the Circuit court was unanimously reversed by this court. The motions in that case and this, though different in form, are, I think, the same in substance. The court no more invades the province of the jury by excluding evidence than by pronouncing it insufficient in law. By one course the evidence is thrown out of the case, and by the other it is destroyed: which, in effect, is the same thing. In *Bell* v. *Morrison*, 1 Peters R. 351, the motion was to exclude the evidence in the very form in which it was made in this case, and the evidence was accordingly excluded. No objection was made by the Supreme court to the form of the motion or instruction in that case.

In the view I have taken of this case, I deem it unnecessary to consider the other questions which arise on the first bill of exceptions. Two of them are important questions; as, 1st, whether the five years limitation to an offset is to be computed from the time of commencing the action or filing the set-off; and, 2d, whether a promise implied from part payment is within the operation of the act of April 1838. In regard to the first question, it was decided by this court in *Trimyer* v. *Pollard*, 5 Gratt. 460, that if the set-off accrued before the action was brought, the limitation is to be computed from the commencement of the action. There may be some doubt as to whether more than two judges so far concurred in that decision as to make it a binding authority. However that may be, and whatever might be my own opinion of the question as an original one, (and I have not so far considered it as to have formed a decided opinion on the subject,) I am willing to consider it as settled by that case: for I consider it more important that the question should be *settled*, than that it should be settled in any particular way. In regard to the second question, it has never been decided by this court, and is one of very great doubt and difficulty. It can never arise under our new Code, and is therefore becoming daily a question of less importance. For the present I forbear to express even the inclination of my own mind upon it.

I think the court erred in overruling the plaintiff's motion for a new trial, for the same reasons for which I think it erred in not excluding the evidence introduced by the defendant in support of the set-off.

On the whole I am for reversing the judgment.

DANIEL, *J.* concurred in the judgment of the court.

ALLEN, *J.* concurred in the opinion of *Moncure*, J.

BALDWIN, *J.* dissented.

The judgment of the court was as follows:

The court is of opinion that the Circuit court did not err in overruling the motion of the plaintiff "to exclude from the jury all evidence introduced by the defendant to prove his set-off, upon the ground that said defendant had not filed with his plea an account of the set-offs, as the statute directs." The defendant, substantially if not literally, complied with the directions of the statute, by filing with his plea the note in writing which was the subject of his set-off, and the record shews that the plaintiff had full notice of the character of the set-off, and that he was not taken by surprise on the trial.

But the court is further of opinion that, upon the facts certified by the said Circuit court as proved in the case, the said set-off is barred by the statute of limitations; and therefore that the said court erred in overruling the motion of the plaintiff to exclude from the

1851.
July
Term.

Bell
v.
Crawford.

jury all the evidence introduced by the defendant in support of the said set-off, on the ground that it is barred by the statute of limitations; and that the said evidence in law is not sufficient to remove that bar; and also erred in·overruling the motion of the plaintiff for a new trial on the ground that the verdict was contrary to the evidence.

Therefore it is considered that the said judgment be reversed and annulled; and that the plaintiff recover against the defendant his costs by him expended in the prosecution of his writ aforesaid here. And this court proceeding to enter such judgment as the said Circuit court ought to have entered, it is further considered that the verdict of the jury be set aside. And the cause is remanded to the said Circuit court for a new trial to be had therein.

---

## Lewisburg.

1851.
July
Term.

### MEEKS' *adm'r*, &c. v. THOMPSON & *als.*

(Absent *Cabell*, P.)

September 10th.

1. Where the charge upon land by will, for the payment of debts, is general, the purchaser from the executor or the administrator with the will annexed is not bound to see to the application of the purchase money.
2. In such case, if the sale was necessary at the time it was made, and was fairly made, and the purchase money has been paid, the failure of the executor or administrator to account for and pay over the proceeds to the creditors of the estate will not impair the title of the vendee.

3. Land in which a widow is entitled to dower being sold by an executor under a charge for payment of debts, he should be credited in his account of the proceeds for the amount he has paid the widow in satisfaction of her dower interest.

1851.
July
Term.

Meeks'
adm'r, &c.
v.
Thompson
& als.

This case was before this court in 1836, and is reported in 7 Leigh 419. That report gives a sufficiently full statement of the case up to the period when that appeal was taken; and the decision of this court only left open the question whether the sale of the land to Joseph Meeks was necessary.

When the case went back, the infant children of James P. Thompson having attained the age of twenty-one years, the suit was carried on in their names, and Joseph Meeks dying, it was revived against his executor, James Meeks, and on his death it was revived in the name of Thomas J. Boyd, administrator of James, and administrator *de bonis non* with the will annexed of Joseph Meeks.

In 1841 the commissioner, John P. Matthews, returned his report of the administration of William P. Thompson upon the estate of James P. Thompson. By this report a balance appeared against the administrator, on the 1st of January 1823, of 1600 dollars 40 cents. In this account the administrator was charged with the purchase money of the land sold Meeks in 1814, and also with the purchase money of other lands sold in 1821 to Adam Waterford, William Hinnegar and James Day, amounting to 981 dollars. There was also a special statement of debts which the defendant insisted were due from the estate of James P. Thompson, amounting to 6843 dollars 46 cents.

At the April term of the court for 1845 the commissioner made another report, in which he stated that at the period of the sale of the land to Meeks there was no personal estate of James P. Thompson unadministered, and that all of the personal estate was charged in the report of 1841. He reported also that at the

1851.
July
Term.

Meeks'
adm'r, &c.
v.
Thompson
& als.

time of the sale to Meeks there was unsold the lands afterwards purchased by Waterford, Hinnegar and Day: And that there was still other lands belonging to the estate, though of very little value; they being in very small parcels, and valued at twenty-five cents an acre; some of which had been sold for taxes.

The report of 1841 was excepted to by both plaintiffs and defendants. The third exception of the plaintiffs was " to allowing any of the claims reported by the commissioner in his special statement, of unsatisfied debts due from the estate of James P. Thompson," as valid or just claims against the estate. Among the claims reported in that special statement is one of 535 dollars, which was paid by Joseph Meeks to H. Smith, the marshal of the Chancery court, under a decree of the court to foreclose a prior mortgage upon a part of the land purchased by Meeks. Another claim reported in that special statement was for 200 dollars which Meeks had paid to Mrs. James P. Thompson for her dower interest in the land purchased by him.

The second exception of Meeks' administrator was to the failure of the commissioner to allow for the deficiency in the quantity of land purchased by Meeks; twenty-two acres of the land so purchased being covered by the better title of Lewis Smith, which, at the average price of the whole tract, amounted to 133 dollars 73 cents. The fourth exception was because the commissioner failed to embrace in his special statement the amount of a bond from James P. Thompson to Robert Sayers, dated the 4th of October 1813, for 180 dollars, the existence of which was proved by Sayers' executor. The fifth exception was to the refusal of the commissioner to allow to Meeks a credit for the 200 dollars paid to Margaret Thompson, the widow of James P. Thompson, for her dower interest in the land sold to him.

1851.
July
Term.

Meeks'
adm'r, &c.
v.
Thompson
& als.

The cause came on to be heard in April 1845, when the court overruled the first and second exceptions of the plaintiffs and sustained the third, and overruled all the exceptions of the defendant Meek's administrator, and made a decree by which the sale of the land to Joseph Meeks was set aside; and an account of the moneys paid by Meeks which went to the extinguishment of the debts of James P. Thompson, and also an account of the rents and profits of the land, together with the permanent improvements made by Meeks thereon, was directed. And the commissioner was directed to ascertain the location and quantity of any of the lands of James P. Thompson, directed to be sold in the first instance for the payment of debts, which remained unsold. From this decree Meeks' administrator applied to this court for an appeal, which was allowed.

*B. R. Johnston*, for the appellant.
*Fulton*, for the appellees.

ALLEN, *J.* delivered the opinion of the court.

It appearing that when this case was before this court on a former occasion, it was held that the grant of administration with the will annexed to William P. Thompson was not a void grant, and that the administrator was empowered to make sale of the land charged by the testator with the payment of his debts; and that, as the will charged all the lands, the administrator was authorized to sell the whole thereof, if such sale became necessary to pay the debts; this court is of opinion that in the case of such a general charge upon the lands, it was not incumbent on the purchaser to look to the application of the purchase money. If the condition of the estate rendered such sale necessary at the time the same was made, and the sale was fair, and the purchase money has been paid, the failure of the administrator to account for and pay over the proceeds to

1851.
July
Term.

Meeks'
adm'r. &c.
v.
Thompson
& als.

the creditors of the estate should not impair the title of
the vendee. The sale in the present case is shewn to
have been for a full price; and the only enquiry left
open by the decree of this court is whether the sale
was necessary for the payment of the debts of the testator. In determining this question it is necessary to
ascertain what debts were chargeable to the estate, and
whether the same could have been discharged without
a sale of the land in the proceedings mentioned sold to
Joseph Meeks. To the debts appearing due and credited
in the administration account, there should, in the opinion of this court, have been added the debt of 535
dollars paid to H. Smith, the marshal, being the amount
of the mortgage on a part of the land sold to Meeks;
and also the debt due to Sayers, designated in the 4th
exception of the appellants. And there should have
been deducted from the amount of assets charged to the
administrator the 200 dollars paid to the widow for her
dower in the land sold, and the sum claimed for the
deficiency in the quantity of the land. It is shewn by
the administration account, as settled since the former
decree of this court, and which was approved by the
Circuit court, that after charging the administrator
with the personal assets and the proceeds arising from
the sale of the real estate, including the land in controversy, he is in arrear the sum of 1600 dollars 40 cents.
This balance would be nearly if not quite extinguished
by the proper charges before referred to. The unsold
lands are proved to be of but little value; so that, without reference to the other debts alleged to have been
outstanding and still unsatisfied, it is manifest that the
condition of the estate required a sale of the whole of
the lands devised, to satisfy the debts of the testator.
The court is therefore of opinion that the Circuit court
erred in holding that such sale was unnecessary, and in
setting the same aside for that cause: And the sale not
being impeached in the bill for any other cause, the bill

of the plaintiffs should have been dismissed as against the representative of Joseph Meeks.

1851.
July
Term.

Meeks'
adm'r, &c.
v.
Thompson
& als.

And the court is further of opinion, as to so much of the bill as seeks an account from the administrator, and the decree in respect to that branch of the case, there is no error in so much thereof as overrules the 1st and 2d exceptions of the appellees and the 1st and 3d exceptions of the appellant to the report of master commissioner Matthews; but the said court erred in overruling the 5th exception of the appellant for the failure to allow the administrator credit for 200 dollars, the sum paid the widow for her relinquishment of dower in the lands sold. The 2d and 4th exceptions of the appellant and the 3d exception of the appellees do not relate to the debits or credits on the administration account, but refer to that branch of the case respecting the indebtedness of the estate and the necessity of a sale of the lands in controversy, and have been before adverted to.

By overruling and sustaining the exceptions applicable to the administration account the balance of 1600 dollars 40 cents ascertained to be due by the report of the master commissioner, and the decree affirming the same, will be reduced by the sum of 200 dollars as aforesaid with interest. For the residue of said sum of 1600 dollars 40 cents, reduced as aforesaid, together with any other sums since received by the administrator, he is responsible.

It is therefore adjudged and ordered that said decree, so far as it conflicts with this opinion and decree, is erroneous, and that the same be reversed, with costs to the appellant; and this court proceeding to render such decree as the said Circuit court should have done, it is further adjudged and ordered that the bill of the appellees be dismissed as against the appellant, the representative of said Joseph Meeks, with costs in the Chancery court.

And the cause is retained as against the said William P. Thompson, the administrator, and remanded with instructions to recommit the same to the commissioner to reform and settle the account according to the principles of this decree, and with instructions to said court to give notice by proper publication to creditors, if any, whose claims are still valid and unsatisfied, to appear, assert and establish their claims, within a period to be prescribed by the court, and for a decree against said administrator for any balance ascertained upon the principles of this decree to be due from him, to be applied to the payment of such debts, or paid over to the appellees, as the rights of the parties may require.

---

## Lewisburg.

### PINCKARD v. WOODS, &c.

(Absent *Cabell*, P.)

September 11th.

An executor, who is also a legatee of one moiety of his testatrix's estate, sells the property and purchases about one half of it himself. He takes bonds from the purchasers of the other part of the estate, which shew upon their face that they are executed to him as executor. Afterwards he sells these bonds at a discount of from eighteen to twenty per cent., the purchaser knowing that the liabilities of the estate of the testatrix were very inconsiderable, and that the sale of the bonds was not necessary for any purposes of the administration. At the time of the sale the executor was solvent and his solvency was not questioned; but he afterwards failed, without paying the legatees of the other moiety of the estate. HELD: That the sale of the bonds at such a discount, when the circumstances of the estate did not require it, was a *devastavit* by the executor; and that the purchaser, having purchased with a knowledge of the fact, will be compelled to pay the amount of the bonds (if they do not amount to more than the *devastavit* of the executor) to the legatees; or if they have been paid by the sureties of the executor, the sureties are entitled to be substituted to the rights of the legatees.

Some time in the year 1836 Mary Crafton died, having first made her will, which was admitted to probat in the Circuit court of Franklin county. No executor being named in the will, Tyree G. Newbill qualified as administrator with the will annexed, and entered into a bond in the penalty of 7000 dollars, with Wiley P. Woods and Joseph Rives as his sureties. By her will, after directing her debts to be paid, she gave one half her estate to Newbill, and the other half to Mary and Catharine Phillips, in equal proportions.

In November 1836 Newbill sold the whole property, all of which was personal, and nearly all of it slaves, upon a credit of twelve months. The sales amounted to 5014 dollars 8 cents, of which Newbill purchased to the amount of 2335 dollars 25 cents. One of the slaves was bought by Hopkins Nowlin at the price of 1200 dollars, and another was purchased by Robert T. Woods for 1250 dollars, and each of them gave his bond with security to Newbill as administrator for his purchases: And on the 10th of February 1837 these bonds were sold by Newbill to Charles Pinckard at a discount of between eighteen and twenty per cent. The debts due from the estate amounted to but about 185 dollars, all of which seems to have been paid off at an early day by the administrator.

Newbill not having paid to Mary and Catharine Phillips their proportion of Mrs. Crafton's estate, they instituted a suit against him and his sureties, Woods and Rives, and in May 1844 they obtained a decree for the sum of 2391 dollars 85 cents, with interest thereon from the 28th day of October 1837 until paid, and their costs. Although Newbill seems to have been in 1836, and for some time afterwards, entirely solvent, and although he was in good credit until the year 1840, yet when this decree was obtained he had become insolvent, and had absconded from the country; and the amount of the decree was paid by the sureties, Woods and Rives, in August 1844.

A few days after the decree in favour of the Phillips had been paid by them, Woods and Rives instituted a suit on the chancery side of the Circuit court of Franklin county against Newbill and Charles Pinckard, seeking to set aside the sale by Newbill to Pinckard of the bonds of Nowlin and Robert T. Woods. In their bill, after stating substantially the foregoing facts, they charged that the condition of the estate of Mary Crafton did not render a sale of the bonds necessary; that Newbill was not in advance to the estate, and that he had purchased at his sale of the property to about the amount of his legacy. They charged that at the time of the purchase of these bonds by Pinckard he knew that he was dealing with an administrator for the assets of his testatrix's estate, and that by the sale the administrator was committing a *devastavit* and a fraud upon the legatees of the testatrix and upon his own sureties; and that independent of this personal knowledge on the part of Pinckard, the bonds shewed on their face that they were due to Newbill in his character of administrator of Mary Crafton deceased, and were thus notice to Pinckard that they were assets of her estate; and that by buying the bonds at a discount he was aiding Newbill to convert the same to his own use, and to commit a *devastavit* and a fraud upon the legatees of his testatrix as well as the sureties of Newbill.

The prayer of the bill was that Pinckard should be compelled to account for and pay to the plaintiffs the amount of money due upon the bonds and received by him, with interest thereon, or so much as should be sufficient to satisfy the plaintiffs for what they had been compelled to pay to Mary and Catharine Phillips, with interest; and for general relief.

The defendant Pinckard in his answer admitted that the bonds of Nowlin and Robert T. Woods were given for purchases of the slaves of the testatrix of Newbill, and were payable to Newbill as administrator with the will annexed of Mary Crafton; and that he purchased the bonds from Newbill at a discount of from eighteen to twenty per cent., which he considered their fair cash value. He said that at the time of purchasing the bonds he knew nothing of the state of the assets of the testatrix's estate, nor of any waste or mismanagement committed by Newbill. He knew that after paying the debts of the testatrix, which he believed to be inconsiderable, that the residue of the estate was to go by one moiety to Newbill and by the other to Mary and Catharine Phillips; and he considered that the bonds purchased as aforesaid would not overgo the part of the estate bequeathed to Newbill. In making the purchase he had no idea of committing a fraud, or of being instrumental in aiding the administrator in committing a *devastavit*.

It is unnecessary to detail the proceedings in the cause. It is enough to say that a commissioner's report ascertained that after crediting on the amount paid by the plaintiffs to the Phillips some small sums of money received by them from the property of Newbill, there remained of that debt the sum of 3542 dollars 66 cents due on the 10th day of June 1847. In August 1848 the court made a decree against Newbill and Pinckard, in favour of the plaintiffs, for this sum, with interest on 3397 dollars 20 cents, a part thereof, from the 10th day of June 1847 until paid, and their costs. And liberty was reserved to Pinckard, if he should pay the said debt to the plaintiffs, hereafter to apply to the court for a decree against Newbill for the amount so paid by him. From this decree Pinckard applied to this court for an appeal, which was allowed.

*Boyd* and *Patton*, for the appellant, insisted that the only ground upon which a purchaser from an executor can be held liable to creditors or legatees, is that the executor was guilty of a fraud in the sale, and the purchaser had, with knowledge, participated in it. That a fraud by the executor was not enough, but that there must have been a participation with knowledge in the execution of the fraud. And they went into an examination of the facts to prove that Pinckard was not a participator in any fraud in the purchase of the bonds, even if Newbill intended to commit a fraud: which they did not admit. They referred to *Nugent* v. *Gifford*, 1 Atk. R. 463, and note; *Mead* v. *Lord Orrery*, 3 Atk. R. 235; *McLeod* v. *Drummond*, 14 Ves. R. 352; *S. C.*, 17 Ves. R. 153; *Field* v. *Schieffelin*, 7 John. Ch. R. 150; 1 Story's Equ. Jur. § 422–23, 580; 1 Lomax Ex'ors 346–7–8, and note.

*Cooke*, for the appellee, admitted there was no doubt of the administrator's right to sell, and that the purchaser was not bound to look to the disposition of the purchase money; but with the exception that if there is anything unfair in the sale, the purchaser is liable for the amount of the property. And he referred to 2 Wms. Ex'ors 611; 1 Story's Equ. Jur. § 422; *Scott* v. *Tyler*, 2 Dick. R. 712. And he reviewed the facts, and insisted that according to *Fisher* v. *Bassett*, 9 Leigh 119, the sale of the bonds at a discount of eighteen per cent. was itself a fraud in the administrator, and that Pinckard participated with knowledge in the fraud.

BALDWIN, *J.* delivered the opinion of the court.

It is the duty of an executor, not to sell, but to collect, the debts due to the estate of his testator, including those arising out of sales of goods made by the executor in the course of his administration; and if he sells such debts at a price below their value, he thereby

1851.
July
Term.

Pinckard
v.
Woods, &c.

commits a *devastavit*, unless he makes it appear that such sale was manifestly required by the interests of the estate: and this he can never do without shewing, in the first place, that the proceeds thereof have been applied to the purposes of the estate. The appropriation by the executor of the proceeds of such a sale to his own individual uses presents the case of a fraudulent breach of trust on his part, for which, of course, he is personally liable to creditors, legatees and others, injuriously affected by such improper diversion of the assets. And the purchaser himself, so acquiring such debt at a profit, if he has reason to believe at the time that the same belongs to the estate, and is so disposed of by the executor for his individual uses, thereby concurs in such fraudulent breach of trust by the executor, and therefore incurs the like liability.

In this case the bonds purchased by the appellant from Newbill, the administrator with the will annexed of Mary Crafton deceased, were executed by the obligors for the prices of certain slaves belonging to the testatrix's estate, and sold by the administrator under the authority of her will; which bonds are on their face payable to Newbill in his character of administrator. The appellant had therefore the best reason to believe that the bonds belonged to the testatrix's estate, when he purchased them from the administrator at a discount of 18 or 20 per cent., and from the profit he was thus allowed to make, he had good reason to believe that the administrator was selling them for his own individual uses; a fact which the result and the condition of the estate have abundantly shewn. Under these circumstances, it was incumbent upon the appellant to stay his hand, until he should ascertain by the requisite enquiries that the sale was to be made for the purposes of the estate, and the sacrifice to be incurred indispensably necessary to prevent some still greater sacrifice. He must have known that it was not in the usual course of administration for an executor to sell debts due the estate at a sacrifice, and he was bound to know that such a sale cannot be tolerated unless under very peculiar emergencies of the estate. If he had made the enquiry, he would have ascertained that the condition of the estate did not require the sale of the bonds. But in truth he knew it without the necessity of enquiry; for he says in his answer that "he was aware that after satisfying the debts of the testatrix, which he believed to be inconsiderable, and the specific legacy of the bed and furniture, the residue of her estate was to go by one moiety to the said Newbill, and by the other to Mary and Catharine Phillips, and he considered that the bonds he was purchasing would not overgo the part of the estate bequeathed to Newbill"; and so defending himself upon the ground that his speculation was warranted, as he believed, by the administrator's individual interest in the estate. But he ought to have known that the administrator had no right to appropriate the assets to the satisfaction of his own legacy, to the entire exclusion of the other legatees; and he was bound to ascertain that Newbill's legacy had not already been satisfied, as in fact it was by his individual purchases at the public sale of the property of the estate; unless, indeed, he chose to apply them by actual payment to the satisfaction of his co-equal legatees.

It is no valid defence for the appellant that at the time he purchased the bonds it was his belief and that of the public generally that the administrator was then in solvent circumstances. Such belief may have induced him to look to the individual responsibility of the administrator as a guarantee against the failure of his speculation, and to that responsibility he must still look, and its having proved abortive furnishes no reason for throwing the consequent loss upon those whom he has aggrieved by his intermeddling with the affairs of the estate, from no other motive than the desire of gain to himself, and careless as to its effects upon the rights of others.

Nor does the statute of limitations afford protection to the appellant, for the appellees have no remedy but in equity, which will not allow its application to such a case as this.

The decree, therefore, of the Circuit court is proper, in holding the appellant responsible to the appellees for the money paid by them as sureties of the administrator to Mary and Catharine Phillips, in discharge of the decree of the Circuit court of Campbell county. But there is error therein to the extent of 38 dollars 75 cents, the costs recovered against the appellees, in their unsuccessful injunction suit with Garland's ex'or, &c., there being no propriety in subjecting the appellant therefor. This error is, however, more than counterbalanced by another against the appellees to the extent of 136 dollars 81 cents, by crediting the appellant twice with that sum on account of the funds received by the appellees for their indemnity as sureties in the administration bond, under the deed of trust from Newbill in the proceedings mentioned, which error is made to appear by a note of appellees' counsel filed with the record, and marked J. R. C.

And the appellees, by their counsel, not desiring to disturb the said decree because of the said error to their prejudice, and the court being of opinion that there is none to the prejudice of the appellant, it is adjudged, ordered and decreed that the same be affirmed, with costs to the appellees.

1851.
July
Term.

# 𝕷𝖊𝖜𝖎𝖘𝖇𝖚𝖗𝖌.

## LEWIS & als. v. CAPERTON's ex'or & als.

(Absent *Cabell*, P. and *Moncure*, J.*)

#### September 22d.

1. A deed executed *bona fide* to secure a loan of money, not to be enforced for ten years, is a valid deed as against creditors of the grantor.

2. A deed which conveys, without a schedule, household furniture, the various kinds of stock on a farm, bacon and lard, to secure a *bona fide* debt, but not to be enforced for eighteen months after its execution, is valid against creditors, though the deed was made without the knowledge of the creditor, and the grantor was indebted to insolvency at the time of the conveyance.

3. A deed which conveys land to secure a *bona fide* debt, which is not to be enforced for two years, and only then or afterwards upon a notice of the sale for one hundred and twenty days, is valid against creditors.

4. Such a deed is valid though the execution of the deed is postponed for five years from the date of the conveyance; and the rents and profits of the property in the meantime is reserved to the grantor.

5. A deed which conveys future rents and profits of property conveyed in other deeds, which were reserved to the grantor in the previous deeds, for the purpose of paying a *bona fide* debt, is valid against creditors of the grantor.

6. A vendor of land retains the title in accordance with the contract. He has a lien on the land for the purchase money, as against creditors or incumbrancers of the vendee; and this though the vendee has subsequently executed a deed by which he conveys other property to secure the purchase money.

7. A post-nuptial settlement made by a husband on his wife, of personal property derived from her father's estate, but of which he retains possession, not having been properly recorded, is void as against the creditors of the husband.

8. A deed made by a husband embarrassed at the time, by which he conveys the proceeds of his wife's land which had been

---

* The cause was argued before Judge *Moncure's* appointment.

1851.
July
Term.

Lewis
& als.
v.
Caperton's
ex'or
& als.

sold, and the note for the purchase money made to him, in trust for himself and his wife for their lives and the life of the survivor, and during his life to be under his control and management, is voluntary and fraudulent as to creditors.

9. A deed which conveys land to secure a *bona fide* debt due to the grantee, and also a debt to the grantor's wife, which is voluntary and fraudulent as to his creditors, and the nature of which debt is known to the grantee, is null and void as a security for the first as well as the last mentioned debt, as against subsequent incumbrancers and creditors of the grantor.

10. The declarations of a wife at the time she executes a deed, or at other times, that she has executed or does execute the deed because her husband had promised that he would settle or because he had settled upon her certain property derived from her father's estate, is not sufficient evidence of a contract between them for such a settlement in consideration of her relinquishment of her right of dower in her husband's land, and thus to support such settlement if made, against creditors or incumbrancers, even to the extent of a reasonable compensation for the right of dower which she relinquished.

11. There being several deeds, conveying in succession the same property, and not merely the equity of redemption therein, every successive incumbrance binds all the property not absorbed in satisfaction of the previous valid incumbrances. And if some of the incumbrances are declared void at the suit of a creditor of the grantor, such creditor is not entitled to have his debt substituted in the place of such void incumbrance to the extent thereof; but the subsequent valid incumbrances have preference.

12. Property covered by various deeds of trust, which may be enforced at different periods, having been sequestrated at the suit of a judgment creditor of the grantor, when the court disposes of the trust subjects, and the rents and profits thereof, the creditor will only be entitled to the rents and profits of the different trust subjects up to the earliest period when either of the valid incumbrances covering such subject was authorized to be enforced. And the different incumbrancers will each be entitled to the rents and profits of the subject covered by his deed from the time he was authorized by the terms of the deed to enforce it.

13. The wife of the grantor not having joined in the first deed, conveying land to secure a debt; but uniting in a second deed, conveying the same land to secure another creditor, the second incumbrancer is entitled to the value of the

1851.
July
Term.

Lewis
& als.
v.
Caperton's
ex'or
& als.

wife's contingent right of dower in the land, to be paid out of its proceeds, as against and in preference to the first incumbrancer.

14. QUÆRE: If the wife's relinquishment of her contingent right of dower in land, where there is no complete alienation of the estate by the husband, but a mere incumbrance given for the security of a debt, constitutes a sufficient consideration for a settlement on the wife.

This was a bill filed in the Circuit court of Monroe county in October 1842 by Hugh Caperton against John B. Lewis and the trustees and *cestuis que trust* in twelve deeds executed by Lewis, eleven of which were charged to be fraudulent and intended to hinder and delay the plaintiff, a creditor of Lewis, in the recovery of his debt. The pleadings and proofs exhibit the following facts:

John Lewis devised to his two sons, John B. Lewis and Thomas P. Lewis, the Sweet springs, in the county of Monroe, with a considerable body of land in Monroe and Alleghany counties; the Sweet springs tract proper containing one hundred and fifty-nine acres. By an agreement under their hands and seals, bearing date the 25th of September 1834, Thomas P. Lewis sold to John B. Lewis all Thomas's right and title in and to the Sweet springs, together with all other lands bequeathed to him by his father, situate in the counties of Monroe and Alleghany, for the sum of 20,000 dollars, with legal interest from the first day of the next January 1835; the amount to be paid by annual payments extending to the year 1846; but no conveyance was made.

By deed poll bearing date the 9th day of February 1837, and prepared and probably executed in South Carolina, John B. Lewis conveyed to William E. Haskell the Sweet springs tract of land, containing one hundred and fifty-nine acres, for the purpose of securing to Haskell the payment of 10,000 dollars, with its interest, which he at that time borrowed from Haskell, and

1851.
July
Term.

Lewis
& als.
v.
Caperton's
ex'or
& als.

for which he gave his bond, with his brother, William L. Lewis, as his surety, payable in ten years; the interest thereon to be paid annually. Mrs. Caroline S. H. Lewis, the wife of John B. Lewis, was not a party to this deed, but she signed it, and her privy examination having been taken before two justices of the peace for the county of Monroe, the deed, with the certificate of the privy examination of Mrs. Lewis, was admitted to record in the clerk's office of the county of Monroe.

By deed poll executed in South Carolina, and bearing date the 11th day of January 1839, John B. Lewis, upon the consideration, as expressed in the deed, of natural love and affection, and of one dollar, conveyed to William L. Lewis twenty-four slaves by name, which the deed stated had been allotted to John B. Lewis in right of his wife, on a division of the negroes of the estate of her father, William R. Thomson, of South Carolina; also the sum of 7000 dollars, then vested in a note drawn by William S. Thomson and others in his favour, the consideration of which was the interest of Mrs. Lewis in the real estate of her father, William R. Thomson. This conveyance was in trust for the use and benefit of himself and wife during their lives and the life of the survivor, and during his life to be under his control and management; and if he should invest the said 7000 dollars in property, the same was to be subject to the same trusts; and upon their death to their children who should survive either of them.

This deed was admitted to record in the Orangeburg district, South Carolina, on the day of its date, upon proof of its execution by a witness thereto; and was recorded in the clerk's office of the County court of Monroe on the 9th of January 1840. The endorsement of the clerk on the deed is: " The foregoing was presented in this office, and which, together with the certificate of its acknowledgment, was admitted to be recorded, which was done." The clerk, who was ex-

1851.
July
Term.

Lewis
& als.
v.
Caperton's
ex'or
& als.

amined as a witness, stated that John B. Lewis took the deed to the clerk's office and handed it to the clerk with a request that he would record it and give it to him before he left; which was done. The deed was not reported to the court or advertised at the courthouse door; but this omission was accidental.

Between the period when John B. Lewis purchased the interest of Thomas P. Lewis in the Sweet springs property, and the end of the year 1841, he proceeded to make improvements upon it at great cost; and in 1841 he was largely indebted: Among his creditors was Hugh Caperton, of Monroe county. In February 1841 Lewis executed to Caperton two single bills, one for 5641 dollars 57 cents, and the other for 13,102 dollars 83 cents. And about the same time he, with James L. Woodville as his surety, executed another single bill to Caperton for about 4520 dollars 25 cents. In December 1841 Caperton instituted suits upon the first two of these single bills, and recovered judgments thereon in May 1842.

Soon after the service of the process upon Lewis at the suit of Caperton, he seems to have visited South Carolina; and whilst there he executed two deeds poll, bearing date the 24th of February 1842. The one reciting that he was indebted to William L. Lewis, of Orangeburg district, South Carolina, as trustee of the wife of John B. Lewis, in the sum of 7000 dollars, by a promissory note bearing date the 1st day of June 1839, with interest, and also in the further sum of 5200 dollars, by a promissory note in favour of William L. Lewis, dated the 1st of September 1841, with interest. For the purpose of securing the said sums of money, with interest, he conveyed to said William L. Lewis a tract of one thousand acres of land, including the Sweet springs tract. This deed was admitted to record in South Carolina; and was also admitted to record in the clerk's office of the County court of Monroe on the

1851.
July
Term.

Lewis
& als.
v.
Caperton's
ex'or
& als.

15th of March 1842, upon the certificate by two justices of the acknowledgment thereof by John B. Lewis. And although Mrs. Lewis was not a party to the deed, and did not sign it, her privy examination was taken and certified.

The other deed, executed at the same time, conveyed to William L. Lewis, for the same purposes, all the grantor's household and kitchen furniture used at his dwelling or other houses on his plantation in Monroe county, and his horses, mules, cattle, hogs, sheep, wagons, gear and all the plantation tools and implements belonging to said plantation. This deed was also recorded in South Carolina, and afterwards in the proper office here, upon the certificate of John B. Lewis' acknowledgment before two justices of the peace for the county of Monroe.

By another deed, which bore date the 11th of March 1842, John B. Lewis, reciting that he was indebted to John Cochran in the sum of 500 dollars, conveyed to Henry Massie all his personal property, described as consisting of household furniture of all the varieties of such property, and bacon, lard, hogs, mules, horses, cattle and sheep, in trust that if the said Lewis should, on or before the 1st day of October 1843, pay to John Cochran the sum of 500 dollars, with interest from the 11th of March 1842, then the indenture to be void; otherwise the trustee should, after the said 1st of October 1843, proceed to sell, &c., and pay to Cochran the said sum of 500 dollars, with the interest due thereon. This deed was duly admitted to record on the 15th of March.

By another deed, dated the 16th of March 1842, Lewis, reciting that he was indebted to Thomas P. Lewis 16,000 dollars, conveyed to Massie the Sweet springs, with all the lands attached thereto either by purchase or inheritance, lying in the counties of Monroe and Alleghany, and all the right, title and estate of the said Lewis therein, and all his hogs, horses, cattle, sheep, plantation utensils of every kind, wagons, &c., bedsteads, beds, mattresses, &c., &c., &c., carriage and harness, kitchen furniture and cooking utensils, and table furniture of every kind, books and paintings, in trust to secure the execution of the agreement between himself and Thomas P. Lewis for the purchase of the moiety of the Sweet springs property. And if the said John B. Lewis failed to comply with that agreement, then the trustee was authorized to sell, after giving six months notice.

On the same day John B. Lewis and Caroline, his wife, conveyed to James L. Woodville the same lands mentioned in the last deed, in trust to secure a debt of 8500 dollars due to the branch of the Bank of Virginia at Buchanan. This deed provided that upon a failure to pay the interest on the 17th of December of each year, or the failure to pay the principal on the 20th of March 1844, the trustee should proceed to sell upon one hundred and twenty days notice; and pay to the bank the said sum, with the interest due.

On the same day Lewis conveyed to Henry Massie the same lands to secure a debt of 5535 dollars due to William P. Phillips, of the town of Charlottesville, with interest from the 1st of October 1841. This trust was not to be executed before the 1st of October 1845, and in the meantime Lewis was to take the profits of the property for his own use and benefit. And the same provision was contained in the preceding deeds. The three last mentioned deeds were admitted to record on the 17th of March 1842.

On the 4th of April 1842 Lewis conveyed the Sweet springs land to Massie for the purpose of indemnifying James L. Woodville as his surety in a bond to Hugh Caperton for 4520 dollars 25 cents, dated the 24th of February 1841. This trust was not to be executed before the 4th of April 1844; and in the meantime Lewis was to take the profits to his own use. This

1851.
July
Term.

Lewis
& als.
v.
Caperton's-
ex'or
& als.

deed was recorded on the 11th of April. And on the 29th of the same month, Lewis, for the purpose of securing the same debt, conveyed to Massie the Sweet springs tract, and also all his lands adjoining the Sweet springs, and especially a tract below the Sweet springs called the lower place, and a tract of four hundred acres above the Sweet springs next the mountain, with all the furniture on the premises at the Sweet springs, upon trust that Lewis should be permitted to retain possession of the property, giving to the trustee, for the further security of Woodville, the profits of said springs for two years from the date of the deed, after defraying the necessary expenses of keeping the same. And if any part of the debt remained due on the 29th of April 1844, then that the trustee should proceed, upon ninety days notice, to sell and pay, &c. This deed was recorded on the 5th of May.

On the 5th of April 1842 Lewis and wife, for the purpose of securing Andrew Allen and numerous other creditors, conveyed to Massie all Lewis's lands in the counties of Monroe and Alleghany, being the same lands before conveyed, upon trust to sell after the 5th of April 1843, for the purpose of paying two small debts due to Samuel Price and Joseph Damron; and in trust to sell after the 5th of April 1847, to pay the other creditors mentioned in the deed. In this deed John B. Lewis warranted the property conveyed against all claims except such persons as claimed under and by virtue of deeds of trust then of record in the clerk's office of the County court of Monroe. This deed was admitted to record on the 11th of April.

On the 1st of May 1842 Lewis, for the purpose of securing a debt of 590 dollars due to John H. Peyton, conveyed to Massie, beds, bedsteads, mattresses, pillows, &c., &c., &c., groceries of every kind, bacon, salt, lard, table furniture, cooking utensils, plantation tools, sheep, cows, calves, stock cattle, together with old hay stand-

1851.
July
Term.

Lewis
& als.
v.
Caperton's
ex'or
& als.

ing in the meadows, also the crop of grain then growing upon the plantation, with the then present growing crop of grass, upon trust to sell after the 1st of May 1844, upon a notice of two months, and to pay the debt. This deed was admitted to record on the 9th of May.

On the 5th of April 1842 John B. Lewis executed another deed to Massie and William L. Lewis, in which, after reciting that his wife, Caroline S. Lewis, in consideration that said John B. Lewis would convey in trust for her use the slaves therein after named, did join in a deed conveying the Sweet springs and all other real estate belonging to John B. Lewis in the counties of Monroe and Alleghany to James L. Woodville, in trust for the benefit of the banks, and that she had, on like consideration, on the same 5th of April 1842, joined to convey the same real estate to Henry Massie, in trust to secure various and numerous creditors, and in a deed conveying to Charles R. Thomson real estate in South Carolina devised to her by her father, William R. Thomson, in consideration of the premises and of one dollar, conveyed to Massie and William L. Lewis twenty-six slaves, by name, being the same mentioned in the deed of 11th of January 1839, upon trust that the said slaves should remain in the joint possession, use and enjoyment of John B. Lewis and his wife, Caroline S., during their joint lives, for their support, and to enable them to support and educate their children, and upon the death of John B. Lewis in the lifetime of his wife, for her support and that of her children, and at her death to be divided among the children. This deed was recorded the 11th of April 1842.

By another deed, bearing date the 18th of August 1842, John B. Lewis, reciting that it was his intention by the deed of the 5th of April to secure the slaves therein mentioned to the exclusive use of Mrs. Lewis and her children, but that by a mistake of the drafts-

1851.
July
Term.

Lewis
& als.
v.
Caperton's
ex'or
& als.

man of that deed an interest was reserved to John B. Lewis, and he considered himself morally and legally bound to secure the said slaves, with their future increase, for the exclusive use and enjoyment of his wife and her children, she having given an ample consideration therefor in the relinquishment of her right of dower in his estate and in the conveyance of her maiden lands in South Carolina, in consideration of the premises and of one dollar, conveyed the same slaves, with their future increase, to Massie and William L. Lewis, for the exclusive use, benefit and enjoyment of the said Caroline S. Lewis and her children by John B. Lewis. This deed was admitted to record the 22d of August 1842.

The deeds to secure Cochran, Peyton and Phillips seem to have been executed without the knowledge of these gentlemen; and Mr. Peyton states in his answer he did not see the deed to secure him until he saw it as an exhibit in this cause; though the debts were no doubt due to them from John B. Lewis. And although some of the creditors in the general deed may have known that Lewis was about to execute a deed to secure them, none of them were informed of or assented to its provisions before the deed was executed

It appears that Mrs. Thomson, the mother of Mrs. John B. Lewis, died in 1838, and that upon her death the land and slaves devised to her for her life passed, under the will of her husband, to his children, of whom Mrs. Lewis was one. Mrs. Lewis's interest in the land was sold to William S. Thomson and two others for 7000 dollars, and they executed their note to John B. Lewis for that sum. The slaves, except perhaps three, mentioned in the deed of January 1839, were slaves derived by Mrs. Lewis from the estate of her father; and it appears that Mrs. Thomson had put into Mrs. Lewis's hands 800 dollars of the assets of her husband's estate, with directions to invest it in negroes, and that this sum

1851.
July
Term.

Lewis
& als.
v.
Caperton's
ex'or
& als.

was invested in the three negroes not derived from Mr. Thomson's estate.

It appears further that about the time of the division of the slaves and the sale of the land, John B. Lewis declared his purpose to convey his wife's property in trust for her; and accordingly, after the division and sale, and before taking actual possession of the slaves, he executed to William L. Lewis the deed of the 11th day of January 1839. And soon thereafter he was permitted to take possession of the slaves and bring them to Virginia; and to receive from the purchasers of the land the 7000 dollars which they owed therefor; he executing to William L. Lewis, as trustee of Mrs. Lewis, his note for the same amount, as a borrower of the trust fund.

The only evidence, other than that furnished by the deeds, that John B. Lewis executed the deeds in favour of his wife upon any valuable consideration, were the declarations of Mrs. Lewis. One witness stated that in May or June 1837 she had heard Mrs. Lewis say, in the presence of her husband, that she had made over her right in the Sweet springs upon the condition that he was to make over to her all the property that was coming to her from her father's estate; and that in 1842 she heard Mrs. Lewis say again, that she made over her right to the Sweet springs in another deed, because her husband had told her he had made over to her by deed the property coming from her father's estate. So the justices of the peace by whom the privy examination of Mrs. Lewis was taken as to her execution of the deeds to Haskell, to Charles R. Thomson for her land in South Carolina, and to secure the Bank of Virginia and the general creditors of her husband, stated that at the time Mrs. Lewis executed the three last deeds, and immediately before signing them, she stated that she was induced to execute them in consideration of Dr. Lewis's securing

1851.
July
Term.

Lewis
& als.
v.
Caperton's
ex'or
& als.

to her the negroes made over in the deed of January 11th, 1839, and the price of her land in South Carolina, but that she made no such statement in relation to the deed to Haskell.

When Caperton recovered judgments against John B. Lewis, in May 1842, he sued out executions both of *fieri facias* and *capias ad satisfaciendum;* but the first were returned " no effects," and the latter " not found." At a subsequent day Thomas P. Lewis, his bail, surrendered him into custody, and he took the benefit of the act for the relief of insolvent debtors, surrendering nothing but his equity of redemption in the deeds herein before mentioned.

When the plaintiff filed his bill he prayed for an injunction to restrain the defendant Lewis and all others from selling, conveying away, or otherwise disposing of the slaves and other personal property mentioned in the deeds aforesaid. This injunction was awarded by one of the judges of the Circuit court; and it was ordered that unless John B. Lewis, or some one for him, should enter into bond with good security in the penalty of 15,000 dollars, with condition to have the slaves and other personal property forthcoming to abide the future order of the court, the sheriff should take possession, and make out an inventory thereof, and hire out the slaves until the next term of the Circuit court of Monroe county; and make report of his proceedings to court.

Subsequently, in December 1842, upon the application of Caperton to the same judge, the prior order was modified so as to authorize Lewis to retain the slaves in his possession until the next term of the Circuit court of Monroe, upon his executing a bond with security in the penalty of 5000 dollars. And it was further ordered that the sheriff should sell the live stock, other than slaves, and the hay and other provender, on a credit of

1851.
July
Term.

Lewis
& als.
v.
Caperton's
ex'or
& als.

six and twelve months; and if John B. Lewis should
consent thereto, that the sheriff should rent out the
springs and the appurtenances and fixtures until the 1st
day of January 1844.

At the October term of the court for 1843 the cause
came on to be heard on a motion to dissolve the injunction, when the court being of opinion that the deed of
the 11th of January 1839 was void as to the creditors
of John B. Lewis, because it was not properly recorded, overruled the motion. And not deciding whether
the deeds of the 5th of April and the 18th of August
1842 were good, either in whole or in part, referred it
to a commissioner to ascertain the value of Mrs. Lewis's
dower interest in the Sweet springs property on the 16th
day of March 1842, the period at which she united in
the deed to secure the debt due to the Bank of Virginia;
and also to ascertain the value of the slaves conveyed
in trust for the benefit of Mrs. Lewis by the said deeds
of the 5th of April and 18th of August 1842, at the
time they were conveyed. And it was further ordered
that A. Dunlap, who was appointed a commissioner for
the purpose, should proceed to hire out the said slaves
for one year from the termination of the period for
which they were then hired out; and also to rent out
the Sweet springs property and the land adjoining, with
the furniture thereto belonging, for one year from the
termination of the then existing lease.

The commissioner appointed to ascertain the value of
Mrs. Lewis's dower interest in the lands, and the value
of the slaves conveyed in trust for her, reported the value of the dower interest of Mrs. Lewis in the property
at 952 dollars 25 cents, and the value of the slaves
conveyed in trust for her at 6900 dollars.

This report was excepted to by the counsel for Mrs.
Lewis; but as this court does not consider or pass upon the question as to the value of Mrs. Lewis's dower

185L.
July
Term.

Lewis
& als.
v.
Caperton's
ex'or
& als.

interest, it is unnecessary to state the principles or facts upon which the commissioner based his report, or the exceptions to it.

The property was regularly rented and hired out from year to year under the directions of the court. And in the progress of the cause, Thomas Henning having recovered a judgment against John B. Lewis for about 188 dollars 90 cents, with interest and costs, on which Lewis took the benefit of the act for the relief of insolvent debtors, said Henning was made a defendant in the suit. And the cause came on to be heard in May 1847, when the court made a decree, by which Mrs. Lewis's exceptions to the commissioner's report were overruled, and the statement fixing Mrs. Lewis's dower interest at 952 dollars 25 cents was confirmed; the deed of the 11th of January 1839 was held to be void as to creditors because not duly recorded; and the deeds of settlement of the 5th of April and the 18th of August 1842, to be valid to the extent, but only to the extent, of the value of Mrs. Lewis's contingent dower interest in the estate of her husband, which appeared to have been the consideration of said deeds. It was further held that Caperton and Henning had liens for the payment of their debts upon the said slaves, subject to the aforesaid claim of Mrs. Lewis, and also upon the equity of redemption in the real and personal property conveyed by John B. Lewis in the deeds herein before mentioned, and also upon any other property held by said Lewis. And it was decreed that Caperton recover from John B. Lewis the sum of 18,758 dollars 88 cents, with interest and costs; and that Henning recover from said Lewis the sum of 205 dollars 54 cents, with like interest and his costs.

The decree further authorized Mrs. Lewis to take slaves to the amount of her interest, or to take the money; and directed a commissioner to sell the slaves not

1851.
July
Term.

Lewis
& als.
v.
Caperton's
ex'or
& als.

taken by Mrs. Lewis, and if she elected not to take slaves, to pay to her from the proceeds of the sale the said sum of 952 dollars 25 cents, with interest from the 1st of January 1843; and to pay the remainder of the proceeds of the sale of said slaves to Caperton and Henning ratably upon their debts aforesaid.

And it was further held that all the other deeds, except the deed given to secure the debt due to John H. Peyton, were valid, and that the creditors in said deeds were entitled to satisfaction of their several debts therein mentioned out of the proceeds of the sale of the property according to their respective priorities; but that Caperton and Henning were entitled to the rents and profits of the said mortgaged and trust property since the same had been sequestered and leased out under the control of the court. And the decree directed the said rents and profits to be paid ratably to them.

It was further held, that the property conveyed to secure the debt of John H. Peyton was of a kind so perishable as to be unfit to be conveyed as a security, and that deed was therefore declared to be void, and the proceeds of the sale of that property and of all the other personal property of John B. Lewis, which was not embraced in any of the deeds declared to be valid, was decreed to be divided ratably between said Caperton and Henning. And the decree then proceeded to direct certain commissioners to sell the real and personal estate conveyed in the several deeds aforesaid in the mode prescribed in the decree; and then proceeded to direct the application of the proceeds of sale among the various creditors mentioned in the deeds, and the remainder after satisfying them to be paid to Caperton and Henning. From this decree separate appeals were obtained; first, by John B. Lewis and his wife and her trustees, William L. Lewis and Henry Massie; second, by Allen T. Caperton, executor of Hugh Caperton; third, by James L. Woodville, who complained that by the

1861.
July
Term.

Lewis
& als.
v.
Caperton's
ex'or
& als.

decree he had been deprived of the rents and profits of
the springs, which had been conveyed in the deed given
to secure him; and fourth, by the Bank of Virginia,
which claimed that as in none of the deeds prior to that
to secure the bank Mrs. Lewis had relinquished her
right of dower, the bank was entitled to have the value
of that interest applied to the payment of its debt.

*Baldwin*, *Price* and *Cooke*, for Mrs. Lewis and her
trustees.

*Eskridge*, *Boyd* and *Price*, for Woodville and the
Bank of Virginia.

*The Attorney General* and *Patton*, for Caperton's
executor.

ALLEN, *J.* delivered the opinion of the court.

The court is of opinion that the mortgage deed to
William E. Haskell, of the 9th February 1837; the
deed of trust to Henry Massie, for the benefit of John
Cochran, of the 11th March 1842; the deed of trust to
James L. Woodville, for the benefit of the Bank of Virginia, of the 16th March 1842; the deed of trust to
Henry Massie, for the benefit of William B. Phillips,
of the 16th March 1842; the deed of trust to H. Massie, for the benefit of James L. Woodville, of the 4th
of April 1842; the deed of trust to H. Massie, for the
benefit of Andrew Allen and others, of the 5th of April
1842; and the deed of trust to H. Massie, for the benefit of James L. Woodville, of the 29th of April 1842,
are valid and binding incumbrances on the property
conveyed by and embraced in said deeds.

The court is further of opinion, that as Thomas P.
Lewis, by the articles of agreement between him and
John B. Lewis, of the date of the 25th September
1834, was not bound to convey the lands thereby contracted to be sold to John B. Lewis until the last instalment of the purchase money was paid, and as he

1851.
July
Term.

Lewis
& als.
v.
Caperton's
ex'or
& als.

still retains the legal title as a security for the purchase
money, he stands on higher ground than a vendor who,
having parted with the legal title, is seeking the aid of
a court of equity to set up and give effect to the implied lien for the purchase money.  Holding the legal
title, the vendor is not claiming an equity; and he cannot be required to surrender that legal title until the
purchase money is paid according to the stipulations of
the contract: and the doctrine of the waiver of the implied equitable lien of the vendor who has parted with
the legal title, when a different security has been taken
for the purchase money, does not apply to such a case.
The court is therefore of opinion that the lien for the
whole of the unpaid purchase money due to Thomas P.
Lewis and his assignees is, so far as regards the property
sold by him, paramount to all the other incumbrances,
and must be first satisfied out of the proceeds arising
from the sale thereof.  And this being so, it is unnecessary to express any opinion as to the deed of trust to
H. Massie, for the benefit of Thomas P. Lewis, of the
16th March 1842.  For if valid, the court, in marshalling the incumbrances, would require him to look to his
first and paramount lien, so as to leave any other fund
embraced in his said deed of trust to be applied to subsequent incumbrances; and as it is manifest the property sold will raise a sum more than sufficient to pay
off the purchase money, the said deed of trust, whether
valid or invalid, can have no effect upon the rights of
the parties.

A majority of the court is further of opinion, that as
the said John H. Peyton has not appealed from said decree, and the decision that the deed of trust in his favour
to Henry Massie, of the 1st May 1842, is null and void,
not being prejudicial to the rights of any of the other
parties before this court, or complained of by them as
erroneous, the correctness of the decree in holding said
deed null and void cannot be enquired into upon the
present appeals.

1851.
July
Term.

Lewis
& als.
v.
Caperton's
ex'or
& als.

The court is further of opinion that the deed of the 11th January 1839, referred to in the answer of John B. Lewis, is void as against the creditors of said John B. Lewis, because the same was not recorded according to the laws of Virginia; and also because the same was a voluntary post-nuptial settlement, made by an embarrassed man, and which, upon its face, attempts to secure the benefit of the property settled for himself during life, and retains the control over the same in his own hands. By the sale of the patrimonial estate of the said Caroline S., his wife, and the payment of the purchase money to him, his marital rights had attached thereon, and he could not by a voluntary deed made in fraud of the rights of his creditors withdraw the same from their reach.

And the court is further of opinion, that as said John B. Lewis was in possession of said slaves in said deed mentioned, the unrecorded and fraudulent deed of the 11th January 1839 could not intercept the marital rights of the husband, so as to exempt the same from the claims of his creditors.

And the court is further of opinion that the deeds of mortgage by John B. Lewis to William L. Lewis, of the 24th February 1842, were fraudulent and void as against the creditors of said John B. Lewis, so far as regards the alleged debt of 7000 dollars, described as being due to said William L. Lewis as trustee of the wife of said John B. Lewis: the said debt being for the price of the maiden lands of said Caroline S., the wife of said John B., received by him and attempted to be settled and secured for the benefit of said Lewis and family by the deed of the 11th of January 1839.

And the court is further of opinion, that although the debt of 5200 dollars, attempted to be secured by said mortgages of the 24th February 1842, was justly due, yet as the mortgagee accepted said mortgages with a knowledge of the fact that said settlement of the

1851.
July
Term.

Lewis
& als.
v.
Caperton's
ex'or
& als.

7000 dollars was a voluntary post-nuptial settlement, reserving the benefit and control of the property to the use of the grantor for life, and as this fact rendered the same fraudulent and void as against creditors so far as respects the 7000 dollars, the same must be regarded as null and void as it respects the debt due to the mortgagee. The court is therefore of opinion that said mortgages of the 24th February 1842, upon the real and personal estate therein described, to said William L. Lewis, as mortgagee, to secure the debts therein set forth, are null and void as against the subsequent incumbrancers and the creditors of said John B. Lewis.

And without deciding the question whether a relinquishment of a contingent right of dower, where there is no complete alienation of the estate by the husband, but a mere incumbrance given for the security of a debt, constitutes a sufficient consideration for a settlement on the wife, as in such case the husband, by discharging the debt and procuring a release of the incumbrance, would be reinvested with his whole estate, in which the wife would have a claim of dower; the court is further of opinion that there is no sufficient evidence of any contract or agreement between said John B. Lewis and his wife, to make upon her a settlement of the slaves named in the deeds of trust to Henry Massie and William L. Lewis, for the benefit of C. S. Lewis, wife of J. B. Lewis, the first of said deeds dated on the 5th April 1842, and the second on the 18th August 1842, in consideration of her release of her contingent dower interest in the estate of her husband. The loose conversations of the parties, as proven, furnishes no evidence of such a contract; and though the wife, when she made such relinquishment, as set forth in the deeds referred to, may have entertained the expectation that a settlement would be made, such hope and expectation cannot detract from the effect of her solemn relinquishment, or entitle her against creditors

1851.
July
Term.

Lewis
& als.
v.
Caperton's
ex'or
& als.

or incumbrancers, without notice of her declarations at the time of making such relinquishment, to any relief against the effect thereof. The relinquishment as to them is to be taken according to its legal effect, as a voluntary act of the wife. The court is therefore of opinion that the deeds of trust to Henry Massie and William L. Lewis, dated the 5th April 1842 and the 18th August 1842, for the benefit of said C. S. Lewis, are null and void as against the creditors of the husband; and cannot be regarded as valid to the extent of the value of her contingent right of dower.

The court is further of opinion, that as the various incumbrances herein declared to be valid were taken upon the property conveyed thereby respectively, and as there is no evidence that any of the subsequent incumbrancers took by express agreement subject to the prior incumbrances, the proceeds arising from the sale of the property are to be applied to the payment of the valid incumbrances according to their several priorities. The judgment creditors have no right to be substituted to the position occupied by any of the incumbrances declared to be null and void: The various incumbrancers, not having contracted with respect to the equity of redemption alone, have a right to charge the whole subject not covered by previous valid incumbrances. Nor is the right of the general creditors secured by the deed to H. Massie of the 5th April 1842, to come in according to the order of their incumbrance, impaired in consequence of the grantor having excepted from his warranty the claims of such persons as claimed under deeds of trust of record: Such exception being merely personal to the grantor and no evidence of any agreement recognizing the validity of all previous incumbrances.

The court is further of opinion that the sequestration made at the instance of the judgment creditors did not change the rights of the parties; and as the incum-

1851.
July
Term.

Lewis
& als.
v.
Caperton's
ex'or
& als

brancers by mortgage or deed of trust were arrested by such sequestration and suit from proceeding to subject said property to sale, they are, as against the judgment creditors, entitled to the rents and profits of the property from the time they could have proceeded under their incumbrances. The rents and profits accruing before that time were interests remaining in the grantor, to which the judgment creditors, in virtue of their judgments, executions and the release of the debtor under the insolvent act, are entitled.

The court is further of opinion that the question as to the claim for the value of the contingent right of dower, raised by the exception of the Bank of Virginia, can only become material in the event of the real estate not producing a sum sufficient to pay Thomas P. Lewis's lien for the purchase money, and the mortgage in favour of Haskell. In that event, and as Haskell's mortgage is subject to the contingent right of dower, there being no valid relinquishment of dower in the deed to him, the Bank of Virginia and the subsequent incumbrancers would be entitled as against Haskell to the contingent value of the dower interest first relinquished by the deed for the benefit of the bank. But the court perceiving that the fund will be certainly ample to pay off the two first incumbrances, there is no necessity to make any enquiry as to the value of such contingent claim of dower.

The court is further of opinion that, in conformity with the principles aforesaid, the proceeds arising and to arise from the sale of the property in the proceedings mentioned, and the interest, rents, hires and profits thereof, should be applied as follows:

1. Out of the proceeds of the sales of the perishable property the debt secured by the deed in favour of John Cochran should be first paid.

2. The residue of the proceeds of the perishable property, other than the furniture rented with the springs

1851.
July
Term.

Lewis
& als.
v.
Caperton's
ex'or
& als.

after the satisfaction of the Cochran debt, should be applied to the judgments of Caperton and Thomas Henning *pro rata.*

3. The proceeds arising from the sales of the slaves and their increase, together with the hires which have accrued or shall accrue, should be applied to the judgments of Caperton and Henning as aforesaid.

4. The rents arising from the springs and other property, up to the 20th March 1844, to be applied to the judgments of Caperton and Henning as aforesaid, subject, however, to a deduction therefrom of a sum sufficient to pay the debts of Samuel Price and Joseph Damron, creditors secured by the deed to Henry Massie for Andrew Allen and others, of the 5th April 1842; the said Price and Damron being authorized to enforce said deed for their benefit on the 5th April 1843.

5. That an account should be taken to ascertain how much of the rents of real estate and furniture should be apportioned, after the 20th March 1844, to each of these subjects, and the rents so ascertained and allowed for the use of the furniture after the 20th March 1844, and also the proceeds arising from the sales of the furniture, to be applied to the payment of the debt secured by the deed of trust to Henry Massie to secure James L. Woodville, of the 29th April 1842; and should there be any residue remaining of such rents and proceeds arising from the sale of the furniture, after satisfying the debt secured by said last mentioned deed, such residue to be paid over to the judgment creditors, Caperton and Henning, as aforesaid.

6. The rents accruing from the realty, to be ascertained as aforesaid, after the 20th of March 1844, to be applied to the debt due to the Bank of Virginia, secured by the deed to J. L. Woodville, of the 16th of March 1842.

7. The proceeds arising from the sale of so much of the real estate as was purchased from Thomas P. Lewis

1851.
July
Term.

Lewis
& als.
v.
Caperton's
ex'or
& als.

to be applied first to the payment of the purchase money payable to the said Thomas P. Lewis and his assignees. And in applying the proceeds aforesaid to the payment of the purchase money, the proceeds arising from the sale of said Thomas P. Lewis's interest in the real estate, other than the tract of 159 acres, known by the name of the Sweet springs, embraced in the mortgage to William E. Haskell of the 9th February 1837, to be first appropriated for that purpose; and if any thing remains unpaid, the balance so remaining to be satisfied out of the proceeds arising from the sale of the moiety of said tract of 159 acres, sold by Thomas to John B. Lewis; the court being of opinion that as Haskell's lien extends to but part of the subject, he has a right to require the application of the proceeds in the manner aforesaid, so as to enlarge the fund out of which he alone can look for satisfaction.

8. After the payment of the purchase money, the residue of the fund arising from the sale of the entire tract of 159 acres, known by the name of the Sweet springs, to be applied to the payment of the debt secured by the mortgage to Haskell.

9. After the satisfaction of the purchase money and the Haskell debt, the residue of the fund arising from the sale of the lands aforesaid, and all the real estate described in the deed of John B. Lewis to James L. Woodville for the Bank of Virginia, of the 16th March 1842, to be applied to the payment of the balance of the debt due to said bank, after crediting the amount applied thereto arising from the rents as aforesaid, and the debt of William B. Phillips, secured by the deed to H. Massie for the benefit of Phillips, of the 16th March 1842; and should the fund be insufficient to discharge both debts, the proceeds to be ratably divided between the debt of Phillips and the balance due to the bank after deducting the credit for rents.

1851.
July
Term:

Lewis
& als.
v.
Caperton's
ex'or
& als.

10. The residue of the proceeds arising from the sale of said real estate to be applied, next after the debts due the Bank of Virginia and Phillips are satisfied, to the satisfaction of the debt secured by the deed to·H. Massie for J. L. Woodville, of the 4th April 1842, or the balance unpaid after crediting the same with the rents and proceeds of the sale of the furniture as aforesaid.

11. The general creditors secured by the deed to H. Massie of the 5th April 1842, except the said Price and Damron, who are to be paid out of the rents as aforesaid, will be next entitled to come in, the fund to be distributed *pro rata* among them, if insufficient to pay all the debts; and if any of such debts have been discharged by any security, he is to be entitled to stand in the shoes of the creditor paid.

12. Next the judgment creditors, Caperton and Henning, will be entitled to payment of any balance due on their judgments, after crediting the same with the proceeds arising from the sales of negroes, hires, personal property and rents, as aforesaid.

13. And the residue, if any remain, after satisfying all the other creditors, to be applied to the debt due William L. Lewis in his own right, and the debt due to him as trustee of C. S. Lewis, secured by his mortgages, which, though void as against subsequent incumbrancers of the whole subject and creditors, is good as between the parties.

14. And lastly, if any surplus should remain after the payment of all of said incumbrances and judgments, the same, or so much thereof as may be equal in value to the price of the slaves and their increase, to be settled and secured upon C. S. Lewis, the wife of John B. Lewis, to be held according to the terms and stipulations of the deed of the 5th of April 1842, as explained by the deed of the 18th August 1842.

1851.
July
Term.

Lewis
& als.
v.
Caperton's
ex'or
& als.

But before any distribution is made, the sums heretofore allowed under interlocutory orders are to be deducted, and all the costs incurred in the prosecution of
these suits in said Circuit court are to be paid out of
the funds arising and to arise from sales and rent of
real estate, the sales and rent of perishable property,
and sales and hires of negroes; the three funds to contribute ratably to the payment of the costs in the Circuit court.

It is therefore adjudged and ordered that said decree,
so far as it conflicts with the principles herein above declared, is erroneous, and that the same be reversed and
annulled; and that the appellees in the case of Lewis
and wife and others against Caperton and others, as the
parties substantially prevailing, recover of the appellants their costs here expended, and that the appellants
in the other cases recover of the appellees their costs
here expended.

And this cause is remanded, with instructions to direct an account to ascertain the proportions of rent to
be credited to the real and personal fund as aforesaid;
and also to ascertain the whole amount of funds in
hand, and arising from the sales to be directed, which
will remain for distribution after deducting the sums
heretofore allowed by the court, and all costs; and the
amount of the several debts towards which the same is
to be applied; that a proper conveyance be executed by
the said Thomas P. Lewis, or a commissioner, to the
said John B., and acknowledged and filed, so that when
a sale is made and confirmed, the same may be withdrawn and recorded; and that in the meantime commissioners to be appointed by the court be decreed to
make sale of the real property embraced in the several
mortgages and deeds of trust herein declared to be valid, and after allowing a proper time to redeem the property by payment of the debts charged thereon, and also
to make sale of the perishable property unsold, the fur-

1851.
July
Term.

Lewis
& als.
v.
Caperton's
ex'or
& als.

niture, and the slaves named in the deeds of January 11, 1839, and of April 5, 1842, together with their increase; the slaves and personal property to be sold for cash, and the real estate to be sold in the following order: first, the tract of 159 acres, known as the Sweet springs tract; second, the residue of the tracts of which said Thomas P. and John B. Lewis were joint owners, dividing such residue in such mode as will be best calculated to enhance the price; third, any other lands of John B. Lewis embraced in the deed of trust to secure the Bank of Virginia; the sales of the real estate to be on a credit of 1, 2, 3 and 4 years, the purchasers giving bond and good security for the amount of the purchase money, and a lien being retained on the lands sold for the security thereof; and that said commissioner report, &c.

DANIEL, J. concurred in all respects in the opinion of the court, except as to the deed of trust of the 11th day of March 1842, made to secure the debt of Cochran. The want of a schedule, the vague manner in which the property is described, the perishable character of said property, the long time given before a sale could be made, and the circumstances under which the deed was executed, rendered it, in his opinion, fraudulent and void as a security for the payment of the debt to secure which it purports to have been made.

BALDWIN, J. dissented from so much of the opinion of the court as avoids the mortgage security given by J. B. Lewis, of the 24th day of February 1842, in regard to the debt due to William L. Lewis.

# Richmond.

1851.
October
Term.

## WADSWORTH & als. v. ALLEN, &c.

(Absent *Cabell*, P.)

**November 10th.**

1. A letter of credit addressed to W & W may be proved to have been intended for W, W & Co., so as to hold the writer bound to the latter upon it.
2. A guarantor may specify in the letter of credit which he gives the terms on which he will be bound; and if these terms are complied with, he is bound, though the law, in the absence of all prescription of terms in his letter of credit, would have prescribed the performance of other acts by the party seeking to subject him upon his guaranty.
3. A guarantor undertaking to pay upon receiving reasonable notice of the failure of the principal debtor to pay the debt when due, dispenses with notice of the acceptance of the guaranty by the parties to whom it is addressed, even if the law would have required such notice.
4. What is reasonable notice of the failure of the principal to pay, is a question for the jury upon the testimony.
5. The fact that the principal gave his bond for the goods he purchased did not release the guarantor.

This was an action brought in the Circuit court of Cumberland county by John E. Wadsworth, Daniel B. Turner and George S Palmer, surviving partners of themselves and Orren Williams, late merchants and partners doing business under the name of Wadsworth, Williams & Co., against Charles B. Allen and William Thaup. The declaration counted on the following letter of credit:

RAINES' TAVERN, October 27th, 1840.

1851.
October
Term.

Wads-
worth
& als.
v.
Allen, &c.

*Messrs. Wadsworth & Williams, Richmond.*

*Gentlemen,*

Please to deliver to Mr. Daniel Totty, or to his order, merchandise to an amount not exceeding in value, in the whole, five hundred dollars; and on your so doing, we hereby hold ourselves accountable to you for the payment of the same, in case Mr. Daniel Totty should not be able so to do, or should make default; of which default you are required to give us reasonable and proper notice.

Your obd't serv'ts,

*Charles B. Allen,*
*William Phaup.*

On the trial of the cause, after the above paper had been read, and the handwriting of the defendants proved, the plaintiffs offered to read the deposition of William B. Isaacs, which had been taken by consent, to be read as evidence on the trial, subject to any legal objections to which the testimony would be subject if given in court. Whereupon the defendants moved the court to strike out the following passages, viz:

" That the said John E. Wadsworth and Orren Williams had, previous to the year 1840, transacted business as merchants and partners under the name of Wadsworth & Williams; which firm was dissolved in the year 1836, and succeeded by the said Wadsworth, Williams and D. B. Turner, under the name of Wadsworth, Williams & Co.; and in 1839 they were succeeded by the same parties and George S. Palmer, the name of the firm continuing as last mentioned. The plaintiffs were frequently addressed and spoken of as Wadsworth & Williams, but that was not the style of the firm in 1840, nor has it been since 1836; but the successors were in the habit of recognizing letters and orders ad-

1851.
October
Term.

Wads-
worth
& als.
v.
Allen, &c.

dressed to Wadsworth & Williams as intended for themselves, and of acting under them. That the said Wadsworth & Williams were not, either jointly or separately,
engaged in the sale of merchandise on their individual
account, or in any other connexion, after the year 1836,
except as members of the firm of Wadsworth, Williams & Co."

The court sustained the motion, and excluded the
evidence; and the plaintiffs excepted.

The plaintiffs then proved, that in the year 1840,
Orren Williams then being alive, Daniel Totty, of the
county of Cumberland, exhibited to the concern of
Wadsworth, Williams & Co. the letter of credit above
given. That on the faith of that letter they sold and
delivered to Totty goods to the value of 395 dollars 47
cents, for which they took his bond dated the 30th of
October, payable in six months. That on the 30th of
April 1841 they wrote to Messrs. Allen and Phaup, referring to the letter of credit, stating the amount of Totty's purchases upon the faith of that letter, and that
the money was due that day and had not been paid:
But there was no proof that the letters had been received. They proved further, that on the 31st of May
1841 their agent called on Phaup, at his house, and informed him that the money had not been paid by Totty,
and asked for payment of it by Phaup. That on the
same day the agent went to the house of Allen, to see
him on the same subject; but he was not at home.
That the agent saw Allen at the March term of the
court for 1842, when he attended as a witness in the
case, when Allen told him that Totty had placed claims
in Allen's hands to pay the said debt. That he saw
Allen again in 1842, when Allen told him that he did
not then have the money to pay the debt, but that he
would pay it in a short time if the agent would have
the suit dismissed. And it was also proved by the plaintiffs' counsel, that either at the June or July term of the

County court of Cumberland in 1841, he met with the
defendant Allen, and exhibited to him the letter of credit and bond of Totty, and informed him that he held
them for collection.

After the plaintiffs had introduced their evidence the
defendants moved the court to exclude from the jury
the letter of credit hereinbefore mentioned, as incompetent to charge the defendants in this cause ; which
motion the court sustained, and excluded the letter ;
and the plaintiffs again excepted.

There was a verdict and judgment for the defendants ; whereupon the plaintiffs applied to this court for
a *supersedeas*, which was allowed.

*Lyons*, for the appellants.
*Garland*, for the appellees.

ALLEN, *J.* delivered the opinion of the court.

It seems to the court here, that although the guaranty offered in evidence by the plaintiffs in error was addressed to Wadsworth & Williams, and not to the
plaintiffs in error, Wadsworth, Williams & Co., yet it
was competent for the plaintiffs in error to prove that at
the time the same was so addressed to Wadsworth &
Williams they were partners in the firm of Wadsworth,
Williams & Co., and were not engaged in the mercantile business on their own account, or in connection
with any other mercantile firm in the city of Richmond ; and that said letter of guaranty being presented
to the plaintiffs in error, the same was accepted by them,
and the goods furnished for the price of which this suit
was brought. The court is therefore of opinion, that
as the evidence set forth in the first bill of exceptions
taken by the plaintiffs in error on the trial of the issue
tended to prove the facts aforesaid, the Circuit court
erred in excluding the same from the jury.

VOL. VIII.—12

1851.
October
Term.

Wads-
worth
& als.
v.
Allen, &c.

1851.
October
Term.

Wads-
worth
& als.
v.
Allen, &c.

And it further seems to the court that said Circuit court erred in excluding from the jury as evidence the said letter of credit, in the second bill of exceptions mentioned, as incompetent to charge the defendants in error. By the terms of the letter of credit the defendants in error waived all right to notice of the acceptance of the guaranty, if they would otherwise have been entitled to require it; a question upon which the court expresses no opinion. By their engagement the defendants in error agreed to hold themselves accountable for the payment of the price of the goods, to an amount not exceeding the sum therein mentioned, in case the purchaser should not be able to pay for the same or make default; of which default they required reasonable and proper notice to be given them. It was competent for the defendants in error to specify the conditions upon which their accountability should depend; and having done so, if those conditions have been complied with, they cannot object the failure of the plaintiffs in error to comply with other terms which the law might have imposed, but a compliance with which the defendants in error have waived.

Whether there was reasonable and proper notice of the default, was a question for the jury upon the testimony, upon proper instructions from the court.

Nor did the fact that the purchaser gave his bond for the price of the goods discharge the defendants in error from liability on their guaranty; the question between them and the plaintiffs in error being, not what evidence of the debt the latter may have taken from the purchaser, but whether the price of the goods has been paid at the time stipulated in the contract of sale.

It is therefore considered that said judgment is erroneous, and that it be reversed, with costs to the plaintiffs in error, and that the verdict be set aside, and the cause remanded for a new trial of the issues joined;

on which trial the part of the deposition of William B. Isaacs, as set forth in the first bill of exceptions, and the letter of guaranty referred to and set forth in the second bill of exceptions, if again offered in evidence, and not objected to for any other cause than is disclosed by said bills of exceptions, are to be permitted to go in evidence to the jury.

1851.
October
Term.

Wads-
worth
& als.
v.
Allen, &c.

## Richmond.

Jones, &c. v. Myrick's *ex'ors.*

Myrick's *ex'ors* v. Epes *& als.*

(Absent *Cabell*, P.)

November 10th.

1851.
October
Term.

1. A forthcoming bond forfeited has the force of a judgment, so as to create a lien upon the lands of the obligors, *only* from the time the bond is returned to the clerk's office.

2. There being no evidence that the bond was returned to the clerk's office before the day on which there was an award of execution thereon by the court, it will be regarded as having been returned to the office on that day.

3. A judgment confessed in court in a pending suit, and the oath of insolvency taken thereon by the debtor upon his surrender by his bail, has relation to the first moment of the first day of the term; but a forfeited forthcoming bond which is not returned to the clerk's office until some day in the term after the first, when there is an award of execution thereon, has no relation; and therefore the assignment by operation of law under the first has preference over the lien of the forthcoming bond.

4. Though a forthcoming bond is forfeited, and not quashed, yet in equity the lien of the original judgment still exists; and if the obligors in the bond prove insolvent, so that the debt is not paid, a court of law will quash the bond so as

1851.
October
Term.

Jones, &c.
v.
Myrick's
ex'ors.

Myrick's
ex'ors
v.
Epes
& als.

to revive the lien of the original judgment. And a court of equity, having jurisdiction of the subject, will treat the bond as a nullity, and proceed to give such relief as the creditor is entitled to under his original judgment.

5. Lands subject to a judgment lien, which have been sold or encumbered by the debtor, are to be subjected to the satisfaction of the judgment in the inverse order in point of time of the alienations and incumbrances: the land last sold or encumbered being first subjected.

6. A judgment creditor, having by his conduct waived or lost his right to subject the land first liable to satisfy his judgment, is not entitled to subject the lands next liable for the whole amount of his judgment, but only for the balance after crediting thereon the value of the land first liable.

7. A judgment creditor, having the prior lien on the lands of his debtor, files a bill against his debtor and other creditors having incumbrances on his debtor's lands. Pending this suit another creditor of the same debtor files a bill against him and his creditors, and among them the judgment creditor, seeking to subject the lands under his lien; and in this suit the proceeds of the whole lands, which were sold by the sheriff under the insolvent laws, or by the trustees in the deeds, are distributed by the decree of the court to other creditors. The judgment creditor afterwards matures his suit and brings it on for hearing.

HELD: That the decree in the other cause concludes him, so that he is not entitled to recover from the creditors who received them, the proceeds of the land sold by the sheriff; nor is he entitled to have the land sold, as against the purchaser thereof.

On the 24th of June 1828 John Myrick instituted a suit in the late District court of chancery at Richmond against William D. Epes and others, the creditors of Epes. The bill was filed at the following August rules, and charged that at the September term of the Superior court of Nottoway county, in the year 1827, he recovered a judgment against Epes for 1160 dollars 1 cent, with interest thereon from the 12th of May 1827, and 7 dollars 51 cents costs. That an execution issued on this judgment and was levied, and a forthcoming bond was given by Epes, with Samuel G. Williams and Joseph G. Williams as his sureties; and was forfeited. That this bond bore date the 25th of October 1827,

1851.
October
Term.

Jones, &c.
v.
Myrick's
ex'ors.

Myrick's
ex'ors
v.
Epes
& als.

and was forfeited on the first Thursday in December following. That a judgment was obtained on this forthcoming bond at the April term of the Superior court in 1828; but that both principal and sureties were insolvent.

The bill further charged that at the time of executing the forthcoming bond Epes was possessed of several tracts of land in the county of Nottoway, in all but one of which he had but a life estate; that was a tract of eight hundred acres on which he resided; and that he also owned a tract in the county of Dinwiddie, in which he had a life estate. And that when the forthcoming bond was forfeited there were no other liens on the land than that created by the forfeiture of the bond. That Epes was very much embarrassed, and from the 14th of February 1828 to the 25th of April he executed five several deeds of trust, which were recorded anterior to the April term of the Superior court. And that at the April term of the court Epes took the oath of an insolvent debtor in several cases.

The bill further stated that the deed conveying the Dinwiddie land was not recorded until two days after the oath of insolvency had been taken by Epes; and that this land had been sold and conveyed by the sheriff to satisfy the judgments on which Epes had taken the oath of insolvency. That although the plaintiff's lien was prior to that under which this land was sold, yet he was not disposed to interfere with said land if he could be decreed his money, to be raised from the other tracts, as they would produce much more than sufficient for this purpose; and as to this matter he submitted to the court to decide as equity should dictate.

The bill further charged that an execution issued on the judgment recovered on the forthcoming bond aforesaid, which went into the hands of the sheriff of Dinwiddie, whose return thereon was referred to as shewing that the plaintiff was entitled to have the slaves

1851.
October
Term.

Jones, &c.
v.
Myrick's
ex'ors.

Myrick's
ex'ors
v.
Epes
& als.

mentioned therein subjected to the satisfaction of his debt, the sheriff returning that he had seen the slaves and endeavoured to levy upon them, but that they had run from him and hid themselves, and had gone into the county of Nottoway. That at the same term of the Superior court of Nottoway the plaintiff had recovered another judgment against Epes; that an execution was issued thereon, which went into the hands of the sheriff of Dinwiddie, and the same return was made upon it as upon the other, except that a part of the money was made. That the slaves mentioned in the return of the sheriff on these executions were not embraced in any deed recorded in Dinwiddie county before the executions went into the hands of the sheriff of that county, in which the slaves were living at the time. That the slaves were therefore liable to satisfy the plaintiff's debts; if not in preference to those creditors at whose suit Epes took the oath of insolvency, certainly he will be entitled to any balance arising from the sale of these slaves, towards the satisfaction of his said executions, and in the first place to the satisfaction of the balance due on the latter.

The bill made William D. Epes, the trustees and creditors in the several deeds, and the creditors at whose suit the insolvent debtor's oath was taken by Epes, defendants, and prayed for a sale of the lands to satisfy any prior liens; that the slaves too might be sold, and the proceeds distributed according to the rights of the parties; and that as the creditors at whose suit Epes took the oath of insolvency had obtained the proceeds of the land in Dinwiddie, that the plaintiff's small judgment might be satisfied out of the proceeds of the slaves; and for general relief.

Of the deeds executed by William D. Epes, one bore date the 14th of February 1828, and by it he conveyed to Francis Epes the tract of eight hundred acres of land in the county of Nottoway, of which he owned

1851.
October
Term.

Jones, &c.
v.
Myrick's
ex'ors.

Myrick's
ex'ors
v.
Epes
& als.

the fee, and a number of slaves, in trust to secure David G. Williams and Edward Bland as his endorsers upon a note for 4300 dollars, discounted at the Bank of Virginia at Petersburg. Another deed bore date the 25th of April 1828, and by it William D. Epes conveyed to Bartelot P. Todd another tract in the county of Nottoway containing four hundred and eighty acres, and the tract in Dinwiddie containing twelve hundred acres, in both of which he held but a life estate, and also a number of slaves, in trust to secure to Archer Jones the payment of a debt of 4420 dollars. And another deed bore the same date, by which William D. Epes conveyed to the same trustee his crops on hand in Nottoway and Dinwiddie, and also the growing crops, with his household and kitchen furniture, stock, &c., and a tract of seventy-five acres of land in which he held a life estate, to secure a debt of 366 dollars 50 cents, due to Edward Bland, and to indemnify Francis Epes as his surety to the amount of 3940 dollars. A fourth deed was of the same date, and conveyed to Todd any balance that might remain in his hands of the proceeds of the property conveyed to secure the debt due to Archer Jones, after the payment of that debt, in trust to secure a number of his creditors, among whom was John Myrick. All these deeds were lodged with the clerk of the County court of Nottoway on the 26th of April, to be recorded.

The Superior court of Nottoway seems to have commenced its term on the next day; and on the 28th William D. Epes was surrendered into custody by his bail in six several actions pending against him in that court, and he thereupon took the oath of an insolvent debtor, and was discharged. On the same day the plaintiff Myrick obtained an award of execution on the forthcoming bond which had been taken upon his execution against Epes, and at the same term he recovered a judgment against Epes for 262 dollars 62 cents, with

1851.
October
Term.

Jones, &c.
v.
Myrick's
ex'ors.

Myrick's
ex'ors
v.
Epes
& als.

interest and costs.   On the first of these executions the sheriff of Dinwiddie returned that he went to the plantation of Epes, in the county of Dinwiddie, on the 3d of May, when he saw several slaves, whom he named in his return ; and that he exerted himself to levy the execution upon them, but that they all ran for the woods and secreted themselves, so that he could not find them.

The deed conveying the land in the county of Dinwiddie, to secure the debt due to Archer Jones, was not recorded in that county until after Epes had taken the oath of insolvency.   The sheriff therefore proceeded, on the 2d of July 1828, to sell the life estate of Epes in the land, when Jones became the purchaser at the price of 753 dollars 75 cents net ; and it was conveyed to him by the sheriff.   It was after this sale and conveyance that the bill of the plaintiff was filed.

The only defendant who answered the bill was David G. Williams, who was the surety secured by the first of the before mentioned deeds.   He, whilst he admitted the facts stated in the bill, denied that the plaintiff had a lien upon the property, real or personal, conveyed to indemnify him.   He insisted that there was no lien by force of a judgment where there was no capacity to take out an execution ; and that consequently the plaintiff lost his lien on the lands of Epes when the forthcoming bond was executed, which, although it is declared by the statute that it shall have the force of a judgment, was nevertheless a judgment on which an execution could not issue until it was awarded by the court: And before that time the deed conveying the eight hundred acres of land for the indemnity of the respondent had been executed and recorded.

In June 1832 the plaintiff Myrick died, and the cause was revived in the name of his executors : And on their motion the case was transferred to the Superior court of Nottoway county.   In April 1833 the cause

1851.
October
Term.

Jones, &c.
v.
Myrick's
ex'ors.

Myrick's
ex'ors
v.
Epes
& als.

came on to be heard in that court, when a commissioner was directed to ascertain and report the yearly
value of the lands in which William D. Epes was interested at the date of the delivery bond referred to in
the bill, and also at the time the original judgment
was obtained.

The case seems to have slept from that time until
April 1839, when it was again heard, and the court, being of opinion that the delivery bond and judgment
thereon operated as a lien on the lands owned and un-
incumbered by William D. Epes at the date of the forfeiture of the bond, directed a commissioner to enquire
into and report the amount of the sales of the real estate of Epes owned by him and not incumbered at the
date of the forfeiture of the bond, the time when the
said lands were sold, to whom sold and conveyed, and
the prices at which each tract was sold, to whom the
purchase money thereof was paid, and the proportion
paid to each. A report was made by a commissioner
in obedience to this order, but it is not in the record.

Before a final decree was made in this case, the record of a cause which had been finally decided in the
same court was filed. This was a case in which
Francis Epes, in his own right, and as administrator of
Thomas R. Epes, and Samuel Scott, as executor of
John F. Epes, were plaintiffs, and William D. Epes
and the trustees and creditors in his several deeds, were
defendants. The plaintiffs claimed as sureties, or representing sureties, of William D. Epes, in a bond
which had been transferred to Joseph Cooper, one of
the creditors at whose suit William D. Epes had taken
the oath of insolvency; and they alleged that Francis
Epes, and Scott as executor of John F. Epes, had been
compelled to pay the debt; and asked to be substituted
to Cooper's rights. The defendants, among whom was
John Myrick, answered, and contested their right to be
substituted to the rights of Cooper. And Myrick stated

1851.
October
Term.

Jones, &c.
v.
Myrick's
ex'ors.

Myrick's
ex'ors
v.
Epes
& als.

the fact that he had obtained two judgments against William D. Epes at the same term at which he had taken the oath of insolvency; and he also stated the facts as to the issue of the executions, and the return of the sheriff thereon. And he claimed to have decreed to him the amount arising from the sale of the slaves made by the sheriff of Nottoway, after satisfying the claims which had preference to his under the assignment of William D. Epes on taking the oath of insolvency.

This case was finally decided in 1834, when the court distributed the proceeds of the Dinwiddie land, 753 dollars 75 cents, and of the slaves sold by the sheriff of Nottoway, 1099 dollars 86 cents, among the creditors at whose suit William D. Epes had taken the oath of an insolvent debtor.

The record of this suit also shewed that all the lands conveyed by William D. Epes, except the Dinwiddie land, had been sold by the trustees, and the proceeds distributed. The Dinwiddie land was sold by the sheriff, and its proceeds distributed as before stated. It appeared that the proceeds of the sale of the tract of eight hundred acres had been paid to D. G. Williams, by the trustee Francis Epes; that Todd had paid to Archer Jones and to Francis Epes the proceeds of the lands conveyed for their benefit, except the Dinwiddie land.

The cause came on to be finally heard in October 1845, when the court being of opinion that the Dinwiddie land, having been sold by the sheriff of said county, under the schedule of said William D. Epes, before the institution of this suit, and the purchaser thereof not having been made a party, no recovery could be had for the said land, or the proceeds thereof, in this cause. And being of opinion also, that the plaintiff had waived his right to the sum of 753 dollars 75 cents, the proceeds of said land, and had no right to

1851.
October
Term.

Jones, &c.
v.
Myrick's
ex'ors.

Myrick's
ex'ors
v.
Epes
& als.

call upon the defendants to pay said amount, on account of the lands sold for their benefit under the deeds of trust exhibited with the bill; and the court being further of opinion that the defendants, Archer Jones and Francis Epes, were liable on account of the lands purchased by them under the deeds made by William D. Epes for their benefit, before the defendant D. G. Williams could be called upon on account of the land sold under the deed of trust for his benefit, the deeds of said Jones and Francis Epes being of posterior dates, decreed that the defendant Jones should pay to the plaintiffs the sum of 906 dollars 68 cents, with interest on 426 dollars 15 cents, part thereof, from the 2d day of October 1845, until paid; and that the defendant Francis Epes should pay to the plaintiffs the sum of 217 dollars 3 cents, with interest on 116 dollars 25 cents, part thereof, from the same date; and that they should pay to the plaintiffs their costs, provided Francis Epes should not be required to pay more than 17 dollars 81 cents, or Jones more than 67 dollars 9 cents, which sums remained in their hands after paying the amounts above decreed to the plaintiffs.    From this decree both the plaintiffs and Jones and Francis Epes applied to this court for an appeal, which was allowed.

The case was argued in writing by *Gholson* and *James Alfred Jones*, for Jones and Epes, and by *Spooner*, for Myrick's executors.

*For Jones and Epes.*

First. If Myrick's executors succeed at all, it must be by force of the lien of the forfeited forthcoming bond.

They do not claim any lien under the original judgment.   On the contrary, they found their claim entirely on the bond: which they do not object to as faulty, but set up as good.   They set forth in their bill that

1851.
October
Term.

Jones, &c.
v.
Myrick's
ex'ors.

Myrick's
ex'ors
v.
Epes
& als.

on the original judgment a *fi. fa.* was issued, and "duly levied"; that "a forthcoming bond was duly executed by W. D. Epes, Joseph G. Williams and Samuel G. Williams, and the said bond was duly forfeited on the first Thursday in December 1827"; and they exhibit copies of the *fi. fa.*, delivery bond, and judgment on the bond, which, they say, was obtained at April term of the Superior court in 1828. They set forth the amount of the judgment on "the delivery bond," and insist that for this amount they have a lien on the lands of W. D. Epes, by reason of their "judgment aforesaid" (*i. e.*, on the delivery bond): which has priority, they say, over the deeds of trust.

The very main object of the suit was to get the benefit of the forthcoming bond. The plaintiff was not content to take merely the amount of the original judgment. It is very clear, then, that in this suit the court cannot proceed to quash the forthcoming bond as faulty, and enforce the lien of the original judgment.

In the court below the plaintiffs did not ask it—it was inconsistent with their bill to ask it; the defendants had no notice that any such thing would be asked, that they might come forward and resist it; and the court, not pretending to quash the bond, enforced the lien claimed under it, and gave a decree for the full amount of the bond.

The forthcoming bond then remaining unquashed, the original judgment is so far satisfied that no new execution could issue on it. *Taylor* v. *Dundas*, 1 Wash. 92; *Downman* v. *Chinn*, 2 Wash. 189; *Garland* v. *Lynch*, 1 Rob. R. 545. And no lien can be claimed by virtue of it, since the lien of a judgment is a mere consequence of the right to sue out an *elegit*. *United States* v. *Morrison*, 4 Peters' R. 124. The executors then are remitted to, and must depend entirely on the lien of the bond.

1851.
October
Term.

Jones, &c.
v.
Myrick's
ex'ors.

Myrick's
ex'ors
v.
Epes
& als.

In the bill it is alleged that the bond was forfeited on 1st Thursday in December 1847, but not that it was returned to the clerk's office. They set forth the judgment on the forthcoming bond, which appears to have been rendered on the 28th day of April 1828.

But where the bond was in the meantime, whether in the clerk's office, or with the sheriff, or the plaintiff, who had the right to demand it of him, (1 Rev. Code 531, § 17,) is not alleged and does not appear. It is argued by the counsel of Myrick's executors that the fact of the return of the forthcoming bond to the clerk's office before the recordation of the deeds of trust sufficiently appeared on the record, and the reasons given to prove it are that the sheriff was bound under a penalty to return the bond on the return day of the execution; that in fact it was in court on the first day of April term 1828; that a copy of it was made by the clerk and filed in this cause; and that no objection was made in the court below that the bond was not returned to the clerk's office according to law.

These reasons are quite unsatisfactory.

In the first place, the sheriff is not bound to return the bond to the clerk's office. He may deliver it to the " creditor, his agent or attorney, or other legal representative," (1 Rev. Code 531, § 17); and whatever may be his duty, it is known to the practitioner in Virginia that the habit of many sheriffs is to retain the forthcoming bonds until court, that they may give the notices of the motion for award of execution.

In the next place, the fact that the bond was in court on the first day of the April term 1848 does not shew where it was before that time. Nor does the fact that a copy was made by the clerk, and filed in this cause, shew anything more than that, at the time when the copy was made, which was long since these transactions took place, the bond was in the office.

1851.
October
Term.

Jones, &c.
v.
Myrick's
ex'ors.

Myrick's
ex'ors
v.
Eps
& als.

Nor can anything be inferred from the failure of the appellants to appear in the court below and object that the bond was not returned to the office before their deeds were delivered there. It was not for them to deny what the plaintiff in his bill did not allege. They had no notice that it was pretended that the bond was returned to the clerk's office before court, or that any benefit was claimed therefrom. The plaintiff can claim the benefit of the admission of the facts alleged, and none other. It is submitted, then, that it by no means appears in the record that the forfeited forthcoming bond was returned to the clerk's office before the deeds were recorded.

But, suppose it did, it is admitted by the counsel that there is not an allegation in the bill that the bond was so returned; and this is plain enough on the face of the bill.

If the fact be material, the omission of the averment in the bill is fatal, and cannot be supplied by proof.

Is it then a material fact in this cause that the forfeited forthcoming bond should have been returned to the clerk's office before the deeds of trust were recorded.

And this turns on the enquiry when a forthcoming bond creates a lien on the land of the obligors. Is it as soon as forfeited, or is it only after being forfeited and also returned to the clerk's office? Or is it even then until execution has been awarded on it?

If the lien is created as soon as the bond is forfeited, then the fact of the return to the clerk's office is not material, and need not be averred; otherwise it is.

The lien of a judgment is a mere consequence of the right to sue out an *elegit* on it and extend the debtor's lands.

When may an *elegit* be sued out on a forthcoming bond? Only after award of execution by the court, made upon motion after notice. Can the lien, which is the mere consequence of the right to sue the *elegit*,

1851.
October
Term.

Jones, &c.
v.
Myrick's
ex'ors.

Myrick's
ex'ors
v.
Epes
& als.

exist before the right to sue the *elegit* exists? It is submitted not. And that if it were conceded that the forthcoming bond had the force of a judgment as soon as forfeited, yet it lacks the quality of a judgment essential to create a lien on lands.

In the language of Tucker, J. in *Lipscomb's adm'r* v. *Davis's adm'r*, 4 Leigh 303: "Admitting, however, that the bond has to some intents the force of a judgment as soon as it is filed, I think it obvious it has not all the effect of a judgment until there has been an award of execution. No execution can be sued out at the mere will of the party; the authority of the court must first be obtained by motion."

But has the bond the force of a judgment to any intent until it has been returned forfeited to the clerk's office? Neither the terms nor the objects nor the policy of the law favour such a conclusion.

The sheriff is to return "the bond to the office of the clerk of the court whence the execution issued, to be there safely kept, and to have the force of a judgment"; *i. e.*, in order to be there safely kept, and have the force of a judgment; for the purpose of being there safely kept and having the force of a judgment. To the argument that the provision as to the return is merely directory to the sheriff, the reply is that the whole proceeding is the proceeding of the sheriff, and for it to have the effect given to it by the law, he must proceed according to law. It is a summary extraordinary proceeding given by statute, and all the provisions of the statute should be complied with to make it valid. If it had been elsewhere declared that the bond should, when forfeited, have the force of a judgment, and then been added that the sheriff should return it to be safely kept and have the force of a judgment, there would be more reason to contend that the provision as to the return and safe keeping was merely directory. But the only words of the law giving the character of a judg-

1851.
October
Term.

Jones, &c.
v.
Myrick's
ex'ors.

Myrick's
ex'ors
v.
Epes
& als.

ment to the bond are those quoted. They follow the provision requiring the return; and there exists between them the relation of an act and its consequence.

And the object of the law was not merely to give the effect of a judgment to the bond.

If the creditor preferred it, the law provided that he might take the bond himself, (1 Rev. Code 531, § 17,) that he might use it as he pleased. That, if he pleased, he might treat it as a common law bond, and sue on it and hold the obligors to bail, and have the other privileges of a bond creditor that do not belong to a judgment creditor. This was the object, and not to convert the bond into a judgment the moment it was forfeited.

The policy of the law, too, in respect to third persons, is averse to creating judgments with their unknown liens and preferences out of these private bonds. Read the remarks of Tucker, J. in *Lipscomb's adm'r* v. *Davis's adm'r*, 4 Leigh 303. Hence our recording acts and our act for docketing judgments, which are in striking contrast with this rule of construction giving a bond in the pocket of the sheriff or creditor the full effect of a docketed judgment.

The counsel of Myrick's executors has cited the law, as it now is, under the new Code, to shew that the opinion of the revisors as to the import of this provision was in support of their position. But it seems to be clearly against it.

By the new Code, " the clerk shall endorse on the bond the date of its return, and against such of the obligors therein as may be alive when it is forfeited and so returned, it shall have the force of a judgment." Under the law, as it is in the Code, the bond is not to have the force of a judgment, even after forfeiture and return, unless the obligor is alive at the return. If he dies after the forfeiture, and before the return, the bond has not the force of a judgment. How, then, can it be

1851.
October
Term.

Jones, &c.
v.
Myrick's
ex'ors.

Myrick's
ex'ors
v.
Epes
& als.

said that from the forfeiture the bond has the force of a judgment?

The apprehension expressed by counsel, " that judgment debtors and securities in forthcoming bonds might play a deep and ruinous game by making and recording deeds in the interval between the forfeiture and return of the bond," is quite unwarranted ; since the creditor has the right to demand the bond of the sheriff and may return it himself.

This view of the statute leads to the conclusion that a forfeited bond has not the force of a judgment in any respect until returned to the clerk's office ; nor even then the force of a lien until there is an award of execution. And therefore that the averment was material, that the bond had been returned when the deeds were lodged for recordation, and also that there had been an award of execution on it : neither of which averments having been made, the bill is materially defective, and should be dismissed.

Secondly. There have been some fluctuations in the decisions as to the question whether alienees of land under the lien of a judgment shall contribute *pro rata*, or in the order of their purchases. If they contribute *pro rata*, the preference to Williams was wrong.

But, if it be conceded that the land last sold is to be first applied to the satisfaction of the judgment, the rule does not justify the preference given to Williams over Jones and Epes.

When the contest is between several deeds of trust, it is a misapplication of it to refer for the preference to the dates of the deeds. Applying the rule, with just regard to the recording acts, we are to look, in determining the question of preference, to the time of the delivery of the bonds to the clerk to be recorded, after due acknowledgment, proof, or certificate.

The act declares that "all deeds of trust and mortgages, whensoever they shall be delivered to the clerk

1851
October
Term.

Jones, &c.
v.
Myrick's
ex'ors.

Myrick's
ex'ors
v.
Epes
& als.

to be recorded, and all other conveyances, &c., shall take effect and be valid, as to all subsequent purchasers for valuable consideration without notice, and as to all creditors, from the time when such deed of trust or mortgage or such other conveyance shall have been so acknowledged, proved, or certified, and delivered to the clerk of the proper court to be recorded, and from that time only."

Now, under the act, the deed of trust first recorded is the first to " take effect " and become " valid " as to the creditors—that is, the deed first recorded first passes the property of the debtor as against the creditor. And the land embraced by the deed first recorded is really the land first aliened ; and the land embraced by the deed last recorded is last aliened, and therefore, under the rule, to be first applied to the satisfaction of the judgment.

The statute fixes the date of the alienation. Equity requires the alienees to pay successively, in the order of their respective alienations.

The rule of equity is thus preserved without frustrating the policy of the statute.

This, too, is in analogy to the law of executions. Suppose the creditor should choose to proceed by *ca. sa.* to make his debt, instead of suing his *elegit.* The land embraced by a deed recorded would be exempt. That embraced by a deed unrecorded, though prior in execution, would go to satisfy the debt.

But if, without reference to the recording of the deeds, the deed last executed must satisfy a judgment lien before one first executed, why does not equity force the last alienee to exonerate the first from the judgment debt, notwithstanding the creditor has chosen to make it by *ca. sa. ?* It is certainly a very ill defined and unsatisfactory equity, as between the several alienees, which depends entirely on the caprice of the judgment creditor in the choice of his execution : so that if he

1851.
October
Term.

Jones, &c.
v.
Myrick's
ex'ors.

Myrick's
ex'ors
v.
Epes
& als.

sues his *elegit* one alienee pays, if he sue his *ca. sa.* another pays.

Very inconsistent consequences will flow from disregarding entirely the recording acts in enforcing the lien of judgments on several alienees.

This case furnishes an illustration. The court held that the proceeds of the Dinwiddie land, 753 dollars 75 cents, were first of all liable to Myrick's lien. Why? Because those proceeds were from lands acquired by the sheriff under the assignment in insolvency, subsequent to the alienation of the other land. He was the last alienee, having no privity with the vendee under the unrecorded deed, but taking in despite of his deed, immediately under the debtor.

It was right that his land should be first subjected. But suppose the deed of trust embracing this Dinwiddie land had been antecedent to the other in date. According to the principle proceeded on by the court, this deed, being antecedent, would shift the lien from this land on the other lands. The lien attached to the other land to the relief of this.

Then when the sheriff took it, he would take it with the lien shifted off. And it would be wrong to hold that the proceeds of the land in his hands were, first of all, liable to the lien. They in fact would not be liable at all, until the other lands were exhausted. And thus, although last aliened, his land would be relieved from the lien, by the lands previously aliened.

This violation of the rule of equity results from holding the unrecorded deed valid against the judgment lien, while it is void as to a *ca. sa.* execution.

It would have been a striking result, in this case, if, when William Dandridge Epes took the oath of an insolvent debtor, the deed of trust, made for the benefit of Williams, had, like the deed embracing the Dinwiddie land, been unrecorded. The land embraced by it would have passed to the sheriff, and Williams would have lost it.

1851.
October
Term.

Jones, &c.
v.
Myrick's
ex'ors.

Myrick's
ex'ors
v.
Epes
& als.

Then, would the judgment lien have been satisfied first out of this land, together with the Dinwiddie land, or first out of the land conveyed to Jones and Epes?

The court below would have held, and held properly, that the land in the sheriff's hands must first be applied to satisfy the lien, because he would be the last alienee. But if, as between Williams on the one hand, and Jones and Epes on the other, their relative responsibility for the lien, in consequence of the land they took, was settled at the date of their deeds, so that the land of Jones and Epes was bound to pay before Williams's land, how could their land be relieved of this obligation and the same be shifted on Williams's land by the mere act of third persons? So that the rule of equity would require the judgment creditor to extend the land conveyed for Williams's benefit, or the lands conveyed for Jones and Epes, not as his deed or their deeds might be first recorded, in conformity with law, but as the judgment debtor might chance to be driven to the oath of insolvency or not.

These inconveniences are easily obviated if, in the application of the rule, courts of equity shall consider no land aliened by deed of trust *quoad* creditors, until the alienee has used the means prescribed by law to make his deed take effect and be valid as to creditors, but remaining in the same plight as to their rights and liens as if the vendor still held it.

If, then, the rule be that the land last sold is to be first applied to the satisfaction of the judgment, it is submitted that it is to the time when delivered to the clerk to be recorded, and not their date, that we must look to determine when lands are aliened by deed of trust; and in this case, as the deeds were delivered on the same day to the clerk, that the beneficiaries under them ought to contribute in proportion to what they severally received.

1861.
October
Term.

Jones, &c.
v.
Myrick's
ex'ors.

Myrick's
ex'ors
v.
Epes
& als.

## MYRICK'S EX'ORS *v.* JONES & EPES.

Thirdly. That portion of the decree which relieves these lands conveyed in trust for Williams and Jones and Epes, from 753 dollars 75 cents of Myrick's debt, seems to be quite defensible.

It is enough to know that, in the case of *Epes and Scott* v. *Epes and als.*, in which Myrick was a party, the question of the disposition of the proceeds of this land was decided; that Myrick appeared, and, without pleading in abatement the pendency of this suit, insisted on his right to those proceeds, by reason of his two judgments, and that a decree was made disposing of those proceeds, which remains unreversed.

So far as the disposition of those proceeds is concerned, it is too late now for Myrick's executors to complain of it or seek to change it.

Nor can they ask, with any propriety, to set aside the sale to Jones. They acquiesced in that sale in the suit of *Epes and Scott* v. *Epes and als.*, and claimed the benefit of it, insisting on a share of the proceeds. And, in this suit, they set forth that sale; and, instead of making the purchaser a party as purchaser, and seeking to set aside the sale, they omit to do it, and again claim the benefit of the sale; praying that they may be allowed a proper amount " of the proceeds of the sales of said land," in part of another judgment of theirs, which they affirm operated a lien on the Dinwiddie land.

It is too late, then, to have the sale set aside.

The enquiry then remains, whether Myrick's executors had a right to charge the 753 dollars 75 cents, or any part of it, on the lands conveyed in trust for Williams and Jones and Epes. And this question depends on another, whether the Dinwiddie land, the proceeds of which amounted to 753 dollars 75 cents, was first liable. If so, a court of equity will turn them over to it.

1851.
October
Term.

Jones, &c.
v.
Myrick's
ex'ors.

Myrick's
ex'ors
v.
Epes
& als.

*Clowes* v. *Dickenson*, 5 John. Ch. R. 235. That land was conveyed by William Dandridge Epes in trust for the benefit of certain creditors; but the deed was not recorded in Dinwiddie, where the land lay, until he took the benefit of the insolvent debtor's oath. The deed, then, never took effect as to creditors.

Nor did the sheriff claim under it, but paramount to it, and by virtue of the assignment in insolvency. This assignment in insolvency to the sheriff was posterior to the execution and recording of the several deeds in trust for Williams and Jones and Epes. If, then, alienees are to pay in the order of their deeds, this Dinwiddie land, being last assigned, must be first applied to the satisfaction of Myrick's judgment; and the court did right to turn his executors off from the lands first aliened, to the extent of the value of this land, 753 dollars 75 cents.

Whether or not, as between other alienees, the rule obtains that the elder is preferred to the junior, it would hardly seem questionable that, as between a prior alienee and a subsequent assignee in insolvency, the alienee would be preferred. For the assignee stands precisely in the shoes of the debtor; taking his property exactly in the plight he held it. And the land in the hands of the debtor is always to be extended in satisfaction of the judgment before the land he has aliened.

*For Myrick's executors.*

As Jones and Epes obtained the first appeal, it seems proper to notice, first, the objections to the decree in the cause, from which both parties have appealed, made by Jones and Epes.

1. The first point made by the appellants, Jones and Epes, is, as to the nature of the lien on the land produced by the execution, and forfeiture, &c., of a forthcoming bond. There is no question as to the original lien on all the lands of William D. Epes, by virtue of

1851.
October
Term.

Jones, &c.
v.
Myrick's
ex'ors.

Myrick's
ex'ors
v.
Epes
& als.

the original judgment. When did that lien cease or expire? The execution and forfeiture of the forthcoming bond did not amount to a payment or satisfaction of the original judgment. The cases of *Taylor* v. *Dundas*, 1 Wash. 92, and *Downman* v. *Chinn*, 2 Wash. 189, do not oppose this view. " The only effect of those decisions is, that a replevin or forthcoming bond, even if defective, is a bar to any further proceedings on the original judgment until quashed." *Randolph* v. *Randolph*, 3 Rand. 490; *Garland* v. *Lynch*, 1 Rob. R. 545.

The original judgment was obtained at September term 1827. The forthcoming bond, taken by virtue of the *fi. fa.* which issued under that judgment, was dated the 25th of October 1827, and was forfeited the first Thursday in December 1827.

The execution aforesaid was returnable to the first Monday in December 1827. If it was returned by the sheriff to the clerk's office on the return day, or before the record of the first deed of trust, April 26th, 1828, even the appellants, in effect, admit the lien of the forthcoming bond would be preferable to the trust deed. Does not the fact of such return sufficiently appear on the record? The sheriff was bound by law, under a penalty, to return the *fi. fa.* on the first Monday in December 1827. He certainly made the return, although he did not date it. There is nowhere in the record an allegation or intimation that the sheriff did not strictly comply with the law and return the forthcoming bond and *fi. fa.* the first Monday in December 1827. It was in court the first day of the April term. D. G. Williams, one of the main defendants, alone answered the bill. He makes no such objection that the bond had not been returned in due time, but relies on a different point, and, as far as any inference as to this point could be drawn from the answer, it would be that the forthcoming bond was duly returned and filed. It is true there is not in the bill a special allegation that the

1851.
October
Term.

Jones. &c.
v.
Myrick's
ex'ors.

Myrick's
ex'ors
v.
Epes
& als.

bond was returned before the month of April 1828. But it was in the clerk's office, and a copy was duly made by and obtained from the clerk, and filed in the cause, and no objection was made, or intimation given, in the court below, that the law had not been strictly complied with. No proof was called for as to this point, and no objection made till the case comes here. The counsel is aware that there were some *dicta* in relation to this point in *Lipscomb's adm'r* v. *Davis' adm'r*, 4 Leigh 303. The point was not discussed by counsel in that case, and the remarks of the judge were *obiter dicta*. It is humbly submitted that the reasons for the opinion expressed by the judge will not bear examination. How could executors or administrators be injured or entrapped? Could it have been possible in a case like this? And as to purchasers, suppose the parties for whose benefit the deeds of trust were executed had gone to the clerk's office in April 1828, when the first deed was recorded, to enquire and ascertain what liens existed on the lands of William D. Epes. Was it possible for them to be entrapped or deceived? They must have ascertained that the original judgment existed and was rendered seven months previously. Surely that would have been notice enough to them. But if more was wanted, they had but to apply to the sheriff, if the execution and forthcoming bond had not been returned. In all such cases the original judgment would be ample notice, and if a case should happen, which would be very rarely, of a forthcoming bond being not returned for 12 months, the same rule perhaps might apply to such bond as would to a common judgment, where no execution was issued within the year. It is true that as to a security in the forthcoming bond the original judgment might not be considered as any notice, but it is generally but a short time between the forfeiting of a forthcoming bond and the judgment on it, and it is believed that rarely, if ever, are the forthcoming bonds in a clerk's office examined by any body for the purpose of ascertaining whether there be any lien on a particular person's land. The counsel in this case has never heard of a single instance of such examination.

1851.
October
Term.

Jones, &c.
v.
Myrick's
ex'ors.

Myrick's
ex'ors
v.
Epes
& als.

It is submitted, however, that in this case the court should not, under the circumstances, require any farther evidence than what appears, that the forthcoming bond was returned with the *fi.fa.* on the first Monday in December 1827.

No objection was made, which, if made, might have enabled the appellees to have proved when the bond was actually returned, if the fact was important. The point made in the answer was not of that character to lead the appellees to believe that any such objection would be made as is now made.

But was the lien of the original judgment in this case suspended after the forfeiture of the forthcoming bond till it was returned to the office, if it was not returned till court, so as to let in the deed of trust executed before the court in April, according to the true meaning of the act of assembly? Could it have been intended that a creditor's lien by judgment should be vacillating and uncertain and depend at all on the strict compliance of the sheriff with the law? The lien to be good if the sheriff did his duty, but lost if he did not. It does not seem reasonable that such should have been the meaning of the legislature, and certainly they have never said so in plain terms. They have said the forthcoming bond shall be returned, and shall have the force of a judgment. The execution of a forthcoming bond is a favour granted the debtor: It is for his accommodation. Landed is generally better than personal security, and it is not reasonable to suppose that the legislature intended to deprive the creditor of his lien without some good cause and by the use of plain terms. The counsel submits with confidence

1851.
October
Term.

Jones, &c.
v.
Myrick's
ex'ors.

Myrick's
ex'ors
v.
Epes
& als.

in this case, that whatever might have been the effect of the forthcoming bond while in the hands of the sheriff after forfeiture, till returned, that when returned it had the force of a judgment from the time it was forfeited. If the lien in such cases, under the then law, did not relate back to the forfeiture, then how easy might this favour to a creditor have been made an instrument of injustice. In large counties and in other places where sales were fixed to take place at points remote from the clerk's office, and frequently fixed to take place after the return day of the execution, it might be very difficult, if not impossible, for the sheriff to return the forthcoming bond to the office for some days after the forfeiture, and creditors then upon the watch had nothing to do but, in the interval between the forfeiture and the return of the bond, to obtain conveyances and have them recorded. According to the doctrine contended for by the appellants Jones and Epes, deeds recorded in such intervals, even the next day after the forfeiture, would overreach the lien of the original judgment, and of the forthcoming bonds forfeited, but still in the sheriff's hands. Judgment debtors and securities in forthcoming bonds might in this way play a deep and ruinous game. The security might have been taken in consequence of his landed estate, and, putting a deed upon record during the interval, the security might become worthless.

The following extract from Judge Roane's opinion in *Lusk* v. *Ramsey*, 3 Munf. 454, seems not to be inappropriate here : " I entirely concur in opinion with one of the judges in the case of *Cook* v. *Piles*, 2 Munf. 153, that a forthcoming bond is no satisfaction of a judgment, until the forfeiture ; and I think it follows that, until such satisfaction has taken place, the lien created under the judgment is not extinguished. The old right does not cease until the new one is authorized to succeed it. No chasm between the two is

1851.
October
Term.

Jones, &c.
v.
Myrick's
ex'ors.

Myrick's
ex'ors
v.
Epes
& als.

to be created by implication or construction." The old law says that a forfeited forthcoming bond shall have the force of a judgment, but it does not say it shall not have that force till returned. Such a meaning can only be made out by implication or construction, and then, it is submitted, against the principles of justice.

Under the law in the new Code, the forthcoming bond is to have the force of a judgment against the obligors who were alive when the bond was forfeited and returned, and the clerk is to note the date of the return of the bond. By the law the sheriff is allowed thirty days to return the bond after it is forfeited. It is evident that the legislature has not given any sanction to the doctrine contended for, by fixing the day of the return of the bond as the commencement of the lien. All the new law requires is, that the obligors shall be alive at the forfeiture and return, to have their lands affected by the lien. The meaning seems clear that the lien relates back to the forfeiture, if the obligors are alive at the return of the bonds.

This record shews that, when the judgment was rendered on the forthcoming bond taken in October 1827, only six months before, all the parties to the bond had become insolvent. It was then in the power of the court, on motion, to have quashed the bond, on account of the insolvency of the obligors; and if the bond had been quashed, it would have restored to the appellees the lien of their original judgment. *Garland* v. *Lynch*, 1 Rob. R. 545. This suit was brought within nine months after the date of the original judgment, and if the forthcoming bond had been then quashed, as it might legally have been, the appellants Jones and Epes could not have complained. It is then submitted, that the court below, sitting as a court of equity, if justice to the appellees required it, had a right to consider the bond as if actually quashed, and as a mere nullity, in a case where all the parties interested were before the court,

4

1851.
October
Term.

Jones. &c.
v.
Myrick's
ex'ors.

Myrick's
ex'ors
v.
Epes
& als.

in accordance with the maxim that a court of equity will frequently consider that as done which could legally have been done, and ought to have been done.

In leaving this point, the counsel submits with confidence to this court, that it is not the true meaning of the act of assembly, taking the plain import of the words, that forthcoming bonds should not have the force of judgments till returned to the clerk's office. The law directs the bonds to be returned with the executions to the office, and says they shall have the force of judgments. If the legislature had intended to restrict the meaning of the words, as contended for, by using the word " there " before the words " force of a judgment," there might have been some ground for the meaning contended for : But such word is wanting. Again, by sec. 17, p. 531, 1 Rev. Code 1819, the sheriff was ordered to deliver the forthcoming bond to the creditor if demanded. If delivered to him, was it not to have the force of a judgment while in his hands, by relation back to the forfeiture, when it should be actually returned to the office ? Could the legislature have intended, when they made such a provision, that the bond should have no force of a judgment till actually in the office? The words directing forthcoming bonds to be returned and to be there kept, seems to be merely directory to the sheriff and clerk, and not intended to restrict the commencement of the lien, or the right to award execution.

The effect of the decision in *Eppes's ex'or* v. *Colley*, 2 Munf. 523, cannot be got rid of by saying the motion is a mere remedy. If the word " thereupon " should be taken in a restrictive sense, and as a sort of precedent condition, the court would not have decided as it did in that case. The Court of appeals, by their decision in that case, shewed that the words directing the forthcoming bond to be returned, &c., should be construed liberally for the creditor; not in a restrictive sense.

1851.
October
Term.

Jones, &c.
v.
Myrick's
ex'ors.

Myrick's
ex'ors
v.
Epes
& als.

## MYRICK'S EX'ORS *v.* EPES, &c.

The main question of dispute relates to the course pursued by the court in reference to the disposition of the proceeds of the sales of the tract of land in Dinwiddie. When the judgment was obtained against Epes in September 1827, and when this suit was instituted in June 1828, that tract of land, in which Epes had but a life estate, was unsold. William D. Epes took the insolvent oath in April 1828, and as no deed of trust had been recorded in Dinwiddie, the whole remaining interest of Epes vested in the sheriff of Dinwiddie for the benefit of certain judgment creditors. One-half of Epes's interest was subject to the lien of the judgment obtained by Myrick's executor in September 1827, and the forthcoming bond taken under it. All the interest which vested in the sheriff of Dinwiddie by virtue of William D. Epes's insolvent assignment was sold by the sheriff in July after this suit was brought, and was bought by Archer Jones, one of the then defendants in this cause. But the bill in this cause was not filed till after said sale. It states the fact of that sale, and submits to the court, in express terms, to decide whether that tract of land, as far as Epes's interest extended and was affected by their judgment and forthcoming bond, should be made liable to help to pay the judgment relied on and set forth in the bill. The deed to Archer Jones for said Dinwiddie land was filed as an exhibit in this cause, and although he was a *pendente lite* purchaser, yet he was at the time also a party in this cause.

It does not appear that any notice was given at the sale of the Dinwiddie land of the lien of the judgment of Myrick's executors, and as far as appears it may be that those present at the sale supposed that the sheriff sold all William D. Epes's life estate in the land. It is

1851.
October
Term.

Jones, &c.
v
Myrick's
ex'ors.

Myrick's
ex'ors
v.
Epes
& als.

true this could not injure the interest of Myrick's executors so far as to cause them any loss, but how far such a sale and conveyance would operate to bring that land within one of the points decided in *McClung* v. *Beirne*, 10 Leigh, 394, is submitted to the decision of the court. It is the fifth point in that cause to which reference is made.

It seems to the counsel that there can be no question that at least one-half of Epes's interest in that land was legally sold and conveyed by the sheriff, and that Myrick's executors had no lien on or claim to more than half, at the time of the sale. And it seems difficult to understand how the court could come to the conclusion that Myrick's executors were entitled to more than half the sales of the Dinwiddie land, if to any part, except by losing sight of the fact that there was no lien on that land but the judgment when the insolvent oath was taken.

The sale made by the sheriff of Dinwiddie could not legally have been of any right, title, or interest which had vested in Myrick's executors under the judgment of September 1827, or the forthcoming bond. Their interest had not been sold, because the sheriff was not called on to sell it, nor was he authorized to sell it, nor did he offer or attempt to sell it. It seems, then, difficult to comprehend on what ground Myrick's executors could claim or be entitled to one cent of the amount of that sale, 800 dollars, net amount 753 dollars 55 cents.

The court decided that Myrick's executors had waived their right to the said sum of 753 dollars 75 cents, the proceeds of the sale of the Dinwiddie land aforesaid. If they had no right to any part of that sum, they could waive nothing. But let us look at the case under the supposition that the executors were entitled to some part or the whole of that sum of 753 dollars 75 cents.

1851.
October
Term.

Jones, &c.
v.
Myrick's
ex'ors.

Myrick's
ex'ors
v.
Epes
& als.

It will not surely be contended that any right to said money was waived in this cause. The question in relation to that land was expressly submitted to the court for decision by the bill, the purchaser was a party and his title deed was an exhibit, and all the exhibits necessary to shew the nature of the interest sold were filed in the cause. If any right, then, was waived by Myrick or his executors, it must have been done in the case of *Epes & Scott* v. *Epes*, &c. That suit was brought in August 1828. It will be seen on examination that the parties in the two cases are the same, except J. D. Royall, sheriff of Nottoway, and E. Watkins, sheriff of Dinwiddie. All the parties interested in that money, being parties in both causes, knew or ought to have known that Myrick had submitted the question about the Dinwiddie land to the decision of the court. The two cases were depending at the same time and were in the same court. Myrick was made a party in the case of Scott and Epes, merely because he was a party in one of the trust deeds. No claim is set up or intimated against his rights by virtue of the lien of the first judgment in 1827 and the forthcoming bond. Was it, then, a fatal error in Myrick that he did not, in Scott and Epes's case, volunteer to state again what he had already done in the suit first brought? If he erred in this, it was certainly not done with any bad intention. In his answer in that cause he expressly refers to his two executions, one on the forthcoming bond and one on the judgment obtained at April term 1828. He did not suppose, nor did his counsel suppose, that any part of the land sales under the insolvent assignment was applicable to the payment of his judgment in 1827, or the forthcoming bond taken under it. If he was mistaken as to this matter, why was he more to blame than Archer Jones, the purchaser and also a creditor under the trust deeds, and D. G. Williams and Francis Epes, all parties in both causes, who remained wholly

1851.
October
Term.

Jones, &c.
v.
Myrick's
ex'ors.

Myrick's
ex'ors
v.
Epes
& als.

silent. Myrick did not obtain a decree for a dollar in Scott's case, and what he did and did not do cannot be construed into an attempt or desire to obtain an undue advantage. No injury was done to any party by the course he pursued.

But if Myrick was entitled to the 753 dollars 75 cents, or any part of it, towards the payment of his forthcoming bond, did not the court commit a grave error in not taking hold of the amount and decreeing it accordingly in this case? True it had been decreed to particular parties in the case of Scott and Epes, but those parties were all before the court in this cause. Surely, then, if they had received moneys to which they were not entitled, and by a decree in a cause brought after this, if that money ought to have been appropriated towards Myrick's forthcoming bond, it was clearly the duty of the court in this cause, which first assumed the control of that fund as far as it could, to have decreed those parties to do justice, to pay back the sums thus received by them, and to which they were not entitled according to the expressed opinion of the court. It was in the full power of the court in this cause to have reached that money and to have had it appropriated in pursuance of its opinion. No part of it was lost, and all might have been still decreed as the court thought it was equitable and legally applicable. It does not seem that any right obtained under that decree in Scott and Epes's case could be a bar in a court of equity to reclaiming the fund thus said to have been waived or abandoned.

It is finally submitted that there is no good ground for deciding in this case that Myrick waived or abandoned his lien on the Dinwiddie land by not urging a claim to the fund of 753 dollars 75 cents, or to one-half of it, more strenuously in *Scott & Epes* v. *Epes*. That money is not lost, and can even now be reached by a future decree in this cause, if indeed any part of it

1851.
October
Term.

Jones, &c.
v.
Myrick's
ex'ors.

Myrick's
ex'ors
v.
Epes
& als.

ought to be applied towards the judgment in question. The counsel has not been able to find any authority tending to sanction the doctrine of waiver or abandonment such as was relied on by the court. This is not a case where a party was present at the sale, and stood by among persons ignorant of his claim, and suffered them innocently and without notice to purchase or in any manner to be injured by his silence. The whole matter was transacted among those who were perfectly informed of all the circumstances attending the matter. No loss was or can be sustained, for if some have to refund, it will be only refunding what they are not and never were entitled to.

BALDWIN, J. delivered the opinion of the court.

The statute concerning executions, (1 Rev. Code 1819, p. 530, § 16,) prescribed, in regard to forthcoming bonds, that in the event of the failure to deliver the property according to the condition of the bond, the sheriff should return it to the office from whence the execution issued, to be there safely kept and to have the force of a judgment; and thereupon it should be lawful for the clerk of the court, where such bond should be lodged, upon motion, &c., to award execution, &c. And by the amendatory act of 1822, (Supp. Rev. Code, p. 270, § 1,) the authority of the clerk to award execution upon the bond was transferred from him to the court. By the true construction of the act of 1819, the forfeited forthcoming bond was to have the force of a judgment, so as to give a lien upon the lands of the obligors, not from the time of the forfeiture, but from the time of the return of the bond to the clerk's office; from which time last mentioned there was a capacity to sue out execution, and whether the same should be awarded by the clerk or the court was immaterial. This construction is warranted by the terms of the statute, and is consonant to its spirit.

VOL. VIII.—14

1851.
October
Term.

Jones, &c.
v.
Myrick's
ex'ors.

Myrick's
ex'ors
v.
Epes
& als.

The *quasi* judgment was, like other judgments, to be deposited in the clerk's office, where it could be seen and inspected by all persons interested in the subject; whereas if it took its force as a judgment lien from the time of the forfeiture, it might be held up, to the great prejudice of creditors and purchasers, for many years, and *that* by the act of the plaintiff himself, for by the 17th section of the same statute it was made the duty of the sheriff to deliver the bond to the plaintiff if required, and there was no period of limitation to the award of execution.

In the present case the execution of Myrick, the testator of the appellants who are first above mentioned, against William D. Epes, upon which the forthcoming bond was taken, issued on the 2d of October 1827, upon a judgment of the Superior court of Nottoway, for 1160 dollars 1 cent, with interest thereon from the 12th of May 1827, and 7 dollars 51 cents costs, and was returnable on the first Monday in December next following. It was levied and the forthcoming bond taken on the 25th of October in the same year; and the bond forfeited on the first Thursday in December 1827, and execution thereupon awarded by the court on the 28th of April 1828. The forthcoming bond must be regarded as returned on the 28th of April 1828 when the motion for award of execution was made upon it, there being no evidence that it was returned at an earlier day. But prior to the 28th of April 1828, the said William D. Epes, by several deeds of trust, conveyed his real estate to secure some of his creditors, which deeds of trust were admitted to record in the county of Nottoway on the 26th of April 1828; one of which deeds, however, embraces a tract of land situate in the county of Dinwiddie, in which county the same was not recorded. And on the 28th of April 1828 the said William D. Epes, in the Superior court of Nottoway county, confessed various judgments, and

1851.
October
Term.

Jones, &c.
v.
Myrick's
ex'ors.

Myrick's
ex'ors
v.
Epes
& als.

being in custody thereupon, by the surrender of his special bail on that day in open court, took the oath of an insolvent debtor, and by his schedule surrendered and transferred to the sheriff all his estate in the property, real and personal, embraced in the deeds of trust aforesaid.

The said deeds of trust, therefore, except in regard to the Dinwiddie land, had priority over the lien of the forthcoming bond, and, with the same exception, over the assignment of the insolvent for the benefit of his schedule creditors ; and the latter must be preferred, in regard to the Dinwiddie land, over the lien of the forthcoming bond, inasmuch as the judgments confessed in open court, and the proceeding thereupon and therein, had relation to the first moment of the first day of the term ; whereas the return of the forthcoming bond must be-treated as an act done in the office and not in the court, and as having no relation at all, and therefore before it was effectual the estate of the insolvent had been assigned by operation of law for the benefit of the schedule creditors.

But although the lien of Myrick by force of his forthcoming bond had thus proved unavailing, as well in regard to the schedule creditors as the incumbrancers, yet that of his original judgment was in equity still subsisting, and, being prior in point of time, paramount to both.  The forthcoming bond, it is true, after its forfeiture operated, while it continued in force, as a discharge of the original judgment; but its purpose was to secure the payment of the debt, and having proved abortive in that respect from the insolvency of the obligors, the court of law would have quashed it, on the motion of the creditor, in order to remit him in all respects to the benefit of his original judgment. And a court of equity, looking to the substance of things, and disregarding mere matters of form, will not, when it has jurisdiction of the subject, require the party

1851.
October
Term.

Jones, &c.
v.
Myrick's
ex'ors.

Myrick's
ex'ors
v.
Epes
& als.

to go through the formality of quashing the bond at
law, but treat the security as a nullity, and proceed to
give such relief as he was entitled to under his original
judgment.

Myrick, therefore, by force of his original judgment,
had at the institution of this suit a lien upon all the
lands of his debtor, William D. Epes, at the time of
the recovery thereof, to the extent of the debt, interest
and costs thereby recovered, and also for the costs and
expenses occasioned by the taking of the forthcoming
bond, which was part of the execution, and proved unavailing without any fault of the creditor. This lien,
by the rules of equity, was to be enforced, in the first
place, as amongst alienees and incumbrancers, against
the land last aliened or incumbered by the debtor, and,
if that should be insufficient, then against the other
lands successively in the inverse order in point of time
of the alienations and incumbrances.

This suit was instituted by Myrick on the 21st of
June 1828, and his bill filed at the August rules next
following. Between those two periods the Dinwiddie
land was sold by the sheriff of that county for the benefit of the schedule creditors. The bill sets forth the
judgment, execution, forfeited forthcoming bond, and
award of execution above mentioned. It also sets forth
the several deeds of trust executed by the debtor, the
judgments confessed by him, his discharge as an insolvent, and his schedule. It asserts the priority of the
plaintiff's judgment lien, and that it is not affected by
the deeds of trust, or the assignment of the debtor on
taking the oath of insolvency. It represents that although the plaintiff's lien upon the Dinwiddie land is
prior to that of the schedule creditors, yet he is not disposed to interfere with that land if he can be decreed
his money to be raised from the other tracts, as they
would produce much more than sufficient for the purpose; and as to this matter submits it to the court to
decide as equity shall dictate.

1851.
October
Term.

Jones, &c.
v.
Myrick's
ex'ors.

Myrick's
ex'ors
v.
Epes
& als.

The bill further represents that the plaintiff obtained another judgment against William D. Epes, in the same court, on the 30th of April 1828, for 262 dollars 62 cents, with interest thereon from the 14th of February 1828, and 7 dollars 15 cents costs; upon which and the forthcoming bond aforesaid writs of *fieri facias* issued, directed to the sheriff of Dinwiddie county, and came to his hands, and thereby created a lien upon the Dinwiddie slaves previously embraced in the schedule aforesaid, at least for any balance remaining after satisfying the schedule creditors, although said writs were never levied upon said slaves, in consequence of their escape from the county of Dinwiddie to the county of Nottoway.

The bill makes defendants the schedule creditors and those secured by the deeds of trust, amongst which defendants are Archer Jones, Francis Epes, in his own right and as administrator of Thomas R. Epes deceased, and Samuel Scott, administrator of John F. Epes deceased; prays satisfaction of the debts due the plaintiff, a sale of the lands and the Dinwiddie slaves, and that if the latter should be applied to the satisfaction of the schedule creditors, then that the plaintiff's smaller judgment should participate in the proceeds of the sale which had been made of the Dinwiddie land, on the ground that it had been obtained at the April term 1828, and, relating back to the first day of the term, operated as a lien upon that land *pro rata* with the judgments of the schedule creditors.

Shortly after the commencement of this suit by Myrick, some of the defendants therein, to wit, Francis Epes, in his own right and as administrator of Thomas R. Epes deceased, and Samuel Scott, administrator of John F. Epes deceased, brought their suit in the same court, in which the bill was filed on the 27th of August 1828. The bill charges that the said Francis Epes, Thomas R. Epes, and John F. Epes became

1851.
October
Term.

Jones, &c.
v.
Myrick's
ex'ors.

Myrick's
ex'ors
v.
Epes
& als.

bound as sureties for William D. Epes in the bond for
1808 dollars, upon which Cooper, one of the schedule
creditors, recovered his judgment; that the judgment
to the extent of 1930 dollars 7 cents had been made by
execution out of the property of Francis Epes; and
that for the small balance still due Cooper was pursuing Samuel Scott, as administrator of John F. Epes.
It sets forth the several deeds of trust above mentioned
by which William D. Epes conveyed his lands and
other property to secure some of his creditors, and represents the failure to record any of them in the county
of Dinwiddie prior to the debtor's oath of insolvency,
and his assignment for the schedule creditors; and that
by this failure they became void as to the Dinwiddie
property, which passed to the sheriff for the benefit of
the schedule creditors.  It states the sale by the sheriff
of Dinwiddie, for the benefit of the schedule creditors,
of the land and some of the other property in that
county; the escape of some of the slaves to the county
of Nottoway, and their liability to be sold there, under
the schedule assignment, by the sheriff of that county.
It seeks the application to the debts due the schedule
creditors of the proceeds of the sale which had been
made by the sheriff of Dinwiddie, and of the sale
which should be made by the sheriff of Nottoway of
the Dinwiddie slaves that had escaped from the latter
to the former county, and the subrogation of the plaintiffs to the interest of said Cooper as one of the schedule creditors in said proceeds:  And it makes the proper defendants, and amongst them the said Myrick;
but it takes no notice of his suit, nor of his paramount
lien upon all the lands of the debtor, and does not
mention the judgments which he had recovered.

To that bill, Myrick, with other defendants, filed a
joint answer, in which they deny the equity to subrogation asserted by the plaintiffs, and allege that the
plaintiff Francis Epes had already received more than

the amount paid on Cooper's judgment from sales of
part of the property conveyed by the trust deeds, one
of which provided for his indemnity as security for the
debt to Cooper, and embraced the Dinwiddie property;
and that its failure as to that property proceeded from
his own *laches*.  Myrick stated separately the recovery of
his two judgments, and reasserted his claim to a lien
upon the Dinwiddie slaves by force of his unlevied
writs of *fieri facias;* but took no notice of his own
pending suit, nor of his lien therein asserted, whether
paramount or *pro rata*, upon the Dinwiddie land, or the
proceeds of the sheriff's sale thereof.

1851.
October
Term.

Jones, &c.
v.
Myrick's
ex'ors.

Myrick's
ex'ors
v.
Epes
& als.

Pending Myrick's suit, sales were made by a trustee
of the property embraced in the trust deeds, in regard
to which they had been duly recorded, and some of it
very shortly after the suit was instituted, and before
the filing of the bill.   In regard to these trust sales, as
well those already made as to those contemplated, the
bill is silent.

The other suit, brought by Francis Epes, &c., was finally heard on the 11th of April 1834, when the court,
by its decree, disposed of the trust sales and the schedule
sales according to the supposed rights of the parties,
substituting the plaintiffs as sureties to the place of
Cooper as one of the schedule creditors, and adjusting
the equities arising amongst some of the parties; and
the design and effect of the decree was to give distri-
butively, as well to the plaintiffs by substitution to the
interest of Cooper, as to some of the other schedule
creditors, the whole proceeds of the schedule sales
made by the sheriffs, including that of the Dinwiddie
land.

It appears that in the Dinwiddie land and the other
lands conveyed by the deeds of trust, the grantor, William D. Epes, had but a life estate, except the tract of
800 acres in Nottoway conveyed by the deed for the
benefit of David G. Williams, in which he had an es-

1851.
October
Term.

Jones, &c.
v.
Myrick's
ex'ors.

Myrick's
ex'ors
v.
Epes
& als.

tate in fee. *That* deed was made on the 14th of February 1828, and the others on the 25th of April next following. It also appears that the proceeds of the trust sales of the lands conveyed for the benefit of Archer Jones and Francis Epes respectively were paid over to them, and that the proceeds of the sale of the 800 acres under the deed of the 14th of February were paid over to Williams; and that the proceeds so paid to said Jones and Epes were rather more than sufficient to pay off the balance of the larger judgment of Myrick, after deducting from it a sum equal to the proceeds of the Dinwiddie land.

Myrick's suit was not finally heard until the 14th of October 1845, when the decree appealed from was rendered, by which the court, declining, for reasons stated, to direct a sale of the Dinwiddie land, held that the plaintiff had waived his right to the proceeds of the sheriff's sale of the Dinwiddie land, and had no right to recover for that amount from the defendants who had received the proceeds of the lands sold for their benefit under the deeds of trust; that the defendants, Archer Jones and Francis Epes, were liable on account of such proceeds before the defendant Williams could be called upon on account of those received by him; and directed payment by said Jones and Epes respectively to the plaintiff of sums together equal to the balance of his larger judgment, after deducting therefrom the amount of the proceeds of the Dinwiddie land.

And so the question arises, whether the appellants, who are the executors of Myrick, ought to recover in this suit the amount of the proceeds of the Dinwiddie land, against those defendants who, as schedule creditors, received the benefit thereof, under the decree of 1834, rendered in the suit brought by Epes and others; and if not, then the further question, whether the executors of Myrick can recover the amount so deducted from his judgment against any of the other defendants.

1851.
October
Term.

Jones, &c.
v.
Myrick's
ex'ors.

Myrick's
ex'ors
v.
Epes
& als.

There is no evidence, nor is there any pretence from any quarter, that the Dinwiddie land did not produce at the sheriff's sale thereof under the schedule the full value of the life estate of William D. Epes therein; nor does it appear that it was sold subject to Myrick's paramount judgment lien, or that the purchaser or the sheriff had any knowledge of the existence of that lien. It would therefore have been competent for the court, while the proceeds of the sale were in the hands of the sheriff or otherwise within its control, to have directed the same to be applied towards the discharge of Myrick's judgment. And that relief would have been required by principles of equity, instead of subjecting the purchaser to the loss of the land; and would have fallen within the scope of the plaintiff's bill, though not designated therein, the object of it being to obtain satisfaction of his demand out of the lands of the debtor, and whether by means of sales thereof to be directed by the court, or of sales already made by competent authority, was immaterial.

It was too late, however, at the hearing of the present suit in 1845, to subject the proceeds of the sheriff's sale of the Dinwiddie land, which proceeds were recovered by the schedule creditors by the decree rendered in 1834 in the suit brought by Epes, &c. That decree is an insuperable bar to the pretension now made by the executors of Myrick, who was a party in that suit, to a recovery against the schedule creditors of the money paid to them under the authority and by the direction of the said decree of 1834. It was a decree not only upon the same matter, the apparent paramount lien and title of the schedule creditors in regard to the Dinwiddie land, which carried with it the negation of a paramount lien or title in all other persons; but it was a recovery of the identical subject, the proceeds of the sale of that land made by the sheriff. Nor was it the less decisive and conclusive that the money was not in the hands of

1851.
October
Term.

Jones, &c.
v.
Myrick's
ex'ors.

Myrick's
ex'ors
v.
Epes
& als.

Myrick, but in the hands of the sheriff, who held it subject to the control and decision of the court; nor that Myrick in his answer did not deny the lien or title asserted in the bill, and asserted no lien or title in himself; nor that the present suit was then pending and the first brought, for it is not the institution of a suit, but the judgment or decree therein, which concludes the rights of the parties. The pendency of the present suit, however, serves to shew, if that were material, that Myrick was not ignorant of his own paramount lien upon the Dinwiddie land, but chose not to insist upon it, preferring and desiring, as would seem from his own bill, to obtain satisfaction of his larger judgment out of his debtor's other lands.

It follows from what has been said, that the Circuit court did not err in failing to decree in the present suit, to the plaintiffs therein, payment by the schedule creditors of the proceeds of the sale of the Dinwiddie land, which they had recovered by the former decree of 1834, rendered in the suit brought by Epes, &c.

Nor did the Circuit court err in refusing to decree against the creditors who had received the proceeds of the sales made under the deeds of trust, so much of the plaintiff's demand as was equal to the proceeds of the sheriff's sale of the Dinwiddie land.

Although Myrick had a paramount judgment lien upon all the lands of his debtor, yet his proper resort was primary as to the Dinwiddie land, secondary as to the Nottoway lands conveyed for the security of Jones and Epes, and ultimate as to the Nottoway land conveyed for the security of Williams; and of these funds he could not subject the second until he had exhausted the first, nor the third until he had exhausted the second. And if by his surrender, waiver, acquiescence, or neglect, he lost the power of proceeding in this order, he thereby incurred the consequences himself, and could not throw the burthen upon others, by whom it

1851.
October
Term.

Jones, &c.
v.
Myrick's
ex'ors.

Myrick's
ex'ors
v.
Epes
& als.

ought not to have been borne.  The facts already stated serve to shew that, with a full knowledge of the priority of his lien, he suffered the proceeds of the Dinwiddie land to remain in the hands of the sheriff for nearly four years without an effort to secure the application thereof to his judgment, and by his wilful waiver or gross neglect submitted to the conflicting pretension of the schedule creditors, and so allowed the fund to be appropriated to their benefit, by an unreversed and irreversible decree in their behalf.  And if, notwithstanding this, he might still have pursued the perishable life estate in the hands of the purchaser at the sheriff's sale, he has not made out a case proper for such relief by evidence, nor by pleading, his bill not having even mentioned the name of the purchaser, who did not stand in the position of a purchaser *pendente lite*, the sale having been made before process served and bill filed.

The court is therefore of opinion that there is no error in the decree of the Circuit court.

DECREE AFFIRMED.

𝕽𝖎𝖈𝖍𝖒𝖔𝖓𝖉.

HUTCHERSON, &c. v. PIGG.

(Absent *Cabell*, P.)

November 10th.

1. The official bond of an executrix only binding the obligors for the due administration of the personal estate, the sureties are to no extent responsible for the rents and profits of the real estate.

2. All the sureties in the official bond of an executrix should be parties to a suit by legatees for distribution, or a sufficient reason should be shewn for failing to make them parties, before a decree is made against one of them.

John Pigg died in 1816, having first duly made his will, which was admitted to record in the County court of Pittsylvania. He left a widow and six children, all of whom were infants. Mrs. Pigg qualified as executrix of the will, with James Adams, Samuel Calland, Nathan Hutcherson, James Hart and Clement Pigg, as her securities. After the qualification of Mrs. Pigg as executrix of John Pigg, she intermarried with Nathan Hutcherson, and he seems to have conducted the administration.

The children seem to have lived with Hutcherson and his wife, on the land belonging to the estate, and no division of the property was made until 1829.

In 1828 Hezekiah Pigg, one of the children of John Pigg deceased, instituted a suit in the County court of Pittsylvania, which was afterwards removed to the Superior court, against Hutcherson and wife and the children of John Pigg, asking for a settlement of Hutcherson's account and a division of the estate. The estate was divided, and the commissioner to whom the executorial accounts were referred made a

1851.
October
Term.

Hutcher-
son, &c.
v.
Pigg.

report, in which he allowed Hutcherson a credit for the support of the children.

Hezekiah Pigg, the plaintiff, excepted to the account of the administratrix, and also to the statement of his account; and the court sustained some of his exceptions, and, among others, the exception to the allowance for his support; and recommitted the report.

In the second account, the commissioner stated the administration account, in which he charged the executor with the rent of the land, and ascertained the balance thereon, and distributed that balance between the widow and the children. Each child's part was 220 dollars 47 cents. He then stated an account between Hutcherson and Hezekiah Pigg, and ascertained the amount due to Pigg to be 211 dollars 88 cents; but he did not state an account with any of the other children; and the court confined its decree to the balance found due Hezekiah Pigg. This decree was in November 1842.

In 1844 John W. Pigg instituted a suit in chancery in the Superior court of Pittsylvania against Hutcherson and Clement Pigg, in which he stated that Hutcherson had administered his father's estate; that Clement Pigg was the only surviving security (though he does not say the others were insolvent). He stated the proceedings in the former suit, and that the commissioner had reported due him the sum of 220 dollars 47 cents, which he was willing to consider as the true sum due him; that no decree had been made in his favour for that sum, and he asked for a decree for it against Hutcherson and Clement Pigg as his surety.

Hutcherson answered the bill, saying that the plaintiff had been fully paid. The bill was taken for confessed as to Clement Pigg.

Hutcherson took testimony to prove that for a part of the time John W. Pigg lived with him, viz., thirteen years, his support was worth 30 dollars a year. He

1851.
October
Term.

Hutcher-
son, &c.
v.
Pigg.

also proved that he paid for John W. Pigg the sum of 75 dollars, and in the suit of Hezekiah Pigg against Hutcherson and als., the first report shewed items not excepted to of 26 dollars 43 cents, paid for John W. Pigg.

The cause came on to be heard in October 1845, when the court made a joint decree against Hutcherson and Clement Pigg for the whole sum of 220 dollars 47 cents, with interest thereon from the 9th of May 1829.

From this decree the defendants applied to this court for an appeal, which was allowed.

*Grattan*, for the appellants, insisted :

1st. That the representatives of the other sureties of Mrs. Hutcherson, as executrix of John Pigg, should have been parties. And for this he cited *Spottswood* v. *Dandridge*, 4 Munf. 289 ; *Taliaferro* v. *Thornton*, 6 Call 21 ; Story's Equ. Jur. § 161, 162, 169 ; *Primrose* v. *Bromley*, 1 Atk. R. 89 ; Calvert on Parties 235, 17 Law Libr.

2d. That it was error to make a joint decree against the executor and the surety, before there had been a decree against the executor and a return of *nulla bona*, or other evidence of his insolvency. *Roberts* v. *Colvin*, 3 Gratt. 358.

*Stanard* and *Bouldin*, for the appellee, insisted :

1st. That it was too late for Clement Pigg to object in this court that the representatives of the other sureties had not been made parties, after he had allowed the case to proceed in the court below upon the bill taken for confessed as to him. They referred to *Chappell* v. *Robertson*, 2 Rob. R. 590, and *Kee's executors* v. *Kee's creditors*, 2 Gratt. 116.

2d. That the case cited by the counsel for the appellant, on the second point, shews that the decree may be

1851.
October
Term.

Hutcher-
son, &c.
v.
Pigg.

against the executor and the surety at the same time; and although it was most proper that the decree should be first against the executor and then against the surety, that was a mere matter of form, which the court will correct without reversing the decree.

DANIEL, *J.* delivered the opinion of the court.

The court is of opinion, that as by the executorial bond given by Mrs. Pigg and her sureties, the obligors bound themselves only for the due administration, by the executrix, of the goods, chattels and credits of the testator, the sureties are, to no extent, responsible for the rents or profits of the real estate; and as it appears that the balance reported by the commissioner in favour of the appellee, and for which the decree was rendered, is composed in part of items for rent of the real estate, received by the appellant Hutcherson in right of his wife, the executrix, it was erroneous in the Circuit court to render a joint decree for said balance against the appellants.

The court is also further of opinion, that as no reason is shewn or alleged for failing to make the representatives of the other sureties to the executorial bond parties to the suit, it was error to render any decree in the cause against the appellant, Clement Pigg, in the absence of said representatives. Decree reversed, with costs to the appellants. Cause remanded, with leave to the appellee to make the proper parties, and for a resettlement of the accounts and further proceedings in order to a final decree.

DECREE REVERSED.

OTT's *ex'x v.* KING *& als.*

(Absent *Cabell*, P.)

**November 10th.**

A debtor contracts to give a lien on two adjoining tenements, to
secure the debt, and the creditor is in possession of one of
the tenements under an agreement by which the rent of
the tenement is to be taken in satisfaction of the interest
on the debt. Afterwards the debtor, becoming embarrassed in his circumstances, conveys all his property in
trust to pay his debts. HELD: The creditor is entitled to
enforce his equitable lien not only against the debtor but
his creditors.

In January 1811 George Ott leased from Miles King
a lot on Main street in Norfolk, for a term of twelve
years, to commence from the 31st of March 1811. Ott
covenanted to build on this lot a good brick house, and
to pay an annual rent of 220 dollars. It was further
agreed that either Ott or King might at any time, not
less than twenty or more than sixty days before the expiration of the term, give the other party notice the lease
would not be renewed, and in that case the buildings
erected by Ott were to be valued, and the amount of
the valuation to be paid by King to Ott before the expiration of the term, and then on such payment the
premises to be surrendered by Ott. Ott entered on the
premises and erected a large double brick tenement,
&c., and continued in possession throughout the term,
which ended on the 31st of March 1823. On the 1st
day of February 1823 Ott gave King a written notice
that he would not renew the lease, and appointed a
valuer of the buildings. King on his part appointed a
valuer, and the two valued the buildings at 8159 dol-

1851.
October
Term.

Ott's ex'x
v.
King
& als.

lars 73 cents. By the agreement of lease, King was to pay Ott the sum ascertained by the valuers, and on the payment Ott was bound to surrender the property at the end of the term. It seems that King was unable to comply with his obligation to pay the value of the buildings. He proposed to Ott to execute two bonds of 2500 dollars each, dated April 1st, 1823, each bearing interest from date, and payable one in four, the other in five years; the residue of 3159 dollars 73 cents payable as King conveniently could after the 1st April 1823. King at various times paid the 3159 dollars 73 cents. He executed his two bonds for 2500 dollars each, according to his proposition, and Ott released possession of one of the houses, and King agreed to execute a deed of trust on the two. Ott retained the possession of one of the houses until his death, as a security for the two notes of 2500 dollars each, and it still is in possession of his executrix and devisee. By an agreement between Ott and King, the rent of the retained tenement was set off against the interest accruing on the bonds; so that only the principal remained due.

In 1831 Ott died, and devised his real and personal estate to Jane Ott, his wife, and appointed her his sole executrix.

Miles King had become much embarrassed in 1835, and executed various assignments on separate portions of his real estate, in which deeds his interest in the land and appurtenances occupied by Mrs. Ott was not conveyed. But by a deed bearing date the 8th day of July 1835 he appointed Newton C. King his trustee for the purpose of receiving all his estate, real and personal, not before conveyed, for the benefit of all his creditors, and added, " I hereby convey the same to him in trust for the purpose aforesaid, he first paying me ten dollars, which I hereby acknowledge to have received."

In July 1840 Mrs. Ott, as executrix of George Ott, filed her bill in the Circuit court of the city of Norfolk

1851.
October
Term.

Ott's ex'x
v.
King
& als.

against Miles King and his wife and N. C. King, in which she set out the foregoing facts and asked that the said two bonds might be decreed to be paid, and in default of payment that a sale of the premises in her possession might be decreed for satisfaction thereof.

Miles King answered the bill, admitting the lease and the agreement by which he was to execute the two bonds, but alleging that they had been nearly paid off; and concurring in the prayer that for the balance due on them they might be held to be a lien on the premises in the possession of the plaintiff. N. C. King answered, averring his ignorance of the matters stated in the bill, except that he had been appointed by Miles King, by his deed of the 8th of July 1835, the trustee and receiver of all his estate not before conveyed, for the benefit of his creditors; and he supposed that by this deed the premises mentioned in the bill passed to him, and whatever rights the creditors had under that deed he submitted to the protection of the court.

In the progress of the cause an account was directed and reported by a commissioner of the court, but when the cause came on to be finally heard in June 1845, the court, being of opinion that the plaintiff was not entitled to the relief prayed for, without acting on the report, dismissed the bill with costs. Whereupon the plaintiff applied to this court for an appeal, which was allowed.

*The Attorney General* and *Cabell*, for the appellant.

1. The agreement between Ott and King should be executed as between them. That agreement is not only fair and certain, but if it had not been reduced to writing, it would have been enforced, because Ott is in possession. 2 Story's Equ. Jur. § 751.

2. If the agreement will not be enforced, then Ott held adversely to King. He held the property as a pledge to secure another contract: and in that state of

1851.
October
Term.

Ott's ex'r
v.
King
& als.

facts King's deed passed nothing. *Hopkins* v. *Ward,*
6 Munf. 38.

3. Independent of the written agreement, Ott had a
vendor's lien on the houses. He built them, and they
were valued and sold to King at the valuation. And
Ott held possession of one of them to secure the payment.

4. The deed of King is a nullity, and cannot affect
Ott's title to specific execution of the contract. The
deed contains no words of conveyance sufficient to pass
real estate or any interest in it. The deed, too, names
no property and no creditor. It is all the property for
all the creditors. *Harvie* v. *Wickam,* 6 Leigh 236;
*Galt* v. *Carter,* 6 Munf. 245. In the case of *Wilkins*
v. *Gordon,* 11 Leigh 547, the deed was sustained; but
there, although the debts were only described as being
about so much, the property was properly described.

It has been frequently held in England that a deed
made without the assent of the *cestuis que trust* is
revocable at the pleasure of the grantor, and void as to
creditors. *Walwyn* v. *Coutts,* 5 Cond. Eng. Ch. R. 7;
*Garrard* v. *Lauderdale,* Id. 1: *Acton* v. *Woodgate,* 8
Id. 97; *Page* v. *Broom,* 3 Id. 543. We have a decision of our own seemingly in conflict with these cases,
*Skipwith* v. *Cunningham,* 8 Leigh 271. This case is,
however, shaken by the later case of *Spencer* v. *Ford,*
1 Rob. 648.

The case has been depending for years, yet no attempt
has been made by creditors to set up the trust as against
the property claimed by Ott. There is no authority in
the deed to the trustee to sell; and the *cestuis que trust*
can only set up their claims by filing a bill to enforce
them: And this they have not done.

5. King did not by his deed to his son, Newton King,
either convey or intend to convey any property but such
as he had a right to dispose of. And as he had no right
to dispose of this property until Ott's claim was satis-

1851.
October
Term.

Ott's ex'x
v.
King
& als.

fied, it is only the remainder after paying that debt
that passed by the deed. *Lacon* v. *Mertens*, 3 Atk.
R. 1; 2 Story's Equ. Jur. § 759; 3 Woodeson's Lect.
281.

There was no counsel for the appellee.

MONCURE, *J.* delivered the opinion of the court.

The court is of opinion that the appellee, Miles King,
having agreed, by contract in writing signed by him, to
give a deed of trust on the lot of land and buildings in
the bill mentioned, to secure the payment of his two
bonds to George Ott, the testator of the appellant, for
two thousand five hundred dollars each, dated the first
day of April 1823, payable four and five years after date,
with interest from the date; and the said George Ott in
his lifetime, and the appellant, as his sole devisee, legatee
and executrix, since his death, having retained possession of a part of the said property, to wit, the western
tenement, since the said contract was entered into, under an agreement with the said Miles King that an annual rent of three hundred dollars should be allowed
therefor and set off against the annual interest on the
said two bonds; the said contract constituted an equitable lien on the said property for the amount of the
said two bonds, which lien a court of equity ought to
enforce not only against Miles King and his heirs, but
against Newton C. King and the creditors, if any, claiming under the general assignment exhibited with the
bill, whether the said assignment be invalid or not, a
question which the court deems it unnecessary, in this
case, to decide. And the court is further of opinion
that the Circuit court, instead of dismissing the plaintiff's bill, should have proceeded to ascertain the balance due upon the said bonds, and then have decreed
that unless the said balance so ascertained, with interest
and costs of suit, should be paid by the defendants, or

some of them, within a reasonable time thereafter, the said property, or so much as might be necessary, commencing with the western tenement aforesaid, should be sold for the purpose of paying the same.   Therefore it is considered that the said decree of the Circuit court be reversed and annulled, and that the appellant recover against the appellee, Miles King, her costs by her expended in the prosecution of her appeal aforesaid here. And the cause is remanded to the said Circuit court to be proceeded in according to the foregoing opinion.

DECREE REVERSED.

1851.
October
Term.

Ott's ex'x
v.
King
& als.

---

## Richmond.

### Ross's *adm'r v.* Reid *& wife.*

(Absent *Cabell*, P. and *Moncure*, J.*)

November 17th.

A party having obtained an injunction to a judgment at law, upon the usual condition of a release of errors, omits to execute the release. Pending the injunction suit, he obtains a *supersedeas* to the judgment at law, but does not perfect the appeal by giving the security. There are repeated applications by him for a renewal of the *supersedeas*, which are granted, but he does not perfect the appeal. The injunction is proceeded in and decided against him; and he afterwards, more than ten years from the date of the judgment, asks that he may have a writ of error to the judgment at law, without giving security, except for costs, which is granted. His *laches* in perfecting his appeal being wilful, deliberate and repeated, and the application for the appeal having been, under the circumstances, improper, the Court of appeals will, upon motion by the appellee, dismiss the appeal.

---

* Judge *Moncure* had been counsel in the cause.

1851.
October
Term.

Ross's
adm'r
v.
Reid
& wife.

This was a motion by Reid and wife, inhabitants of the kingdom of Scotland, to dismiss a writ of error to a judgment of the Circuit court of Spottsylvania, recovered by them against Ross. All the facts of the case are stated by Judge *Baldwin* in his opinion.

*Morson*, for the motion.

There can be no doubt that if Ross had executed a release of errors at law when he obtained his injunction, as he was required to do, that release would have been a good bar to his writ of error to the judgment at law against him; and might have been pleaded in bar. *Hite* v. *Wilson*, 2 Hen. & Munf. 268. So if not given, if inadvertently omitted to be required when the injunction was granted, and the party attempted to take advantage of it in the chancery suit, the court would prevent him. *Ashby* v. *Kiger*, Gilm. 153. Indeed, a court of equity will consider that a party has abandoned his remedy at law by proceeding in equity. *Fairfax* v. *Muse*, 4 Munf. 124. If, then, this was an appeal in equity, there would clearly be no difficulty in having it dismissed.

The remedy in the present case is by summary motion in the nature of a writ of *audita querela*. That writ is now obsolete, and a motion is substituted for it. The nature of the writ is stated in 3 Chitty's Black. 405–6, and the notes. The remedy by this writ applies wherever anything has occurred since the judgment entitling the defendant to relief. It is in the nature of a bill in equity, a writ of a most remedial nature, and intended for the relief of parties who have a good defence, but have no opportunity to make it in the ordinary forms of law.

Here, then, is a case in which we have a good defence, because, as we have seen, in equity the appeal would be a nullity. And the party has had no opportunity to make defence to this writ of error, because it was not

1861.
October
Term.

Ross's
adm'r
v.
Reid
& wife.

proceeded on until the injunction suit was ended. If, pending that suit, notice had been given to the defendants, Reid and wife, Ross would have been compelled to abandon his application for a writ of error.

The gross negligence of the appellant in the prosecution of this writ of error will well justify its dismissal. Without stating the several steps of this proceeding to obtain the writ, it is enough to say that the present and only writ now pending has been obtained more than ten years after the judgment, and is therefore barred by the statute of limitations. In the case of an action at law, or bill in equity, to which the statute of limitations applies, a party cannot rely upon a former action or suit which has gone off, to remove the bar of the statute. *Braxton* v. *Woods*, 4 Gratt. 25. And why not in this case, as the writ of error now pending is another and distinct writ from that formerly allowed, which was a writ of *supersedeas*.

*Patton*, in opposition to the motion.

This motion proceeds upon the *concessum* that there has been no release of errors by the appellant. And I suppose we must presume upon this motion that the judgment appealed from is erroneous.

It seems to be supposed that Reid and wife might have enjoined the prosecution of this appeal; and therefore that this court will now grant relief upon the equitable grounds. And it is argued in the next place that the appeal is not rightfully pending here now. I shall consider the last proposition first.

The application for the writ of error in this case was made out of court, and the record was not left with the clerk, because it was not recollected that the law required it. The application was then made to the court; and such applications are made here every day without notice. The writ of error was then awarded by the court, and was not given for more than five

1851.
October
Term.

Ross's
adm'r
v.
Reid
& wife.

years. But this court has decided, upon mature consideration, that if that order now stood, Ross being dead, his administrator could now prosecute that appeal, though no bond had ever been given.

It is supposed the appellant is barred of his right to prosecute this appeal from what has occurred in this case: And that is that Mr. Ross, being unable to give the appeal bond required of him, applied for leave to prosecute the appeal without giving security, except for costs. That is all he asked, and all that was granted to him. But it is said by the counsel for this motion that the writ of *supersedeas* was, on his motion, set aside, and that a new writ was awarded. Ross had a legal right to have the judgment against him reviewed by this court. The basis of his suit here is the petition for an appeal; and when that was allowed his appeal was pending. The writ is mere process to give notice to the other party. If the writ is the commencement of the proceeding in the case of an appeal, no appeal is pending until the appeal bond is given: And that is expressly denied by the case of *Williamson v. Gayle*, 4 Gratt. 180. But it is said the *supersedeas* was set aside. What is the difference between a *supersedeas* and a writ of error? The first is a writ of error, and gives notice to the other party of the pendency of the appeal. But it is something more, and suspends proceedings on the judgment in the court below upon condition of giving security. It was this part of the process that Ross asked to have set aside; and not that which constituted the writ of error.

The great complaint here is that Ross obtained an injunction to the judgment at law. In fact there was no injunction. That was granted only on the condition precedent of a release of errors at law. That release was as necessary as an injunction bond; and not having been executed, there has been no injunction. Whether that release had or had not been executed,

1851.
October
Term.

Ross's
adm'r
v.
Reid
& wife.

could be known by Reid and wife by a simple enquiry in the clerk's office; and I reckon there has been some studious sleeping on their part in the hope that the five years would elapse so as to prevent an appeal from the judgment. They answered the bill, objecting to the jurisdiction of the Chancery court, and stating grounds of defence which were conclusive unless disproved: And Ross had said in his bill that he had no proof. If, therefore, there was delay in the termination of that suit, it was their own *laches*. And if they delayed to sue out execution on their judgment, it is to be attributed, not to the injunction, which had no existence, but to the decision of this court in the case of *Ross* v. *Milne*, 12 Leigh 204; a case founded on the same paper as is this suit, and which shewed that there was error in this judgment for which it would necessarily be reversed upon appeal.

Reid and wife have now all the rights they ever had; or if they have lost any by not proceeding earlier, they have only themselves to blame. They had all their rights unimpaired by any proceeding either in this or the injunction case. And having slept on their rights they come here to complain that Ross asked for aid, which was offered to him on terms which he could not or did not choose to comply with; and now they seek to deprive him of his legal rights upon the principles of the writ of *audita querela*. This is a writ of extensive application; but I question if any case can be found in which it has been employed to support a judgment illegal at law.

. BALDWIN, *J.* The ground of this motion is the alleged misconduct and *laches* of the plaintiff in error, as disclosed by the record of the appellate proceedings in this court, and the record of the injunction suit prosecuted by him in the court below, to be relieved against the judgment now sought to be reversed.

1851.
October
Term.

Ross's
adm'r
v.
Reid
& wife.

It appears that the judgment was recovered by Reid and wife, the defendants in error, against Ross, the plaintiff in error, on the 13th of September 1838, in an action of debt brought by the former against the latter. Ross filed his bill in equity for a discovery and relief against the judgment, and on the 20th of September 1838 obtained an injunction order restraining all proceedings upon the judgment until the further order of the court; which injunction was granted upon the usual condition of giving bond and security to pay and satisfy the judgment if the injunction should be dissolved, and of filing a release of all errors in the judgment and proceedings at law. The bond and security was given the 29th of the same month, but no release of errors was ever filed. The injunction suit, however, proceeded in like manner as if the release of errors required had been filed, and was heard on the 27th of May 1848, when a decree was rendered by which the injunction was dissolved and the bill dismissed. The fair presumption is, that during the whole period of its pendency the defendants therein were ignorant that the condition of the injunction order had not been fully complied with, inasmuch as they made no effort to sue out process of execution upon their judgment, nor to exact the filing of a release of errors.

It may be that the failure of Ross to give the release of errors was in the first instance from inadvertence; but pending the injunction cause, to wit, on the 27th of June 1842, he applied to and obtained from a judge of this court a vacation order awarding a writ of *supersedeas* to the judgment at law upon the usual terms. At that time he could not have been ignorant that he had not given a release of errors, for he must have known that if he had the attempt to reverse the judgment in the appellate court was utterly hopeless.

After obtaining from the judge the order for a writ of *supersedeas*, it was incumbent upon Ross to return

1851.
October
Term.

Ross's
adm'r
v.
Reid
& wife.

it, with the record upon which it was obtained, to the office of the appellate court; and our statute law prescribed that if the party praying such writ of *supersedeas* should not deliver the record, with the order allowing the same, within thirty days thereafter, to the clerk of the Court of appeals, the same should not be received thereafter, unless good cause should be shewn to the contrary; and that after such dismission no appeal, writ of error, or *supersedeas* should be allowed. Supp. Rev. Code, p. 155, § 53. Ross, however, did not return the record, with the judge's order endorsed, within the time required by law, nor attempt to shew cause against the dismission of the case, until the 27th of April 1843, a period of ten months, when, on his motion, and for reasons appearing to the court, the writ of *supersedeas* awarded by the judge in vacation was directed to issue on bond and security being given. This order of the court was made *ex parte*, no notice being required by the act of assembly or the rules of the court; and it is known that such orders are usually made without evidence, and upon the mere suggestion of some excuse for the delay.

I cannot doubt that if it had been made known to the judge in vacation, when the petition for the writ of *supersedeas* was presented, that Ross was then prosecuting an injunction bill to be relieved against the judgment, that he would not have awarded the writ, whether upon the supposition that the condition of the injunction order requiring a release of errors had or had not been performed: if the former, he would have seen that the appellate proceedings were idle; if the latter, that an abuse was attempted which would have induced him to require performance of the condition before acting upon the subject. And if the same fact had been made known to this court when the petitioner applied for leave to perfect his appellate proceedings, his motion would doubtless have been overruled and his case dis-

1851.
October
Term.

Ross's
adm'r
v.
Reid
& wife.

missed, or he would at least have been laid under the condition of dismissing his bill of injunction.

Under this order of the court, of the 27th of April 1843, it seems that a writ of *supersedeas* issued, but what became of it does not appear. It is certain that the condition of giving bond and security was never complied with. If it had been, then the endorsement of the fact by the clerk of the court below upon the writ would have authorized its service upon the adverse parties, and such service would have led them to the enquiry whether a release of errors had been given, and, upon ascertaining that it had not, to the proper course of proceeding in order to exact it.

Ross, however, on the 29th of February 1848, while the injunction suit was still pending, and more than five years after the order of the 27th of April 1843, obtained on his *ex parte* motion an order of this court, suggesting that the writ of *supersedeas* had not been returned executed, and awarding a new writ. But the new writ of *supersedeas* was not sued out until the 14th of August 1848, after the decree had been rendered dissolving his injunction and dismissing his bill. And upon the 17th of October following, upon his petition, without notice, stating his inability to give bond and security in double the amount of the judgment, he obtained an order of this court, founded upon the act of 1825, Supp. Rev. Code, p. 127, setting aside the order allowing him the writ of *supersedeas*, and awarding a writ of error, upon giving bond and security for the costs thereof only. Although by the literal terms of this last order, it would seem that the appellate cause was dismissed and a new one instituted, the inevitable result of which would be to bar the latter by the operation of the statute of limitations, yet I think a fair and reasonable construction of the order is that it was intended, in conformtiy with the prayer of the petition, to discharge the *supersedeas* of the appellate

1851.
October
Term.

Ross's
adm'r
v.
Reid
& wife.

proceeding, and allow it as a mere writ of error to be continued and renewed.

It thus appears that Ross did not perfect his appellate proceeding, so as to enable him to ask to be heard thereupon in this court, until since the order of the 17th of October 1848, (made more than ten years after the date of the judgment,) allowing him to renew his writ of error, on giving security for costs only: And the question is whether, under the circumstances of the case, he ought to be now heard, for the purpose of reversing the judgment for some error of law therein, though he has exhausted in another forum the remedy he prosecuted there upon the principles of equity. And if he ought not to be heard, then it follows that the writ of error must be discharged, and the parties dismissed from this court.

It is true that by the construction which has been given to our statute law, (as it stood prior to the new Code, and which was thereby adopted,) a writ of error or *supersedeas* was not barred by the statute of limitations, though bond and security was not given within five years from the date of the judgment, if the order allowing the writ, or even the application therefor, was made within that time. Still, however, the appellate proceeding, though considered as pending, was not made effectual for the purpose of staying execution of the judgment, or of being brought to a hearing by the plaintiff in error, until the bond and security was given. And it cannot be doubted that it is the duty of the party to perfect the same within a reasonable time, and if he should fail to do so when required by the court, that his appellate proceedings should be dismissed. And it is equally clear that when the party has been guilty of great *laches*, the court may refuse him its aid, or its leave, to perfect his appellate proceeding, and discontinue the same. *Anderson* v. *Lively*, 6 Leigh 77; *Williamson* v. *Gayle*, 4 Gratt. 180.

1851.
October
Term.

Ross's
adm'r
v.
Reid
& wife.

Whether, if this were a case of mere *laches*, *that* would appear to have been sufficient to call for the dismissal of the writ of error, I deem it unnecessary to consider. This, it seems to me, is not a case of mere *laches*, on the part of the plaintiff in error, but of *laches* wilful, deliberate and repeated; and moreover, of misconduct in the instituting and prosecuting of a wrongful appellate proceeding, for the purpose of securing an undue advantage arising solely out of his own failure of duty, a duty which if it had been performed would have excluded him inevitably from the appellate forum.

In the first place, it was the duty of Ross, if his omission to perform one of the conditions upon which he obtained the injunction to the judgment was inadvertent, to have supplied the defect, so soon as he discovered it, by executing and depositing with the proper officer a release of all errors at law; and if he did not choose to do this, to have dismissed his injunction bill, or to have disclosed the omission to the court or the adverse party, which would have led to the exaction of the release of errors. Instead of taking this obvious course, he still pursues his remedy in equity, and availing himself at the same time of his knowledge that the errors at law, if any, had not been formally released, he obtains the vacation order of June 1842, for a writ of *supersedeas*, nearly three years after the date of the judgment; and thus secures himself in the appellate forum from the bar by further lapse of time of the statute of limitations. It was not his interest, however, for the reason already suggested, to perform the condition of that order, nor of the order of this court of April 1843, founded upon his not having returned the record within the time prescribed by law. But it *was* his interest, shortly before the expiration of five years from the order last mentioned, to guard against the imputation of *laches*, by procuring the order of February 1848, suggesting that the writ of *supersedeas* thereto-

COURT OF APPEALS OF VIRGINIA.

1851.
October
Term.

Ross's
adm'r
v.
Reid
& wife.

fore issued had not been returned executed ; and after
the decree in the Circuit court of May 1848, to sue out
his writ of *supersedeas* of August 1848, to prevent the
execution of the judgment, provided he could give the
required security ; and failing in that, to obtain the
order of October 1848, dispensing with security except
for costs.   These several steps, it will be seen, so far
from repelling, confirm strongly the imputation of
*laches ;* but are more important as serving to shew that
being *ex parte*, and so furnishing no notice to the defendants in error, most of them were, if not designed,
at least calculated, to place the appellate proceeding in
a condition to be rendered available, if the bill of injunction should fail.

   It is true that Reid might by much vigilance have
discovered the failure of Ross to give the release of
errors, but it is plain that he did not discover it, and
that Ross availed himself of his adversary's ignorance
to pursue the two incompatible remedies at the same
time ; which ignorance on the part of Reid, and his
consequent belief that his hands were tied by the injunction order, rendered it impracticable for him to enforce his judgment by process of execution.

   I need not, I think, step aside to enquire by what
analogies this court may proceed, upon motion, or without, to protect its jurisdiction and process from abuse,
instead of sending them to the guardianship of a different forum ; and in the case before us, it seems to me,
the shortest and most effectual remedy compatible with
a due hearing and consideration is the best.

   Judges ALLEN and DANIEL concurred in the opinion
of *Baldwin*, J.

   The following is the order entered in the cause:
   This court, having maturely considered the motion
of the surviving defendant, James Reid, by counsel, and

1851.
October
Term.

Ross's
adm'r
v.
Reid
& wife.

the evidence submitted in its support; and having also maturely considered the cause shewn against the said motion, and the evidence relied on in support of that cause by John S. Caldwell, as committee administrator of the plaintiff, James Ross, who is now deceased, and whose said administrator appeared by counsel to shew cause as aforesaid; and upon such consideration, as well as upon consideration of the arguments of counsel, who were fully heard upon both sides, *this court*, being of opinion that the said Caldwell, as committee administrator as aforesaid, has not shewn good cause *against* the said motion, but that the said James Reid, surviving defendant as aforesaid, has shewn good cause *in its support*, thereupon doth grant the said motion of the said surviving defendant, James Reid, and doth order that the writ of error heretofore allowed in this case to the said James Ross, who is now deceased, be abated and dismissed, and that the said Caldwell, as committee administrator as aforesaid, be barred and precluded forever from suing out any writ of *sci. fa.*, or other process to revive the same, or from, in any way whatsoever, farther prosecuting the said writ of error. And it is farther considered and adjudged by this court, that the said Caldwell, as committee administrator as aforesaid, out of any assets of the said James Ross deceased, in the said administrator's hands to be administered, do pay unto the said James Reid, surviving defendant as aforesaid, his costs by him about his motion in this behalf expended.

## 𝕽𝖎𝖈𝖍𝖒𝖔𝖓𝖉.

### BRYAN *v.* STUMP, *&c.*

(Absent *Cabell*, P.)

**November 17th.**

1851.
October
Term.

1. A brother and sister, both of whom are married, own a tract of land jointly. In 1802 the brother and his wife and the sister and her husband unite in a deed of partition of the land, and from thence to the present time the land is held in severalty by the parties respectively and those claiming under them. The partition is valid and binding on the parties, though no certificate of the privy examination of the wives is annexed to the deed.

2. A trustee in a deed, the trusts of which have been satisfied, executes a power of attorney to a third person with authority to release the deed. The attorney executes a deed which commences in the name of the trustee *by* the attorney, but it is signed in the name of the attorney *for* the trustee; and it releases the land not to the grantor in the trust deed, but to a purchaser under him. HELD: The deed of trust is duly and regularly released.

3. QUÆRE: If the certificate of the privy examination of a *feme covert*, made under the act of 1792, which purports in the body of the certificate to be under the seals of the justices, but in fact no seals or scrolls are affixed to their names, is valid so as to bar the *feme*.

4. Whether or not such certificate be valid, it is at least so doubtful as to cast a cloud upon the title; and the husband being dead, and the interest of the *feme* in the land having been the fee, and her title not being barred by lapse of time, a sale of the land under a deed of trust should not be made. until the cloud is removed, though neither the *feme* during her life nor her heirs since have set up any claim to the land.

In September 1843 Thomas Bryan filed his bill in the Circuit court of Hampshire county, to enjoin the sale of a tract of land under a deed of trust executed by himself to Isaac Baker, to secure a sum of money which he owed to Jacob Stump for the purchase money

of the land.   The grounds of the injunction as they
appear upon the pleadings and proofs are as follows:
Sometime previous to September 1802 Michael Cresap was the owner of a tract of two hundred and fifty
acres of land in the county of Hampshire, which on his
death descended to his two children, Thomas Cresap and
Abigail, who married James Cresap.   By deed of partition bearing date the 23d of September 1802, made between Thomas Cresap and Mary, his wife, and James
Cresap and Abigail, his wife, this tract of land was divided between them by metes and bounds; but there
was no privy examination of either of the *femes covert*.
The parties, however, took possession of the part of the
land assigned to them, and held it without molestation.
On the 27th of April 1814 James Cresap and Abigail,
his wife, conveyed to James M. Cresap, with special warranty against themselves and all claiming under them,
the land assigned and conveyed to them by the deed of
September 1802.   It appears that James Cresap and his
wife lived in the State of Maryland, and a commission
issued to three persons by name, who were described as
justices of the peace for the county of Alleghany, in
the State of Maryland, authorizing any two of them to
take the privy examination of Abigail Cresap, and certify it under their seals to the County court of Hampshire.   The certificate of the two who acted under
this commission stated the fact of the privy examination properly; and it purported to be under their hands
and seals, but no seals or scrolls were affixed to their
names; and they did not, nor were they required by the
commission to certify that they were justices.

On the death of James M. Cresap this land descended
to his son, Luther M. Cresap, and he and his mother,
Mary Cresap, united in a deed bearing date on the 29th
of November 1834, by which they conveyed it to
James Prather, in trust to secure a debt of 1100 dollars
which they owed to John J. Jacob.   They afterwards

in 1835 sold the land to Jacob Stump, and conveyed it
to him by deed bearing date the 4th of April 1843;
having previously, as early as 1835, paid off the debt
to Jacob by the assignment to him of one of Stump's
bonds.

In May 1842 an agreement was entered into between
Stump and Thomas Bryan, by which Stump agreed to
sell to Bryan this land for 7000 dollars; of which 3000
dollars was to be paid on the 1st of the next April, and
the balance in two equal annual payments; and upon
the receipt of the first payment Stump was to convey
the land clear of all incumbrances; and Bryan was to
execute his bonds for the deferred payments, and a deed
of trust upon the land to secure them. Bryan paid a
part of the first payment, and executed his bond for
1750 dollars, payable on the 1st of July 1843, and the
other two bonds as provided for in the agreement. And
on the 6th of April 1843 Stump and wife, by a deed
which traced the title from the deed of September 1802,
conveyed the land to Bryan; and they covenanted that
they had an indefeasible estate in fee simple in the premises, and good right to convey, and they conveyed
with general warranty. And on the same day Bryan
conveyed the land to Isaac Baker in trust to secure the
balance of the purchase money, with power to sell upon
the failure to pay any one of the bonds.

In July 1843 James Prather, then residing in Illinois,
the trustee in the deed to secure the debt to Jacob, executed a power of attorney to William Donaldson, of
Hampshire, by which, after reciting the conveyance to
himself, and the several subsequent conveyances, he
authorized Donaldson to execute for him and in his name
a deed of release to the person legally entitled to receive the same. And accordingly Donaldson, on the
19th of July 1843, executed a deed which commenced
in the name of James Prather, by William Donaldson,
his attorney in fact, but was signed William Donaldson,

attorney in fact for James Prather; and the seal was attached to his name. He released and conveyed the land to the trustee Baker.

Bryan having failed to pay the bond for 1750 dollars, which fell due the 1st of July 1843, the trustee advertised the land for sale; and Bryan applied for and obtained an injunction, relying upon the want of the certificate of the privy examination of the *femes covert* who executed the deed of partition in 1802; the insufficiency of the certificate accompanying the deed of 1814; and that the deed of trust to Prather was still outstanding, the conveyance by Donaldson not being, as he contended, valid to release it.

The defendants answered the bill. It appeared from the proofs that James Cresap lived until about 1836, and he was survived by his wife Abigail, who lived until 1843; and that they and those claiming under them had held quiet and undisputed possession of the land from 1802 down to the hearing of the cause. It further appeared that their children were the heirs of both of them, and that they derived from their father an estate of more than three times the value of the land sold and conveyed by Stump to Bryan.

In April 1844 the court dissolved the injunction; and the plaintiff applied for and obtained an appeal to this court.

*Robinson*, for the appellant, relied,

1st. On the defect in the certificate of the privy examination of Mrs. Abigail Cresap, attached to the deed of 27th April 1814, which he insisted should have been under the seals of the justices. For which he referred to the act, Old Rev. Code, edi. of 1814, p. 221; *Tod v. Baylor*, 4 Leigh 498; *Hairston* v. *Randolph*, 12 Leigh 445.

2d. He insisted that the warranty of James Cresap was not such a security as a court of equity would compel a purchaser to take as a security for a clearly defective title. For which he referred to *Keytons* v. *Brawford*, 5 Leigh 39.

3d. That at least the case came within the principle of the class of cases which reprobates a sale of lands under a trust deed whilst there is a cloud upon the title. And he referred to *Miller* v. *Argyle*, 5 Leigh 460.

4th. That the time which had elapsed since the conveyance in 1814 was not a bar to an action by the heirs of Abigail Cresap to recover the land, either on the ground of *laches* or of the statute of limitations. That the purchasers were entitled to possession under the conveyance from James Cresap until his death in 1836; and only seven years had passed after his death before this bill was filed. And he referred to *Hairston* v. *Randolph*, 12 Leigh 445.

*Patton*, for the appellee.

Bryan accepted the conveyance from Stump with full knowledge of all the defects in the title, as a compliance with Stump's covenant. And he was so well satisfied with the title that he conveyed to the trustee with general warranty, and then comes to complain of these irregularities without an intimation of Stump's insolvency, or of an apprehension that he will be disturbed in his possession of the land. The irregularity of which he complains is, moreover, merely technical, and the provision of the statute requiring the justices to certify under their seals may well be considered as merely directory. *Bank of the U. S.* v. *Dandridge*, 12 Wheat. R. 6.

But if this formal defect exists, will a court of equity enjoin the payment of the purchase money under the circumstances of this case? Clearly it will not be done in England where there is a deed with general warranty, unless, possibly, the grantor be insolvent. Here the grantor is not insolvent, no suit has been brought or is threatened, and the vendee has taken the conveyance with a full knowledge of the defects in the title. If a court of equity should interfere in such a case, it would aid in the perpetration of a fraud by the vendee in taking the possession and the title, and then, upon the pretence of these defects, of which he was before informed, refusing to pay the purchase money. 2 Lomax Dig. 282, and the cases there cited.

MONCURE, *J.* delivered the opinion of the court.

The court is of opinion that the partition made between Thomas Cresap and Mary, his wife, and James Cresap and Abigail, his wife, on the 23d day of September 1802, as appears by their indenture of that date, followed, as it has been ever since, by the possession in severalty of the said parties, and those claiming under them, is a valid and binding partition, although no certificate of the privy examination and acknowledgment of the said Mary and Abigail is annexed to the said indenture.

The court is also of opinion that the deed of trust of the 29th of November 1834 was duly and regularly released by the deed of the 19th of July 1843.

The court is also of opinion that the certificate of the privy examination and acknowledgment of the said Abigail, annexed to thei ndenture of the 27th day of April 1814, substantially and sufficiently conforms to the requisitions of the statute of 1792, in regard to conveyances by husband and wife, except that the said statute requires the certificate of the justices to be returned under their hands and seals, and no seals or scrolls appear to be affixed to the names of the justices in this case, though they state in their certificate that it is given under their hands and seals. The court, without deciding whether the apparent omission of seals or scrolls as aforesaid rendered the title of the appellee Stump to the land sold and conveyed by him to the ap-

1851.
October
Term.

Bryan
v.
Stump, &c.

pellant defective, is yet of opinion that, as the said Abigail survived her husband, who did not die until 1836, and therefore when the injunction awarded in this case was dissolved she was not barred by the statute of limitations from asserting any claim to the said land, such omission of seals or scrolls raised a cloud over the title which, according to the case of *Miller* v. *Argyle;* 5 Leigh 460, and other cases therein referred to, ought to be removed before any sale is made under the deed of trust to secure the purchase money; and that the said injunction should have been retained until the said cloud was removed by a release of any claim of the heirs of said Abigail to said land, or by the decision of a court of competent jurisdiction adversely to such claim in a suit to which the said heirs were parties, or by the lapse of fifteen years from the death of her said husband, which would bar the right of entry of her heirs, or by some other effective means. Therefore it is decreed and ordered that the order of the Circuit court dissolving the said injunction be reversed and annulled, with costs to the appellant against the appellee Stump; and that the cause be remanded to the said Circuit court to be further proceeded in according to the foregoing opinion.

## 𝕽𝖎𝖈𝖍𝖒𝖔𝖓𝖉.

## BROOKE *v.* WASHINGTON.

(Absent *Cabell,* P.)

**December 1st.**

A partnership for the manufacture of iron is composed of four persons, the names of two of whom do not appear; and they live at a distance. The acting partners buy land in their own name for the purpose of obtaining from it wood to be used in the manufacture of iron, and so far as it is paid for it is paid for out of the partnership effects. The land is partnership property, and the partnership having failed, the two dormant partners are liable to the vendor for the balance of the purchase money.

This was a suit instituted in 1843 in the Circuit court of Jefferson county by Thomas B. Washington against Thomas H. Perdue, William Nichols, Charles Brooke and Leonard Jewell, as partners under the style of Perdue, Nichols & Co., to recover from them the purchase money of a tract of land which the plaintiff alleged he had sold to the partnership. The question in controversy was, whether the land had been sold to the two first named partners as individuals or had been sold to the partnership. The facts and the proceedings in the case are stated by the judge in delivering the opinion of the court. The decree in the court below was in favour of the plaintiff; and Brooke obtained an appeal to this court.

*Patton,* for the appellant, contended:

1st. That Brooke was not a secret partner, and yet that Washington had contracted with Perdue and Nichols as individuals, and not with the firm ; and therefore, whatever use was made of the property purchased

1851.
October
Term.

Brooke
v.
Washing-
ton.

the partnership was not bound by the contract.   Gow. on Part. 183–4 ; Collyer on Part. 266 ; *Emily* v. *Lye*, 15 East's R. 7; *Jacques* v. *Marquand*, 6 Cow. R. 497; *Ex parte Hunter*, 1 Atk. R. 223.

2d.  That the partnership was only for the manufacture of iron ; and that the purchase of land was therefore not within the scope of the partnership : And the several partners can only be bound by the contract by their consent to it.   If indeed all the partners had consented to this purchase, it still would not be partnership property ; but it would be held as real estate, in which they were tenants in common.   *Wheatley* v. *Calhoun*, 12 Leigh 264.

3d.  That even if Brooke and Jewell had been secret partners, and the contract had been made with Perdue and Nichols as partners, and for the use of the partnership, they had no authority to bind the other partners in a purchase of land, if they intended to do it.   By the statute of frauds no man is chargeable on any contract concerning the sale of lands, but on some memorandum in writing signed by himself or his agent lawfully authorized.   *Pitts* v. *Waugh*, 4 Mass. R. 424 ; Tucker's opinion in *Wheatley* v. *Calhoun*, 12 Leigh 273.

*Cooke*, for the appellee, insisted :

1st.  That Brooke was a secret partner ; but that the question was immaterial, as he was bound whether a secret or known partner.   *Williams* v. *Donaghe's ex'or*, 1 Rand. 300.

2d.  That the land was essential to enable the partners to carry on their business, as is proved by the fact that in eighteen months they cut off it five thousand cords of wood.   And that whatever doubts may have existed as to the light in which real property is to be considered when bought and used by a partnership for partnership purposes, it is now well settled that it is to be

1851.
October
Term.

Brooke
v.
Washing-
ton.

considered as forming a part of the partnership funds. *Phillips* v. *Phillips*, 7 Cond. Eng. Ch. R. 208; *Broom* v. *Broom*, 9 Id. 118; *Randall* v. *Randall*, 10 Id. 52; *Pierce's adm'r* v. *Trigg's heirs*, 10 Leigh 406.

3d. That the statute of frauds did not apply, as there had been part performance, the purchasers having taken possession of the land, and taken off it a large quantity of wood, thereby materially diminishing its value. *Whitchurch* v. *Bevis*, 2 Bro. Ch. R. 559; 1 Fonb. Equ., Book 1, ch. 3, § 8, note e.

MONCURE, *J.* delivered the opinion of the court.

The suit in which the decree from which the appeal in this case was taken, was rendered, was a suit brought to recover of dormant partners a debt for which the ostensible partners had given their bonds, but which the latter had become unable to pay by reason of their insolvency. The following appear to be the facts of the case so far as it is material to state them. In 1841 Perdue, Nichols, Brooke and Jewell entered into partnership for carrying on the iron making business in the county of Jefferson; and accordingly carried it on for about two years. Perdue and Nichols resided in the county of Jefferson, and were the ostensible partners; Brooke and Jewell were non-residents of the State, and their names did not appear in the style of the firm, which was "Perdue, Nichols & Company." It does not appear to have been known to the appellee, nor generally, that Brooke and Jewell were partners; and it was proved that several suits were brought by different attorneys against Perdue and Nichols alone as constituting the firm of "Perdue, Nichols & Company," though it does not appear that there was any designed concealment of the fact that Brooke and Jewell were members of the firm. In May 1841 the appellee Washington sold and conveyed to Perdue and Nichols 843 acres of land in Jefferson for 6200 dollars; of

1851.
October
Term.

Brooke
v.
Washing-
ton.

which 1100 dollars was paid at the time, and for the
balance they gave their bonds, payable in five annual
instalments, and gave a deed of trust on the land to secure the payment of the same.    The cash payment
was made by the check of " Perdue, Nichols & Co.," and
entries were made on their books, bearing the same
date with the deeds and bonds, to wit, the 1st of May
1841, crediting Washington in account with the firm
for 6200 dollars, the purchase money of the land, and
debiting him in the same account with 1100 dollars,
the cash payment.  During the operations of the partnership for some eighteen months after the purchase, about
five thousand cords of wood were cut from the land
and used in the said operations.    Portions of the land
were also rented out and the rents were received by the
firm and entered on their books.    Brooke had access to
the books and looked into them, though it did not appear that he ever examined any account but his own.
In December 1842 Perdue and Nichols, in their individual names and by the partnership name of Perdue,
Nichols & Co., executed a deed of trust to secure the
debts of the firm, which are enumerated.    Three parcels of land, besides other property, were embraced in
the deed, but the land bought of Washington was not
included, and the debt due to him was not mentioned
in the deed.    In March 1843 Washington filed his bill,
charging that a large portion of the value of the land
consisted in the timber and trees standing on it; that
the object of the purchasers in buying it was to cut
off the timber for fuel to supply their iron works; that
they had cut down and carried off the timber and trees
on the land until it was of very little value; that he had
no other security for the purchase money than the land
itself under the deed of trust; that the partnership had
become insolvent and made a general assignment of
their effects for the benefit of their creditors; and his
only mode of redress to recover the balance due him

was to charge the same on the individual partners; and that Brooke was a partner at the time of the sale, though he was then ignorant of the fact, the name of Brooke being withheld from the public; and seeking to charge said Brooke as a member of the firm for the balance of said debt. Afterwards an amended bill was filed, charging that Jewell also was a secret partner of the firm; and seeking to make him liable. Of all the defendants, Brooke alone filed an answer. He placed his defence upon the ground that the purchase was not made on account or upon the credit of the firm, or by his authority, and was not within the scope of the partnership; and in the absence of any knowledge on the subject at the time it was made, "presumes it was made by Perdue and Nichols with the view of bringing it into the firm as a part of their share of the capital"; and he also objected to the jurisdiction of the court.

The Circuit court, being of opinion that Brooke and Jewell were secret members of the firm; that that fact was unknown to the appellee at the time of the sale; that the land was purchased for partnership purposes; that the chief value thereof consisted in its timber required as fuel for the iron works; and therefore that such purchase was a transaction in the ordinary course of business in conducting the iron works, rendered a decree against all the parties for the balance due to Washington after crediting the proceeds of the sale of the land. From that decree the appeal in this case was taken.

The case of *Weaver* v. *Tapscott*, 9 Leigh 424, seems to rule this case, and to shew that there is no error in the decree of the Circuit court. In that case Weaver and Trimble were partners in the boating business upon James river, between Rockbridge and Richmond. Trimble went to Buckingham and hired hands to be employed in the business, which were actually so employed during a portion of the time that

1851.
October
Term.

Brooke
v.
Washing-
ton.

the partnership continued ; and for the hire he executed his bond with Tapscott as surety. Trimble, the principal obligor, having become embarrassed, and left the State, Tapscott, the surety, was compelled to pay the money, and filed his bill to recover it of the other partner, Weaver, who had not signed the bonds. He obtained a decree ; and this court, consisting of five judges, unanimously affirmed it. Many expressions used by the judges in that case are very apposite to this. Parker, Judge, says : " A dormant partner, to whom a vendor gives no credit, and whose responsibility constituted no part of the consideration moving him to sell, is liable to the whole extent of engagement in matters which, according to the usual course of dealing, have reference to the business transacted by the firm. *Robinson* v. *Wilkinson*, 3 Price's Exch. R. 538 ; *Saville* v. *Robertson*, 4 T. R. 720. There can be no doubt that the hiring of hands to be employed in the boating business had immediate reference to the nature of the dealings between Trimble and Weaver. The trade in which they were engaged could not be carried on without hands any more than without boats." " If Tapscott was ignorant of Weaver's being a partner, it brings this case within the influence of those upon secret partnership. Gow. 176. If he knew it, but dealt with Trimble alone, without intending to release the partnership, it must be governed by the cases of *Bond* v. *Gibson*, 1 Camp. R. 185, and *Gouthwaite* v. *Duckworth*, 12 East's R. 421. It is only, I think, in cases where a separate credit is clearly given to one of the partners, *to the exclusion of the rest,* that the latter are absolved." " When one deals with a partner in matters relating to the partnership business, it ought to be inferred that he deals on the credit of the partnership, unless the circumstances prove that though apprised of the partnership he meant to give individual credit. It would be hard to hold him bound to prove that he knew

1851.
October
Term.

Brooke
v.
Washing-
ton.

of the partnership and dealt on its credit." " The presumption is in the affirmative; and to discharge the firm it ought to appear clearly that he gave credit to the individual alone, and intended to absolve the other partners." Cabell, Judge, says: " It is perfectly clear that Weaver was equally liable with Trimble even if Tapscott at the time of the contract was ignorant of the fact that Weaver was a partner. And if the fact of the partnership was known to Tapscott, Weaver is *a fortiori* liable; unless, indeed, it can be shewn that Tapscott, with this knowledge, contracted on the individual credit of Trimble, in exclusion of that of Weaver. Nothing of the kind is attempted to be proved, and it cannot be presumed without proof. Weaver, therefore, was clearly liable on the hiring; and the cases of *Sale* v. *Dishman*, 3 Leigh 548, and *McCullough* v. *Somerville*, 8 Leigh 415, shew that this obligation was not extinguished by the execution of a bond by his partner." Tucker, P., referring to the arrangement alleged, that Weaver should find the hands and Trimble the boats, says that even if it was made between the parties, yet the public had nothing to do with that arrangement, and as Weaver was to get half the profits he was responsible for the hires, since that interest in the profits *ipso facto* constituted him a partner." Again he says: " 'It is possible,' says Chief Baron Macdonald, in *Barton* v. *Hauson*, 2 Camp. R. 97, ' that separate credit may be given to one of two partners individually, but the presumption of law is otherwise, and that presumption must be rebutted by very clear evidence. And this is reasonable; for why should the partner desire to bind himself and absolve the concern; or why should the dealer with him prefer to bind him individually, when, if bound as a partner, he is personally not less bound, and there is the additional security of his partner?' In this case it is absurd to suppose that Tapscott took Trimble's individual responsibility, if he knew of Wea-

1851.
October
Term.

Brooke
v.
Washing-
ton.

ver's connexion with him ; and if he did not know of it, then the execution of a sealed instrument could not have been with a view to indicate his individual responsibility in contradistinction to that of the concern."

These copious extracts are made from the opinions of the judges in *Weaver* v. *Tapscott*, because, *nomine mutato*, they are as applicable to this case as they were to that, and because they leave little or nothing more to be said in this case. It seems to be difficult to find a distinction between that case and this, unless it be in the fact that in that case the bonds were given for negro hire, and in this they were given for the purchase money of land ; and that is a distinction without a difference, at least in principle. Land is not ordinarily a subject of partnership operation, and therefore stronger evidence is required to shew an intent to convert real estate into partnership stock. But it is capable of being so converted; and an intention to make such conversion being shewn by sufficient evidence, it becomes as completely a part of the social effects as if it were personal estate. In the case of *Wheatley* v. *Calhoun*, 12 Leigh 264, this court said, that "whatever doubts may have heretofore existed as to the light in which real property is to be considered, when brought and used by a commercial partnership for the purposes of the concern, it is now well settled that it is to be looked upon as forming a part of the partnership funds. Such is at present the received doctrine in England, and so this court has decided." In that case Wheatley and Calhoun had purchased a mill and tract of land jointly, and for some time conducted a partnership milling business. The question was whether there was sufficient evidence of an intention to convert the mill and land into partnership stock, or whether they merely intended to carry on the milling business in partnership. Tucker, P., in delivering the opinion of the court, said : "There may, indeed, be partnerships in the business of milling or mi-

1851.
October
Term.

Brooke
v.
Washing-
ton.

ning or farming; but unless the intent of the joint owners to throw their real estate into the fund as partnership stock is distinctly manifested, or unless the real property is bought out of the social funds, for partnership purposes, it must still retain its character of realty." "In this case I see nothing from whence to infer that there was any design on the part of these joint purchasers to convert their real estate into partnership stock." In the case now under consideration the evidence is conclusive that the land was bought for partnership purposes, paid for in part, and intended by the purchasers to be paid for entirely, out of partnership funds, and applied to partnership purposes. The purchase was within the scope of the partnership, for the operations of the furnace could not be carried on without fuel; and the best mode of obtaining it was to purchase land in the neighborhood, well covered with wood, as was the land of Washington. All the partners are therefore bound for the purchase money, on the authority of the cases before cited. The case of *Pitts* v. *Waugh*, 4 Mass. R. 424, was a very different case from this. It was a case of speculation in lands, and the question was, whether, not being a subject of trade and commerce, the mercantile law in regard to dormant partners was applicable thereto; and the court thought not. That case was decided in 1808, since which time the partnership law in regard to real estate has undergone great changes. Collyer on Partnership, § 135 and notes. But in this case the land was not purchased for speculation, but for the purpose of carrying on a business which was an ordinary and legitimate subject of commercial partnership. There is nothing in the objection of the statute of frauds. The purchase being within the scope of the partnership, the partners who made it were agents for the partnership, which became bound by a valid contract made by their agents. It would also be bound on the doctrine of part performance.

The jurisdiction of a court of equity in this case is fully sustained by the cases of *Sale* v. *Dishman*, 3 Leigh 548; *Weaver* v. *Tapscott*, 9 Leigh 424; *Williams* v. *Donaghe's ex'or*, 1 Rand. 300; *Galt* v. *Calland*, 7 Leigh 594; *Parker* v. *Cousins*, 2 Gratt. 372.

The court is therefore of opinion to affirm the decree.

DECREE AFFIRMED.

1851.<br>October<br>Term.<br><br>Brooke<br>v.<br>Washing-<br>ton.

---

## Richmond.

### ISLER *& wife* v. GROVE *& wife*.

(Absent *Cabell, P.*)

**December 6th.**

Where the subject matter in controversy is of the nature of estimated and unliquidated damages, and the accuracy and credit of the witnesses is impeached, an issue should be directed.

1851.<br>October<br>Term.

Benjamin Beeler, of Jefferson county, died in 1827, leaving a widow and several children; three of whom were by his last wife. Mrs. Beeler lived on the land on which her husband had lived, without any assignment of dower, until 1833, when she married Abraham Isler. During her widowhood her three children lived with her, and on her marriage Isler qualified as their guardian; and at that time the daughter, Mary W. Beeler, was about fifteen years old. In 1835 the land was divided, and Isler held the share of his ward, Mary W. Beeler, until she arrived at the age of twenty-one years; and soon after that period she was married to George G. Grove. Isler settled his guardianship accounts in 1836 and 1839, the last time after Mary W. Beeler had come of age; and according to these ac-

1851
October
Term.

Isler
& wife
v.
Grove
& wife.

counts he was in advance to his ward 109 dollars 24 cents.

In 1839 George G. Grove and his wife filed their bill in the Circuit court of Jefferson county, against Isler and wife, in which they charged that the accounts had been improperly settled; and asked for a settlement of the account of Mrs. Isler whilst she acted as guardian *de facto* of the female plaintiff; and of the account of Isler after his qualification.

The defendants demurred to the bill for multifariousness, and also answered; but the court overruled the demurrer, and directed the accounts as asked for in the bill. Under this decree the commissioner reported that the plaintiffs had not required him to take an account of Mrs. Isler's actings before her marriage, and it therefore had not been taken. He reported an account of Isler's actings as guardian, based upon the accounts previously settled, lessening a credit to the guardian for the board for a period of six months, when she was absent from his house, and adding several charges for wood cut and rails removed from the land of his ward; and by these alterations in the account bringing Isler in debt to his ward, on the 1st of January 1839, 174 dollars 12 cents.

To this report Isler filed eight exceptions, all of them having reference to the charges for the wood and rails alleged to have been taken from the land of the female plaintiff. The commissioner returned with his report the depositions taken upon this subject; and they shewed that there were numerous witnesses, whose testimony was conflicting and contradictory; and one of the most important witnesses for the plaintiffs was impeached.

The cause came on to be heard in October 1844, when the court reduced the price at which the rails were charged to 2 dollars 50 cents a hundred, making due from Isler 152 dollars 87 cents, and overruling all

1851.
October
Term.

Isler
& wife
v.
Grove
& wife.

the other exceptions, gave the plaintiffs a decree for that sum, with interest from the 1st of January 1839 until paid, and their costs. From this decree Isler and wife applied to this court for an appeal, which was allowed.

*Cook*, for the appellants.
*Watkins*, for the appellees.

ALLEN, *J.* delivered the opinion of the court.

The court is of opinion, that as the accuracy and credit of the testimony relied upon to sustain the items of the master commissioner's report, which were excepted to in the eight exceptions filed by the appellants to said report, were impeached, an issue should have been directed, as a jury, with the witnesses before them, would have been better enabled to test their accuracy and weigh their credit than a commissioner or the court. The case, too, from the character of the claim, was peculiarly proper for an issue; for although it was competent for the appellees to make the alleged profits received and made by the guardian from the use and sale of the timber taken from the ward's estate a matter of account, yet the extent of the charge on this account, if any was proper, depends upon estimate, and is in the nature of unliquidated damages, and therefore should have been submitted to a jury. The court is therefore of opinion that the decree is erroneous, and the same is reversed with costs. And the cause is remanded, with instructions to direct an issue to ascertain and try whether any timber, not accounted for by the appellant in his accounts rendered, was taken by him from the lands of the ward, and sold or converted to his own use; and what sum would be a proper charge against the guardian for such timber so taken and sold or converted to his own use.

DECREE REVERSED.

# Richmond.

CARRINGTON & als. v. DIDIER, NORVELL & Co.

(Absent *Cabell*, P.)

December 6th.

1. Creditor of a deceased debtor may proceed, by foreign attachment against the heirs residing abroad, to subject land or its proceeds, in the State, descended to them from the debtor.
2. So he may proceed against them as absent defendants in equity to marshal the assets, and thus subject the land descended to them.
3. Heirs residing out of the State, having instituted a suit for a sale of land descended to them, and the same having been sold, and the proceeds being in the hands of a commissioner directed by the court to collect them, a creditor of the ancestor, seeking to subject these proceeds to the payment of his debt, should apply by petition to the court to be made a party in the cause, and to have the fund applied by proceedings in that cause to the payment of his debt. Or if he proceeds by foreign attachment, the commissioner should be a party, and be restrained by the endorsement on the process from disposing of the proceeds. Or if the creditor proceeds against the heirs to marshal the assets, there should be an injunction to restrain the commissioner from paying away the money in his hands. And the commissioner, though a party, as administrator of the debtor, to the creditor's suit, but having in fact no knowledge of the object of it, paying over the money to the heirs under the order of the court whose commissioner he was, will not be affected by the *lis pendens* of the creditor's suit so as to be held liable to pay it over again to the creditor.

This was a suit in chancery, brought in July 1841 in the Circuit court of Halifax, by Didier, Norvell & Co. against Henry Carrington, administrator of John A. Morton deceased, and the four children of John A. Morton. The facts are fully stated in the opinion of the court. There was a joint decree against Henry Carrington and the other defendants. And they thereupon applied to this court for an appeal, which was allowed.

1861
October
Term.

Carrington
& als
v
Didier,
Norvell
& Co

*N. Taylor*, for the appellants.

*Stanard* and *Bouldin*, for the appellees.

ALLEN, J. delivered the opinion of the court.

It appears that the appellees, on the 30th July 1841, sued out of the Circuit court a *subpœna* in chancery against the appellant, Henry Carrington, as administrator, and the other appellants as children and heirs of John A. Morton deceased, which was returned executed August 7th, 1841, on Henry Carrington, and the rest no inhabitants. On the 21st August 1841 they filed their bill, in which they charge that they are creditors of the intestate; that the administrator alleged there were not assets in his hands sufficient to pay them; but the personal estate had been exhausted in the payment of bond debts binding the heirs; that the real estate of which the intestate had died seized, in the county of Halifax, had been sold under a decree of the county court of said county, for the purpose of dividing the proceeds amongst the heirs; that said Carrington had been appointed by the said court collector of the proceeds of sale, and had collected and then held part thereof, and the residue would be due at a future day. They seek to marshal the assets and to be substituted to the rights of the bond creditors, and satisfied out of the real assets; and pray that Carrington, as administrator and as such collector, be made defendant; that as administrator he render an account, and as collector be restrained from paying away or disposing of the funds in his hands or which may come into his hands; and ask that the proceeds arising from the sale be applied to the payment of their debt, and for general relief. Two of the children and heirs were proceeded against as non-residents, by publication; a guardian *ad litem* was appointed to defend the other two children and heirs as infants, who in December 1842 put in an answer for them.

1851.
October
Term.

Carrington
& als.
v.
Didier,
Norvell
& Co.

At November rules 1841 the bill was taken for confessed as to Carrington, and as to him the cause set for hearing.    At April rules 1843 it was set for hearing as to the non-resident defendants, and came on for hearing at April term 1843, upon the order of publication, the answer of the infants by the guardian *ad litem*, and the bill taken for confessed as to Henry Carrington; and an interlocutory order for an account was rendered. At the April term 1844 the cause was heard upon exceptions to the report and recommitted.    Henry Carrington answered in April 1845; and on the 13th April 1846 the decree appealed from was rendered.    In his answer Carrington avers that all the assets which came to his hands as administrator have been paid out to the creditors ; an averment which is sustained by the report of the master commissioner, which shews he is in advance to the estate.    He further avers that the money arising from the sale of the land descended to the heirs, and which came to his hands as collector, had been paid out by him to the parties respectively entitled to receive it, in virtue of two orders of the County court made in the suit in which he was appointed collector ; that he acted in obedience to the orders of the court whose commissioner he was.    And he alleges that he had no recollection that the *subpœna* in this cause had been ever served on him; and that he had no knowledge of the existence of the suit at the time he paid out the money.    The record of the County court, which he files as an exhibit with his answer, shews that a friendly suit for the sale of the land and distribution of the proceeds was brought in November 1839, and a decree appointing commissioners to sell was rendered during the same term.    In January 1841 H. Carrington was appointed collector.    At August term 1841 the report of sale was confirmed, and the collector ordered to pay over the amount of the first instalment, after deducting certain allowances to the **widow**

1851.
October
Term.

Carrington
& als
v
Didier,
Norvell
& Co.

children, in the proportions fixed by the decree; and March term 1842 he was ordered to pay over the ond instalment: and the report of the commissioner was that the money was all paid out by him between 1st February and the 1st November 1842.

In September 1841, after the institution of this suit, appellees obtained a judgment against the administor for their debt, subject to a credit of 108 dollars 91 cts, paid on the 27th September 1841. By the commissioner's report it appears that assets to the value of ? dollars had been applied by the administrator in the ?ment of debts binding the heirs.

From the foregoing statement of the facts it is evit that the appellees had a right to be substituted to shoes of the creditors whose debts bound the heirs, l that the assets should have been marshalled for their ?efit. The land had been sold by a decree of the ort at the time they instituted their suit; and it was ?petent for them to follow the proceeds. Their bill ? out that their debtor was late of the city of New rk: the original subpœna is returned no inhabitant to all the defendants except the administrator; and ? of the children and heirs being adults, were proded against as non-residents; and from the return on subpœna and the other circumstances, it is fair to ?sume the infant children and heirs were also non-resits. The heirs were debtors to the value of the as? descended, and if non-residents, it would have been ?petent to have proceeded against them by way of ?eign attachment, and by a restraining order, or an en?ement on the subpœna, which stands in place of ?h order, to have attached the proceeds arising ?n the sale of land. The appellees did not adopt this ?rse. The heirs were not treated as debtors; but proceeding was to subject the land descended, or proceeds arising from the sale thereof, as the estate their deceased debtor within the jurisdiction of the

1851.
October
Term.

Carrington
& als.
v.
Didier,
Norvell
& Co.

court. The heirs were made defendants, not as debtors, but as absent defendants, having an interest in the subject which the creditor was seeking directly to charge under the equitable jurisdiction of the court to marshal the assets of a decedent. They were warranted in this course by the case of *Tennent* v. *Patton*, 6 Leigh 196, where, in a case to marshal the assets, one of the heirs, being a non-resident, was proceeded against as an absent defendant. But their bill cannot be treated as tantamount to a foreign attachment with a restraining order. Regularly, they should have enjoined the resident defendant from paying over the funds in his hands to those entitled thereto, or have obtained some order from the court restraining the resident defendant from paying away the funds. This was not done. The resident defendant avers he did not know of the existence of the suit at the time the money was paid away, and that he did not remember the *subpœna* had ever been served upon him. The *subpœna* was sued out against him in his character of administrator only, and not against him as collector. It gave him no notice of a proceeding against him for the money in his hands as collector. There is no evidence of actual notice to him, and as he could have had no motive in paying to one in preference to the other claimant, it seems manifest that he has acted in good faith, in obedience to the orders of the court from which he derived his authority, and to which he was responsible, and in ignorance of the claim of the appellees. There is nothing to affect his conscience. If he is to be compelled to pay the money over again, it must result from the application of some stern and inflexible rule of equity, which from reasons of public policy fixes a liability upon him, though he was free from all blame. This, it is maintained on the part of the appellees, is the case here. The money was paid *lite pendente ;* and therefore there could be no change of subject by the voluntary act of the party, so as to af-

the right of the party suing. The doctrine of *lis* *pens* does not depend upon the presumption of no- but upon reasons of public policy; and where it ates, applies although there was no possibility of e of the suit. *Newman* v. *Chapman*, 2 Rand. 93. eating this as a subject which would be affected e *lis pendens*, how does the appellant Carrington ? No fraud is imputable to him; he has collected d as an officer of court. He was the mere agent e court, having no interest in the subject; the t made an order for him to pay it away, and he ed it. Can this be treated as a voluntary act of arty calculated to defeat the rights of a suitor in her case? It is said he should have communicated endency of the suit to the County court; but this similar arguments are based on the assumption that presumed to have notice of the suit and the pray- the bill: and presuming he had notice, he is then treated as if he actually had it, and his conscience be affected thereby. But notice in fact is denied, t proved, and is against all the presumptions of the ; nor is notice, actual or presumptive, at all neces- if this is a case for the application of the doctrine *s pendens*. But where, as in this case, an officer court is made a defendant, who, as agent of the t, collects money to be held subject to its control, is liable to attachment instantly for disobedience to ders, the duty of obedience is a paramount obliga- ; and he cannot be held responsible for such obe- e by the application of the general doctrine of *lis* *ens*. The creditors were the parties in default, and ot invoke the application of the principle where it operate so harshly. Their suit was originally irreg- y instituted. They should have made themselves, etition or bill, parties to the proceeding in the ty court, in which court the fund had been rea- ; and then proper measures would have been taken

1851.
October
Term

Carrington
& als.
v.
Didier,
Norvell
& Co.

1851.
October
Term.

Carrington
& als.
v.
Didier,
Norvell
& Co.

to secure it. They had full notice of this proceeding, for they refer to it in their bill. Failing in this, they should either have proceeded by foreign attachment and obtained a restraining order, or made the proper endorsement on the *subpœna;* or, if they elected to proceed to charge the subject and treat the heirs as absent defendants, they should have enjoined the defendant from paying over the money, or taken some measures to secure the fund in his hands or to have it paid into court. Instead of doing so, they seem to have contented themselves with the institution of their suit, relying upon the doctrine of the *lis pendens*, whilst the collector, in ignorance of any claim, was permitted to go on and pay away the money. The claim to charge him has little foundation in equity, and I think his duty to obey the decrees of the court, whose agent he was, was a paramount obligation, and relieves him from all liability growing out of the doctrine of *lis pendens*. And therefore that so much of the decree as charges Henry Carrington for the money paid out by him as collector, in obedience to the orders of the County court, is erroneous. The decree was also erroneous in not giving the infants a day to shew cause against it after arriving at full age; but as the decree against Carrington and the various defendants is joint, and must be reversed, and such decree entered as the court below should have done, the leave can still be reserved.

Reversed with costs; and this court, proceeding to render such decree, &c.; bill dismissed as to Henry Carrington without costs. It is further adjudged and ordered that the plaintiffs recover (as in former decree from several defendants, leaving out Carrington), and leave is reserved to the infants to shew cause against this decree within six months after they respectively attain full age.

# Richmond.

## NUCKOLS's adm'r v. JONES.

(Absent Cabell, P.)

December 6th.

1851.
October
Term.

case of probat the deposition of an aged witness, taken
in bene esse, allowed to be read, upon proof, either by wit-
esses or his own affidavit, of his inability to attend the
court.

case of probat, a witness unable to attend the court is
xamined as to the hand writing of a testamentary paper
hich had been shewn to him by the propounder of the
ill, but which was not before him at the time he gave his
eposition. HELD: That the testimony is admissible; its
eight depending upon the certainty of the proof that the
aper propounded for probat is the paper that was shewn
the witness.

tness called to prove the hand writing of a paper offered
r probat may be impeached by proof of what she has
id about that paper at another time: But neither her
apacity to judge of the hand writing or her credit is to be
apeached by what she may have said about some other
aper.

w trial will not be granted on the ground of after discov-
ed evidence, upon the affidavit of a party that he has
een informed and believes that certain witnesses will give
nportant testimony, without proof, by affidavit of the per-
ns or others who have heard them, of what they will
ate; and especially if their evidence will be not of new
cts, but merely cumulative, and the cause has been
epending for a length of time, and these newly discov-
ed witnesses live in the county and within a few miles
the party who makes the application.

he April term 1848 of the Circuit court of Han-
ounty, John B. Jones offered for probat a paper
g as the will of Ann W. Nuckols, when, on the
of Nathaniel Nuckols, he was permitted to enter
f a party to contest the probat of the paper; and
use was continued. In the same year Nathaniel
ls died, and the cause was revived in the name of

1851.
October
Term.

Nuckols's
adm'r
v.
Jones.

Edward W. Morris, as his administrator, and after repeated continuances came on to be tried before a jury in April 1850.

The paper contains but a single clause, and is as follows:

" I give to brother John all my hole estate, real and personal. By so doing give all my brother's children one hundred dollars apeace. This is my last will and testament.

"ANN W. NUCKOLS, 1847."

It appears that Nathaniel Nuckols married Ann W. Jones in 1838, and that there was a marriage agreement between them, by which she was authorized to dispose of her property by will, subject to a life estate in her husband; that they lived unhappily together, and frequently separated, and a short time before her death she informed one of the witnesses that Nuckols had threatened to break open her trunk, looking for papers and money; and added, " Let him break it open; he will find nothing there."

It appeared further that Ann W. Nuckols died on the 6th of November 1847; that on the day of her death a small box was taken from a press in the room in which she was lying very ill, and then supposed to be dying, by her female servant, and handed to the wife of the propounder of the will, who took it, without any remark being made by either her or the slave. That about a week, or probably more, afterwards, in the latter part of November 1847, the wife of the propounder of the will, being in the porch of the house and residence of her husband, who is the brother of the testatrix, called to a son of hers then engaged in the garden, a few yards distant, and asked him if he did not wish to see the locket of his deceased aunt, meaning Ann W. Nuckols; that he replied he did, and went

1851.
October
Term.

Nuckols's
adm'r
v.
Jones.

e porch, where she opened a small box, where
ket was, and which he had seen worn by his de-
aunt frequently before; that in attempting to re-
he locket the hinge was attached to a pad of
on which the locket rested, and in taking the
out the cotton came out with it, and the paper
for probat was there found, folded up and con-
a ten cent piece; which box, locket and pad of
were produced in court, and exhibited to the
d used as evidence. That this paper being ta-
t and read by the wife of the propounder, she
ately handed it to another son, and directed him
it to his father, who was then at his mill, about
miles off. That the propounder of the will was
the 22d day of November 1847 in the road,
from towards his mill, when about three quarters
ile from the mill, in company with the son last
I to; that he remarked to the person who met
it he was glad to see him, he had a paper he
to shew him, and intended to go to see him
; and then shewed him the paper propounded
obat, stating it was the will of Mrs. Nuckols.
e paper was examined then and on the next day
person met by the propounder, which person
a contiguous farm, and was a magistrate of the
of Louisa; and he proved on the trial that the
is unchanged and was then as it was at that

ral exceptions were taken in the progress of the
y the opponent of the probat of the paper;
and the facts on which they are based, are stated
opinion of Judge *Allen*. After the verdict in fa-
the will was rendered, the defendant applied to
rt for a new trial, on the ground that the ver-
is contrary to evidence, and also on the ground
r discovered evidence; but the court overruled
tion, and on the motion of the defendant certi-

1851.
October
Term.

Nuckols's
adm'r
v.
Jones.

fied the facts proved. These, however, are not given, except so far as they relate to the production of the paper. The court admitted the paper to probat; and the administrator of Nathaniel Nuckols applied to this court for an appeal, which was allowed.

*Meredith* and *Robert G. Scott*, for the appellant, insisted:

1st. That the evidence of the witness Glenn's inability to attend the court was not sufficient. His own testimony was not admissible, and the other evidence did not prove his inability to attend.

2d. That a part of this witness' deposition, which related to the paper propounded for probat, should have been excluded, because the paper was not before him when he gave his evidence; and there was no proof to identify the paper which had been shewn to him as the paper which was propounded for probat. If this testimony was illegal, the judgment should be reversed. *Poindexter* v. *Davis*, 6 Gratt. 481: *Wiley* v. *Givens*, Id. 277.

3d. That Harding's testimony as to what was said by the witness, Elizabeth Glenn, was improperly excluded. 1 Stark. Evi. 134, 164; 2 Stark. Evi. part 1, 222, 223.

4th. That the court should have granted a new trial on the ground of the after discovered evidence. *Delima* v. *Glassell*, 4 Hen. & Munf. 369; *Arthur* v. *Chavis*, 6 Rand. 142; *Culaghan* v. *Kippers*, 7 Leigh 608.

*Lyons*, for the appellee,

On the first point made by the counsel for the appellants, referred to *Pollard's heirs* v. *Lively*, 2 Gratt. 216, in which it was held that the testimony of the witness was competent to prove his inability to attend the trial of the cause.

1851.
October
Term.

Nuckols's
adm'r
v.
Jones.

the second point he referred to the evidence to
that the paper propounded for probat was the pa-
ewn to the witness Glenn. And he insisted that
jection did not go to the admissibility of the evi-
, but its weight; and that was a question for the
And he insisted further, that the court would not
e a judgment for the admission of illegal testimony
other evidence was ample to sustain the verdict,
was in this case. *Doe ex dem. Teynham* v.
, 19 Eng. C. L. R. 165.

the third point he insisted, that as the appellees
xamined the witness, Elizabeth Glenn, as to what
ad said, they were not authorized to contradict
y other testimony. *Daniels* v. *Conrad*, 4 Leigh
1 Stark. Evi. 134; 3 Stark. Evi. 1753; 2 Philip's
Cow. & Hill's edi. 726; 3 Id. 132, 136; *Cle-
v. Tulledge*, 19 Eng. C. L. R. 247; *Harris* v.
m, 7 Wend. R. 57.

the fourth point he insisted that a new trial is
granted on the ground of after discovered evi-
upon the mere affidavit of the party asking it.
na v. *Glassell*, 4 Hen. & Munf. 369; *Arthur* v.
is, 6 Rand. 142. The principles on which the
trial is granted on this ground are, first, that there
een no *laches* on the part of the party asking it;
d, that the evidence is not merely cumulative;
third, the affidavit of the witnesses discovered,
ing that their evidence will be material. *Williams
ldwin*, 18 John R. 489; *Bunn* v. *Riker*, 4 John.
!6; *Wheelwright* v. *Beers*, 2 Hall's N. Y. R. 391;
le of New York v. Superior Court of New York,
Vend. R. 286; *Calaghan* v. *Kippers*,. 7 Leigh
Smith v. *Brush*, 8 John. R. 84; *Pike* v. *Evans*,
ohn. R. 210.

LLEN, *J.* At a Circuit court held for the county of
over, on the 7th April 1848, the appellee exhibited

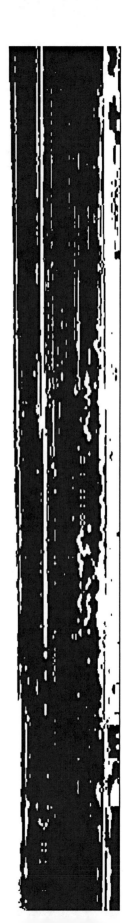

1851.
October
Term.

Nuckols's
adm'r
v.
Jones

a paper writing purporting to be the last will and testament of Ann W. Nuckols, and offered the same for probat. There was no subscribing witness to the paper, and the validity of the instrument as the will of the deceased depended mainly on the proof of her hand writing. The deceased at the time of her death was a married woman, but by the terms of a marriage agreement possessed the power of disposing of her separate estate at her death. Her husband, who survived her, appeared and contested the probat; and having died during the pendency of the controversy, his administrator with the will annexed appeared and was permitted to enter himself as the opponent of the probat. On motion of the contestant, a jury was ordered to be empanneled to ascertain and determine whether the paper writing propounded was the true last will and testament of the deceased. After some continuances the controversy came on for trial at the April term 1850, and the jury found that the paper propounded was the true last will and testament of the deceased.

Several exceptions were taken to decisions of the court during the progress of the trial; and after the verdict a motion was made for a new trial upon the ground of after discovered testimony, and also upon the ground that the finding of the jury was contrary to evidence. Both motions were overruled, and the appellant excepted. The first exception taken during the trial was to a decision of the court overruling a motion to exclude the deposition of William Glenn, taken by the appellee to be read *de bene esse*, because there was no sufficient evidence to shew the inability of the witness to attend. It was proved by the magistrate who took the deposition that the witness was an old man, probably between seventy-five and eighty years of age; that he complained of ill health, stating that his physicians represented he was labouring under rheumatism of the heart, and the witness was of opinion that Glenn was unable to ride on

1851.
October
Term.

Nuckols's
adm'r
v.
Jones.

back from his house to the court house; and an-
witness testifies to the age of Glenn, and gives
his opinion he could not travel to the court house
out danger to his health and probably his life.
testimony of itself proves sufficient inability to
ad to warrant the reading of the deposition; and
orce is not weakened by the evidence on the other
that some two or three years before Glenn was in
habit of riding to the city of Richmond, and that
witness who deposes to this fact, when he last saw
did not perceive any change in his general appear-
and health. In addition to this evidence is the
avit of Glenn, given immediately before the trial, in
h he swears that from sickness and infirmity he
unable to attend the court. This of itself would
justified the reading of the deposition, as was deci-
by this court in *Pollard v. Lively*, 2 Gratt. 216.
he objection to the whole deposition being overruled,
appellant moved the court to exclude from the jury
e parts of the deposition in which the witness testi-
hat a paper writing, purporting to be the last will
he deceased, and which had been shewn to him, as
witness stated, by the propounder of the will some
before the taking of the depositions, was in the
d writing of the deceased; because those parts of
deposition are not legal and competent evidence, and
irrelevant and unconnected with the issue. The
position presented by the exception, is whether it
competent for the witness to give evidence of the
d writing of a paper shewn to him previously by the
ellee as the will of the deceased, without having the
er before him when he gave his deposition, or without
inct proof that the paper shewn to him was the paper
red for probat. The objections, it seems to me, go
er to the weight of the evidence than to the com-
ency of the witness. The paper, when exhibited for
bat, becomes part of the records of the court, and

1851
October
Term

Nicholas's
adm'r
v.
Jones

it would not be in the power of the party, in many cases, to procure the original, so that a witness at a distance from the office where it was deposited could inspect it when giving his testimony.   In such case he would necessarily be constrained to speak from his recollection of the paper if formerly examined by him.   Whether the testimony proved the identity of the paper was a question for the jury.   The witness had been cross examined on each occasion when his deposition was taken.   But no intimation was given that the paper shewn to and seen by the witness was not the one exhibited for probat.   Nor does any exception appear to have been filed to the reading of the depositions, or these portions of them, before the jury was sworn.   Under these circumstances it would have operated as a surprise on the other side to have excluded the deposition from the jury entirely.   The weight they would allow to it would depend upon the question whether the paper spoken of by the witness was sufficiently identified, by all the testimony in the cause, with the paper offered for probat.

Another witness, Elizabeth Glenn, having testified in her examination in chief that she believed the paper offered for probat and the signature thereto to be in the hand writing of the deceased, and that she had seen the deceased write often, and had frequently seen her hand writing, was asked on her cross examination if she had seen another paper purporting to be in the hand writing of the deceased.   She answered that she had, and that it had been shewn to her by Mr. Harding.   And being asked if she did not say that the paper so exhibited to her was in the hand writing of the deceased, replied she had not, but thought the signature to it was like the hand writing of the deceased. The appellant, after all the evidence had been adduced for the propounder of the will, introduced a witness, Harding, who testified, among other things, that after the death of the alleged testatrix, having become inter-

1851.
October
Term.

Nuckols's
adm'r
v.
Jones.

ed in her property by a purchase from her husband,
t which interest he had released, and having heard of
e existence of the paper offered for probat, and that
e witnesses, E. Glenn and her father, were relied on to
ove the hand writing, called to see them, and under-
inding from them that they were acquainted with the
nd writing of the deceased, and that they had seen
e paper offered for probat and believed it to be in her
nd writing, for the purpose of testing the accuracy
their knowledge in regard to the hand writing of the
ceased, exhibited to them a paper which he had pre-
red, imitating the writing of the deceased and pur-
rting to be signed by her. And the witness was then
ced what was said by E. Glenn and her father in re-
·ence to the paper so exhibited to them by the wit-
ss; but the propounder of the will objected to any
swer being given by the witness to the question; and
e objection being sustained by the court, no answer
is given by the witness; to which decision the ap-
llant excepted. The answer to the question must
ve been intended to contradict what the witness, E.
enn, had said on her cross examination, and so to im-
ach her credit; or must have been intended to weak-
confidence in the ability· and skill of the witnesses
judging of the hand writing of the deceased, by
ewing that they were imposed upon by the spurious
per prepared by the witness and exhibited to them.
does not appear that E. Glenn alluded to this paper
her examination in chief. The question before the
ry was whether the paper offered for probat was in
e hand writing of the deceased. Any statements made
another time by the witness, touching the matter in
ue and contradicting her evidence in chief in regard
the paper, to the hand writing of which she had de-
sed, would have been proper, as tending to impeach
e credit ·of the witness. But what she may have
id about any other paper at any other time, having no

1851.
October
Term.

Nuckols's
adm'r
v.
Jones.

relation to the paper offered for probat, was a distinct collateral fact, as to which she could not be examined for the purpose of impeaching her testimony by contradicting her; nor was it competent, after such question was put and answered, to adduce evidence to contradict the answer. *Harris* v. *Wilson*, 7 Wend. R. 57; *Charlton* v. *Unis*, 4 Gratt. 58. Such a course of examination would raise different issues and tend to divert the minds of the jury from the real enquiry before them; for if the statement so made in regard to any collateral paper was contradicted, the other side would be authorized to sustain it; and so the genuineness of every collateral paper would be put in issue.

Still less was it competent to offer such evidence to test the skill and ability of the witness to speak as to the hand writing of the deceased. The circumstances under and the purposes for which it was prepared shew a design to circumvent and entrap the witness by exhibiting a forged paper, a fact which of itself justified the rejection of the evidence; and as the paper so exhibited to the witness was not produced, the evidence would not have furnished any test of skill. For that would have depended upon the success with which the hand writing of the deceased had been imitated in the paper exhibited to the witness.

After the verdict the appellant moved for a new trial, upon the ground of after discovered testimony unknown to him when he went into the trial; and in support of the motion filed his affidavit, in which, after stating that he had made diligent enquiries for evidence to prove that the paper offered for probat was not in the hand writing of the deceased, before the trial, he had since the trial been informed and believed that the paper had been shewn by the propounder to two females, who were acquainted with the hand writing of the deceased, and would, if examined, have testified that they did not believe the paper was in her hand writing. The

1851.
October
Term.

Nuckols's
adm'r
v.
Jones

ersons referred to, it appeared, resided in the county nd within six miles of the appellant. This affidavit id not furnish any ground for setting aside the verdict. Ie had not seen or conversed with the persons whose estimony is deemed material; his affidavit is based on nere reports derived from others, and there is nothing o shew that the persons referred to would testify in the nanner supposed. Even if the affidavits of the sup-osed witnesses were dispensed with, there should have een the affidavit of some person who had seen and onversed with them. It would lead to endless litigation f verdicts fairly rendered should be set aside upon a nere rumor that other testimony might be procured. The controversy had been pending in court for two ears, the administrator had made himself a party to he contest eighteen months before the trial, and the ause turned upon the proof of hand writing. The par-ies went into the trial prepared with their evidence on his question, and the testimony supposed to be since iscovered is not evidence of any new fact, but merely umulative evidence bearing upon the question in regard o which the parties had been at issue from the begin-ing. This is a species of evidence which has not gen-rally been regarded as a good ground for granting a ew trial. *Callaghan* v. *Kippers,* 7 Leigh 608.

A different practice would hold out inducements to a egligent or fraudulent suitor to omit the use of proper liligence in preparing for trial, or to withhold a portion f his testimony until he had discovered the strength f his adversary's case, with the expectation of being ble to overthrow it by preponderating testimony at a ubsequent trial. Upon both grounds, the absence of ny direct evidence from the persons referred to, or from ny person having communication with them, and the haracter of the testimony it was reported they would jive, the motion was properly overruled.

1851
October
Term.

Nuckols's
adm'r
v.
Jones.

There was an additional reason for refusing to set aside the verdict in this case. A motion for a new trial is addressed to the sound discretion of the court, to be exercised in view of all the facts developed on the trial. Judge Cabell, in the case of *Callaghan v. Kippers*, 7 Leigh 608, observes that courts exercise the power of granting new trials, upon the ground of after discovered testimony, rarely, and with great caution; and never but under very special circumstances. The party asking its exercise must shew he was ignorant of the existence of the evidence, that he was guiltless of negligence, and that the new evidence, if it had been before the jury, ought to have produced a different verdict. In this case the bill of exceptions sets out the facts proved at the trial, which this court held, in the case referred to, was essential in order that the appellate court might be furnished with the means of ascertaining whether the court below clearly erred. From this certificate of the facts it appears that five witnesses introduced by the appellee deposed that they believed the paper to be wholly in the hand writing of the deceased. One of these was a magistrate residing in her neighbourhood; another a store keeper near her residence, who had often seen her write, and had often received orders from her, which she recognized as genuine; and a third her brother, who had gone to school with her for five years, had spent much time with her since she was a woman, and some time since she was married, had corresponded with her and knew her hand writing well. On the other side two witnesses were examined as to this question, one of whom would not at first have taken it to be the hand writing of the deceased, but upon closer inspection, and his attention being called to the manner in which some letters were formed and their disconnection, doubted whether it was in her hand writing or not; so that his testimony as to this matter could have

1851.
October
Term.

Nuckols's
adm'r
v.
Jones.

influence.    The second witness who did not believe
e paper to be in her handwriting was one of those
o at one time had acquired an interest in the proper-
by purchase from the surviving husband, but the
tract was afterwards cancelled : A fact which, though
might not have affected his credit, may have insensi-
 influenced his judgment.    If the two females refer-
 to in the affidavit had concurred with this witness,
re would have been three witnesses to five upon the
estion of hand writing ; so that the new evidence re-
rted to exist, if it had been before the jury, ought not,
 anything disclosed by the record, to have produced
lifferent verdict ; for the weight of evidence on the
estion of hand writing would have inclined in favour
 the verdict as found.

On the merits the case is free from difficulty.    The
per on its face gives conclusive evidence of testamen-
y intent.    It disposes of the whole estate, and states
t it is her last will and testament : And being proved,
 the satisfaction of the jury and the court, to be
olly in the hand writing of the testatrix, and being
ned by her, it is a complete statutory disposition of
 property.    That the jury was justified by the evi-
ce in finding it to be wholly in her hand writing,
 could not properly have arrived at any other con-
sion if they believed the witnesses, appears from
at has already been said in reference to the testi-
ny on the question of hand writing.    The objections
wing out of the appearance of the paper and the cir-
nstances attending its discovery might with some
e rise to suspicion ; whilst others, in view of the
racter and temperament of this old woman, her fear
 distrust of her besotted husband, with whom she
d unhappily, and from whom she frequently separa-
, her repeated declarations of her wish that no part
her property should be enjoyed by him, her com-

1851
October
Term

Nuckols's
adm'r
v
Jones

plaints that he had threatened to break open her trunk, and her fears that he might do it, would probably conclude that the mode adopted to preserve her will, and have it placed in the hands of her brother, was natural and characteristic. All this, however, is matter of speculation, and can have but little influence when it is satisfactorily shewn that the paper left by her shews upon its face a testamentary intent, is a completed instrument, and is wholly in her hand writing. I think there was no error in any of the decisions of the court during the progress of the trial which have been excepted to; that the motion for a new trial, upon both the grounds relied on, was properly overruled; and that the sentence should be affirmed.

BALDWIN and MONCURE, *J's*, concurred in *Allen's* opinion.

DANIEL, *J.* dissented. He thought that, under the circumstances of suspicion which existed in the case, there should have been a new trial to let in the after discovered evidence.

JUDGMENT AFFIRMED.

# Richmond.

## Ball & *als.* v. Johnson's *ex'or* & *als.*

1851. October Term.

(Absent *Cabell*, P.)

December 6th.

he statute of limitations does not commence to run against the owners of the remainder in slaves, in favour of the purchaser of the life estate, until the death of the life tenant.

ı a bill by persons claiming to be legatees or assignees of legatees, against defendants as other legatees and assignees of legatees, under the same will, for distribution of the slaves bequeathed to the legatees jointly, the presumption is, in the absence of all pleading and proof to the contrary, that the persons made parties to the suit as legatees are not fictitious persons, or mere pretenders to the characters assumed in the proceedings.

ı such case, the case being a proper one upon its merits for distribution of the subject amongst those entitled thereto, the bill should not be dismissed for want of parties, or of proof that the parties were what they professed to be; but the court should direct the plaintiffs to amend their bill and make the proper parties, and should direct a commissioner to ascertain and report the persons entitled to the several distributive shares.

n March 1844 a bill was filed in the Circuit court of g William county, in which the plaintiffs stated nselves to be Peggy Minor, widow of Richard Minor d, and who before her marriage was Peggy Powers; hard Gwathmey, sheriff and committee of the estate James Powers deceased, and Samuel B. Lipscomb, claimed as purchaser from Delila and Sally Powchildren of William Powers deceased. The bill rged that David Powers, after providing for the payt of his debts, left the remainder of his property to wife for her life, and at her death to be equally did among his eight children and the child of his wife former husband, who was to share equally with

1851
October
Term.

Hall
& als
v.
Johnson's
ex'or
& als

his own children. That the plaintiff, Peggy Minor, was one of the children; that Gwathmey was the representative of James Powers deceased, who was another of them, and that Lipscomb claimed the interest of William Powers, another child of David, by purchase from Delila and Sally Powers, the children of William; and the deeds from them to him were made exhibits with the bill. That among the negroes left by David Powers to his wife for life was one named Esther, who had since had some four or five children. That Mrs. Powers sold her life estate in this slave to Christopher Johnson, who, as plaintiffs had heard, had purchased the interest of several of the legatees in said slave. That Johnson died in possession of said slave and her increase, in the life time of Mrs. Powers, who had since died. That there has been no division of this slave and her increase, but that they were then in the possession of one or more of Johnson's legatees.

The bill stated that the names of the other legatees of David Powers were Thomas Toler and Sally, his wife, who was Sally Powers; Polly Reid, who was the daughter of Mrs. Powers by her first husband; Richard Gwathmey, sheriff and committee administrator of David Powers deceased, and also of Alexander Powers; Betsey Powers, and Catharine Allen, who was Catharine Powers, and Fielding Slater, who claimed as purchaser of the interest of Thomas Toler and Sally, his wife. And making these and the surviving executor of Christopher Johnson, and his legatees, parties defendants, they asked for a discovery of the names, sexes and ages of the children of Esther, and for a division of the said slaves either by a sale or in kind: for their share of the hires of said slaves since the death of Mrs. Powers; and for general relief.

Sherwin McRae, the surviving executor of Johnson, and the guardian of his two younger children, answered the bill for himself and his wards. He stated that the

1851.
October
Term.

Ball
& als.
v.
Johnson's
ex'or
& als.

eft by Christopher Johnson had been distributed
his legatees. That the bequests of the slaves
bsolute and unconditional, recognizing no pro-
r title in any other person. That Esther was in
ssession of Johnson many years before his death;
at she and her children have been in possession
legatees ever since; a possession which had been
nd undisturbed, and adversary to all the world.
his possession had continued more than five
n Christopher Johnson before his death, and he
1832; and had continued ever since in those
1g under him. And they therefore relied on the
of limitations. He further stated that Esther
r children were, with other slaves, bequeathed by
pher Johnson to his wife for her life, and then
three youngest children; and had been divided
st them according to the will. And he called for
of the identity of the Esther mentioned in the
th the slave in the possession of Johnson, and
thed by his will; and strict proof of the title of
intiffs in all other respects. And it was objected
e administrator or executor of William Powers
t a party to the suit.

pears from the evidence that David Powers died
is to July 1806, and that a negro girl named
was allotted to Mrs. Powers, as a part of her
itable interest in her husband's estate. That
me afterwards, (the time is not stated, but it was
is to 1825,) Mrs. Powers sold her life estate in
ve to Christopher Johnson, and that since John-
urchase of her all her children, five in number,
en born. Johnson seems also to have purchased
e interest of some of the remaindermen in this
And in 1832 he bequeathed these slaves to his
oungest children. Mrs. Powers died in 1843.
cause came on to be heard in May 1846, when
irt dismissed the plaintiffs' bill with costs.

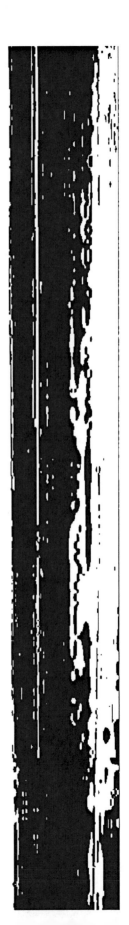

1851.
October
Term.

Ball
& als.
v.
Johnson's
ex'or
& als.

At the same term of the court there was an application for a rehearing of the cause, on the ground of after discovered evidence, and the affidavits of several witnesses were filed with the petition, to prove that Johnson had only a partial interest in the slaves. But the court refused to rehear the cause. And thereupon the plaintiffs (one of whom, Peggy Minor, had married Achilles Ball) applied to this court for an appeal, which was allowed.

*Lyons*, for the appellants, insisted that their title to an interest in the slaves was fully made out. And that Mrs. Powers, the life tenant, having lived until 1843, until that time the possession of the purchaser from her, and those claiming under him, was not adversary, but under her title: and therefore that the statute of limitations was no bar. He referred to *Lynch* v. *Thomas*, 3 Leigh 682; *Merrit* v. *Smith*, 6 Id. 486.

*Daniel*, for the appellees, insisted:

1st. That the answer having put in issue the identity of both the plaintiffs and the property claimed, that identity must be proved; and that there was a total absence of proof that the plaintiffs were the persons whom they claimed to be. So there was no proof of the assignment to Lipscomb. And upon the necessity of proof of the assignment, he referred to *Corbin* v. *Emmerson*, 10 Leigh 663; *Tennant* v. *Patton*, 6 Leigh 229.

He insisted further, if there had been proof of the title of the assignors and of the assignment, that Lipscomb was not the proper party to sue, but William Powers's administrator. And he insisted that the joinder of an improper party was fatal. For which he cited *Cuff* v. *Platall*, 3 Cond. Eng. Ch. R. 651; *Makepeace* v. *Haythorne*, Id. 652; *King of Spain* v. *Machado*, Id. 643; *Dickenson* v. *Davis*, 2 Leigh 401.

1851.
October
Term.

Ball
& als.
v.
Johnson's-
ex'or
& als.

wis, J. delivered the opinion of the court.

pears to the court that the slave Esther, in the
ings mentioned, was the property of David
deceased, in his life time, and was by his last
d testament bequeathed to his wife, Elizabeth
during the term of her natural life, and after
ath in remainder jointly to his eight children
named and the daughter of his said wife by a
husband. That Christopher Johnson, the father
of the appellees, purchased from the said Eliza-
owers her life estate in the said slave, and also
sed the undivided interest therein of some of the
s in remainder, but whose or how many does not
ly appear. That the said Johnson, at the time
purchase from the said Elizabeth Powers, ac-
possession of said slave, and held her and her in-
until his death; and that since his death she and
rease have been held by his widow during her
d since her death by some of his children and
s, under his will. That the said Elizabeth Pow-
l a year and some months before the institution
suit, and thereupon her life estate, which she had
the said Christopher Johnson, was determined;
se claiming under him have thenceforth had no
s in the subject, beyond those acquired by the
ristopher Johnson by purchase from some of the
s in remainder as aforesaid.

the court is of opinion that the legatees in re-
r of the said David Powers, whose interests in
ject were not purchased by the said Christopher
n, had no cause of action or suit to recover the
ntil the determination of the life estate by the
f the said Elizabeth Powers, until which time
session of the said Christopher Johnson, and of
claiming under him, was not adversary to, but
ent with, and in support of, the title in remain-
And the persons so entitled are not therefore

1851
October
Term

Hull
& als.
v
Johnson's
ex'or
& als.

barred by the statute of limitations; nor does the lapse of time furnish any presumption against their right to recover their respective interests in the subject.

It also appears that the object of this suit is to obtain distribution amongst those entitled in remainder of the said slave Esther and her increase, and of their hires since the expiration of the life estate. The bill purports to make as the proper parties thereto, some as plaintiffs and the rest as defendants, those interested in the subject, whether as legatees or as representing or deriving title from legatees: And it represents that the said Esther and her increase are in possession of some one or more of the heirs and legatees of the said Christopher Johnson, and it makes them and his surviving executor defendants; and it further represents that the plaintiffs have heard that the said Johnson in his life time purchased the interests of some of the legatees in remainder.

And the court is of opinion that the parties in this suit, both plaintiffs and defendants, are to be treated as occupying the position of persons claiming a common right in the same subject, derived from the same original source: and the jurisdiction of the court is invoked for the purpose of causing the proper distribution in severalty to be made amongst them. There is no conflict, so far as yet appears, of pretensions in the cause in regard to the ownership of the several distributive shares; and if there be any difficulty in making the distribution sought, it must arise from mere absence of proof as to the identity of persons made parties as legatees, or as to the representative character of parties in relation to deceased legatees, or as to the fact of assignment to parties claiming to be purchasers from legatees. These are matters in which the appellees have no interests beyond those acquired by the said Christopher Johnson in his life time. The distributive shares in point of number are fixed, and the persons to take them

1851.
October
Term.

Ball
& als.
v.
Johnson's
ex'or
& als.

tively designated by the will of the said David
rs.    To such of the shares as were purchased by
Christopher, when ascertained, the appellees or
of them will as his representatives be entitled;
heir shares cannot be enlarged or diminished by
ailure of proof as to other distributive shares not
red by their testator.    The only legitimate conse-
ce of a failure of proof as to some of the distribu-
hares would be to suspend the action of the court
e disposition thereof until the defect be supplied;
t is the province of the court to direct the proper
to be taken for that purpose.    It could furnish no
reason for dismissing the suit, and thereby defeat-
he rights of parties who appear to be entitled to
· distributive shares.

le presumption is, in the absence of all pleading or
f to the contrary, that the persons made parties to
uit as legatees, or personal representatives of lega-
named in the will, are not fictitious persons or mere
inders to the characters assumed in the proceedings;
this presumption is applicable to most of the parties
e cause.    It is only in reference to parties claiming
ititled to distributive shares by purchase that the
eedings and proofs are defective: these are the
itiff Lipscomb, the defendant Slater, and the appel-
as representatives of Christopher Johnson.    Lips-
b claims the share of the legatee, William Powers
ased, by purchase from Delila and Sally Powers, his
lren; but the said Delila and Sally, and the person-
ipresentatives, if any, of the said William Powers
ased, are not made parties either as plaintiffs or de-
ants, and there are no averments or proofs tending
iew that the distributive share of the said William
'ers became vested in his said children; nor is there
evidence of the execution of the papers purporting
ie assignments from them to the said Lipscomb.
defendant Slater is stated in the bill to claim by

1851.
October
Term

Ball
& als.
v
Johnson's
ex'or
& als

purchase, as the plaintiffs have been informed, the interests of the defendants, Thomas Toler and Sally, his wife, one of the legatees named in the will; but neither Slater nor Toler and wife have answered, and there is no evidence of such purchase. The appellees, or some of them, as representatives of Christopher Johnson, are entitled to such of the distributive shares as he may have acquired by purchase from legatees; but such of his representatives as have answered are silent upon that subject, and no written or other definite evidence in relation to it has as yet been produced.

The case being a proper one upon its merits for distribution of the subject amongst those entitled thereto, and as such distribution must be accomplished through the agency of one or more commissioners, the decree upon the hearing ought of course to have been interlocutory only, and to have directed the measures requisite for supplying the defects above mentioned in the pleadings and proofs. For this purpose the court ought to have directed the plaintiffs to amend their bill, and make the proper additional parties, and a commissioner or commissioners to ascertain and report the persons entitled to the several distributive shares, the number, sexes, names and ages of the slaves and their estimated values, the hires of them accruing since the expiration of the life estate, and the persons accountable therefor, with the credits to be allowed for charges incurred since that time in the care and maintenance of any of tender years, or otherwise incapable of labour, and to ascertain and report whether the slaves could be distributed in kind, and if so, to apportion the respective shares of the persons entitled. And upon the coming in of such report, it would have been proper for the court, by its further directions, to accomplish a distribution of the slaves in kind, or of the proceeds of a sale of them, if that should be necessary; and finally to dispose of the cause according to the rights of the parties.

e court is therefore of opinion that the decree of ircuit court, dismissing the bill of the plaintiffs, is eous.   Reversed with costs, and remanded with ictions to reinstate the cause, and proceed accord- ) the principles above declared.

CREE REVERSED.

## 𝕽𝖎𝖈𝖍𝖒𝖔𝖓𝖉.

## Vance v. McLaughlin's *adm'r.*

(Absent *Cabell*, P.)

### December 6th.

rife's interest as legatee in her father's estate, in the hands of the executor, may be subjected by the creditor of her husband, by a proceeding by foreign attachment, when the husband resides out of the State.

)ugh the service of the process upon the executor creates a lien upon the wife's interest in favour of the creditor, yet if the husband dies pending the proceedings, leaving his wife surviving him, the lien of the creditor is defeated, and the property belongs to the wife.

egularities in a decree which do not injure the appellant are not sufficient grounds for reversing it.

is was a proceeding by foreign attachment in the ty court of Hampshire, commenced in April 1830, 'illiam Vance against John Collins as an absent )r and William McLaughlin, executor of Daniel aughlin deceased, as a home defendant, in which laintiff sought to subject the interest of the defen- Collins, in right of his wife, in the estate of her

1851.
October
Term

Vance
v.
McLaugh-
lin's
adm'r

late father Daniel McLaughlin, to the satisfaction of his debt. The bill was afterwards amended and all the legatees of Daniel McLaughlin were made parties; and an account of the administration of William McLaughlin on the estate of his testator was taken, which ascertained the amount in his hands to which Collins and wife were entitled to be 106 dollars 85 cents, with interest on 88 dollars 2 cents, a part thereof, from the 21st of September 1833 until paid.

In 1834, though the death of the executor, William McLaughlin, was not suggested, the suit was revived against Daniel McLaughlin as administrator *de bonis non* with the will annexed of Daniel McLaughlin deceased. And in 1837 there was a decree against Collins for the amount of the debt due the plaintiff, viz., 80 dollars 39 cents, with interest on 75 dollars, a part thereof, from the 14th of May 1817 until paid; and there was a personal decree against Daniel McLaughlin, the administrator, for the amount reported to be in the hands of William McLaughlin due to Collins and wife. From this decree McLaughlin applied to the Circuit court of Hampshire for an appeal, which was allowed.

In 1838 the cause came on to be heard in the Circuit court, when the decree of the County court was reversed, and the cause was retained for further proceedings. Whilst the case was pending in the Circuit court the defendant Collins died, leaving his wife surviving him. And without a revival of the cause against the representatives of Collins and William McLaughlin, it came on to be heard in September 1840, when the court dismissed the bill, with costs to the defendant, Daniel McLaughlin, administrator of William McLaughlin, executor of Daniel McLaughlin. And it appearing that the plaintiff had issued execution upon the decree of the County court, and made the money out of the defendant, Daniel McLaughlin, before the appeal was allowed,

ie court gave McLaughlin a decree against him for
ie sum of 125 dollars 27 cents, the amount so made,
ith interest thereon from the 21st day of April 1837,
iat being the return day of the execution. From this
ecree Vance applied to this court for an appeal, which
as allowed.

1851.
October
Term.

Vance
v.
McLaugh
lin's
adm'r.

*Cooke,* for the appellant.
*Patton,* for the appellee.

DANIEL, *J.* delivered the opinion of the court.

The court is of opinion that the rights and interests
f the absent defendant Collins in and to the share of
is wife in the personal estate of her father in the hands
f the executor, William McLaughlin, were liable to be
roceeded against and charged by the creditors of said
ollins, by way of foreign attachment; and consequently
iat the proceedings in this case were properly com-
ienced.

The court is, however, also further of opinion that
ie commencement of such proceedings by the creditor
' the husband are not in legal contemplation equiva-
nt to the reduction into possession by the latter of the
ibject sought to be charged, but creates only a lien in
.vour of the creditor, which is liable to be defeated by
ie husband's dying pending the proceeding, leaving
.s wife surviving him. That by the death of Collins
iring the progress of the suit the whole right to his
ife's share in the property or balance in the hands of
ie executor of her father devolved on her; and that
ie.right of the creditor Vance to have his demand sat-
fied out of it terminated with the life of his debtor.

The court is also further of opinion, that though it
as not regular to render a final decree without first re-
iving the cause against the representative of Collins,
r to give a decree for costs in favour of Daniel McLaugh-
n, as administrator of William McLaughlin, executor of

1831
October
Term.

Vance
v.
McLaugh-
lin's
adm'r.

Daniel McLaughlin, yet that these irregularities do not, under the circumstances of the case, constitute sufficient grounds for the reversal of the decree.

The court is therefore of opinion to affirm the decree, with costs, &c., to the appellee.

DECREE AFFIRMED.

---

## Richmond.

### FLEMING & als. v. BOLLING & als.

(Absent *Cabell*, P.)

**December 6th.**

A decree which passes upon the whole subject in issue, so as to be final in its nature, is not converted into an interlocutory decree by the addition thereto of an order suspending the decree as to the amount of an item of the account involved in the cause, until the decision of another suit brought by another party against both the plaintiffs and defendants in the first suit, in which the amount of that item is claimed by the plaintiff.

Thomas M. Fleming, of the county of Goochland, died in 1801, leaving a widow and three infant children. By his will he gave his land to his wife for her life, and at her death to his children. He emancipated his slaves, except those he had received by his wife; and these he gave to her. And he appointed several executors, of whom Edward Bolling, the brother of Mrs. Fleming, alone qualified.

Bolling seems to have acted not only as executor, but as agent for Mrs. Fleming for a number of years. The stock on the farm and the household furniture, he left

n the farm for the use of Mrs. Fleming, according to
he directions of the will; and he sold all the slaves
mancipated by the will, and applied the proceeds of
ale to the payment of debts. Some of these slaves
e sold at private sale, and two of them he seems to
ave purchased back himself, selling them, as was in-
isted in the progress of the cause, at much less than
hey would have brought at auction.

In 1815 Mrs. Fleming and her children instituted
his suit in the late Chancery court at Richmond,
gainst Bolling, as executor of Thomas M. Fleming,
nd his official sureties. In their bill, after stating the
rovisions of the will and the qualification of Bolling,
ley charge that he received and disposed of the crops
rown on the land for a number of years, sold a large
umber of slaves, and that he had failed to apply the
inds which came to his hands to the payment of the
ebts of the estate, and had not settled his accounts.
.nd they pray for a settlement of the account; that the
xecutor may be compelled to apply the assets in his
ands to the payment of the debts of the estate; and
iat the balance remaining after discharging the debts
iay be paid over to them; and for general relief.

Bolling and his sureties answered the bill; and the
ccounts were referred to a commissioner. The report
f the commissioner was twice recommitted. In the
iird report, which was returned in January 1826, the
ommissioner made alternate statements, presenting the
iews of the plaintiffs and defendants. On this last re-
ort the controverted questions were reduced to three:
ie was in relation to the price of the slaves sold by
ie executor at private sale; another was in relation to
debt which the executor claimed to have been due to
im from Thomas M. Fleming at his death; and the
iird was in relation to a credit claimed by the execu-
r for a sum of money paid to James Lyle on account
f a debt due to him by Thomas M. Fleming in his life

1851.
October
Term.

Fleming
& als.
v.
Bolling
& als.

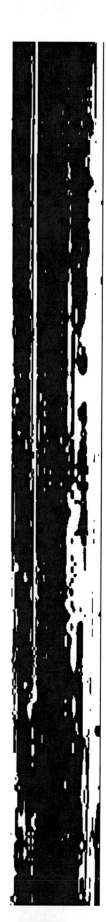

1851.
October
Term.

Fleming
& als.
v.
Bolling
& als

time.  It appeared that a certain William R. Fleming
had, in December 1806, executed to the executor Bolling his bond for £226, for slaves purchased by him;
and that Bolling had assigned this bond to Lyle in part
discharge of the debt due from Thomas M. Fleming to
Lyle.  William R. Fleming became insolvent, so that
Lyle failed to recover the amount of the bond from
him; and he insisted upon his right to have the
amount paid to him either by Bolling, the executor, or
out of the land of Thomas M. Fleming, upon which he
held a mortgage from Fleming for the security of his
debt, which he was then seeking to enforce in the
United States court.

By the statement A of the report, which gave the
executor credit for this payment to Lyle, there was due
to him from his testator's estate, on the 31st of December
1808, the sum of 1129 dollars 29 cents; and it appeared by a former report that he was indebted on his account as agent, at the same date, the sum of 665 dollars
34 cents.

At the June term 1826 the cause came on to be
heard upon the report, when the court made an entry
that "the court not being advised what decree should
be rendered in the premises, time was taken until the
next term to consider thereof."

On the 6th of February 1828 James Lyle, as administrator *de bonis non* with the will annexed of James
Lyle sen'r, deceased, filed his bill in the late Chancery
court at Richmond against Edward Bolling, as executor
of Thomas M. Fleming, and the children of Thomas
M. Fleming and others, in which he stated the indebtedness of Thomas M. Fleming to his testator, and that
the debt was secured by a mortgage on Fleming's land;
that in 1804 his testator had instituted a suit in equity
in the Circuit court of the United States, against these
same parties, to have the mortgage foreclosed; and that
an objection had been taken to the jurisdiction of the

1851.
October
Term.

Fleming
& als.
v.
Bolling
& als.

ourt, upon which the plaintiff was advised that he must be turned out of court. He further stated the assignment by Bolling, as executor of Fleming, of William R. Fleming's bond, which had not been paid, owing to the insolvency of the obligor, and that he was entitled to have satisfaction for the amount of said bond from Bolling and his sureties, or out of the land. That he had understood that in the suit of Thomas M. Fleming's devisees against Bolling and his sureties, Bolling was claiming a credit for the amount of this bond, and that it had been allowed him by the commissioner. He therefore prayed that the court would suspend rendering a decision on the credit claimed by Bolling for the amount of this bond until the matters contained in his bill could be fully heard and decided on in equity; that the court would decree a foreclosure of the mortgage and the payment of the balance due thereon out of the proceeds of the mortgaged subject, or would decree the said balance of principal money, interest and costs, to be paid by the defendants, or such of them as were liable to pay the same; and for general relief.

Before this bill was answered by any of the parties, the case of Fleming against Bolling and others came on to be heard on the 16th of February 1828, when the court made a decree, whereby the statement A of the commissioner's report was approved, and the other statements were disallowed; and considering that against the balance of 1129 dollars 29 cents, found due to the executor by that statement, ought to be set off the balance on the agency account stated in the commissioner's former report, of 665 dollars 34 cents, which would still leave due to the defendant, Edward Bolling, a balance of 463 dollars 95 cents, with interest thereon from the 31st of December 1808, it was decreed that the plaintiff, Tarlton Fleming, in his own right, and the other plaintiffs, should severally pay to the defendant,

1851.
October
Term.

Fleming
& als.
v.
Bolling
& als.

Edward Bolling, each a third part of the said balance last mentioned, as their respective portions, with interest thereon at the rate of six *per cent. per annum*, from the 31st of December 1808 until paid; and that they should pay to the defendants their costs. " But this decree, as to the amount due on a bond executed by William R. Fleming to the defendant, Edward Bolling, executor of Thomas M. Fleming deceased, dated the 19th of December 1806, which bond was assigned by the defendant, Edward Bolling, to James Lyle, on the 22d of December 1806, and for the amount of which bond the said Edward Bolling has received a credit in his administration account settled in this cause, say for seven hundred and fifty-three dollars and thirty-three cents, with interest thereon from the 7th day of April 1806, is to be suspended until the cause depending in this court between Lyle and Fleming's executor and others shall be decided "

After this decree was entered, the defendants to Lyle's suit answered the bill, contesting his right to recover the amount of William R. Fleming's bond; and it appeared that allowing them a credit for that bond, the whole of Lyle's debt was discharged.

In the progress of that cause a decree was entered in both causes in 1829, directing the plaintiffs in the first cause to pay into bank the amount decreed against them. There were also orders made in the causes removing them first to the Circuit court for the county of Henrico, and afterwards to the Circuit court of the town of Petersburg.

The case of *Lyle* v. *Bolling, ex'or, and others,* came on finally to be heard on the 14th of July 1842, when the court dismissed the bill with costs. And in June 1843 the plaintiffs in the first cause applied to the court for leave to file a bill of review to the decree of February 1828; or if the court should not consider that decree final, then for a rehearing of that cause. But e court rejected both motions; the decree having en pronounced according to the admissions of the aintiffs' counsel ten years before the motion was subitted. Whereupon the plaintiffs applied to this court r an appeal, which was allowed.

*Stanard* and *Bouldin*, for the appellants.
*Grattan* and *Patton*, for the appellees.

MONCURE, *J.* delivered the opinion of the court.

The petition for the appeal in this case was preferred 1844, and complains of errors in a decree of the late iperior court of chancery for the Richmond district, ndered on the 16th of February 1828—sixteen years fore the petition was preferred. The question which st presents itself for the decision of the court is, 1ether the decree was final or interlocutory. If final, e appeal when applied for was barred by the limita-n prescribed by law, and must be dismissed as having en improvidently allowed; if interlocutory, it will en be necessary to decide the other questions arising the case.

It will be admitted on all hands that the decree )uld have been final in form and substance but for e suspending order contained in the latter part of it. ie former part of the decree bears every mark of ality upon its face. In the report of the commis-ner, on which the decree was rendered, alternative itements were made embracing all the subjects of ntroversy in the case; and the court, approving of e of the statements and disallowing the others, ascer-ned a balance due from the plaintiffs to the defen-nt, apportioned it among the plaintiffs, and decreed e payment of the same and the costs of the suit by em to the defendant. At the conclusion of the de-ee an order of suspension was made in these words: But this decree, as to the amount due on a bond exe-

1851.
October
Term.

Fleming
& als.
v.
Bolling
& als.

1851.
October
Term.

Fleming
& als.
v.
Bolling
& als.

cuted by William R. Fleming to the defendant, Edward Bolling, executor of Thomas M. Fleming deceased, dated the 19th of December 1806, which bond was assigned by the defendant, Edward Bolling, to James Lyle, on the 22d of December 1806, and for the amount of which bond the said Edward Bolling has received a credit in his administration account settled in this cause, say for seven hundred and fifty-three dollars and thirty-three cents, with interest thereon from the 7th day of April 1806, is to be suspended until the cause depending in this court between Lyle and Fleming's executor and others shall be decided." Does this order of suspension make the decree interlocutory?

The distinction between final and interlocutory decrees has been often considered by this court, and there are many cases on the subject in our reports. In the case of *Thorntons* v. *Fitzhugh*, 4 Leigh 209, Judge Carr, after referring to some of the previous cases, and repeating expressions which had fallen from some of the judges in deciding them, says: " These cases seem to me to take the true and clear distinction ; where any thing is reserved by the court for future adjudication, in order to settle the matters in controversy, the decree is interlocutory ; but where upon the hearing all these matters are settled by the decree, such decree is final, though much may remain to be done before it can be completely carried into execution, and though to effectuate such execution the cause is retained and leave given the parties to apply for the future aid of the court." In the case of *Cocke* v. *Gilpin*, 1 Rob. R. 20, Judge Baldwin investigated the subject very fully, and after adverting to the necessity of resorting to some criterion by which the distinction between the two kinds of decree may be preserved, remarks : " For my own part I am aware of no proper criterion but this: Where the further action of the court *in* the cause (which he contradistinguishes from the action of the

urt *beyond* the cause, to which he afterwards adverts)
necessary to give completely the relief contemplated
the court, there the decree upon which the question
ises is to be regarded, not as final, but as interlocutory."
Let us apply these rules laid down by Judge Carr
d Judge Baldwin (and approved by this court) to
is case, and enquire, in the language of the former,
whether any thing was reserved by the court, in the
cree in question, for future adjudication in order to
ttle the matters in controversy "; or, in the language of
e latter, " whether the future action of the court *in*
e cause was necessary to give completely the relief
ntemplated by the court "?  To ascertain what was
ntemplated by the court in making the suspending
der before mentioned, it will be necessary to take
me notice of the facts and proceedings in the case.
homas M. Fleming died in 1801, and Edward Bolling
ialified as his executor.  In 1815 the widow and chil-
en, devisees and legatees of Fleming, exhibited their
ll against Bolling and his securities, in the late Supe-
or court of chancery for the Richmond district, for
e purpose of obtaining a settlement of the execu-
rial account, and a decree for the balance that might
found due thereon.  This suit was pending in said
urt until the 16th of February 1828, when the de-
ee before mentioned was rendered.  During the pro-
ess of the suit three different reports were made by
e commissioner, under different orders of the court;
e last of which reports bears date in January 1826.
mong the subjects of controversy before the commis-
oner and the court was the right of the executor to
credit for the amount of William R. Fleming's bond,
entioned in the order of suspension aforesaid.  That
nd had been given for the purchase of slaves belong-
g to the testator's estate, and on the 22d of Decem-
r 1806 was assigned by Bolling as executor to Lyle,
account of a mortgage on the testator's real estate.

1851.
October
Term.

Fleming
& als.
v.
Bolling
& als.

1851.
October
Term.

Fleming
& als.
v.
Bolling
& als.

Suit was not brought on the bond until 1808 ; judgment was not obtained until 1810 ; and after several executions had been sued out on the judgment, one of which had been levied on slaves, which were discharged for want of an indemnifying bond, a *fi. fa.* was returned *nulla bona.* On the one hand Lyle contended that this bond was assigned to him with the understanding that Miller would sign it as surety, and that the proceeds, when collected, and not till then, were to be applied to the payment of the mortgage, and insisted that Miller having refused to sign the bond, Bolling was bound to take it back, but refused or failed, though required to do so ; whereupon he brought suit on the bond, &c., but having failed to recover the money, credit should not be given therefor. While on the other hand Bolling contended that the bond was assigned by him to Lyle in part payment of the mortgage ; that Lyle's only recourse was upon the assignment, and that he had lost that recourse by want of due diligence. To the last report of the commissioner in the case an exception was taken by the plaintiffs for allowing credit to the executor for the said payment to Lyle, " because (in the language of the exception) that payment is not established, and a suit is now actually pending in the Circuit court of the United States at Richmond, to compel the payment of that very amount from the representatives of Thomas M. Fleming, and, if allowed on this account, the estate may be compelled to pay the same twice ; and plaintiffs refer to the proceedings in said suit." That suit had been instituted in 1804 to foreclose the mortgage, was then pending, and in it a controversy was then going on about the propriety of a credit for the said bond of William R. Fleming. It would seem that the court suspended the decision of this case for some time, with a view of ascertaining what would be the decision in that suit in regard to the said credit ; for in July 1826, the next term after the

1851.
October
Term.

Fleming
& als.
v.
Bolling
& als.

d last report was returned, an entry was made
it " the court not being advised what decree should
rendered in the premises, time is taken until the
xt term to consider thereof": And the next order
iich was made in the case was the decree of the 16th
February 1828. When that decree was rendered it
d been ascertained that the suit in the Federal court
uld be dismissed for want of jurisdiction. And in
ε same month in which the said decree was rendered,
d a few days before, to wit, on the 6th of February
28, Lyle exhibited his bill in the said late Superior
irt of chancery, where this case was then pending,
king Bolling, the executor, and his sureties, and the
rs of Thomas M. Fleming defendants, giving an ac-
int of the case in the Federal court, and of the as-
nment of William R. Fleming's bond, and the pro-
dings thereon; and praying a foreclosure of the
rtgage, a sale of the mortgaged premises, and pay-
nt of the balance due on the mortgage debt out of
ε proceeds of sale, or by such of the defendants as
ght be liable therefor. He refers to the bill in this
ie, states that he had been informed that in an ac-
int taken in the case Bolling had improperly claimed
d been allowed a credit for the amount of said bond,
ich said Lyle was ready to shew said Bolling was
t entitled to, and prays the court to suspend render-
; any decision on the said credit until the matters
itained in said bill could be fully heard and decided
in equity.

In this state of things the decree of the 16th of
bruary 1828 was rendered, and the question recurs, did
ε court which rendered it contemplate any further
licial action in the case to settle the matters in con-
versy therein? This court is of opinion that it did
t. The case had been pending about thirteen years.
involved the settlement of old transactions, some of
ich had been subjects of much controversy; and it

1851
October
Term

Fleming
& als
v
Hulling
& als

was doubtless desirable, both to the court and the parties, that the case should be ended; provided it could
be ended without detriment to any of the parties arising from the pretensions of Lyle in regard to the credit
for the amount of William R. Fleming's bond. The
suit in the Federal court being about to be dismissed,
and a new suit having just been commenced by Lyle,
which might last, as it actually did, some thirteen years
longer, the court seems to have determined to decide
this case, and turn the parties over to the suit just
brought by Lyle for any further adjustment of their
rights and liabilities in regard to the said bond which
the result of that suit might render proper. The right
of the executor to a credit for the amount of said bond
was a question legitimately raised and regularly controverted in the case: being maintained by the executor
on the one side, and denied by the legatees on the
other. The proper parties were all before the court.
Lyle was neither a necessary nor a proper party to the
case. The case was therefore in a situation to be decided, (if it was not the duty of the court to decide it,
if desired by the parties,) without waiting for the decision of Lyle's suit. In deciding it, the court was of
opinion that the executor was entitled to credit for the
amount of said bond, and therefore allowed it; the
effect of which allowance was to give the executor a
decree against the legatees for 463 dollars 95 cents,
with interest from the 31st of December 1808. The
amount of the credit was 753 dollars 33 cents, with interest from the 7th of April 1806; and if it had been
disallowed, the decree would have been the other way
for the difference between the two sums and interest.
While, however, the court deemed it proper to decide
the case, yet, as Lyle was not a party to it, and therefore not bound by the decree, it deemed it also proper
to protect the legatees against the possible consequences
of a different decision in Lyle's suit of the question in

1851.
October
Term.

Fleming
& als.
v.
Bolling
& als.

gard to the propriety of the credit for the amount of illiam R. Fleming's bond. Therefore the suspend- g order was added to the decree; the object of which ems to have been, not to reserve the question for fu- re decision by the court in this case, but to prevent e enforcement of the decree until Lyle's suit was de- led; and to subject the parties to such directions as ght seem proper to the court in that suit, when it ould be decided.

That the court did not intend to reserve the question regard to the propriety of said credit for future deci- n in the case seems to be manifest from the terms of e decree. By it the court expressly approved the count of the commissioner containing the credit, dis- lowed the accounts from which the credit was ex- ided, ascertained the balance due to the executor, d decreed the payment of the same with costs. This s a plain action of the judicial mind upon this ques- n, between these parties; and seems to be wholly consistent with an intention in the same decree to spend judicial action on the same question. If, how- er, the court intended to say, that while it judicially ted upon the question in this case, and between these rties, it did so without prejudice to any judicial ac- n which might appear to the court in Lyle's suit to proper, then the decree is consistent and reasonable itself. If the court intended to suspend judicial ac- n on the question, why was any decree made in the se? Or, if there was any advantage in deciding on l the questions in controversy except that in regard to illiam R. Fleming's bond, why was not the report nfirmed as to all other matters, and left open as to at? Or, if the court intended to decree on the whole atter, but reserve to itself the power of reforming the cree on motion, if the decision of Lyle's suit should nder such reformation proper, why was not such res- vation expressly made in the decree? Whether such

1851.
October
Term.

Fleming
& als.
v.
Bolling
& als.

a reservation would have made the decree interlocutory is a question which need not be considered, as no such reservation is contained in the decree. The object which the court seems to have had in view could better be attained by rendering a final decree in the case, without prejudice to any order that might be proper to be made in Lyle's suit in regard to the single matter of William R. Fleming's bond. By that course old and troublesome transactions would be settled by a decree, which, as the law then was, could not be disturbed after the lapse of three years; while, at the same time, the plaintiffs would be secured against all possible danger by the suspension of the decree until Lyle's suit should be decided. That danger was a remote one, to say the most of it. If Lyle should fail in his suit, as the court when it rendered the decree must have expected he would, and as turned out to be the case, then there would be an end of the suspension, and the decree in this case might be enforced. If Lyle should succeed, his first recourse would be against Bolling and his sureties, who in that case would undoubtedly be bound in the first place for the amount of William R. Fleming's bond; and, upon payment by them, they would be entitled to enforce the said decree. The only contingency upon which it would be necessary to resort to the plaintiffs in this case was the success of Lyle in the suit, and the inability of Bolling and his sureties to pay the amount of the recovery. In that double contingency the mortgage would be enforced for the payment of the amount, and the heirs of the mortgagor (the plaintiffs in this case) would be protected by a perpetual injunction of the decree in Bolling's favour, and by a decree over against Bolling and his sureties, to such extent as might be proper. All the parties concerned being before the court in Lyle's suit, the principles of equity would enable and require it to do justice among them by laying the burden at once on

1851.
October
Term.

Fleming
& als.
v.
Bolling
& als.

e right shoulders, or giving one defendant a decree over
ainst another, or by the exercise of its restraining
wers, as might seem to be just and proper.

But it is said that the period of suspension was infinite, and that the court could not have intended to
ive it to the clerk to determine when the suspension
is ended, but must have intended to decide that
estion itself. The period of suspension being capable
being rendered certain, is in effect as definite as if it
d been for a given time. And in the event which
curred, to wit, the decision of Lyle's suit against him,
was only necessary to exhibit an official copy of the
cision to enable the clerk to issue execution on the
cree. That was, in point of fact, the very course pur-
ed; and the execution was quashed only because
ore than a year had elapsed after the decree was ren-
red before execution was sued out. On a *scire facias*
erwards issued, the execution was awarded by the
irt. Had Lyle's suit been decided differently, and
y occasion had arisen for preventing the execution of
e decree in this case, such order would have been made
the court in that case as would have relieved the
rk from all embarrassment in regard to the propriety
suing out the execution. And even if it had been
cessary to refer to the court the decision of the ques-
n whether the period of suspension was ended, or
iether an execution might be issued on the decree,
is not perceived that such necessity would render the
cree less final, being matter relating only to the ex-
ition of the decree.

Again it is said that the decree was treated as inter-
:utory by the court and counsel; orders having been af-
·wards made in the case. The only orders afterwards
ide in the case were in relation to the transfer of it,
different times, to courts which succeeded to the late
perior court of chancery of the Richmond district,

1851
October
Term

Fleming
& al.
v.
Bolling
& al.

and in 1840 to the Circuit court of Petersburg; and in relation to the payment of the amount of the decree into bank. On the other hand, the court treated the decree as final on the ground assigned for overruling the motion for leave to file a bill of review, and in awarding execution upon the *scire facias*. But if the decree was in fact final, its character could not be changed by the manner in which it was afterwards treated by the court.

And again, it is said that to treat the decree, under the circumstances of this case, as final, would operate a surprise upon the appellants, and subject them, at the same time, to great and irremediable injury. If this be so, the necessity of so treating the decree must be matter of extreme regret to the court. But might it not, on the other hand, be said that to treat the decree as interlocutory would subject the appellees to at least as great and irremediable injury. The law limiting the right of appeal was intended to remedy a great evil, and to put an end to litigation. The period of limitation, when the decree in this case was rendered, was three years; but has been since extended to five years. More than five times the former, and three times the latter period elapsed after the rendition of the decree before the appeal was applied for. Had the decree been interlocutory in keeping open a single matter, yet, being certainly intended to be final as to all other matters, the appellants could at once have appealed from it; and no good reason appears for their not having done so. Were this court now to set aside a decree made twenty-five years ago, and require a resettlement of transactions which commenced fifty years ago, which could not be settled without great difficulty when they were comparatively fresh, and the parties and their witnesses alive, and which, now that the parties and witnesses may all be dead and the vouchers lost, could not be expected to be correctly settled at all, great and irremediable injury might be done to the appellees. But it is the duty of

ie court to decide the question of law, whether the de-
·ee is interlocutory or final, without being influenced by
ie consequences of the decision, except so far as they
ay throw light on the question to be decided. And
ie court being of opinion that the decree is final, the
·ppeal must therefore be dismissed.

DANIEL, *J.* dissented.

APPEAL DISMISSED.

---

## Richmond.

### MOORE *v.* MOORE's *ex'or & als.*

(Absent *Cabell,* P.)

#### December 9th.

ℋERE: Whether an attestation of a will out of the room in
    which the testator is lying. and out of his sight, but in a
    case in which the testator was able, and might have placed
    himself in a position to see the witnesses when they signed
    the paper, is a valid attestation? A court of four judges
    equally divided upon the question.

This was a bill filed in the Circuit court of King
id Queen county, by James E. Moore, to set aside the
ill of his father, Richard Moore deceased, which had
en admitted to probat in the County court of that
·unty in October 1834. An issue *devisavit vel non*
as directed ; and upon the trial the jury found a spe-
al verdict.

The only question in the cause was as to the attes-
tion of the testamentary paper. It was attested by

1841.
October
Term

Moor
v.
Moore's
ex'or
& als

three witnesses; and the special verdict finds that the will was written on the day on which it bears date, the 23d of July 1834, at the request and dictation of Richard Moore; and after it was written was read to him, and then read by him carefully; and was then signed by him in the presence of all the attesting witnesses, who were by him requested to sign it as witnesses. That the will was then taken by the witnesses into the passage, and there signed by them in the presence of each other; after which they carried it back and handed it open, with their names subscribed to it, to the testator, who held it a minute or more and looked at it, and then gave it to one of them to be folded up for preservation.

The testator, lying in his ordinary position in his bed, could not have seen the attesting witnesses sign their names; but he might have seen them if he had got out of bed, or by changing his position in the bed so as to lean over the foot of it; and his state of health and strength was such at the time that he might have got out of bed, or have so changed his position in bed if he had desired to do so: But the testator did not get out of bed, nor change his position in the bed so as to lean out at the foot of it.

Upon this special verdict the court below made a decree establishing the will; whereupon James E. Moore applied to one of the judges of this court for an appeal, which was allowed.

*R. T. Daniel*, for the appellant.

This case turns upon the true meaning of the words "in the presence," in the act of 1823 concerning wills. That act uses the words as to the witnesses to a will "subscribing in his presence," the presence of the testator. The special verdict shews that the will was not signed in the presence of the testator, nor in the room where the testator lay.

1851.
October
Term.

Moore
v.
Moore's
ex'or
& als.

The principle established by the cases is, that where ᵉ witnesses attest the will out of the room in which ᵉ testator is, he must be in such a position as that he s the capacity, without changing that position, to see ᵉ witnesses when they subscribe the paper. The ᵢes on this subject are reviewed in *Neal* v. *Neal*, 1 igh 6. Although in that case the judges differed on the question whether an attestation in the room ᵢs in all cases good, they were all of opinion that ᵢere an attestation is made out of the room it must made so that the testator has a capacity to see the tnesses attest without changing his position.

It will be urged that the testator looked at the paper ᵉr it was attested. It does not appear that a word ᵢs said at that time : And what passed then might ve been a publication ; but cannot be made a sub-ᵢption by the witnesses in the presence of the testa-·. *Doe* v. *Manifold*, 1 Maule & Selw. 294.

*Griswold*, for the appellee.

The counsel for the appellant has taken no distinc-n between the paper as a will of realty and a will of rsonalty. The will was admitted to probat in 1834, fore our statute requiring attesting witnesses to wills personalty. Sess. Acts of 1834–5, ch. 6, p. 47 ; *Red-ᵣd* v. *Peggy*, 6 Rand. 316.

It must be conceded that the statute in relation to lls of real estate is broad enough in its terms to ex-ᵢde all wills where the witnesses did not subscribe in ᵉ actual presence of the testator : But the courts ve established a constructive presence. The authori-s on the subject are cited in *Neal* v. *Neal*, 1 Leigh

All these authorities concur in declaring that it was ᵉ object of the statute to prevent imposition upon the ᵢtator. And viewing this as the object of the law, ᵉ courts have gone far to uphold fair wills by giving iberal construction to the words " in the presence of "

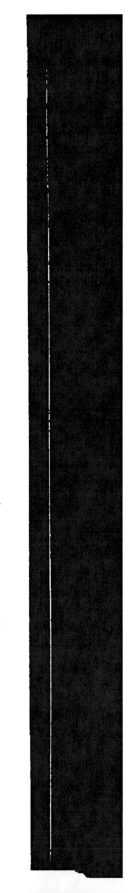

1861.
October
Term.

Moore
v.
Moore's
ex'or
& als

the testator. In the case before us all the objects of the statute have been attained: The witnesses relied upon by the testator have subscribed the paper; and the paper is the very paper which he executed as his will, and requested the witnesses to attest. If, therefore, this paper is declared not to be the will of the testator, that decision must be based upon some merely technical ground, to which the declared purposes, objects and wishes of the testator are to fall a sacrifice.

All that the case of *Neal* v. *Neal* decided was, that a paper attested in the same room with the testator was *prima facie* attested in his presence; and if attested out of the room in which the testator was, it was *prima facie* out of his presence. This was no new law, and yet there are many cases in which it has been held that a will attested out of the room in which the testator was, was valid, upon the principle of a constructive presence. The true principle, as held in the English cases, and in *Neal* v. *Neal*, is, that if the testator could, by his own volition, and without a material change in his position, place the witnesses within range of his vision whilst they were attesting the paper, they were, in the contemplation of the statute, in his presence. In this case the testator was able to change his position at his pleasure without assistance; and by a slight change in his position he might have seen the witnesses whilst they were attesting the will.

These cases of wills stand each upon its own circumstances; and when the circumstances afford the security against imposition intended by the statute, they are to be held sufficient to sustain the will. In the case of *Neal* v. *Neal* the court distinguished between the cases where the testator can change his position himself, and those in which he is unable to do it: And this will explain the seeming conflicts in the opinions of the judges in that case. When he cannot move himself without help, then he must be able in his then position

1851.
October
Term.

Moore
v.
Moore's
ex'or
& als.

see the witnesses whilst they are attesting the paper. hen he can move himself without help, then it is not cessary that he shall be able to see them in the pre- e position which he then occupies. The court is ferred to 4 Kent's Com. 516; *Davy* v. *Smith*, 3 lk. R. 395.

But if the attestation of the witnesses out of the om in which the testator was, was not a subscribing his presence, the delivery of the will, subscribed by e witnesses, open to the testator, and his examination it in their presence, was equivalent to a signing in s presence. An acknowledgment by a testator that a per is his will is an acknowledgment that the signa- re is his. And although the witnesses are required prove every fact necessary to constitute the paper a ll, and signing by a testator is necessary, yet proof them that the testator acknowledged the paper to be s will is sufficient proof that he signed it. *Burwell Corbin*, 1 Rand. 131. On this point the court is re- red to *Burwell* v. *Corbin*, 1 Rand. 131; *Dudleys* v. udleys, 3 Leigh 436; *Pollock* v. *Glassell*, 2 Gratt. 9; *Rosser* v. *Franklin*, 6 Gratt. 1.

*R. T. Daniel*, in reply.

As to the proposition that this is a good will of per- nalty, that depends upon the dates.

The counsel on the other side says, in relation to all ese cases upon the attestation of wills, that there was inability of the testator to change his position.— iswold: No. I said that was the distinction taken the judges in *Neal* v. *Neal*.—Daniel: In all the ses the whole question was whether the attestation s or was not in the room where the testator was. nd when the attestation takes place out of the room, the cases hold it must be within the range of the tator's vision. The controversy in *Neal* v. *Neal* s as to an attestation in the testator's room. Brooke

and Carr, J's, held that where it was in the same room, and there was no suspicion of fraud, it was enough. But where the attestation was out of the room, the question was not whether the testator had power to move himself, but whether the attestation was within the range of his vision. And so is *Winchilsea v. Wauchope*, 3 Cond. Eng. Ch. R. 474.

In *Neal* v. *Neal* the question was upon the sufficiency of an attestation in the same room with the testator, when he was so placed that he could not see the witnesses sign, and was not able to turn himself. There was no suspicion of fraud in that case. There was no doubt that the paper contained the true will of the testator; yet a majority of the court held that it was not attested in the presence of the testator.

Judge Carr, after considering the question really involved in the case, proceeds to refer to another class of cases, where the attestation was out of the room; and he says many decided cases held that the attestation in these cases must be within the vision of the testator: And he refers to *Doe* v. *Manifold*, 1 Maule & Sel. 294 In our case it is admitted that the testator did not see, and could not see, the attestation by the witnesses where he was lying.

But it is said that the presentation of the will by the witnesses, after they had signed it, to the testator, and his examination of it, is equivalent to a signing in his presence. The paper was not a will when it was taken from the room, and a thousand acknowledgments by the testator, without the attesting witnesses, would not make it his will. It was then no will when it left the room or when it returned, but the mere fact that the testator looked at it when it was presented to him has had the talismanic effect of making it a will, though not a word passed between the witnesses and the testator on the occasion. They did not say that they had attested it; he did not say the attestation was theirs;

1851.
Octobel
Term.

Moore
v.
Moore's
ex'or
& al.

t a mere look is to convert the paper into a will, duly
ested in his presence.

DANIEL, *J.* The writing, the probat of which is con-
ted, is dated the 23d of July 1834, and was ordered
be recorded by the County court of King and Queen
the October term in the same year. A bill being
d in the Superior court, contesting the probat, an
ne was directed, on the trial of which the jury found
pecial verdict, to the effect that the said paper writing
s written on the day on which it bears date, at the
quest and dictation of the deceased, and after it was
itten was read to him, and then read by him carefully;
d was then signed by him in the presence of the three
bscribing witnesses, who were by him requested to
n it as witnesses; that the will was then taken by
e witnesses into the passage, and there signed by them
the presence of each other: after which they carried
back and handed it open, with their names subscribed
it, to the testator, who held it a minute or more and
ked at it, and then gave it to one of them to be folded
for preservation. That the testator, lying in his or-
ary position in his bed, could not have seen the at-
ting witnesses sign their names, but he might have
n them if he had gotten out of bed, or by changing
position in the bed so as to lean out over the foot of
e bed; and that his state of health and strength was
h at the time that he might have gotten out of bed,
have so changed his position in it, if he had desired
do so; but that the testator did not get out of bed,
r change his position in the bed so as to lean out at
e foot of it; and that the testator at the time was of
nd and disposing mind and memory, and of lawful
e to make a will.

It is conceded that the paper in question is a good
ll of personal property, as prior to the passage of the
t of the 4th March 1835, entitled " An act prescribing

1851.
October
Term.

Moore
v.
Moore's
ex'or
& als.

the manner of making wills and testaments of personalty," the attestation by the witnesses was not one of
the requisites of the due execution of wills of personals. The only question here is whether it was duly
executed as a will of realty; and turns upon the construction of the words of the last clause of the second
section of the act of the 17th February 1823, entitled
"An act concerning the probat of wills in certain cases."
The second section of the act is in these words : " That
no last will and testament shall be good and valid to
pass any estate, right, title or interest in possession, re-
version or remainder, in lands, tenements or heredita-
ments, or annuities or rents charged upon or issuing out
of them, unless such last will and testament be signed
by the testator, or testatrix, or by some other person in
his or her presence, and by his or her direction, and
moreover, if *not wholly written by himself or herself, be
attested by two or more credible witnesses subscribing
their names in his or her presence.*"

The only difference between the language of this section and that of the first section of the act of the 3d
March 1819, entitled " An act reducing into one the several acts concerning wills," &c., in regard to the attestation, is that the act of 1823 requires the will to " be attested by two or more credible witnesses *subscribing
their names* in the presence " of the testator, whilst
that of 1819 simply requires that it " be attested by
two or more credible witnesses in the presence," &c.

The only reported case in which the meaning to be
given to the words " attested in the presence of the testator " has been heretofore directly before this court for
adjudication is that of *Neal* v. *Neal*, 1 Leigh 6.

In that case it was proved that the testator, who was
very weak and not able to rise from his bed or turn himself without assistance, was raised up and placed on the
side of his bed, and a small table set by, and the will
placed on it: and that the testator, supported there,

gned it, after which the table was removed and he
aced in his bed ; that he was laid with his back to the
ble on which the will was laid, when two of the at-
sting witnesses subscribed their names ; and that the
stator could not see the witnesses attest the will, or
e will itself, being unable to turn his face towards
em ; that the third witness came into the room
metime after this, and put his signature, as he said,
a situation where the testator could have seen
m, though other witnesses said they thought differ-
tly. It was also proved that, before any of the wit-
sses subscribed, the testator was asked if he acknow-
dged the paper to be his last will and testament, and if
desired that the witnesses should respectively attest
; to which questions he answered in the affirmative.
On an appeal from a decision sustaining the will, all
e English cases bearing upon the construction of the
ause of the statute of 29 Charles 2, (from which our
atute of 1819 is taken,) requiring the attestation of
e witnesses in the presence of the testator, were cited
d reviewed by the judges of this court in their opin-
ns. The case, it is true, was one of a will attested in
e same room with the testator, yet the circumstances
the case and the nature of the question not only jus-
ied, but necessarily called for, the declaration of cer-
in rules and definitions equally as controlling in ques-
ns arising on attestations out of the room. The con-
nction, therefore, of the words " in the presence of the
stator," drawn by the court as well from the cases
here the attestation was out of the room, as from those
which the attesting witnesses and the testator were,
the time of the attestation, in the same room, carries
ith it the same weight as a decision, when sought to
applied to a case like the one before us, as if it had
en pronounced in one of the same class. The true
eaning and objects of the requirement of the statute
e, I think, more fully developed in the case just cited

1831
October
Term

Moore
v.
Moore's
ex'or
& als.

than in any of the English cases on the same subject;
and in a recent work, Modern Probate of Wills, the opinion of Judge Cabell is referred to as containing one of
the best commentaries on the construction of the word
" presence " in the statute, to be found.   With such
views of the character of that case, I do not deem it necessary to repeat here an extended notice of the English decisions preceding it, and shall content myself with
citing such portions of the opinions of the judges as I
think particularly applicable to this case, and with endeavouring to shew that the authority of *Neal* v. *Neal*
is not only not impaired, but is fully sustained by decisions of a more recent date.

  " The object of this requisition (says Judge Cabell in
his opinion) is to enable the testator to see that those
who attest the will are the persons in whom he confides,
and to prevent a false paper from being surreptitiously
imposed on the witnesses."   " The object of the law
will be completely effected, and can only be effected, by
the testator's being in such a situation in relation to the
will and the witnesses that he *may*, if he *will*, see from
that situation both the will and the witnesses in the act
of attestation.   This capacity in the testator is unquestionably the test of *presence*, in all cases of attestation
*out of the room* in which the testator may be, for all the
cases shew that an attestation *out of the room* of the
testator is held to be in his presence if he *might* see
it, and not in his presence if he *could not* see it.   Now,
as the reason of the law in requiring an attestation to
be in the presence of the testator is precisely the same
whether that attestation be in the same room or in a
different room, the law will apply the same test of presence to both cases.   An attestation, therefore, in the
same room with the testator will, as in the case of an attestation in a different room, be held to be in his presence
or not in his presence, according to the capacity or want
of capacity in the testator to supervise the transaction.

1851.
October
Term.

Moore
v.
Moore's
ex'or
& als.

'here is, however, one important difference between an
ttestation in the same room and one not in the same
oom with the testator: In the absence of all proof, a
ian is presumed to be able to see what is done in the
ame room with him, and to be unable to see what is
one in a different room. An attestation, therefore, in
he same room is *prima facie* good; an attestation in a
ifferent room is *prima facie* bad. But this presump-
ion must yield to positive proof. An attestation, there-
ore, out of the room of the testator, but proved to be
rithin the scope of his vision, becomes good as being
i his presence; and an attestation in the same room,
ut proved to be out of the scope of his vision, becomes
ad as not being in his presence."

Judge Coalter says that the words and intention of
he statute are satisfied only when it is proved " that
he testator was so *present* to the witnesses and *they* to
*im* as that he *might*, and therefore probably *did*, see the
ttestation."

Judges Carr and Brooke, who thought that the will
ad been duly attested, endeavoured to maintain that
hough the testator was not able to change his position
rithout the aid of others, yet as the attestation was in
he same room, and the testator could by his attendants
ave caused himself at any moment to be turned so as
o bring the will and witnesses in full view, and so near
o him as to afford him an opportunity to distinguish a
alse will if such had been substituted, the attestation
ught to be held to be virtually in the presence of the
estator; that a knowledge on the part of all present
hat the testator could in an instant cause the transac-
ion to be subjected to the test of his senses, united with
he fear which guilt always feels, would give to any
arty meditating such a fraud a consciousness so strong
f the presence and power of detection of the testator
s to furnish substantially those guards intended by the
tatute.

1851.
October
Term.

Moore
v.
Moore's
ex'or
&.als.

But a majority of the court held that this capacity of the testator to cause the relative position of himself and the witnesses to be changed was of no avail. " A power of that sort (said Judge Cabell) exists in every case: in every case the testator may cause his own situation, or that of the witnesses, to be so changed as that he may see the attestation. Such a power was expressly held to be insufficient in the cases of *Doe* v. *Manifold* and *Tod* v. *The Earl of Winchilsea.*"

Judge Coalter, in reply to the same view, said : " If the doctrine contended for be tenable, why shall not a will executed in an adjoining room be good, when the testator could direct the table to be set out within his view, whereat to attest it ? Why not if attested in an obscure corner in the same room, because he might have ordered it to be done in a part of the room where he could see what was doing ? The law is not that it shall be attested in his presence *if* he thinks it proper to superintend the act himself, otherwise he may trust to the honesty of his friends and the witnesses to see for him that no fraud is done. No ; the law requires him to be present himself, body and mind. If he can by turning his eye see what is doing, he will be presumed to have seen it, and no further proof that he *did see* is necessary ; but if interposing walls or other obstructions render it doubtful whether he could see or not, the *power* to see must be made apparent ; as that a door or window *was open*, (not that it might have been opened if requested,) and that his position in bed *was such* (not *might have been* such had he desired to be raised or turned) as that he had it in his power, by simply looking on, to see."

The reasoning of Judge Green, the other member of the majority of the court, was to the like effect, and need not be repeated.

In the three cases of *Shires* v. *Glasscock*, 2 Salk. 688, *Davy* v. *Smith*, 3 Salk. 395, and *Casson* v.

1851.
October
Term.

Moore
v.
Moore's
ex'or
& als.

*Dade,* 1 Bro. Ch. R. 99, (cited in *Neal* v. *Neal,*) in which attestations out of the room were sustained, it was shewn that the witnesses and the testator were so situated in proximity and relation of situations that the testator might have seen the act of attestation. And Judge Carr admitted that all the attempts made to support wills out of the room of the testator, and also out of his sight, had failed ; and that in many cases it had been decided that though the signing was in a room contiguous, yet the devise would be void *unless the testator was in a position from which he might, if he chose, see the witnesses subscribe without changing his position.* The cases of *Eccleston* v. *Speke,* Carth. 79 ; *Broderick* v. *Broderick,* 1 P. Wms. 239 ; *Machell* v. *Temple,* 2 Show. 288, and *Doe* v. *Manifold,* 1 Mau. & Selw. 294, referred to by him and cited by the bar here, are all of that class.

In looking to more recent cases it will be found that the rule has been in no degree relaxed. In the case of *Reynolds* v. *Reynolds,* 1 Spears' R. 253, decided by the Supreme court of South Carolina in 1843, the witnesses, after seeing the testator sign, being ignorant that it was necessary that the testator should see them subscribe, withdrew for convenience to a table in the hall and subscribed their names. It was proved that the testator could not as he lay in his bed have seen them so subscribe. But it was also proved that if he had risen from his posture, and sat on the side anywhere from the centre to the foot of the bed, he might have seen them ; and it appeared that he had strength enough to have done so ; but it was also proved that he did not alter his recumbent posture at all. It was held that the attestation was not good ; that although the testator need not actually see the witnesses sign the will, yet they must have stood in a position to let him see their subscribing ; which means that they must not withdraw themselves from the continued observance of his senses, although

1851.
October
Term.

Moore
v.
Moore's
ex'or
& als.

the testator may himself refrain from using such senses ; that such discretion is with *him*, but not for the witnesses to avoid the opportunity of his doing so.

In the case of *Edward Colman*, 7 Eng. Eccl. R. 392, the will was signed by the deceased in the presence of two witnesses; but subscribed by them in an adjoining room communicating with it by folding doors, which were open, the witnesses being in such a situation that the testator could not, without a change of position, see them. The motion for probat was rejected.

So in the case of *Alexander Ellis*, 7 Eng. Eccl. R. 150, it was proved that the will was signed by the testator in the presence of the witnesses, who took the paper into another room which communicated with the testator's by two separate doors, both of which were open, and there subscribed it in a situation where the testator could not see the witnesses, nor they him, yet so near to the testator that they could hear him breathe. The court held that the will was not attested in the presence of the testator, actual or constructive. They said that the case was a hard one, but the law was imperative; and the probat was refused. No case has been cited at the bar, and I have not been able to find one, in which a will attested out of the testator's room, and in a situation where the testator could not see the act of attestation, has been sustained. 'In the case before us it is not only found that the testator could not see the witnesses attest without a change of position, but all inference of such a change of position, deducible from the fact that the state of the testator's health and strength admitted of his altering his situation, is cut off by the express finding of the jury that he did not get out of bed nor change his position in it. I cannot, therefore, perceive on what ground the due attestation of the paper is to be maintained.

COURT OF APPEALS OF VIRGINIA.

1851.
October
Term.

Moore
v.
Moore's
ex'or
& als.

It is suggested that such a ground may be discovered in the circumstances which transpired after the witnesses had subscribed. It is difficult to conceive what further validity can be imparted to the paper by those circumstances ; which are, as already set forth in the statement of the facts, that after the witnesses signed their names, they carried back the will and handed it open, with their names subscribed to it, to the testator, who held it a minute or more and looked at it, and then gave it to one of them to be folded up for preservation. It is to be borne in mind that the verdict of the jury is a special one, and therefore there is no room for presumption ; and as the circumstances just detailed do not of themselves import a second attestation by the witnesses after their return into the presence of the testator, I cannot perceive that they are of any value in the controversy.

If, however, it is to be inferred that the testator intended by what he did to approve of the manner in which the witnesses had discharged the office they had been requested to perform, such inference would, I think, be of no legal weight. In the most of such controversies it might be doubtless shewn that the testator was satisfied with the attestation, as otherwise he would cause it to be so made as to conform to his views. The mode of attestation is one of the safeguards which the law has enacted for the protection of the testator, and it does not permit him to dispense with it by substituting it by another, however well he may approve of the latter, or however fair and free from all suspicion it may in fact be shewn to be.

All implications and inferences favourable to the will, which could in any way be deduced from the conduct of the witnesses and the testator, after the subscribing by the former, (supposing that it were allowable to imply facts not found in the verdict,) are, I think, fully met by adjudicated cases.

VOL. VIII.—21

1851
October
Term.

Moore
v.
Moore's
ex'or
& als.

In the case of *Edelen* v. *Hardey's lessee*, 7 Har. &
John. 63, which was an action of ejectment, the case
turned upon the due execution of a will which was offered as evidence on the trial. It appeared that after
the testator had signed the will, the witnesses by *his*
request went out of the room into an adjoining room,
and there signed. After it was so signed by the witnesses, a friend of the testator, who had written it, carried it back to the testator and read it to him; informed
him that the witnesses had attested it, shewing him at
the same time their hand writing, at which the testator
nodded his head by way of assent, appeared quite satisfied, and added, as witness thought, " well " or " very
well." The court was asked to instruct the jury that
this evidence, if believed by them, furnished presumptive proof of a compliance with the requisites of the
statute. This instruction the court refused to give;
and on an appeal its refusal was sustained. The case
was, I think, a stronger one for the will than the one
under consideration.

Even were it considered that the conduct of the witnesses after their return into the room of the testator
implied a reacknowledgment by them of their signatures
to the will as witnesses, such reacknowledgment would
not, I think, according to the decisions on the subject,
cure the defective attestation. In the case of *Ragland*
v. *Huntingdon*, 1 Iredell R. 561, it was proved by one
of the subscribing witnesses that he was requested by
the testator to prepare his will according to his instructions, and he did so, and signed his name as a witness
before the testator signed, but not in his presence, and
then read the will to the testator and told him he had
signed as a witness; and the testator approved and executed it; and the other witness then signed in the presence of the testator. It was held not a valid execution of the will—the statute requiring *both* witnesses
to *sign in the presence of the testator*.

1851.
October
Term.

Moore
v.
Moore's
ex'or
& als.

The ninth section of ch. 26, Victoria 1, declares that no will shall be valid unless signed at the end or foot thereof by the testator, or by some other person in his presence and by his direction; and such signature shall be made or acknowledged by the testator in the presence of two or more witnesses *present at the same time,* and such witnesses shall attest and shall subscribe the will in the presence of the testator, &c.

In a case arising under this law, *Moore* v. *King,* 7 Eng. Eccl. R. 429, the Ecclesiastical court held, that though both the witnesses attested and subscribed in the presence of the testator, yet, as the law required the witnesses to be present at the same time, that the attesting and subscribing by one of the witnesses on one day and the attesting and subscribing by the other on another day, though the first witness on the latter occasion acknowledged his signature in the presence of the testator and of the other witness, did not fulfil the requirements of the law. The facts as stated were, that the testator signed a codicil in the presence of a witness (his sister). On a subsequent day, when his sister and another person were present, he desired her to bring him the codicil, and requested the other person present to attest and subscribe it, saying in the presence of both parties and pointing to his signature, "This is a codicil signed by myself and by my sister, as you see; you will oblige me if you will add your signature, two witnesses being necessary." The second witness then subscribed in the presence of the testator and of his sister; the latter, who was standing by him, pointing to her signature and saying, "There is my signature; you had better place yours underneath." She however did not resubscribe.

If this case is entitled to respect as authority, it seems to me decisive of the question under discussion, as it is manifest that the only thing causing it to fall short of a literal compliance with the requisitions of

1851.
October
Term.

Moore
v.
Moore's
ex'or
& als.

the statute was the substituting the acknowledgment by the first witness of her signature in the place of a resubscribing.

As before intimated, however, I do not deem it necessary to the decision of this case to rely on such decisions, the character of the verdict forbidding, in my opinion, any inferences or implications that make it necessary for those denying the validity of the will to invoke the aid of such authority.

Nor do I think that the decisions in relation to the proof by the witnesses of the signing by the testator tend in any measure to impair the force of the authorities I have cited. There is no question here as to the execution of the will on the part of the testator, but the case turns on the manner in which the act of attestation has been performed by the witnesses; and the requirements of the law in relation to the two things are of a wholly different character, for whilst it is positive in requiring that the will shall be attested by the witnesses subscribing their names in the presence of the testator, it does not require that the testator shall sign the will, or cause it to be signed for him, in the presence of the witnesses. The kind or degree of proof by which the fact of signing by the testator, or some one for him, is to be established, is not prescribed. No doubt, therefore, is thrown on the proposition which I have endeavoured to maintain, nor any inconsistency in the opinions of judges exhibited, by shewing that a long series of decisions, commencing at an early period, declare that it is not necessary for the witnesses to see the testator sign, and that the fact of signing may be inferred from his acknowledgment of the instrument to be proved as his will; whilst it is at the same time shewn that a uniform current of decisions, emanating from the same tribunals, announce in effect that the witnesses can attest under the immediate supervision of the testator. For these reasons I am of opinion that the will was not duly attested, and that the sentence of the court below should be reversed, and that the instrument should be admitted to record as a will of personals and rejected as a will of real estate.

1851.
October
Term.

Moore
v.
Moore's
ex'or
& als.

BALDWIN, J. The point of the objection taken to the probat of this will is, not that the attestation of the subscribing witnesses was made out of the room where the testator was at the time, nor that the testator did not see the witnesses in the act of signing their names to the instrument, nor that he was incapable, either mentally or physically, of observing, understanding and controlling the act which they thus performed ; but it is that the position of the testator's body was such at the time that the attestation did not fall within the scope of his vision, and could not without a change of that position, which, although he was fully capable of making, he did not in point of fact make. If, therefore, the objection prevails in this case, it must be fatal to every will in regard to which it occurs, under all conceivable circumstances. We are at liberty, therefore, to make the case, strong as it is, if possible still stronger. We may suppose that a testator, in a perfect state of health both of body and mind, and actively engaged in the pursuits of life, sends for his most confidential friends to attend and witness his will ; that he dictates it to one of them, who writes it at his side ; that he forthwith reads it over, signs and acknowledges it to the witnesses, they sitting or standing around him ; that it being more convenient, from the condition of the room, or the furniture, or any other cause, they then, at his request or by his permission, pass into an adjoining room, through a door between the two rooms, kept wide open during the entire transaction, immediately subscribe their names to the instrument, and instantly return with it to the testator, presenting it to him open and pointing to their signature with the ink thereof still wet ; that he there-

1851.
October
Term.

Moore
v.
Moore's
ex'or
& als.

upon receives it, carefully inspects it, expresses his approbation, folds it up and puts it away amongst his papers, or deposits it with one of the witnesses for safe keeping; that while the witnesses are signing their names, the testator remains in the room from which they passed, without the slightest impediment to his seeing through the open door every stroke of the pen with which they wrote, except only that he happens at the moment to stand or sit or lie with his back towards the witnesses, instead of his face. Is such a will so made and attested null and void under the provisions of our statute, 1 Rev. Code, p. 365, because the witnesses, when in the act of subscribing, did not fall within the range of the testator's vision?

The terms of the statute require that if the will be not wholly written by the testator, it shall " be attested by two or more credible witnesses in his presence." It is not prescribed that the testator shall see the witnesses sign, nor is the character of the place of attestation designated : it may be done in a small chamber or a spacious hall, a public street or an open field. The word " presence " is rather indefinite in its signification, but may be somewhat explained by contrasting it with its opposite, " absence." The attestation must not be in the absence of the testator. It is adequate to preventing the mischief of a will being brought already drawn and subscribed with the names of witnesses, and obtaining the testator's signature or acknowledgment in a brief space of time, or of procuring such signature or acknowledgment, and taking it away to be thereafter subscribed by witnesses according to their own convenience or purposes. It may also present some slight impediment to the foisting of a false paper upon the testator or the witnesses about the time of attestation; but it is obvious that there can be no absolute security against such a fraud, which can be best detected by looking to all the circumstances of the transaction; and

1851.
October
Term.

Moore
v.
Moore's
ex'or
& als.

it is clear that the legislature did not intend by a rigid formality to impair seriously the testamentary power. And it surely is not competent for the courts to interpolate words not found in the statute, and, by an inexorable adherence to them, defeat fair wills, liable to no suspicion of fraud or malpractice, and so sacrifice the object to be attained, the safe exercise of the testamentary power, to mere slips in matters of form.

It is conceded by every one that it is unnecessary the testator should actually see the witnesses sign, if he could do so from the situation in which he was, by the mere exercise of his volition ; and the question is placed upon the narrow ground whether that volition is to be accomplished without a change of place, or position, or posture, in the room where he sits or stands or lies. There is no warrant, I think, either in reason or authority, for the proposition that subscribing witnesses must be within the range of the testator's vision from the spot of the room where he is at the time, as he happens to sit or lie or stand, if he is mentally and physically capable of changing his position in his bed or chair or room, so as to enable him to see the subscribing witnesses in the adjoining room.

In the present case there is a strong and controlling feature not to be found in any other that I have seen. The will, after being signed by the witnesses, was brought by them to the testator, and inspected and identified by him, and their attestation fully approved. This, in connection with the other circumstances of the transaction, for which I refer to the special verdict, made the attestation one entire, continuous act, substantially in the testator's presence, and in conformity with the fair interpretation and true spirit of the statute. And the establishment of this will cannot introduce any injurious principle or precedent : whereas its rejection would, as I conceive, tend to such a result.

1851.
October
Term.

Moore
v.
Moore's
ex'or
& als.

ALLEN, J. The facts found by the special verdict raise the question whether the will was so subscribed by the attesting witnesses in the presence of the testator as to constitute a valid will of realty under the statute. The cases in the English courts in reference to the subject are fully examined and commented on by Judge Carr in the case of *Neal* v. *Neal*, 1 Leigh 6, and the result to be deduced from them is that an attestation in the same room is *prima facie* good, and that an attestation out of the room is *prima facie* bad; but that in the latter case such attestation becomes good if shewn to be within the scope of the testator's vision. In the latter proposition all the judges of this court concurred. The statute intended to protect the testator from witnesses in whom he did not confide, and to prevent a false paper from being fraudulently imposed upon him and the witnesses: And hence the necessity of such a presence as will give him a control over the attestation during the whole progress of the transaction. Where they are in the same room they are mutually present, and if the testator has the capacity by his own unaided power to see what is transpiring, he has the control over the attestation which the statute designed to give him. He may not choose to overlook the transaction, but the power to do so at any instant is a sufficient security against fraud, and constitutes such a presence as conforms to the requisitions of the statute as construed by the courts.

But where the attestation is not in the same room, sight comes in place of the mutual presence in the same room. If without a material change of position the attestation comes within the scope of his vision, if by the exercise of his own volition he may in his then position see what is passing at any instant of time the act is in progress, the attestation is in his presence though he may not in fact see it. The knowledge of the fact that he has the capacity to overlook the trans-

October
Term.

Moore
v.
Moore's
ex'or
& als.

action gives him the same control over the attestation which is afforded by mutual presence in the same room. It is found in this case by the jury that the testator, lying in his ordinary position in his bed, could not have seen the attesting witnesses sign their names, the witnesses having carried the will out of the room into a passage and there subscribed it; but that he might have seen them if he had got out of his bed, or by changing his position so as to lean out over the foot of the bed, and that he had the physical capacity to have done either if he had so desired, but that he did neither.

I have found no case, and we have been referred to none, in which the question turned upon the physical capacity of the testator to have followed the witnesses, where the attestation was out of the room, or to have materially changed his position in his room so as to bring the subscribing witnesses within the scope of his vision during the attestation. If such enquiry were proper, then it would follow that an attestation, no matter where made, would have been sufficient, provided the testator had the capacity to supervise it if he desired to do so. This would be to substitute the confidence of the testator in the witnesses and friends about him for the actual presence and control provided by the statute.

If the will in this case had been attested in the same room, in the presence of the testator, it would have been a valid instrument, for it had been signed and published as his last will, and nothing was wanting to its completion but a legal attestation. No subsequent inspection or recognition was required to add to its legal effect. But how would it have been if, the attestation having been made in the manner disclosed by this record, one of the witnesses, by the previous request of the testator, or of his own accord, had folded it up and placed it away in the testator's desk or taken charge of it himself? Would it be maintained that a paper so

1851.
October
Term.

Moore
v.
Moore's
ex'or
& als.

attested out of the room and out of his sight could be sustained as conforming to the law ? If not, then it must be conceded that the attestation here alone would not have sufficed to give validity to the instrument: something must be superadded, or substituted rather, in the place of a regular attestation. This would be adding a new term to the statute, and declaring in effect that the will should either be attested in his presence, or if not, that the witnesses, after subscribing their names, should exhibit the will so subscribed to the testator and acknowledge their signatures. It is unnecessary to inquire whether such a provision would have furnished as great a security against the imposition of a surreptitious paper on a man *in extremis* as the actual safeguards thrown around him by the statute. It is sufficient to say that the law contains no such provision, and it is the province of this court to declare what the law is, and not to enact new laws.

Our statute of wills, so far as respects attestation, was copied from the statute of 29 Charles 2, and it is a well established principle that where an English statute is copied, the decisions of the courts at Westminster may be considered as having been adopted with the text they expounded.

The case of *Eccleston* v. *Speke* or *Petty*, Carthew 79, occurred in 1st William and Mary, not very long after the passage of the English statute. In that case the testatrix signed the will in the presence of the subscribing witnesses in her bed chamber, the witnesses subscribed it in a hall, and it appeared that it was not possible to see from her chamber what the witnesses did at the table in the hall. The testatrix continued in her chamber all the time they were subscribing. And it was held that the attestation did not conform to the statute. Nothing was said as to the physical power of the testatrix to have left her chamber. The case established *that* not being in her chamber, where she could

1851.
October
Term.

Moore
v.
Moore's
ex'or
& als.

have seen if she had chosen, and being out of her chamber and without the scope of her vision, the attestation was invalid. This has been recognized as the leading case on this point, giving a construction to the statute soon after its enactment, and, so far as I have seen, has never been controverted by any subsequent case in the English courts or the courts of the different States. The principle of the case was distinctly recognized by all the judges of this court in *Neal* v. *Neal*, and it seems to me is conclusive against the attestation in this case, if the case is to be decided upon the regularity of the attestation alone, as I think it must be. The facts found —that the witnesses, after subscribing their names in the passage, carried it back and handed it open, with their names subscribed to it, to the testator, who held it a minute or more and looked at it, and then gave it to one of the witnesses to be folded up for preservation— whilst they furnish a moral certainty that no fraud or imposition was practiced on the testator, do not amount to an attestation in his presence, the only security against fraud which will satisfy the requisitions of the law. A will not wholly in the hand writing of the testator may be acknowledged in the most solemn form before any number of witnesses, and under circumstances excluding the possibility of fraud, yet the law presumes it fraudulent, and, in the language of one of the judges in *Neal* v. *Neal*, no proof of actual fairness can avail to supply the requisites of the statute.

The will being dated, and the testator having died before the passage of the act of March 4, 1835, Sess. Acts 43, requiring the same kind of proof as to wills of personalty that was requisite to the validity of a devise of realty, I think the facts found are sufficient to authorize its admission to probat as a will of personalty, (*Redford* v. *Peggy*, 6 Rand. 316,) and am therefore of opinion that the sentence, so far as it admits it to probat

1851.
October
Term.

Moore
v.
Moore's
ex'or
& als.

as a will of personalty, should be affirmed, and reversed so far as it was admitted to probat as a devise of realty.

MONCURE, *J.* thought the will attested in the presence of the testator within the meaning of the statute; and concurred fully with Judge *Baldwin.*

---

## Richmond.

### GLAZEBROOK'S *adm'r v.* RAGLAND'S *adm'r.*

(Absent *Cabell,* P.)

#### December 9th.

A deed of trust by husband in favour of himself and wife was not duly recorded; but the land was sold by the trustee under a decree of the court in a friendly suit by the *cestuis que trust* against the trustee, and conveyed to the purchaser by deed duly recorded. Years afterwards, but before all the purchase money was paid, the purchaser became the surety of the husband in a forthcoming bond, and was compelled to pay the money. In an action on the bond for the purchase money by the trustee against the administratrix of the purchaser, she pleaded as a set-off the debt paid by the purchaser as surety of the husband. HELD:

1st. That though the trust deed was not duly recorded, yet under the circumstances it was valid; and neither the land nor the purchase money was liable for the husband's debts.

2d. The deed of trust being valid, the interest of the husband in the trust subject is a joint interest, and therefore cannot be set off by a debt due from himself.

This was an action of debt, brought originally in the County court of Hanover in the year 1825, by John Glazebrook against Sarah Ragland, administratrix of Absalom Ragland deceased. The facts of the case

1851.
October
Term.

Glaze-
brook's
adm'r
v.
Ragland's
adm'r.

In the year 1807 Oliver Cross executed to Doswell and Day, trustees, a deed conveying to them a tract of land in the county of Hanover and other property, in trust to sell the land, and out of the proceeds to pay a moiety to said Oliver Cross, and with the other moiety to purchase other land for the use of Sarah, wife of Oliver Cross, during her widowhood, or dispose of the money as they may think most advantageous, paying her the interest on such moiety, if not appropriated to the purchase of land; and at the death of said Sarah, or her marriage, the land or money to be divided among the children of Oliver and Sarah Cross. The deed was made expressly " to secure to the children and their heirs a fee simple estate, and also to provide for his wife a competent and decent maintenance during her widowhood."

The deed was proved in Hanover County court on the 27th of May and the 26th of August 1807, by the oaths of two witnesses as to the grantor, and on the said 27th of May was acknowledged in court by the trustees.

On the 28th of February 1811 friendly proceedings were had between Oliver Cross and Sarah, his wife, and James Doswell as trustee (Day being dead), whereby John Glazebrook was substituted as trustee in lieu of Doswell, and empowered and directed by the decree then pronounced " to sell and convey the title " of the land embraced in said trust deed, and to report to the court.

Under authority of this decree Glazebrook sold the land, and Absalom Ragland (the intestate of the defendant) purchased it, and executed for the purchase money a bond of £546, conditioned to pay £273 on demand to " John Glazebrook, acting as trustee under a decree of the worshipful Court of Hanover, bearing date the 28th day of February 1811, in the room of James Doswell, for selling lands belonging to Oli-

1851.
October
Term.

Glaze-
brook's
adm'r
v.
Ragland's
adm'r.

ver Cross and Sarah C
bears date 11th January
veyed the land to the pu

By an endorsement o
substituted as trustee for
credited a payment of $
July 1823. When that
not appear.

On the 7th of Februa
action of debt) was insti
name of Glazebrook, the
benefit of John Darracot
Sarah Ragland, administ
The suit in its progress
William L. White, as adi
the benefit of the admin
cott, and of John B. Tin
Ragland.

The defendant Timbe
county of Hanover on tl
continued to the 27th c
plea of "*payment*" previ
the cause had been once i
record states, " thereupoi
no assets, and fully admi
the plaintiff's demand in

On the 25th of July 1
from the County to the
None of the pleas were i
other form than the abov
any issue ever joined on

The cause was tried oi
a verdict was found for t
dollars 67 cents, with in
1823; the recovery being
sion of an off-set, to th
court *the plaintiff* filed t

1851.
October
Term.

Glaze-
brook's
adm'r
v.
Ragland's
adm'r.

By the first exception it appears that after the plaintiff had given in evidence the bond on which the suit was brought, the defendant introduced and offered as an offset to the plaintiff's demand a copy of a judgment in the name of Joel Cross, executor of Joseph Cross, against Oliver Cross and Absalom Ragland, defendant's intestate, rendered in Hanover County court on the 22d of May 1816, upon a motion for a judgment on a forthcoming bond for £295. 2. 6., to be discharged by £147. 11. 3., with interest from the 20th of March 1816, and the costs, with a statement endorsed of the amount due, (503 dollars 75 cents,) interest being calculated in said statement up to the 1st of August 1816 ; and also an endorsement thereon, signed " C. P. Goodall," to the effect that " the within judgment was for the benefit of the within named A. Ragland, he having paid me the same "; but that said Goodall " was *not* to be liable in any respect for the amount thereof, should the within Oliver Cross prove insolvent." To the introduction of which as an offset, the plaintiff objected. But the defendant stated he intended to follow up that evidence with proof that Absalom Ragland paid the money to Goodall (who had authority to receive it) as security for Oliver Cross ; that the said bond was given by him for the purchase of the land embraced in the deed aforesaid from Oliver Cross to Day and Doswell ; that the deed was irregularly recorded, not being proved by the requisite number of witnesses, and was for that reason void as to the creditors of Oliver Cross. Whereupon, " the court being of opinion, upon the case stated, that the deed from Oliver Cross to Doswell and Day, not having been recorded, passed no title as against Joseph Cross's executor, and constituted no barrier to the recovery of the debt due to him out of the fund thereby conveyed ; that Glazebrook should be considered, as regards the creditors of Oliver Cross, as a mere trustee for him ; that A. Ragland is entitled to

1851.
October
Term.

Glaze-
brook's
adm'r
v.
Ragland's
adm'r.

be substituted to all the rights of Joseph Cross's executor, and is therefore entitled to set off the debt which he has paid for Oliver Cross against the demand here asserted "; admitted the said copy and endorsement to go to the jury as evidence, should the defendant exhibit to the jury the proof with which he proposed to support the offer of said copy and endorsement.

By the second exception it appears that the defendant " did support his offer of said copy and endorsement " by the proof " that the defendant, Absalom Ragland, did, on the 1st of August 1816, pay as security for Oliver Cross, on said judgment in favour of Joseph Cross's executor, the sum of 503 dollars 75 cents, which is the amount of the set-off so insisted on by the defendant." Whereupon the plaintiff objected to said set-off, that it was barred by the statute of limitations, and should not be allowed for that reason ; and moreover, that if it appeared to be due more than five years before the death of Glazebrook, the plaintiff, it should be disregarded ; and asked the court so to instruct the jury. But the court being of opinion that Ragland was substituted to the rights of Cross's executor as a judgment creditor of his principal, Oliver Cross, and for that reason, and because the said claim had been relied on as an offset in this cause before the judgment was barred, the said offset is not barred by the statute.

The court having entered up a judgment according to the verdict, the plaintiff applied to this court for a writ of error, which was allowed.

*R. T. Daniel*, for the appellant.
*Lyons*, for the appellee.

MONCURE, *J.* I concur in the results of Judge *Baldwin's* opinion in this case, and in much of his reasoning ; but as I am not prepared to assent to or dissent from some of the views expressed by him, it may be proper that I should give the reasons which have led me to the same results to which he has arrived.

1851.
October
Term.

Glaze-
brook's
adm'r
v.
Ragland's
adm'r.

In 1807 Oliver Cross conveyed 600 acres of land and certain slaves to Doswell and Day, in trust for the benefit of himself and his wife and children. In the same year the deed was acknowledged by and recorded as to the trustees, and was proved by two witnesses as to the grantor; but never having been further proved, though there were four subscribing witnesses to the deed, it was never recorded as to him. In 1811 Day, the acting trustee, having died, and Doswell being unwilling to act, a suit in chancery was brought by Cross and wife to have a trustee substituted and the trusts of the deed carried into execution; and a decree was accordingly made substituting Glazebrook as trustee and authorizing him to sell and convey the land, and further to act in all respects as trustee under the deed. In 1812 Glazebrook, acting as trustee under the said decree, sold 277½ acres of the said land by metes and bounds to Ragland, who executed his bond for the purchase money, payable on demand, to said Glazebrook as trustee aforesaid. The decree was particularly referred to both in the deed to Ragland and in his bond; and the deed was duly recorded. In 1816 Ragland became the surety of Oliver Cross in a forthcoming bond to Joseph Cross, on which a judgment was obtained, which was paid by Ragland. In 1825 suit was brought in the name of Glazebrook for the benefit of Darracott, (who it seems had been substituted as trustee in Glazebrook's place,) against Ragland's administratrix, upon Ragland's bond for the purchase money of the land bought by him as aforesaid. In 1832 the claim of Ragland for the payment made by him of the judgment on the forthcoming bond aforesaid was filed by his administratrix as a set-off to the plaintiff's demand. In 1845 the suit was tried, and the Circuit court being of opinion that the deed from Oliver Cross to Dos-

well and Day, not having been reco
title as against Joseph Cross's exect
tuted no barrier to the recovery of the
out of the fund thereby conveyed ; t
should be considered, as against the cr
Cross, as a mere trustee for him ; that
titled to be substituted to all the r.
Cross's executor, and was therefore e
the debt which he had paid for Oliver (
demand asserted by the plaintiff in th
the evidence offered by the defendant o
which was thereupon allowed by the j
and judgment were rendered for the
plaintiff's demand, after deducting the
set-off.   Was the set-off a good one?
now to be considered.

It is not necessary to consider in th
to an action brought by a trustee, a
made of money due from the *cestui qu*
ther the law on this subject was correct
the cases of *Bottomley* v. *Brook* and *J*
cited in Babington on Set-off, p. 60.   ]
ted by all, that debts which are not m
set off at law ; nor in equity, withou
for so doing.   If Oliver Cross had an
bond to Glazebrook as trustee, it seems
interest in common with his wife and
the bond been payable to the *cestuis q*
of the trustee—to Oliver Cross, and h
dren, instead of to Glazebrook—mon
land on account of Oliver Cross alone
been set off in a suit at law upon the bo

tion brought by a trustee, a set-off may be made of money due to the *cestui que trust?* "

1851.
October
Term.

Glaze-
brook's
adm'r
v.
Ragland's
adm'r.

But the opinion of the court below does not controvert the proposition that debts which are not mutual cannot be set off against each other. On the contrary, it proceeds upon the supposition that the debts in this case are mutual; that the deed from Oliver Cross to Doswell and Day, not having been recorded, passed no title as against the creditors of said Oliver; that Glazebrook should be considered, as against said creditors, as a mere trustee for said Oliver; and that Ragland was entitled to be substituted to all the rights of Joseph Cross, a judgment creditor of said Oliver, and to set off the judgment paid by him against the demand of the plaintiff.

If it were true that Joseph Cross was entitled to have the amount of his judgment against Oliver Cross paid out of the purchase money due by Ragland, without regard to any rights or interests of the wife and children of Oliver Cross, under the deed of trust of 1807, then it would follow that Ragland, having paid the judgment as surety, would have a right to be substituted to all the rights of Joseph Cross, the judgment creditor. But was Joseph Cross so entitled? I think not. The deed of trust of 1807 is not impeached as fraudulent or voluntary, and therefore void as to creditors. It does not appear that Joseph Cross was a creditor, or that there were any creditors of Oliver Cross when that deed was executed. It is assailed solely on the ground that it was never recorded. But, though unrecorded, it was good against the grantor and his heirs; and good against his creditors also until judgments were obtained by them. The judgment of Joseph Cross was not obtained until nine years after the execution of the deed of trust; nor until Ragland had become a purchaser of the land under a decree of a court of chancery, received his deed, had it recorded, and been four years in possession of the

1851.
October
Term.

Glass-
brook's
adm'r
v.
Ragland's
adm'r.

land. Under these circumstances I think the judgment was a lien or charge neither upon the land nor upon the purchase money; and that the *cestuis que trust* under the deed of 1807 are entitled to receive and hold the said purchase money against any claim of Joseph Cross founded on the said judgment, and of course against any claim of Ragland to stand in his place; except that to the extent of any interest of Oliver Cross in the said purchase money, a court of equity may, for special reasons, afford relief, as it might in any case in which it is sought to set off a several against a joint demand. I regard the institution of the suit in chancery for the appointment of a trustee and the execution of the trust; the rendition of the decree in that suit; and the sale and conveyance under the decree, and the recordation of such conveyance, as equivalent to the recordation of the deed of trust: and I think the cases of *Childers* v. *Smith*, Gilm. 196, and *Dabney* v. *Kennedy*, 7 Gratt. 317, fully sustain this view of the case.

It is not pretended that the land itself is bound by the lien of Joseph Cross's judgment; but it is insisted that the purchase money yet remaining in the hands of Ragland is bound in place of the land. The purchase money was payable on demand four years before the judgment was obtained. If it had been actually paid before the judgment was obtained, it would hardly be contended that it would have been bound by the judgment, in the hands of the *cestuis que trust*. And yet it is not perceived how the default of the purchaser in not paying the purchase money until after the judgment was obtained could give any right to the judgment creditor, or take any away from the *cestuis que trust*. If such default could have the effect of giving any right to the judgment creditor, it would seem that the loss should fall on him who committed the default; and that the lien of the judgment should operate on the land rather than the purchase money.

1851.
October
Term.

Glaze-
brook's
adm'r
v.
Ragland's
adm'r.

If the land could be considered as bound, in the hands of the purchaser, for the judgment of Joseph Cross, Ragland could not, I think, claim to have it paid out of the purchase money; first, because he bought with notice that the deed was unrecorded, and might have protected himself by having it recorded at any time before the judgment was obtained. When he bought the title was perfect, and it became imperfect, if at all, only by his suffering the deed to remain unrecorded until after Joseph Cross had obtained his judgment. And secondly, because Ragland purchased with special warranty only, and the covenants contained in the deed to him do not extend to the incumbrance of the judgment.

I think, therefore, that the evidence of the set-off was improperly admitted; and being of that opinion it is unnecessary to consider the other questions presented by the record.

BALDWIN, J. It appears that a set-off was claimed at the trial for a sum of money paid by Ragland, the defendant's intestate, in discharge of a judgment on a forthcoming bond in which he was surety for Oliver Cross, on the ground that the bond on which the action is founded was executed to Glazebrook, the plaintiff's intestate, in trust to secure a debt due to the said Cross: And in proof of these facts, evidence was introduced of a deed of trust made in the year 1807 by Cross, conveying a tract of land and other property to trustees, in trust to sell the land, and out of the proceeds pay a moiety to Cross, and with the other moiety to purchase other land for the separate use of Sarah, the wife of Cross, or dispose of the money as the trustees should deem most advantageous, paying her interest on her moiety of the money if not appropriated to the purchase of land, and on the death or future marriage of said Sarah, her moiety of the money, or the land therewith purchased, to be divided amongst the

1851.
October
Term.

Glaze-
brook's
adm'r
v.
Ragland's
adm'r

children of the said Oliver and Sarah Cross; and it was
proved that in the year 1812 a sale was made by
Glazebrook, as substituted trustee, under the trust deed,
of part of the land thereby conveyed, and Ragland becoming the purchaser, he executed the bond on which
the action is founded to Glazebrook, and received from
him a deed of conveyance. The set off so claimed
was objected to by the defendant, but allowed by permission of the court.

I can perceive no sound objection, where an action is
brought on a bond or note executed to the plaintiff to
secure a debt due to another, to allowing the defendant
to prove payment to, or a good set off against, the person so beneficially entitled. But such a set-off must
be governed by the rules in regard to mutuality prevailing at law, and for the most part in equity, which
inhibit the set off of a joint against a separate, or a
separate against a joint debt. And in this case it does
not appear that Oliver Cross was entitled to the whole
proceeds of the sale under the deed of trust; and to
ascertain whether the fact be so would require a settlement of the trust subject and transactions by means of
a suit in equity, to which all the *cestuis que trust* would
be necessary parties. To obviate this objection it is
contended on the part of the appellee that the deed of
trust, which was not admitted to record, was therefore
void as against Ragland, who became a subsequent
creditor of Oliver Cross, the grantor, by the payment
in the year 1816 of the judgment on the forthcoming
bond. And this presents the question, whether the
provision in our registry law, declaring deeds of trust
and mortgages not duly recorded void as to creditors
and subsequent purchasers without notice, is applicable
to a case such as the one before us.

It might be proper to consider here whether it is
competent for Ragland, he having purchased under the
trust deed, to impeach in his character of creditor the

1851.
October
Term.

Glase-
brook's
adm'r
v.
Ragland's
adm'r.

title which he holds and enjoys in his character of purchaser. But waiving that enquiry as unnecessary in
this case, let us proceed to the question above stated, as
it concerns the creditors in general of Oliver Cross.
And in considering that question we must first ascertain what purchasers are contemplated by the statute;
for if a purchaser under and by force of an unrecorded
deed of trust acquires a perfect title, then he holds the
property subject only to his own debts, and not to those
of any other person.

The statute, 1 Rev. Code, p. 362, § 4, provides that
all bargains, sales and other conveyances whatsoever, of
any lands, and all deeds of trust and mortgages, shall be
void as to all creditors and subsequent purchasers for
valuable consideration without notice, unless they shall
be acknowledged or proved and lodged with the clerk
to be recorded, &c.

Now this enactment does not embrace purchasers
under and by force of the very deed from which they
derive their title. It is directed against purchasers
subsequent to the deed required to be recorded, who
acquire their right or title from some other instrument,
for example, a subsequent deed from the same grantor.
This is manifest in regard to a purchaser by an absolute
deed: he is not, in reference thereto, a subsequent purchaser, and it would be absurd to talk of his having or
not having notice of his own deed. It is equally true
in regard to a purchaser under and by virtue of a mortgage or deed of trust: he cannot be considered a subsequent purchaser in reference to that deed, and it
would be idle to discriminate in reference to him between purchasers with and without notice. He always
has notice of the deed under and by the authority of
which he purchases. It will be seen at a glance that
the notice spoken of by the statute is not of the fact
that the deed is unrecorded, but of the deed itself, in
reference to a title subsequently acquired, and which

1851.
October
Term.

Glase-
brook's
adm'r
v.
Ragland's
adm'r.

could not have been good if the prior deed *against* which the second purchaser claims had been duly recorded.

It is true that the terms of the statute, and its spirit too, embrace unrecorded deeds of trust and mortgages while they continue incumbrances, while they remain executory, but not after they have ceased to be incumbrances; not after they have been executed and extinguished by a sale or foreclosure, and a conveyance of the title to the purchaser. While they continue executory, they may be successfully impeached or resisted by creditors of the grantor, whether prior or subsequent, with or without notice, or by subsequent purchasers without notice; but not afterwards by creditors who had acquired no specific lien or incumbrance, nor by purchasers from the grantor, after he by himself, or his trustee, or judicial authority, had become denuded of all title.

A man, however much embarrassed with debt, may make a fair sale of his property, and convey a good title thereto beyond the reach of his creditors; and so long as he can do this by himself, he may do it by his agent, (and his trustee authorized to sell is his agent,) and the power or authority to his agent need not be recorded. A mortgagee or *cestui que trust* for value is a creditor, and the deed, though unrecorded, being good between the parties, is only void in the preference which it gives over other creditors; and the title therefore passes, subject to the priorities which they may gain by a due course of proceeding. But the law does not shove the mortgagee or *cestui que trust* aside, and place the creditors at large in his seat. The latter may never assert their demands, and while they choose to lie dormant, the incumbrancer is not bound to sleep also. The deed being good between the parties, they may proceed to enforce it, otherwise it would be good for nothing. If the creditors at large ever come, they

1851.
October
Term.

Glaze-
brook's
adm'r
v.
Ragland's
adm'r.

must come in time, and not after the property has been sold under the authority of the deed to a *bona fide* purchaser, who has paid his money and received his title, and thereby extinguished, *quoad* that property, the incumbrancer on the one hand, and the creditors at large on the other. The property is thenceforth his, and he may defy them all. In this case, it is true, the whole of the purchase money has not been paid by Ragland, the purchaser under the trust deed, and this action is brought to recover the balance due; but, as already shewn, it does not appear that Oliver Cross is exclusively entitled to it.

The payment above mentioned by Ragland in 1816, of the judgment against him and Cross on the forthcoming bond, in which Cross was the principal and he was the surety, thereby created a simple contract debt from Cross to Ragland, recoverable in *assumpsit*, which was barred when this action was brought in 1825 on Ragland's bond to Glazebrook; and so, for that reason also, was not a good set-off against that bond. Ragland by that payment did not acquire the right of being substituted at law to the judgment creditor. The doctrine of substitution is the mere creature of equity, and if introduced into the courts of common law, must carry with it the marshalling of assets, and other kindred doctrines, and so tend to a confusion of jurisdictions. Of these subtle and pervading equities, the common law is ignorant. They have been devised by courts of equity for their own purposes of justice, and are administered by means of their own peculiar powers, by which all parties in interest may be convened before them, all matters of account and trust adjusted, and new life infused into extinguished securities. To such purposes and means the common law forum, by reason of its forms, its technicalities and its modes of trial, is but ill adapted.

1851.
October
Term.

Glaze-
brook's
adm'r
v.
Ragland's
adm'r.

These views of the merits dispense with the necessity of considering the formal errors assigned by the plaintiff in error.

It seems to me, therefore, that the Circuit court erred in permitting the evidence of set-off in the bills of exception mentioned to go to the jury; and that its judgment is therefore erroneous.

ALLEN, J. concurred in the opinion of Judge *Moncure*.

DANIEL, J. concurred in the opinion of Judge *Baldwin*.

JUDGMENT REVERSED.

---

## Richmond.

### NOWLIN & *wife* v. WINFREE.

(Absent *Cabell*, P.)

**January 19th.**

Prior to 1819 a testator devises to his three daughters by name his estate, " both real and personal," " to them and their heirs lawfully begotten of their bodies." "And in case either of my daughters should die without heir or heirs as above mentioned, the surviving ones to enjoy their equal part." This is an estate tail, which by the statute is converted into a fee. And the limitation over is after an indefinite failure of issue, and void.

This was an action of *detinue* brought in 1845 in the Circuit court of Halifax county, by Hopkins Nowlin and Cloe Irby, his wife, against Matthew Winfree, to recover a number of slaves. On the trial the jury found a special verdict, which presented the case as follows :

1852.
January
Term.

Nowlin
& wife
v.
Winfree.

Benjamin Hall died in the year 1803, leaving a will which was duly admitted to probat in the County court of Halifax.   After directing his debts to be paid, and giving to his wife for her life certain real estate, slaves and other property, he gave to each of his three sons, by separate clauses of his will, certain parts of his estate, in fee, including in the gift to one of them the land given to his wife for life ; and he declared that they were not to have any further interest in his estate. Then comes the two following clauses :

" I give and bequeath to my three daughters, to-wit, Caty Miller, Sally Hall and Cloe Irby Hall, all that part of my estate not hereinbefore mentioned, both real and personal, after the payment of my debts before mentioned, to them and their heirs lawfully begotten of their bodies : The above mentioned Caty Miller to account for all that part of my estate which she hath heretofore had in possession when a division is made."

" Also it is my will and desire that all that part of my estate which I have lent to my wife, and not herein otherwise given, should after her death be divided as above mentioned ; and in case either of my daughters should die without heir or heirs as above mentioned, the surviving ones to enjoy their equal part."

Of the three daughters of the testator, Caty Miller died first, leaving children.   Sally Hall married the defendant Winfree, and died before the institution of this suit, leaving no child or other descendant ; and Cloe Irby married the plaintiff Nowlin, and is yet living. The slaves claimed in the action are either the slaves received by Mrs. Winfree from her father's estate or their descendants.

Upon the special verdict the court rendered a judgment for the defendant.   Whereupon the plaintiffs applied to this court for a *supersedeas*, which was granted.

1852.
January
Term.

Nowlin
& wife
v.
Winfree.

The cause was elaborately argued by *Stanard* and *Bouldin*, for the appellants, and *Robinson*, for the appellee; but the authorities have been given in two late cases, and the question has almost ceased to be of any practical importance.

ALLEN, *J.* delivered the opinion of the court.

The question presented by the special verdict, as to the proper construction of the will of Benjamin Hall deceased, has been frequently under consideration in this court. The case of *Bells* v. *Gillespie*, 5 Rand. 273, presented precisely the same question, and the principle there settled rules this case. That case conformed to the earlier decisions of this court, giving a construction to the laws docking entails; and it has been recognized and followed in the subsequent cases of *Broaddus & wife* v. *Turner*, 5 Rand. 308; *Griffith* v. *Thomson*, 1 Leigh 321; *Callava* v. *Pope*, 3 Leigh 103; and *Deane* v. *Hansford*, 9 Leigh 253. The principle thus firmly established by a series of adjudications has become a rule of property in the construction of wills made prior to 1819, and ought not now to be questioned, the more especially as but few cases are likely to occur hereafter in which the question can arise. According to these authorities the will in this case created an estate tail in the first taker by express words; and the bequest over after the death of the daughter without heirs was an executory limitation after an indefinite failure of issue, and therefore void, and the daughters took the slaves in absolute property.

Judgment affirmed with costs.

BALDWIN, *J.* dissented.

## 𝕽𝖎𝖈𝖍𝖒𝖔𝖓𝖉.

### LENOWS *v.* LENOW.

(Absent *Cabell*, P.)

February 2d.

1852.
January
Term.

A proceeding by foreign attachment is instituted against two persons, as jointly indebted to the plaintiff. One of them appears and answers the bill; but the other is regularly proceeded against as an absent debtor, and there is a joint decree against both defendants. HELD:

  1st. That the absent defendant who did not appear cannot appeal.

  2d. But the decree being a joint decree, and being erroneous, the appellate court will, upon the appeal of the absent defendant who did appear and answer, reverse the decree as to both.

This was a case of foreign attachment, brought in the Circuit court of Southampton county, by Jacob Lenow against Joseph and James Lenow as absent debtors, and Frances Lenow as a home defendant having effects of Joseph Lenow in her hands. The bill charged that Joseph and James Lenow were indebted to the plaintiff by a bond in which they were both bound for 1600 dollars. Frances Lenow answered the bill, admitting that she had in her hands effects of Joseph Lenow. Joseph Lenow appeared and was permitted to file his answer, in which he denied that he or James owed the plaintiff anything. He admitted that the bond for 1600 dollars had existed, but that upon a settlement it had been delivered up and a bond for 700 dollars, the balance due, was executed by James Lenow, who was the principal debtor; and that this bond had been afterwards discharged by him. James Lenow was proceeded against as an absent defendant, and the bill was taken for confessed as to him.

Whether anything was due to the plaintiff from the defendants, Joseph and James Lenow, was a mere question of fact, and this court thought there was nothing due. The court below directed a commissioner to state an account of the payments made upon the bond, and according to the commissioner's last report there was due the sum of 368 dollars 83 cents, with interest thereon from the 6th of October 1841 ; and for this sum, with its interest, the court gave to the plaintiff a joint decree against Joseph and James Lenow ; and directed the sheriff to sell the interest of Joseph Lenow in the slaves in the possession of Frances Lenow, and out of the proceeds to pay the debt, interest and costs. From this decree Joseph and James Lenow applied to this court for an appeal, which was allowed.

*Stanard* and *Bouldin*, for the appellant.

Although the absent defendant, James Lenow, who did not appear in the court below, could not appeal from that decree, as it has been held by this court in *Platt* v. *Howland*, 10 Leigh 507, and *Barbee* v. *Pannill*, 6 Gratt. 442, yet Joseph Lenow did appear and answer, and his appeal is properly here. The decree appealed from is a joint decree against both Joseph and James Lenow. Joseph Lenow is interested to have the whole decree reversed, because, if affirmed as to James, when he pays the money he may call upon Joseph for contribution. But further, as we have said, the decree is a joint decree against both ; and if the court reverses the decree, from the necessity of its nature, the whole decree is reversed : And as James Lenow is not before the court upon this appeal, the court cannot enter another decree against him.

*Macfarland*, for the appellee, referred to *Platt* v. *Howland*, 10 Leigh 507, to shew that if there was error against the absent defendants it could not be corrected by appeal. He also referred to *Heffernan* v. *Grymes*, 2 Leigh 512, to shew that the home defendant could not correct the decree as to the absent defendants, by appeal to this court. Then the question is whether one of two absent defendants can come in and make himself a party and contest the plaintiff's claim as to both. There is no principle which will authorize him to defend the case for the other absent defendant, that did not equally apply to a defence made by a home defendant for the absent defendant. The policy of the statute, too, forbids the relief to the one upon the appearance and defence of the other. It is enabling one to make defence without giving to the plaintiff the security to which the law entitles him. Moreover, although the party appealing is bound if the decree is affirmed, yet the other absent defendant is not bound. And he thus plays the safe game, of heads I win, tails you lose: If the decree is reversed, he has the full benefit of it; if it is affirmed, and it may be affirmed by a divided court, he is not bound.

DANIEL, *J.* delivered the opinion of the court.

The court is satisfied, by the pleadings and proofs in the cause, that the bond of sixteen hundred dollars, in the bill and proceedings mentioned, had been reduced prior to the 1st September 1840, by payments, to about the sum of seven hundred dollars; that on the day last mentioned a new bond (whether executed by James Lenow or Joseph Lenow does not distinctly appear) for the said balance of seven hundred dollars was delivered by the said Joseph to the appellee, Jacob Lenow, and accepted by the latter in satisfaction and discharge of the said balance, and that the said bond of sixteen hundred dollars was thereupon surrendered by the said Jacob to the said Joseph; and that thereafter and prior to the institution of this suit the said bond of seven hundred dollars was fully satisfied, by payments made by the said James and Joseph. The court is therefore of opinion that the Circuit court erred in adopting the special statement of the commissioner as the basis of its decree, and in rendering a decree against the appellants for the balance reported in said statement, and in ordering a sale of the property attached; and that it ought, instead thereof, to have confirmed the original report of the commissioner, and dismissed the bill. The court is also further of opinion, that notwithstanding James Lenow was regularly proceeded against as an absent defendant, and therefore, according to the decisions of this court in the cases of *Platt* v. *Howland*, 10 Leigh 507, and of *Barbee* v. *Pannill*, 6 Gratt. 442, had no right to appeal to this court on account of any error in the decree against him ; yet that as Joseph Lenow filed his answer under the permission of the court, and thus entitled himself to the privileges of a home defendant, and succeeded, in the opinion of this court, as above indicated, in proving a defence which was in no respect personal, but established the satisfaction and discharge of the joint obligation on which the suit was founded, the appeal of the said Joseph necessarily brings under review the propriety of the whole decree, and devolves upon this court the duty of correcting and reversing it, in favour as well of the said James as of the said Joseph. The court is therefore of opinion to reverse the whole decree, with costs to the appellant, Joseph Lenow. And this court, proceeding to render such decree as the Circuit court ought to have rendered, doth confirm the original report of the commissioner, and dismiss the bill with costs to the said Joseph Lenow.

DECREE REVERSED.

# 𝕽𝖎𝖈𝖍𝖒𝖔𝖓𝖉.

### DICKINSON *v.* HOOMES'S *adm'r & als.*

(Absent *Cabell,* P )

**February 2d.**

1852.
January
Term.

There is a devise to J, with a limitation over, upon his dying without issue at his death, to his brother R if he should survive him, or his representatives, and R dies in the lifetime of J. J sells and conveys the land to A; and R, though he does not convey the land, is a party to the deed, and J and R covenant as follows : That the said J, for himself and his heirs, and the said R, as contingent devisee under the will of Col. J, by whom said land was devised to J, do hereby covenant and agree to and with the said A, that they will warrant and defend the fee simple estate, &c., to said land, to him and his heirs forever, against the claim of themselves and their heirs, and the claim of any person claiming under them by virtue of the will aforesaid, and do relinquish and fully confirm to said A all the right they or their heirs now have or may hereafter have to said land or any part thereof, to him and his heirs, free from the claim of the said J and R and their heirs, and of all other persons in the whole world. HELD:

   1st. That this covenant of R extends to the claim of his children to the land, though they claim not as his heirs, but as devisees under the will of Col. J.

   2d. That the covenant of R is a covenant running with the land, and a purchaser claiming under A, a portion thereof, by a regular chain of conveyances, is entitled to the benefit of said covenant for his indemnity against said claims.

   3d. That the children of R having inherited from him lands in Kentucky, and as by the laws of that State lands descended may be subjected to the payment of the debts of the ancestor, and the heir is bound by such a covenant of warranty by the ancestor, a court of equity in the State of Virginia may compel the children of R residing within the jurisdiction to account for any lands in Kentucky descended to them as his heirs, as a trust subject for the payment of his debts : And under the circumstances of this case, the power should be exerted.

1852.
January
Term.

Dickinson
v.
Hoomes's
adm'r
& als.

4th. Under the circumstances of the case, the heirs held
    bound to account for only so much of the Ken-
    tucky lands as they have actually gotten or may
    get possession of, with the rents and profits derived
    therefrom, deducting the cost and expense of re-
    covering the lands.

John Hoomes the elder died in 1805, leaving a will
dated in 1804, whereby he gave to each of his sons,
John, William, Richard and Armistead, to his daughter
Sophia, and grandson John Waller Hoomes, land and
slaves in fee simple; but directed that if any of them
should die without issue living at his death, his estate
should be divided equally between the survivors, or their
representatives, according to the principles of the law
of descents. All of them survived the testator, and
took possession of the estates devised to them. In 1819
John Hoomes the younger sold and conveyed the land
devised to him to Samuel A. Apperson; and Richard
Hoomes and the other children of John Hoomes the elder united in the covenants contained in the deed.

These covenants are as follows: "And the said John
Hoomes, for himself and his heirs, and the said William
Hoomes, Richard Hoomes, Armistead Hoomes and Wilson Allen and Sophia, his wife, for themselves and their
heirs, as contingent devisees or legatees under the will
of Col. John Hoomes, late of the Bowling Green, deceased, by whom said land was devised to John Hoomes,
do hereby covenant and agree to and with the said Samuel A. Apperson, that they will warrant and defend the
fee simple estate and complete right and title to said two
tracts of land, to him and his heirs and assigns forever,
against themselves and their heirs, and against the claim
and demand of any person or persons claiming from, by
or under them, in virtue of the will aforesaid, and do relinquish and fully confirm to said S. A. Apperson all
the right they or their heirs now have, or might or may
hereafter have, to said land, or any part thereof, to him
and his heirs and assigns forever, free from them, the said

1852.
January
Term.

Dickinson
v.
Hoomes's
adm'r
& als.

John Hoomes, William Hoomes, Richard Hoomes, Armistead Hoomes, Wilson Allen and Sophia, his wife, late Sophia Hoomes, and their heirs, and of all other persons in the whole world."

This land, or the greater part of it, passed by a regular chain of conveyances from Apperson to William W. Dickinson. John Hoomes the younger died in 1825, without issue. William and Richard died in the lifetime of John, the former without issue, the latter leaving several children. In 1827 the children of Richard filed their bill against Dickinson, claiming to be entitled as purchasers under the will of their grandfather, John Hoomes the elder, to one undivided fourth of the land devised to John Hoomes the younger; and praying for partition thereof and an account of rents and profits. Their claim was sustained by the Circuit court, and also by this court on appeal; and the decision of this court is reported in 1 Gratt. 302.

As to the construction and effect of the covenant of warranty in the deed of conveyance embracing the land in question, executed by the said Richard and others, if coupled with the descent of assets from him to the appellees, this court deemed it irrelevant to go into the consideration thereof, inasmuch as no such defence was made in the court below; nor could any cause of action founded upon said warranty be prejudiced by the decision aforesaid.

After the case went back to the Circuit court, to wit, in 1844, Dickinson filed a cross bill, charging that a tract of land called Ruffin's, of greater value than the land in controversy, had come by descent from Richard Hoomes to his children, and had been divided among them; and that the said children, except one of them, who had intermarried with Alfred H. Garnett, of whose circumstances said Dickinson knew nothing, were wholly insolvent; and praying an injunction of the in-

1852.
January
Term.

Dickinson
v.
Hoomes's
adm'r
& als.

terlocutory decree which had been affirmed as afore-said, and for general relief.

The injunction was granted; but was afterwards dissolved; it appearing that the tract of land called Ruffin's had been sold under a decree of a court of chancery, and the entire proceeds of sale applied to the discharge of the debts of Richard Hoomes.

In 1845 Dickinson filed a supplemental bill, charging that since the filing of his original bill he had ascertained that lands in Kentucky, which had been devised by John Hoomes the elder to the said Richard, had come by descent from Richard to his said children, and greatly exceeded in value the subject of controversy in the suit, and praying that the injunction should be reinstated, and for general relief. The injunction was accordingly reinstated. The children of Richard Hoomes filed their answer, relying on various grounds of defence. Dickinson afterwards answered the original bill of the said children, relying on the same grounds which he had taken in his supplemental cross bill.

In May 1849 the two causes were heard together; and the Circuit court being of opinion that it had not been shewn in the cases that assets had descended from Richard Hoomes to his children, therefore dismissed the bills of Dickinson with costs.

From this decree Dickinson applied to this court for an appeal, which was allowed.

The facts in relation to the liability of the heirs of Richard Hoomes upon his covenant of warranty, for lands descended to them, will be found stated in the opinion of Judge *Moncure.*

*R. T. Daniel,* for the appellant.

The first enquiry which arises in this case is, as to the extent of the covenant of Richard Hoomes in the deed to Apperson; and what is its effect as against his heirs. The exposition of the clause in the will of John

1852.
January
Term.

Dickinson
v.
Hoomes's
adm'r
& als.

Hoomes the elder, under which these appellees claim an interest in the land conveyed in the deed to Apperson, was made by this court in the case of *Dickinson* v. *Hoomes*, 1 Gratt. 302. In that case the court held that the children of Richard took as purchasers under the will of John Hoomes the elder. And the question is, Did Richard Hoomes mean to covenant against the claim of his children merely as his heirs, or also as devisees under the will of John Hoomes. We say it was plainly his object and purpose to covenant for a good title out and out.

In construing the covenant it is to be taken most strongly against the covenantor. *Iggulden* v. *May*, 7 East's R. 241. And the intention of the parties was, obviously, to unite in confirming to John Hoomes the younger a good title. This covenant was one running with the land; and was, in the language of the books, an inherent covenant. The distinction between a pure technical warranty and a covenant to warrant is stated in 2 Thom. Coke 361, 362, and *Tabb* v. *Binford*, 4 Leigh 132. A covenant to warrant may be made by a stranger even, if the covenantee has an interest in the land. For the doctrine in relation to covenants running with the land, the court is referred to *Spencer's Case*, Smith's Leading Cas., 43 Law Libr. 75, 82.

The fact, if it was so, that the land has been sold to several alienees, does not impair the effect of the covenant. There is, however, no proof that all the land was not conveyed to Dickinson. It is true that it is stated in 3 Preston on Abstracts of Title 58, that a covenant cannot be divided and split up. But he cites no authority for the proposition; and on the next page of his book he seems to contradict it. It is moreover opposed to the decision in *Twynam* v. *Pickard*, 2 Barn. & Ald. 105, and to the doctrine as stated in Platt on Covenants 495, 496; and 2 Thom. Coke 362, seems also to assert a doctrine in conflict with it.

1852.
January
Term.

Dickinson
v.
Hoomes's
adm'r
& als.

It will be said that a court of equity in Virginia cannot make a decree subjecting these appellees for assets derived from the lands in Kentucky. It is true that a court of equity in Virginia cannot make a decree to subject lands in Kentucky by sale or sequestration. But the court has power over the parties to this suit, and may deny them relief, except on condition that they will account for these lands. Or a court of equity may by a decree *in personam* compel these parties to do whatever it is equitable they shall do either with respect to the lands or their proceeds. *Mussie* v. *Watts*, 5 Cranch 148. It is said that there is no proof of what is the law of Kentucky on this subject. If the proof is not authenticated in strict accordance with the statute, it is too late to take the objection in this court; and it should have been made in the court below, when it might have been readily obviated.

*Morson*, for the appellees.

The appellees claim as purchasers under John Hoomes the elder, and not from, by, through, or under Richard Hoomes. And yet it is claimed that this warranty bound them as the heirs of Richard Hoomes so far as they had assets; and the bill alleged that they had assets descended to them from Richard in Virginia. This turned out not to be the fact, and then an amended bill was filed alleging that the heirs of Richard Hoomes had received assets by descent in Kentucky. To this bill various defences were set up. The court below regarded the defence that no such assets had descended to these appellees from their father, in Kentucky, as supported by the proofs; and upon that ground mainly, if not entirely, rested its decree. In this opinion the court was fully warranted by the proofs, which shew that, upon an enquiry made before a commissioner as early as 1826, the assets of Richard Hoomes's estate

1852
January
Term.

Dickinson
v.
Hoomes's
adm'r
& als.

were exhausted, leaving many debts unpaid; and which shew further that they never were entitled to the lands in Kentucky, as the lands of Richard Hoomes, but of John Hoomes the elder; and that they never in fact obtained possession of them either as the lands of John or Richard Hoomes; but after the division among the heirs of John Hoomes, and without any possession of them having been taken under that division, they were a second time forfeited for non-payment of taxes; and if they got them at all, they obtained them by purchase under the delinquent land laws of the State of Kentucky.

Is it to be contended that these appellees were bound to redeem these forfeited lands in Kentucky for the benefit of the creditors of Richard Hoomes? If they are under any such obligation the position of heirs would be one of grievous hardship. But such a proposition is against all law and justice.—*Bouldin*, counsel for the appellants: I shall contend that the lands were not forfeited at the time of the death of Richard Hoomes; and that the heirs, by forfeiting them, subjected themselves personally to creditors for their value, as for so much real assets descended.—*Morson:* This proposition of law cannot be sustained. The heirs were not bound to take or accept the lands as heirs; but might permit the lands to be forfeited; and then had as good a right to purchase them from the State as any other person.

Richard Hoomes was never seized of these lands; and by the common law "*seisina facit stipitem*." The common law did not, therefore, give the appellees these lands as heirs. Ram on Assets 155, 8 Law Lib. But if the appellees did have lands by descent in Kentucky, they are not liable therefor to the appellant in this suit. The covenant of Richard Hoomes in the deed to Apperson has not been broken, and cannot

1853.
January
Term.

Dickinson
v.
Hoomes's
adm'r
& als.

therefore be enforced against his heirs. Richard Hoomes does not convey the land : That was devised to John Hoomes the younger with a contingent interest over to Richard Hoomes and the other brothers and sisters. And the object of the deed was not to convey a perfect title to the land, but to convey, so far as Richard Hoomes was concerned, his contingent rights and interests ; or rather, to covenant against these contingent rights and interests. That the covenant has not been broken is *res adjudicata*, as appears from the case between these same parties, 1 Gratt. 302. That case shews that the appellees claim under John Hoomes the elder, not under their father, Richard Hoomes : They claim over and above him.

Again. The covenant is not a covenant running with the land. It is clearly not such a covenant as by assignment would confer on the assignee a right to sue in his own name. See *Spencer's Case*, and the American notes, 43 Law Libr. 75 to 108 ; *Randolph* v. *Kinney*, 3 Rand. 394 ; Shephard's Touch. 316, 330, 30 Law Libr. Assignees are not bound except by inherent covenants running with the land. And if the grantor does not deliver possession, and conveys no title, any covenant he makes does not run with the land. See 2 Lomax Dig., p. 82, § 25, and p. 242 ; 2 Sugden on Vend., p. 90 top, 79 margin ; *Urquhart* v. *Clarke*, 2 Rand. 549. This was a case of the sale of a wife's land by the husband and wife. The children claiming were the children of the husband Dunkinson. On the face of the deed Dunkinson and wife claimed to convey and warrant a fee simple estate. Mrs. Dunkinson had not conveyed properly ; and it was held that as the land descended from the mother, the claimants were not barred by the deed and warranty of the father. And it was further held, that though real assets descended to the children from the father, they were not

1852.
January
Term.

Dickinson
v.
Hoomes's
adm'r
& als.

bound. The assignee cannot recover in his own name where there is no estate conveyed by the covenantor. By the warranty which we are considering, the covenantor only covenants against himself and his heirs, and those claiming by, through, or under him. And the appellees do not claim by, through, or under him. The warranty, therefore, is not broken. 2 Lomax Dig. 263.

Even if it was established that lands had descended in Kentucky to the appellees, still no recovery could be had against them in Virginia in a Virginia forum. Story's Conf. of Laws, § 551, 555. Each State and country has exclusive jurisdiction over the real and immovable estate within its territories. Each State has its own rules with regard to the disposition of such estate. Story's Conf. of Laws, § 523. The *lex loci rei sitæ* governs creditors, the *lex domicilii* governs the succession. Real assets abroad cannot be reached in Virginia. In Ram on Assets, p. 236, 8 Law Libr., will be found an English statute making lands in the colonies liable to specialty debts; and another statute extending the like provisions to the English possessions in India. Why were such statutes necessary there, if the heir in England was liable for real assets descended to him in the colonies? Are not our States separate and independent of each other—more so than the colonies of the mother country?

At common law the seisin of the ancestor was necessary to enable an heir to maintain a writ of right. 1 Lomax Dig. 617; 2 Tuck. Com. 181. And unless, therefore, there is such a statute in Kentucky as our Virginia statute, 1 Rev. Code, ch. 128, § 90, the heirs could not have recovered these lands in Kentucky. 2 Lomax Dig. 246–7.

The appellees are not bound for profits, if bound for the value of the land. *Blow* v. *Maynard*, 2 Leigh 29; *Hobson* v. *Yancey*, 2 Gratt. 73.

1832
January
Term.

Dickinson
v.
Hoomes's
adm'r
& als.

*Barton*, on the same side, submitted a printed argument.

For the appellees, we humbly contend that the decree is right in its effect, and ought to be affirmed:

1. Because we say that the covenant of Richard Hoomes, made to Apperson in the deed to him by John Hoomes, jr., has never been broken: at least that it was not broken by our recovering the land in controversy as purchasers from Col. John Hoomes.

We contend that the covenant of Richard Hoomes is a special covenant of a most limited nature; and that so far from the insertion of the words " as contingent devisees or legatees under the will of Colonel John Hoomes, late of the Bowling Green, deceased, by whom said land was devised to John Hoomes," enlarging the covenant, that, taken in their proper meaning, they restrict and limit still further what was without them a mere special warranty, or covenant of warranty. If we leave out these words the covenant reads thus:

" And the said John Hoomes, for himself and his heirs, and· said William Hoomes, Richard Hoomes, Armistead Hoomes, and Wilson Allen and Sophia, his wife, for themselves and their heirs, do hereby covenant and agree, to and with the said Samuel A. Apperson, that they will warrant and defend the fee simple estate and full and complete right and title to said two tracts of land, to him and his heirs and assigns forever, against themselves and their heirs, and against the claim and demand of any person or persons claiming by, from, or under them."

Now this is a mere special covenant of warranty, guarding against the covenantors, their heirs, and those claiming by, from, or under the covenantors; and this covenant would clearly not have been broken by our recovery of the land. For we succeeded not as heirs of Richard, nor as claiming by, from, or under Rich-

1852.
January
Term.

Dickinson
v.
Hoomes's
adm'r
& als.

ard Hoomes, but as purchasers from Col. John Hoomes. It is true the appellees were the children of Richard Hoomes ; but it is not true that *quoad* this land they were the heirs of Richard Hoomes. And the words " by," " from," and " under " do not refer to kin or blood relationship, but to the derivation of title and interest in or to the land.

If we insert the words before given, we then see that the covenant becomes more special and restricted. John Hoomes, the grantor, covenants for himself and his heirs generally. The others covenant for themselves and their heirs, as contingent devisees or legatees, &c. Why insert these words unless some meaning was designed to be conveyed by them ? It is obvious that they did not intend to covenant in any other character than as contingent devisees or legatees ; and this becomes very plain hereafter. They warrant and defend against themselves and their heirs, and all claiming by, from, or under them, in virtue of the will aforesaid. It is not *or by* virtue of the will, &c.

This does not enlarge the class of claimants guarded against to all who may claim by virtue of the will, whether by, from, or under the covenantors or not. But it requires that the claimant, to be included in the covenant, shall not only claim by, from, or under the covenantors, but also in virtue of the will aforesaid. So that a claimant might claim by, from, or under the covenantor, and the covenant would not be broken ; or he might claim in virtue of the will, and the covenant would not be broken. His claim only would be covenanted against who claimed both by, from, or under the covenantor, and in virtue of the will aforesaid.

The appellees have not claimed this land either as heirs, or by, from, or under the covenantor ; much less, in either of those ways, in virtue of the will aforesaid. Can this covenant, then, be said to be broken by the appellees taking the land as purchasers from Col. John

1852.
January
Term.

Dickinson
v.
Hoomes's
adm'r
& als.

Hoomes—a contingency which is not included in the obligation ?

While surrounding facts are properly admissible to explain or remove ambiguities or difficulties caused by matters extraneous to the instrument, there is no ground for the introduction of loose speculations as to the probable meaning or intention of parties in such an instrument as this. In its interpretation we must look to the language in which the meaning of the parties is expressed—the terms of the obligation.

If extraneous matters were admissible, we might very reasonably contend that these parties having received no portion of the consideration, all of which appears upon the face of the deed to have been paid or secured to John Hoomes, that the terms of their covenant should not be enlarged by construction to create an obligation that was not intended.

The covenantors might have chosen to yield all rights which they then had, or might thereafter acquire, to enable their brother to obtain a higher price for the land; and they might be willing to covenant against themselves and their heirs, and claimants by, from, or under them, &c., and yet not be willing to surrender rights which their children might acquire, or being unable to surrender them, to covenant against their children claiming rights acquired from other sources.

This distinction is the very one made in this case, and which the language of the covenant necessarily leads to.

Nor can it be said that it was the avowed object of this conveyance to give a fee simple estate, and full and complete right and title to the land, as against all persons, when John Waller Hoomes, a grandson of Col. John Hoomes, and who occupied the same position to this land that Richard Hoomes did, does not join in the covenant, nor is his name mentioned as one to join; and when all of those whose names are mentioned

1852.
January
Term.

Dickinson
v.
Hoomes's
adm'r
& als.

did not execute or sign the instrument. And the purchaser's taking a deed with the relinquishment and covenant from only a portion of those having this contingent interest shews that he was running a risk with
his eyes open, and that he did not understand the covenant to be as comprehensive as is now claimed by the
appellant; else he would have insisted upon its protection from all, by requiring all to sign.

The relinquishment and confirmation, though no part
of the covenant, and only operating as to the rights of
the parties thereto, and their heirs, as heirs—a proposition which will not be controverted, and is indeed settled by the court in the case in 1 Gratt. 302—throws
some light upon the meaning of the covenant. When
they meant to use general terms, language of a comprehensive signification, they knew what terms, what language, to use. And the very difference in the terms
used in the covenant and the relinquishment leads us
to the conclusion that their own rights the parties were
willing to yield in the amplest and most generous manner; but when it came to the imposition of obligations
upon others, that the most guarded and limited engagement only would be entered into; only that, indeed,
which would carry out the object of the relinquishment. For it is true, that had Richard survived John
his contingent interest would have become a vested interest in him, and if the relinquishment would not
have transferred it to the purchaser, yet his covenant
would have protected against his heirs; for they would
have claimed by, from, and under him, in virtue of the
will aforesaid: And this, we insist, was the true and
only object of the parties.

If it had been intended to give to this covenant a
large and comprehensive character, how easy to have
expressed it, by inserting at the end of the covenant,
"and all other persons whatsoever." Or to have guarded against the contingency of John's surviving Rich-

1852.
January
Term.

Dickinson
v.
Hoomes's
adm'r
& als.

ard Hoomes, by merely changing the words, " in virtue of the will aforesaid," to " or by virtue of the will aforesaid," or, indeed, by merely inserting the word " or " before the words " in virtue," &c.   Had any of these changes been made, there would have been some ground for the allegation of a broken covenant.   But as they were not made, and the covenant is in the words we have mentioned, we humbly submit that it is clear that the covenant of Richard Hoomes has not been broken.

2. We contend that the appellant, as assignee, has no right of action upon this obligation, for the reasons assigned in the answer of the appellees and the opinion of the court below.   2 Lomax Dig. 242–3, 277; 1 Smith's Lead. Ca., notes, 107, 43 Law Libr.

There is no proof of this land having passed by a regular chain of conveyances with general warranty to the appellant.

3. In order to hold us responsible on account of assets descended, it is necessary that we should have received real estate by descent, not by purchase or gift; and that by descent from the same ancestor that made the warranty.   2 Lomax Dig. 246, § 8.   And we contend that it is also necessary that the land should lie within the territorial jurisdiction of the courts whose tribunals are appealed to.

Real estate is universally conceded to be exclusively under the control of the *lex loci sitæ;* and no other country can take cognizance of controversies concerning it, or bind it in any way.   Story's Conf. of Laws, § 363–4 and 5, § 445, 543, § 551–5–6.

From the principles stated by Judge Story, we must infer necessarily that if this claim of the appellant was on a bond binding the heirs of Richard Hoomes, that our courts could not enter judgment against them so as to bind lands in Kentucky; and if it should appear in an action at law that there were no real assets in Vir-

1852.
January
Term.

Dickinson
v.
Hoomes's
adm'r
& als.

ginia, that judgment would necessarily be entered for the defendants. That such is the correct view, the court is respectfully referred to 3 Vin. Abr. 142; *Earl of Kildare* v. *Sir Morrice Eustace*, 1 Vern. R. 419; where Sir John Holt, *arguendo*, says " that it was resolved in *Evans and Ascough's Case*, Latch, fol. 234, and *Dowdale's Case*, 6 Coke 46, that land in Ireland should be assets to satisfy a bond debt here, but otherwise of lands in Scotland." And just above he stated the reason for the distinction, viz. : that Ireland was a conquered country, and hath courts of its own by the King's grant, but not exclusive of the King's courts here.

Now Kentucky is certainly as much of a foreign country to Virginia, and as much entitled to exclusive jurisdiction over lands within her limits, as Scotland was to England in 1686, when this was cited as law by Sir John Holt, who was seeking to establish the jurisdiction of the English court.

And in *Dowdale's Case*, 6 Coke 46, it was gravely questioned and decided by the court, whether lands lying in one county in England could be held to be assets by descent on a suit brought against the heir in another county, where he resided. And while it was of course decided that lands thus situated were to be considered assets, yet that such a point should have been mooted intimates very clearly what the decision would have been on the question of lands lying in a foreign country.

The doctrine, as applied to bonds binding the heirs, of course applies equally to covenants binding the heirs. And upon these authorities, and the exclusiveness of the territorial jurisdiction over lands, we contend that inasmuch as the courts of Virginia, in an action brought against an heir on a covenant or bond binding the heirs, could create no lien, impose no liability, nor give any redress for a violated obligation, against lands lying in

1852.
January
Term.

Dickinson
v.
Hoomes's
adm'r
& als.

Kentucky, that a covenant binding heirs does so only in respect to lands within the territorial jurisdiction of the country whose tribunals are appealed to.

The English court of chancery has certainly stretched its jurisdiction to the uttermost limits, and never favours an attempt to circumscribe it, yet I have seen no case where, in respect to controversies concerning lands in foreign countries, the English chancellor has ever asserted this extraterritorial jurisdiction, save when fraud was charged. And it has been happily said, " that the jurisdiction over fraud, like that over piracy, knew no territorial bounds or restrictions."

The contract between the parties thus fixing and settling their legal rights, the appellant can occupy no better position here than if he were attempting to impose a liability by an original suit of his own. And if he could not hold us responsible in such a suit, we contend that he has no right to use this defence in a suit of ours, even though it be in equity. We are seeking legal rights in an equity suit, and the rights of both parties to this controversy are ascertained by law. And while the maxim that " he who seeks equity must do equity " is a very good one, when applicable, there is another more germain to the matter, that " equity follows the law."

If, however, the position of the counsel for the appellant be correct, and, by acting *in personam*, a court of chancery in Virginia can indirectly operate on lands in Kentucky, in a case where no fraud can be alleged, yet, upon the previous references to Story's Conflict of Laws, and perfectly well established principles, it will not and cannot be controverted, that the courts here can give no further or other remedy than would be given in Kentucky, can impose no other obligations than are imposed in Kentucky ; and that the liabilities of the heirs are to be established here exactly as they would be in Kentucky. That is, that our courts are to ascer-

1852.
January
Term.

Dickinson
v.
Hoomes's
adm'r
& als.

tain what is the law of Kentucky, and apply it to the case. Now what is the law of Kentucky in regard to the liability of heirs on account of obligations under seal binding heirs?

The courts of Virginia will not take judicial notice of the laws of a foreign State, but they must be proved as facts. Story's Conf. of Laws, § 637. If they b written laws, copies proved and authenticated must be produced. § 641.

The laws of Kentucky on this point are written or statute law. The appellant has sought to introduce no evidence of the law of Kentucky upon this point, except that contained in Mr. Herndon's deposition, which is not admissible evidence to prove what the law is. Story's Conf. of Laws, § 641. The appellant has therefore entirely failed to prove an indispensable point of his case, were we to concede every point of law and fact to be as he claims. That this deficiency exists in his case is his own fault, and proceeds from his own *laches*. He had had full time and opportunity to obtain any evidence or legal instrument that he might have desired.

4. The second auditor of the State of Kentucky, in whose office are kept the land books of non-resident proprietors, proves that the lands in the name of Col. John Hoomes, in the State of Kentucky, as appears by the books in his office, amounted to 19,725⅜ acres, divided into various tracts, and lying in different parts of the State. Of this number that 1008½ acres were lost by prior claims, leaving 18,717⅜. Two tracts, one of 1001¾, the other of 300 acres, were discontinued as the property of citizens of Kentucky. When they were transferred does not appear. It seems, however, to have been prior to 1826. And they may be the lands referred to as sold by Samuel Chiles, of which we knew nothing, as we were infants at the time, even if it were after Richard Hoomes's death; thus leaving

1852.
January
Term

Dickinson
v
Hoomes's
adm'r
& als.

17,415 acres, of which it is proved that various tracts, amounting to 14,535 acres, were forfeited for non-payment of taxes, prior to 1828, mostly prior to 1826: leaving a tract of 2880 acres which was discontinued, as it was found upon survey to contain 400 acres surplus; 2573 acres of this were afterwards re-entered for taxation, and the taxes becoming in arrears, were afterwards sold by Draffin, agent of the State, and at this sale purchased by Richard H. Hoomes.

It appears very distinctly from the report of the decision and Draffin's deed, and this deposition of the auditor, that the same tract that was divided was afterwards sold for the taxes and bought by R. H. Hoomes.

The discrepancy in the quantity exists only in appearance; for when the portion allotted to Williamson Tally, for his services in having the decision made, is subtracted, the balance amounts so nearly to the number of acres conveyed by Draffin to R. H. Hoomes as to shew that they must be the same tract, and that the slight difference in number of acres is to be traced to different surveys, &c. The appellant has fallen into the mistake as to the identity from not understanding the facts. It appears from the record that in May 1833 the only tract of land in Kentucky that had belonged to Col. John Hoomes, then remaining, was laid off by commissioners, and after deducting the large portion that went to Tally for his services, the remainder was divided among the children of Richard Hoomes, the assignee of Armistead Hoomes and Wilson Allen. No change was made in the names on the non-resident books in the second auditor's office: and when this tract was afterwards forfeited for non-payment of taxes, Tally, being a resident of Kentucky, had taken care that his portion should not be included in the forfeiture. The number of acres was thus reduced, and was sold by John Draffin as being in the name of John Hoomes, and bought by Richard H. Hoomes, who thus took his

1862.
January
Term.

Dickinson
v.
Hoomes's
adm'r
& als.

title directly from the State of Kentucky; and afterwards, *ex gratia*, as a gratuity on his part, allowed the others who had been mentioned in the division made some twelve years before, to purchase from him, by the payment of their proportionate shares of the purchase money paid by him, the tracts that had been originally assigned to them.

The land stood on the land books of Kentucky, so far as we know or have any reason to believe, in the name of John Hoomes. Richard did not there appear ever to have had any title even, much less possession, and unless the common law doctrine, that "*non jus sed seisina stipitem facit*," was changed in Kentucky by a statute, they would not have taken any land as heirs of Richard Hoomes, but as heirs of their grandfather, John Hoomes. Brown's Legal Maxims 227. And if any such change has been made in the law of Kentucky, it was the duty of the appellant to shew the change, which he has not attempted to shew. So that as appears by this record the appellees were right in saying that they took from their grandfather, and not from their father. Indeed, however this point might be decided, they took a large portion of that assigned to them directly from their grandfather's will, precisely as they took the land in controversy in this case, in this State; for John Hoomes, and it is believed William Hoomes also, survived Richard and died childless and unmarried.

It being shewn, then, that this is the same tract divided in 1833, sold to Richard H. Hoomes in 1835, and from whom the other appellees derived their title, and that this is the only tract of land in Kentucky that has ever or could ever come to our possession, we submit, that as our only beneficial title was obtained from the State of Kentucky, that there is no foundation to charge us with the value of these lands, even were the

1852.
January
Term.

Dickinson
v.
Hoomes's
adm'r
& als.

original title, which was lost, derived from Richard Hoomes.

For the appellees we contend, therefore, that the decree of the court below should be affirmed:

1. Because the covenant of Richard Hoomes has not been broken.

2. Because, if broken, the right of action did not pass to the assignee Dickinson.

3. Because lands descended in Kentucky are not assets in Virginia, and could not in any case be so claimed, whether in a court of law or equity, without shewing that they would be assets in Kentucky; which has not been done.

4. Because we have inherited no lands, in Kentucky or elsewhere, from Richard Hoomes, but derived a title from John Hoomes, and have derived our possession and only beneficial title directly from the State of Kentucky.

*Bouldin*, for the appellant, in reply.

I shall consider first the extent and effect of the covenant of Richard Hoomes. What was its object and what its effect? Before entering upon these enquiries, however, it may be well to state some general rules of construction, by which the meaning of the covenant may be ascertained.

1. " Covenants are to be construed according to the obvious intention of the parties as collected from the whole context of the instrument, *et antecedentibus et consequentibus*, and according to the reasonable sense of the words."

2. " If there be any ambiguity, then such construction shall be made as is most strong against the covenantor; for he might have expressed himself more clearly." 1 Wheaton's Selwyn 376; 2 Lomax Dig. 251; Platt on Covenants, 3 Law Libr. 61, 63.

1852.
January
Term.

Dickinson
v.
Hoomes's
adm'r
& als.

With these principles in view, let us return to the question, What is the object and effect of Richard Hoomes's covenant? To aid in ascertaining its object we may refer to the situation of the parties, to their relation to the property, and to the business they were transacting, when the covenant was made. John Hoomes was in possession of and held in the property a base or qualified fee. Richard Hoomes held a contingent interest therein under the will of Col. John Hoomes, dependent on the death of John Hoomes without children living at his death. The children of Richard Hoomes also held a contingent interest in the same property under the will of Col. John Hoomes, depending on the death of John Hoomes without issue, and of their father Richard, in the lifetime of John. Such was the state of things when John Hoomes sold and conveyed the property to Apperson.

Now what, according to the dictates of common sense, and from our knowledge of the motives and conduct of men, would be a leading object with parties thus situated? Obviously it would be the first wish of Apperson, the purchaser, to secure a good title to the property, freed from the contingent interest of Richard Hoomes and his children; and it would as clearly be to the interest of John Hoomes, the vendor, if possible, to secure him such a title. This, I insist, would naturally be the object of parties thus situated: and that such was in fact their intention is plainly to be gathered from the terms of the covenant, construed "according to the reasonable sense of the words" used. (Mr. B. here read the covenant and commented on its terms.) He insisted that there was nothing in the narrow and hypercritical construction placed on the words of the covenant by the learned counsel for the appellees, to prevent the court from carrying into effect the obvious intent of the parties. That a covenant could not well be drawn more clearly indicating a pur-

1862.
January
Term.

Dickinson
v.
Hoomes's
adm'r
& als.

pose to guard against the very contingency that has happened than the one under consideration. viz., to protect the purchaser not only against the claim of Richard Hoomes himself, but also against the claim of his children or "heirs," not *as heirs*, but "as contingent devisees or legatees under the will of Col. John Hoomes," claiming the property "in virtue of the will aforesaid," and connecting themselves with the testator through the said Richard Hoomes. He insisted that it was the obvious purpose and effect of this covenant to extinguish the entire contingent interest of Richard Hoomes himself, and to guard against the contingent interest of his children claiming through him " in virtue of the will aforesaid." And that such was the understanding of the parties is manifest from the clause of confirmation which follows immediately after the covenant.

If, however, the terms of the covenant are ambiguous, which I submit is the most that can be said of them, then they must be construed most favorably to the covenantee, and most strongly against the covenantor, for it was his duty to " have expressed himself more clearly," and this would lead us to the same result. *Quacunque via*, then, the appellees are bound by the covenant of their ancestor to indemnify the plaintiff against this demand to the extent of the real assets descended to them, provided this is a covenant which runs with the land. And this brings us to the next question.

2. Does this covenant run with the land and pass to the appellant?

Gentlemen say not; because, say they, Richard Hoomes conveyed nothing by the deed containing the covenant, and only covenanted against a possibility. That possibility, however, that contingent interest, I insist, is in fact, and in contemplation of law, both an interest and an estate; an interest and estate, appreciable, valuable, and transmissible by deed, devise, or

1852.
January
Term.

Dickinson
v.
Hoomes's
adm'r
& als.

descent; and the extinction of which was most beneficial to the holder of the land.   1 Lomax Dig. 467; 3
Id. 323–4; and the cases there cited.   And this brings
the covenant directly within the influence of the principle quoted by the gentlemen on the other side from
the American notes to *Spencer's Case*, 1 Smith's Leading Cases 75, 107, that a covenant affects and runs
with the land, " although not to be directly performed
upon it, provided it tend to diminish or increase its
value in the hands of the holder "; and this too when
there is no tenure or privity of estate between the covenantor and the covenantee.   In such case, however,
it runs with the land for its benefit; but not to charge
it.   To do the latter there must be tenure or privity.
1 Smith's Leading Cases 107–8; *Plymouth* v. *Carver*,
16 Pick. R. 183.   It might in this case, if necessary,
be insisted that there *was* privity between the covenantor and covenantee—privity of estate to support a
charge.   But it is not necessary to contend for that
proposition, as this covenant is clearly beneficial to the
estate and not a charge upon it.   It increased the value
of the estate in the hands of the holder, and therefore
affected and run with the land.

The objection urged on the other side is not tenable for another reason.   An estate of freehold was created by the deed in which the covenant is contained;
and that estate continued and was not defeated until
after the land came to the hands of the appellant.
Here, then, is a case in which an estate of freehold was
created in the covenantee by the deed containing the
covenant, and the covenantee put in possession of the
land; and in which, as is apparent to all, the land was
made more valuable in his hands by the covenant: and
this land, by a regular and unbroken chain of conveyance, has come to the possession of the appellant.

The principle established by the cases commented on
by the learned gentlemen on the other side has no ap-

1852.
January
Term.

Dickinson
v.
Hoomes's
adm'r
& als.

plication to such a case.  It is an error to suppose that they shew that the covenantor must grant to, or create an estate in, the covenantee.  They only shew that the covenantee must have an assignable estate to support the covenant, either pre-existing or created by the instrument containing the covenant.  The existence of an estate in the covenantee, to which the covenant may attach, is the important requisite.  It is wholly unimportant how or from whom he may have derived it.  An examination of the cases cited on the other side will shew that they were all cases in which there was no pre-existing estate in the covenantee, and none created by the instrument containing the covenant.  The first is a leading case on the question.  *Awder* v. *Noke*, Cro. Eliz. 373, 436–7, 1 Smith's Leading Cases 99.  In this case there was no estate in the first grantor, and of course no estate created in or passing to the first grantee.  There being, then, no estate pre-existing or created in the grantee, there was of course nothing upon which the assignment by the grantee could operate, and nothing to which the covenant could attach : and it was so decided.

The next case is *Andrew* v. *Pearce*, 4 Bos. & Pul. 158, 1 Smith's Lead. Cas. 99.  There the estate, which was a term of years carved out of an estate tail, was avoided by the death of the tenant in tail.  After the death of the tenant in tail, the assignee of the term, when it had ceased to exist, assigned over.  Held, that a naked covenant could not pass as incident to a term of years which had ceased to exist; and therefore did not pass by the assignment.  This is the same principle with *Awder* v. *Noke*.

And so with *Nesbit* v. *Montgomery*, 1 Taylor 84, 1 Smith's Lead. Cas. 99.  The declaration stated want of title at the date of the original demise, and of course the grantee acquired nothing and could assign nothing.

1852.
January
Term.

Dickinson
v.
Hoomes's
adm'r
& als.

All, then, that these cases require is an estate in the covenantee, to which the covenant may attach, created or existing at the date of the covenant, and continuing at the time of the assignment: and our case comes fully up to these requisitions.

In New York it has been decided, and it is submitted with good sense, that whenever possession accompanies a grant or conveyance, the covenants do pass with the land to the grantee and his assignees, notwithstanding no actual title was created. *Beddoe* v. *Wadsworth*, 21 Wend. R. 120. This, I submit, is a rational decision, for it makes a covenant answer the purpose for which it was designed, namely, to support a defective title.

The only Virginia cases commented on by the counsel on the other side are *Randolph* v. *Kinney*, 3 Rand. 394, and *Urquhart* v. *Clarke*, 2 Rand. 549. *Randolph* v. *Kinney* is precisely the same in principle with the cases of *Awder* v. *Noke* and *Nesbit* v. *Montgomery*. There was no estate pre-existing in, or passing by, the original deed to the first grantee, and of course nothing passed by the grant of the latter to which the covenant could attach itself. When, however, such an estate does exist in or pass to the grantee, then a covenant may be made with him, to run with the land, even by a stranger to the title and the original deed. 2 Thomas's Coke 362; *Spencer's Case*, Smith's Lead. Cases, p. 82, 83; 2 Lomax Dig. 260. The case of *Urquhart* v. *Clarke* has no application to this case: The question under consideration did not arise.

But if the covenant did not run with the land, and an action at law could not be maintained by the appellant, still a court of equity ought to give relief. *Nesbit* v. *Brown*, 1 Dev. Equ. R. 30.

It is unnecessary, however, to press this latter view, as the covenant unquestionably runs with the land.

1852.
January
Term.

Dickinson
v.
Hoomes's
adm'r
& als.

To shew this more conclusively, let us ask whether an action of covenant could not be maintained by the appellant against the principal grantor, John Hoomes, or his heirs, on his covenant for title. That it could will not be denied. But the covenant of John and Richard Hoomes is a joint covenant, in the same deed, couched in the same words, and precisely for the same thing. Now if it runs with the land against John, the same covenant being Richard's too, must also run with the land as to him. It would be strange that under such circumstances the covenant should run with the land as to one co-covenantor, and be in gross as to the other.

3. But it is objected, in the third place, that a part of the land has been aliened, and that covenant will not lie for an assignee of a part of the subject, because the covenant is an entire thing, and the remedy on it cannot be apportioned. For this proposition the only authority cited is a remark of Mr. Preston, quoted in a note to 2 Lom. Dig., p. 263. On this subject it is enough to say that Mr. Preston, in this remark, if it is properly construed on the other side, contradicts himself, (see the first part of the remark quoted,) and is contradicted by authority. 2 Thomas's Coke 362; Platt on Covenants 495; *Stevenson* v. *Lambard*, 2 East's R. 575.

We have thus ascertained: 1. That the covenant bound the heirs of the covenantors to protect Apperson and his assignees against the claim of the appellees. 2. That this covenant runs with the land. 3. That it is not extinguished by the alienation of part of the land.

4. Let us enquire, in the fourth place, whether this court can hold the appellees responsible for the real assets descended to them in the State of Kentucky, by repelling to the extent of those assets their demand in this case?

We say the jurisdiction unquestionably exists; and

1852.
January
Term.

Dickinson
v.
Hoomes's
adm'r
& als.

it would be difficult to find a case demonstrating more forcibly than this the necessity of its existence and the propriety of its exercise.

I shall not deny that real estate always, (and even personal estate to the extent stated by the opposite counsel,) must be governed by the *lex rei sitæ.* Nor will I deny that, in the exercise of the jurisdiction now claimed for this court, it must, to some extent, enquire into the laws of other countries. But do these admissions concede inconveniences and difficulties of a character to prevent the exercise of the jurisdiction invoked?

Before considering the question, let us look a little to the facts of the case, and the relative position of the home and foreign jurisdiction.

Here was the domicil through life of the original testator, Col. John Hoomes. Here was the domicil of Richard Hoomes, the ancestor of the appellees. Here is the domicil of the appellant; of the appellees; of the administrator, and of all the creditors of Richard Hoomes of whom we have any knowledge. In this court and in this suit can they all be convened. In addition to all this, the appellees who have converted the foreign assets are irresponsible. The real assets alone are beyond the jurisdiction of this court, and subject to a foreign jurisdiction. And the question is, where, under such circumstances, can justice and equity be most safely and conveniently administered? In Kentucky, where the real assets alone are, or here, where all the parties are, where all the important evidence is, where the creditors are, and where all the decedents lived and died? The answer can only be in favour of the jurisdiction of this court.

Is there any thing, then, to prevent the exercise of this obviously wholesome jurisdiction? It has been suggested from the bench that there is: that the foreign assets may have been subjected, under the foreign

1852.
January
Term.

Dickinson
v.
Hoomes's
adm'r
& als.

jurisdiction, or may now be subject, to the claims of creditors of Richard Hoomes; and thus the appellees would be made to lose their father's lands in Kentucky and their own land here.

The difficulty is, in this case at least, merely an abstract one; for Richard Hoomes has been dead for nearly thirty years, and no claim has been presented against the land or the heirs in Kentucky. But the difficulty is in fact more specious than real. It would apply with precisely the same force were the lands in Virginia and not in Kentucky; and in each case the protection against it is alike simple and the same. It is simply to plead and prove the fact that the lands descended have been subjected, or are subject, to claims against the ancestor, having precedence over the claim asserted. A failure to plead and prove it, were the whole of the Kentucky lands now in Virginia, would subject the appellees in this very cause to all the evils suggested; whilst, on the other hand, the appellees may, in the same cause, secure to themselves complete protection from the claim of the appellant by proving the fact suggested, if it exists. I see, therefore, no difficulty in the suggestion. 1 Wheaton's Selwyn 490, 492; 2 Tuck. Com. 112; 3 Tuck. Black 421, in notes. It is true, that in an action at law against an heir on the bond of his ancestor, the court cannot notice lands descended in a foreign State. The reason is, that on admission by the heir of lands by descent, the judgment and execution at law is against the lands, and not against the heir personally: and the lands will be extended. But as legal process cannot run into a foreign jurisdiction, proof of lands there would be unavailing. But a court of equity, acting on the person, may compel the heir to convey land in a foreign country, or, if already conveyed, may require him, as a condition upon which the aid of the court will be extended to him, to account for the proceeds: And this is what we ask.

1852.
January
Term.

Dickinson
v.
Hoomes's
adm'r
& als.

The creditors, if any, being made parties, all equities would be settled in one suit, by a court of competent jurisdiction; and the decree could be pleaded in Kentucky against any creditor renewing his claim against the heir in that State. And this court would enjoin the proceeding, if the creditor should be within its jurisdiction. *Wedderburn* v. *Wedderburn*, 17 Cond. Eng. Ch. R. 208; affirmed on appeal; 18 Id. 585. There could not well be a stronger case of the exercise of the power under consideration than the case cited. So, too, a proceeding by a creditor in Kentucky might be arrested there, at the instance of the heir, on his shewing to the court that the matter was "*res adjudicata*" in Virginia. *Booth* v. *Leycester*, 15 Cond. Eng. Ch. R. 580; and cases cited in the note to that case.

The general doctrine of equity on this subject is "that the court of chancery, having authority to act upon the person, may indirectly act upon real estate, situate in a foreign country, through the instrumentality of this authority over the person; and that it may compel him to give effect to its decree respecting such property, whether it goes to the entire disposition of it or only to affect it with liens or burthens." Story on Conf. of Laws, § 544, 545; *Brodie* v. *Barry*, 2 Ves. & Beame 127; *Massie* v. *Watts*, 5 Cranch's R. 148; *Farley* v. *Shippen*, Wythe's Rep.; *Guerrant* v. *Fowler*, 1 Hen. & Munf. 5.

Now we do not ask this court to act directly on the Kentucky lands; all that we ask is, that the appellees, who are seeking the aid of this court, shall be compelled to perform the covenant of their ancestor, to the extent of the value of the lands received by descent from him in the foreign jurisdiction. And we do this with the greater confidence in this case, because there is in truth no conflict of law in relation to these Kentucky lands. The Kentucky law of descents and our

1852
January
Term.

Dickinson
v.
Hoomes's
adm'r
& als.

own is the same ; and in administering the foreign law in this case we are but administering our own.

But it is objected, by Mr. Barton, that parol proof of a written or statute law is inadmissible. The objection comes too late. It was not made in the court below by exception, and cannot be made in argument here. But if in time, the objection is untenable. The laws of a foreign country, written or unwritten, may be proved by an expert, as a fact. *Baron De Rodes' Case*, 55 Eng. C. L. R. 246 to 254; *Cocks* v. *Purday*, 61 Id. 269.

5. And, lastly, as to the fact of lands in Kentucky by descent from Richard Hoomes.

It will be observed that the appellees had no claim to the Kentucky lands under their grandfather, Col. John Hoomes. He died testate, and in the events which have occurred these Kentucky lands vested absolutely in Richard Hoomes, as he complied with the conditions of the devise, by leaving children. His title to the lands being thus consummate, he had constructive seisin thereof, (if seisin was necessary,) without actual *pedis positio*. *Green* v. *Liter*, 8 Cranch's R. 228, 248-9. And by his death intestate, the law cast the seisin on his heirs, (the appellees,) and they became at once constructively seised of all the lands then unsold. (Same case.)

But neither actual nor constructive seisin is necessary to support a descent. The rule " *seisina facit stipitem* " has been abolished both in this State and in Kentucky; not, as contended by Mr. Morson, by reason of the statutory provision in relation to writs of right, (1 Rev. Code, ch. 128, § 90, p. 510,) but as a rule of descent, by the first section of the act of descents. 1 Rev. Code 355, ch. 96, § 1; 1 Lomax Dig. 594; 2 Tuck. Com. 189. And the Kentucky statute in relation to this matter is proved to be a literal transcript of our own.

The idea that the heirs, by suffering their *own lands*

1852.
January
Term.

Dickinson
v.
Hoomes's
adm'r
& als.

to be sold for taxes and themselves becoming the purchasers, could thereby break the descent and cease to be heirs, does not seem to require a grave refutation at our hands. I submit that the decree is erroneous and should be reversed.

MONCURE, J., after stating the case, proceeded:

This case has been argued in this court with great ability by the counsel on both sides. Various questions of law and fact were raised and discussed in the case, as

1st. Whether the covenant of Richard Hoomes had been broken? And if broken,

2d. Whether the right of action therefor passed to the assignee Dickinson? If so,

3d. Whether lands descended in Kentucky could be regarded as assets by descent in any proceeding in Virginia? And if so,

4th. Whether in fact any lands in Kentucky descended from Richard Hoomes to his children; and if they did, whether they were not forfeited for non-payment of taxes, and whether such of them as were held by the children were held by them as purchasers from the State of Kentucky, and not as heirs of their father?

I will now proceed to consider the question first above stated, that is, Whether the covenant of Richard Hoomes has been broken? The only ground on which it is contended to have been broken is, that his children have recovered, as purchasers, under the will of John Hoomes the elder, one fourth of the land claimed by Dickinson to have been derived under the deed from John Hoomes the younger to Apperson, in which the said covenant is contained. And whether broken or not depends upon the proper construction of the covenant. If it be a covenant of general warranty, or a covenant of special warranty against the claims of the said children, then it has been broken. But if it be a

1852.
January
Term.

Dickinson
v.
Hoomes's
adm'r
& als.

covenant of special warranty only against the claims of the covenantor and his heirs, (technically and properly speaking,) and all persons claiming by, from, or under them, then it has not been broken. Let us now see what is its proper construction.

The covenant is in these words : " And the said John Hoomes, for himself and his heirs, and said William Hoomes, Richard Hoomes, Armistead Hoomes, and Wilson Allen and Sophia, his wife, for themselves and their heirs, as contingent devisees or legatees under the will of Col. John Hoomes, late of the Bowling Green, deceased, by whom said land was devised to John Hoomes, do hereby covenant and agree to and with the said Samuel A. Apperson, that they will warrant and defend the fee simple estate and full and complete right and title to said two tracts of land, to him and his heirs and assigns forever, against themselves and their heirs, and against the claim and demand of any person or persons claiming by, from, or under them, in virtue of the will aforesaid, and do relinquish and fully confirm to said S. A. Apperson all the right they or their heirs now have, or might or may hereafter have, to said land or any part thereof, to him and his heirs and assigns for-ever, free from them, said John Hoomes, William Hoomes, Richard Hoomes, Armistead Hoomes, and Wilson Allen and Sophia, his wife, late Sophia Hoomes, and their heirs, and of all other persons in the world."

If the latter branch of the clause, commencing at the words, " and do relinquish and fully confirm," had been omitted in the deed, there would have been no ground whatever for contending that there was any covenant of general warranty on the part of Richard Hoomes. The only question then would have been, whether the covenant of special warranty contained in the former branch of the clause was confined to the claims of the covenantor and those claiming under him, or extended to the claims of his children, whether

1852.
January
Term.

Dickinson
v.
Hoomes's
adm'r
& als.

claiming under him or otherwise.   Let us first consider
the former branch of the clause separately, and ascertain
the nature and extent of the covenant therein contained.
There is nothing peculiar in that branch of the clause
but the words " as contingent devisees or legatees under the will of Col. John Hoomes," and the words
" in virtue of the will aforesaid."   Strike out those
words, and the covenant is clearly confined to the claims
of the covenantor and those claiming under him.   The
remaining words are precisely those which are generally
used to express such a covenant of special warranty:
"And the said Richard Hoomes, &c., for themselves
and their heirs, covenant with the said Apperson that
they will warrant and defend the estate to him, and
his heirs and assigns forever, against themselves and
their heirs, and against the claim and demand of any
person claiming by, from, or under them."   These, in
substance, are the remaining words used, and by no
other words or form of expression could such a covenant of special warranty be more plainly or appropri-
ately expressed.   In this construction every word has
its proper signification.   The covenantors intended to
bind their heirs, and therefore covenanted for themselves " and their heirs "; and they covenanted to warrant the estate against the claims of " their heirs," not
as purchasers from John Hoomes the elder, but in the
technical and proper sense of the word, as persons claiming by descent from them.   Greenleaf, in his treatise on
evidence, vol. 1, § 287, note 3, properly says that " the
rules of interpretation of wills, laid down by Mr. Wi-
gram in his admirable treatise on that subject, may be
safely applied, *mutato nomine*, to all other private instruments."   They are contained in seven propositions
as the result both of principle and authority, of which
the two first are as follows:

" I. A testator is always presumed to use the words
in which he expresses himself according to their strict

1852.
January
Term.

Dickinson
v.
Hoomes's
adm'r
& als.

and primary acceptation, unless from the context of the will it appears that he has used them in a different sense; in which case the sense in which he thus appears to have used them will be the sense in which they are to be construed.

"II. Where there is nothing in the context of a will from which it is apparent that a testator has used the words in which he has expressed himself in any other than their strict and primary sense, and where his words so interpreted are sensible with reference to extrinsic circumstances, it is an inflexible rule of construction that the words of the will shall be interpreted in their strict and primary sense, and in no other, although they may be capable of some popular or secondary interpretation, and although the most conclusive evidence of intention to use them in such popular or secondary sense be tendered."

The word "heirs," in its strict and primary sense, is a word of limitation; and although it may be capable of some popular or secondary interpretation, yet, being in this case sensible with reference to extrinsic circumstances, it must, according to the foregoing rules, be construed in its strict and primary sense, unless, from the context of the instrument, it appears to have been used in a different sense. Does it appear, from the context, to have been used in a different sense? I am now confining my remarks to the former branch of the clause aforesaid. We have seen that the only peculiarity therein consists in the words, "as contingent devisees or legatees under the will of Col. John Hoomes," and the words "in the will aforesaid." Do these words take from the word "heirs," in the context, its strict and primary meaning, and give it a popular and secondary signification? The covenant with the addition of these words is in substance as follows: "And the said Richard Hoomes, &c., for themselves and their heirs, *as contingent devisees or legatees under the*

1852.
January
Term.

Dickinson
v.
Hoomes's
adm'r.
& als.

*will of Col. John Hoomes*, covenant with the said Apperson, that they will warrant and defend the estate to him and his heirs and assigns forever, against themselves and their heirs, and against the claim and demand of any person claiming by, from, or under him, *in virtue of the will aforesaid.*" I do not think the additional words were intended to enlarge the covenant, or to extend it to persons not claiming by, through, or under the covenantors. I rather think, if they were intended to have any effect at all on the covenant, they were intended to restrict it to persons claiming as contingent devisees, or in virtue of the will, and by, through, or under the covenantors. So that a claim of the covenantors or their heirs in any other right than in virtue of the will would not come within the scope of the covenant. The chief object in using these words doubtless was to shew the interest of Richard Hoomes and others in the subject, and their reason for uniting in the execution of the deed. The land had been devised to John Hoomes the younger in fee; and he had sold and conveyed it to Apperson, and received the purchase money. But Richard Hoomes and others were devisees in remainder on the contingency of their surviving John Hoomes the younger, and of his dying without issue: And they were willing to relinquish to the purchaser their contingent rights, and to warrant the title against all persons claiming under them in virtue of those rights. They therefore covenant " as contingent devisees," and against claims under them " in virtue of the will." To give to these additional words the effect of extending the covenant to persons not " claiming by, through, or under " the covenantors, would be to render inoperative the words " by, through, or under." And thus words which are plain, usual, and well understood would be rendered ineffectual by a strained construction of words which are at least very equivocal. Now it is a settled rule of con-

1852.
January
Term.

Dickinson
v.
Hoomes's
adm'r
& als.

struction that effect should be given, if possible, to every word contained in the instrument; and especially that words of common and settled signification should have their full force and effect.

I will present another view of this part of the subject. The covenant can be extended to the claims of the children as purchasers under the will of John Hoomes the elder, only, I presume, by construing the word "heirs" as "children." The word "heirs," as referring to Richard Hoomes &c., occurs twice in that part of the covenant now under consideration. . Where it first occurs it clearly is used in its strict and primary sense, and does not mean "children." The covenantors bind themselves and their "heirs." If the word in this connection be not construed in its strict and primary sense, then there is nothing in the covenant to bind the heirs, whether they have assets by descent or not. The same word where it again occurs in the same sentence ought to receive the same construction; at least, without very strong reasons for giving it a different one; and none such appear in this case.

I think, therefore, it may fairly be concluded that the former branch of the clause before quoted, construed by itself, contains no more than a covenant of special warranty against the claims of persons claiming under the covenantors. Let us now see whether it contains any thing more when construed in connection with the latter branch of the clause. That branch is separated from the former only by a comma, and is in these words:

"And do relinquish and fully confirm to said S. A. Apperson all the right they or their heirs now have, or might or may hereafter have, to said land or any part thereof, to him and his heirs and assigns forever, free from the said John Hoomes, &c., and their heirs, and of all other persons in the world."

If the words of this latter branch of the covenant were such as, taken alone, would be construed to

1852.
January
Term.

Dickinson
v.
Hoomes's
adm'r
& als.

import a covenant of general warranty, they would not be so construed, taken in connection with the former branch of the covenant. Otherwise the two branches of the clause would be inconsistent with each other, and the former would contain a covenant of special, and the latter a covenant of general warranty. A deed should be construed according to the intention of the parties, as the same may be gathered from the whole instrument. It would be absurd to suppose that the covenantors intended to give a general warranty against all the world, after carefully giving a special warranty only against persons claiming under them in virtue of the will. All covenants of warranty have the same object, but to a greater or less extent; and the rule, as laid down by Sugden in his Law of Vendors, vol. 2, p. 94, is that " where restrictive words are inserted in the first of several covenants having the same object, they will be construed as extending to all the covenants, although they are distinct." This rule is supported by the following authorities: *Nervin* v. *Munns*, 3 Lev. 46; *Broughton* v. *Conway*, Dyer's R. 240; *Browning* v. *Wright*, 2 Bos. & Pul. 13; *Foord* v. *Wilson*, 4 Eng. C. L. R. 205; *Nind* v. *Marshall*, 5 Id. 95. In the last cited case some of the covenants were restrictive, but one of them was general against "all persons whatsoever." Dallas, C. J., said: " I think ' all persons whatsoever' must be construed to mean persons of the description in the other covenants, that is, persons claiming under the covenantor, or persons claiming under them ; and that they are in the nature of sweeping and comprehensive words, introduced to give the largest effect to the special words; reference being had to their special nature, and as such ranging under known rules of construction, and to be explained and applied as I have already stated." The same might be said of the expression, " all other persons in the world," if the words of the latter branch of the clause were such as, taken alone, would import a cove-

1852.
January
Term.

Dickinson
v.
Hoomes's
adm'r
& als.

nant of general warranty in the broadest sense of the term.

But suppose the latter branch of the clause, taken alone, could be regarded as importing a general warranty, what is the subject to which the warranty refers? Is it the land itself, or is it merely the right of the covenantors thereto? Unquestionably the latter. "And do relinquish and fully confirm to the said Apperson all the right, &c., to said land," are the words used. Richard Hoomes, &c., were contingent devisees; they covenanted as contingent devisees; and they relinquished to the purchaser from John Hoomes the younger their right as contingent devisees. And if this relinquishment imports a covenant of general warranty, it is only of their right as contingent devisees. In *Sweet* v. *Brown*, 12 Metc. R. 175, A conveyed to B all his right, title and interest in and to certain real estate described by metes and bounds, with the usual covenants of seisin and warranty. It was held that the covenants were limited to the estate and interest of A in the granted premises; and were not general covenants extending to the whole parcel described in the deed. In *Allen* v. *Holton*, 20 Pick. R. 458, a similar decision was made. See also *Blanchard* v *Brooks*, 12 Pick. R. 47. If Richard Hoomes only warranted his right as contingent devisee, his warranty was of course not broken by the claim of his children to their rights as contingent devisees and purchasers under the will of their grandfather.

But does the latter branch of the clause import any covenant at all; or, at least, any covenant as separate and distinct from the covenant of special warranty contained in the former? I rather think not. I think its only office was to shew that the relinquishment and confirmation were intended to be as full and complete as possible.

Whether, therefore, the two branches of the clause be construed separately or together, I think they import

1852.
January
Term.

Dickinson
v.
Hoomes's
adm'r
& als.

no more than a covenant of special warranty on the part of Richard Hoomes against the claims of persons claiming under him. This construction, instead of being weakened, will be strengthened and confirmed if we look to the whole deed, to the situation of the parties, and the relation which they respectively bore to the subject of the conveyance. It is not pretended that Richard Hoomes participated in any way whatever in the consideration which was paid for the land. He seems to have had no interest in the sale. He had a contingent interest in the land, which he was willing to relinquish to the purchaser; and he was willing also to warrant the land against all persons claiming under him as contingent devisee. He therefore joined in the execution of a deed containing such a relinquishment and covenant, expressed in words as apt and suitable as any that could have been used to express them. Would it be reasonable to depart from the strict and primary sense of these words, and place upon them a strained construction, for the purpose of making him relinquish, not only his own contingent right, but also the contingent rights of others; and covenant, not only against all persons claiming under him, but also against his children claiming as purchasers under their grandfather, and even against the whole world? It was an act of liberality on his part to have relinquished his own right without consideration. While he was willing to do that, he might not have been willing, and probably was not willing, to relinquish the rights of others or incur a personal liability on account of rights over which he had no control. An intention to make a relinquishment or incur a liability so extensive should be plainly expressed. If the words used are equivocal, and import, at least as strongly, a more limited and reasonable intention, they should be construed according to such latter intention. In this case we have seen that they import more strongly, if not plainly, an intention on

1852.
January
Term.

Dickinson
v.
Hoomes's
adm'r
& als.

the part of Richard Hoomes only to relinquish his own rights, and covenant against persons claiming under him.

It is quite probable that when Richard Hoomes executed the deed he had no idea that his children could have any claim as purchasers under their grandfather's will; but supposed, if he thought at all on the subject, that, in the event which has happened, they could only claim by descent from him. If he had then supposed that they would be entitled as purchasers in the event that has happened, and had intended· to relinquish their right, or rather to covenant against it, he would have expressed his intention in plain language, and not in words which import an intention only to relinquish his own right, and to covenant against persons claiming under him. The fact that he has used such words, I think conclusively shews that he intended only to relinquish his own right, and to covenant against persons claiming under him: and that, whether he supposed, or did not suppose, that his children would be entitled as purchasers in the event that has happened. If he so supposed, we have already seen that he would have used different language to have relinquished their right or covenanted against it. If he did not so suppose, then of course he only intended to relinquish his own right, and to covenant against persons claiming under him; for, not being aware of any right of his children, he could not have intended to relinquish or covenant against it. And considering himself the proprietor of the right which this court has since decided to be theirs, he must have considered the relinquishment of his own right and covenant against persons claiming under him as covering the whole ground.

Supposing that Richard Hoomes when he executed the deed was not aware of the rights of his children; whether or not he would have covenanted against it if he had been aware of it, is matter of conjecture mere-

1852.
January
Term.

Dickinson
v.
Hoomes's
adm'r
& als.

ly, and can have no influence in the decision of the question we are now endeavouring to solve; which is, whether he did actually covenant against it.

It has been argued with some force that John Hoomes, the vendor, having joined in the same covenant with the contingent devisees, it cannot be restricted as to the latter without being also restricted as to the former; which, it is thought, would be unreasonable. It does not, I think, follow, as a necessary consequence, that because the covenant of the vendor and contingent devisees is contained in the same clause, or even in the same words, it must therefore have the same extent as to both. Suppose, for example, that the latter part of the clause before quoted could be considered as importing a general warranty. *Redendo singula singulis*, the vendor, having conveyed the estate itself, might be considered as intending to warrant the estate itself, while the contingent devisees, having only relinquished their right as such, might be considered as intending to warrant only that right. But without deciding whether the covenant of warranty on the part of the vendor was general or special, I do not admit that an intention on his part to give a special covenant only would have been unreasonable; nor, if it would, that that consideration can have much, if any, effect on the construction of the covenant on the part of the contingent devisees. In England the covenants of the vendor are generally of a restricted nature. Lord Eldon, in *Browning* v. *Wright*, 2 Bos. & Pul. 23, thus describes the common course of business in such a case: "An abstract is laid before the purchaser's counsel; and though to a certain extent he relies on the vendor's covenants, still his chief attention is directed to ascertaining what is the estate, and how far it is supported by the title. The purchaser, therefore, not being misled by the vendor, makes up his mind whether he will complete his bargain or not, and if any doubts arise on the

1852.
January
Term.

Dickinson
v.
Hoomes's
adm'r
& als.

title, it rests with the vendor to determine whether he will satisfy those doubts by covenants more or less extensive. *Prima facie*, therefore, in the conveyance of an estate, we are led to expect no other covenants than those which guard against the acts of the vendor and his heirs." In Virginia the practice is different: and while, on the one hand, less attention is directed to the title than in England, so, on the other, a covenant of general warranty is usually required and given. Such a covenant seems not to be entitled to the importance which is attached to it by our practice; and it would doubtless be better, as in England, to pay more attention to the title, if not to attach less importance to a general warranty. But why in this case should a covenant of general warranty have been given? It was known both to vendor and vendee that the title of the former was not absolute. The vendor claimed under a will which was exhibited to the vendee, and under which his estate was subject to be defeated by his death without issue. Now, whether he intended to sell precisely such estate as he had, or to sell and warrant a greater estate than he had, was matter of contract between the parties: *Prima facie*, a vendor intends only to sell such estate as he has, where his estate is of a limited nature, or subject to a contingency. In this case the vendee might choose to run the risk of losing the estate in the event of the vendor's dying without issue, receiving, of course, an equivalent in an abatement of the price, rather than pay the price of the absolute estate, and rely on the covenant of the vendor for his indemnity. Unless the vendor had other estate than that devised to him by his father, his covenant of general warranty would have afforded little or no indemnity against the claim of the contingent devisees; for the same contingency which would occasion a breach of his covenant would deprive him of the means of paying damages therefor. The vendee would

1852.
January
Term.

Dickinson
v.
Hoomes's
adm'r
& als.

place little or no reliance on the covenant of the vendor as a means of indemnity in such a case, and unless
the contingent devisees would join in the deed, would
of course require an abatement of the price.   The contingent devisees did not all join in the deed, and to the
extent of the interest of those that did not join a proportionable abatement was doubtless made.   Whether
any abatement was made on account of the contingent
interest of the children of Richard Hoomes does not
appear.   Probably not, because probably no such contingent interest was known to exist.   But if no such
interest was known to exist, it is on that account more
probable that the vendee relied on the relinquishment
and covenant of Richard Hoomes, than on any covenant of John Hoomes, to protect him against an interest
which he then supposed to be vested entirely in Richard Hoomes.   In this case, therefore, a special covenant
on the part of John Hoomes would at least not have
been unreasonable.   But even if it would, it certainly
would not have been more so than a general covenant
on the part of Richard Hoomes.

I am therefore of opinion that the covenant of Richard Hoomes has not been broken; and if the other, or
even one of the other, judges agreed with me in this
opinion, it would be unnecessary for me to say anything
more; but as that is not the case, I must now proceed
to examine and consider the other questions.

2d.  Did the covenant run with the land; or has
Dickinson, the assignee of the land, a right of action for
a breach of the covenant?

It is a general rule of the common law that *choses
in action* are not assignable.   But to this general rule
there are exceptions, one of which is, that covenants
running with land pass with the land to the assignee
thereof.   Of the covenants usually contained in a conveyance of land, some run with the land and some do
not.   Those which are broken, if at all, at the instant

1852.
January
Term.

Dickinson
v.
Hoomes's
adm'r
& als.

of their being made, such as the covenant of *seisin*, of *right to convey*, or *against incumbrances*, do not run with the land; while those which may be broken afterwards, such as the covenant of *warranty*, for *quiet enjoyment*, or for *further assurance*, do run with the land. But even the latter, when broken, cease to run with the land from the time they are broken; for a broken covenant is a mere *chose in action*, which by the common law is not assignable; being no longer inherent in the land, which alone gives to the covenant its assignable quality. The covenant of Richard Hoomes was a covenant of warranty, and was not broken at the time of the assignment of the land to Dickinson; it therefore passed with the land to him, unless prevented from so passing by the objection that the estate conveyed to him was insufficient to support the covenant, or the objection that no estate at all passed to him from Richard Hoomes, the covenantor. Let us first examine the objection (if in fact such an objection can be considered as having been made) that the estate conveyed to Dickinson was insufficient to support the covenant of warranty, even on the part of John Hoomes, the grantor of the estate. That it is necessary that some estate should be vested in the covenantee, to make a covenant of warranty effectual even between the contracting parties, is undoubtedly true, and results from the very nature of that covenant. The covenants of *seisin* and of *right to convey* are effectual covenants, though no estate be vested in the covenantee; because they are broken, if at all, at the instant of their being made, without any further act or default of the covenantor. But the covenant of warranty and of quiet enjoyment, which are the same in effect, can only be broken by an eviction or ouster by title paramount. They therefore presuppose the *possession* of an estate by the covenantee, and of course cannot be effectual where no such possession has passed to him. A deed

1852.
January
Term.

Dickinson
v.
Hoomes's-
adm'r
& als.

purporting to convey land which is in the adverse possession of a third person will not only not support a
covenant of warranty, but is altogether null and void.
But if the grantor be in possession of the land at the
time of the execution of the deed, his possession and
his estate, whatever it may be, will pass to the grantee,
and will support a covenant of warranty contained in
the deed. This distinction is well illustrated by the
case of *Slater* v. *Rawson*, 1 Metc. R. 450, and again
in 6 Metc. 439. By the deed, in which a covenant of
general warranty was contained, in that case, a tract of
land containing 130 acres was conveyed by metes and
bounds. A man named Jacobs had a title paramount to
22 acres of the land, which was therefore yielded up to
him by the assignee of the land; who thereupon
brought an action on the covenant of warranty. The
defendant contended that he was never seised of the
land in controversy, and that therefore nothing passed
by his deed. A verdict was rendered for the plaintiff
on a question reserved by the judge. The Supreme
court awarded a new trial. Dewey, J., in delivering the
opinion of the court, after stating that the defendant
at the time of making his conveyance had no legal title
to the 22 acres of land, proceeds to enquire whether
the defendant was seised in fact, and uses the following
language: " The case as stated by the parties, in the
report, finds that the premises, which are the subject of
this controversy, were a part of a large tract of wood
land unenclosed by fences, and of which there had
been no actual occupation by any of the parties. Taking these facts to be correctly stated, there was clearly
no seisin in fact in the defendant, acquired by an entry
and adverse possession. The rule as to lands that are
vacant and unoccupied, that the legal seisin follows the
title, seems to be applicable here; and having ascertained in whom is the legal title, that also determines
in whom the seisin is." " The covenant of warranty

1852.
January
Term

Dickinson
v.
Hoomes's
adm'r
& als.

is wholly ineffectual, as no land passed to which it could be annexed; and the result, therefore, from this view of the case, is that the plaintiff cannot maintain his action." 1 Metc. R. 456–7. On the new trial evidence was offered to prove that the defendant and his father, under whom he claimed, had exercised acts of ownership on the land, and that he was in fact seised and possessed thereof at the time of the execution of the deed. A verdict was rendered for the plaintiff as before, subject to the opinion of the Supreme court. That court rendered judgment on the verdict. Wilde, J., in delivering the opinion of the court, after reviewing the evidence, says: " It therefore clearly appears by the evidence that the defendant, at the time of his conveyance, had the actual possession of the premises, and that he had a valid title against all the world, except the true owner of the Jacobs lot. If any other person had entered on the land in dispute, he might have maintained trespass against him; or if he had been ousted he might have maintained a writ of entry. But the defendant's counsel contend that although he had possession of the land in dispute, yet he had not such a possession as would amount to a disseisin of Jacobs, who afterwards entered on the premises and ousted the plaintiffs; and therefore that the defendant was never actually seised of the land in dispute, and that no title thereto passed by his deed to the grantees; so that the covenant of warranty could not run with the land and pass to their assignees." The learned judge, after making several observations and citing various authorities relating to the legal difference between seisin and possession, further says: " It is not necessary, however, in the present case to decide the question whether there is any legal distinction between the words *seisin* and *possession*; for if the defendant was in possession when he conveyed, &c., claiming to hold the whole land conveyed, he had a good right to convey his title,

1852.
January
Term.

Dickinson
v.
Hoomes's
adm'r
& als.

whatever it was. His estate passed by his deed to the grantees, and all his covenants were binding." "It is universally true that a party in possession of land, claiming title, may make a legal conveyance, and his title by possession will pass to his grantee. Actual possession of property gives a good title against a stranger having no title."

In *Beddoe* v. *Wadsworth*, 21 Wend. R. 120, the Supreme court of New York decided that "an assignee of covenants of warranty and for quiet enjoyment may maintain an action on the covenants where possession is taken under the deed and there is a subsequent eviction, although at the time of the execution of the deed the grantor had no title." To the same effect also is the case of *Fowler* v. *Poling*, 2 Barb. R. 300, and 6 Barb. R. 165.

If a covenant of warranty contained in a deed executed by a person in possession of land did not run with the land, where there is an outstanding paramount title, the most serious inconveniences would follow. The covenant of warranty is the only covenant inserted in many, if not most, of the deeds that are executed in this country, and, according to the general understanding of our people, it runs with the land, and may be resorted to for the indemnity of the holder whenever he is evicted by title paramount. As I have already had occasion to remark, more attention is paid to the covenant of warranty and less to the title with us than in England. A purchaser is often satisfied, without looking further into title, when he finds that several of the deeds under which he claims contain the covenants of warranty of persons, in the continuance of whose responsibility he has perfect confidence. But of what value would be these covenants if an outstanding paramount title would render them ineffectual? They could only be broken by an eviction or ouster by title paramount; and yet the very existence of such an out-

1852.
January
Term.

Dickinson
v.
Hoomes's
adm'r
& als.

standing title would render the covenant ineffectual! So far from affording any protection to the assignee, they would afford none even to the covenantee. In some cases they might be of benefit, as, for instance, where an actual disseisin of the rightful owner by the grantor could be proved. But this limitation would so curtail the operation of the covenant, and throw so much doubt and difficulty over it, as to render it of little value.

I think, therefore, that reason and authority unite in shewing that wherever the deed passes the possession the covenant of warranty is effectual and runs with the land.

The case of *Randolph* v. *Kinney*, 3 Rand. 394, is not in conflict, but in accordance, with the distinction I have referred to. In that case all the parties claimed under Stuart, who was the proprietor of 331 acres of land. In 1748 Stuart conveyed 57 acres of the land to James Miller. In 1763 Stuart conveyed the whole 331 acres to John Miller; thus including the 57 acres he had before conveyed to James Miller. In 1784 John Miller conveyed the whole 331 acres to Randolph, who in 1808 conveyed it to Kinney. Judge Carr, in his opinion, in which the other judges concurred, uses the following language: "Those claiming the 57 acre tract, under the deed of 1748 from Stuart to James Miller, were in possession by virtue of that conveyance. The subsequent deed, therefore, from Stuart to John Miller, for the whole tract, although it included these 57 acres, could pass neither the possession nor the title: and as Miller had neither possession nor title to these 57 acres, he could convey neither to Randolph, nor Randolph to Kinney. The clauses of general warranty in the deeds from Stuart to John Miller, and from Randolph to Kinney, could not operate as real covenants, unless the vendees entered; and could pass to the assignee only along with the land and as

1852.
January
Term.

Dickinson
v.
Hoomes's
adm'r
& als.

incident to it. But here, the land not passing, the warranty could not pass. A disseisor may convey and warrant the land; for there may be a fee simple in a disseisor. But a person against whom there is an adversary possession cannot make a warranty which will pass to an assignee, because he cannot convey." Thus it is manifest that the opinion of Judge Carr, that the warranty in that case was ineffectual, was based entirely on the fact that the possession of the land in controversy, at the time of the conveyance, was adversary, and therefore did not pass to the grantee.

If a covenant of warranty contained in a conveyance from a person in possession, but without title, is effectual and will run with the land, it would seem, *a fortiori*, that where the grantor is not only in possession, but has a title to the land, though not such a title as is conveyed and warranted to the purchaser, the covenant of warranty will be effectual and will run with the land. On this subject see the notes of the American editor to Smith's Leading Cases, 43 Law Lib., p. 122, citing the case of *Balley* v. *Wells*, 3 Wils. P. 36. The case of *Andrew* v. *Pearce*, 4 Bos. & Pul. 158, might seem at first view to be a contrary decision. But in that case the lease for years by a tenant in tail had become void by the termination of the estate in tail, and after it had thus become void it was assigned to the plaintiff. The land was not conveyed, but the lease was assigned to the assignee. And Sir James Mansfield, Ch. J., said: " The lease is stated to have become absolutely void by the death of Peter Best, without heir male. The lease, then, having become absolutely void, what could be the operation of the assignment by Bennett to Andrew? He could neither assign the lease nor any interest under it, because the lease was gone. What right of any sort had Bennett? If any thing, it could only be a right of ac-

1852.
January
Term.

Dickinson
v.
Hoomes's
adm'r
& als.

tion on the covenant, and that could not be assigned by law," &c. Now, in the case under consideration, John Hoomes the younger, at the time of his conveyance, was seised of an estate in fee, though defeasible; and he conveyed an estate in fee simple with covenant of warranty. So far, therefore, as John Hoomes, the grantor of the estate, is concerned, it seems to be as strong a case as well could be to make a covenant of warranty effectual, and run with the land.

But it is objected that the covenant under consideration was made by Richard Hoomes, and that no estate passed from him to the covenantee. Let us now examine this objection, which was chiefly relied on in the argument. It can hardly be said that no estate passed from Richard Hoomes; or, at all events, that he was a stranger to the subject matter of the contract and the conveyance. He had in fact an interest in the subject—an interest which depended on the double contingency of John's dying without issue living at his death, and of Richard's surviving him. The parties doubtless supposed that his interest was even greater than it was, and that it depended on the single contingency of John's dying without issue living at his death. This court, however, has decided that his interest depended on the double contingency aforesaid. 1 Gratt., p. 302. If that double contingency had occurred, the deed would have operated, at least by estoppel, to pass the interest of Richard Hoomes to the purchaser, and the covenant would then undoubtedly have run with the land. But as John was seised with the estate in fee, and conveyed it with covenant of warranty, Richard's joining in the deed was a confirmation of the conveyance, so far as he was concerned; and if it be necessary, to make a covenant run with the land, that some estate should pass from the covenantor to the covenantee, I think it might well be contended that this case comes up to the requisition.

1852.
January
Term.

Dickinson
v.
Hoomes's
adm'r
& als.

But is it necessary that some estate should pass from the covenantor to the covenantee in order that the covenant may run with the land? I think not. In the notes of the learned English annotator to *Spencer's Case*, 43 Law Lib., p. 99, he says: " Where such a covenant (that is a covenant for something relating to the land) is made, it seems to be of no consequence whether the covenantor be the person who conveyed the land to the covenantee, or be a mere stranger. Thus in the *Prior's Case* reported in the text, and in Co. Litt. 384 b, the Prior was a stranger to the land of the covenantee; and there is a good reason for this assigned in the above passage in Co. Litt., where the law is said to be so, *to give damages to the party grieved ;* in other words, in order that the person who is injured by the non-performance of the covenant, who is always the owner of the land *pro tempore*, may be also the person entitled to the remedy upon it by action." But while, on the one hand, it seems that the *benefit* of a covenant runs with the land, though the covenantor be a stranger to the land ; so, on the other, it would seem that the *burden* of a covenant in no case runs with the land ; in no case, I mean, in which the relation of landlord and tenant is not created by the deed. In regard to covenants entered into by the owners of land, the same learned annotator says: " Great doubt exists whether these in any case run with the lands so as to bind the assignees of the covenantor. One inconvenience which would be the result of holding them to do so is, that the assignee would frequently find himself liable to contracts of the very existence of which he was ignorant, and which perhaps would have deterred him from accepting a conveyance of the land, if he had known of them ; and the reason assigned in the first Institute for allowing the *benefit* of a covenant relating to the land to run therewith, viz., to give the remedy to the *party grieved,* does not apply to the question respecting the

1852.
January
Term.

Dickinson
v.
Hoomes's
adm'r
& als.

*burden* thereof." Id., p. 101. See also the notes of the American annotator. Id., p. 137. The law is laid down to the same effect in 2 Lomax's Dig., p. 260, § 29, 30, 31. The principle thus stated by these profound jurists is opposed by no authority I have met with, and is most consonant with reason and conscience. There may have been good reason under the feudal constitution for requiring that the warranty should accompany the estate and exist only between the donor and donee. But the technical warranty which formerly existed has been altogether disused, if not abolished; and its place is now supplied by covenants, which better suit the present condition of things. I can see no reason why these covenants, if in their nature they are such as can run with the land, should not run with the land as well when they are made by a stranger as when they are made by the donor; but I can see many reasons for the contrary. A person may be willing to purchase land notwithstanding a flaw in the title, if he can fortify it by proper covenants. The owner may not be sufficiently responsible, but may be able to procure the assistance of responsible friends, or creditors, or others may have sufficient interest to join him in the covenants. But what would these covenants be worth if they could not be enforced by an assignee of the land? A covenant of *seisin*, or of *right to convey*, would never be given in such a case, because it would be known to the parties that as soon as made it would be *ipso facto* broken. A covenant of *warranty*, or for *quiet enjoyment*, would be the most appropriate covenant for such a case; and yet, to make that covenant effectual, it would be necessary, according to the doctrine contended for, that the covenantee should always retain the property.

I am therefore of opinion that the covenant of Richard Hoomes runs with the land, even though he should be considered as a stranger to the land. It is perhaps proper that I should express the opinion I entertain, that

1852.
January
Term.

Dickinson
v.
Hoomes's
adm'r
& als.

even if the covenant did not run with the land, an assignee would have a right to enforce it for his benefit
in the name of the covenantee. " Where the covenants
entered into with a purchaser are covenants in gross,
and he afterwards sells, the purchaser from him, being
entitled to the benefit of the former covenants, can compel him to allow his name to be used for the purpose of
enforcing the covenants." This is the language of Sir
Edward Sugden, 2 Sug. on Vend. 726; and the authority he cites for it is *Riddell* v. *Riddell*, 10 Cond.
Eng. Ch. R. 183. I am also of opinion that if there be
an unbroken chain of covenants of the same kind, run-
ing through all the *mesne* conveyances, even though
they be not covenants running with the land, a court
of equity will give the assignee the benefit of any of
the remoter ones. " A court of equity will make the
party immediately liable who is or may be, at law or
in equity, made ultimately liable. Thus, for example,
if a *chose in action*, not negotiable at all, or not negotiable by the local law, except to create a legal right of
action between the immediate debtor or endorser and
his immediate endorser or assignee, should be passed to
a remote assignee or endorsee, the latter would be entitled in equity directly to sue the party who was ultimately or circuitously liable for the debt to the antecedent holder or creditor." This is the language of Story,
2 Equ. Jur. § 1250; and the authority he cites in illustration of it is the case of *Riddle* v. *Mandeville*, 5
Cranch's R. 322. See also 43 Law Library, p. 122, and
the case there cited of *Nesbit* v. *Brown*, 1 Dev. Eq. R.
30. This equitable doctrine is not opposed by the case
of *Randolph* v. *Kinney*, 3 Rand. 394. In that case
there was not an unbroken chain of covenants of the
same kind. The only covenant which appears to have
been contained in the deed to Randolph, who asserted
the equity, was a covenant for quiet enjoyment. And
that was never of any effect, because the land in con-

1852.
January
Term.

Dickinson
v.
Hoomes's
adm'r
& als.

troversy never came to the possession of Randolph, but remained in the adversary possession of another, in whose possession it was when conveyed to Randolph. There was, then, no starting point; no foundation for the equity to rest upon.

But it is said that only a portion, though much the greater portion, of the land conveyed by John Hoomes the younger to Apperson, was conveyed by the latter to Dickinson; and one of the learned counsel for the appellees relies on a defence, which he admits to be technical, and for which no authority is to be found except in a work of Preston, viz., that a covenant cannot be apportioned. That writer, who, as the counsel properly says, is a very great authority, does certainly say that " when the property is subdivided by sales it seems to follow from a maxim in law that the purchasers lose the benefit of the former covenants, on the ground that the remedy cannot be apportioned; or, in more correct terms, the covenantor cannot be subjected to several actions. Thus when a man sells two farms to A, and covenants with him, his heirs and assigns, and one of these farms is sold by A to B, B can never sue on this covenant, since it would subject the covenantor to several actions." 3 Preston Abstr. 56, 58; 2 Lomax 263–4, note. But, as one of the learned counsel for the appellants properly remarked, Preston seems to contradict this position in another part of his work, when he says that covenants which run with the land are not extinguished by apportionment of the land into parcels among several purchasers and owners. The position is not only unsupported by any other authority than that of Preston, but it is opposed by an array of authority no less imposing than his. Sugden, after quoting the observation of Preston, says: " The better opinion, however, seems to be, that an alienee of one of the estates could maintain covenant against the covenantor where the covenants run with the land." It does not seem that any injus-

1852.
January
Term.

Dickinson
v.
Hoomes's
adm'r
& als.

tice would arise by suffering several covenants to lie, although it might expose the covenantor to inconvenience; whereas the denial of the right to each assignee might lead to positive injustice, or, if not, to greater inconvenience on their part." 2 Sug. on Vend. 743, pl. 91, 92. See also *Kane* v. *Sanger*, 14 John R. 89, and authorities cited; *Van Horne* v. *Crain*, 1 Paige's R. 455; *Astor* v. *Miller*, 2 Paige's R. 68. It is true, as a general principle of law, that covenants are not apportionable; and so also is it true, as a general principle of law, that covenants are not assignable. But as covenants which run with land are assignable, because the land itself is assignable, so also it would seem that covenants which run with land are apportionable, because the land itself is apportionable. A covenant running with land would be of very little value if it ceased to run with the land whenever the land was divided, whether by act of law or by the act of the owner. We know that covenants for the payment of rent are apportionable, both by act of law and by the acts of parties. 8 Bac. Abr., Rent., M. And for the same reason why may not other covenants be apportioned? The rule of law that covenants are not apportionable is founded on convenience. But injustice is a greater evil than inconvenience. And wherever justice, or even greater convenience, requires that a covenant should be apportioned, it would seem to be reasonable that the general rule should bend and admit of an exception.

3dly. I come now to the consideration of the question, "whether lands descended in Kentucky could be regarded as assets by descent in any proceeding in Virginia?"

"Freehold land of inheritance, descended to a person's heir at law, is, by the common law, assets for the payment of the ancestor's debts by specialty, as by bond or covenant, in which his heirs are bound." Ram on Assets 214, 8 Law Library 144. The common law in

1852.
January
Term.

Dickinson
v.
Hoomes's
adm'r
& als.

this respect was the law of Virginia when it embraced
the territory which now constitutes the State of Kentucky.  It has been the policy of all, or nearly all, the
States of the Union to extend, and not to restrict, the
liability of land for the payment of debts.  While in
our own State that policy has not progressed so rapidly
as in some of the other, and especially in most of the
western States, it has at length reached the point of
subjecting an intestate's land to the payment of all his
debts.  In the absence, therefore, of all evidence on the
subject, it would be presumable that in Kentucky land
is liable for the payment of debts, at least to the extent
to which it is liable at the common law; especially if
that liability sought to be enforced by the bill should
not be denied by the answer.  But in this case it is
proved affirmatively by John C. Herndon, a lawyer of
that State, that by the law of that State, which existed
in 1823 when Richard Hoomes died, and has ever since
existed, freehold land of inheritance descending from
an intestate " can be subjected to the payment of the
intestate's debts, either by proceedings in law or chancery."  It is also proved by him that as early as 1798 an
act was passed, which is still in force in that State, containing a provision similar to 1 Rev. Code, ch. 99, § 21,
that " if the deed of the alienor doth mention that he
and his heirs be bound to warranty, and if any heritage
descend to the demandant of the side of the alienor,
then he shall be bound for the value of the heritage
that is to him descended," &c.  This last provision having been the law of Virginia when Kentucky was or-
ganized as an independent State, the probability is that
it never ceased for a moment to be the law of the latter State, and that the said act of 1798 was merely a
continuation or re-enactment of an existing law.  Without any proof of such re-enactment it would have been
fair to presume that the provision continued to exist as
a part of the Kentucky law.  It is contended by one

1852.
January
Term.

Dickinson
v.
Hoomes's
adm'r
& als.

of the counsel for the appellees that the Kentucky laws
in question being statute laws, the evidence of Herndon
is inadmissible ; no foundation having been laid for its
introduction as secondary evidence, by proof of inability to obtain copies of the statutes.   The citation from
Story's Conflict of Laws, § 637, 641, certainly gives
support to the position that, as a general rule, a foreign
statute law must be proved by an authentic copy, if to
be had.   The courts of some of the States, and the
Supreme court of the United States, are of opinion
" that the connexion, intercourse and constitutional ties
which bind together these several States, require some
relaxation of the strictness of this rule," and " have accordingly held that a printed volume, purporting on the
face of it to contain the laws of a sister State, is admissible as *prima facie* evidence to prove the statute laws
of that State."   1 Greenl. Ev. § 489, and cases cited
in note 2, among which is the case of *Taylor* v. *Bank
of Alexandria*, 5 Leigh 471.   But I incline to think
that the doctrine of primary and secondary evidence
does not apply to the case, and that a foreign law,
whether written or unwritten, may be proved by a person who is learned in that law, without laying any
foundation for the introduction of secondary evidence.
This is the principle of a late decision of the Court of
Queen's Bench, cited by one of the counsel for the appellants from 55 Eng. C. L. R. 250, 267.   As was said
by one of the judges in that case, " the general principle
does not seem to apply to the case.   What, in truth, is
it that we ask the witness?   Not to tell us what the
written law states ; but, generally, what the law is.
The question is not as to the language of the written
law : For when that language is before us we have no
means by which we are to construe it."   " How many
errors might result if a foreign court attempted to collect the law from the language of some of our statutes
which declare instruments in particular cases to be null

1852.
January
Term.

Dickinson
v.
Hoomes's
adm'r
& als.

and void to all intents and purposes, while an English lawyer would state that they are good against the grantor, and that the courts have so expounded the statutes! It is no answer to say that other evidence by word of mouth may be added for the purpose of giving the interpretation of the written law. I am merely shewing that our courts require, not the actual written words of a foreign law, but the law itself; for which purpose a professional witness is required to expound it." But the evidence of Herndon not having been objected to in the court below, (in which case authenticated copies of the statutes might have been exhibited,) it would seem to be too late to make the objection in this court.

Whether, therefore, we look to the evidence of Herndon or not, I think it must be regarded as the law of Kentucky, that any land in that State which may have descended from Richard Hoomes to his heirs at law is assets for the payment of what may be due upon his covenant of warranty in this case; and that if the land to which the covenant is annexed were situate in the State of Kentucky, the heirs of the covenantor, in an action brought by them to recover that land, would be barred for the value of the land to them descended.

But the land to which the covenant is annexed being situate, and the suit for its recovery by the heirs of the covenantor being brought, in Virginia, the question is, whether the land descended to them in Kentucky is assets, and whether they ought to be bound for the value of the said land descended to them, at least to the extent to which it has actually come to their hands.

I think this question should be answered in the affirmative. It is undoubtedly true that real estate, or immovable property, is exclusively subject to the laws of the government within whose territory it is situate; and that no writ of sequestration or execution, or any order, judgment, or decree of a foreign court, can be en-

1852.
January
Term.

Dickinson
v.
Hoomes's
adm'r
& als.

forced against it. But I think it is no less true "that equity, as it acts primarily *in personam*, and not merely *in rem*, may, where a person against whom relief is sought is within the jurisdiction, make a decree upon the ground of a contract, or any equity subsisting between the parties respecting property situated out of the jurisdiction." In this very language the principle is stated by White and Tudor in their notes to leading equity cases, Law Library, May 1851, p. 319; and the authorities to which they and the American editors refer seem fully to sustain the principle.

In the case of *Massie* v. *Watts*, 6 Cranch's R. 148, Marshall, Ch. J. reviews the principal cases, commencing with the celebrated case of *Penn* v. *Lord Baltimore*, 1 Ves. sr. 444, and concludes, "upon the authority of these cases, and of others which are to be found in the books, as well as upon general principles, that in a case of fraud, of trust, or of contract, the jurisdiction of a court of chancery is sustainable wherever the person may be found, although lands not within the jurisdiction of that court may be affected by the decree." "The circumstance," to use his language in another part of the case, "that a question of title may be involved in the enquiry, and may even constitute the essential point on which the case depends, does not seem sufficient to arrest that jurisdiction." In the case of *Mitchell* v. *Burch*, 2 Paige's R. 615, the chancellor says : "Although the property of a defendant is beyond the reach of the court, so that it can neither be sequestered or taken in execution, the court does not lose its jurisdiction in relation to that property, provided the person of the defendant is within the jurisdiction. By the ordinary course of proceeding, the defendant may be compelled either to bring the property in dispute, or to which the complainant claims an equitable title, within the jurisdiction of the court, or to execute such a conveyance or transfer thereof as will be sufficient to vest the legal

1852.
January
Term.

Dickinson
v.
Hoomes's
adm'r
& als.

title, as well as the possession of the property, according
to the *lex loci rei sitæ.*  See also *Mead* v. *Merrit*, Id.
404.  These principles have been recognized in Virginia, so far as we have had any adjudications on the
subject.  In the case of *Farley* v. *Shippen*, Wythe's
R. 135, Chancellor Wythe decreed that the defendants,
who resided in Virginia, were trustees for the benefit of
the plaintiffs of certain lands in North Carolina, and
should convey the same to them.  " If," said the chancellor in that case, " an act performed by a party in
Virginia, who ought to perform it, will be effectual to
convey land in North Carolina, why may not a court
of equity in Virginia decree that party, regularly
brought before that tribunal, to perform the act ?  Some
of the defendant's counsel supposed that such a decree
would be deemed by our brethren of North Carolina an
invasion of their sovereignty.  To this shall be allowed
the force of a good objection, if those who urge it will
prove that the sovereignty of that State will be violated
by the Virginia court of equity decreeing a party
within its jurisdiction to perform an act there, which
act voluntarily performed any where would not be
such a violation.  The defendant's counsel objected
also, that the court cannot, in execution of its decree,
award a writ of sequestration against the lands in North
Carolina, because its precepts are not authorities there.
But this, which is admitted to be true, doth not prove
that the court cannot make the decree ; because, although it cannot award such a writ of sequestration, it
hath power confessedly to award an attachment for
contempt in refusing to perform the decree."  In
*Guerrant* v. *Fowler*, 1 Hen. & Munf. 5, Chancellor
Taylor approved the principles of the case of *Farley*
v. *Shippen*, and decreed accordingly.

Immovable property being subject to the laws of the
government within whose territory it is situate, the
question whether and to what extent it is liable to the

claims of a plaintiff must of course be determined according to those laws. Therefore, where the suit is brought in a country different from that in which the property is situate, the court, in giving relief, must to that extent administer foreign law. This may be an inconvenience, but it is no objection to the jurisdiction of the court, and is preferable to that failure of justice which would arise from a refusal to interfere in such cases. Courts, in the administration of justice, are in many cases bound to execute foreign laws. Where a suit is brought in one country on a contract made in another, the *lex loci contractus* governs the case. Where a citizen of one country dies, leaving personal property in another, the *lex domicilii* governs the succession and distribution of the property. In the latter case the domiciliary administrator cannot recover property situated out of the limits of the jurisdiction from which he derived his appointment. An auxiliary administrator must be appointed by the jurisdiction in whose limits the property is situate; and he is responsible for the property, not to the domiciliary administrator, but directly to creditors, legatees and distributees. In a suit brought by legatees or distributees to enforce that responsibility, the *lex domicilii* must be ascertained and administered by the court. *Harvey* v. *Richards*, 1 Mason's R. 381, was such a suit, and in it the law of Bengal, which was the place of the domicil, was ascertained and administered.

An heir who has assets by descent, which are liable by the *lex loci* to the payment of the ancestor's debts, may be considered, to the extent of the assets, as a debtor by contract to the creditors, and also as a trustee of the subject for their benefit. His case, therefore, as well upon the ground of trust as of contract, seems to be embraced by the principle as laid down by the Chief Justice in *Massie* v. *Watts*, "that in a case of fraud, of trust, or of contract, the jurisdiction of a court of chan-

1852.
January
Term.

Dickinson
v.
Hoomes's
adm'r
& als.

1852.
January
Term.

Dickinson
v.
Hoomes's
adm'r
& als.

cery is sustainable wherever the person may be found, although lands not within the jurisdiction of that court may be affected by the decree." It is true the creditors have no lien upon the land descended, and a *bona fide* purchaser of it from the heir is entitled to hold it against the claims of creditors. But the heir was always bound in equity, and for a long time has been bound at law, to the extent of the purchase money. An heir, in regard to the assets descended, is as much a debtor by contract, and a trustee for the benefit of the creditors whose claims bind the heirs, as an executor is in regard to the assets in his hands. In the case of *Tunstall* v. *Pollard*, 11 Leigh 1, it was decided by this court that an executor having taken probat of the testator's will and letters testamentary in England, and collected the assets of the testator's estate there, and brought them with him to Virginia, but having never qualified as executor in Virginia, is liable to be sued by the legatees in the court of chancery of Virginia for an account of his administration, and for the legacies that remain unpaid. There would seem to be less difficulty in maintaining a suit against an heir in respect of foreign assets than a suit against a foreign executor, even in respect of assets brought with him to the country in which the suit is brought. An heir is a *quasi* personal debtor, liable to be sued in the *debet* and *detinet*. His obligation attaches to his person, and follows him wherever he goes. The only difference between him and an ordinary debtor is the extent of his responsibility, which is limited not only by the nominal amount of the contract, but also by the value of the assets descended. He holds the assets in his own right, and as his own property. An executor, on the other hand, acts under a commission, and is accountable to the jurisdiction from which he received it. It was contended with very great force, in the case of *Tunstall* v. *Pollard*, that the executor is accountable exclusively to the jurisdiction from which he receives his commission. But the court overruled the objection. President Tucker, in delivering an opinion in which a majority of the court concurred, after admitting that the administration of the assets must be governed by foreign law, and repelling the objection arising from the difficulty of ascertaining that law, remarks: " Whatever of difficulty or inconvenience may be fancied to exist in the execution of this duty, it weighs little in the balance in comparison with the burden which would be imposed upon creditors and distributees by refusing cognizance of their cases here, though the person and the property are both in our power, and sending them to sue in a foreign country from which the executor has absconded with the whole of the assets in his pocket. How shall they sue him there when he is not within the jurisdiction? How shall they reach the assets there when he has eloigned them ?" P. 29. " Upon the whole, then, it appears that in subjecting the executor to suit, who has brought the assets into this jurisdiction, no mischief will arise; while the contrary doctrine will protect an executor (who quits the country where he administered and comes over to this country with the assets) from all claim whatsoever. If he cannot be sued here, he can be sued nowhere; since the foreign court can have no longer power over him when his person and his effects are both beyond its reach."

1852.
January
Term.

Dickinson
v.
Hoomes's
adm'r
& als.

An heir cannot be sued at law in respect of foreign assets, because the writ of *extendi facias*, which is the only execution against the heir on a judgment at law, cannot be enforced *extra territorium*. But courts of law and equity have concurrent jurisdiction of suits against heirs. And though some of the modern means whereby a decree of a court of equity may be enforced can have no operation *extra territorium*, yet the ancient process of attachment may still be resorted to for the purpose of enforcing the performance of a decree ; and will gen-

1852.
January
Term.

Dickinson
v.
Hoomes's
adm'r
& als.

erally be found effectual whenever the person who is
to perform the decree is within the jurisdiction of the
court. The court will give to the suitor all the redress
within its power, and will not be deterred from doing so
by the consideration that it cannot act *in rem* as well
as *in personam*. I think, therefore, a suit in equity may
be maintained against the heir whenever his person is
within the jurisdiction of the court. Ordinarily, the
court in whose jurisdiction the defendant resides would
be the most convenient court for him; for, in the language of Chancellor Wythe in *Farley* v. *Shippen*, "a
case can rarely if ever occur, the discussion of which
can be so convenient to the defendant in any other as
in his own country." But cases may sometimes occur
in which, all things considered, it may be more convenient to turn over the parties to a foreign jurisdiction.
The ancestor may reside and die abroad, leaving all
his family and estate in the place of his domicil. One
of his heirs may remove to this country or be casually
here, and be sued here for a debt binding the heirs. In
such a case justice as well as convenience would require that the suit should be brought where most of the
heirs reside, where the executor resides, where the property is situate, and where, therefore, the accounts can
more conveniently be settled, the law which governs
the case be better ascertained, and the decree be more
effectually enforced. "It may be admitted," says Story, Justice, in the case of *Harvey* v. *Richards*, 1 Mason's R. 381, 409, "that a court of equity ought not
to be the instrument of injustice, and that if, in the
given case, such would be the effect of its interposition,
it ought to withhold its arm. This, however, would be
an objection, not to the general authority, but to the exercise of it under particular circumstances." Under
such circumstances the court, in the exercise of a sound
discretion, should dismiss a creditor's bill against the
heir, without prejudice to any suit he may bring in the

1852.
January
Term.

Dickinson
v.
Hoomes's
adm'r
& als.

place of the domicil. But, on the other hand, cases may occur in which justice as well as convenience would require the suit to be brought in the country in which the heirs reside; though the land sought to be affected is situated in another country. Nay, cases may occur in which there would be an absolute failure of justice if the suit were not so brought. Suppose the ancestor lives and dies in Virginia, leaving all his heirs here, and all his creditors here, and all his estate here except some wild lands in another State, and suppose the heirs sell these lands, receive the proceeds and bring them to Virginia, could not a suit in equity be maintained in Virginia by the creditors against the heirs? In the language of Story, J., in the case of *Harvey* v. *Richards*, "the property is here, the parties are here, and the rule of distribution is fixed. What reason then exists why the court should not proceed to decree according to the rights of the parties? Why should it send our own citizens to a foreign tribunal to seek that justice which it is in its own power to administer without injustice to any other person." Indeed it may be said, in language similar to that of Tucker, President, in *Tunstall* v. *Pollard*, " if the heirs in the case supposed cannot be sued here, they can be sued nowhere; since the foreign court can have no longer power over them when their persons and effects are both beyond its reach." But suppose further, that the heirs, having sold the lands and brought the proceeds here, bring a suit in equity in this State to recover land conveyed by their ancestor with covenant of warranty binding the heirs, could not the defendant in that suit defend himself by averring and shewing that the value of the land was already in the hands of the heirs in the form of money arising from the sale of lands in another State descended to them from the same ancestor and liable by the laws of that State for the payment of the ancestor's debts? It may be said that the cases supposed are extreme cases.

1852.
January
Term.

Dickinson
v.
Hoomes's
adm'r
& als.

And yet they are very much like the case under consideration, if lands in Kentucky in fact descended from Richard Hoomes to his heirs at law; a question which will be presently considered. To say that because in some cases it might be inconvenient to exercise such a jurisdiction, it should therefore be exercised in no case whatever, would be to say that positive and certain injustice should be permitted to be done for the purpose of avoiding a possible inconvenience. The question whether the court will give relief in any given case is, in the language of Story, J., in *Harvey* v. *Richards*, " a matter, not of jurisdiction, but of judicial discretion, depending upon the particular circumstances of each case."

The exercise of such a jurisdiction would be no invasion of the sovereignty in whose jurisdiction the property is situate, and no violation or obstruction of its laws. On the contrary, it would rather tend to execute and enforce those laws. Its object is to enforce a contract, or trust, or liability, created, or recognized, or permitted by those laws, against persons who are out of the limits of the jurisdiction where the property is situate. It supplies a remedy when otherwise there might be none, and is auxiliary, instead of adversary, to the foreign jurisdiction. No sovereignty would object to the exercise of such a jurisdiction. The citizens of that sovereignty might be deeply interested in its exercise. Suppose the ancestor dies in another State, leaving his land, his heir and his creditors there; and that the heir sells the land, receives the money and comes to our State to reside. Would our court of equity deny relief to the creditors in such a case? Would not national comity as well as justice require it to give such relief? And yet the motives and reasons for giving relief would be much stronger in a case in which the ancestor, heir and creditors all resided in our own country. If the sovereignty of the *situs* would not, as it could not, object to the exercise of jurisdiction by our court in the former case, it certainly would not in the latter.

1852.
January
Term.

Dickinson
v.
Hoomes's
adm'r
& als.

Nor would the exercise of such a jurisdiction be apt
to produce any conflict of authority between the tribunals of different States; or to expose the defendant to
a multiplicity of suits or a double liability.   As was
well said by one of the counsel for the appellant, the
heir may protect himself by his pleas, whether the land
lies in Virginia or elsewhere; and where the land lies
elsewhere, a court of equity will take especial care that
he be not subjected to a double charge.   That court is
armed with power, and it is its duty, to direct all proper
accounts and enquiries, and use all precautions which
may be necessary for the attainment of complete justice to all the parties.   It professes, in such a case, in
good faith to administer the law of the *situs*.   And the
sovereignty of the *situs* will give full faith and credit
to its judgments.   In the case of *Tunstall* v. *Pollard*
the same objection of conflict of jurisdiction was made.
But it was answered by the president in this way: "It
is said, indeed, that peradventure there might be a conflict between the decisions of the foreign court and
ours, and that between the two the executor might suf-
fer.   I think not.   While this court would be bound
in its decision to conform to the law of the forum which
granted administration, the foreign court, on its part,
would consider the party protected for what he is compelled to do by us.   No court, it must be presumed,
could ever charge an executor with a *devastavit* because he has paid a debt decreed *in invitum* by a foreign tribunal, although the domestic *forum* may consider the decree erroneous."   He then proceeds to shew
by authority that this is the established principle of
public law, as recognized both in England and the United States.   An heir who pays the debt of the ancestor binding the heir is protected to the extent of such
payment, and may plead it for his protection in any suit
brought against him by another creditor of the ancestor.   This he may do, even though the payment be

1852.
January
Term.

Dickinson
v.
Hoomes's
adm'r
& als.

voluntary; and, *a fortiori*, he may do it if the payment be made by compulsion. If the heir reside here, the suit must be brought here, in which case, of course, our courts would give the heir the benefit of his payment. But if the suit could be brought in a court of the *situs*, such court would give at least as much effect to a payment by compulsion as to a voluntary payment, and this would be sufficient for the protection of the heir.

There is then no danger in any case of any injury to the heir arising from a conflict of jurisdiction. But if there were any danger in any case, there can certainly be none in this, in which the ancestor and all the heirs always resided in Virginia; in which the ancestor has been dead nearly thirty years; and in which it is not pretended in the answer of the heirs that any suit has ever been brought in Kentucky to subject the assets descended from the ancestor to the payment of his debts, or that any creditor of the ancestor ever existed in that State. If it be said that there is a possibility of the existence of such a creditor, or the institution of such a suit, it is so bare and remote as not to be a feather in the scale against the positive injustice which would be inflicted on the appellant by compelling him to surrender land warranted to him by the ancestor, to heirs who are in possession of assets by descent from the same ancestor, and to turn him over to the possibility of obtaining relief in Kentucky, where none of the heirs reside, and where now there may be no remaining assets.

The comity which authorizes, if not the necessity which requires, the exercise of such a jurisdiction in countries generally, applies with greatly increased force to the United States as among themselves. Their close political union, their local proximity to each other, and the frequent social and commercial intercourse of their inhabitants, render it absolutely necessary that the prin-

1852.
January
Term.

Dickinson
v.
Hoomes's
adm'r
& als.

ciples of comity among themselves should be carried to the fullest extent; while the similarity of their institutions and laws render it comparatively convenient and easy to enforce in one State a contract or trust governed by the laws of another. It may be said that, in some of the States, and especially of the new States, land has been made assets for the payment of all the debts of a decedent, and is subject to sale for that purpose by his personal representative, though the descent is not broken. This, so far from diminishing, increases the propriety of affording equitable relief in other States, where the heir may be found by the creditors with the proceeds of the land in his pocket. The giving of such relief may involve the necessity of taking an account of the assets, real and personal, and of the administration thereof by the foreign representative; but it no more involves that necessity where the real estate is placed on the footing of personal assets by the local law, than where it is liable as at common law; for the personal, being the primary fund for the payment of debts at common law, must be exhausted before the real estate can be taken for that purpose: so that an account of the personal estate must generally be taken before the common law liability of the real estate can be enforced. Indeed, where the real estate is placed entirely on the footing of personal assets, and subjected to primary liability, the necessity for the settlement of an account of the personal estate, before the real can be taken, would seem to be thereby obviated. But the necessity for such a settlement, where it exists, is no objection to the jurisdiction, but addresses itself entirely to the judicial discretion of the court. It may be a reason for "declining to exercise the jurisdiction in particular cases," but is no reason "against the existence of the jurisdiction itself." 1 Mason's R. 414 and 415. As was said by the learned judge in that case, in speaking of a kindred subject, whether the court will

1852.
January
Term.

Dickinson
v.
Hoomes's
adm'r
& als.

give relief or not "must depend on the circumstances
of each case"; and it is incumbent on those who resist
the giving of relief "to establish in the given case that
it may work injustice or public mischief." Id. 430.
But, reverting to the policy which has prevailed in most
if not all of the States to increase and facilitate the liability of real estate for the payment of debts, it would
be strange indeed if it should be a fruit of that policy
to discharge the heir from all liability for the ancestor's
debt, in a case in which the plainest equity requires
that he should be made liable, and in which he might
be made liable without the least injustice or the slightest inconvenience to any body in the world. I imagine
that in no State of the Union is the estate of a decedent discharged from liability merely because it has
passed from the hands of the personal representative
and reached the hands of heirs or distributees. I imagine that in every State, as at common law, the claims
of creditors attach to the estate as a trust subject, and
(though from necessity *bona fide* purchasers must acquire a good title) follow it into the hands of heirs and
distributees, and may be enforced wherever their persons are to be found and the doctrines of the English
chancery prevail.

Reason and authority are alike in favour of the jurisdiction of a court of equity in such cases. While the
general principle that that court has jurisdiction over
the person, wherever it may be found, to enforce a contract or a trust, though land in a foreign country may
be affected thereby, is sustained by many cases, and is
now a well settled doctrine of equity: and while the
case of an heir having in his hands foreign assets by
descent, whether in the form of land or money, which,
by the contract of the ancestor and the law of the *situs*,
are bound for the debts of the ancestor, is clearly within the reason of those cases and of that doctrine; I
have yet seen no case, ancient or modern, in which it

1852.
January
Term.

Dickinson
v.
Hoomes's
adm'r
& als.

was decided that a court of equity, having jurisdiction over the person of the heir, had no power to enforce such a liability. In the earlier ages of English equity law, before it was well defined and established on the broad basis of justice on which it now stands, there was a struggle between the common law lawyers and the equity lawyers, not on the particular question of the liability of an heir for foreign assets by descent, but on the general question of the jurisdiction of a court of equity *in personam*, though the decree might indirectly affect land situated in a foreign country. The case of *Arglasse* v. *Muschamp*, 1 Vern. R. 75, decided in 1682, was a suit in equity to be relieved against a fraudulent conveyance of lands in Ireland. The defendant pleaded to the jurisdiction. The Lord Chancellor, after saying, " This is surely only a jest put upon the jurisdiction of this court by the common lawyers; for when you go about to bind the lands, and grant a sequestration to execute a decree, then they readily tell you that the authority of this court is only to regulate a man's conscience, and ought not to affect the estate, but that this court must *agere in personam* only; and when, as in this case, you prosecute the person for a fraud, they tell you, you must not intermeddle here, because the fraud, though committed here, concerns lands that lie in Ireland, which makes the jurisdiction local; and so would wholly elude the jurisdiction of this court," overruled the plea, and ordered the defendant to pay costs " for endeavouring to oust the court of its jurisdiction." The case of the *Earl of Kildare* v. *Sir Morrice Eustace*, Id. 419, cited by Mr. Barton, was a suit in equity to enforce a trust of lands in Ireland. Sir John Holt, the counsel for the plaintiff, maintained the jurisdiction of the court. The defendant's counsel " in a manner waived," and thus conceded, " the preliminary point" of jurisdiction, " and would not enter into the debate whether the court might not decree

1852.
January
Term.

Dickinson
v.
Hoomer's
adm'r
& als.

the trust of lands in Ireland, the trustee being in England." But they insisted that it was certainly a matter discretionary in the court, whether they would do it or not; and that as this case was circumstanced, they apprehended the court would not interpose. And among the reasons assigned for not interposing in the case were the following: " 1st. That in this case there had been no less than two judgments in the courts of law in Ireland, and no less than three bills in equity "; and " 2dly. That Sir Morrice Eustace, the trustee, did not live in England, but came here occasionally upon other business; and that it would be unreasonable to keep him from his own country and from all his other concerns, to attend this suit." But the court, consisting of the Lord Chancellor and the judges, overruled the objection, and decided not only that the court had jurisdiction of the case, but that it was a proper one for the exercise of its judicial discretion. It is true, as stated by Mr. Barton, that Sir John Holt, in arguing the case, said " it was resolved in *Evans & Ascough's Case*, Latch, fol. 234, and *Dowdale's Case*, in 6 Coke's R. 348, that lands in Ireland shall be assets to satisfy a bond debt here, but otherwise of lands in Scotland "; and it is also true that in 3 Vin. Abr. 141, also cited by Mr. Barton, the following passage appears: " Lands in Ireland are assets to satisfy a bond debt in England, but it is otherwise of lands in Scotland "; to which passage is appended, as the only authority on which it rests, a reference to the argument of Sir John Holt, in 1 Vern. 419, " citing it as resolved in *Evans & Ascough's*, Latch 233, and *Dowdale's Case*, 6 Coke's R. 348." The only authorities for the passage, then, are the cases cited from Latch and Coke. These were both common law cases—the former being an action of trespass in the Court of King's Bench, and the latter of debt in the Court of common pleas: and nothing which could have been said in them, however plainly expressed,

1852.
January
Term.

Dickinson
v.
Hoomes's
adm'r
& als.

would have been regarded as authority on the question of
the jurisdiction of a court of chancery *in personam.*
The case in Latch was decided in the reign of James the
first; and the only edition of the report I have seen
is the original one by Walpole, written in Norman
French, which I do not understand. I cannot therefore undertake to say what was said in the case in relation to assets by descent, or in what connection it
was said. The case in 6 Coke 348, *Dowdale's Case,*
was decided in the same reign. But nothing was said
in it about assets by descent in a foreign country. It
was an action of debt against an executor, who plead
*plene administravit.* The jury found that there were
assets, but that they were beyond sea or in Ireland.
It was resolved, " that the jurors have found the substance of the issue, that is to say, assets; and the finding that they are beyond sea is surplusage. For if the
executors have goods of the testator's in any part of
the world, they shall be charged in respect of them, for
many merchants and other men, who have stocks and
goods to a great value beyond sea, are indebted here in
England; and God forbid that those goods should not
be liable to their debts, for otherwise there would be a
great defect in the law." In *Dowdale's Case* the question was as to the difference between local and transitory actions, and whether a jury could find transitory
things in another country. It was necessary for the
parties in pleading to name a certain place for a venue,
and the question in the case was whether the evidence
of the parties and finding of the jury must be literally
confined to the place named in the issue, or might be applied to any other place. It was in reference to that question that it was said by counsel in argument to have
been decided, in an action of debt against an heir on the
bond of his ancestor, in which the defendant pleaded
" nothing by descent," and the plaintiff averred assets
by descent in *London,* and gave in evidence assets in

1852.
January
Term.

Dickinson
v.
Hoomes's
adm'r
& als.

*Cornwall,* that the jury could not find this local matter in a foreign country. But the court, in answer to this argument, said: "God forbid but that the jury may find assets by descent in any other county within England; for the law is that the plaintiff in such case shall have in execution all the lands which the heir has, and perhaps he has lands in divers counties; and therefore, although one place be named for necessity, yet the jury may find all that which by law shall be chargeable in such case, in what town or county soever it lies."

The distinction between Ireland and Scotland referred to *arguendo* by Sir John Holt was founded on the idea that seems at that time to have existed that Ireland, being a "conquered kingdom," the judgments and decrees of the English Superior courts could be enforced by them in that country. And therefore Lord Holt said: "That Ireland hath its courts of its own by grant from the King; but not exclusive of the King's courts here, for Ireland is a conquered kingdom; and a decree of this court may as well bind land in Ireland as by every day's practice it doth lands that lie in foreign plantations: and for precedents cited the case of a *scire facias* brought in the chancery here to repeal a patent of lands in Ireland. If a man that is beneficed here is made a bishop in Ireland, that comes within the statute of II. 8, against pluralities, and shall make void his living here in Ireland; and it was resolved in *Evans & Ascough's Case,* Latch, fol. 233, and *Dowdale's Case,* 6 Coke's R. 348, that lands in Ireland shall be assets to satisfy a bond debt here, but otherwise of lands in Scotland." And in the case of *Sir John Fryer* v. *Bernard,* 2 P. Wms. 261, referred to in Raithby's note to 1 Vernon 76, it seems that a sequestration was awarded by the English court of chancery against defendant's real and personal estate in Ireland, a sequestration having been first taken out in England and returned *nulla bona.*

1852.
January
Term.

Dickinson
v.
Hoomes's-
adm'r
& als.

Now it is not pretended by any that the courts of one State can enforce their judgments in another; and therefore, in a suit at law against an heir, land descended to him in another State cannot be regarded as assets by descent, because the writ of *extendi facias* cannot be enforced against it. But the question in this case is not whether land descended in another State can be regarded as " assets by descent," technically speaking, here, for what is to be regarded as " assets by descent," in a technical sense, must be only such as are made so by our own law and as are within the reach of our own courts. The question is whether a trust created by or under the laws of another State can be enforced against a trustee residing here? And I think it clearly can. It matters not whether the trust be created by the act of the parties, or by the local law. In either case the *lex loci* is administered. Nor does it matter that the trust relates to an immovable subject in another State, provided the decree does not invade the jurisdiction or the sovereignty of that State. And there can be no invasion of that jurisdiction or sovereignty where we only require our own resident citizens to do that which if voluntarily done would be valid in that State. *A fortiori*, there can be none where the subject has been sold and the money is in their hands.

As to the statutes of 5 George II, ch. 7, and 9 George IV, ch. 33, mentioned in Ram on Assets, 8 Law Lib. 158, referred to by Mr. Morson, they were not passed because they were considered necessary to enable an English court of chancery to enforce, against a trustee residing in its jurisdiction, the execution of a trust concerning foreign land; nor for the purpose of giving that court any jurisdiction in regard to such land descending to a person residing in its limits. Those statutes merely make real estate in certain colonies and provinces of England assets by descent for the payment of debts generally, instead of certain specialty debts

1852.
January
Term.

Dickinson
v.
Hoomes's
adm'r
& als.

only, as at common law, and provide remedies against those assets, to be had in the colonial and provincial courts, and not the courts of England. This was a mere exercise of legislative power over a part of the British dominions, and I do not see how it can affect the question under consideration.

I will now proceed to consider the last question arising in the case; and that is,

4thly. Whether, in fact, any lands in Kentucky descended from Richard Hoomes to his children; and if they did, whether they were not forfeited for non-payment of taxes; and whether such of them as were held by the children were held by them as purchasers from the State of Kentucky, and not as heirs of their father?

When John Hoomes the elder died, in 1805, he appears to have been entitled to 18,000 or 20,000 acres of land in Kentucky, which, as a part of the residuum of his estate, he charged by his will with the payment of his debts; and the surplus of which he devised to his five children, John, William, Richard, Armistead and Sophia, " to hold the same in fee simple, subject to the condition or contingency to which their other property was subject." So that to one undivided fifth of these lands, subject to the charge aforesaid, Richard Hoomes became entitled as devisee of John Hoomes the elder. These lands, or the greater part of them, seem to have remained undisposed of at the death of Richard Hoomes in 1823, eighteen years after the death of his father, John Hoomes. The appellant contends that the portion of these lands to which Richard was entitled at the time of his death descended to his children, and became assets by descent liable for his debts by the law of Kentucky. To this claim several objections are made by the appellees.

1st. They insist that Richard had never any actual seisin of the Kentucky lands. That by the common

1852.
January
Term.

Dickinson
v.
Hoomes's
adm'r
& als.

law he could not be the stock of the descent of any portion of the said lands to his children, who must claim, if at all, under the ancestor last actually seised, according to the maxim, *non jus, sed seisina facit stipitem :* and that this rule of the common law, so far as appears from the record, is still the law of Kentucky.

I do not think this objection is well founded, for several reasons. 1st. I think, as was said by the Supreme court of the United States, in the case of *Green* v. *Liter,* 8 Cranch's R. 229, " that even if, at common law, an actual *pedis positio,* followed up by an actual perception of the profits, were necessary to maintain a writ of right, (or, in this case, to constitute a stock of descent,) which we do not admit, the doctrine would be inapplicable to the waste and vacant lands of our country (such as were the lands in Kentucky owned by John Hoomes the elder at his death). The common law itself in many cases dispenses with such a rule ; and the reason of the rule itself ceases when applied to a mere wilderness." And I therefore think that if John Hoomes the elder was seised of these lands at the time of his death, and they were not in the adverse possession of others at the time of Richard Hoomes's death, he was sufficiently seised of his portion of them to make him a stock of descent on common law principles as modified by the condition of the country. 2dly. If John Hoomes the elder was seised of them at the time of his death, which is not denied, he had a right to devise them even according to the English statute of wills, and his devisees became by the devise seised in deed, without any actual *pedis positio* or taking of the *esplees.* The maxim *seisina facit stipitem* is inapplicable to such a case. The children of Richard Hoomes must take his portion of the lands as his heirs, or not at all. They cannot take it as heirs at law of John Hoomes the elder, because it was effectually devised by him to Richard. The de-

1852.
January
Term.

Dickinson
v.
Hoomes's
adm'r
& als.

vise broke the descent. Suppose the devise had been to a stranger instead of a son, the heirs of the stranger could not claim under the testator as a stock of descent, and could only claim by inheritance from their father. The law having authorized the devise, the estate thereby conferred was as perfect as if it had been conferred by the common law feoffment with livery of seisin. The will operates like a deed of bargain and sale or other conveyance under the statute of uses, by virtue of which the bargainee has a complete seisin in deed, without actual entry or livery of seisin. 3dly. It is proved by Herndon, and would have been presumable if not proved, for reasons which I have before stated, that the statute of descents of Kentucky is similar to the statute of descents of Virginia, in declaring " that henceforth when any person having a *title* to any real estate of inheritance shall die intestate as to such estate, it shall descend," &c. I think that " the common law rule, *seisina facit stipitem*, may now, therefore, be regarded as abrogated " in Kentucky as well as "in Virginia "; and that there, as well as here, " having *title* to any real estate is alone sufficient to make the intestate the root of the inheritance." 1 Lomax's Dig. 594, § 2.

2dly. They insist that none of these lands have come to their hands, except 635 acres, which they contend was afterwards forfeited for non-payment of taxes, and sold and conveyed by the agent of the State to Richard H. Hoomes, one of the heirs of Richard Hoomes, who thereby acquired " a title in the said lands by purchase from the State, and not by descent from his ancestor."

The answer of the appellees, the heirs of Richard Hoomes, to the supplemental bill of the appellant, expressly admits that on the 6th of May 1833, 2726 acres of these Kentucky lands were divided among the parties entitled thereto by commissioners appointed for the purpose; and that 635 acres thereof were allotted to

1852
January
Term.

Dickinson
v.
Hoomes's
adm'r
& als.

the said heirs of Richard Hoomes, of which 75 acres were apportioned to Williamson Tally as compensation for his services in procuring the same to be divided and allotted. They further say that, from the best information they have been able to obtain, the land allotted to them did not exceed the value of 1 dollar 25 cents per acre; and that they did not realize from their sale a greater sum. They further say they have good reason to believe that other lands in the State of Kentucky were in the seisin and possession of their grandfather, John Hoomes, but such have never come to their pos-. session.

Now here is a solemn admission that 635, minus 75, acres of these lands have not only come to their hands, but been by them converted into money. To be sure, they "insist that these lands were derived by them under the will of their grandfather, and were not inherited from their father." But this is a question of law, about which I think, and have endeavoured to shew, they are mistaken; at least as to so much of the land as their father was entitled to at the time of his death; for they were themselves entitled to a portion of it as contingent devisees of their grandfather, according to the decision of this court in the case reported in 1 Grattan.

How is the force of this admission to be avoided, if I am right on the question of law aforesaid?

After the answer had been written and signed, an addition was made thereto, to the following effect: " Your respondents beg leave further to state to your honour a fact omitted to be stated in the body of their answer; that is to say, that on the      day of      1842, a certain tract of land containing 2086 acres, and situated in the county of Anderson and State of Kentucky, and entered for taxation in the name of John Hoomes, was struck off to the State of Kentucky for the non-payment of the tax due thereon; which said land was after-

1852.
January
Term.

Dickinson
v.
Hoomes's
adm'r
& als.

wards, to wit, on the 21st of May 1845, sold and conveyed by John Draffin, agent for the Commonwealth, to
your respondent, Richard H. Hoomes, by the name of
Richard Hoomes, for the sum of 80 dollars 71 cents,
by reason whereof the title to the said land became
vested in him as purchaser from the State of Kentucky.
Your respondents believe, and therefore aver and charge,
that the said 2086 acres are the same lands, or parcel of
the same lands, mentioned in the report of commissioners McBrayer and Herndon mentioned in this answer.
All which will more fully and at large appear by reference to an attested copy of the said report, and a like
copy of the said deed, filed with this answer and prayed
to be taken as part thereof."

The Circuit court was of opinion, and the appellees'
counsel contend, that the 2086 acres above mentioned
were in fact, as believed by the said respondents, to be
parcel of the 2726 acres which were divided as aforesaid; while, on the other hand, the counsel for the appellant contend that they are different lands. The respondents were not themselves certain that they are the
same lands, but only believed so; and on that account,
as well as on account of the doubt in which the evidence leaves the question, it would have been proper, I
think, to have referred it to a commissioner, even if the
right of the appellant to relief had depended upon it.

But does the right of the appellant to relief depend
upon the question whether they are the same or different lands. Suppose they are the same lands; what
effect can that fact have on the rights of the parties?
None, I conceive; unless it be to make the land which
was allotted to the heirs of Richard Hoomes, as aforesaid, chargeable with a due proportion of the 80 dollars and 71 cents, paid by Richard H. Hoomes in discharge of the arrears of tax due upon the 2086 acres
sold and conveyed by the agent of the State of Kentucky for the non-payment of the tax due thereon as

1852.
January
Term.

Dickinson
v.
Hoomes's
adm'r
& als.

aforesaid.　The 2726 acres of land aforesaid had come to the hands of the parties, and been divided.　Arrears of taxes are suffered to accrue thereon ; and in 1842, nine years after the division, they are struck off to the State for non-payment of the taxes.　In 1845, twelve years after the division, they are sold and conveyed by the agent of the State, for the " amount of tax, interest and charges due thereon, to Richard H. Hoomes, one of the heirs of Richard Hoomes.　I am now supposing that they are in fact the same lands.　Can these heirs now say that their responsibility for these lands as assets by descent was discharged by this forfeiture and sale, and conveyance to one of them?　Had that one any right to redeem these lands from forfeiture, or purchase them for his own benefit, in exclusion of his coparceners?　If he had any such right, did he do it?　Is there any pretension that they or their assigns have surrendered the land to him, or accounted to him for the proceeds of sale ; or paid to him anything more than their aliquot portions of the said sum of 80 dollars and 71 cents, if even they have paid that?　The probability, from the pleadings and the evidence, is that Richard H. Hoomes went out to Kentucky to look after these lands, as agent for the heirs of his father or grandfather ; and finding that 2086 acres of land standing on the tax-book in the name of his grandfather had been struck off to the State, he redeemed or purchased it from the agent of the State by paying the amount of tax, &c., due thereon.　He and his principals and co-heirs probably doubted whether it was the same land or not, which had been divided between them.　But, whether the same land or not, it was prudent to redeem it, and obtain a conveyance from the State.　For if it was the same land, their title to what they had already obtained would be thus confirmed.　And if it was different land, they would thus obtain so much more.　Whether it was the same or different land, seems to have been re-

1852.
January
Term.

Dickinson
v.
Hoomes's
adm'r
& als

garded by the appellees as a question of little importance; for, in the preparation of the body of their answer, they overlooked it altogether, and acknowledged
themselves unconditionally to have received 635, minus
75, acres of the land.

Without pursuing this examination any further, I am
very decidedly of opinion that the court below should
not have dismissed the appellant's bill for want of proof
of assets descended to the appellees from their father in
Kentucky; but that, it appearing from the evidence
that 18,000 or 20,000 acres of land in that State actually belonged to John Hoomes the elder at the time of
his death; that though much the larger portion of it
appears to have been forfeited for non-payment of taxes,
yet these taxes all accrued, not only since the death of
John Hoomes the elder in 1805, but since the death of
Richard Hoomes in 1823; that the heirs of John Hoomes
the elder and of Richard Hoomes have by their agents
from time to time looked after these lands, and surveyed,
divided and made sales of portions of them; it should
have been referred to a commissioner of the court to
enquire, ascertain and report what lands in Kentucky
descended from Richard Hoomes to his heirs at law,
and came to their possession: and the value and disposition which has been made thereof; and how much
has been or is to be, and when, received by them for the
said lands, or such part thereof as may have been sold
by them, or for the rents and profits of any of the said
lands; and what expenses have been necessarily incurred by them in looking after, obtaining possession of,
dividing and selling the same, and collecting the proceeds of sale; and any other facts which, in the opinion of the court below, might have been necessary to
shew what benefit the heirs of Richard Hoomes have
derived from his land in Kentucky. To the extent of
that benefit I think they are, in equity, bound to in.
demnify the appellant against the recovery from him of

1862.
January
Term.

Dickinson
v.
Hoomes's
adm'r
& als.

that portion of the land warranted by their father, to
which this court has decided them to be entitled as
purchasers under the will of their grandfather, and of
the rents and profits thereof. If the amount of that
benefit is equal to, or greater than, the value of the said
portion, and its rents and profits, then the said recovery should be altogether barred and enjoined. But if
the amount of that benefit is less than that value, the
portion of the warranted land to which the appellees
are entitled should be subject to a charge for the said
amount, and, if the same be not paid in a reasonable
time, should be sold for its payment.

Under the statute of 1798 of Kentucky, which we
have seen is similar to 1 Rev. Code, ch. 99, § 21, if the
warranted land were situate, and the suit to recover it
were pending, in that State, the heirs would be bound
for the value of the lands to them descended. So that,
if at the death of the ancestor the lands descended were
of greater value than the land warranted, the title of
the warrantee and his assigns would then be good
against the heirs of the warrantor, and could not be defeated by the forfeiture of the land descended for non-
payment of taxes thereafter accruing, nor by any dis-
parity that might thereafter arise between the relative
value of the land descended and the land warranted.
It was contended by Mr. Morson that heirs are not
bound to pay taxes for the benefit of creditors, and
that if, by non-payment of taxes, the descended land is
forfeited, the heirs will not thereby become liable to
creditors for the value of the land. This may be so, as
a general rule at least. But where there are no unsatisfied creditors of the ancestor except the warrantee, and
he becomes a creditor by a breach of the warranty occasioned by the recovery of the land from him by the
heirs, I think the period of the ancestor's death is that
at which the rights of the parties become fixed, and
the relative values of the lands descended and warrant-

1852.
January
Term.

Dickinson
v.
Hoomes's
adm'r
& als.

ed are to be ascertained, under the provisions of the statute above mentioned. It would be too strict, however, to apply the latter rule to this case. The heirs resided in Virginia, and the lands were wild and uncultivated, and scattered over the State of Kentucky. The quantity and locality of the lands were probably unknown to the heirs, who were infants at their father's death; and cannot properly be considered as in default, by suffering any of the lands to be forfeited for non-payment of taxes, or by not having afterwards redeemed them from forfeiture. The appellant is seeking to enforce an equity against the heirs, and the just measure of that equity cannot exceed the benefit derived by them from the Kentucky land. But while on the one hand the heirs should not be charged with the value of such of the said land as may have been lost by forfeiture; so on the other they should be charged with any rents and profits which may have been received by them on account of the said land. For though, as the law has been settled in Virginia, heirs are not bound for rents and profits accruing before a judgment or decree has been rendered against them, yet, as in this case we are departing from the letter of the Kentucky statute of 1798 for the purpose of doing equity between the parties, and as an account has been decreed against the appellant in the court below for rents and profits, it would seem to be just and right that a corresponding account of rents and profits received by the heirs should also be taken. Otherwise, if the heirs were entitled to recover, but were not accountable for, rents and profits, they might, by delaying their suit until the amount of rents and profits of the warranted land was equal to the value of the land descended, recover the whole of the warranted land; whereas, if they had sued immediately after the ancestor's death, they might have been barred of any recovery whatever. If the heirs prefer to account for the value of all the land de-

1852.
January
Term.

Dickinson
v.
Hoomes's
adm'r
& als.

scended, instead of the value of such of it as has come to their hands, with rents and profits actually received, of course they have a right so to account. But I imagine they would greatly prefer to account for the value of the descended land which has come to their hands, with rents and profits actually received, and interest on the price of such as they may have sold. Indeed I doubt whether any rents and profits have been actually received by them. But if any have, it is right they should account for them.

But it is contended by the counsel for the appellees that as the assets of Richard Hoomes were marshalled in a suit in Caroline, which was commenced in 1826 and ended in 1842, the style of which was *Collins* v. *Garrett*, and as the creditors in that suit were not entirely satisfied, they, if any creditors of Richard Hoomes, and not the appellant, are entitled to charge the appellees for the value of the Kentucky lands descended to the latter. The answer to this objection is, that a final decree was rendered in that suit in 1842. That the appellant was not a party to that suit, not considering himself a creditor until the decision of the case in 1 Gratt. 302, in 1844, and is therefore not bound by the decree. That by the Kentucky statute of 1798 the heirs are bound for the value of any land descended to them, and if this charge be not in its nature paramount to the claims of all other creditors of the ancestor, it would seem at least to be good against any claims which may not have been asserted before such charge is enforced by judgment or decree. And that at all events the appellant would be entitled to recover out of the Kentucky assets a proportion of his claim equal to that which other creditors of equal degree have recovered of their claims out of the Virginia assets, before they could participate with him in the application of the former; which would doubtless give to him the whole of the Kentucky assets.

1852.
January
Term.

Dickinson
v.
Hoomes's
adm'r
& als.

I have now considered all the questions presented by the record. My opinion has been protracted, perhaps, to too great length. But the number, novelty, difficulty and importance of the questions involved, and the fullness and ability with which they were discussed by the counsel on both sides, seemed to render a long opinion necessary.

ALLEN, J. I am of opinion that the heirs cannot be called to account in a Virginia court for real estate descended to them in another State, unless it shall appear that the heirs have disposed of the land and received the proceeds. That as to immovable property the *lex rei sitæ* controls, and if subjected to the debts of the ancestor, it must be by the laws and through the tribunals of the country where it lies. That the mode of proceeding being *in rem*, to subject the thing itself, the courts of a foreign jurisdiction can take no cognizance of it; nor would the courts of the local jurisdiction, in a proceeding by creditors to subject the property itself in the mode prescribed by the local law, pay any respect to a proceeding in a foreign jurisdiction against the heir personally.

I am further of opinion that it is not incumbent on the heir to redeem for the benefit of creditors waste lands descended to him, and which may have been forfeited for taxes accrued either before or after the death of the ancestor; and that if such forfeited land be thereafter sold for the non-payment of taxes, it is competent for the heir to purchase and hold as any other purchaser.

And being of opinion that it does not appear that the heirs have received anything from the Kentucky lands descended, except in respect to lands as to which the descent was broken by a sale for taxes, I should on that ground be for affirming the decree.

On the other questions involved, I think the covenants in the deed bound the heirs, and that the recovery referred to constituted a breach; and that the covenants run with the land, and that the assignee, by deed, of the whole or a portion thereof, is entitled to the benefit of the covenants, and may recover for the breach.

1852.
January
Term.

Dickinson
v.
Hoomes's
adm'r
& als.

The decree was as follows:

A majority of the court is of opinion,

First. That the covenant of Richard Hoomes in the deed to Samuel A. Apperson, in the proceedings mentioned, extends to the claim of the children of said Richard, which was sustained by this court in the case of *Dickinson* v. *Hoomes*, 1 Gratt. 302; and will therefore be broken by an eviction under said claim.

Secondly. That it is a covenant running with the land; and the appellant, as assignee of a portion thereof by a regular chain of conveyances, is entitled to the benefit of the said covenant for his indemnity against the said claim.

Thirdly. That as by the law of Kentucky, as it existed at the death of said Richard Hoomes, and still continues to exist, lands in that State descending from an intestate can be subjected to the payment of his debts, by proceedings either in law or chancery; and " if the deed of an alienor doth mention that he and his heirs be bound to warranty, and if any heritage descend to the demandant of the side of the alienor, then he shall be barred for the value of the heritage that is to him descended "; a court of equity of this State may compel the children of said Richard Hoomes, residing within its jurisdiction, to account for any lands in Kentucky descended to them as his heirs, as a trust subject for the payment of his debts. And although a court of equity of one State, in the exercise of a sound judicial discretion, may in some cases decline to act on

1852.
January
Term.

Dickinson
v.
Hoomes's
adm'r
& als.

persons residing or found within its jurisdiction, where the subject sought to be affected is situated in another State, yet, in this case, it would be an exercise of sound judicial discretion on the part of the Circuit court of Caroline to compel the said heirs, as a condition of the relief they are seeking as aforesaid against the appellant, to account to him, so far as may be necessary for his indemnity against the breach of said covenant, for any benefit they may have received from any land in Kentucky descended to them from the said Richard.

Fourthly.   That it appearing to the court that John Hoomes the elder was entitled at his death to eighteen or twenty thousand acres of land in Kentucky, to one fifth of which the said Richard became entitled as devisee of the said John, and remained so entitled at the death of him, the said Richard, in 1823, the said one fifth descended from the said Richard to his said children.   And although it further appears to the court that the greater part of these lands were forfeited to the State of Kentucky for non-payment of taxes accruing thereon after the death of said Richard, and so may be forever lost to the said heirs; and although it would be too strict, under the circumstances of this case, to hold the said heirs accountable, as for assets by descent, for the value of any lands so lost; yet, as it appears that a portion of said lands has actually come to the hands of the said heirs, and been by them converted into money, and that they may yet be entitled to other portions of them, the said Circuit court, instead of dismissing the bills of the appellant, should have directed one of its commissioners to enquire, ascertain and report what lands in Kentucky descended from the said Richard to his heirs, and have come to their hands or been sold by them, and the value or amount of sales thereof; what rents and profits, if any, have been received by them on account of any of the said lands; when any such

1852.
January
Term.

Dickinson
v.
Hoomes's
adm'r
& als.

amount of sales, or rents and profits, were so received; what expenses have been incurred by them, or any of them, in redeeming, obtaining possession of, surveying, dividing, or selling any of the said lands, or collecting the rents and profits or proceeds of sale of any of them; and any other facts which may, in the opinion of the said Circuit court, be necessary to ascertain the extent of any benefit received by the said heirs from the said lands. And if it should appear that the amount of said benefit is equal to, or greater than, the value of the land which the said heirs are entitled to recover of the appellant, and the rents and profits thereof, they should be altogether barred and enjoined from such recovery. But if the said amount should be less than the said value, rents and profits, then the payment of the same by them to him should be made a condition of their said recovery; and unless such payment be made in a reasonable time, the said land, or so much thereof as may be necessary, should be sold therefor.

Therefore it is considered that the said decree is erroneous; that it be reversed and annulled, with costs; and that the cause be remanded to be further proceeded in on the principles above indicated.

## Richmond.

1852.
January
Term.

TRICE v. COCKRAN.

(Absent *Cabell, P.*)

February 10th.

1. Case is a proper remedy for the breach of an express warranty of soundness of a slave or other personal chattel sold.
2. In case for the breach of a warranty of soundness of a personal chattel, it is not necessary to allege the defendant's knowledge of the unsoundness: And if it is alleged, it is not necessary to prove it.

B. F. Cockran instituted an action upon the *case* against George W. Trice in the Hustings court of the city of Richmond, and filed a declaration containing two counts. The first count charged that the defendant falsely and fraudulently induced the plaintiff to purchase of him a slave, " by then and there falsely and fraudulently warranting the said slave to be sound," when in fact the said slave was unsound, and died of the disease then upon him, and that the plaintiff had sustained damage to the amount of 500 dollars, for medical attendance, &c.; and concludes with an averment in the following words: " And so the plaintiff saith that the said defendant falsely and fraudulently deceived him, the said plaintiff, in the sale of the said slave as aforesaid."

The second count charges that the defendant being possessed of the slave, and well knowing that he was unsound, " did nevertheless falsely, fraudulently and deceitfully, then and there, represent the said last mentioned slave to be sound, and did, then and there, by means of the said false, fraudulent and deceitful representations, induce the said plaintiff to buy the said

slave of the said defendant." It then charges the unsoundness of the slave, and his consequent death and
damage to the plaintiff.

To this declaration the defendant demurred generally,
and pleaded "not guilty," and there was joinder in the
demurrer and issue on the plea. The court overruled
the demurrer, and the case was tried upon the plea.

Upon the trial the plaintiff offered evidence of the
unsoundness of the slave and his death, and exhibited
and proved a bill of sale for him *under seal*, by the defendant, containing a warranty of the soundness.

The defendant offered evidence to prove that the
slave was placed by the defendant in the hands of an
auctioneer in Richmond to be sold, and that at the time
he so placed him with the auctioneer, the defendant
told him that he had been sold before he became the
property of the defendant, and was returned by the
purchaser because he was believed to be unsound, and
that he (the auctioneer) must not sell him to any one
without making that fact known to him; that the slave
remained for some time at the auction house in Richmond, where he was seen by all the dealers, and among
them the plaintiff, and finally he was exposed to public
sale, proclamation being made by the auctioneer that a
doubt was entertained of his soundness, but he would
warrant him sound, and if the purchaser did not like
him he might return him; that at this sale (made in
the absence of the defendant, who was in the country,
the sale being made in Richmond) the plaintiff became
the purchaser of him at 470 dollars. This was in
July.

The plaintiff, after the purchase and a full statement
by the auctioneer of all that the defendant had told
him as to the former sale of the slave and the return of
him, declined to keep him, and returned him; and the
slave remained at the auction house, where the plaintiff
frequently saw him, until the 12th of September, when

the plaintiff proposed to the auctioneer to sell him again, saying that if he would do so, and warrant him sound, he (the plaintiff) would bid 400 dollars for him; that accordingly the auctioneer did put him up to sale again, and, in the absence of the defendant, warranted him sound, and the plaintiff purchased him at a single bid of 400 dollars, took possession of him, gave a note at ninety days for the purchase money, which he paid at maturity, and shipped the slave to the south.

The bill of sale was partly printed and partly written. The warranty was printed. It was in blank as to the price and name of the purchaser when left with the auctioneer, and he filled up the blanks.

It was also proved by the auctioneer that the slave was sold for less than the price of a sound slave; that if sound he would have commanded at least 550 dollars, which price was offered for him by another purchaser, but was withdrawn when the auctioneer communicated to him what the defendant had directed him to communicate to all purchasers before he sold him.

Upon this proof the defendant by his counsel asked the court to instruct the jury, "that to entitle the plaintiff to recover, they must be satisfied from the evidence that the slave was unsound at the time of the sale to the plaintiff, and the defendant knew of the unsoundness, and fraudulently concealed it, or falsely and fraudulently represented him to be sound; and the plaintiff is not entitled to recover by the force of the warranty merely, if one was made": which instruction the court gave.

The plaintiff then asked the court to instruct the jury that he was entitled to recover upon the first count, if he proved to their satisfaction the unsoundness at the time of the sale, and an express warranty: which instruction the court refused to give.

The plaintiff excepted and spread the whole testimony upon the record.

The jury found for the defendant, and judgment was rendered accordingly. Thereupon the plaintiff applied to the Circuit court for a *supersedeas*, which was awarded: And when the cause was heard in that court the judgment of the Hustings court was reversed, and the cause remanded, with instructions that at any future trial of the cause, in case such question should arise as at the former trial, not to give the instruction it then gave at the instance of the defendant, but to give that which was moved by the plaintiff. To this judgment Trice obtained a *supersedeas* from this court.

*Lyons*, for the appellant.

1st. The action was *case* for the fraudulent representations charged in the declaration, and the fraud was therefore the gist of the action, without proof of which the plaintiff was not entitled to recover. *Bayard* v. *Malcolm*, 1 John. R. 452.

The declaration plainly shews this, and the issue found in the cause does also. That issue was upon the plea of not guilty. If the action had been upon the warranty, it would have been *assumpsit* and not *case*, and the plea would have been *non assumpsit*. 1 Chitt. Pl. 106; *Stuart* v. *Wilkins*, Doug. R. 18; Saund. Plead. and Evi. 913; *Langridge* v. *Levy*, 2 Mees. & Welsb. 519; *S. C.*, 4 Id. 337.

2d. The action could not have been upon the warranty, because the warranty was under seal, and covenant and not *case* was the proper action upon it. 1 Chitt. Pl. 118. That the auctioneer, if he had authority to warrant, might, under his parol authority to warrant, fill up the blanks in the bill of sale, is abundantly proved by the cases of *Texira* v. *Evans*, cited Anstr. R. 229; *Zouch* v. *Claye*, 2 Levintz R. 35; *Speake* v. *United States*, 9 Cranch's R. 28; *Smith* v. *Crooker*, 5 Mass. R. 538; *Woolley* v. *Constant*, 4 John. R. 54; *Knapp* v. *Maltby*, 13 Wend. R. 587; *Wiley* v. *Moor*, 17 Serg. & Rawle 438.

3d. Because if the first count in the declaration was to be considered against its frame as a count on the warranty, because the term warrant is used, although it is not charged that the defendant assumed or promised any thing, but only that he made false, fraudulent and deceitful representations and warranty, and so deceived the plaintiff, then there was a misjoinder of actions, because *case* and *assumpsit* cannot be joined in the same declaration, and the demurrer to the declaration should have been sustained. 1 Chitt. Pl. 201; *Corbit* v. *Packington*, 13 Eng. C. L. R. 170; *Wilson* v. *Marcy*, 1 John. R. 503.

So incompatible are the two forms of action that in *assumpsit* upon the warranty evidence of fraud is not admissible. *Evertson's ex'ors* v. *Miles*, 6 John. R. 138.

The plaintiff might have sued upon his warranty, or he might sue, as he did, for the imputed fraud; but he must sue for one or the other, and not for both. If there had been a warranty by parol, *assumpsit* might have been maintained, but if under seal, as here it was, if there was any, covenant only could be maintained, or *case* for the deceit; and therefore, in a suit not founded upon the warranty, because not in covenant, it was perfectly right to instruct the jury that the plaintiff must prove the imputed fraud, or fail, and could not recover on the warranty. To determine otherwise would be to declare that a covenant is evidence in *case* or *assumpsit*, and recovery may be had for breach of covenant by action on the *case*, and that without averring the existence of any covenant.

But the evidence shews clearly that there was no warranty obligatory upon the appellant, because it was proved distinctly that he ordered his agent not to sell the slave without making known his defects; that the agent did so, and the purchaser had full notice of every thing in respect to the soundness of the slave prior to the purchase of him by the appellant, and the warranty could not properly be held, therefore, to apply to any unsoundness existing prior to that purchase, but must be construed, like a warranty of soundness where there is a visible defect, as not covering that defect. If the slave had been seised with small-pox or measles, or some other disease which impaired his value, so soon after the sale as to shew that he contracted it before the purchase by the appellant, such defect might have been covered by the warranty. *Bayley* v. *Merrill*, Cro. Jac. 386; *Dyer* v. *Hargrave*, 10 Ves. R. 507; Buller N. P. 31.

The error of the Circuit court was occasioned by relying upon and misapplying the case in 2 East. That case affirms that in *case* on the warranty the *scienter*, if laid, need not be proved. Let that be admitted, and yet the authority does not rule this case; for this is not a suit on the warranty, as already shewn. This case is like that of *Dowding* v. *Mortimer*, decided by Lord Kenyon, and admitted in 2 East to be law. The gravamen is the deceit.

The instruction asked for by the counsel for the appellee shews that the instruction given was correct, for by it he limits his right to recover to the first count, and to the warranty, shewing that unless entitled to recover on the warranty, he could not recover at all; and not being entitled to recover in *case* upon a warranty in covenant, it followed necessarily that he could not recover at all in this suit.

*R. T. Daniel*, for the appellee.

The instructions asked and refused were relevant to the evidence, which presented to the jury the questions of fact, Was the slave unsound when sold? Had there been a warranty; or had there been a false representation or concealment of that unsoundness if it existed?

The effect of the instruction given was that under the declaration, there could be no recovery unless the plaintiff established a fraud in the sale; that even if he proved an express warranty of soundness, and unsoundness at the date of the warranty, he could not recover.

The declaration is in *case*, and the first count is in the common form of declaring in *case* for a breach of warranty, whilst the second count is in the common form of declaring where deceit is alleged, and is expected to be proved, that is, where the *scienter* of unsoundness is alleged and expected to be proved. 2 Chitt. Pl. 277, 278. It has been decided long since that *case* may be maintained upon a warranty; and that it is not necessary to allege the *scienter:* or if it is alleged, it need not be proved. *Williamson* v. *Allison*, 2 East's R. 446. If, therefore, the jury were satisfied that there was a warranty of the slave, and that he was unsound, the plaintiff was entitled to recover on the first count of the declaration. But the instruction given by the Hustings court forbade his recovery in that case.

The question whether the warranty was not by a covenant was not made in the Hustings court, and therefore cannot be raised or considered here. *Newsum* v. *Newsum*, 1 Leigh 86; *Barrett* v. *Wills*, 4 Id. 114. If the defendant below had intended to rely on the ground that the action should have been covenant, he should have moved to exclude the paper when it was offered in evidence to the jury.

But the bill of sale having been in blank when it was left by the appellant with the auctioneer, and having been filled up without the proper legal authority, was of no validity. *United States* v. *Nelson & Myers*, 2 Brock. R. 64, in which the cases cited on the other side are reviewed; *McKee* v. *Hicks*, 2 Dev. R. 379; *Davenport* v. *Sleight*, 2 Dev. & Bat. 381; *Cleaton* v. *Chambliss*, 6 Rand. 86.

1852.
January
Term.

Trice
v.
Cockran.

BALDWIN, *J.* delivered the opinion of the court.

In this case the instruction given at the trial, on the motion of the defendant, was not in reference to the form of the action or the form of the evidence of warranty. The defendant did not assert or concede that there was a warranty by deed, or any warranty at all. On the contrary, his own evidence presented the question, whether the bill of sale for the slave, executed by the defendant, before the sale, and in blank as to the name of the vendee and other particulars, and left with his agent in that condition, to be filled up by the latter after a sale should be made by him for the defendant, and so filled up by the agent, without any authority from the defendant by deed, or any other authority than as above mentioned, was in point of law the deed of the defendant. And also the further question, whether the verbal authority to the agent to fill up the blanks in the bill of sale still existed at the time therein mentioned, or had been exhausted by a prior sale by the agent to the plaintiff, which was rescinded by agreement between them, without consultation with the defendant. And if the bill of sale was not upon either ground the deed of the defendant, or whether it was so or not, still an ulterior question was presented by the evidence, whether the plaintiff could avail himself of a parol warranty of soundness made by the agent at his last sale aforesaid.

The instruction given for the defendant was not upon any of those points. The court was not called upon to say to the jury that if they believed the evidence the verbal authority from the defendant to his agent to fill up the blanks in the bill of sale was sufficient in law, or that it was not exhausted by the first sale made by the agent, or that the bill of sale was the deed of the defendant, or that covenant and not *case* was the plaintiff's only remedy, unless there was actual fraud in the sale of the slave, or that the plaintiff could not recover upon the parol warranty made by the agent. But the broad instruction given to the jury was in effect that, whether the warranty was by deed or by parol, the plaintiff could not recover upon either count of his declaration, without proving moreover, not only that the slave was unsound at the time of the sale, but that the defendant knew of the unsoundness, and fraudulently concealed it, or falsely and fraudulently represented the slave to be sound. This instruction was clearly wrong, in regard to the first count of the declaration, which was not founded upon actual fraud, but upon a mere warranty only.

The action of *trespass on the case* is a proper remedy for the breach of an express warranty of soundness of a slave or other personal chattel sold, as much so as the action of *assumpsit*, with which it is a concurrent remedy, and the party aggrieved may elect between them. In both forms of action the gravamen is the breach of the warranty, which in the former is treated as a tort, with the appropriate language in declaring for a tort; but a *scienter* or knowledge of the defendant of unsoundness is immaterial, and need not be alleged in the declaration, nor if alleged need it be proved. This is the firmly established doctrine of the courts, both in England and in this country, ever since its adjudication in *Williamson* v. *Allison*, 2 East's R. 446. It seems, however, that the directly opposite proposition was asserted by the defendant, and that it was contended on his part at the trial that in *case* upon an express warranty actual fraud is the gist of the action, and must be established, though a breach of the warranty be proved.

It is true that upon the second count of the declaration actual fraud, which involved the *scienter* of the defendant, was essential to the plaintiff's recovery; that count not being founded upon the warranty, but upon a fraudulent concealment or misrepresentation of unsound-

ness: but in the first count a *scienter* of the unsoundness is not even alleged, and the substantial grievance
complained of is, that the plaintiff was deceived and
injured by the falseness or wrongfulness of the warranty itself. Upon the second count the plaintiff was
entitled to recover on proof of actual fraud, whether
the warranty was by deed or by parol: And upon the
first count the defendant seems to have silently waived the question whether the warranty was by deed or
by parol. This it was competent for him to do, and if
a verdict had been rendered for the plaintiff on that
count and a new trial asked for, it could not have been
properly granted on the ground that the warranty was
by deed.

This court cannot undertake to say that the instruction given for the defendant was correct, because the
warranty was not by parol but by deed. The bill of
exceptions cannot be treated as a demurrer to evidence,
and a point raised which was not asserted in the motion for instruction to the jury. There was evidence
before the jury tending to prove a warranty by parol as
well as by deed, and it would be improper to infer the
correctness of the broad proposition as applicable to the
sale, that actual fraud was necessary to maintain the
action, by inference from a narrower proposition not asserted, that the warranty was by deed and not by parol, and therefore that in the absence of actual fraud
the proper remedy was in covenant and not in *case*. A
party moving an instruction ought to lay his finger upon the very point, and not leave the correctness of his
proposition upon the silent assumption of another proposition unasserted though presented by the evidence.
Such a practice might tend to surprise the court and
mislead the jury. In this case the jury might have inferred, and most probably did infer, from the instruction
given, that the only question for their consideration was
whether actual fraud was proved by the evidence.

It seems therefore to the court, that the instruction given to the jury by the Hustings court was erroneous, and that its judgment was therefore correctly reversed by the Circuit court.

But it further seems to the court that the Circuit court erred in its direction that upon the new trial to be had the instruction moved by the plaintiff and rejected by the Hustings court should be given to the jury, which direction must be treated as part of the judgment of the Circuit court. The instruction so directed, in effect, assumes that whether the warranty was by deed or by parol, the plaintiff is entitled to recover without proof of actual fraud on the part of the defendant.

Both judgments reversed with costs, and case remanded for a new trial upon the evidence which may be adduced by the parties, and such proper instructions as the court may thereupon give to the jury.

JUDGMENT REVERSED.

## 𝕽𝖎𝖈𝖍𝖒𝖔𝖓𝖉.

MONTAGUE'S *ex'x* v. TURPIN'S *adm'x & als.*

1852.
January
Term.

(Absent *Cabell,* P.)

**February 16th.**

1. A judgment rendered against an administratrix upon the bond of her intestate is conclusive evidence of the validity of the debt as against the administratrix.
2. Where two of three obligors in a bond are dead insolvent, and there is no personal representative of either of them, the obligee, coming into equity to enforce the payment of the debt against the personal representative of the other obligor, is not bound to have personal representatives of the deceased insolvent obligors appointed, and make them parties. And this especially where the defendant has not, by his answer or in any other mode of pleading, objected to the failure to make them parties.

In December 1841 the executrix of William Montague recovered a judgment against the administratrix of Miles Turpin deceased, in the Circuit court of Henrico county, for 920 dollars debt and 280 dollars damages. .This judgment was rendered upon a bond executed on the 19th of May 1814 by Benjamin Haley, George Williamson and Miles Turpin to William Montague for the sum of 460 dollars, for the hire of several slaves for the year 1815, and was in the penalty of 920 dollars. An execution was issued upon the judgment and was returned "no effects." The executrix thereupon, in 1842, filed her bill in the Circuit court of chancery for the Richmond circuit, against Miles Turpin's administratrix and heirs, and the sureties of the administratrix, in which she charged that the adimnistratrix had wasted the assets of her intestate's estate ; and she asked for a settlement of the administration account and satisfaction of her judgment.

1852.
January
Term.

Monta-
gue's ex'x
v.
Turpin's
adm'x
& als.

Turpin's administratrix, in her answer, stated that the bond on which the plaintiff's judgment was founded had been paid as early as 1825 by Benjamin Haley, who she insisted was the principal in the bond, by letting William Montague have a wagon and team of mules; and that she was ignorant of this fact until after the judgment was recovered.

The court directed an account of the administration on Turpin's estate, and it appeared by the report of the commissioner that the personal assets in the hands of the administratrix were more than sufficient to satisfy the judgment.

The defendants took the evidence of a witness to prove that Benjamin Haley had let Montague have a wagon and mules in payment of the debt, and the witness swore to the fact. It appeared, however, that this witness had been examined on the first trial of the action on the bond, when a verdict was rendered for Turpin's administratrix, which was set aside by the court. On the second trial the witness was not examined, for what reason does not appear, and there was a verdict and judgment for the plaintiff.

In the progress of the cause it was suggested by the counsel of Turpin's administratrix that the representatives of Benjamin Haley and George Williamson should be made parties. It appeared, however, from the record of a cause between *Turpin's adm'x* v. *Sheppard & als.*, the same reported 3 Gratt. 373, filed by the administratrix, that she had alleged in her bill in that case, and the allegation was sustained by the proofs, that Benjamin Haley and George Williamson were both dead insolvent, and that there was no representative of either of them.

The cause came on to be heard in March 1846, whereupon the court being of opinion that whatever relief, if any, the plaintiff was entitled to, it was proper, in order to obtain the same, that she should amend

1852.
January
Term.

Monta-
gue's ex'x
v.
Turpin's
adm'x
& als.

her bill and make parties to this suit the representatives of Benjamin Haley, the principal debtor, and of George Williamson, who was co-surety with Miles Turpin in the bond sought to be enforced by the plaintiff, and also joint trustee with the said Miles Turpin in the trust deed from the said Benjamin Haley, securing, among other debts, the said bond; and leave being then given to the plaintiff, as heretofore had been done, to amend her bill, and she, by her counsel in court, declining to do so, the said counsel alleging there were no such representatives in existence, the court decreed that the bill of the plaintiff should be dismissed with costs. From this decree Montague's executrix applied to this court for an appeal, which was allowed.

*Walter Harrison*, for the appellant.
*Stanard & Bouldin* and *R. T. Daniel* for the appellees.

ALLEN, *J*. delivered the opinion of the court.

The court is of opinion that as it appears that the appellant had obtained a judgment against the appellee, F. J. Turpin, administratrix of Miles Turpin, upon the joint and several bond executed to the testator of the appellant by the said Miles Turpin, together with Benjamin Haley and George Williamson, the said judgment was conclusive evidence of the validity of the debt as against the personal representative of said Miles Turpin. And it furthermore appearing from the record of the case of *Turpin* v. *Sheppard & others*, made an exhibit in this cause, and the exhibits filed in said cause, that said Haley and Williamson, who were jointly bound with said Miles Turpin, are both dead insolvent, and have no personal representatives, it was not incumbent on the appellant, under such circumstances, to have representatives appointed, and make them parties; more

1852.
January
Term.

Monta-
gue's ex'x
v.
Turpin's
adm'x
& als.

especially as the appellee, the administratrix of said Miles Turpin, did not, by her answer or in any other mode, object to the failure to make them parties. The court is therefore of opinion that the Circuit court erred in dismissing the bill because the appellant declined to amend her bill and make the representatives of said Benjamin Haley and George Williamson parties.

The court is further of opinion that the evidence in the record does not shew that any part of the debt for which the judgment was obtained was ever paid by the said Benjamin Haley, and as the cause came on for final hearing it would have been proper as the case was presented to proceed to decree in favour of the appellant; but as no decree was rendered upon the merits by the court below, and a decree by this court, proceeding to pronounce now such a decree as the court below should have done, might operate as a surprise on the appellees, it is adjudged and ordered that the decree be reversed with costs, and the cause remanded for further proceedings in order to a final decree.

## 𝕽𝖎𝖈𝖍𝖒𝖔𝖓𝖉.

### PHIPPEN *v.* DURHAM *& als.*

1852.
January
Term.

(Absent *Cabell*, P.)

**March 1st.**

1. A deed which conveys all the property of the grantor in trust for the payment of his debts, is valid, though it contains a provision that no creditor shall take any benefit under the deed who does not, within thirty days from its date, signify his acceptance of its terms and conditions; and further agree to release and acquit the grantor from all further claim for the debt acknowledged therein.

2. The creditors named in such a deed, being dissatisfied with the trusts therein declared. it is agreed between each other and the debtor that none of them will sign it, and that when the thirty days expires, another deed shall be executed by the debtor with other provisions. The day before the thirty days expires two of the creditors execute the deed, with the avowed purpose to each other of securing the benefit of the deed to all the creditors. After the thirty days has expired, one of these signing creditors files a bill against the other and the trustee, to have the trust executed for the exclusive benefit of the two; which the other resists. The other creditors having sued the debtor and obtained judgments by confession, on which the debtor took the oath of an insolvent debtor, filed their bill in the same court against the debtor and signing creditors, charging that the deed was void as to them, and that the plaintiff in the first suit was guilty of a fraud in signing the deed. On the hearing the first bill should be dismissed with costs; and the deed being in fact valid. the fund should be distributed among all the creditors according to its provisions.

On the 12th of May 1837 John Durham, a boot and shoe maker residing in the city of Richmond, having been sued for a debt which he considered he did not owe, and apprehending that a judgment might be recovered against him during the term of the court which

1852.
January
Term.

Phippen
v.
Durham
& als.

had then commenced, executed a deed of trust on his property for the benefit of his other creditors by name; providing in the deed, however, that no creditor who should not, within thirty days from its date, signify his assent to, and acceptance of, its terms and conditions, and further agree to release and acquit the said Durham from all further claim on account of the debt acknowledged by said deed to be due to such creditor, should take any benefit under the deed; and that the surplus, after paying the debts of the accepting and releasing creditors, should be paid over to the said Durham. This deed appears to have been executed without the knowledge of the creditors for whose benefit it was made, and was never signed by the trustee. On the day after its execution it was acknowledged by Durham in the clerk's office. On the 10th of June 1837, the day before the expiration of the thirty days mentioned in the deed, it was signed and acknowledged by two of the creditors, to wit, Thomas Mieure and Phippen & Mallory, by B. W. Mallory. It was never signed by any of the other creditors.

On the 17th of June 1837 Mallory & Phippen exhibited their bill in chancery against Durham, Pulliam the trustee, and Mieure; claiming that they and Mieure, as the only accepting creditors, were exclusively entitled to the benefit of the deed, and praying for an injunction, that a trustee might be substituted to the place of Pulliam, who declined to act, and that the trust might be executed. On the same day the injunction was awarded; and, under the order awarding it, the sheriff took possession of the property.

On the 23d of the same month, June 1837, Durham confessed judgments in the clerk's office at the suits of his other creditors, and, being prayed in custody, took the oath of an insolvent debtor; surrendering in his schedule (besides some other subjects, apparently of little value) whatever interest he might have in the property conveyed by said deed of trust.

1852.
January
Term.

Phippen
v.
Durham
& als.

At July rules thereafter, Stevens and others, the schedule creditors, exhibited their bill in chancery in the same court, against Mallory & Phippen, Pulliam, Mieure and Durham, and William D. Wren, sergeant of the city of Richmond, charging that after the execution of the deed, and before the expiration of the 30 days, it was agreed by all the parties, including Mallory & Phippen, that the recorded deed should not be adopted, but should become inoperative by the expiration of the 30 days, and a new deed should be made and different provisions introduced. That afterwards, to wit, on the 10th of June, the day before the expiration of the 30 days, Mieure, thinking that some benefit might result to Durham and his creditors by a mere formal signature of the deed by one or more of the creditors, proposed to Mallory to sign the deed, with the understanding that such signature should be for the benefit of all the other creditors, if it should become necessary to avail themselves of the same; with the design, however, that if no judgment should be obtained against Durham, as was apprehended by him, the deed should be cancelled, and another made carrying out the new agreement and understanding between the parties. That Mallory assented to these views of Mieure, and it was understood between them that, should a judgment go against Durham at the then term of the court, all the trust property should be sold and applied to the payment of all the debts mentioned in the deed, as if it had been signed by all the creditors. That with these views and this express understanding, Mieure and Mallory proceeded to the clerk's office to sign the deed; and at or about the time of getting there Mallory proposed to Mieure to sign the deed and claim the whole amount of proceeds, (as the same would not very much exceed the amount of their respective debts,) in exclusion of all the other creditors; that Mieure indignantly rejected this proposition as a fraud on the other credi-

1852.
January
Term.

Phippen
v.
Durham
& als.

tors, and on Durham also, and a plain and flagrant violation of the then subsisting understanding among all
the parties; and further admonished Mallory that if he
persisted in any such design, he had yet time and would
inform Durham and every creditor, so that they might
on that and the succeeding day come in and sign the
deed, and defeat the purposes of Mallory.  That finding
Mieure inflexible in this respect, Mallory yielded and
signed the deed with the distinct agreement and understanding that the acceptance, if operative at all, was to
be for the joint benefit of all the creditors.  That such
was, and is yet, the understanding of Mieure, who has
a clear pecuniary interest to take under the deed in exclusion of, and not in participation with, the other
creditors; as in the one case he would get all of his
debt, and in the other little more than one half of the
same, if so much: and that in consequence of this
agreement Mieure gave no notice to Durham nor to the
other creditors.  And they insisted that by reason of
the premises the said deed was void as to them, and the
said property was vested by law in the said sergeant of
Richmond for their benefit; and praying that the said
deed might be declared fraudulent and void as to them,
and the property sold, and the proceeds applied to the
payment of the debts due to them; or that such other
or further decree might be made as upon all the facts of
the case might seem just and equitable.

At August rules in the same year, 1837, Mieure filed
his answer to the bill of Mallory & Phippen, making
substantially the same statement as was made in the
bill of the schedule creditors, in regard to the agreement of the parties not to accept the deed, and the subsequent execution thereof by himself and Mallory, and
the purposes for which it was so executed, and declining to participate in what he considered to be a fraud.

On the 2d of August 1837 there was an order of sale
in Mallory & Phippen's suit, and on the 1st of January
1838 the report of sale was returned.

On the 19th of April 1838 the depositions of Mieure and Durham were returned and filed in the suit of the schedule creditors. Mieure proved substantially what he had stated in his answer to Mallory & Phippen's bill. Durham proved that about ten days after the deed had been admitted to record, Mr. James C. Crane, of the firm of James C. Crane & Co., creditors named therein, stated to him that he had examined the said deed, was not satisfied with it, and did not consider it good for anything, or words to that effect, and proposed that another deed with different provisions should be made and executed. That to this deponent consented; and at the instance of said Crane went to see all the creditors named in the deed who resided in Richmond. The first of them he called on was George Phippen, of the firm of Mallory & Phippen, to whom he stated what had occurred between Mr. Crane and himself. That said Phippen declared he thought the arrangement proposed by Mr. Crane the best that could be made; that he was willing to do whatever the other creditors thought most advisable, and would not sign the deed that had been admitted to record. That deponent considered said Phippen as agreeing for Mallory & Phippen not to sign the said deed, but that another deed with different provisions was to be prepared and executed for the benefit of all the creditors named in the deed. That a day or two after the expiration of the said term of 30 days, Mallory called on deponent and informed him he had signed said deed. Deponent enquired why he had done so after the agreement and understanding aforesaid. Mallory replied that he had never committed himself in the affair, and had signed the deed with a view to secure himself; and that he had it in contemplation from the first—that is, from the time of the interview between deponent and Mr. Phippen—that, if none of the other creditors signed the said deed, he would sign it himself and take the benefit thereof, to

1852.
January
Term.

Phippen
v.
Durham
& als.

1852.
January
Term.

Phippen
v.
Durham
& als.

the exclusion of the other creditors, and thus secure his debt.

Although the bill of the schedule creditors was filed in July 1837, the *subpœna* issued thereon was returned executed on Mallory & Phippen on the 1st of November 1837, the answer of Mieure to the bill of Mallory & Phippen was filed in August 1837, and the depositions of Mieure and Durham were returned and filed in April 1838, no answer was ever filed by Mallory to the bill of the schedule creditors, and none by Phippen until June 1842—five years after the bill was filed. In his answer he denies that Mallory & Phippen in any manner released or renounced their claim to the benefits of. the said deed; or that they ever accepted it on any other terms than those expressed in the deed; or that Mallory accepted and signed it in the manner and upon the terms set forth in the bill; or that Mallory had any right or authority to renounce the said deed for the firm and to surrender, without consideration valuable in law, the rights of the firm under the deed.

The two suits were never formally consolidated; but after 1838 the orders made in them were joint orders—among which was an order of continuance on the motion of Mallory & Phippen, and the affidavit of Phippen made in March 1843. On the 28th of June 1843 they came on to be heard together, and the decree was made from which the appeal was taken. By that decree the bill of Mallory & Phippen was dismissed with costs; the court being of opinion that the deed was fraudulent and void: and one of its commissioners was ordered to state an account of the claims of all the creditors of Durham in the suit of the schedule creditors, and apportion the fund among them according to the amount of their respective claims, making alternative apportionments, in one of which the debts due to Mallory & Phippen and Mieure shall be embraced, and from the other they shall be excluded, and to report, &c.

185:.
January
Term.

Phippen
v.
Durham
& als

On the day after the said decree was rendered, to wit, the 29th of June 1843, the deposition of Mallory was returned and filed in both of the cases. It was taken in Missouri. The deposition, though a short one, was taken in parcels on three different days. On the first day the witness stated, "I recollect that sometime in the year 1837 I did sign a deed executed by John Durham for the benefit of certain creditors named therein, by the signing of which I, as one of the firm of Mallory & Phippen, which firm was a creditor of said Durham, agreed to the stipulations therein contained for the benefit of the creditors." On the 2d day he stated, "I recollect that in the month of June 1837 I went, in company with Thomas Mieure, from the Bank of Virginia to the Hustings court office, and then and there each of us, in each other's presence, signed the deed made by Durham as I before referred to; and the said Mieure remarked at the same time, that he should not avail himself of its benefits to the exclusion of other creditors, but merely signed it so as to make the same binding on the said Durham. I did not give my assent to that or any other remark which went to show that I signed it for the same purpose." And on the 3d day he stated, "I signed the aforementioned deed with the intention of securing whatever advantages the said deed would give. Some time after signing the deed I was astonished to learn that the aforesaid Mieure said I assented to any thing that would compromit my interest, or deprive me of the full benefit of said deed." The deposition was objected to by the schedule creditors on the ground that Mallory, the witness, was a party on the record and interested in the subject in contest, and that the same was taken without leave of the court.

On the next day, June 30th, 1843, a motion was made by Mallory & Phippen to set aside the decree; in support of which motion they offered the said depo-

1852.
January
Term.

Phippen
v.
Durham
& als.

sition of Mallory : but the motion was overruled.  The court at the same time certified that, on the calling of the causes, the counsel for Mallory & Phippen moved the court to continue them, in order that they might have the benefit of the deposition above mentioned, which they were in daily expectation of receiving ; but the court overruled the said motion, and entered the decree aforesaid.

Phippen applied to this court for an appeal, which was allowed.

*Lyons*, for the appellant.
*Robert G. Scott*, for the appellees.

MONCURE, *J.*, after stating the case, proceeded :

If the question were *res integra*, " Whether a deed of trust, conveying all the property of a debtor for the benefit of such of his creditors as may within a specified time release him from all further claims, and providing that the surplus of the trust fund after satisfying the accepting creditors should be paid to the debtor, is valid against the creditors who do not accept ?" I would be inclined to answer it in the negative.  While the many cases on this subject are conflicting, I think the preponderance is against the validity of such a deed.  The cases are collected in 1 American Leading Cases, p. 69–85.  This court, however, has decided in favour of the validity of such a deed (*Skipwith's ex'or* v. *Cunningham*, 8 Leigh 271); and while I do not approve, I yet bow to the authority of that decision.  That case expressly recognizes the distinction taken by Chancellor Kent in *Seaving* v. *Brinkerhoff*, 5 John. Ch. R. 239, that to make such a deed valid it must convey all, and not a part only, of the debtor's property.  And as the deed in this case does not profess to convey, and did not in fact convey, all of the debtor's property, it might be contended that the deed

1852.
January
Term.

Phippen
v.
Durham
& als.

was on that ground invalid. The property, however, not included in the deed, was probably of small value, consisting, as appears from the schedule, of *choses in action* to the amount of 131 dollars 65 cents, an interest in lands lying in western Virginia, forfeited for non-payment of taxes, three old stoves, &c., and it would therefore perhaps be proper to say in this case, as was said in the case of *Skipwith's ex'or* v. *Cunningham*, that " the deed essentially complies with the requirements of the law."

But conceding that such a deed may be valid, it is certainly important to its validity that the creditors who claim the benefit of it should take no unfair advantage of the other creditors. The transaction, in its very nature, requires the utmost fairness in the dealings of the parties with each other. A debtor in failing circumstances proposes to surrender all his property for the equal benefit of all his creditors who will release him from all further claims ; and he executes and puts on record a deed for that purpose. His object is to obtain a release from all his creditors, and to be disembarrassed in his future operations ; and he offers, as the price of this relief, to make a full and fair surrender of all his property, and to place his creditors on the footing of equality. It is proper that his creditors should be notified of his offer a reasonable time before the expiration of the period limited for its acceptance, in order that they may obtain such information as will enable them to exercise their choice with discretion. It is proper that the creditors should have an opportunity of acting in concert ; and it is natural and reasonable that they should so act. In this case it was especially so ; as, when the deed was executed, it was extremely doubtful whether it would be valid if accepted. The deed bears date the 12th of May 1837. The case of *Skip-with* v. *Cunningham* was decided at April term 1837. If decided at the date of the deed, the decision was not

1852.
January
Term.

Phippen
v.
Durham
& als.

then reported, and could only have been known to a very few. At that time many counsel would have advised that such a deed would be invalid; and all would have advised that its validity would at least be extremely doubtful. Whether such a deed would be invalid, or of doubtful validity, it would have been unwise in the creditors to accept it; for by accepting it they would have tied their own hands, and might have defeated the very object they had in view. In this case, therefore, there was a double motive for concert among the creditors; and accordingly the evidence shews that they did act in concert; at least so far as to determine among themselves that they would not accept the deed. Durham proves that about ten days after the deed was executed, Mr. Crane, a creditor, stated that he had examined the deed, was not satisfied with it, and did not consider it good for anything; and proposed that another deed with different provisions should be executed. To this proposition Durham assented, and at Crane's instance went to see the other creditors. The first he saw was Phippen, who approved the arrangement proposed by Mr. Crane, expressed his willingness to do whatever the other creditors thought most advisable, and declared that he would not sign the deed that had been admitted to record. After this express disclaimer of the deed by Phippen, it may be doubted whether he could retract his disclaimer and accept the deed. But certainly he could not do so without informing the other creditors in time to enable them to accept the deed within the 30 days.

Now if the claim of the schedule creditors stood alone upon the evidence of Durham, supported as it is by corroborating circumstances, I would regard it as not overthrown by the only countervailing evidence in the case, which is to be found in the answer of Phippen. It is contended that that answer is responsive to the bill, and can only be overthrown by the evidence of

1852.
January
Term.

Phippen
v.
Durham
& als.

at least two witnesses, or one witness and corroborating circumstances. I do not consider that answer entitled to so much weight. It was not filed until about five years after the bill and the answer of Mieure, and four years after the depositions of Durham and Mieure were filed. In all of these documents it was expressly charged or proved that Phippen, or Mallory & Phippen, had consented that the deed should be inoperative, and that they were guilty of a fraud in afterwards accepting the deed or attempting to set it up for their benefit against the other creditors. Such a charge, if untrue, should be promptly denied; and if the denial be long postponed, it must lose its weight in the same proportion. The answer, too, is brief and general, though the charge is full and specific. On the other hand, the evidence of Durham is corroborated by the circumstance already stated, that what he proves might naturally and reasonably have been expected to occur; and by the further circumstance, that the conduct of the non-accepting creditors is almost inexplicable on any other hypothesis. They probably would not have remained quiet but for an agreement or understanding among all the creditors that the deed would not be accepted. But for such an agreement or understanding, it is hardly credible that (the debtor and creditors residing in Richmond, where the deed was recorded) the debtor and non-accepting creditors, or some of them, would not have gone to the clerk's office on the last of the 30 days to see if any of the creditors had signed the deed.

But the claim of the schedule creditors does not stand alone on the evidence of Durham, supported as it is by corroborating circumstances. Mieure proved that some days previous to the last day upon which, according to the terms of the deed, the creditors had a right to sign it, all the creditors therein named, as deponent believed, and certainly Mallory & Phip-

1852.
January
Term.

Phippen
v.
Durham
& als.

pen, determined not to accept the deed, but to suf-
fer it to be inoperative by the expiration of the 30 days
without signing the same. Deponent was confident
that this was the understanding and agreement among
all the said creditors.

Now here are two witnesses positively testifying to a
fact which is decisive of this case, to wit, the fact that
within the 30 days the creditors, and certainly Phippen,
agreed not to accept the deed; and if the answer of
Phippen had denied this fact in the most positive and
explicit terms, and were entitled to all the weight to
which an answer can be entitled, it would be insufficient
to resist the force of the concurring testimony of these
two witnesses.

But Mieure proved another fact which is decisive of
this case, to wit, that he and Mallory signed the deed
with the express understanding and agreement that,
if carried out by a sale of the property therein mentioned, it should enure to the benefit of every creditor who
should think proper to take under the same, in the same
manner and to the same extent as though they had also
on that day signed said deed. What evidence is there
in the case to disprove this decisive fact thus proved
by the evidence of Mieure? Not a particle, unless the
deposition of Mallory, which will be presently noticed,
be considered as evidence in the case. It is true that
Phippen in his answer denies that Mallory accepted and
signed the deed in the manner and upon the terms set
forth in the bill. But that denial was not made on the
personal knowledge of Phippen; and if made on any
information at all, such information must have been
derived from Mallory. The denial, therefore, is not evidence; and certainly cannot weigh down the evidence
of Mieure.

It will not do for Mallory to say that Phippen could
not bind him by agreeing not to accept the deed; nor
for Phippen to say that Mallory had no right " to re-

1852.
January
Term.

Phippen
v.
Durham
& als.

nounce the said deed for the firm, and to surrender, without consideration valuable in law, the rights of the firm under the deed." If these parties were right in saying that one could not bind the other, yet certainly each could bind himself, and as each did bind himself by agreeing to that which is decisive against the claim of the firm, therefore the firm is as much bound as if they had both expressly agreed not to accept the deed, or to accept it for the benefit of all the creditors. But I apprehend they are not right in so saying; and that the said several agreements of Mallory and Phippen for the firm are binding on the firm and each member of it.

Durham and Mieure are both competent witnesses. Durham is disinterested; and the interest of Mieure is against his testimony.

But it is contended that the court below erred in overruling the motion of Mallory & Phippen to continue the case, in order that they might have the benefit of the deposition of Mallory, which they were in daily expectation of receiving, and also in overruling their motion to set aside the decree after said deposition was returned.

The suits were instituted in 1837. The charges made in the bill of the schedule creditors were of such a nature as to render it proper that if they could be disproved by Mallory, his deposition should be taken and filed without any unnecessary delay. He was at that time in Richmond; for in November 1837 the *subpœna* was returned executed upon him. When he left Richmond or the State does not appear; nor is there any trace in the record of any effort to take his deposition until March 1843, six years after the filing of the bill, when the suits were continued on the motion of Mallory & Phippen, and on the affidavit of Phippen that he had, in the preceding December, sent the necessary papers to St. Louis, Missouri, for the purpose of taking

1852.
January
Term.

Phippen
v.
Durham
& als.

Mallory's deposition, but that they had miscarried, and therefore the deposition had not been taken. At the next term, to wit, on the 28th of June 1843, when the suits were again called for hearing, Mallory & Phippen moved for another continuance for the same cause, and the court overruled the motion. It seems to me that, without accounting for the great apparent default which had occurred in not taking the deposition before, Mallory & Phippen had no right to have the trial of the suits longer delayed on that ground, and that the court, in its discretion, might properly overrule the motion.

But let us consider the deposition as *in* the case; and enquire, first, whether it be competent evidence, and secondly, what is its effect, if competent. First, is he a competent witness? He certainly is not, unless he be rendered so by a release or assignment of his interest; and there is no evidence in the record of any such release or assignment, or that his interest, which certainly once existed, has ever, in any manner, been extinguished. The only allusion to the subject of his interest is contained in the affidavit of Phippen before referred to, in which he says, " that the said Mallory has now no interest in them (the suits) whatever, his whole interest having been long since transferred to this affiant," &c. But this is certainly not sufficient to disprove his interest. Secondly, suppose that he is a competent witness, what is the effect of his evidence? It might be supposed to be unnecessary to answer this question, supposing the witness to be incompetent, as he undoubtedly is, on the record as it now stands. But it is to be remembered that the deposition of Mallory was not filed, and the exception to the competency of the witness taken, until after the dismission of the bill of Mallory & Phippen. Mallory may in fact have no interest in the controversy, as is stated in the affidavit of Phippen before mentioned; and the fact that he has none may have been, or may yet be, proved in the suit of the

1852.
January
Term.

Phippen
v.
Durham
& als.

schedule creditors, which is still pending in the court below. In this view of the case it becomes important to answer the question as to the effect of Mallory's evidence, supposing him to be competent; and I will therefore now proceed to do so. He testifies under very unfavourable circumstances. In 1837, when the deed was executed and the transactions connected with it were all fresh, a full and specific detail of them was made in the bill of the schedule creditors, and the answer of Mieure to the bill of Mallory & Phippen, and the conduct of Mallory was thereby deeply implicated. He never answered the charges made against him; and never gave his deposition in the suits until June 1843, six years after the suits were instituted, when his deposition was taken in Missouri. The deposition is equivocal and unsatisfactory; and under the circumstances can have little weight against the testimony of a witness testifying against his interest and at a time when the transactions to which the testimony relates were all fresh in the memory of the witness. But admit the statement of Mallory to be strictly and literally true, and what does it shew? "I recollect," says the witness, "that in the month of June 1837 I went, in company with Thomas Mieure, from the Bank of Virginia to the Hustings court office, and then and there each of us, in each other's presence, signed the deed made by Durham, as I before referred to; and the said Mieure remarked at the same time that he should not avail himself of its benefits to the exclusion of other creditors, but merely signed it so as to make the same binding on the said Durham. *I did not give my assent to that or any other remark which went to shew that I signed it for the same purpose.*" But did he express his dissent to that remark of Mieure? He does not say that he did, as he certainly would have said had the fact been so. Then, when the remark was made by Mieure, Mallory, according to his own admission, was silent: And his silence was

1852.
January
Term.

Durham
v.
Phippen
& als.

either designed to give consent, or to induce Mieure to believe that he consented, and prevent him from informing the other creditors. For Mallory must have known that if he had given the slightest intimation of dissent Mieure would have at once informed the other creditors, so that they might, by signing the deed in time, defeat the object of Mallory and accomplish that of Mieure. If the silence of Mallory was designed to give consent, then Mallory & Phippen are bound by such consent. If it was designed to deceive Mieure, it was a fraud which can give Mallory & Phippen no advantage over the other creditors.

If, therefore, the case stood alone upon the statement of Mallory, that statement would be fatal to the pretensions of Mallory & Phippen to the whole of the trust fund in exclusion of the schedule creditors.

The great difficulty I have had in this case has been in determining whether Mallory & Phippen should be allowed to participate at all in the distribution of the fund.

In attempting to secure to themselves the benefit of the deed of trust in exclusion of the schedule creditors, they attempted to perpetrate a fraud. They came into a court of equity with unclean hands; and one of the established maxims of that court required it, I think, to dismiss their bill, "for the court will never assist a wrong-doer in effectuating his wrongful and illegal purpose." 1 Story's Equ. Jur. § 64, e. But it must be remembered that the schedule creditors also came into a court of equity; and though they came in with clean hands, yet they came asking equity. And another maxim of the court, one which, of all others, it perhaps most delights to enforce, certainly most often enforces, declares that "he who asks equity must do equity." Then the question is, Is there any equity which these schedule creditors should be required to do to the accepting creditors, as the price of that equity which is

1852.
January
Term.

Phippen
v.
Durham
& als.

demanded by the former? I think there is. The deed of trust was not in itself fraudulent; and was accepted by Mieure, if not Mallory also, with the understanding that it should enure to the benefit of all the creditors. They seem, therefore, to have acquired a legal advantage, and to have some equity. And the schedule creditors cannot deprive them of that legal advantage without the aid of a court of equity, and cannot obtain that aid without doing equity. But what is the measure of that equity? Certainly not the payment of the whole of the claims of the accepting creditors, for that would exhaust the whole trust subject, and be against the understanding with which the deed was accepted, besides giving effect to the unlawful purpose to which Mallory & Phippen afterwards sought to pervert their acceptance of the deed. The answer to the question is given by another maxim of the court, that " equality is equity "; or, as it is sometimes expressed, " equity delighteth in equality." 1 Story's Equ. Jur. § 64, f. The application of this maxim to the case will carry into effect the understanding with which the deed was accepted, and will do equal justice to all the creditors.

But a question still remains to be answered, and that is, whether the creditors shall be required to release their debtor Durham from all further claim on account of the debts due them after the fund aforesaid shall have been exhausted in the payment of said debts, according to a provision to that effect in the deed? With all deference for the opinions of those of my brethren who differ in opinion with me on this question, I think the creditors should not be so required. To require them to do so would be to give effect to the deed against the express agreement of all the creditors that it should be ineffectual; would be to take away from the schedule creditors rights acquired by legal diligence, without any necessity whatever for so doing. All that the accepting creditors can require is to be allowed to

1852.
January
Term.

Phippen
v
Durham
& als.

participate *pro rata* in the distribution of the fund.
When that is accorded to them, why should any other
terms be imposed on the schedule creditors? Why
should they be required to release the debtor? The
accepting creditors will not be benefitted by the release
of the debtor. Their interest is the other way. The
schedule creditors ask no equity against the debtor:
against him their rights both at law and in equity are
complete. He not only has no equity, but demands no
equity in the case. He is a defendant in both of the
bills, and answers neither of them. According to the
pretensions of Mallory & Phippen, they and Mieure
would get the whole trust fund and release the debtor,
while the entire claims of the schedule creditors would
be left unsatisfied and liable to be enforced against him.
According to the pretensions of the schedule creditors,
they would get the whole trust fund, leaving the balance of their claims, and the entire claims of the accepting creditors, or at least of Mallory & Phippen, unsatisfied and liable to be enforced against the debtor.
In this conflict of pretensions the debtor has no legal or
equitable interest, and claims none. In his deposition
he maintains the pretensions of the schedule creditors,
which leave him bound for the entire amount of the
claims against him after applying the trust fund to their
payment. The only question is whether the schedule
creditors should get all under their execution liens, or
allow the accepting creditors to participate with them.
These two classes of creditors are alone interested in the
solution of this question. It is a matter of indifference
to the debtor whether the balance due by him after the
application of the trust fund be due to one class or other
of his creditors. Why, then, should a release be required
of the creditors? Why should this measure of relief
be forced upon a debtor not seeking it—not entitled to
it according to his own evidence in the case? I am for
giving no effect whatever to the deed of trust, except

1852.
January
Term.

Phippen
v.
Durham
& als.

to the extent of affording an opportunity to a court of equity for the application of its favourite maxims, that " he who asks equity must do equity," and " equality is equity," and it is with great difficulty that I go even to that extent in this case.

The court below, in dismissing the bill of Mallory & Phippen, did not intend to decide that they were not entitled to participate in the distribution of the fund, but reserved that question for future decision in the suit of the schedule creditors. In that suit, to which all the parties to this suit are defendants, the fund can, and ought, I think, to be apportioned *pro rata* among all the creditors.

I am for affirming the decree.

DANIEL, *J.* I have not been able to discover anything on the face of the deed out of which this controversy has arisen, or in the history of the case, from which to draw the conclusions that the said deed is fraudulent in fact or in law. The right of a debtor, in making a deed of trust upon all of his estate for the benefit of his creditors, to insert in the deed the condition that all who should accept its provisions should release him from all further demand on account of the debts secured, was recognized by this court in the case of *Skipwith's ex'or* v. *Cunningham,* 8 Leigh 271; and reason and authority are there furnished for the distinction made between the conveyance of the *whole* and the conveyance of *part* only of the debtor's property upon such condition.

There is, I think, nothing in the case from which to infer that the deed made by Durham originated in any purpose or design to conceal from his creditors or secure to himself any portion of his property. It is true that the schedule rendered by him on taking the oath of an insolvent debtor contains a list of small debts due to him, and a few articles of personal property of trifling

1852.
January
Term.

Phippen
v.
Durham
& als.

value, not mentioned in his deed. There is no proof, however, that these debts existed, or that he owned these articles of property, at the date of the deed. And if such proof existed, or the probability of the existence of the fact is to be inferred from the short space of time that elapsed between the date of the deed and the time of surrendering the schedule, it would, in the absence of all other evidence of fraud, and in view of the inconsiderable value of the subjects in question, be harsh, I think, to refer the failure to embrace them in the deed to any dishonest purpose on the part of the grantor. The charitable and fair presumption is that he omitted them from forgetfulness, if indeed he was the owner of them when he made the deed.

The deed may therefore be justly treated as one devoting the whole of the debtor's property to the demands of his creditors, and the objection made to the condition which it imposes on the creditors is answered by the decision of this court in the case above cited. The deed is, I think, unassailable on this ground, or on any other, so far as the grantor is concerned; and the Circuit court erred in dismissing the plaintiff's bill *on the ground that the deed was fraudulent and void.* The conduct of the plaintiffs has, however, been such as, in my opinion, to debar them of all claim to the interference of a court of equity to enforce, at their suit, any right which they acquired by virtue of their having signed and accepted the deed within the time prescribed. They and Mieure only of the creditors having executed the deed, stand, according to its provisions, as preferred creditors, and entitled to appropriate the whole of the trust fund, if necessary, to the satisfaction of their debts. The testimony taken in the suit of Stevens and the other schedule creditors, however, discloses the fact that the deed was signed by Mieure, and by Mallory, in the name of Phippen & Mallory, with the express understanding that the deed should enure to

1852.
January
Term.

Phippen
v.
Durham.
& als.

the benefit of all the creditors as fully as if each of the others had also signed the deed. Phippen & Mallory now repudiate this understanding, and avail themselves of their position to claim for themselves and Mieure the whole of the trust fund to the exclusion of the other creditors. This conduct, taken in connection with the fact, disclosed in the testimony of Mieure, that Mallory had proposed to him that they should sign the deed and claim the benefit of it to the exclusion of the other creditors, and only consented to the understanding above mentioned upon being warned by Mieure that if he did not the other creditors should be notified of his course, and thus have an opportunity also of signing the deed, furnishes, I think, sufficient proof that the use now sought to be made of the deed by Mallory was one contemplated by him at the time he became a party to it. Such being the origin and nature of their claim, Phippen & Mallory, as plaintiffs in a court of equity, were, in my opinion, entitled to no aid or relief whatever; and the chancellor, for the reasons I have stated, did right, I think, in dismissing their bill. Whether their position as defendants in the suit brought by the schedule creditors will so far avail them as to give them the right to insist that they shall not be compelled to yield their place in the deed, except on the condition of being allowed to receive, according to the understanding with Mieure, their *pro rata* share of the fund, is a question reserved by the chancellor for a future adjudication, which I do not wish to anticipate by any expression of opinion further than what has been rendered necessary in passing upon their rights in their own suit. As yet no step has been taken in either branch of the proceedings of which the appellants have, in my opinion, any right to complain; and I am for affirming the decree.

1842.
January
Term.

Phippen
v.
Durham
& als.

BALDWIN, J. This is an appeal from a joint decree, rendered in two suits embracing the same subject and involving the same controversy, and heard together without objection; and the appeal has therefore brought up both causes for adjudication here. In one of them, that first instituted, Mallory & Phippen are the plaintiffs; and in consequence of the omission as defendants of all the creditors secured by the trust deed in question, except Mieure, the merits of the controversy are not fully developed in that suit. But in the other, brought by nearly all the creditors secured by the deed, very shortly after the first, the merits of the controversy have been fully developed, by the pleadings, proceedings and proofs, between the proper parties. It is not to be supposed for a moment that it would be proper, from separate and unconnected views of the two cases, to render a decree repugnant and conflicting in itself in regard to the rights of the parties and the relief consequent thereupon. We must, therefore, of necessity, look in the first place to the suit in which the merits have been fully developed, for the consideration and determination thereof, and the result will then designate the disposition to be made of the other case.

In Virginia the principle is established that a deed of trust made by a debtor, conveying his property for the security of creditors, which is in all other respects fair and *bona fide*, is not to be treated as fraudulent because it imposes upon the creditors intended to be secured the condition of releasing to the grantor so much of their respective demands as may remain unsatisfied after the application thereto of the proceeds of the trust subject, and requires of them their acceptance of the provisions of the deed within a given time. *Skipwith's ex'or* v. *Cunningham*, 8 Leigh 271. The effect of such a condition is to give the whole benefit of the trust to the creditors who comply with it, to the exclusion of those who fail to do so within ·the prescribed period. It has somewhat the nature of a forfeiture, and there ought to be perfect fairness and good faith on the part of the creditors seeking to avail themselves of it.   If, therefore, some of the creditors, with the design of excluding the rest, resort to false representations or other deceptive arts, by which the latter are surprised or deluded, and so prevented from acceding to the terms proposed in the deed, such misconduct furnishes a proper ground for relief in a court of equity.

I think it appears from the record that, by common understanding and agreement amongst the creditors, including the defendants, Mallory & Phippen, it was determined, in consequence of apprehensions entertained in respect to the validity of the deed, that none of them would become parties to the instrument, but that the same should be suffered to become inoperative by their failure to affix their signatures within the prescribed period of thirty days; that in conformity with this understanding and agreement, the deed was not signed by any of the creditors, with the exception of Mallory & Phippen and the defendant Mieure; that within a day or two before the expiration of the time limited, Mallory and Mieure went together to the clerk's office, where the deed was deposited and recorded, and then and there signed the same, the latter individually, and the former for himself and his partner Phippen; that Mieure acted for the honest purpose of preserving to the creditors in general intended to be secured by the deed the benefit of its provisions, by admitting them to a participation therein, and Mallory for the dishonest purpose, and with the preconceived design, of taking the other creditors by surprise, excluding them from all resort to the property, and appropriating it to the satisfaction of the debt due to himself and partner; and that Mallory accomplished his purpose by taking advantage of the general delusion and general expectation of

1852.
January
Term.

Phippen
v.
Durham
& als.

1852.
January
Term.

Phippen
v.
Durham
& als.

the creditors to which he had contributed, by lying by
until it was too late to warn the other creditors, unless
by the vigilance and diligence of Mieure ; and by quiet-
ing the latter (who had indignantly rejected a proposition to become his confederate, and threatened to
rouse the other creditors,) by consenting to concur with
him in admitting them to participation in the benefits
of the trust.

These facts, I think, are established by the deposition of Mieure, of whose competency there can be no
doubt, his evidence being directly against his own pecuniary interest, which, like that of Mallory, is to exclude
the other creditors from all participation in the trust
subject.   The testimony of Mieure is strongly corroborated and sustained by the deposition of Durham, if
the latter be a competent witness, which is a question
of some difficulty, from the peculiar nature of the case.
It is a question which I do not deem it necessary to
consider, and I shall therefore not rely upon the evidence of Durham, but treat Mieure as the only witness
for the plaintiffs.

The credibility of Mieure is quite obvious, and the
weight of his testimony is not impaired by the rule of
evidence that requires a responsive answer, negativing
allegations of the bill, to be overcome by two witnesses,
or one witness and corroborating circumstances.   The
rule is not applicable to a case like this, in which
the respondent does not speak from his own personal
knowledge.   The answer, though purporting to be that
of Mallory & Phippen, is in fact the answer of Phippen
alone ; and was sworn to and filed by him only, and
not by Mallory, against whom the bill is taken for
confessed.   It is a sweeping answer, putting in issue by
denial general allegations of the bill, but evading the
details therein set forth in regard to the misconduct of
Mallory, as to which the respondent Phippen knew
nothing personally, though seeking to avail himself of

1852.
January
Term.

Phippen
v.
Durham
& als

it, and in regard to which he does not undertake to express any knowledge or even belief.

The veracious testimony of Mieure is therefore sufficient in itself, and I need not even refer to the circumstances of the case by which it is corroborated. In regard to the deposition of Mallory, one of the plaintiffs, filed after the rendition of the decree, if the matter of it were entitled to any weight, it is so obviously irregular and incompetent that in my view of the case it would be a waste of words to make any remarks upon it.

It seems to me clear that the plaintiffs are entitled to relief within the scope of the allegations of their bill, but not to that specifically designated in the bill, which seeks to set aside the deed of trust altogether, and enforce their supposed rights as schedule creditors subsequently acquired when Durham took the oath of insolvency. But that relief would, I think, be improper; the sound objection being not to the validity, but the abuse of the deed, which was regularly accepted by both Mieure and Mallory, and avowedly with the view of admitting the other trust creditors into participation with them of its benefits. The purpose of Mieure was *bona fide*, and though that of Mallory was not so, it may be treated as if it had been; and it cannot be doubted that it was competent for them to waive any exclusive advantage to themselves, and constitute themselves trustees for the other creditors intended to be secured. To abrogate the deed would be wrong and injurious in regard to some of the trust creditors, who were not also schedule creditors, including Mallory & Phippen, and against them the plaintiffs are entitled to relief only upon the condition of doing equity, according to the well established rule which operates in favour of wrong doers, however iniquitous and fraudulent their conduct may have been. It would be improper also in

Vol. viii.—31

1852.
January
Term.

Phippen
v.
Durham
& als.

respect to Durham, against whom the trust ought to be
carried out upon the prescribed condition of his being
released from the demands of the creditors so far as unsatisfied by the application of the trust subject.

Mallory & Phippen, for the reasons already stated,
are not aggrieved by so much of the chancellor's decree as dismisses their bill with costs, that being the
legitimate consequence of a decision against them upon
the merits in the other suit, in which any equities on
their part are reserved for the final decree, by which
complete justice may be done all round amongst the
parties.   It is true the reason for dismissing the bill of
Mallory & Phippen is stated to be that the deed of trust
is fraudulent and void; but the presumption is that the
chancellor had in mind the fraudulent operation sought
to be given to the deed, and that he did not mean to
treat the provisions of the deed as nought, directly in
the teeth of the express decision of this court in the
case of *Skipwith's ex'or* v. *Cunningham*.   And however this may be, the decree is merely interlocutory,
with the proper reservation, and we are not to anticipate
that it will be carried out by the final decree upon
erroneous principles.

I think there is no error in the decree to the prejudice of the appellants, and that it ought to be affirmed.

ALLEN, J.   The case of *Skipwith* v. *Cunningham*
has affirmed the right of the debtor, conveying all his
property for the benefit of his creditors, to exact a general release from the creditors accepting the provisions of
the deed, as the condition on which they shall participate in the fund provided.   The deed in this case cannot be assailed on that ground; nor is there any evidence of actual fraud in its execution.   The evidence,
however, I think, shews that there was an understanding on the part of the creditors, including the appellants,
that the proceeds of the property embraced in the trust

1852.
January
Term.

Phippen
v.
Durham
& als.

should be applied to the payment of all the debts named in the deed in the same manner as if all had signed it.  The appellants, therefore, have been guilty of the fraudulent attempt to acquire an unfair advantage over the other creditors, in the effort to exclude them from the benefits of the deed.  Still it seems to me the court below erred in dismissing the bill filed by the appellants to enforce the execution of the deed.  Though the case came on for hearing together with the bill filed by the judgment creditors to impeach the deed for fraud, there was no necessary connection between the causes.  The decree dismissing the bill is a final adjudication against the appellants.  Mallory & Phippen are not judgment creditors.  Their whole claim to satisfaction of their debt, or any part of it, out of this property, rests upon the deed, and this the court by its decree declares to be fraudulent and void, and therefore dismisses the bill.  If this decree stands, of what avail is the instruction of the court in the case of the creditors, directing the commissioner to make alternative apportionments of the fund amongst the creditors, one embracing, the other excluding the debt of Mallory & Phippen?  Resting, as they must do, on the deed alone, and that being adjudged in so many words to be fraudulent and void, it is difficult to perceive how they can be let in to participate in the fund.  The general creditors claim, not under but against the deed; they assert their legal lien; and when by the decree in the case of the appellants the deed is put out of the way as utterly void, the property must of necessity be distributed amongst the creditors at whose suit the debtor has taken the insolvent oath.  Considering the deed as valid, and that the conduct of the appellants in asserting an exclusive claim to the benefits of it, though improper as it regards the other creditors, could not avoid the deed or do away with the effect of an acceptance of its provisions, it only remained for the court to carry into

1852.
January
Term.

Phippen
v.
Durham
& als.

execution the agreement and understanding of the parties; and to apply the proceeds to the debts named, in
the same way as if the creditors had signed it. If they
had signed they would have released their debtor for
the residue of their debts. This has been done by
Mallory & Phippen.

The debtor, having made a fair dedication of his property, upon terms which the law justified him in imposing, has a right to insist upon a release from all who
claim to participate. And the fund should have been
divided between the creditors who have .signed and
such of those named in the deed as may agree to the
terms prescribed. Such a distribution of the trust fund
can only be made in the suit instituted by Mallory &
Phippen to execute the trust; and would be totally inconsistent with the case made by the general creditors,
who rely on their legal lien alone, and repudiate the
deed. And it would present a most anomalous case
were the court, after a solemn decree declaring the
deed fraudulent and void in a suit brought to enforce it, to proceed, in a suit brought to impeach it, to
distribute the trust fund as though the deed were a
valid security.

The rule that the party, to entitle himself to relief,
must appear with clean hands, cannot be applied to this
case without injustice to others as well as the appellants,
the plaintiffs in the court below. The deed, if valid,
divested the debtor of his property and vested it in the
trustee for the benefit of the creditors who signed within the period prescribed. The signatures of Mallory &
Phippen and Mieure imparted vitality to the deed; and
the fund could only be administered by the trustee or
under the direction of a court of equity. When, therefore, the trustee declined to act, a court of equity was
constrained, upon the application of any party interested, to interpose and protect the fund. And its jurisdiction having once attached, it must go on to dispose of

1852.
January
Term.

Phippen
v.
Durham
& als.

the subject according to the rights of the parties. The bill was not filed to set up a fraudulent deed—that is conceded to be good and valid; the claim, therefore, as preferred by the bill, was proper, and the objection goes, not to the validity of the deed, but to the extent of the rights of the creditors named, as modified by the understanding and agreement amongst them. This, therefore, is nothing more than the ordinary case of a party, who has rights proper to be enforced in a court of equity, claiming more than the proof shews him entitled to. The court in such cases may, in the exercise of its discretion, subject the party to costs; but it cannot refuse relief of some kind. This will appear more clearly if the case is viewed by itself and without reference to the bill filed by the creditors after the institution of the suit by Mallory & Phippen. Could the court, if that were the sole case pending, have dismissed the bill after its jurisdiction had attached and it had actually taken possession of the trust fund? It must of necessity go on to dispose of the fund. If the deed is sustained it could not be restored to the debtor, for he had parted with all right to it. Nor would it be proper to place it in the hands of the trustee, even if, as in this case, he had not declined to act. Nothing would remain for the court to do but to enquire into the rights of the parties and to distribute the fund accordingly. A dismissal of the bill would have been erroneous in the case supposed, and there does not seem to be any distinction between that and the case before us. But in this case the error is aggravated by the decree declaring the deed fraudulent and void; thus precluding the court from ever treating it as a valid subsisting security for any purpose, as between these parties, in any subsequent proceeding. I think the decree should be reversed, and the cause remanded with instructions to hear both causes together, and to distribute the trust fund amongst

1852.
January
Term.

Phippen
v.
Durham
& als.

the creditors who have signed the deed and such others of the creditors named therein as may elect to come in and release the debtor according to the terms of the deed.

But the other judges differ from me, and the decree is therefore affirmed.

# Richmond.

## CHARLES v. CHARLES.

(Absent *Cabell*, P.)

March 4th.

1. The rights of a husband to the property of his intended wife may be intercepted by his agreement to that effect. And where by express contract before and in contemplation of marriage, for which the marriage is a sufficient consideration, he agrees to surrender his right to the enjoyment of the property during the coverture, and his right to take as survivor, there remains nothing to which his marital rights can attach during the coverture, or after the death of the wife. In such a case the wife is to all intents to be regarded as a *feme sole* in respect to such property; and there is no necessity that the marriage contract or settlement should limit the property to her next of kin upon her failure to appoint, but it will pass as if the wife died *sole* and intestate.

2. If the husband has relinquished his marital rights to his wife's property, he is not entitled to administration upon her estate.

A marriage being about to take place between Henry H. Charles, of the county of York, and Martha P. Wynne, widow of Richard Wynne deceased, a deed, bearing date the 8th day of October 1835, was executed by the parties for the settlement of her property. This deed recited that it had been agreed between the parties that Mrs. Wynne should, after the marriage, receive and enjoy, during the joint lives of the said Wynne and Charles, the interest and occupation of her personal estate ; and also that the same, and the interest and profit thereof, from and after the decease of such of them as should first happen to die, should be at the sole and only disposal of the said M. P. Wynne, notwithstanding her coverture.   And that it had been also agreed, that in case the said Charles should, after the marriage, happen to survive the said M. P. Wynne, that he should not claim any part of the real or personal estate whereof the said M. P. Wynne should be seised or possessed or entitled to at any time during the coverture ;  and that the said real and personal estate of the said M. P. Wynne should be in no wise under the control of said Charles, nor in any manner or at any time subject to his debts.

The deed then proceeds to convey in the name of M. P. Wynne to James Kirby sr., with the consent and approbation of Charles, which is witnessed by his sealing the deed, all her property, both real and personal, in trust for Mrs. Wynne until the marriage; then upon trust that Kirby will permit her to enjoy the sole, separate and exclusive use of the said property for her own separate and special use ; and upon the further trust that the trustee will permit the said M. P. Wynne to dispose of the said property by deed, will, or otherwise, as she shall think proper ; and that he will convey a legal title to the person or persons to whom she may convey the property.   This deed was executed by Charles, Mrs. Wynne and the trustee, and duly admitted to record : And the marriage took place.

In December 1849 Mrs. Charles died, leaving her husband surviving her, without having disposed of her estate either by deed or will, or otherwise.   She left no child surviving her or descendant of a child, though she had had children by her two former marriages; but they had died before her marriage with Henry H.

Charles.   Her distributees, if her husband was not entitled to her personal estate, were her nieces, descendants of sisters, of whom one was married to William H. Charles.

The slaves belonging to Mrs. M. P. Charles at the time of her marriage never went into the possession of the trustee, but always remained in the possession and enjoyment of Henry H. Charles, during the coverture.

At the April term 1850 of the Circuit court of York county, Henry H. Charles moved the court to be permitted to qualify as the administrator of his late wife, Martha P. Charles; which motion was opposed by William H. Charles, who asked for the administration for himself, on the ground of his marriage with one of the nieces of Martha P. Charles, entitled, as he insisted, to a portion of the estate.   These motions came on to be heard together in April 1851, when the court overruled the motion of Henry H. Charles, and granted the administration to William H. Charles.   And thereupon an exception was taken to the opinion of the court, and Henry H. Charles applied to this court for a *supersedeas*, which was awarded.

*Morson*, for the appellant.

It is submitted that the decision of the Circuit court was erroneous and prejudicial to Henry H. Charles, and ought to be set aside and reversed.   He must, by operation of law, be entitled to the property, unless the deed has intercepted the rule of law, and, by substituting a rule of its own and a rule intended to apply to the emergency which has occurred, has clearly not only taken the property from him, but given it to others.   For where, upon a given state of facts, the rule of law turns property over to one man, it cannot be turned over to another by any compact, agreement, or declaration of any party or parties which stops short of clearly giving and manifesting an intention to give it to such other.

Heirs cannot be disinherited by the strongest declarations in a will that they shall not take : the will must go further, and designate others who shall take. *Boisseau* v. *Aldridges*, 5 Leigh 222. By similar reasoning, husbands cannot be deprived of their rights of property arising "*jure mariti*" by a deed which shall even declare that they should not have them, unless the deed further provided that they should go to others. If they be not by the deed, in the event that has occurred, turned over to any body, then it is not a "*casus fœderis*," not a case which the deed has provided for, but a "*casus omissus*," one for which a rule must be found, not in the deed, but in the general principles of the law. And these general principles give the property to the husband ; enable him to qualify as the wife's administrator, and afterwards to keep possession absolutely for his own benefit, subject only to the payment of her debts. See 1 Lomax's Ex'rs 135, 136, 310, 311 ; Tate's Dig. 394-5, § 7. See also Code of Virginia of 1849, p. 541, § 4.

Even should it be held, then, that the words of the deed manifested an intention to take the subject from the husband upon the contingency that has happened, they failed to give it to others and only authorized the wife so to give it ; and this she has never done. Of consequence neither the deed nor the wife has ever yet given the subject to others ; and if given to others it can only be by operation of law. But there certainly is no rule of law which, under the circumstances, can give the property to others ; though there is the general rule of law which does give it to the surviving husband.

It is worthy of remark that, in the recital of the deed, as well as in the express declarations of trust, while great care is evinced to secure the property to the separate use of the wife, and to give her the power to dispose of it, there is an utter absence of any expression or provision to point out how it is to go in case of her making no such disposition. The trustee, "his executors, administrators and assigns," are to permit the *feme* (studiously omitting, apparently, her executors or administrators) to enjoy the separate use of the property, and to dispose of it by deed, will, or otherwise; and they are required to convey the legal title to the person or persons to whom she may convey the property. Now this omission is very strong to shew (made as it was in a deliberate deed) that, as against the husband, the only parties intended to be preferred, certainly the only parties expressly preferred, were the *feme* and her appointees; and it is unnecessary to dwell upon the essential distinction between such appointees and the present antagonists of the husband. Indeed, it can scarcely be doubted that in the case of *Bray* v. *Dudgeon*, 6 Munf. 132, the introduction of expression, where here there is omission, was the turning point of the adjudication. There the deed expressly provided that, upon the failure of the wife to appoint, " her proper and legal heirs" should take; and it is manifest that it was this provision which excluded the husband alike from the administration and the property. A similar commentary obviously occurs in reviewing the case of *Ward* v. *Thompson*, 6 Gill & John. 349, in which the rights of the husband were held to be extinguished by the stipulation that without his interference in any manner the trust subject should be under the exclusive and entire management and control of the wife, " her heirs, executors, administrators, or assigns," who, it was agreed, should " receive and enjoy the rents, issues and profits." The case of *Marshall* v. *Beall*, 6 How. S. C. R. 71, is explicable in the same way. And the governing principles applicable to the present case, and similar cases, are very luminously illustrated by Chancellor Kent in *Stewart* v. *Stewart*, 7 John. Ch. R. 229, 245, 246, 247, a case which takes what seems to be the true ground, that the marital rights of the husband, over the property of his wife, can only be extinguished by plainly and clearly giving that property to others, or by conferring on the wife, or her representatives, other than the husband, the power to make and accomplish such gift, and an execution by her or them of such power.

Besides it is submitted that the true construction of the recitals in the deed does not authorize the inference that they are intended to deprive the husband entirely, at all events, and upon every contingency, of all rights of property in the trust subject. That passage in the recital, (omitted in the declaration of trusts,) which provides that the husband, in case of surviving the wife, should not claim any part of the trust subject, ought to be taken in connection with the rest of the deed : and so taken cannot properly be made to do more than stipulate that the husband, as against the claims of the appointees under the wife, (so appointed in conformity with the deed,) should not assert any conflicting or repugnant rights. This would reconcile all parts of the deed. Anything else would bring them in conflict. But should such conflict be brought on, the recital would have to give way to the declarations of trust. Mere matter of introduction could not over-ride the solemn provisions in the conveyance and the declarations of the trusts therein. *Stewart* v. *Stewart*, 7 John. Ch. R. 229; Sheph. Touch., ch. 5, p. 75, 76, note 62, 78, 77, 88, in 30 Law Libr.

If not precluded from taking the property, of course he is entitled to the administration.

*Meredith*, for the appellee.

The whole question is, who is entitled to the estate of Mrs. Charles? On the question who is entitled to administration there has been some vacillation in the decisions on the English statutes; but when the case came up between the husband and the next of kin, it was decided in favour of the husband; but he took the administration because he was entitled to the property, and only when entitled. *Fielder* v. *Hanger*, 5 Eng. Eccl. R. 265; *Watt* v. *Watt*, 3 Ves. R. 244; *Bailey* v. *Wright*, 18 Ves. R. 49; *Fettiplace* v. *Gorges*, 1 Ves. jr. 46; 1 Wms. Ex'ors 244; Toller's Ex'ors 85, 116; *Cutchin* v. *Wilkinson*, 1 Call 1; *Hendren* v. *Colgin*, 4 Munf. 231; *Bray* v. *Dudgeon*, 6 Munf. 132; *Thornton* v. *Winston*, 4 Leigh 152. These cases shew that the person entitled to the property is entitled to administration on the wife's estate.

The enquiry then is, what interest did Henry H. Charles take in his wife's estate. And this depends on the construction of the deed of the 8th of October 1835, executed by the parties. Pending the treaty of marriage the husband covenanted that she should have her own estate; and that he would not claim any interest in it if he survived her. The property of the wife was not property in possession, in which the title of the husband was perfected by marriage; or there would have been no necessity for administration on her estate. But the legal title was in the trustee and the beneficial interest was in the wife; and as there must be a joint interest, in order that one may take as survivor, there could be no title by survivorship in the separate property of the wife.

It is insisted by the counsel on the other side that though it is true that the husband excludes himself, he should have gone further and pointed out some one else to take the property in the event of the intestacy of the wife. And *Boisseau* v. *Aldridges*, 5 Leigh 222, is relied on for the proposition. But there the son was no party to the instrument; here the husband is a party to the deed; and he, in consideration of the marriage, covenants that he will not take anything either during the marriage or if he survives the wife. This is all the husband could do. He had no right to say how the property should go; nor had he any interest which he could convey. All that he had was such an interest as he could only release and only release to her; and that he did, and thereby her title became perfect. *King* v. *Bettesworth*, 2 Strange's R. 1118; 2 Story's Equ. Jur. § 1382. This last authority, and the cases there cited, shew that all the husband has to do, to exclude himself, is to create a separate estate in the wife, and that excludes him.

It is said that the wife should have made an appointment; and that it is only her appointee who can exclude the husband. The wife here stands as a *feme sole*, and has the power and the estate of a *feme sole;* and an appointment is unnecessary to pass her property. Here Mrs. Charles had a separate estate, on which there was no limitation as to time; and therefore she had the power to dispose of it without regard to the power of appointment. *Tappenden* v. *Walsh*, 1 Eng. Eccl. R. 100; *Fettiplace* v. *Gorges*, 1 Ves. jr. 46; 2 Story's Equ. Jur. § 1389, 1390, 1394. In such a case it is not necessary that the deed or marriage agreement should direct who shall take the estate after the death of the wife without making an appointment. *Bradley* v. *Westcott*, 13 Ves. R. 445, 451; *Barford* v. *Street*, 16 Ves. R. 135; *Anderson* v. *Dawson*, 15 Ves. R. 532; *Gackenbach* v. *Brouse*, 4 Watts & Serg. 546.

ALLEN, *J.* delivered the opinion of the court.

The deed of marriage settlement, duly executed by the parties and their trustee before marriage, recited amongst other things that it hath also been *agreed*, that in case the said Charles should after the intended marriage happen to survive the said Martha, that he should not claim any part of the real or personal estate whereof the said Martha should be seised or possessed or entitled to at any time during the coverture between them; and that the said real and personal estate of the said Martha should be in no wise under the control of the said Charles, nor in any manner or at any time subject to his debts. The deed then proceeds to grant the property of the intended wife to the trustee, and by the declaration of trust the separate and exclusive use of the property is secured to the wife; the trustee was to permit her to dispose of it by will or otherwise, and to convey the property to such appointee or alienee: but in the declarations of trust there is no express provision excluding the husband in the event of his surviving, and in default of any appointment or disposition by the wife. And it is contended that by operation of law the husband surviving is entitled, in virtue of his marital rights, to take the property, as she did not dispose of it or appoint the uses to which it should be applied after her death. The rights of the husband to the property of his intended wife may be intercepted by his agreement to that effect; and where by express contract, for which the marriage is a sufficient consideration, he agrees to surrender his right to the enjoyment of the property during the coverture, and his right to take as survivor, there remains nothing to which his marital rights can attach during the coverture or after the death of the wife. In such case the wife is to all intents to be regarded as a *feme sole* in respect to such property; and there would seem to be no necessity for any limitation over to her next of kin in the event of a failure to appoint during her lifetime. The husband having by contract for a good consideration released his rights as survivor, the property must pass as though she had died *sole* and intestate. That such was the intent of the parties in this case is clear from the deed. The contingency of his surviving was foreseen, and the agreement as recited in the deed signed by all the parties provided for it. By that agreement so recited, he bound himself not to claim the property should he happen to survive his wife. There is nothing to indicate

1852.
January
Term.

Charles
v.
Charles.

an intention to restrict the claim as against the appointees of the wife. The expressions refer not to persons against whom he would not claim, but to the subject as to which in that contingency he released all claim ; and to shew more clearly that such was the intent of the agreement, it is furthermore recited that the property was not to be under his control, or in any manner or at *any time* subject to his debts, not restricting the time to the continuance of the coverture.

Having thus by contract intercepted the marital rights of the husband either to enjoy during coverture or to take by survivorship, and this intention appearing on the face of the deed, it was only necessary that the declarations of trust should provide for the control and authority of the wife during the coverture. And the property, if not disposed of, passed to her personal representative for the benefit of her next of kin, as if no marriage had ever taken place, and she had died *sole* and intestate.

The right of the husband to administer depending on the question whether in virtue of the marital right he is entitled to the property, and as by the agreement recited in the deed of settlement he relinquished and renounced such right, his motion to administer was properly overruled, and the administration granted to the appellee, one of the distributees of the deceased. The order should be affirmed.

## Richmond.

### CRALLE & *als.* *v.* MEEM & *als.*

(Absent *Cabell*, P. and *Daniel*, J.\*)

**March 4th.**

1. D being the endorser of C on several notes discounted at bank, and it being expected that he will endorse other notes for C, the latter executes a bond binding his heirs to D, with a condition that he will, when required by the bank or D, pay off all such notes, and thus indemnify and save D harmless. C dies whilst D is his endorser on several notes, which, by an arrangement with the bank, D takes up by the discount of his own note; and subsequently the administrator of C pays up the whole amount of the notes, principal and interest, out of the personal estate. HELD: That this bond was a valid security to D, binding the heirs of C; and that the notes, to the extent of the penalty, having been paid out of the personal assets, the simple contract creditors of C are entitled to have the assets marshalled, and to be substituted, to the extent of the penalty of the bond, to the rights of D upon the real estate in the hands of the heirs of C.

2. Upon a bill by simple contract creditors to marshal assets, it is competent for the court, in its discretion, to decree a sale of the real estate in the hands of the heirs, some of whom are infants, for the payment of the debts: But it is premature to decree a sale before adjudicating the claims of the creditors, and so ascertaining the amount of indebtedness chargeable upon the lands of the decedent.

3. Though such a decree for a sale of land has been prematurely made, yet if the sale is made and confirmed, the court will not set the sale aside on the petition of the purchasers, if upon the hearing it appears that the sale is beneficial to the infants.

4. The application of the purchasers, in such a case, to have the sale set aside, should be by petition in the cause. And if they proceed by bill to enjoin the collection of the pur-

---

\* Judge *Daniel* had been counsel in the cause in the Circuit court.

1852.
January
Term.

Cralle
& als.
v.
Meem
& als.

chase money, and have the sale set aside, the bill should be treated as a petition in the cause, and be brought to a hearing with it.

5. The court having made the decree for a sale of the real estate. on the petition of the adult heirs, and with the assent of the creditors, it is erroneous to proceed to sequestrate the rents of the other real estate in the hands of the heirs for the payment of the debts, before deciding upon the claim of the purchasers to have the sale set aside.

This was a suit in the Circuit court of Lynchburg, by John G. Meem and others, simple contract creditors of John J. Cabell deceased, against his administrator and heirs, to marshal the assets, and have payment of their debts out of the real estate of the deceased. The bills, after setting out the debts of the plaintiffs, and the qualification of Thomas R. Friend as the administrator of John J. Cabell, stated that he had disposed of all the personal estate, and had exhausted it in payment of debts, many of which bound the heirs of his intestate; and that he had rendered no account of his transactions. That among the claims which should be regarded as binding the real estate, and which had been discharged by the administrator out of the personal assets, were sundry negotiable notes, made by John J. Cabell in his life time, and endorsed by Henry Davis. That to secure himself from loss Davis had taken from Cabell a bond binding his heirs in the penalty of 10,000 dollars, with condition to pay off and discharge these notes, when required by Davis or by the bank at which they were made payable, so as to save harmless and indemnify Davis from loss or damage on his endorsements. That after the death of Cabell these notes were protested for non-payment, and subsequently discharged by the administrator out of the personal assets, to an amount exceeding the penalty of the bond.

The prayer of the bills is for a settlement of the accounts of the administrator, and that the assets may be marshalled, so as to subject the real estate descended to

1852.
January
Term.

Cralle
& als.
v.
Meem
& als.

the heirs to the payment of the outstanding simple contract debts; and for general relief.

The administrator, widow and heirs answered the bill, and called for proof of the complainants' debts. They admitted that John J. Cabell was largely indebted at the Bank of Virginia and the Farmers Bank at Lynchburg, by notes endorsed by Henry Davis, and that Davis held the bond referred to in the bill; but they denied that the condition of that bond had been broken; the notes on which Davis was endorser having been paid by the administrator, so that Davis had sustained no loss or damage by his endorsements.

They admitted that Cabell died seised of a large real estate, which was then held by his widow and heirs; and they asked that if it should be held that it was liable for the payment of the debts of the complainants, the defendants might be allowed to select such parts of the estate as they may desire to be disposed of, so that the satisfaction of the plaintiffs may be attended with as little injury to them as practicable.

In October 1837 a commissioner was directed to settle the accounts of the administrator, designating the grade and dignity of debts paid by him; and also to state an account of the real estate of which John J. Cabell died seised, the annual value thereof, and in whose possession it was at the time of the decree; and also an account of the debts due to the respective plaintiffs.

The report of the commissioner was made, and was recommitted for the purpose of correcting some errors in the calculation of interest on the complainants' debts, and was again returned to the June term 1839. At this term of the court Richard K. Cralle, who had married one of the daughters of John J. Cabell, then deceased, leaving children, the widow of John J. Cabell, and S. W. Ward, a daughter, the two first in their own right and as guardians of some of the infant heirs, filed

1852.
January
Term.

Cralle
& als.
v.
Meem
& als.

a petition in the cause, in which, after referring to the debts of the complainants, they say they have no reason to doubt that their debts are really due; and that they at all times anticipated that a resort to John J. Cabell's real estate, for their payment, would become necessary, and they had therefore in their answers prayed that when a decree should be made, subjecting the real estate, they might be permitted to designate the portion thereof to be so subjected, and the manner and mode of doing it.

They stated that a division of the real estate (except a tract of land in Bedford owned jointly by Cabell and Leftwich) had been made among the heirs at law and widow, under an order of the Hustings court of Lynchburg, but had not been confirmed, owing to the pendency of this suit; but that since the division the several heirs had held and enjoyed their respective portions thereof. That there was a tract of land lying on the Kanawha river, containing one thousand acres, which was divided into equal portions of two hundred and fifty acres to each one of the heirs of John J. Cabell, each part being regarded as of equal value. That this land, though deemed very valuable, was not productive in rents or profits to the heirs, and could be sold without affecting the division of the balance of the estate among them. That the other property divided yielded a large rent, which they were compelled to apply to purposes of present support. That the debts to be paid were of such magnitude that if the court should sequester these rents and annual profits for the payment of the debts, that the petitioners would be wholly deprived of their resources for living for an indefinite period, and thereby be subjected to serious inconvenience. They pray that the court will decree a sale of the Kanawha land, upon such a credit as will ensure the greatest possible price, and that the proceeds may be applied to the payment of the debts of the complain-

1852.
January
Term.

Cralle
& als.
v.
Meem
& als.

ants. They think such a sale would be beneficial to all concerned; and will be entirely agreeable to Thomas R. Friend, who was then absent, and who had married a daughter of John J. Cabell, then deceased, leaving three children, all of whom were infants. This petition was accompanied by an affidavit of Richard K. Cralle verifying the facts therein stated.

The infant defendants to the bills were made parties defendants to this petition, and an answer was filed for them by a guardian *ad litem*.

Upon the filing of the petition and the answer, the cause came on to be heard, when the court pronounced its opinion, declaring that when the parol contract creditor is decreed to have satisfaction out of the real assets of his deceased debtor's estate, he is but substituted to the right of some creditor whose debt bound such real assets: that these rights by substitution cannot be greater than the originals for which they are substituted; and that in either case the land ought not to be sold if the debt can otherwise be paid in a reasonable time. And it appearing to the court, from the report of the commissioner, that the rents arising from the real estate would, in all probability, be sufficient to discharge the respective demands of the several simple contract creditors aforesaid in a reasonable time, the court accordingly was about to proceed to sequester the rents of the real estate, with a view of applying the same to the payment of said debts; but the defendants, the heirs at law and distributees of the said John J. Cabell deceased, thereupon presented to the court their petition, with the answer of the infant heirs, by their guadian *ad litem* thereto, praying, for certain reasons therein set forth, a sale of a portion of the lands whereof the said John J. Cabell died seised and possessed, in satisfaction of said debts, in lieu of the payment of the same out of the rents. And the court, on consideration of said petition and of the answer thereto, together with an ex-

1852.
January
Term.

Cralle
& als.
v.
Meem
& als.

hibit (the report of the commissioners for the division of the estate among the heirs), and the affidavit of Richard K. Cralle, filed therewith, is of opinion, from the facts therein disclosed, that it would be most conducive to the interest of said heirs and distributees, some of whom are infants, to proceed to sell the real estate designated in said petition, rather than to sequester the rents, since by the latter proceeding said heirs and distributees would be deprived of their property, and consequently of their chief means of support, until said debts should be paid, which in all probability could not be effected for some three or four years. And not at that time deciding upon any other matter, the court, with the assent of the plaintiffs, decreed that Richard K. Cralle and Samuel Hannah, either of whom might act, should proceed to sell at public auction, upon the premises, the said Kanawha land, on a credit of one, two, three and four years, in equal payments, taking from the purchasers bonds with good personal security for the purchase money, and retaining the lien as a further security, subject to be resold if default should be made in the payment of the bonds as they fell due; and report their or his proceedings to the court. And liberty was reserved to the infant defendants to shew cause against the decree at any time within six months after they should respectively attain the age of twenty-one years.

At the May term of the court for 1840 Richard K. Cralle returned his report of the sale of the Kanawha land, by which it appeared that he had sold one undivided moiety of the Kanawha land for 18,000 dollars, to Joseph Friend and Thomas R. Friend. One of these purchasers, Thomas R. Friend, was the owner of one fourth of this tract of land, by purchase from Mrs. Ward, one of the daughters of John J. Cabell, and he held another fourth in right of his deceased wife, who was another daughter of said Cabell; and by agreement with

1852.
January
Term.

Cralle
& als.
v.
Meem
& als.

the commissioner before the sale of the undivided moiety, they were to take the one moiety at the price the other should bring. At the same term of the court this report was confirmed; and the report of the commissioner upon the accounts was recommitted, with the exceptions thereto, to a special commissioner, who was directed to call in all the outstanding creditors of John J. Cabell.

In October 1841, on motion of the plaintiffs, and by consent of the counsel of all the parties, Cralle and Hannah, or either of them, were directed to collect the outstanding bonds given for the Kanawha lands, then due and in arrear, and the other bonds as they should fall due, and, after paying all the costs of the suit, to deposit the residue in one of the savings banks in Lynchburg. In June 1842 the report of the special commissioner was recommitted, with the exceptions thereto, to one of the commissioners of the court. And again, on the motion of the plaintiffs, the court directed Cralle and Hannah forthwith to proceed to collect the bonds then due for the purchase money of the Kanawha land, and to pay the money arising therefrom into one of the banks at Lynchburg to the credit of this cause.

In May 1844 Commissioner Davis returned his report, to which there were various exceptions by the administrators and heirs of Cabell. Some of these exceptions were to particular debts reported as due from John J. Cabell; and to all of them for the mode in which the commissioner charged interest upon them. The only exceptions, however, which it is necessary to notice, refer first to the notes secured by the bond mentioned in the bill as having been executed by John J. Cabell to his endorser, Henry Davis, for his security. This bond bears date the 15th of August 1821, and is in the penalty of 10,000 dollars. The condition is set out at length in the opinion of the court. The facts connected with this exception were, that at the time of the

1852.
January
Term.

Cralle
& als.
v.
Meem
& als.

death of John J. Cabell, which occurred between the 6th and the 20th of August 1834, Henry Davis was his endorser on three notes, which had been discounted at the Bank of Virginia at Lynchburg, for 2500 dollars, 5000 dollars, and 3000 dollars; and on one, which had been discounted at the Farmers Bank, for 3000 dollars. On the 20th of August 1834 the directors of the Bank of Virginia made an entry upon their minutes, that " on the application of Henry Davis, he is permitted to assume the payment of John J. Cabell's note endorsed by him for 2500 dollars, and due at this day; he, the said Davis, giving his note for the same amount at sixty days, endorsed by Peter Dudley, and further securing the payment of the same by the deposit of the notes aforesaid of the said Cabell (protested), and an indemnifying bond executed to him by the said Cabell in the penalty of ten thousand dollars." Subsequently the same arrangement was made as to the other two notes discounted at that bank. It does not certainly appear what arrangement was made by Davis with the Farmers Bank; but he took up the note at that bank by a discount of his own with Peter Dudley as endorser, leaving Cabell's note with the bank as collateral security.

The arrangement with the Bank of Virginia was executed; the note of Cabell being taken up after it was protested by the proceeds of the note of Davis endorsed by Dudley; and the notes of Cabell and his bond were deposited with the bank as collateral security: the endorsement of Dudley being considered as merely nominal, and only intended to put the note in form. And it was the understanding between the bank and Davis that he could not be coerced to pay his notes until Cabell's means were exhausted. The discount on Davis's notes were paid by him from time to time as they were renewed, until they were paid off by Thomas R. Friend, the administrator of Cabell, out of the personal assets of the estate. Friend paid on the first note

1837.
January
Term

Craik
& als.
v.
Meem
& als.

784 dollars 20 cents on the 24th December 1834: and he paid on the second note 500 dollars on the 19th of November of the same year.  On the 13th of February 1835 Friend deposited in the Bank of Virginia bonds amounting to 14,391 dollars, proceeds of the personal estate of his intestate, for the purposes following:  The proceeds of such as should be first paid were to be applied to the extinguishment of a note of 3000 dollars, which Dr. Cabell owed the Farmers Bank at Lynchburg, endorsed by Henry Davis, and assumed by him at Cabell's death, with all discounts and charges on the same.  The proceeds of such as should be next collected were to be applied to the extinguishment of the three notes which Cabell owed to the Bank of Virginia at Lynchburg, endorsed by Henry Davis, and by him assumed as they severally fell due after Cabell's death, with all discounts and charges thereon.  And if anything should remain after satisfying these claims, with all discounts and charges, it was to be applied to the payment of a debt of 379 dollars 9 cents due from Cabell to Davis.  These bonds were collected, and the debts for which Davis was bound as endorser, with all discounts and charges thereon, were paid in December 1835 and January 1836.  Previous thereto, viz., in November 1834, judgments were recovered by Davis, suing for the benefit of the banks, against the administrator of Cabell upon the notes which had been protested as they fell due after Cabell's death.

It appears that the only payments made by Davis as endorser for Cabell, except by the discount of his note, were the discounts upon the first making and the renewal of his notes; and these advances had been repaid at the times and in the manner hereinbefore stated.

Another exception referred to a note of 5000 dollars, made by John J. Cabell and endorsed by Richard E. Putney.  On the 9th of March 1834 Cabell and Putney entered into a covenant binding their heirs each to

1852.
January
Term.

Cralle
& als.
v.
Meem
& als.

pay to the other the sum of 10,000 dollars, or so much as would secure him for his endorsement for the other. This covenant is set out in the opinion of the court. At the time of Cabell's death Putney was his endorser on a note for 5000 dollars, dated the 6th of August 1834; but it does not clearly appear from the evidence that this was for the same debt for which Putney was Cabell's endorser at the date of the covenant. The Bank of Virginia at Charleston sued Putney upon his endorsement, and in October 1834 he confessed a judgment: And thereupon the bank agreed to suspend execution of this judgment for two years from that time, upon his executing his bond, with David Ruffner as his surety, with condition for the payment of the judgment, interest and costs at the end of the two years. This bond was executed; and the debt was afterwards paid by the administrator of Cabell out of the personal estate.

Pending the proceedings in this cause, Joseph Friend and Thomas R. Friend in September 1842 filed their bill in the same court for an injunction to restrain the collection of the purchase money of the Kanawha land. After referring to the suit of the creditors of John J. Cabell against his administrator and heirs, and the proceedings therein up to the time of filing their bill, they state that the accounts ordered, except the administration account, had not been taken, and especially that the order directing the account of the debts due the complainants had not been completed, but was then in progress of execution; nor, as they believed, had any account been taken of the real estate or its annual rents.

They referred to the petition filed by Richard K. Cralle and others and the proceedings therein, and the sale of the land made by Cralle to themselves, and the confirmation of that sale by the court.

1852.
January
Term.

Cralle
& als.
v
Me·m
& als.

They further represent that at the time of their purchase they made no enquiry into the title to the land,
or the authority under which it was offered for sale.
That since the sale they have come to the knowledge
of facts which they are advised renders their title worthless and unavailing, at the election of the infant heirs
of John J. Cabell, when they shall attain full age.
That the sale was made for the payment of simple contract debts, which had not as yet been proved and established so as to authorize a sale of the real estate.
That the admission of the justice of the debts by the
petitioning heirs did not give any additional validity to
the sale ; as among them Mrs. Sally W. Ward was the
only adult heir, and she had previously sold her interest
in the land to the complainant, Thomas R. Friend.
That the other petitioners were infants of very tender
years, who could not, as the complainants were advised,
be bound by their express assent, and much less by the
merely negative admissions of their guardians or next
friends.

They further represent that from the best information they had been able to obtain the debts to which
John J. Cabell's estate may be subjected cannot exceed
five or six thousand dollars; and that the real estate would
in ordinary times yield an annual rent of 7000 dollars,
which would, if applied under the directions of the court,
in a short time discharge all the debts which bound the
land.   And they further represent that a tract of land
lying in Bedford county, belonging in the greater part
to the estate of John J. Cabell, has since his death been
sold by commissioners under a decree of the County
court of Bedford, for a large sum of money, which had
been applied, or was in a course of application, to the
payment of the debts binding the heirs of Cabell.
That notwithstanding all this Richard K. Cralle, acting
under an order of the court, had instituted actions at

1852.
January
Term.

Cralle
& als.
v.
Meem
& als.

law upon the bonds of the complainants against them and their sureties, in the Circuit court of Kanawha county, where the same were then pending.

And making the heirs of John J. Cabell and the complainants in the creditor's suit defendants, they ask that the decree of the 7th of June 1839, for the sale of the Kanawha land, and all proceedings had under it, may be set aside, rescinded and annulled; that their bonds for the purchase money may be delivered up to be cancelled; that Cralle, as commissioner of the court, may be enjoined from proceeding to collect the amount of said bonds; and for general relief. The injunction was awarded.

Richard K. Cralle, Mrs. Ward and Henry Ann Cabell, the youngest daughter of John J. Cabell, and who had then attained the age of twenty-one years, answered the bill. They insisted upon the necessity of the sale of the land, and that it was advantageous to the infant heirs, and should be enforced. A number of the creditors also answered, insisting upon the validity of the sale, and that it should be enforced; and testimony was taken on both sides to sustain their pretensions.

On the 21st of November 1846 the case of the creditors of John J. Cabell against his administrator and heirs was brought on to be heard, upon the papers formerly read and the report of the commissioner Davis, with the exceptions thereto, when the court, being of opinion that the simple contract creditors of John J. Cabell, upon the principle of marshalling assets, have the right to occupy the shoes of Henry Davis and Richard E. Putney, who held two securities, each binding as well the personal assets as also the heirs, which were paid off and satisfied by the defendant, Thomas R. Friend, administrator of John J. Cabell, out of the personal assets of his intestate's estate; and being further of opinion that the creditors should not longer be hindered and delayed by the sale of the Kanawha

1852
January
Term.

Cralle
& als.
v.
Meem
& als.

land, made upon the petition of the heirs of John J. Cabell, for their own easement, under the decree of the 7th of November 1839, though it appears on the face of said decree that it was made with the assent of the plaintiffs, after the court had pronounced its opinion, and was in the act of sequestering the rents and profits of the said John J. Cabell's real estate, which had descended upon them; which rents and profits before this time would probably have paid off and satisfied all the debts: And this is the more equitable, because the validity of that sale, and the title to the land sold under it, being questioned by one or more injunctions in this court between the alleged purchasers of the lands and Cabell's heirs, (the record of which injunctions is filed among the papers in this cause,) and they having made no movement in it, the court will leave this family matter to be settled among themselves, and will now restore the creditors to the position they occupied at the date of the decision in June 1839. Wherefore the court doth adjudge and decree that the rents and profits of all the lands and tenements of which the said John J. Cabell died seised and possessed, save the Kanawha and Bedford lands, which have been sold by the procurement of the adult heirs, be sequestered to create a fund as well for the payment of the simple contract creditors in the proceedings mentioned, to the extent that they may be entitled by marshalling the assets, as for the payment of the bond debts proper.

The decree then proceeded to appoint a receiver, with power, by distress or otherwise, to collect all the rents then due or to become due upon the real estate remaining unsold as aforesaid, and to rent out the property from year to year, and collect the rents; and after paying all the taxes, costs, charges and necessary repairs, to deposit the residue in one of the savings banks in Lynchburg to the credit of the cause.

1852.
January
Term.

Cralle
& als.
v.
Meem
& als.

The decree further ordered that one of the commissioners of the court should take an account of the moneys arising from the sales of the Bedford lands aforesaid, shewing what had become of the same; and that he should examine and report upon the exceptions taken to the administrator's account, and make any changes in the report of Commissioner Davis warranted by the proofs in the cause; and also that he should take a further account of the simple contract creditors. From this decree the heirs of John J. Cabell, except the children of Mrs. Friend, applied to this court for an appeal, which was allowed.

*Stanard* and *Bouldin*, for the appellants.

One of the questions in the cause, and the principal one, is that arising upon the effort to charge the real estate, upon the principle of marshalling assets, with the amount of the bond executed by Dr. Cabell to Davis, and upon the covenant between Cabell and Putney.

First. Did the bond from Cabell to Davis constitute a claim upon the real estate of Cabell in the hands of his heirs, of which, under the circumstances of this case, the simple contract creditors may avail themselves? By the act of 1831, Sup. Rev. Code, p. 220, the notes endorsed by Davis ranked with specialties in the administration of the assets of Dr. Cabell's estate, and the notes, with all costs and charges, were paid by Cabell's administrator out of these assets. The question then is, has the bond been forfeited so as to enable Davis, or any one else, to maintain an action upon it; and if it has been so forfeited, what is the extent of the damages which can be recovered in such an action? And the further question is, whether by means of this bond the simple contract creditors can claim on the real estate of Cabell; Davis himself never having been subjected to loss?

Let us try this question of forfeiture as if in a court of law; and let us enquire whether there has been a

1852
January
Term.

Cralle
& als.
v.
Meem
& als.

forfeiture of the bond which would have given Davis a right of action upon it.

Before a forfeiture can be established two facts must be made out. First. That Cabell or his administrator was requested to pay the notes on which Davis was bound as Cabell's endorser. And, second. That being requested, they failed to pay, so that Davis suffered loss.

To sustain an action at law on the bond, it would have been necessary to aver and prove a special request. The court will observe the language of the bond; and will observe that the request may be made by Davis or his representative, but it is to be made to Cabell alone. But passing by this, it is clear the request should have been made to the administrator of Cabell, as it should have been made to himself in his lifetime. Now where a request is required to do a collateral act, especially to create a forfeiture, it must be a special request. Otherwise, if a note for fifty dollars had not been paid, Cabell or his administrator might have been sued. This, then, is a case in which a precedent request is necessary and must be averred. *Birks* v. *Trippet*, 1 Wms. Saunds. 36; *Hill* v. *Wade*, Cro. Jac. 523; *Bowdell* v. *Parsons*, 10 East's R. 359; *Carter* v. *Ring*, 3 Camp. R. 459.

If the demand was necessary, was it made? It may be said the note was protested: But this was no demand. The protest is sufficient to charge an endorser on a note; but to forfeit a bond the demand must be personal. 5 Viner's Abr. 207, P. B.

It may be said that Davis was compelled to renew the notes, and pay the discounts upon the renewals; and that this was a forfeiture of the bond. But the condition of the bond is to pay the notes when thereto required. Davis did not require the payment of the notes by the administrator: And if he chose to have the notes renewed and to pay discounts upon them, without

1852.
January
Term.

Cralle
& als.
v
Meem
& als.

giving notice to the administrator, and requiring him to pay them, that was his own act, for which he can blame no one but himself.

It will be said, however, that suits were brought upon the notes. It seems that some time after the arrangement was made with the bank by Davis, there was a judgment by confession by the administrator, in a suit brought in the name of Davis for the benefit of the bank. But whenever an actual request is necessary a suit is not sufficient. In some cases, where the condition of the bond is to pay money, a suit has been held sufficient; but where a collateral act is to be done an actual request is necessary. If the bank had sued Davis on the notes, it might have been a question whether that created a forfeiture of the bond. But before notice to the administrator, the bank agreed with Davis that they would not sue him until their remedies against Cabell's estate were exhausted : And as a part of the consideration for that agreement Davis deposited with the bank Cabell's bond. Davis, therefore, had no right of action against Cabell's administrator until all the notes were paid. What could he have averred and proved? What damage could he have laid? Could he aver he had been sued? No. Could he aver that he was liable to be sued? No. Could he say he had sustained damage? No. Would it not have been a complete defence, even after the judgments on the notes, that the administrator was prepared to pay, and had paid, the whole amount of these debts?

There was, then, but one state of facts under which Davis was entitled to sue upon the bond of Dr. Cabell : And that was that the bank had been unable to make the money out of Cabell's estate upon the notes. If the bank had failed to make the money by proceedings against the administrator upon the notes, and had required Davis to pay, and he had paid it, then he might have required the bank to return to him the bond, that

1852.
January
Term.

Cralle
& als.
v.
Meem
& als.

he might hold Cabell's heirs liable to him. But until he had paid off the whole amount to the bank, he was not entitled to the bond. Then, in the state of things as they really existed, Davis could not sue upon the bond. The bank could not have sued upon it, because it was not given to them or for their indemnity. And yet, although no person had a right to sue upon the bond, and no steps were ever taken to forfeit it, this is now attempted by these simple contract creditors, through the agency of a court of equity. But in the case of *Webster* v. *Bannister*, Doug. R. 393, it was held that even if an actual forfeiture has occurred, the parties may waive it; and it cannot be enforced by third persons; and that especially by the aid of a court of equity.

If, as we contend, a demand was necessary to entitle Davis to the benefit of the bond, the question arises, when should that request be made? The suits on the notes were brought after they had all fallen due. It is true generally that a suit is a demand; but here the demand is a condition precedent, which must be complied with strictly *modo et forma*. Davis or the bank might claim upon the notes or the bond, but if he intended to claim upon the bond, then he must comply with the condition.

But if the suits upon the notes is a demand so as to enable Davis to sue on the bond, this right of action gave only the right to recover for the amount of actual damages sustained. This is not a bond for money, but with a collateral condition; a bond of indemnity. This condition is to pay the notes so as to indemnify and save Davis harmless. And if the notes, with all the costs and damages actually incurred by him, are paid before a suit is brought upon the bond, no action can be sustained upon it. To shew that this is a bond of indemnity, I refer to *Pond* v. *Warner*, 2 Verm. R. 532; *Douglass* v. *Clarke*, 14 John. R. 177; *St. Albans*

1852.
January
Term.

Cralle
& als.
v.
Meem
& als.

v. *Curtis*, 1 D. Chip. R. 164. And the condition, being for the benefit of the obligor, shall be construed favourably. 2 Lomax Dig. 113. Let us suppose that Davis had brought a suit on the bond after the suits against the administrator upon the notes, what damage could he have averred that he had sustained? Will it be said he was damnified by being fixed for his liability as endorser? The bond does not protect him from that damnification. And moreover, his giving his own note was voluntary on his part, without notice to the administrator. And so too was his payment of discounts upon the notes.

Again, Davis could not have sued before December 1835, that being the time when the suits were brought against the administrator; and in December 1834 the administrator had deposited five hundred dollars in the bank; and he deposited much more in January and February 1835—indeed more than enough to pay all the discounts. Davis never paid Cabell's note. The bank never surrendered that or intended to do it. The giving his own note did not pay it, because one security will not extinguish another of the same grade. *Manhood* v. *Crick*, Cro. Eliz. 716; *Norwood* v. *Grype*, Id. 727. This is the state of things if Davis had sued upon the bond. But he did not sue upon it, and has not claimed the benefit of the forfeiture. And if he could and did not, how can third persons insist upon enforcing it in equity.

If a court of equity could take jurisdiction to enforce the forfeiture of the bond, it could not be acted on without pleadings and a jury. Cabell's heirs had a right to the verdict of a jury and judgment of a court on the question whether the condition of the bond was forfeited; and also on the extent of the damages. If the suits on the notes was a demand, the judgments may have been confessed upon the express condition that the suits should not be considered. Upon a plea stating the

1852
January
Term.

Cralle
& als.
v.
Meem
& als.

facts it would have been a good defence at law; and
will a court of equity undertake to decide the question
upon an exception to a commissioner's report. If the
court will take jurisdiction of this question, all it could
do would be to direct an issue of *quantum damnificatus*,
or an issue as to the forfeiture of the bond.

Again. These plaintiffs come here upon the ground of
marshalling assets. But in this case they cannot come
to marshal assets without violating the principle that
a court of equity will never actively aid in enforcing a
penalty or forfeiture. 2 Story's Equ. Jur. § 1319, p.
551. But if this penalty had been actually incurred,
might not the heirs have come into equity to be relieved
from it, by paying the notes and the damages sustained
by Davis.

As to the covenant with Putney, that only applies to
the notes in being at the time of its execution, without
any provision as to their renewal. And these plaintiffs
seek to charge Cabell's heirs on account of a note for
5000 dollars, endorsed by Putney, dated the 6th of August 1834, after the date of the covenant. This particular note was certainly not in existence when the
covenant was executed; and there is neither a provision in the covenant for the renewal of the notes, nor
proof that this note was a renewal of any note in existence at the time the covenant was executed. It might
have been renewed twice at sixty days. Hurlstone on
Bonds, p. 94, 9 Law. Libr.; *Union Bank* v. *Ridgely*,
1 Har. & Gill 324.

The court below clearly erred in making a decree for
the sequestration of the rents, after having decreed a
sale of a part of the lands, not only at the request of
the heirs, but with the concurrence of the plaintiffs; and
after, too, that sale had been made and confirmed, and
orders have been made, on the motion of the plaintiffs,
directing the commissioner to proceed to collect the purchase money. The court in its decree says it was

1852.
January
Term.

Cralle
& als.
v.
Meem
& als.

about to make a decree to sequestrate the rents, when the heirs applied to have a sale of a part of the lands. If the court was about to make such a decree, it was about to do what it had no right to do. For the court will not sequestrate the rents where a sale of a part of the land will pay the debts. And in this case the sequestration was certainly improper until the court had decided whether that sale should stand.

*Robinson,* for the creditors.

It is very clear that the heirs had not intended to raise the first and second questions discussed by the counsel, in 1839, when they filed their petition for the sale of the land.

At the death of Dr. Cabell, Davis was his endorser on four notes; and it is beyond all question that if Cabell's administrator failed to pay these notes, and Davis paid them, that Davis would have a remedy against Cabell's heirs upon his bond. We say both facts are shewn to have occurred.

First. Cabell's administrator failed to pay the notes, and they were regularly protested. But it is argued that a special request is necessary to give Davis a right of action on the bond; and that none was made. I need not go beyond 2 Lomax Dig. 113, to shew that any words evincing an intention to make the request is sufficient. The condition of the bond is that payment should be made when required by the bank or Davis. And we say he was required to pay exactly in the mode contemplated by the parties. Of course they contemplated that the demand of payment was to be made in the mode applicable to such a case. Here there was a demand of payment, protest and notice, which was the usual and regular mode of making the demand in such a case. All this doctrine, therefore, about a special request, is beside the case. We have an action and a judgment; and the latter is an adjudication of the fact

1853.
January
Term.

Cralle
& als.
v.
Meem
& als.

that the administrator of Cabell had been required to pay, and had not paid, the notes on which Davis was Cabell's endorser.

It is said Davis was not sued. The object of the bond was to prevent his being sued. But Davis paid the notes; and from that moment he had a right of action on the bond. Counsel asks what Davis could have averred in an action on the bond. He could have averred that the administrator had not paid off the notes when required, and that they had been paid by himself: And he could have proved his case as easily as he could plead it. The protest would have shewed both demand and refusal to pay; and the production of the notes by Davis would have proved his payment of them: And the true measure of damages would have been the whole amount of the notes not paid by the administrator, and paid by Davis. Upon the proof of these facts the recovery would have been certain. Could it have been prevented by shewing that Davis had paid the amount of the notes by the proceeds of his own notes. Of what consequence is that. It is every day's mode of payment by an endorser called on suddenly to take up a note. Nor can it make any difference that the bank was informed when it discounted Davis's note that the proceeds would be applied to pay Cabell's note; or that they were informed that they should have the security of Cabell's notes and the bond. It is said that Davis at no time had possession of Cabell's notes. They belonged to him, and he only transferred them back to the bank as collateral security. And then it is asked how Davis could maintain an action on the notes when he was not entitled to them. The best answer is that he did maintain an action against the administrator on the notes; and the judgment decided that he had the right of action upon them. And if he had a right of action on the notes, he had a right of action on the bond; because he could

1852.
January
Term.

Cralle
& als.
v.
Meem
& als.

not have a right of action on the notes unless upon demand and neglect to pay, and payment by Davis; and these would entitle him to sue on the bond. The right to sue upon the bond is so clear that I presume no question would have been made of Davis's right to sue if he had found it necessary to sue the heirs; but the administrator paid him, and therefore rendered a suit by him unnecessary.

It is said that when the administrator paid the notes he was entitled to them and the bond. That is true. But that is the case always; every administrator is entitled to a bond when he pays it. But that cannot impair the right of the simple contract creditors to come into equity to marshal the assets: And we have but the common case of the bond creditor having two funds and the simple contract creditor having but one; and the first taking that which was subject to satisfy the last, the last is entitled to go against the other fund.

The next question is as to the effect of the covenant with Putney. Putney was on a note of Cabell's which was protested, and Putney was sued; and then gave security for the payment of the amount. It is in proof that the debt evidenced by the note on which Putney was endorser had been contracted some time before that note was made; and construing the covenant according to the intention of the parties, the court will construe it to include the renewed notes. It is true that it does not positively appear that the debt was in existence when the covenant was executed, but the court will not require strict proof when the question was not made in the court below. If, however, the court has any difficulty as to the fact, it will direct that when the case goes back there may be an enquiry upon this point. In truth, all that the court below has done is to decide that the simple contract creditors have the right to stand in the shoes of Davis and Putney to the extent they have been paid out of the personal assets.

1852.
January
Term.

Cralle
& als.
v.
Meem
& als.

It is said that by agreement the obligee may waive the forfeiture. But here he has taken pains to exclude the conclusion that he had waived it. So it is said that the plaintiffs have no right to come into equity to enforce a forfeiture. A court of equity will enforce the forfeiture of a mortgage; and this is like that case. So, in the case of a bond binding the heirs, a court of equity will enforce a payment out of the real estate: And now by the late statute the only remedy on a bond against the heirs is in equity. It is said further that the doctrine of marshalling assets is the creature of equity; and that equity will not do injustice. But I would enquire what injustice there can be in compelling these parties to pay the debts of their ancestor out of his large estate.

It will be seen that the court below was about to sequestrate the rents of the real estate in the hands of the heirs, when they asked for a sale of a part of it, and selected the part that they preferred to have sold. After the sale the purchasers filed their bill objecting to the sale, on the ground that there were infant heirs, whose lands were improperly sold, and for other irregularities. The injunction was an irregular proceeding, and the purchasers should have proceeded by petition in the cause. The creditors had gotten nothing, though the decree for the sale was made in 1839. What, then, were they to do? The debts bind the whole estate; and if there is any difficulty in subjecting one part of it, they may resort to another part. The heirs are no worse off if they are allowed to have the benefit of the sale. It would have been improper to set aside the sale, because the heirs may wish to enforce it. And the court only says, this sale was made at your instance, and you may enforce it; but creditors are not to be delayed in the recovery of their debts.

*Patton*, for Friend and his children.

1852.
January
Term.

Cralle
& als.
v.
Meem
& als.

Mr. Robinson says the heirs had no intention to raise the question arising on the bonds of Cabell to Davis, and on his covenant with Putney, when they filed their petition in the cause. But their answer, filed before the petition, expressly denies the liability of the real estate under this bond : And this is the great question of controversy. There are infant parties too; and therefore there could be no waiver or admission of the liability of their estate under this bond and covenant. As to Putney's covenant, no bill claims to subject the real estate on account of this covenant; and it is only brought into the cause by the commissioner's report.

The argument of the counsel for the creditors is that the bond became forfeited whenever there was a failure to pay when demand of payment of the notes was made at the banks. But this argument is in utter disregard of the terms, objects and stipulations of the bond. The stipulation is to pay when required, so as to indemnify and save harmless Henry Davis from loss or damage. If the demand at the bank for payment of the note was all that was necessary, why was Henry Davis to make a demand of Dr. Cabell. The demand at the bank was certainly usual; but the demand provided for in the bond was to create a new and original obligation. This will be manifest by a single enquiry : Was the bond forfeited by a demand at the bank, or by a demand by either Davis or the bank on Dr. Cabell? No demand was necessary to fix Dr. Cabell's liability on the note; that is only necessary as to endorsers. Suppose the note had been demanded and protested, and even sued upon, not only against Dr. Cabell's estate but Davis, and judgment had been rendered against Davis; would this bond be forfeited? Certainly not. It cannot be forfeited until Davis has sustained actual damage by payment.

1852
January
Term.

Cra'le
& als.
v
Meem
& als.

The necessity of a demand in this case is a rule of law, and is founded in reason and justice. The bond was not necessary as a security in the lifetime of Dr. Cabell: He was bound to pay his notes, and all his property was liable. The bond was only necessary after his death, to provide for the contingency of his dying without leaving personal assets sufficient to pay his debts: And he gave the bond, in which he binds his whole estate to guard his surety from loss, provided the surety gave him notice. The bond was not given to bind Cabell to pay the note at maturity, but to guard his surety from loss.

As the law then was, the heirs of Cabell were not bound to pay the notes on which Davis was endorser: and they had a right to have the notice and demand before they should become bound. Their interest is entitled to the same protection and security as if they held by an independent title; and they are therefore entitled to have the protection provided for them by the bond.

The counsel for the creditors says it has been adjudged that the demand made by the suit was all that was necessary. But the question is not whether there had been a demand made upon the note; for no such demand was necessary: Dr. Cabell was bound without a demand. It is the bond which provides for and requires a demand in order to raise the obligation therein provided for, and it is that demand for the proof of which we ask, and the proof of which is wanting.

It is further contended that Davis has paid these notes, and that he is therefore entitled to hold Dr. Cabell's estate bound on the bond. The actions were brought on the notes as subsisting liabilities against Dr. Cabell's administrator, and judgments were rendered upon them. As to all the parties to these suits, therefore, that was an adjudication that the notes had not

1852.
January
Term.

Cralle
& als.
v.
Meem
& als.

been paid : And this is what is made out by the proof. Indeed every thing that was done was to hold Dr. Cabell's estate liable, and give them time to pay the debt. The counsel refers to the note of Davis endorsed by Dudley, and discounted at the bank, as a payment of Dr. Cabell's notes by Davis. But we are looking not to the form, but the substance of things; and all the proofs shew that the notes of Dr. Cabell were not paid, or intended to be paid, by that arrangement. We insist that nothing but actual payment can operate as a forfeiture of a bond which stipulates to protect the party from all loss and damage from the endorsement; and when there is a forfeiture, it extends only to the amount of the damage sustained. If, then, we shew that there has been no actual payment of the notes, and only payment of one or two discounts upon his own note, we shew at the same time that this is the extent of his loss and damage.

Formerly, on the forfeiture of a bond, the penalty was all payable; and the obligor could only be relieved by a resort to a court of equity, which would relieve him on its own principles. Now this is changed, and by our statute the plaintiff, in an action on a bond for the non-performance of covenants or agreements, is only entitled to a verdict and judgment for such damages as he may prove he has sustained. 1 Rev. Code of 1819, p. 509, § 82. This is the doctrine now, and no other sum can be recovered than what will indemnify the plaintiff for his actual loss. Sedgwick on Measure of Damages, p. 415, 416. In this case Davis's loss is what he has actually paid. Even where a surety has been taken into custody, yet he can only recover to the extent of the injury he has sustained, and not to the amount of the debt, unless he has paid it. *Rodman v. Hedden*, 10 Wend. R. 498. In that case it was said that if the surety give a negotiable note in satisfaction of the debt, so as to discharge the principal, he may re-

1852.
January
Term.

Cralle
& als.
v.
Meem
& als.

cover the amount of the debt. But to authorize him to do this he must discharge the principal, and his note must be taken as payment. But the giving a negotiable note as a collateral security will not entitle him to sue for the amount of the debt for which he was surety.

There is a distinction taken in the books between cases where there is a condition to pay at all events, and a condition to indemnify and save harmless. Our case falls within the latter class : And in such a case there is no forfeiture until damage is sustained. If any other authority is wanted in the case, the court is referred to *Hopewell* v. *Cumberland Bank*, 10 Leigh 206, and *May* v. *Boisseau*, 12 Leigh 512. But the cases of the first class are not conformable to principle. Sedgwick on Measure of Damages, p. 311. Indeed, the doctrine that a surety may sue whilst the principal remains bound cannot be carried out in this first class of cases without great enormity. The bond is to the surety, and according to these cases the surety may sue upon it directly there is a failure to pay. The creditor may sue on the obligation or note executed to him. And thus the principal debtor may be compelled to pay twice. But on a covenant to indemnify and save harmless, the damages must be proved to have been sustained   Sedgwick, p. 312.

We submit, then, that actual loss must be proved; and that the recovery by the surety can only be to the extent of that loss. And to entitle the surety to recover he must prove payment. What, then, is payment? In Sedgwick on the Measure of Damages, p. 317 and onwards, it will be seen that neither bond nor note nor judgment nor security on land will amount to a payment. It is said that a negotiable note is an exception ; but there is no ground for this distinction either in law or common sense. Though a bond or note or conveyance of real estate is not damage, yet, if taken in satisfaction of the debt, it is payment or damage; and will

1852.
January
Term.

Cralle
& als.
v.
Meem
& als.

authorize the surety to sue. So a negotiable note if taken as a discharge or extinguishment of the principal's liability, will authorize the surety to sue; and only when so taken. And this must be so. There can be no remedy on an indemnifying bond until the first is discharged. They cannot both exist at once; and it is only the extinguishment of the one which brings the other into existence. And this is the result of the authorities as stated by Sedgwick, p. 319. The reason given for holding the giving a negotiable note a payment is that it is treated as money. But that is not the true reason. The true reason is that the debt for which it is given has been thereby discharged; and it matters not in what way or by what means the debt is discharged, that is a payment.

To constitute a negotiable note a payment it is essential that it shall be given and accepted in full payment of the debt. Sedgwick on Measure of Damages, p. 326. If this be so, there is an end of the question in this case. Here there was no satisfaction of Cabell's notes; but it was agreed by both Davis and the bank that the notes were not to be discharged; and by the act of the bank and Davis actions were brought against the administrator of Cabell upon these notes as subsisting securities; and judgments were recovered and the money paid upon these judgments by the administrator.

The counsel for the creditors seems to admit, that upon the record as it now stands, the heirs cannot be subjected upon the covenant with Putney. In truth no additional proof can subject them. Not a cent was paid by Putney upon the note on which he was endorser. The covenant is to indemnify against loss; and all the surety did was to give a bond with security to pay the debt in two years. The debt was in fact paid by the administrator of Cabell.

It certainly is a matter too plain for argument that after the court has sold property to more than is needed to pay all the debts of the estate, and the proceeds are under the control of the court, then to sequestrate the rents and profits of all that remains in the hands of the heirs, is erroneous. Besides, there was a tract of land sold in Bedford county; and in the decree sequestra- ting the estate a direction is given to enquire as to the proceeds of this land. And whilst there are these two tracts of land sold, and before a dollar has been ascer- tained to bind the heirs, this sequestration was ordered.

It has been suggested that the court may put the in- junction suit out of the way. But that is an indepen- dent suit, and is not in this court: therefore this court cannot judicially know whether the injunction is proper or improper, or what disposition should be made of it. It is said the application to suspend the collection of the purchase money should have been by petition in the cause. The reason for that is not perceived. Suits were brought on the bonds for the purchase money of the land, the sale having been confirmed: and the only mode of protecting themselves left to the purchasers was by injunction. That suit not having been acted on by the court below, and not being here, this court cannot act on it, and cannot know whether the injunc- tion was proper or improper.

*Bouldin*, for the appellants, on the last point consid- ered by Mr. Patton.

There having been a sale of the land reported and confirmed in this cause, and there being no objection to it by the heirs, but the sale being proved to be favoura- ble to them, and a copy of the injunction cause being filed, it was competent for the court to direct the col- lection of the purchase money of the land sold. The injunction cause being ready, the court below should have acted on both causes at once, and should have dis- solved the injunction and directed the payment of the money. And this court will direct the court below to

1852.
January
Term.

Cralle
& als.
v.
Meem
& als.

dispose of the injunction case before any steps are taken against the heirs. And the plaintiffs in the injunction being heirs in part, and parties in this suit, their bill will be considered as a petition, and may be treated as a proceeding in the cause.

BALDWIN, J. delivered the opinion of the court.

The bond with collateral condition executed by Dr. Cabell to Davis may be treated as a covenant, and its purpose seems mainly to have been to provide a security which, in the event that has happened of Cabell's death, would subject his real as well as personal assets. The covenant was of comparatively little value in the lifetime of Cabell, inasmuch as legal proceedings against his person and property could not be materially affected by the dignity of the demand, and would be substantially the same whether it were evidenced by specialty or by simple contract. But the security afforded by a specialty binding his heirs might become all important upon the occurrence of his death. It appears that Davis had incurred responsibilities to a large amount as his endorser in bank, and that renewals of the notes, and other future liabilities of the like kind, were contemplated. The death of Cabell without having discharged these debts would, without a specialty binding his heirs, leave Davis exposed to the hazard of loss by the inadequacy of the decedent's personal estate, though the owner of real property of great value.

The condition of the obligation is as follows: "Whereas the above named Henry Davis hath endorsed sundry notes, which have been discounted for the accommodation of the said John J. Cabell, at the office of discount and deposit of the Bank of Virginia in Lynchburg, and it is in contemplation to renew said notes, from time to time, according to the custom of said bank; now therefore, in case the said John J. Cabell shall, whenever thereto required by said bank, or

1852.
January
Term.

Cralle
& als.
v.
Meem
& als.

by said Henry Davis, or his legal representative, well and truly pay and discharge all such notes as now are or hereafter may be endorsed for his accommodation by said Henry Davis, whether the said endorsement be made for the renewal of the notes already endorsed, or for obtaining from said office of discount and deposit, or elsewhere, further loans for the accommodation of the said John J. Cabell, on either notes, bills, or otherwise, so as fully to indemnify and save harmless the said Henry Davis and his legal representatives from all loss or damage on account of the said endorsements, then the above obligation to be void, else to remain in full force and virtue."

This was not a covenant of mere indemnity, but a covenant to pay the notes, &c., whenever required by the bank or by Davis. It was not in the alternative, either to pay the notes or to indemnify and save harmless, but a direct and positive engagement to pay, and by that means indemnify and save harmless: and thus in effect it was a stipulation that by payment of the debts Davis should be relieved from all responsibility as surety therefor. Nor was any formal demand or notice from the bank or from Davis necessary to give effect to the covenant. It is not pretended that the bank was bound by any contract with Cabell to extend to him credit beyond the period stipulated in the notes, nor that Davis was so bound to continue his endorser. By the uniform usage and custom of banks, and the universal understanding of those who deal with them, notes negotiable and payable there must be paid at maturity, or within the three days of grace thereafter. And the failure to obtain such extension of credit, or the disapproval of the person offered as endorser, would be the most decisive requisition of payment that could be made by the bank. And so the withholding by Davis of a renewed endorsement would be equally a requisition on his part that the notes should be paid by Cabell.

1852.
January
Term.

Cralle
& als.
v.
Meem
& als.

It is clear, therefore, that the covenant would have been broken by the failure of Cabell in his lifetime to pay the notes at maturity, and that Davis could in that event have maintained an action at law against him upon his obligation. The only difficulty, if any, in such an action would have been in regard to the extent of the recovery. It being incompetent for the legal forum to enforce a specific execution of the contract, a question might have arisen as to the *quantum* of damages, if the notes had not been paid by Davis, or had been paid by Cabell, before verdict. That is a subject which we need not consider, there having been no breach of the covenant in the lifetime of Cabell (the notes not having reached maturity until after his death), and it serving to throw no light upon the present suit in equity.

The covenant of Cabell to pay the notes not only devolved at his death upon his personal representative, but also descended upon his heirs at law, and the latter became as much bound to pay them out of the real assets as the former to pay them out of the personal assets. And the death of Cabell and the arrival of the notes at maturity without payment thereof out of his estate constituted by inevitable necessity a breach of the covenant, as well on the part of his heirs as on the part of his administrator. It will be seen from the condition of the bond that it was not in the contemplation of the parties to renew the notes after the death of Cabell. There was no authority on the part of his administrator or his heirs to renew them in their representative character; and in point of fact they were not renewed. On the contrary, they were taken up at maturity by Davis, the endorser, which he could not have failed to do but at the expense of his credit and the harrassment of a suit.

It appears that by an arrangement with the banks Davis obtained the means of relieving himself from his

1852.
January
Term.

Cralle
& als.
v.
Meem
& als.

liabilities to them as Cabell's endorser. This was accomplished by his giving his own notes with a nominal endorser, and pledging as collateral securities the notes of Cabell and his obligation aforesaid. Davis's notes were discounted by the banks, and the proceeds applied to the credit of Cabell's notes, and the banks consented to indulge Davis upon his notes so discounted until the collateral securities were exhausted. This transaction was perfectly fair and legitimate, and conformable to the rule of equity by which a creditor is entitled to avail himself of any counter bonds or other securities given by the principal debtor to those bound with him as sureties; and the principle is not varied by his consenting to take the surety as his principal debtor, with a transfer of such securities so previously acquired. We need not consider whether this adjustment was equivalent to a payment to the banks of Cabell's notes by Davis, the endorser; for the result, as it affects the merits of this suit, is the same either way. The full amount of the notes was afterwards paid by Cabell's administrator out of the personal assets of the estate, and whether in reimbursement of Davis, or in satisfaction of the banks, who stood in his place and held his securities, is wholly immaterial.

The merits of the case, however, do not depend upon the enquiry, when or by whom the notes of Cabell have been actually paid, or whether they have been paid at all; but upon the force and obligation of the covenant and the condition of the assets. The counter bond of Cabell, by which he bound himself and his heirs to pay off his notes in bank, to the exoneration of Davis, his endorser, placed the latter in the position of a specialty creditor, entitled to performance of the obligation from the heirs as well as the administrator. He had two funds for the satisfaction of his demand, the real assets in the hands of the heirs and the personal assets in the hands of the administrator: the simple

contract creditors had but one, the personal assets only. 1852.
January
Term.

Cralle
& als.
v.
Meem
& als. The well established and familiar rules of equity, derived from considerations of natural justice, required a resort by the specialty creditor to that fund to which the simple contract creditors could not look ; or if he should exhaust the personal assets, in the whole or in part, that they should be placed in his stead, and relieved out of the real assets to the same extent. And in a suit for marshalling the assets, it matters not whether the debts binding the heirs have been actually paid or remain to be satisfied, or whether they are evidenced by direct obligations or collateral covenants, or whether the former have not yet fallen due, or the latter have not yet been broken. These are all matters of detail in the arrangement, application and distribution of the assets by the equitable forum, and do not in any wise impair the principles belonging to the subject.

The right of the plaintiffs as simple contract creditors to marshal the assets, and obtain satisfaction of their demands out of the realty in the hands of the heirs, in relation to the covenant with Putney, stands upon the same footing and is governed by the same principles as in regard to the covenant with Davis. The contract between Cabell and Putney is in the following words : "Memorandum of agreement between R. E. Putney and John J. Cabell, all of the county of Kanawha, Virginia : That whereas the said John J. Cabell is endorser for the said Putney in a large sum at the Bank of Virginia, and being desirous to secure said Cabell as endorser, hereby binds himself, his heirs, &c., to pay to the said Cabell the sum of 10,000 dollars, or so much as the said Putney may be in default to the said bank ; and whereas the said Putney is endorser for the said John J. Cabell in a like large sum at the Bank of Virginia at Charleston, Kanawha, and the said Cabell being desirous of securing said Putney in the aforesaid undertaking as endorser, hereby binds himself, his

1852.
January
Term.

Cralle
& als.
v.
Meem
& als.

heirs, &c., in the sum of ten thousand dollars, or so much as the said Cabell may be in default to the said bank, to be paid to the said Putney whenever such default shall happen."

The covenant on the part of Cabell with Putney varies from his covenant with Davis only in point of form, except that the former stipulates in the event of Cabell's default with the bank, to make payment thereupon to Putney; and the effect of the two covenants respectively in regard to the real assets of the covenantors, and the consequent equities of the simple contract creditors, is essentially the same. The only difficulty in relation to the covenant with Putney is from the absence of direct evidence to prove that Cabell's note for 5000 dollars, subsequently made, endorsed and discounted, falls within its provision. The presumption, however, is that said note was not made for a new consideration originating after the covenant, but for the renewal of a note of that amount made by Cabell, with Putney as endorser, and discounted at the bank prior to the covenant. It is a matter, however, which can in all probability be reduced to a certainty, one way or the other, upon a reference to a commissioner, and such an enquiry ought to have been directed by the court below.

In proceeding to give relief to the plaintiffs as simple contract creditors entitled to marshal the assets, the court below had competent authority to decree, at the proper time, a sale of the real estate in the hands of the heirs, so far as requisite for that purpose: But it was premature to do so before adjudicating their several demands, and so ascertaining the amount of indebtedness chargeable upon the lands of the decedent. It is true that the sale which the court directed of land in Kanawha was upon the petition of the adult heirs and by consent of the plaintiffs; but no such consent could be given on the part of the infant heirs, and their rights

1852.
January
Term.

Cralle
& als.
v.
Meem
& als.

and interests were under the protection of the court. A sale, however, was had under the decree, which was reported to and confirmed by the court, and an order made for the collection of the proceeds; and although it was competent for the court, these proceedings being interlocutory, to set them aside in the further progress of the cause, upon its appearing that they were prejudicial to the interests of the infants, yet, on the other hand, if appearing to be beneficial to them, there could be no good reason for disturbing them in behalf of any other party. But a bill was filed in the same court by the purchasers at the sale, praying an injunction (which was granted) to judgments recovered on the bonds given by them for the purchase money, and seeking to set aside the decree for sale, and the proceedings under it, on the ground that the same being irregular and unwarranted as against the infant heirs, and subject to future impeachment by them, they (the purchasers) were exposed to the hazard of great loss, if compelled to pay up the purchase money.

To this bill of the purchasers the numerous creditors, the heirs of Cabell as well adults as infants, and other persons, were made defendants. Some of the defendants answered, and evidence was taken *pro* and *con* upon the question whether the land was sold at a price prejudicial or advantageous to the heirs, and that case is still pending and undetermined. The proceeding was, however, irregular and improper as a separate suit, and the bill ought to have been treated by the court as a mere adjunct of the original cause, and in the nature of a petition, and to have been brought to hearing therewith. And if so treated, it would have presented to the consideration of the court the enquiry whether the sale made under its decree was advantageous or injurious to the infant heirs.

Instead of taking this course, the original suit was again brought to a separate hearing, and the court.

1852.
January
Term.

Cralle
& als.
v.
Meem
& als.

without adjudicating any of the demands of the creditors, or making any disposition of the proceeds of sale of the Kanawha land, but leaving the injunction which had been granted to the purchasers in full force, and the land itself in their possession, and the objections which had been made to the sale thereof unadjudicated, rendered another interlocutory decree, by which the whole rents and profits of all the other real estate of the decedent were sequestered.

And the court is of opinion that there is no error in so much of the decree of the Circuit court as declares the principles upon which the assets, real and personal, of the intestate ought to be marshalled, but that it is erroneous in not directing the injunction bill of the purchasers of the Kanawha land and the proceedings thereupon to be heard together with and as a part of the proceedings of this suit, and in not adjudicating the question whether the sale of the Kanawha land ought to be established or set aside, and in not adjudicating and marshalling the respective claims of the creditors, and in all other respects wherein it conflicts with the principles above declared. It is therefore adjudged, ordered and decreed that so much of the decree of the Circuit court as is above declared to be erroneous be reversed and annulled, and that the residue thereof be affirmed, with costs to the appellants. And the cause is remanded to the Circuit court to be proceeded in conformably to the principles of this opinion and decree, and upon such further proofs as may be adduced by the parties.

## 𝔅𝔦𝔠𝔥𝔪𝔬𝔫𝔡.

### SCHOFIELD v. COX & als.

(Absent *Cabell*, P.)

1852.
January
Term.

March 4th.

1. A owns a tract of land on which there is a deed of trust to secure a large debt. A sells two thirds of the land to B, and
   for the purchase money takes from B eleven bonds payable at successive periods, and a deed of trust upon the
   property sold to secure them. A assigns to C the fifth,
   sixth and seventh bonds due; and B pays to A, either before the assignment or afterwards, without notice of it,
   rather more than enough to discharge the first four bonds;
   and then A and B become insolvent. HELD:

    1st. That C, as assignee of A, is entitled, as between him
   and A, to the benefit of the deed of trust given by
   B to secure the payment of his bonds.

    2d. That C is entitled to have the one third of the land
   not embraced in his security applied in the first
   place to satisfy the first incumbrance, to the relief
   of the two thirds of the land conveyed by B to secure his bonds.

    3d. That the payments beyond the amount of the first
   four bonds, made by B to A without notice of the
   assignment, having been made on account, are not
   to be treated as applicable to the first bond assigned to C, but to the bonds held by A.

2. A living out of the State, D sues out a foreign attachment
   against him, and attaches the one third of the land which
   was not sold to B, and also the debt due from B to A; the
   attachment being issued after the assignment to C. HELD:

    1st. As between the attaching creditor and the assignee,
   the latter has the preference.

    2d. The whole land being sold together, the one third
   and so much of the two thirds of the purchase
   money as is necessary, will be applied to discharge
   the first incumbrance; and the balance will be applied to pay the assignee.

    3d. The attaching creditor proving his debt, is entitled
   to a personal decree against his absent debtor,
   though the property attached may be adjudged to
   the assignee.

1852.
January
Term.

Schofield
v.
Cox
& als.

This was a proceeding by foreign attachment, commenced in July 1841, in the Circuit court of Jefferson county, by Jesse Schofield against Luther J. Cox as an absent debtor, and Benjamin Ford and Daniel Snyder home defendants, having estate of the absent debtor in their hands. In the progress of the cause J. & A. H. Herr were, on their petition, admitted as parties defendants, and claimed the fund in the hands of Ford & Snyder, under assignment from Cox. The facts are as follows:

Cox being seised of certain mill property, subject to an incumbrance for 11,537 dollars, sold and conveyed two undivided thirds of it, free from incumbrance, to Snyder & Ford for 21,466 dollars 71 cents, payable in eleven instalments; two of which were for 2333 dollars 34 cents each, and payable on the 28th of March in the years 1841 and 1842, with interest from the date, which was on the 28th of November 1840; and the other nine were for 1866 dollars 67 cents each, and payable at 2, 4, 6, 8, 10, 12, 14, 16 and 18 months after date. To secure the payment of these instalments, Snyder & Ford executed their bonds and a deed of trust on the said two thirds of the property. On the 13th of April 1841 Cox assigned three of the intermediate bonds, to wit, the bonds payable at 8, 10 and 12 months after date, amounting together to 5600 dollars, to J. & A. H. Herr. After the assignment, to wit, in July 1841, Schofield, to whom Cox was indebted in the principal sum of 2317 dollars 89 cents, instituted a foreign attachment suit therefor against Cox, who was a non-resident of the State; and attached Cox's remaining one third of the property, and the debts due him by Snyder & Ford for the other two thirds. Snyder & Ford paid to Cox the two first instalments of 1866 dollars 67 cents each, and made various other payments at different times between the 18th of January and 27th of November 1841 inclusive, to the amount of 5630 dol-

1852.
January
Term.

Schofield
v.
Cox
& als.

lars 15 cents, making the aggregate of payments made by Snyder & Ford to Cox 9363 dollars 49 cents, of which 4733 dollars 34 cents appear to have been paid before, and 4630 dollars 15 cents after the assignment. Nothing appears to have been paid on account of the assigned bonds. Cox and Snyder & Ford became insolvent, and the whole of the property was sold to satisfy the prior incumbrance. The amount of the sale was 14,000 dollars; of which, after paying expenses and satisfying the prior incumbrance, a surplus remained of 2037 dollars 38 cents, to be paid to the assignees or the attaching creditor, according as the court should be of opinion that the one or the other was entitled to the same.

The cause came on to be heard in June 1844, when the court, being of opinion that the assignees, J. & A. H. Herr, were entitled in preference to the plaintiff, dismissed his bill; whereupon he applied to this court for an appeal, which was allowed.

*Cooke*, for the appellant.
*A. Hunter*, for the appellees.

MONCURE, *J.*, after stating the case, proceeded:

The court below was of opinion that the assignees were entitled, and dismissed the bill of the attaching creditor. I think the court below was right.

Let us enquire, first, how the case stands between Cox and his assignees. And secondly, how it is affected by the intervention of the attaching creditor.

First. How does the case stand between Cox and his assignees? There appears to have been no agreement between Cox and Snyder & Ford for the payment of the prior incumbrance by the latter out of the purchase money; though Cox may have looked to that as the source from which he was to derive the means of making such payment; and Snyder & Ford had a

1852.
January
Term.

Schofield
v.
Cox
& als.

right to rely upon it as their indemnity against such incumbrance.    But Cox on the one hand was bound to
discharge the incumbrance, and (dependent on that obligation) Snyder & Ford on the other were bound to
pay off their bonds as they became due : and there was
a lien by deed of trust on two undivided thirds of the
property to secure the payment of these bonds as they
became due to Cox or his assigns.   *Gwathmeys* v.
*Ragland*, 1 Rand. 466.   Of the eleven bonds given by
Snyder & Ford to Cox, four, amounting together to the
sum of 7933 dollars 35 cents, became due before the
three bonds assigned to J. & A. H. Herr became due ;
and four, amounting together to the same sum, became
due afterwards.   Snyder & Ford having, as before stated, paid to Cox 9363 dollars 49 cents, had more than
extinguished the four bonds which became due before
the three bonds assigned to J. & A. H. Herr.   So that,
at the time of the sale of the property under the prior
incumbrance, two undivided thirds of it were, as between Cox and his said assignees, bound in the first
place for the payment of the three assigned bonds ; and
if Cox had discharged his obligation by paying off the
prior incumbrance. the three assigned bonds would have
been fully paid out of the proceeds of sale of the said
two thirds.

The case then stood thus :  The prior incumbrancer
had a lien on the whole property.   The assignees had
a lien on two thirds of it.   And the property was insufficient to satisfy both liens.   In this state of things
a court of equity, on the familiar principle of marshalling securities. would charge the prior incumbrance first
upon the third of the property on which the assignees
had no lien. and then upon the other two thirds ; so
that the property left, after satisfying the prior incumbrance, would be property on which the assignees had
a lien, and would be applicable to its discharge.   And
if, as was the case here, the whole property was sold

1852.
January
Term.

Schofield
v.
Cox
& als.

and the proceeds applied to the payment of the prior
incumbrance, the surplus would be considered as arising
from the sale of the subject on which the assignees had
a lien, and be therefore applicable to the payment of
the assigned bonds.　Cox certainly could not object to
this mode of marshalling the securities for the benefit
of his assignees.　He was bound to indemnify not only
them, but the obligors, against the prior incumbrance.

It is contended by the counsel for the appellant that
J. & A. H. Herr must recover as assignees of the bonds
at 8, 10 and 12 months, or not at all ; and that the record shews that the greater part of these three bonds
was paid by Snyder & Ford to Cox without notice of
the assignment.　I do not think so.　The two bonds
at two and four months were discharged.　The other
payments, amounting to 5630 dollars 15 cents, appear
not to have been applied to any particular bonds.　If
they were applicable to the bonds as they became due,
they would still leave due the whole of two and part of
the third of the assigned bonds ; which would greatly
exceed the amount of the surplus in controversy ; and
the right of the assignees to such surplus would therefore not be affected.　But while it might be proper, so
far as the obligors are concerned, to apply their payments to the bonds in the order in which they became
due, without regard to the assignment of any of them,
supposing they had no notice of such assignment, it
would not be proper, as between the assignor and the
assignees, to apply any of the payments to the assigned
bonds.　And if such application were made for the
benefit of the obligors, the assignees would be entitled
to be indemnified out of the bonds remaining in the
hands of the assignor.

But secondly, How is the case affected by the intervention of the attaching creditor?　I think not at all.
It is well settled that the attaching creditor stands on
no better footing as to the thing attached than that on

1852.
January
Term.

Schofield
v.
Cox
& als.

which his debtor stood at the time of the attachment. 2 Rob. Pr. 207, and the cases cited by the counsel for the appellees. In this case, therefore, the attaching creditor Schofield can no more object than can his debtor Cox to the marshalling of the securities for the benefit of the assignees as before stated.

I think the decree ought to be affirmed; at least so far as it gives priority to the assignees over the attaching creditor. But instead of dismissing the bill of the latter, the court should have given him a personal decree against the absent debtor, according to the case of *Williamson* v. *Gayle*, 7 Gratt. 152.

ALLEN and DANIEL, *J's,* concurred in the opinion of *Moncure,* J.

BALDWIN, *J.* did not see the opinion, but concurred in the decree; which was as follows:

The court is of opinion, that on the principle of the decision of this court in the case of *Williamson* v. *Gayle & al.,* 7 Gratt. 152, there is error in the decree appealed from in this case, as between the appellant and the appellee Cox, in dismissing his bill as to the said Cox, instead of giving him a personal decree against that defendant for the amount of his demand and his costs in the Circuit court; but that there is no error in the residue of the said decree. It is therefore decreed and ordered that so much of the said decree as is above declared to be erroneous be reversed and annulled, with costs to the appellant against the appellee Cox; and that the residue of the said decree be affirmed, with costs to the appellees, J. & A. H. Herr. And this court proceeding to render such decree as the said Circuit court ought to have rendered in lieu of so much of the decree aforesaid as is above declared to be erroneous, it is further decreed and ordered that the appellant do recover against the appellee Cox the sum of two thousand three hundred and seventeen dollars and eighty-nine cents, with interest thereon from the 11th day of November 1840 till paid, and his costs by him expended in the prosecution of his suit in the said Circuit superior court.

1852.
January
Term.

Schofield
v.
Cox
& als.

---

## Richmond.

### Archer *v.* Archer's *adm'r.*

(Absent *Cabell,* P. and *Baldwin,* J.)

April 26th.

1. The plea of " *non damnificatus* " is a good plea only where the condition is to indemnify and save harmless. The plea should go to the right of action, not to the question of damages.

2. Wherever the plea of "*non damnificatus*" is a good plea, it is equivalent to the plea of "*conditions performed.*" And if this last mentioned plea has been filed in a cause, it is no error to refuse the application, at a subsequent term, to file the former.

3. A testator devises a tract of land for the payment of a particular debt, and the land is sold; but the creditor receives only the first payment of the purchase money, and refuses to take the balance, which is applied to the payment of other debts of the testator. Whether the land was the primary fund for the payment of the particular debt, or not, that debt was in fact the debt of the testator's estate, for which a legatee was responsible under his refunding bond.

4. In an action by an executor upon a refunding bond, he offers in evidence the record of the cause in which the decree was rendered against him, on account of which his action is brought; and he then offers in evidence the execution which had issued on the decree, and the return thereon, which were objected to by the defendant, but were admitted by the court. To the admission of the evidence the defendant excepted, but the exception did not contain the

1852.
April
Term.

———

Archer
v.
Archer's
adm'r.

execution. HELD: That the relevancy of the evidence being obvious without an inspection of the execution, it was not essential that it should be contained in the bill of exceptions.

This was an action of debt instituted in the Circuit court of Chesterfield county in June 1838 by William S. Archer against John Archer. The declaration merely set out the bond on which the action was instituted, without referring to the condition. The defendant appeared at the March term for 1841, craved oyer of the bond and condition, and pleaded "conditions performed."

The bond was executed by John Archer with a surety to William S. Archer, administrator of John Archer deceased, of Amelia, who was one of the acting executors of John Archer of Bermuda Hundred, in the county of Chesterfield, in the penalty of 2600 dollars, with a condition that the obligor, John Archer, who was one of the distributees of John Archer of Bermuda Hundred, and who had received his due proportion of the said estate from John Archer of Amelia, should refund his due proportion of all sums of money which might, at any time thereafter, be recovered of or against the said William S. Archer, his executors or administrators, in manner as aforesaid.

The plaintiff replied, and set out three assignments of breaches, all of which were intended to present the same subject matter. That was that in July 1837 a debt which John Archer of Bermuda Hundred had owed, in his lifetime, to Judith Archer, in her lifetime, amounting to 2148 dollars 7 cents, with interest at five per cent. on 1272 dollars 96 cents, a part thereof, from the 31st of December 1820 till paid, and 139 dollars 5 cents costs, had been recovered by the administrator of Judith Archer against the plaintiff, as the administrator of John Archer of Amelia, who in his lifetime had been the executor of John Archer of Bermuda Hundred, by the decree of the Circuit court of Henrico, of which the

1852.
April
Term.

Archer
v.
Archer's
adm'r.

defendant had notice and had been requested to pay his proportion, which was one fifth of the amount so recovered.

At the November term 1842 the defendant tendered a plea of " *non damnificatus*," in addition to the plea previously pleaded ; but it was objected to by the plaintiff, and rejected by the court. The defendant then tendered a rejoinder to the plaintiff's replication ; which was also objected to by the plaintiff, but the court overruled the objection. The defence set up in the rejoinder was, that the debt which was decreed to be paid by the plaintiff, as the administrator of John Archer of Amelia, to the administrator of Judith Archer, was not a debt, at the time of pronouncing said decree, due from the estate of John Archer of Bermuda Hundred, but was a debt from the said John Archer of Amelia to the estate of Judith Archer. Upon this rejoinder there was an issue.

The cause came on to be tried at the March term for 1843, when the defendant took two exceptions, one for the admission of testimony, and the other for the refusal of the court to give an instruction to the jury. The facts in relation to both the subjects of exception are stated in the opinion of Judge *Moncure*. There was a verdict and judgment for the plaintiff for the sum of 673 dollars 82 cents, with six *per cent. per annum* interest thereon, from the 3d day of January 1838 until paid. Whereupon the defendant applied to this court for a *supersedeas*, which was awarded.

*Stanard & Bouldin* and *Cooke*, for the appellant.
*Taylor, Macfarland* and *Rhodes*, for the appellee.

MONCURE, *J.* Two errors are assigned in this case. The first is the rejection of the plea of *non damnificatus*. Did the Circuit court err in rejecting that plea? The condition of the bond was for the payment of one

1852.
April
Term.

Archer
v.
Archer's
adm'r.

fifth of all sums of money which might at any time
thereafter be claimed or recovered of or against the
said William S. Archer, &c. According to the rule laid
down in Stephen on Pleading, p. 386, that a general
mode of pleading is often sufficient where the allegation on the other side must reduce the matter to a certainty, the plea of " conditions performed," generally,
was an admissible plea in this case. But not the plea
of *non damnificatus.* As was said by the Supreme
court of New York, in the case of *McClure* v. *Erwin,*
3 Cow. R. 313, 332 : " This is a good plea in all cases
where the condition is to indemnify and save harmless ;
because it answers the condition in terms. But it is
good in that case only. The plea should go to the
right of action, not to the question of damages. The
plaintiff, so far as it depends upon the pleadings, shews
his right to recover by setting forth the bond with its
condition, and alleging a breach of that condition,
either general or special, as the case may require. If
the defendant by his plea admit that the condition has
been broken, he concedes the plaintiff's right to recover ;
and, by not denying the breach assigned, but, instead of
doing this, interposing the general plea of *non damnificatus,* he, in effect, admits the breach."

But if the plea of *non damnificatus* had been originally admissible in this case, the court was right in rejecting it at the time it was offered. On the 27th of
March 1841 the defendant plead " conditions performed," to which the plaintiff replied specially, by three
several assignments of breaches. On the 1st of November 1842 the defendant tendered the plea of *non
damnificatus,* in addition to his former plea of " conditions performed," which was objected to by the plaintiff and rejected by the court. And thereupon the defendant rejoined to the replication to his former plea.
Now, wherever the plea of *non damnificatus* is a good
plea, it is because it is in the nature of a plea of per-

1852.
April
Term.

Archer
v
Archer's
adm'r.

formance; "being used," as Stephen on Pleading, p. 388, says, "where the defendant means to allege that the plaintiff has been kept harmless and indemnified, according to the tenor of the condition." Where, then, the plea of *non damnificatus* is a good plea, it is equivalent to the plea of "conditions performed." And the latter plea having been put in more than eighteen months before the former was tendered, there could have been no necessity for the former. If the former had been also put in, the replication and issue thereon would have been the same as on the plea of "conditions performed." The defendant has had every benefit under the issue made up on the plea of "conditions performed" which he could have had under the same issue made up on the plea of *non damnificatus*. The question involved in the issue was whether the debt decreed to be paid by William S. Archer, as administrator of John Archer of Amelia, to the administrator of Judith Archer, was, at the time of pronouncing the decree, a debt due from the estate of John Archer of Chesterfield, or a debt due from the estate of John Archer of Amelia. If the former, then it is certain not only that the condition was broken, but that the plaintiff was damnified to the extent of one fifth of the amount of the said decree.

The other error assigned is the refusal of the court to give the instruction asked for on the trial of the cause. That instruction was "that as John Archer of Chesterfield devised a tract of land for the payment of the debt due Judith Archer, that debt did not create a lien on the personal estate of the testator, unless the land proved insufficient for that purpose." I think that the question involved in that instruction was an abstract one, and its solution by the court was not necessary to a proper decision of the case, and might have embarrassed the jury. The only issue was whether the debt decreed to Judith Archer was, at the time of the decree,

1852.
April
Term.

Archer
v.
Archer's
adm'r.

due from the estate of John Archer of Chesterfield, or from the estate of John Archer of Amelia. It was at one time, undoubtedly, the debt of the former. When and how did it cease to be so? The defendant contended that the land devised was the primary fund for the payment of this debt; that it was sold and the proceeds received by the executor; and that when the proceeds were so received, *pro tanto* at least, the debt to Judith Archer became the debt of the executor. On the other hand, the executor contended that he had paid the first instalment of the purchase money of the land to Judith Archer, but she refused to receive the other two instalments; and he had accordingly applied them to the payment of other debts of his testator's estate; had credited them in his executorial account, on which there was a balance due to him by the estate; and that thus the residue of the debt to Judith Archer was in fact the debt of his testator's estate, whether the land was the primary fund for the payment of said debt or not. In support of his pretensions, the defendant exhibited the record in the case of *Archer's adm'r* v. *Robertson, &c.*, reported in the name of *Robertson* v. *Archer*, 5 Rand. 319. That was a suit brought by William S. Archer, administrator of John Archer of Amelia, against the legatees of John Archer of Chesterfield, to recover a balance alleged to be due by the estate of the latter to the estate of his executor, John Archer of Amelia; and to obtain indemnity against any outstanding claims against the said testator's estate. In that suit the executorial account was settled; the proceeds of the sale of the land devised for the payment of Judith Archer's claim were credited, and the payment of the first instalment on account of that claim was debited to the estate; and a balance was ascertained to be due to the executor of 3061 dollars and 13 cents; for proportionable parts of which, and interest, a decree was rendered against the legatees respectively. From

1852.
April
Term.

Archer
v.
Archer's
adm'r.

that decree an appeal was taken, and this court dismissed the bill as to every purpose, except for the purpose of having proper refunding bonds taken from the legatees or their representatives, to indemnify the estate of John Archer, the executor, against any sums which had been or might be recovered against the estate of John Archer of Chesterfield since the death of the executor. The court in its opinion said that the most certain way of obtaining justice in this case is to consider all matters between the executor and legatees, so far as relates to actual receipts and disbursements by the executor up to the time of his death, as finally closed," &c. In the account of these receipts and disbursements, we have seen that while the whole purchase money of the land was credited to the estate, the amount of the first instalment only was charged as having been paid to Judith Archer. The balance of her claim was reported as an outstanding claim against the estate, and no other outstanding claim was reported. The effect of the decision of this court was to confirm the settlement of the executorial account (except that the balance reported to be due by the estate to the executor was extinguished), and of course to leave the balance due to Judith Archer an outstanding debt of the estate. The main, if not the only, object of requiring a refunding bond doubtless was to provide indemnity against that debt, for which a suit was then pending, and, ten years thereafter, a decree was rendered against William S. Archer, administrator of John Archer of Amelia. There is nothing in that decree which can prejudice the right of William S. Archer to recover on the refunding bonds of the legatees of John Archer of Chesterfield. The court declined giving a decree over against them, expressly on the ground that the remedy was at law on the refunding bonds.

The counsel for the appellant also contended that the opinion of the Circuit court set forth in the second

Vol. VIII.—35

1852.
April
Term.

Archer
v.
Archer's
adm'r.

bill of exceptions taken on the trial of the case was erroneous. After the plaintiff had offered in evidence the bond on which the suit was instituted, and the record in the case of *Archer's adm'r* v. *Archer's adm'r & als.*, and the defendant had offered in evidence the record in the suit of *Archer's adm'r* v. *Robertson & als.*, (which bond and records are inserted in the bill of exceptions,) the plaintiff offered in evidence an execution and the return thereon, issued in the former suit; to which execution going in evidence to the jury the defendant objected, but the court overruled the objection and permitted the execution to go as evidence to the jury; to which opinion of the court the defendant excepted. The execution is not inserted in the bill of exceptions. It is true, as a general rule, that when an exception is taken to the admission of evidence, its admissibility must appear upon the record, or the judgment will be reversed. And it is also true that where the evidence is documentary, the insertion of the document in the bill of exceptions is generally the best mode of shewing its admissibility. But the insertion of the document in the bill of exceptions is not necessary, if its admissibility otherwise appears upon the record. The case of *Hairston* v. *Cole*, 1 Rand. 461, was relied on in the argument. But that case materially differs from this. The opinion of the court in that case is very short, and is in these words: " The statement in the bill of exceptions that a manuscript *purporting to be a copy of an act of the general assembly of Virginia, entitled an act, &c.,* is too imperfect to enable the court to pronounce any opinion thereon, it not being stated that the said copy was authenticated and how authenticated, nor is the said transcript set out in the bill of exceptions. The judgment is therefore reversed and the cause remanded for a new trial." There it did not appear on the record that the manuscript purporting to be

1852.
April
Term.

Archer
v.
Archer's
adm'r.

a copy, &c., was duly authenticated. If it had so appeared, it is obvious, from the language of the court, that the said manuscript would have been considered admissible evidence. Its relevancy to the matter in controversy seems not to have been questioned; and was probably apparent on the record. Whether it was a duly authenticated copy or not appears to have been the only question on which its admissibility depended. But here the original execution and return thereon, and not a copy, much less a manuscript purporting to be a copy, were offered in evidence, and the only question on which their admissibility depended was as to their relevancy. Were they relevant? I think they were. The suit was brought by a personal representative, on a refunding bond, for a just proportion, being one fifth, of a debt of John Archer of Chesterfield that had been recovered against the plaintiff. The record of the suit in which the recovery had been obtained was offered in evidence by the plaintiff, without objection from the defendant. The execution on the decree rendered in that suit, and the return thereon, were then offered in evidence by the plaintiff, and were objected to; but no ground of objection is stated. The record of the suit being admissible, indeed necessary, evidence in the case, it seems to follow, as a matter of course, that the execution and return, which are matters of record, and in some sense at least a part of the record of the suit, are also admissible, if not necessary evidence in the case, to shew whether the amount of the decree was paid or not, and what was the amount, if paid. The objection in this case must be regarded as a general objection to the admissibility of an execution and return in such a case, without reference to any particular ground of objection; and so regarded, it was properly overruled. If there had been any such ground of objection in this case, it behooved the exceptant to set it forth; and not having done so, it is fair to presume that none existed.

1852.
April
Term.

Archer
v.
Archer's
adm'r.

The counsel for the appellant also contended that the Circuit court should have rendered judgment for the defendant, *non obstante veredicto;* or, at least, to have awarded a repleader; on the ground that the breaches assigned in the replication were insufficient, and the issue on which the verdict was found was immaterial. It was contended that the condition of the bond, properly construed, was referrible only to any recovery which might be had against William S. Archer as the representative of John Archer of Chesterfield; and that the recovery in this case, as set out in the replication and shewn by the record therein vouched, being a recovery against him as administrator of John Archer of Amelia, though on account of assets received by the latter as executor of John Archer of Chesterfield, the condition was not broken. I think the condition of the bond refers to such a recovery as is shewn by the replication and record; and that the bond was intended, and properly so, to indemnify the estate of John Archer of Amelia against any recovery which might be had against it in respect of the assets of his testator by him received and distributed among the legatees. The testator had been long since dead, and his estate fully administered by his executor. There was no occasion for an administrator *de bonis non,* for there were no remaining assets to be administered. If there were any outstanding creditors, their recourse would properly be against the estate of the executor, who as to them had committed a *devastavit;* and whose representative, in the event of a recovery against him by any such creditors, should have recourse over against the legatees, for whose benefit the *devastavit* was committed. The bond was intended to provide for that recourse against the legatees. William S. Archer, the representative of the executor, in effect, if not in form, represented that portion of the estate of the testator for which the estate of the executor was responsible to the creditors of the testator; and the de-

1852.
April
Term

Archer
v.
Archer's
adm'r.

cree of Judith Archer, before mentioned, was a recovery against William S. Archer as representing the estate of John Archer of Chesterfield within the meaning of the bond. I think the breaches, or at least the second and third of them, were well assigned, and that the issue was material.

I am for affirming the decree.

The other judges concurred in the opinion of Judge *Moncure*.

JUDGMENT AFFIRMED.

---

### Richmond.

## CLARK *v.* BROWN.

(Absent *Cabell*, P. and *Baldwin*, J.)

#### April 26th.

1. Where an appeal or *supersedeas* is applied for since the Code of 1849 went into operation, the application must be governed by the act in the Code, ch. 182, § 2, p. 683.
2. In an action on the case for an injury done to plaintiff's land by the mill dam of the defendant, though the freehold or franchise was drawn in question, yet if the damages found by the jury are under $200, the Court of appeals has no jurisdiction of the case.

This was an action of trespass on the case in the Circuit court of Patrick county, brought by Abram Brown against Jacob Clark, for a nuisance in erecting a mill dam on his own land, whereby the water is thrown back and overflows the adjoining land of Brown. Issue was joined on the pleas of not guilty and the statute of limitations.   On the trial an exception was taken by Clark to the refusal of the court to give an instruction to the jury asked for by him; and the jury having found for Brown, and assessed his damages to twenty dollars, Clark moved the court to set aside the verdict and grant a new trial, on the ground that the finding of the jury was contrary to the law as applicable to the facts proved on the trial.   The motion was overruled, and an exception being taken, the court certified such of the facts proved in relation to which the finding of the jury was supposed to be erroneous.   From these two exceptions it appears that Clark, amongst other things, relied for his defence upon the fact that he and those under whom he claimed had exercised, for more than twenty years before the institution of the suit, an exclusive, adversary and uncontested right of keeping up a dam at the place, and of the height of the dam in the declaration mentioned; and that such right had never been lost or abandoned.   Judgment was rendered by the court below on the 21st June 1850, and a *supersedeas* thereto was granted after the 1st July 1850.

*Patton*, for the appellant.
*Grattan*, for the appellee.

ALLEN, *J.*, after stating the case, proceeded:

The *supersedeas* being awarded after the new Code went into operation, it must, according to the case of *Yarborough* v. *Deshazo*, 7 Gratt. 374, be regulated by its provisions.   And it is contended that by the new Code, although it may appear that a freehold or franchise was drawn in question upon the trial, yet, as the damages found are under two hundred dollars, this court has no jurisdiction.   The Code, ch. 182, § 2, p. 683, provides that no petition for an appeal from, or writ of error or *supersedeas* to, a judgment, decree, or order of an inferior court shall be presented when the matter in con-

1852.
April
Term.

Clark
v.
Brown.

troversy is merely pecuniary and not of greater amount than two hundred dollars, exclusive of costs. Upon this provision it becomes necessary to ascertain what is meant by the phrase, the matter in controversy merely. Is it restricted to that which, in the language of Judge Roane, in *Lewis* v. *Long*, 3 Munf. 136, 154, is of the essence and substance of the judgment, and by which the party may discharge himself; or is it to be construed as embracing any other matter which may be incidentally and collaterally drawn in question? In this case we are relieved from the necessity of going into a laborious investigation as to the meaning of the words and the intent of the legislature in making use of them. The phrase, "the matter in controversy," when used in relation to the appellate jurisdiction of this court, has already received a judicial exposition leading to special legislation. The legislature was familiar with this construction; and when, therefore, words are used which in the same connection had received a judicial construction, it must be intended that the words are used in the sense which had been given to them.

The act of 1792, concerning the Court of appeals, provided that the court should have jurisdiction, if the matter in controversy should be equal in value, exclusive of costs, to 100 dollars, if a judgment of the District court, or be a freehold or a franchise. Under this act it was determined in the cases of *Hutchinson* v. *Kellam* and *Lymbrick* v. *Seldon*, 3 Munf. 202, that to give the court jurisdiction on the ground that the matter in controversy was a freehold or franchise, the right to the freehold or franchise must be *directly* the subject of the action; and not have been incidentally or collaterally drawn in question. In both cases the action was trespass *quare clausum fregit*, and the damages recovered less than 100 dollars; but it appeared from the records that the titles or bounds of land were drawn in question. "To give this court jurisdiction," Judge

Cabell observed, " the matter in controversy must be equal in value to 100 dollars, or must be a freehold or franchise. The action of trespass is one in which damages only are recovered, and although the title or bounds of land may be incidentally and collaterally brought in question, yet the value of the matter in controversy is, from the nature of the action, the value of the damages sustained by the trespass ; and this as well where the title or bounds of land may be drawn in question as where they may in no manner be involved in the dispute." Roane and Fleming concurred with Cabell, and Roane adverted to the considerations which may have operated in inducing the legislature to make a distinction between this court and the District courts in respect to the appellate jurisdiction of the latter from judgments of the County courts. The act of 1792, regulating the jurisdiction of the District court, had authorized an appeal from the County courts where the debt or damages or other thing recovered or claimed, exclusive of costs, should be of the value of 100 dollars, or where the title or bounds of land should be drawn in question. Coalter, who dissented from the other judges, had argued that, as this act was in *pari materia*, and had passed at the same session, both acts should be construed together as forming one system. Alluding to these different provisions, Roane remarked, " That the District courts, being skilled in the law, might, in the opinion of the legislature, well be trusted with the final decision of questions of that nature, except where the sum found is over the limits of the act, or where the controversy is for the freehold or franchise itself."

The case of *Lewis v. Long*, 3 Munf. 136, was an action of debt on a single bill for more than 100 dollars. The jury found for the plaintiff the debt in the declaration mentioned, to be discharged by less than 100 dollars ; and the judgment followed the verdict. Upon

1852.
April
Term.

Clark
v.
Brown.

appeal it was determined that the smaller sum found by the jury, and not the nominal sum for which judgment was entered, was the matter in controversy between the parties. The matter in controversy, Judge Roane observes, is that which is the essence and substance of the judgment, and by which the party may discharge himself.

A similar expression in the act of Congress establishing the Federal courts was construed in the same manner in the case of the *United States* v. *McDowell*, 4 Cranch's R. 316. That was an action for 20,000 dollars, the penalty of an official bond of the marshal, alleging as a breach the failure to pay over to the United States 320 dollars. There was a decision against the United States, and upon error to the Supreme court it was decided that, the matter in dispute being of less value than 2000 dollars, the court had no jurisdiction. Some years after these decisions, the case of *Skipwith* v. *Young*, 5 Munf. 276, was brought up. It was, like the present case, an action of trespass on the case for injury to the land of the plaintiff by the erection of a mill dam. The defendant, besides the plea of not guilty, filed a special plea setting out that those under whom he claimed had many years before a mill and dam at the same place, &c. The plea was withdrawn by consent, but with leave on both sides to give in evidence the special matter in support or avoidance of the matter contained in the plea. There was a verdict for the plaintiff for one penny damages, subject to the opinion of the court on a point reserved involving the right of the defendant to build a mill under the circumstances set forth. It thus appeared, as well from the pleadings as the finding, that the questions between the parties were the right and title to the land overflowed, and the right to erect and continue the mill and dam— the same questions which, from the instruction moved for and the certificate of facts, would seem to have been drawn in question in the case under consideration. But notwithstanding the imposing form in which the questions were there presented, and although it was argued and authorities adduced to prove that a verdict and judgment in an action of trespass *quare clausum fregit*, in which the pleadings put the freehold in issue, were conclusive as to the right, and could be pleaded by way of estoppel, this court determined that, as the damages were less than 100 dollars, the defendant could not appeal to this tribunal. In the course of his opinion in this case, Brooke, Judge, remarked, " That the matter in controversy is that for which the suit is brought, and not that which may or may not come in question. In the case relied on in 3 East, Lord Ellenborough says, the judgment is the fruit of the action, and can only follow the particular right claimed, and injury complained of. The injury in the case before the court is emphatically the matter in controversy, though other matters may have been put in issue ; the finding of which by the jury may, if pleaded, estop the party in another action."

In his opinion the judge adverted to the consequences of so construing the statute as to extend the appellate jurisdiction to decisions of the inferior courts in which matters not directly in controversy may have been indirectly drawn in question ; and argued to shew that under such a construction few cases would escape the jurisdiction of the appellate court. In consequence of these decisions, the law was amended at the revisal of 1819, and after the words " or be a freehold or franchise," there were inserted the words, " or where such freehold or franchise, or the title or bounds of land, are drawn in question." Thus the law stood until the new Code superseded it. The appellate jurisdiction was limited to cases where the matter in controversy should be equal to a particular sum or be a freehold or franchise : or cases in which a freehold or fran-

chise or the title or bounds of land, though not the
matter in controversy, should be drawn in question.  It
was argued that the provision of the new Code was intended to re-enact the former law and carry out its principles, merely increasing the amount from 100 to 200 dollars, exclusive of costs, where the matter in controversy
was merely pecuniary.   The intention of the legislature must be collected from the expressions used where
they are free from ambiguity.   One object of the
change was to impose a further limitation on the jurisdiction of this court, and to exclude from it cases of
minor importance where the matter in controversy is
merely pecuniary.  If the matter in controversy for which
the action is brought be not merely pecuniary, but embraces something besides, which would be covered by
the judgment, an appeal would lie.   But we cannot
suppose that the legislature, after the repeated adjudications of this court and the legislation in consequence
thereof, could have contemplated embracing, by the
terms used, every case where any matter not merely
pecuniary was drawn in question.  Such a construction,
instead of carrying out the manifest intent to restrict
the jurisdiction, would enlarge it, and leave the court
with almost unlimited appellate jurisdiction.

As the law stood before, the court could not take
jurisdiction where other matters were drawn in question collaterally, except in a few specified cases involving a freehold or franchise or the title or bounds of
land.   But if, in consequence of the use of the word
" merely," the law is to be construed as still extending
to those excepted cases, what is to confine it to them ?
The exposition which would embrace the matters provided for by the former law would equally embrace
every other matter not merely pecuniary when drawn
in question; although the direct object of the action
was the recovery of damages only.   And in almost
every action, matters in addition to the mere pecuniary

amount sought to be recovered may be incidentally drawn into question during the trial. To suppose that the legislature intended to enlarge the jurisdiction of this court, so as to extend to all such cases, would be imputing to them an intention to give an undefined and almost unlimited jurisdiction, whilst at the same time they were professing to restrict it within narrower limits. It may be that the effect of the present enactment upon the few excepted cases provided for by the revisal of 1819 was not adverted to; but this court cannot look beyond the law to ascertain the intent of the legislature; and confining itself to that, it is constrained to say that in an action like this, sounding in damages merely, those damages are, according to the adjudications of the court, the only matter in controversy; and the amount recovered being less than 200 dollars, the court cannot take jurisdiction, it not being competent to take jurisdiction under the law now in force because a matter not directly in controversy may have been incidentally drawn in question.

The appeal should be dismissed as being improvidently allowed.

The other judges concurred in Judge *Allen's* opinion.

APPEAL DISMISSED.

## Richmond.

Rice's *ex'or v.* Annatt's *adm'r.*

1852.
April
Term.

(Absent *Cabell, P.* and *Baldwin, J.*)

May 4th.

1. In an action of debt, under the plea of payment the defendant
   may give in evidence parol admissions of the plaintiff that
   but a portion of the debt claimed is really due.
2. Where the defendant relies upon a specific payment or set-off
   by way of discount against a debt, an account stating distinctly the nature of such payment or set-off, and the several items thereof, must be filed with the plea; though the
   defendant may rely upon the parol admissions of the plaintiff to prove such payment. But this is not necessary
   where no specific payment is relied on; but the defendant
   offers proof of the admissions of the plaintiff that but a portion of the debt is due.

This was an action of debt in the Circuit court of
Halifax county, by the administrator of John Annatt
against the executor of Jesse Rice. The action was
founded on a bond for 109 dollars 38 cents, dated and
payable on the 13th of May 1829, executed by Jesse
Rice to John Annatt; and the only defence was payment by the defendant's testator. With the plea of payment the defendant filed an account of payment and
offsets, the first item in which was, 1829, May 13, paid
109 dollars 38 cents. The other items were set-offs.

On the trial of the cause there was a verdict for the
plaintiff under an instruction from the court; and the
defendant then applied for a new trial on the ground of
misdirection. It appeared that on the trial the defendant introduced a witness, who stated that he heard the
plaintiff, some time before the institution of this suit,
tell the defendant that 25 dollars only of the bond declared upon remained unpaid. And this being the only

1852
April
Term.

Rice's
ex'or
v.
Annatt's
adm'r.

direct evidence of a payment, the plaintiff's counsel moved the court to exclude it from the jury, on the ground that no such payment as that indicated by the testimony was stated in the account of payments filed with the plea. This motion the court overruled, but instructed the jury, that as no such payment was stated in the account filed with the plea, they could not, on that testimony, find a partial payment of the bond declared upon; but that they might use the testimony, along with the other evidence, to fortify the presumption of payment arising from the length of time.

The court overruled the motion for a new trial, and rendered a judgment upon the verdict for the plaintiff. Whereupon the defendant, having excepted to the opinion of the court overruling his motion for a new trial, applied to this court for a *supersedeas*, which was awarded.

*Stanard & Bouldin*, for the appellant.
*Patton*, for the appellee.

ALLEN, *J.* delivered the opinion of the court.

The court is of opinion, that as by the act of assembly, 1 Rev. Code 509, § 84, it was provided that if before action brought the defendant hath paid the principal and interest due by the defeasance or condition, he may plead payment in bar, it would have been competent to give in evidence the parol admissions of the plaintiff that nothing was due, in support of such plea of payment. And as by the act of assembly, 1 Rev. Code 487, ch. 127, it was provided that in an action of debt, due by judgment, bond, bill, or otherwise, the defendant shall have liberty, upon the trial thereof, to make all the discount he can against such debt, and upon proof thereof the same shall be allowed in court, it is competent under the plea of payment to give in evidence parol admissions of the plaintiff that but a por-

1852.
April
Term.

Rice's
ex'or
v.
Annatt's
adm'r.

tion of the debt claimed was really due. Where the
defendant relies upon a specific payment or set-off by
way of discount against the debt, an account stating
distinctly the nature of such payment or set-off, and
the several items thereof, must be filed with the plea;
though the defendant may rely on parol admissions of
the plaintiff to prove such payments. But this does not
apply to a case where no specific payment is relied on;
as the defendant may be destitute of any evidence to
prove the same, and still be enabled to prove by the admissions of the plaintiff that but a portion of the debt
sued for is due. Unless such proof be admissible under
the general plea of payment, the defendant would be
deprived of a defence which the justice of the case required.

The court is therefore of opinion that the Circuit
court erred in instructing the jury that, upon evidence
of the declarations of the plaintiff in the action some
time before the institution of the suit, that 25 dollars
only of the bond mentioned in the declaration remained
unpaid, they could not on that testimony find a partial
payment of the bond in the declaration mentioned, because no such payment was stated in the account filed
with the plea, and in overruling the motion of the plaintiff in error to set aside the verdict and grant him a new
trial on account of such misdirection. It is therefore
considered that said judgment be reversed with costs;
and the cause is remanded with instructions to set aside
the verdict and award a new trial upon the usual terms.


JUDGMENT REVERSED.

## 𝕽𝖎𝖈𝖍𝖒𝖔𝖓𝖉.

1852.
April
Term.

### BOOTH *v.* KINSEY.

(Absent *Cabell*, P. and *Baldwin*, J.)

**May 4th.**

A debtor in execution executes a forthcoming bond to the creditor, and a third person and the obligee execute the bond
with the debtor, as his sureties. The bond being forfeited,
the obligee gives notice to the principal obligor and the
other surety of a motion for award of execution upon the
bond against them; but the notice does not mention the
obligee as a co-obligor. HELD:

1st. That the bond is a valid bond to bind the other
surety, but that he is only liable as a co-surety
with the obligee.

2d. That if the principal creditor proves insolvent, the
surety may be relieved to the extent of one moiety
of the debt, either by bill in equity, or by motion
under the statute for the relief of sureties.

3d. The notice is not defective for failing to mention the
obligee as a co-obligor.

The case is stated by Judge *Moncure* in the commencement of his opinion.

*Lyons*, for the appellant.
*Grattan*, for the appellee.

MONCURE, *J.* Otey Kinsey sued out a *ca. sa.* against
Henry Shoemaker; who, being arrested and committed
to jail, gave a forthcoming bond, with the appellant,
Moses G. Booth, and the same Otey Kinsey, the obligee
in the bond, as his sureties. A motion was made by
Kinsey against Shoemaker and Booth, the other two
obligors, for award of execution on the bond; and it
was proved that in due time a written notice of the
motion, addressed to Shoemaker and Booth, and full

and specific in all respects, except that the name of Kinsey was not mentioned as a co-obligor in the bond, had been served on Booth, and a verbal notice of the motion had been given to Shoemaker. And it was admitted on both sides that the Otey Kinsey whose name was signed to the bond as an obligor was the same person who was the obligee in the bond; and it was proved on the part of the defendants that Shoemaker had been discharged from custody under the *ca. sa.* by the execution of the bond aforesaid by Booth and Kinsey, without in fact having delivered up the property specified in the bond, or any other property whatever. The defendants opposed the motion on the grounds, 1st, that there was a variance between the written notice and the bond; 2dly, that they had not received sufficient notice of the motion, and 3dly, because the plaintiff, being a joint obligor with the defendants, could not legally recover judgment against them, and the bond was nugatory and void. But the court being satisfied that there was no substantial variance between the written notice and the bond, and that both defendants had had legal notice of the motion; and being of opinion that the said bond was the bond of the defendants alone, and was not vitiated by the fact that the plaintiff also signed it; overruled the objections of the defendants and gave judgment against them. The defendants excepted, and obtained a *supersedeas* to the judgment.

In regard to the 1st and 2d objections, I will only say that I concur in the opinion of the court below thereon, and think they were rightly overruled. In regard to the 3d, I have had much difficulty, and will have to express my opinion somewhat at length.

That a man cannot be both debtor and creditor at the same time is undoubtedly true, as applied to an individual in his own right, without any person associated with him, either on the debtor or creditor side.

There is an inherent impossibility in the thing; and all instruments, whether in the form of specialties or simple contracts, made for the purpose of producing these inconsistent characters of debtor and creditor in one and the same person must of necessity be void. The defect in such cases is *substantial and radical.*

But a man, either severally or jointly with others, can be creditor or debtor to himself and others. This is of every day occurrence in cases of partnership, where a member of a firm is creditor or debtor of the firm, or where the same person is a member of creditor and debtor partnerships. The same principle applies to other cases, for in every case of the kind there is a *quasi* partnership between the parties associated on either side, limited to the purposes of the contract; but just as effectual, *quoad* those purposes, as a full mercantile partnership would be.

That a man cannot be both plaintiff and defendant in the same suit at law, whether others be associated with him or not, is also true. But this is a *technical,* and not a *substantial* or *radical* defect. It applies to the remedy and not to the right; and may be obviated by resorting to a court of equity, in which a man can be both plaintiff and defendant in the same suit; or by introducing a new party to the contract, in whose name a suit at law may be brought without violating the technical rule; or by suing at law in such manner (if the form of the contract or the law will admit of it) as not to exhibit the apparent inconsistency of making the same person both plaintiff and defendant.

Thus a bill of exchange or negotiable note, payable by a firm to a member of it or order, becomes an available security at law in the hands of an endorsee, who may sue the drawer or maker as well as the endorser. It can hardly be necessary to cite authorities on this subject. The doctrine is stated and many of the cases cited in *Smith* v. *Lusher,* 5 Cow. R. 688.

COURT OF APPEALS OF VIRGINIA.

COURT OF APPEALS OF VIRGINIA.

So also where a statute authorizes the assignee of a bond to sue in his own name, he may maintain a suit thereon at law, though the same person be both obligor and obligee in the bond. This was expressly and unanimously decided by the Supreme court of the United States in the case of *Bradford* v. *Williams*, 4 How. U. S. R. 576. There is a statute in Florida authorizing an assignment of bonds, and the assignee to sue at law in his own name, similar to our statute on the same subject. The Supreme court held, under this statute, that where a joint and several bond was signed by three obligors and made payable to three obligees, one of whom was also one of the obligors, and the obligees assigned the bond, the fact that one of the obligors was also an obligee was no valid defence in a suit brought by the assignee against one of the other obligors, and that the inability of one of the obligees to sue himself did not impair the vitality of the bond, but amounted only to an objection to a recovery in a court of law; and the assignment and ability of the assignee to sue in his own name removed this difficulty. There is no doubt but that if the case of *Bradford* v. *Williams* had gone up from this State, instead of Florida, the Supreme court would have decided the case under our statute in the same way, for our statute goes at least as far in favour of the assignee of a bond as does the statute of Florida.

So also when the bond is joint and several, and the obligee is one of the obligors, he may, I think, maintain an action at law in his own name against one of the other obligors. The principle of the decision of *Bradford* v. *Williams* seems to apply to the case; for it may be here said, as was in effect said by the court in that case, that the inability of the obligee to sue himself does not impair the vitality of the bond, but amounts only to an objection to a recovery in a court of law; and as the assignment and ability of the assignee to sue in his own name removed the difficulty in that case, so here the ability of the obligee to sue one of the other obligors in his own name in like manner removes the difficulty. In that case it was unnecessary to decide this particular question, because the suit was brought in the name of the assignee; and the case, in the opinion of the court, fell within the principle of the case of a partner drawing a bill upon his own firm, or making a note, in the name of the firm, payable to his own order; both of which are valid in the hands of a *bona fide* holder. But it is manifest that if it had been necessary to decide this particular question in that case, the court would have decided it in favour of the right of the obligee to sue. For Mr. Justice Nelson, in delivering the opinion of the court, said: "Whether the obligees of the bonds in question could have maintained an action at law against the defendant is a question we need not determine; though it is not easy to perceive the force of the objection urged against it, namely, that Craig, one of the co-obligors, is also an obligee. The bond is joint and several, and the suit against Judge, one of the obligors; and if it had been brought in the name of the obligees, Craig would not have been a party plaintiff and defendant, which creates the technical difficulty in maintaining the action at law. It would have been otherwise if the obligation had been joint and not several; for then the suit must have been brought jointly against all the obligors."

An action at common law on a joint and several bond must be against one or all of the obligors, and not an intermediate number of them. It cannot be against all of them where the obligee is also one of the obligors, for then the same person would be both plaintiff and defendant in the same suit at law. And if it were brought against the other obligors, the fact that the obligee was one of the obligors might, it seems, be

1852.
April
Term.

Booth
v.
Kinsey.

plead in bar of the action; and indeed could not be
plead in abatement, as in other cases of non-joinder of
defendants; "because a plea in abatement ought to
give a better writ, not to shew that the plaintiff can
have no action at all," as he cannot in such case have
against all of the obligors. *Mainwaring* v. *Newman*,
2 Bos. & Pul. 120. The rule that an action cannot be
maintained against an intermediate number of joint and
several obligors does not apply to a motion on a forthcoming bond; the statute authorizing execution thereon
to be awarded " against the obligor, or obligors, or any
of them": And this it seems may be done even where
the notice is against all of them. *Glassell* v. *Delima*,
2 Call 368. It seems to follow, therefore, on principles
before stated, that where the obligee in a forthcoming
bond is one of the obligors, he may maintain a motion
on the bond against the other obligors. In the case
under consideration the notice, motion and judgment
were all against the other obligors only.

There are several decisions of the Supreme court of
North Carolina which assume the position that whenever the same person is an obligor and an obligee in the
same bond it is void, and no action can be maintained
upon it against any of the obligors, whether the bond
be joint, or joint and several. I have very high respect for the court by which these decisions were made,
but think the position assumed in them is not sustained
by reason or authority. They were made about the
same time, and rest upon each other. In only one of
them, and that the fourth of the series, was it necessary
to decide the question, as the decisions were sufficiently
sustained by other grounds. The only English case
cited in support of the position is the case of *Mainwaring* v. *Newman*, 2 Bos. & Pul. 120, in which the contract was joint only, and it was necessary therefore that
the action should be joint. That, too, was the case of
a negotiable note executed to a firm by a member of it;

which was certainly not void, and would have been actionable at law in the name of an endorsee who was not also a defendant. I really do not see on what principle it can be said that the whole bond is void merely because one of the obligors is also the obligee. There might be some reason for saying (though I do not admit, but deny it) that the bond is void as to the obligor who is obligee, and good as to the other obligors only, on the principle that where a *feme covert* or other person incompetent to make a contract signs a bond as one of the obligors, it is void only as to her; or that where a partner executes a bond in the name of the firm, it is good as to him and the other obligors, and void only as to the partners who do not execute the bond. But why should a person who is competent to bind himself, and does bind himself, by the execution of a bond, be allowed to avoid the bond merely because it is also executed by a person who cannot be sued at law on the bond? It is admitted by Ruffin, Judge, in one of the North Carolina cases, 3 Dev. R. 290, that the coverture, or other personal incapacity of one of the obligors, does not affect the other obligors who are able to contract; and that the latter are bound as if they alone had executed the bond. Why are they not, *a fortiori*, bound where they execute the bond with another who is capable of contracting, but cannot be sued at law on the bond because he is also an obligee in the same bond? The reason given by the Judge for their not being bound in the latter case is, that " the parties intended to have contribution," and " it never could have been intended that one of the persons who sealed the instrument should alone pay to the other the money mentioned in it. And because it cannot be enforced without that construction, it must be taken to be void altogether." Now this reason applies with great force to the former, but little or none to the latter case. Where one of the obligors is a *feme covert*, or otherwise incompetent, it is evident that the other obligors intended to have contribution ; and yet certain they can never have it in any form of action or in any forum. Where one of the obligors, though competent, yet happens to be an obligee, it is also evident that the other obligors "intended to have contribution," and it must be admitted on all hands they can have it by suit at law or in equity. In the former case the other obligors altogether lose the contribution intended. In the latter it could at most be only postponed; and even the evil of postponement would in many cases be avoided by allowing an assignee to bring an action at law in his own name against all the obligors. Another reason given by the learned Judge is, that " there can be no delivery to an obligee by himself; nor by one obligor to another obligor." This is a strictly technical reason, and ought to be sustained by good authority, but none is cited for the purpose. I do not see why there should be any difference between a bond and promissory note in this respect. A man is incapable of contracting with himself, whether by bond or simple contract. In this respect there is no difference between the two forms of contracting. The incapacity results from the inherent impossibility of the thing itself; not from anything in the nature or dignity of the form of the contract. Though delivery be necessary to make a good deed, yet almost any act or word shewing an intention to deliver is sufficient for the purpose. But suppose it were universally true that "there can be no delivery to an obligee by himself, nor by one obligor to another obligor "; would it not follow, as a necessary consequence, that a bond ineffectually executed by one party would not be void as to other parties who had effectually executed it? Suppose a bond effectually executed by one obligor is merely signed by another person; would it not be the bond of the former, though not of the latter? Suppose it is signed and sealed, but not delivered by the latter; would it not still be the bond of the former?   And would the fact that from the character of the parties there could not be a delivery by the latter make any difference?

But these North Carolina cases were cited and relied on in the argument of the case of *Bradford* v. *Williams*, 4 How. U. S. R. 576, decided in 1846, and yet the Supreme court made the decision and expressed the opinion before mentioned.   I think that decision and opinion are unopposed by authority, are reasonable, and tend to the promotion of justice.   I am therefore disposed to follow them.

Pothier on Obligations has been referred to by the counsel for the appellant; but, in looking to the references to that work, I see nothing which is opposed to the view I have expressed.   1st. As to the right of a surety to substitution.   That right is not affected by the view I take of the case.   According to that view, a surety would have the same right of contribution against a co-surety who is also an obligee as against any other co-surety.   2dly.   As to the effect of a release of one of the obligors.   According to Pothier there are two kinds of release, one called " a real release," the other a " personal discharge."   A real release is where the creditor declares that he considers the debt as acquitted; it is equivalent to a payment, and renders the thing no longer due; " consequently it liberates all the debtors of it, as there can be no debtors without something due."   A personal release merely discharges the debtor from his obligation, and extinguishes the debt indirectly where the debtor to whom it is granted was the sole principal, because there can be no debt without a debtor."   " But if there are two or more debtors *in solido*, a discharge to one of them does not extinguish the debt; it only liberates the person to whom it is given, and not his co-debtor; the debt is extinguished, however, as to the part of the person to whom the discharge was given, and the other only remains obliged for the remainder.'

Pothier, p. 111, ch. 3, art. 11, § 1 and 11. Now if the case of one of the obligors being also an obligee is analogous to either of the releases described by Pothier, it is that called a personal discharge. 3dly. As to the effect of " confusion," which, in its application to this case, " is the concurrence of the characters of creditor and debtor of the same debt in the same person," whereby the two characters are mutually destroyed. It is answer enough to say, in the language of Pothier, that " in order to induce a confusion of the debt, the characters not only of debtor and creditor, but of sole debtor and sole creditor, must concur in the same person"; and that " if a creditor of the whole becomes heir of the debtor for part, the confusion only takes place with respect to that part." Id., p. 111, ch. 5. In most countries complete justice may be done by one and the same court in one and the same suit; so that in a case of partial personal " release " or " confusion," the obligation of the debtors as thereby modified can at once be enforced without difficulty. But where the difference exists, as with us, between law and equity, and common law and chancery courts, the strict and technical rules of the common law sometimes prevent the common law courts from doing complete justice, or even justice at all; and a resort to a court of chancery becomes necessary. By one of those rules we have seen that the same person cannot be both plaintiff and defendant in the same suit; so that wherever the form of the contract is such as to render it necessary in a suit thereon to make the same person both plaintiff and defendant, a court of common law can take no cognizance of the case, whatever may be the rights and obligations of the parties; and resort must be had at once to a court of chancery. By another of those rules it would seem that a court of common law must enforce the obligation of the debtors, if at all, in its original form, and not as modified by a partial " release " or "confusion." So that wherever in such case the form or state of the contract is such as that a suit may be brought thereon without making the same person both plaintiff and defendant, a court of common law, though it may take cognizance of the case, cannot do complete justice in it; but must render judgment for the whole amount of the obligation, leaving the debtors to resort for ultimate relief to a court of chancery, or to a subsequent motion to the court of law as hereinafter mentioned.

So much for the law of this case; and though there may be some doubt about the law, there can, I think, be none about the justice of the case. It is not pretended by Moses G. Booth that his signature to the bond was obtained by fraud, or that he signed it by mistake, or did not understand it. If he had had any meritorious defence he would have relied upon it, and not have relied alone on the defences of variance between the notice and bond, and insufficiency of notice, and the technical objection that the obligee in the bond was also a co-obligor. He intended when he signed the bond to incur the obligation which it plainly imports. He intended to be bound jointly with his co-obligors, and severally, for the forthcoming of the property therein mentioned on the day of sale. The bond has been forfeited. Shall he be released from his obligation, or shall he be compelled to perform it? If his obligation can be enforced according to his intention, and consistently with the rules of law, it is our duty to enforce it. It can be enforced according to his intention. He intended to be bound precisely as if some other person, instead of Otey Kinsey, had signed the bond as co-surety with him. Suppose that had been the case, a judgment could then have been recovered against him severally; or against him and the principal jointly, as has been actually done in this case: and on payment of the debt he could have recovered one half

1852.
April
Term.

Booth
v.
Kinsey.

of the amount by motion against his co-surety. Are not his rights and obligations precisely the same in the case that has occurred, with this single exception, which makes this case more favourable to him, that his co-surety being also obligee, he would not be required to go through the form of paying the whole debt to the obligee to recover one half of it back from him; but, if the debt cannot be made of the principal obligee, will be relieved on motion by paying one half of it into court. Of what injustice, then, can he complain if his obligation be enforced precisely according to his intention? But look at the other side; and see what injustice may be done to the obligee by declaring the bond to be void. It was insisted by the defendants, the principal obligor and surety Booth, by their counsel, on the trial of the motion in the court below, not only that the bond was void, but that the plaintiff had by his own act discharged the principal obligor from custody under the *ca. sa.*, and thereby released him from all liability for the debt. Suppose the bond be declared void, then the debt has either been altogether released, as insisted by defendants' counsel, or the obligee will lose the benefit of the forthcoming bond, will be subjected to the expense and delay of the proceedings in the court below and this court, and will have to sue out a new execution on his judgment. And all this against the express obligation of the defendants, incurred with their eyes open and on valuable consideration; and when the obligee has acted in good faith, and has performed his part of the contract! The obligee had the body of his debtor in custody for the debt. The appellant was willing to become the surety of the debtor if another person would become co-surety. The obligee was himself willing to become such co-surety. And accordingly, the forthcoming bond was executed and the debtor was discharged from custody. Here was a valuable consideration moving from the obligee, whose conduct in the transaction, in that view of it, was not only blameless but meritorious. Indulgence to the debtor may have formed a further consideration; for the bond bears date in January 1844, whilst the notice bears date in September 1845, about eighteen months thereafter. This is the case which the record seems to present; and these are the consequences which would result from a reversal of the judgment. The law should be plainly written which would require us to encounter consequences like these. If there be any such law, it can only be the technical rule that a person cannot be obligor and obligee in the same bond, or plaintiff and defendant in the same suit. I do not think that rule requires it; and I am therefore for affirming the judgment; though I do not concur in the opinion expressed by the court below, that the bond "is the bond of the defendants alone." I think it is the bond of all the persons whose names are thereto signed as obligors; and that Kinsey is equally bound for contribution as co-surety with Booth, unless such obligation, which the bond imports, was varied by an express agreement between them; and that the obligation of Kinsey, whatever it may be, may be enforced by a court of equity, or by motion to the court which rendered the judgment.

Daniel, J. The third reason or cause for reversing the judgment assigned by the plaintiff in error in his petition for an appeal, viz., that the bond is void because of the fact that Kinsey, who is the obligee, is also one of the obligors, is, upon a first view of the case, apparently very strongly favoured by the decisions of the Supreme court of North Carolina in the cases of *Justices* v. *Dozier* and *Justices* v. *Bonner*, 3 Dev. R. 287, 288.

In each of these cases the bond of a guardian, payable to the justices of a county, was declared void, on the ground that some of the obligees were also obligors in the bond; and the general principle was then asserted that, in all cases of joint bonds or of bonds joint and several, where one of the parties occupies the double relation of obligor and obligee, the instruments are at law wholly void. The soundness of this principle, however, as extended to the cases of joint and several bonds, is denied by Justice Nelson in delivering the opinion of the Supreme court of the United States in the case of *Bradford* v. *Williams*, 4 How. U. S. R. 576, and the counter opinion expressed, that when the bond is joint and several, the fact that one of the obligors is also an obligee does not render the bond wholly void, or stand in the way of a recovery against any one of the obligors who is not also an obligee.

In accordance with the latter opinion is that of the Supreme court of Kentucky as announced in the case of *Daniel* v. *Crooks*, 3 Dana's R. 64. It appears from the statement of that case, as given by Marshall, Judge, in delivering the opinion of the court, that the appellant had entered into a bond, with Magowan as security, payable to Stockton and many others, stockholders of the Mount Sterling Bank. The appellee was one of the obligees, and the appellant and his security, the obligors, were also among the obligees. The condition of the bond recited that the appellant, the principal obligor, had undertaken to settle up the business of the bank, to pay its debts to individuals, and *to redeem the stock* at one hundred dollars per share; to enable him to do which he was to have all the debts and property of the bank in his own right; and on performing the condition, the bond was to be void. The appeal was from a decree rendered against the principal in the bond alone, in a suit in chancery brought by the appellee, to compel him to redeem certain shares of the stock held by the appellee; and the case turned upon the question whether the chancellor had properly taken jurisdiction. The Supreme court held that he had not. Judge Marshall, in delivering the opinion, said that the jurisdiction was asserted only on the ground that, in consequence of the obligors being also obligees, the bond was either not obligatory at all, or, if obligatory, would not sustain an action at law in which the defendants would also be plaintiffs.   The suit, he said, had been entertained and the decree founded on the idea that the bond was not · obligatory : that the chancellor had proceeded on the ground that the security was to be considered as being entirely discharged from liability for the principal's performance of the condition ; and on the further ground that the principal was to be held liable, not by force of his bond, but of the fact that he had acquired all the property of the bank, and was therefore bound to pay the stockholders.   For this idea he said there was no foundation ; that whatever difficulties there might be in maintaining an action at law on those stipulations, in the performance of which the stockholders as a body were interested, the stipulation for the redemption of the stock was one for the breach of which, in relation to himself, each obligee towards whom there could be a breach had an easy and perfect remedy at law by a separate action of covenant.   And the decree was reversed and the bill dismissed for want of jurisdiction in the chancellor.

The reasons given by the Supreme court of North Carolina in *Justices* v. *Dozier* and *Justices* v. *Bonner*, before cited, for asserting the nullity of the bonds in those cases, are mainly of a technical character, and have, it seems to me, very little application to the case before us, when they come to be considered in connection with the peculiar nature of a delivery bond, the manner in which it is taken, the remedies upon it, and the statutory provisions for the summary relief of sureties against their principals and co-sureties.

Those reasons are briefly, first, that the bonds cannot be enforced without naming some of the parties both as plaintiffs and defendants. Secondly, that there can be no delivery to an obligee by himself, nor by one obligor to another obligor. And, thirdly, that inasmuch as the bond for these reasons must be held naught as to those who are both obligors and obligees, it ought to be declared void *in toto;* as otherwise the intention of the parties to the contract would be violated: For that the sureties must have intended to have contribution; that it could not have been intended that one of the persons who sealed the instrument should alone pay to the other the money mentioned in it; and because it could not be enforced without that construction, it should be taken to be void altogether.

The delivery bond here taken is in pursuance of the laws authorizing a debtor under the service of a *ca. sa.* to tender to the sheriff property in discharge of his person, and then, if he chooses to do so, to give bond with security, payable to the creditor, for the forthcoming of the property at the day appointed by the sheriff for its sale. If the bond is forfeited by a failure of the debtor to deliver the property according to the condition, the law requires the sheriff to return the bond to the office of the clerk of the court from whence the execution issued, to be there safely kept and to have the force of a judgment. And the court, to whose office the bond is returned, is authorized upon motion, on ten days' notice, to award execution thereupon for principal, interest and costs against the obligor or obligors, *or any of them,* in behalf of the obligee or obligees.

It will be seen that whilst the statute requires the bond to be made *payable* to the creditor, a *delivery* to him is by no means essential to its validity. On the contrary, the sheriff is required to return the bond to the clerk's office; and in the case of *Eppes' ex'ors* v. *Colley,* 2 Munf. 523, the objection was taken (though overruled by this court) that the sheriff, before notice of the motion was given, had delivered the bond to the creditor, instead of returning it to the clerk's office according to the act. And in the case of *Turnbull, ex'or* v. *Claibornes*, 3 Leigh 392, the forthcoming bond was held to be good though taken after the death of the creditor in the execution, to whom it was made payable. No question about the delivery, therefore, can arise here, out of the fact that Kinsey, who is the obligee, is also one of the sureties.

The bond is a joint and several bond, and it will be seen also from the above recital of the provisions of the law that the obligee is authorized to proceed against " any of the obligors." If, therefore, some other person than Kinsey had been the third obligor to the bond, Shoemaker and Booth would have had no right to complain that the proceedings were against those two alone. It is consequently difficult to perceive how they are injuriously affected in this particular by the incapacity of the third obligor (Kinsey) to be united with them. In obtaining a judgment against Shoemaker and Booth alone, Kinsey has done no more than he would have had a perfect right under the statute to do, no matter how many other obligors there might have been in the bond; and in his proceedings no party has been placed on the record in the attitude of both plaintiff and defendant.

The technical difficulties with respect to the delivery of the bond and the form of the proceeding upon it being thus obviated, I do not see why the judgment upon it was not proper; nor why Booth might not proceed to redress himself by the surety's summary proceeding under the statute, either against the principal in the bond or against his co-surety, who is Kinsey, as the circumstances of the case may require, exactly as he would or might have proceeded had some other person than Kinsey been the other surety.

In this aspect of the case no injustice is done to any one. Booth's liabilities as a surety are in no respect either enhanced or diminished, and Kinsey certainly cannot complain that full efficacy is given to the bond by treating him as, what he has represented himself in the bond to be, a co-surety with Booth.

The laws in regard to delivery bonds have been made in ease, and for the relief, of debtors, and this court has been constant in refusing to permit any slight irregularities, either in the form of the bonds or in the mode of proceeding on them, to stand in the way of a prompt recovery upon them by the creditor. And I think that we can in this case enforce what may be fairly supposed to be the true intention of the parties, without encountering any legal absurdity or doing violence to any of the forms of pleading, in proceeding to a judgment on the bond. Concurring, therefore, as I do, with the judge of the Circuit court, that the notice was regular, and that there is no variance between it and the bond, and that a judgment could be rendered upon it against Shoemaker and Booth, I am for affirming his judgment against them.

I think, however, that Booth may legally treat Kinsey as a co-surety, and may, by proceedings in equity or by motion in the Circuit court, upon proving the insolvency of Shoemaker, be relieved by paying one half of the debt.

ALLEN, *J.* concurred in the opinions of *Moncure* and *Daniel*, J's.

The following was the entry:

The court is of opinion that there is no error in the judgment of the Circuit court; and the same is therefore affirmed with costs. The court is, however, also further of opinion that it is competent for the plaintiff in error, Booth, to treat the defendant in error, Kinsey, as a co-surety in the forthcoming bond in the proceedings and judgment mentioned; and in the event of the insolvency of the principal, to proceed, either by bill in equity or by motion before the said Circuit court, under the provisions of the act, 1 Rev. Code 460, for the relief of securities, to obtain against said Kinsey such an order for contribution as, modified by the fact that the said Kinsey is also the obligee in the bond, will operate to discharge the said Booth from the judgment on payment of one half of the debt and costs. This judgment is therefore without prejudice to the right of the said Booth to pursue any steps he may be advised to take, either at law or in equity, for obtaining relief to the extent above indicated.

---

## Richmond.

### HUNT's *adm'r* *v*. MARTIN's *adm'r*.

(Absent *Cabell*, P. and *Baldwin*, J.)

**May 13th.**

1. A plea which professes to go to the whole action, but answers only to a part of it, is defective and demurrable.
2. Where a defendant in detinue dies, and the action is revived against his administrator with the will annexed, the plaintiff is entitled to demand from the administrator, not only the property sued for, but damages for its detention, and the costs incurred in prosecuting the original action against the testator in his lifetime.
3. The *scire facias* to revive the action of detinue against the administrator should suggest the coming of the property into the hands of the administrator since the death of the testator. And the *scire facias* not being in the record, nor in the clerk's office of the court below, and no objection appearing to have been taken to it in that court, this court will presume that it was in all respects regular.
4. Where an action of detinue is revived against an administrator with the will annexed, and a judgment is recovered, the judgment for the damages for detention of the property

1852.
April
Term.

Hunt's
adm'r
v.
Martin's
adm'r.

and the costs should not be against the administrator personally, but against him as administrator, to be levied of the goods, &c., of his testator in his hands to be administered.

In June 1845 Sims, as administrator of Martin, instituted an action of detinue against Eustace Hunt for the recovery of a number of slaves. The process does not seem to have been served upon Hunt, and an attachment to enforce an appearance was issued and levied on slaves. A judgment was confirmed against Hunt in the office; and at the October term of the court his death was suggested. At the May term 1846 the suit was revived against Coleman, as administrator with the will annexed to Eustace Hunt, upon a *scire facias* said to be issued on the 11th of March, but it is not in the record, and the clerk of the Circuit court certified that it was not among the papers in the cause in his office. At the May term of the court Coleman appeared and pleaded the general issue, and offered three special pleas, which were objected to by the plaintiff, and rejected by the court; to the rejection of which the defendant excepted. The third plea avers that after the suit was brought, and between the death of Hunt and the issue of process to revive the suit against the defendant, he had delivered all the slaves but one to the plaintiff, and that the plaintiff had accepted them. The first and second pleas, as to the slaves claimed in the declaration, aver that after the suit was brought, and between the death of Hunt and the issue of the process to revive the suit against the defendant, he had delivered all the slaves but one to the plaintiff, who had accepted them; and as to that one the defendant did not detain him.

At the May term of the court the cause was tried, when the jury found a verdict for the plaintiff for all except one slave, and his damages were assessed at 2000 dollars. Whereupon the defendant moved the court for a new trial, but the plaintiff releasing 500 dol-

1853.
April
Term.

Hunt's
adm'r
v.
Martin's
adm'r.

lars of the damages, the court overruled the motion, and gave a personal judgment against the defendant for the slaves and 1500 dollars damages. But the plaintiff afterwards released on the record the slaves and their alternative values.

The defendant applied to this court for a *supersedeas*, which was awarded.

*Grattan*, for the appellant.
*Griswold*, for the appellee.

DANIEL, *J.* delivered the opinion of the court.

The third special plea tendered by the plaintiff in error, whilst it professes in its commencement to be a plea to the whole action, answers only as to the slaves in the declaration mentioned, and is wholly silent as to the damages for detention, and as to the costs of the action against Hunt. On the death of Hunt the defendant in error had a right to demand of his administrator, not only the slaves, but also the damages for their detention and the costs incurred in prosecuting the original action against Hunt in his lifetime. A plea, therefore, averring the delivery of the slaves to the defendant in error, and the acceptance of them by him, was no answer to so much of the *scire facias* as claimed the damages and costs aforesaid. The court is of opinion that the said plea was therefore defective, and that the Circuit court did not err in refusing to receive it.

The first and second special pleas do not profess in terms to answer the whole action, and might perhaps have been properly received by the court as pleas to so much of the *scire facias* as demanded the slaves therein mentioned. The error (if any), however, in refusing to receive said pleas was cured by the release of his recovery as to the slaves and their values, subsequently made by the defendant in error; and there is now no injury arising from the refusal of the court to receive said pleas, of which the plaintiff in error can complain.

1852.
April
Term.

Hunt's
adm'r
v.
Martin's
adm'r.

The objection taken here in argument, for the first time, by the counsel of the plaintiff in error, that there is no *scire facias* nor declaration alleging that the slaves in controversy have, since the death of Hunt, come into the possession of his administrator, cannot avail him. From an inspection of the certificate of the clerk of the Circuit court, which has been read by the agreement and consent of the counsel, it appears that the *scire facias* which issued on the 11th March 1846 is no longer on file in his office. In the absence of the said *scire facias*, the record being silent as to any objection having been taken to it in the Circuit court, it must be presumed by this court that the said *scire facias* was in all respects regular, and that it suggested, as it ought to have done, the coming of the slaves into the possession of the administrator since the death of the testator, in which case there was no need of any such allegation by a formal declaration.

The court is, however, of opinion that the Circuit court erred in rendering a personal judgment against the plaintiff in error for the damages for the detention of the slaves and the costs, instead of rendering a judgment for said damages and costs against the plaintiff in error as administrator, to be levied of the goods, &c., of the testator in his hands to be administered. The said judgment is therefore reversed, with costs, &c., and this court proceeding to render such judgment as ought to have been rendered, and it appearing that the defendant in error has released to the plaintiff in error the slaves, together with their respective values, it is adjudged, &c., that the said defendant in error recover against the said plaintiff in error 1500 dollars, the damages aforesaid, and the costs in the court below, to be levied of the goods, &c., of the testator in his hands to be administered.

# REPORTS OF CASES

DECIDED BY

# THE GENERAL COURT

OF

# VIRGINIA,

AT

## DECEMBER TERM 1851,

AND

## JUNE TERM 1852.

SECOND EDITION.

RICHMOND:
J. H. O'BANNON, SUP'T PUBLIC PRINTING.
1898.

# CASES

### DECIDED BY

## THE GENERAL COURT

### OF

## VIRGINIA.

---

## DECEMBER TERM 1851.

---

### JUDGES PRESENT.

*Field,*

| *Lomax,* | *Thompson,* |
| *Leigh,* | *Estill.* |

---

COMMONWEALTH *v.* FEAZLE.

**December 4th.**

A storehouse in a village, late at night, after persons cease to
come to the store to purchase goods, and the door is locked,
is not a public place, within the meaning of the statute
against gaming.

This was a presentment in the Circuit court of Cabell county, at the September term 1848, against Everett

Feazle, for unlawful gaming, by playing at a game of cards in the storehouse of Irvin Lusher, a public place in the county of Cabell. The defendant pleaded " not guilty "; and on the trial the jury found a special verdict as follows:

That the defendant, some time in the month of March 1848, did play at a game of cards, in company with others, in the town of Barboursville, in the county of Cabell, at the storehouse of Irvin Lusher, mentioned in the presentment; that the persons engaged in playing at the time had gathered together late in the evening at the said storehouse, and sat about the fire until the customers had retired, and until it was believed that no person would come that night for the purpose of trading; and until the tavern across the street had been closed, and the people in town had gone to bed. The door and windows being closed, some person having proposed a game, the door of the storehouse was locked, the key-hole stopped, and every place through which it was supposed light might escape or be seen outside of the house was closed, and a blanket or other cloth was thrown over the box upon which they played so as to prevent noise.

At the time of the playing said Irvin Lusher had in his storehouse spirituous liquors, crackers, cheese, raisins, &c., and the persons playing would draw liquor and drink it, and take crackers, &c., and eat them, without asking for them; he being present and not object. ing. And the said Irvin Lusher refusing to take any pay for the things thus taken, and also furnishing candles and fuel, the persons engaged in playing withdrew money from the common stock, and gave it to him for the light and fuel.

Through the spring and winter of 1848, before the playing mentioned in the presentment, sundry persons had gone to said storehouse, and there played at cards three or four times: And at these times the doors, windows, &c., were closed in the same manner as before mentioned.

On the night when the defendant played as above stated, when the proposal to play was first made Lusher objected, on the ground that it was too early in the night; that persons might be up who might desire to come into the house.

Upon this special verdict the court, with the consent of the defendant, adjourned to this court the following questions:

First. From the foregoing facts, is the place at which the playing took place a public place, within the meaning of the law to suppress gaming?

Second. What judgment ought the court to give on the special verdict?

LOMAX, J. delivered the opinion of the court.

The court is of opinion that the place in the proceedings mentioned is not a public place, within the meaning of the law to suppress gaming.

2d. That judgment should be rendered on the special verdict in favour of the defendant.

FIELD and ESTILL, J's, dissented.

COMMONWEALTH *v.* HALL.

December 6th.

A license to one man to keep a tavern at his house in a village will not authorize another, who formed a partnership with the first in the sale of the spiritous liquors, which the first was authorized to sell under his license, to sell liquors at a house on the same lot and within the same enclosure with the tavern.

This was an indictment in the Circuit court of Gilmer county, at its September term for 1850, against Hannibal Hall, for selling by retail ardent spirits without a license. The first count in the indictment charged the selling to be drank at the place where sold; the second charged it not to be drank where sold.

The parties agreed the facts, and submitted the question of law arising thereon to the court. The facts were, that on the 29th of May 1849 the County court of Gilmer granted a license to Thomas Marshall to keep an ordinary at the house where he was then living, in the town of Glenville, until the May term of the County court 1850. Under this license Marshall commenced and kept an ordinary: the liquors were kept, sold and drank in a small building on the same lot, and in the same enclosure in which the main building was situated, and about ten feet from it. On the 8th of December 1849 Marshall and the defendant, by an agreement under seal, formed what is termed in the agreement a partnership in the bar attached to the ordinary, by which, in consideration of the amount that Marshall had paid for the license to keep an ordinary and for the rent of the small building, the defendant bound himself to furnish and keep constantly on hand a supply of liquors suitable for the customers of said ordinary: And the profits were to be divided in proportion to the sums advanced by each party.

On the 1st of March 1850 the County court, with the consent of Marshall, transferred his license to Stephen W. Ratcliff, who had rented and removed to the property occupied by Marshall as an ordinary. On the 11th of April Ratcliff and the defendant entered into an agreement in all respects like that between Marshall and the defendant; and on the 12th day of April the defendant sold liquors by retail at the small building above described as being the place where Marshall had kept and sold liquors.

With the consent of the defendant the Circuit court adjourned to this court the following question:

What judgment ought this court to give on the facts agreed?

By the Court: Judgment ought to be given against the defendant for 30 dollars and the costs.

COMMONWEALTH *v.* McKINNEY.

**December 8th.**

An indictment for a wilful trespass was against Joseph McKinney. It was endorsed by the grand jury, an indictment against Thomas McKinney, "a true bill," and so it was noted upon the record. A writ was issued and served on Joseph, who appeared and moved to quash it. HELD:

   1st. The writ should be quashed.

   2d. The court cannot alter the record so as to make it conform to the indictment.

This was an indictment for a wilful trespass to personal property in the Circuit court of Preston county; and the facts were agreed as follows: At the September term of the court for 1850 an indictment for a

1861.
December
Term.

McKin-
ney's
Case.

wilful trespass to personal property, against Luke McKinney, John McKinney and Joseph McKinney, was sent to the grand jury; which indictment they returned to the court with the following endorsement:

"*Commonwealth* v. *Luke McKinney, Thomas McKinney* and *John McKinney.*"

" Indictment for wilful trespass to personal property. A true bill.

"*William Royse*, Foreman."

The record of the court set out that: The grand jury adjourned on yesterday appeared pursuant to the order of adjournment, and retired to their room; and after some time returned into court, and presented an indictment against Thomas McKinney, Luke McKinney and John McKinney for wilful trespass to personal property—a true bill.

A writ of *venire facias* was issued against the parties, which was served on Luke, John and Joseph McKinney; and thereupon Joseph McKinney appeared and moved the court to quash the said indictment as to him, or to set aside the service of the *venire facias* upon him, and discharge him from further prosecution in this cause, for want of any sufficient record of the finding of a bill of indictment against him. Whereupon the court, with the consent of the said Joseph McKinney, adjourned to this court the following questions:

1st. Whether the said record of the finding of an indictment against Luke McKinney, Thomas McKinney and John McKinney is a sufficient record of the finding of a bill against the said Joseph McKinney to put him to answer the same?

2d. What is the legal effect of the variance between the record of the finding of said indictment and the indictment itself?

1851.
December
Term.

McKin-
ney's
Case.

3d. Is it competent for the court, by an order now to be made, to correct the error in the record of the finding of the said bill, so as to make the same conform thereto, and to cause the said prosecution to proceed against the said Joseph McKinney with or without further process against him?

4th. Ought the court to quash the said indictment as to the said Joseph McKinney, or to set aside the service of said *venire facias* upon him, and discharge him from further prosecution in this case?

5th. What judgment ought the court to render in the premises?

FIELD, *J.* delivered the opinion of the court.

The court is of opinion and decides that the sheriff's return of the *venire facias* as to Joseph McKinney should be quashed, and the said Joseph discharged from further prosecution upon the indictment, because it does not appear from the record that the said Joseph has been indicted; and it is not competent for the court to alter or amend the record in that respect. *Cawood's Case,* 2 Va. Cas. 527, and others referred to in 3 Rob. Pr. 98.

We deem it unnecessary to decide any other question.

1851.
December .
Term.

### COMMONWEALTH *v.* SHELTON *& others.*

**December 11th.**

Betting on a horse race is not within the meaning of the 5th section of the 10th chapter of the act of the 14th March 1848, concerning crimes and punishments, and proceedings in criminal cases.*

At the October term for 1849 the grand jury for the county of Cabell presented Jerome Shelton, Ballard McComas, David Shelton, Rowland Bias, Johnson Lusher and Thomas A. Childers for unlawful gaming, by betting on a horse race, at a race field on the lands of Thomas McComas, in the county of Cabell.

The prosecution against Bias was dismissed; and when the trial of the other defendants came on the jury found a special verdict as follows:

That some time within twelve months before the finding the presentment in this cause, a horse race was run in a field belonging to Thomas McComas, in the county of Cabell, for twenty or twenty-two dollars; that one of the horses belonged to one Ray and the other to a man named Hodge. That the agreement to run the race and the amount for which it was to be run was agreed upon at the house of Andrew McComas, about a mile distant from the place where the race was run, and on the opposite side of the river. That David Shelton made the agreement for the bet, and

---

* That section is as follows: " Any free person who at any ordinary, race field, or public place, shall play at any game whatever, except bowls, chess, backgammon, draughts, or any licensed game, or bet on the hands or sides of others who do play, shall be punished by fine of thirty dollars, and give security, in such sum as the court may require, to be of good behaviour for twelve months; but no person shall be imprisoned in default of such security more than three months."

was interested in the race one fifth of the amount of the bet for which it was run.

That about a month previous to the time of running the race above referred to, a like race was run at the same place, for the sum of fifty dollars, in which the defendant Ballard McComas agreed to become interested to the extent of one third of the bet. This bet was also made at the house of Andrew McComas.

That at another time a third horse race was run at the same place, by the defendants Thomas Childers and Johnson Lusher, for the sum of one dollar; which bet was also made at the house of Andrew McComas. That these bets were all made and the races run within a year before the finding of the presentment in this case. That all the defendants were on the ground at the time when the several races were run. There was a verdict in favour of Jerome Shelton; and as to the other defendants the question was submitted to the court upon the special verdict.

With the consent of the defendants the Circuit court adjourned to this court the following questions:

1st. Is betting on a horse race gaming, within the meaning of the 5th section of the 10th chapter of the act of 1848, passed March 14th, 1848, entitled an act to reduce into one the several acts concerning crimes and punishments and proceedings in criminal cases?

2d. If not included in the 5th section, is betting upon a horse race included within the meaning of the 6th section of the 10th chapter of said act?

3d. If betting upon a horse race be indictable upon either of said sections, is a person interested in said race to a less amount than 20 dollars, where such bet exceeds that sum, guilty of unlawful gaming or wagering.

4th. Where the presentment charges, as in this case, that the betting took place at the race field, is the presentment sustained by proof of a betting at another and different place?

Vol. viii.—38

5th. If the case set out in the presentment be unlawful gaming as aforesaid, is proof that one of the defendants agreed to become interested, without proof
that he staked any money, sufficient to sustain the presentment on that point?

6th. What judgment ought the court to render in
the premises?

LOMAX, J. delivered the opinion of the court.

The presentment charges that the defendants, "on
the 1st of August 1849, at a race field on the lands of
Thomas McComas, in the said county of Cabell, unlawfully did game by betting on a horse race then and
there run over the paths in said race field, contrary to
the form of the statute," &c.

The 5th section of the 10th chapter of the act passed
14th March 1848, entitled an act to reduce into one the
several acts concerning crimes, &c., enacts as follows:
"Any free person who at any ordinary, race field, or
public place, shall play at any game whatever, except
bowls, &c., or bet on the hands or sides of others who
do play, shall be punished by fine of 30 dollars, and
give security," &c.

The first question in the case adjourned submits to
this court the consideration whether "is betting on a
horse race gaming, within the meaning of the section
which has just been quoted." And the answer to it
must depend on this, whether a horse race is a playing
at a game, so that betting upon the race is a betting on
the hands or sides of others who do play.

In the construction of the English statute, 9 Ann, ch.
14, for preventing of excessive and deceitful gaming,
it was held by the courts in England that the word
games used in that act comprehended horse races. That
statute was understood, as it would seem, to comprehend the games embraced by the preceding statute of
16 Car. 2, ch. 7, which was entitled an act against de-

ceitful, disorderly and excessive gaming. And in this statute horse races are expressly mentioned; and persons winning by fraud, or cheating at " cards, dice, tables, tennis, bowls, kittles, shovel board, cock fightings, horse races, dog matches, foot races, and all other games and pastimes," were to forfeit treble the sum or value of money so won. When, therefore, the statute of Ann spoke of playing or betting, it was considered that it had relation to games or plays in former statutes against gaming; that foot races and horse races and the like had been expressly mentioned as games in the statute of Charles, and that the two statutes were to be taken together. *Lynall* v. *Longbotham*, 2 Wils. R. 36; *Bloxton* v. *Pye*, 2 Wils. R. 309. The first statute in Virginia relating to gaming was passed in February 1727. 4 Hen. Stat. 214. This statute was mainly a transcript of 9 Ann, ch. 14, above referred to. There was, however, for the construction of the word games, or playing or betting at games, no prior statute in Virginia, as there was in England, that could be referred to to illustrate the meaning of this language. Hence the assembly found it necessary to pass the second statute in Virginia, in 1740. 5 Hen. Stat. 102. It recites that the former act of 1727 had been construed not to extend to horse racing and cock fighting, which had been found to produce as great mischiefs as any of the games in said act mentioned, and therefore it enacted, as in the former act, that all promises, agreements, mortgages, securities, &c., where the consideration was money won, laid, or betted at horse races, cock fights, or any other sports or pastimes, or any wager whatsoever, should be void," &c., &c.; adopting pretty much the very same provisions in regard to these sports and pastimes as in regard to gaming in the former statute. These provisions in both statutes related only to civil rights and civil remedies, without at all affecting gaming as a criminal offence. For the first time, gaming was made an offence in Virginia by the 4th section of this act of 1740, which prohibited gaming at ordinaries; and inflicted a penalty on ordinary keepers for permitting gaming at their ordinaries. In the revision of the laws in 1748 both of the preceding acts of 1727 and 1740 were embodied in one act; and that act vacates promises, agreements, mortgages, &c., where the consideration was " money or other valuable thing laid or betted at cards, dice, tables, tennis, bowls, or any other game or games whatsoever, or at any horse race, cock fighting, or any other sport or pastime, or on any wager whatsoever." It will be observed that, as well in this statute as in that of 1740, horse racing was not included in the list enumerated as gaming; but is added in a list seemingly distinct from the former list, and denominated sports or pastimes. A provision was made in the 5th section of this act of 1748 against the offence of gaming at ordinaries or other public places; and it enacted that " any person playing in an ordinary, race field, or other public place, at any game or games whatsoever, except billiards, bowls, backgammon, chess, or drafts, or who shall bet on the sides or hands of such as do game, every person, on conviction thereof," in the mode prescribed, should be liable to certain penalties. The offence of ordinary keepers permitting gaming was also re-enacted; and justices were subjected to penalties for neglecting to put the act in force; and punishments inflicted upon cheats, &c. In 1792, (1 St. at Large N. S. 106,) there was a re-enactment of the provisions in the same language as to the enumerated list of acts designated as gaming, and as to horse races and other sports or pastimes; and so again in the revisal of 1819, 1 Rev. Code, ch. 147, vacating all contracts, &c., made upon consideration of games, and sports or pastimes, and any wager whatsoever, as in the former laws: And in regard to the criminal offence of gaming at ordinaries and other public places, retaining the very same language, (so far as is pertinent to the offence,) as that which was used in regard to the same offence in the statute of 1748; and which was used in the former revisals.

Now it is remarkable in the same laws relating both to civil consequences of gaming, or contracts founded on gaming considerations, the laws take the amplest scope of expression, embracing what is denominated games or gaming, sports or pastimes, and all wagers whatsoever, vacating all contracts upon considerations arising out of such acts: Nevertheless the phraseology of those clauses which treat of gaming *criminaliter*, as offences, the language is much more circumscribed. The clause respecting gaming at ordinaries and other public places dropped horse racing, cock fighting, or other sport or pastime, "or any wager whatsoever," which had been included in the civil provisions enacted in the same law; and enacted that if any person shall at any time play in an ordinary, race field, or any public place, at any game or games whatsoever, except bowls, backgammon, &c., or shall bet on the sides or hands of such as do game, every person, upon conviction thereof, &c., shall be subjected to a penalty denounced. This omission of what the statute had in preceding clauses under the denomination of sports and pastimes, and seemingly distinguished by the legislature from what was denominated gaming, and the omission of the comprehensive word "wagers" generally, does seem to be very significant of an intention not to include the two latter classes of cases within the games or gaming to be treated *criminaliter*. In the following section (the 6th section) 147, revisal of 1819, which inflicts a penalty for winning or losing more than 20 dollars at any time within twenty-four hours, the language is "playing or betting at any game," (not at any sport or pastime,) with an enlargement by the words, "or wager whatsoever," which last words were

omitted in the preceding section, as has just been noticed.    What may be the effect, within the 6th section,
of a wager upon a horse race, is not within the scope
of an enquiry confined to the 5th section of chap. 10,
in the act of 1847–8, by the question which is adjourned to this court by the judge below.    It seems
also not to be without much significance, that the legislature, in the very clause now under consideration, in
describing public places where the gaming was made
offensive, should mention a race field as one of them.
For if horse racing was one of the species of the games
which were made criminally offensive, no public race
field could legally be contemplated as having existence.
It would have been as inappropriate as to have spoken
in a law as to gaming or other offence in a billiard room
during that period when the law had entirely forbidden
billiard tables to be kept or billiards to be played.    The
whole history of our legislation in regard to the subject
of gaming, and the uniform peculiarity of the language
in which that legislation has been expressed, seem most
strongly to discriminate horse racing or other sport or
pastime from the gaming which was made criminal ;
and to exclude it from the operation of this section of
the law.    In confirmation of this construction of the
law comes the history of this Commonwealth for more
than a century since the law was passed making it penal to play at any game in an ordinary, race field, or any
other public place.    No sport or pastime has, during all
that time, been more favourably and more extensively
indulged by all ranks and professions of society in
Virginia than horse racing.    It seems to have been universally regarded as a licensed amusement to all classes ;
which none in former times more encouraged than those
holding official stations, the obligations of which would
have constrained them to have enforced the denuncia-
tions of the law against the amusements which they were
patronising and enjoying, if the same had been illegal.

It would seem most wonderful if the terrors of this law had remained latent so long, ever since 1740, under the construction of it supposed or doubted upon this record, and now to be roused into activity in the year 1850.

This court responds to the first question adjourned, that betting on a horse race is not within the meaning of the 5th section of the 10th chapter of the act passed March 14th, 1848, entitled an act to reduce into one the several acts concerning crimes and punishments and proceedings in criminal cases. The decision upon this point in the case renders it unnecessary, upon this record, with the special verdict found therein, to answer the second question which has been adjourned; because it appears that the losing or winning in the present case, in any of the bets charged in the presentment, was not of a sum or anything of greater value than 20 dollars. And moreover, that any answer to the third, fourth and fifth questions is rendered unnecessary in this case, after the decision of this court hereinbefore given upon the first question. And in regard to the last question adjourned, it is considered by this court that judgment should be entered for the defendants: Which is ordered to be certified.

BELL *v.* THE COMMONWEALTH.

December 11th.

1. In prosecutions for felonies and other serious offences, the court will not, on the motion of the prisoner, quash the indictment, unless where the court has no jurisdiction, where no indictable offence is charged, or where there is some other substantial and material defect. In other cases he will be left to his demurrer, motion in arrest of judgment, or writ of error.

2. QUÆRE: If the statement in the commencement of the indictment, of the name of the court and the term at which the indictment was found, is not surplusage. If not surplusage it is useless.

3. Where the indictment in the caption names one county, and in the body of it speaks of the defendant as of another county, the charging the offence to have been committed in the county aforesaid, is error, it not being alleged with sufficient certainty that the offence was committed in the county in which the indictment was found.

4. A prisoner being sent on for further trial by an examining court, which sat during the session of the Circuit court to which he is sent for further trial, that term of the Circuit court is not one of the two at which the statute directs that he shall be indicted, or that he shall be discharged from imprisonment.

Alonzo G. Bell was indicted in the Circuit court of Campbell county, for stealing a horse. When brought to the bar, before pleading, he moved the court to quash the indictment, on two grounds. 1st. Because the caption of the indictment recites the court as " the Circuit Superior court of law and chancery for Campbell county," when in fact there is no court in the Commonwealth bearing that title; the true name of the court being " the Circuit court of Campbell county." 2d. Because the indictment on its face declares that it was found by the grand jury at the October term of the Circuit Superior court of law and chancery holden in and for the county of Campbell aforesaid, in the year of our Lord one thousand eight hundred and fifty; when in fact no such court was then held, and no such indictment was found at the October term 1850 of the Circuit court of Campbell county.

The record states in its commencement the name of the court, and the term, correctly; and these are also stated correctly when recording the fact that the indictment was found against the prisoner. But in the indictment itself the errors relied on as the ground of the motion are found; and an inspection of the record of the court for the October term 1850 shewed that no indictment was found at that term against Bell. But the court overruled the motion; and the prisoner excepted.

The prisoner then offered a special plea, which was, in substance, that on the 13th of May he was examined before the County court of Campbell for the supposed felony in the indictment mentioned, and was remanded for trial in the Circuit Superior court of law and chancery for the county of Campbell. That said Circuit Superior court was in session on the said 13th of May 1850, when the prisoner was so remanded, and had been in session from the 8th day of May, and continued its session until the 18th day of May 1850. That the next term of said court (its name having been changed in the mean time to "the Circuit court of the county of Campbell") was commenced on the 8th day of October 1850, and continued its session until the 19th of October, when it again adjourned until its next regular term in May 1851. And that the prisoner was not indicted at either of the said terms of May or October 1850; nor did the failure to indict him arise from any of the causes stated in the statute; and so the prisoner was not lawfully indicted for said supposed offence set out in the indictment. This plea the court rejected; and the prisoner again excepted.

The prisoner then pleaded "not guilty," and upon

his trial was convicted and sentenced to two years and six months imprisonment in the penitentiary.

In the caption of the indictment the court is stated as of the county of Campbell. It then proceeds to state that the grand jury for the county aforesaid present Alonzo G. Bell, late of the county of Roanoke, in the State of Virginia, and at the parish of Russell and in the county aforesaid; one bay mare of the value, &c.

The prisoner applied to this court at its June term 1851 for a writ of error to the judgment, which was awarded.

*Irving*, for the prisoner.
*The Attorney General*, for the Commonwealth.

LEIGH, *J.* delivered the opinion of the court.

Alonzo G. Bell was indicted at the May term 1851 of the Circuit court of Campbell, and at the same term he was tried and convicted. Before a jury was empanneled for his trial, he moved to quash the indictment. This motion was overruled, and he excepted to the opinion of the court. He also offered a plea, which was rejected, and he again excepted to the opinion of the court.

At the last term of this court he applied for a writ of error. The record then before the court did not shew that the indictment had been found by the grand jury, and a writ of error was awarded. A full record has been certified to this court, from which it appears that the indictment was found by a grand jury regularly empanneled. And we are now to enquire whether there is any error in the proceedings and judgment in the Circuit court.

In the indictment the court is styled " the Circuit Superior court of law and chancery," and it is stated that the grand jury was empanneled at the October term 1850 of the court; whereas the true style of the court is, the Circuit court, and in point of fact the grand jury which found the indictment was empanneled at the May term 1851 of the said court. And it is insisted by the prisoner's counsel that for the misdescription of the court, and the misstatement as to the term at which the indictment was found, in the indictment, the court ought to have quashed the indictment. And to sustain this position the court was referred to passages in Stark. on Cri. Plead. 258, and Archb. Plead. and Ev. in Criminal Cases 33. The passages cited from these authors apply to captions of records certified to the Court of King's Bench from inferior courts, and point out what the captions of such certified records ought to contain. But the caption in the present case is in proper form, and therefore these authorities do not apply to the question under consideration. There is in this case nothing wrong in the caption, and the defects, if defects there be, are in the indictment alone. Still the question remains whether the court ought to have quashed the indictment for the misnomer of the court and for the misstatement of the term at which the indictment was found.

A motion to quash an indictment is addressed to the discretion of the court, and in cases of felony and other serious offences, courts, when the motion is made by the defendant, usually refuse to quash, unless upon the plainest and clearest grounds, but leave the party to a demurrer, or motion in arrest of judgment, or writ of error. 1 Chit. Cr. Law 246, top paging, Phila. Edi. 1819. And the cases in which the court, on the motion of the party accused, ought to quash are, where the court has no jurisdiction, where no indictable offence is charged, or where there is some other substantial and material defect. 1 Chit. Cr. Law 248. Upon this authority, we are of opinion that the Circuit court rightly refused to quash the indictment for the defects above mentioned.   For these defects shew no want of jurisdiction, and an indictable offence is plainly set forth, and the defects complained of are merely formal, not affecting in the least the guilt or innocence of the accused, and not calculated to embarrass him.   Indeed, they are so wholly unconnected with the charge that they ought perhaps to be regarded as surplusage.   We have looked to the forms of indictments given in Starkie on Criminal Pleading; and in none of them is the style of the court, or the term of the court at which the indictment was found, set forth.   And the setting them forth in this indictment, if it be not surplusage, was certainly useless, and for the insertion of useless matter an indictment ought not to be quashed.

The facts set forth in the rejected plea were before this court at the last December term, on the application of the prisoner for the writ of *habeas corpus*, in order that he might be discharged by reason that he had not been indicted within two terms after he had been remanded to the Circuit court to be tried.   On that occasion after great consideration this court was of opinion that two terms, such as the law contemplates, had not elapsed; and that the prisoner had no right to claim his discharge on this ground.   We have at this term reconsidered the question, and we have come to the same conclusion.   We are therefore of opinion that the matter set forth in the plea was no ground of defence, and that the Circuit court rightly rejected the plea.

But there is a defect in the indictment, in not setting forth with sufficient certainty the county in which the larceny was committed, for which the judgment must be reversed.   Campbell county is mentioned in the caption, and in the body of the indictment the county in which the larceny was committed is set forth in the following words, "that Alonzo G. Bell, late of the county of Roanoke, in the State of Virginia, labourer, on the 10th day of March, in the year of our Lord one thousand eight hundred and fifty, with force and arms, at the parish of Russell and in the county aforesaid." So that two counties had been previously mentioned before the county in which the larceny was committed is stated, and then the county where the larceny was committed is stated by the words " in the county aforesaid," without stating to which of the previously named counties the word " aforesaid " had reference. This manner of stating the county where the theft was committed is insufficient. 1 Chit. Cr. Law 160 ; Archbold's Pleadings and Evidence in Criminal Cases 49 ; 2 Gabbett's Cr. Law 205 ; 1 Wms. Saund. 308, n. 1. According to some of these authorities, the word " aforesaid " refers to the county last before named. If this be the correct construction, the word " aforesaid " referred to the county of Roanoke ; and then the Circuit court of Campbell had no jurisdiction. And according to a part of these authorities, it is uncertain to which of the counties before named the word referred ; and the court cannot say in which county the offence was committed. But whichever of these may be the true construction, all the authorities agree that the indictment is bad. And for this error the judgment must be reversed.

The judgment was as follows :

It seems to the court here that there is error in the said judgment in this, that it is not sufficiently alleged in the indictment that the stealing of the mare was committed in the county of Campbell. Wherefore it is considered that the said judgment be reversed and annulled. And this court proceeding to give such judgment as the Circuit court ought to have rendered, it is further considered that the said Alonzo G. Bell go quit of the said indictment. And on the prayer of the attorney general that the said Alonzo G. Bell may be held in custody to answer a good and sufficient indictment to be exhibited against him in the Circuit court of Campbell, for the felonious stealing, taking and carrying away the mare in the aforesaid first indictment mentioned, it is ordered accordingly, unless the said Alonzo G. Bell shall be discharged by the said Circuit court, or otherwise, by reason that there have been three regular terms of the said court since his examination without his being tried, or unless he shall be otherwise legally entitled to be discharged.

## CLORE'S *Case.*

(Absent *Field,* J.*)

December 12th.

1. After a prisoner has been tried by an examining court and remanded for further trial before the Circuit court, and an indictment has been found against him, it is too late to plead in abatement that, or move to quash the indictment because, there were irregularities in his examination before the committing magistrate.

2. If it may be fairly understood from the record of the examining court that the crime for which the prisoner is indicted is the offence for which he was examined, that is sufficient.

3. QUÆRE: If the setting aside a person called upon the *venire,* on the motion of the attorney for the Commonwealth, is a ground of exception by the prisoner.

4. Upon a trial for murder a venireman, when called, states that he has conscientious scruples about the propriety of capital punishment, and is opposed to it; and being asked by the Commonwealth's attorney whether, if the testimony in the cause proved the prisoner to be guilty of murder in the first degree, he would convict him of it, replies, " I do not know." He is properly challenged for cause by the attorney, and set aside by the court.

5. A venireman when called stated, " that he had not heard any

___

*He had tried the cause in the Circuit court.

of the evidence, nor had he heard any report of it from those who had heard it; but from the rumour of the neighbourhood he had formed an opinion which was at the time he spoke existing on his mind, and which he should stick to, unless the evidence should turn out to be different from what rumour had reported it to be. That he had no prejudice nor partiality for or against the prisoner, and believed he could give him a fair and impartial trial according to the evidence that should be given in." He is a competent juror, and challenge of him for cause by the prisoner was properly overruled.

1851.
December
Term.

Clore's
Case.

In the Circuit court of Madison county, at its May term 1851, Edmund Clore was indicted for the murder of Thomas Carpenter. At the same term of the court he offered two pleas in abatement. In the first he alleged that he was committed to prison by Thomas A. Gordon, Esq., a justice of the peace for the county of Madison, without any enquiry or examination into the truth of the offence wherewith he was charged or for which he was committed. In the second he alleged that the offence wherewith he stood charged was never examined into by a justice of the peace in his presence. The court rejected his pleas.

The prisoner then moved the court to quash the indictment in consequence of the same irregularity of proceeding before the committing magistrate as set forth in the pleas in abatement, and because the prisoner had not been duly examined before a court of examination upon the charge of murder set forth in the indictment. And he furthermore moved the court, in the event of refusing to quash the indictment, to defer all further proceedings therein until the prisoner should be regularly committed for examination by a justice of the peace of Madison county, upon the charge of murder set forth in the indictment, and should be duly examined therefor by the proper court of examination and remanded to this court for trial. Upon this motion the record of the examining court was inspected by the court. This record contains the warrant of the justice to arrest the prisoner for the murder of Thomas Carpenter; and the *mittimus* of the same justice committing the prisoner to the jail of the county to be examined for the same murder. The record further states, that Edmund Clore, who stands charged with the murder of Thomas Carpenter, was brought to the bar of the court in custody, &c.; that witnesses were sworn and examined on the part of the Commonwealth; that the arguments of counsel were heard; and then proceeds: " On consideration whereof, it appears to the court that a felony has been committed, and that there is probable cause to charge the accused therewith; the said Edmund Clore is remanded for trial in the Circuit court of this county; and he is remanded to the jail of this county, there to remain till the sitting of said Circuit court." The court overruled the motions. To the several opinions of the court, 1st, in rejecting the said pleas; 2d, in refusing to quash the said indictment; 3d, in refusing to defer all further proceedings at present upon said indictment, the prisoner excepted.

Upon the trial of the case James W. Twyman, one of the *venire*, being called and sworn, stated, " that he had not heard any of the evidence, nor any report of it; but from what he had heard spoken of the case in the neighbourhood, he had formed an opinion to a certain extent. The court asked him if there was partiality or prejudice on his mind for or against the prisoner. He replied that he could not say there was any, but if any, it was in favour of the prisoner."

" Upon further interrogation by the attorney for the Commonwealth, the venireman stated that he had conscientious scruples about the propriety of capital punishment, and was opposed to it. He was then asked by the attorney for the Commonwealth whether, if the testimony in the cause proved the prisoner to be guilty of murder in the first degree, he would convict him of it. He replied that he did not know." He was there-

1851.
December
Term.

Clore's
Case.

upon challenged by the attorney for the Commonwealth for cause, and the challenge was sustained by the court. To which the prisoner excepted.

Another venireman, Henry Huffman, being called and sworn, stated, "that he had not heard any of the evidence, nor had he heard any report of it from those who had heard it; but from the rumour of the neighbourhood he had formed an opinion which was now existing upon his mind, and which he should stick to, unless the evidence should turn out to be different. from what rumour had reported it to be. That he had no prejudice nor partiality for or against the prisoner, and believed he could give him a fair and impartial trial according to the evidence that should be given in." The juror was objected to by the prisoner for cause, but the objection was overruled by the court; and the prisoner again excepted.

The jury found the prisoner guilty of murder in the first degree; when he moved the court to set the verdict aside, and grant him a new trial; but the court overruled the motion, and having spread the facts upon the record, sentenced the prisoner to be hung. Whereupon he applied to this court for a writ of error; and in his petition stated as ground of error:

1st. The rejection by the Circuit court of both and each of his pleas in abatement.

2d. The refusal of the court to quash the indictment upon the grounds stated in his motion.

3d. The refusal to defer proceedings upon the indictment.

4th. The court's setting aside as a juror James W. Twyman.

5th. The refusal of the court to set aside as a juror Henry Huffman.

6th. The refusal of the court to set aside the verdict and award a new trial.

VOL. VIII.—39

The facts spread upon the record are not stated here. because they do not present a case which can be of any importance in defining what constitutes murder in the first degree.

*William Green,* for the prisoner.

LOMAX, *J.* delivered the opinion of the court.

The three first grounds of error alleged in the petition of the prisoner may be considered together. They are:

1st. The rejection of the two pleas in abatement that were tendered by the prisoner.

2d. The refusal of the court to quash, upon motion, the indictment, upon grounds the same that are stated in the pleas in abatement, with an additional ground, that the prisoner had not been duly examined before a court of examination upon the charge of murder set forth in the indictment.

3d. The refusal of the court to defer proceedings upon the indictment, in the event of the refusal to quash, till there should be a regular commitment of the prisoner before a justice and a due examination before the proper court of examination.

The objection urged in this defence upon the motion to quash, because the prisoner had not been duly examined before an examining court, is at once disposed of by reference to the record of the proceedings of the examining court, which was submitted to the inspection of the court, and forms a part of the record in the case. It is stated in the former, that " Edmund Clore, who stands charged with the murder of Thomas Carpenter, was brought to the bar in custody," &c., &c. Now although in the final sentence of the examining court he is not remanded for trial of the said murder, yet the judgment is sufficiently certain, when it is therein stated that witnesses had been examined and

1851.
Decem' er
Term.

Clore's
Case.

the arguments of counsel heard, upon consideration whereof, that it appeared to the court that *a felony* had been committed, and that there was probable cause to charge the accused therewith ; and that the said Edmund Clore be remanded for trial, &c. The felony can fairly be understood only to have reference to the murder, wherewith it was before stated he had been charged, and upon which charge the examination had been held.

The matters embraced in the pleas, which were the same matters taken as grounds for quashing the indictment, besides that above noticed, were irregularities alleged to have been committed by the justice of the peace before awarding the warrant of commitment. No. precedent has been referred to for sustaining either a plea in abatement or a motion to quash, upon the ground of such irregularities in the initiatory proceedings of the justice, which are designed merely to ascertain that there is a degree of suspicion against the accused, requiring that he should be held in custody until a more solemn examination can be had as to the probabilities of the charge, and a trial had of his guilt or innocence. Whatever inconveniences he may complain of as to the examination, or want of examination, before the justice, they can have no relevancy as objections to the indictment, which has given the sanction of the grand inquest of the county to the charge for which the justice committed him. At that stage of the proceedings, after the finding of the grand jury upon the examinations and proofs before them, charging him with the murder, what defence, in reason or in law, can or ought it to be to the prisoner, that the justice who committed him for the crime with which the grand jury have charged him, did not, in his prior examination, examine the case according to legal rules of evidence? The answer to that question is so decisively pronounced in the case of the *Commonwealth* v. *Murray*, 2 Va. Cas. 504, as to

render any discussion upon the subject wholly unnecessary.  In that case, upon a motion to quash the indictment, among other grounds, upon objection taken to
the warrant of commitment, the General court pronounced the opinion, "that even if the warrant of
commitment were bad in the particular adverted to, it
would be no ground to quash the indictment : because
the indictment charges the prisoner with an offence for
which he had been previously examined : And whether
the original *mittimus* was legal or not ; yet clearly, after
he had been remanded to jail by the examining court,
his second commitment was entirely regular."  The
principle of that decision is not at all varied because of
any subsequent amendments of the law in chap. 204,
Code of 1849, relating to arrest, commitment and bail.
It was not error, therefore, in the refusal of the court
below to admit the pleas, or in the refusal to quash the
indictment, even supposing the grounds stated for quashing were established by proper proofs, whatever might
be in such cases the proper proofs ; but in this case no
proof at all was offered to sustain the grounds or to defer
the proceedings, as was asked for upon the indictment.

The fourth error insisted upon is the setting aside as
a juror James M. Twyman.

When, upon the Commonwealth's challenge, one of
the *venire* is erroneously excluded from the panel of
the jury, the effect upon the trial is materially different
from that produced by erroneously overruling the prisoner's challenge to a venireman.  In the former case the
exclusion of a particular man from the jury does not
throw any obstacle in the way of empanneling an impartial jury of qualified jurors.  The effect is only to set
aside one alleged to be disqualified, and to put in his
place one that is qualified.  This exclusion and substitution can in no wise affect the fairness and impartiality
of the trial ; because the trial is still had before a jury
all the members of which are free from exception.  Not

so in the other case. Then a disqualified juror is imposed upon the accused. He has not been tried by twelve qualified jurors, as the law entitled him; and the disqualification of the juror, thus imposed upon him, vitiates the verdict. Overruling his challenge, therefore, is a just ground of exception on his part; and he is allowed to complain of the error, because he has thereby been aggrieved. He has not been tried, as he was entitled to be, by twelve duly qualified jurors. But in the other case, notwithstanding the exclusion complained of, of one of the *venire*, he has had all that any prisoner can be entitled to demand—a fair and impartial trial before twelve jurors, free from all exception. And again, if the exclusion of the venireman upon the Commonwealth's challenge be a matter of exception and a ground of error on the part of the accused, how can the supposed wrong that the error has inflicted upon him be repaired? It is only upon reversal of the judgment to award a new *venire facias;* not that he may have the excluded venireman empanneled on his jury, but that he may again be tried by twelve qualified jurors; in other words, that he may have another trial, such precisely in all respects as that fair and impartial trial, before a jury free from exception, that he has already had. Even if we could suppose that the law entitles him in any sense to an election of his jurors out of the panel of the *venire*, so that the judge ought not arbitrarily to deprive him of it, yet if he has enjoyed the benefit of the great object of all trials, his wrong can at most amount only to *damnum absque injuria*. We are strongly disposed to think that the exclusion of a venireman upon the Commonwealth's challenge, as stated in this record, ought not to have been allowed as a matter of exception, or to be entertained as error. *Henry's Case,* 4 Humphr. R. 270, (Tennessee,) and *Arthur's Case,* 2 Dev. R. 217, (N. Carolina,) are strong to support these views of the court. The remarks made by Henderson, Ch. J., in the latter of these cases, are exceedingly forcible.

But was there any error in excluding Twyman from the jury? This venireman, "being called and sworn, stated that he had not heard any of the evidence, nor any report of it; but from what he had heard spoken of in the case in the neighbourhood, he had formed an opinion to a certain extent." Thereupon "the court asked him if there was partiality or prejudice on his mind for or against the prisoner? He replied that he could not say there was any, but if any, it was in favour of the prisoner." Now, as to the opinion stated upon this examination, this court, upon the principles herein afterwards stated, does not think that such opinion, as it is presented in the bill of exceptions, could furnish a ground for the Commonwealth's challenge. But the interrogatory, propounded by the court, seems to be upon a matter distinct from the formation of a preconceived opinion; it is in regard to his feelings. It might be a question deserving grave consideration whether any degree of favour towards the accused, however doubtfully felt or expressed, ought not to exclude the juror, upon the Commonwealth's challenge, from sitting upon the jury; because if it should not, the correlative challenge on the part of the prisoner, because of a prejudice similarly felt, might be forestalled in all cases hereafter, and precluded by our decision. That point is therefore waived, to consider another ground of challenge for cause on the part of the Commonwealth. Upon further interrogation by the Commonwealth's attorney, Twyman "stated that he had conscientious scruples about the propriety of capital punishment, and was opposed to it. He was then asked by the Commonwealth's attorney whether, if the testimony in the cause proved the prisoner to be guilty of murder in the first degree, he would convict him of it. He replied that he did not know." He was thereupon challenged for cause by the Commonwealth, and the challenge sustained. No case has been found in the English books, deciding the question upon this last mentioned matter of conscientious scruples, as a cause of challenge for the crown. It is not often that the crown, according to the English practice under their statutes, is put to the necessity of shewing cause of challenge. The postponement of the cause of challenge and setting aside the jurors excepted to by the crown, until the panel is entirely gone through without obtaining a qualified jury from the rest of the *venire,* operates generally, perhaps in all cases, as a sort of peremptory challenge by the crown, though it be restricted to challenge for cause only. In New Hampshire, in a case of misdemeanor, (*Pierce* v. *State,* 13 New Hamp. R. 555-6,) and in Pennsylvania, in a case of murder, (*Commonwealth* v. *Lisher,* 17 Serg. & Rawle 155,) such cause of challenge, independent of statute, has been allowed. A recent provision in a statute in Virginia, Code of 1849, ch. 208, § 8, declares that " any person whose opinions are such as to prevent his convicting any one of an offence punishable with death shall not be allowed to serve as a juror on a trial for such offence." Now what is a conscientious scruple, as spoken of by the venireman, but an opinion, and more than an opinion. For it is not merely a speculation established in the mind, but it has pierced into the conscience and fastened itself there, as a scruple to regulate his life and actions, and stirring opposition to the propriety of capital punishments which had been enacted by law. And so deeply rooted was this conscientious scruple opposed to a legal punishment, that he did not know whether even the sacredness of the oath to decide in his verdict according to the evidence could overcome this conscientious scruple. Was this opinion or scruple of such influence as to " prevent " him from " convicting the prisoner ?" The court could not know ; and the juror himself, according to his examination, did not know that the evidence proving murder in the first degree, or his loyalty, or the obligations of the oath to find according to evidence, would control or overcome the influence of his conscientious scruples. Such being the state of the juror's mind, it was most proper to regard him as excluded, by the spirit and even by the terms of the provision of the act referred to, from serving as a juror.

The 5th error assigned is the refusal of the court to set aside as a juror Henry Huffman.

We are again brought to the consideration of the question of the disqualification of veniremen to be sworn as jurors, in consequence of their preconceived impressions or opinions in regard to the crime or to the accused to be tried. To secure, as far as possible, the impartiality of jurors, such only should be empanneled as will strictly decide, according to the proofs offered at the trial, and according to them alone. Whatever considerations may have recommended juries of the vicinage, it is, if it were practicable, desirable that the men constituting the jury should never, previously to the trial, have heard of the offence or the offender.

When the venireman is called before the court and offered as a juror, it seems to be a fair presumption that he has intelligence to know his duty and integrity to perform it; and that he is under no influences impelling him to do wrong. That presumption is not less fair and reasonable though it should be deemed proper to test the state of his mind and of his feelings in regard to the matter to be tried through the more searching detection of an examination upon oath. If there be no extraneous proofs offered, as in this case, we are bound, according to every principle of justice and of law, to credit the disclosures which he makes, as to his own belief of the state of his mind, which can only be known to himself; and not to disbelieve an unimpeached witness, made a witness, not by his own act, but by the act of

1851.
December
Term.

Clore's
Case.

the court, and who is subjected to those sanctions of truth, the most solemn that can be applied to the consciences of men. Where no positive inconsistencies appear in his examination, suspicion should not be indulged in unnecessarily creating them. At the same time, that there should be no overstrained efforts to overlook inconsistencies, the whole of the examination should receive a candid and a reasonable construction. If there be no irreconcilable inconsistencies discovered, then there is a concurrence of presumption and of testimony which should overrule and silence every objection to the qualification of the juror.

When, therefore, the juror states, as he does in this case, "that he had no prejudice or partiality for or against the prisoner, and he believed he could give the prisoner a fair and impartial trial according to the evidence that should be given in," we are bound so far to regard that to be true which he has so stated. The credit paid to that statement must be conclusive, unless repelled by other parts of the examination, that may conflict with and disprove it. Is there any such conflicting disclosure made by the juror?

He states "that he had formed an opinion." It is not expressly stated the extent of that opinion; whether it was an opinion extending to the whole case, in all its facts and circumstances as it would be expected to be submitted to the jury upon the trial, or extending only to some part of the case: nor does he expressly describe the nature of that opinion, in the power and influence that it would be likely to have over his judgment, as being a *decided* or *substantial* opinion : nor does he state that its power and influence, whatever they might be, had derived any adventitious strength from the circumstance that the opinion had been expressed to others. There are infinite shades of opinion between that degree in which it is an impression too slight to restrain the free exercise of the judgment when called to a graver consideration of the case, and that degree amounting to a deep settled conviction. When it is stated merely that an opinion has been formed, in which of these classes would a fair presumption place that opinion, in its operations and its influence upon the judgment of a man who swears, notwithstanding the formation of that opinion, " he believes he can give the prisoner a fair and impartial trial, according to the evidence that should be given in " ? If it was of the latter kind, the juror must have been perjured in the statement which he makes of his impartiality, or infatuated into an unnatural dullness in the statement which he makes of his belief. It would seem, therefore, a reasonable presumption to place the opinion alluded to in the former class, and thereby give consistency to this sworn examination in all its parts : and moreover, as the juror felt conscious that, notwithstanding the opinion, he retained the power to give an impartial trial to the case made out according to the evidence that should be given in, it would be fair to presume that the opinion was limited in its extent ; or was based, not upon the facts and circumstances which the trial would develope, but upon facts and circumstances he had heard that might be materially different. So that the opinion could not be regarded as one formed of the true case, which he may not yet have heard, and as to which, therefore, his judgment had not as yet been compromised.

In the anxiety of the courts to select impartial and upright jurors, a test has been applied to ascertain the extent and nature of the preconceived opinion, by ascertaining what had been the sources of the information which had given birth to the opinion : Not that a decided or substantial opinion, when stated to be decided and substantial, would be reduced to anything less, in the consideration of the court, according to the means of information. Such an opinion, howsoever

1851.
December
Term.

Clore's
Case.

formed, with or without any information, will always
be a disqualification of a juror.   But that state of opinion is not to be presumed where such is not stated to
be the case ; for such a prejudication of the criminality
of a fellow being is not consistent with ordinary humanity, and is regarded as offensive to the law.   But
where the nature and influence and extent of the opinion are undisclosed, the test alluded to may very properly be referred to.   If the opinion of the juror was
formed upon hearing the evidence upon some former occasion, it would be in vain to believe otherwise than
that it was a decided and substantial opinion.   He had
had the facts and circumstances of the case, the credibility of the testimony and every thing materially tending to produce a fixed judgment in the case, all of
them, under consideration, and the decision in which
they resulted in his own mind would not be likely to
be changed upon a repetition of the same proofs at the
trial upon which he was to be placed ; nor should the
preconceived opinion be otherwise regarded when it
was formed upon conversations with the prosecutor or
the witnesses, or upon reports communicated to him of
what had been testified or would be testified, and a
full credence had been given to the statements, through
whatever channel so made to him.   In making these
enquiries into the state of the juror's mind, the degree of
credence which he reposed in the persons from whom,
or through whom, he has derived the information leading to his decision, is also a consideration which must
always be entitled to much weight.   But in the present
case the juror swears that he had not heard any of the
evidence, nor had he heard any report of it from those
who had heard it ; nor does he say that he had placed any
credence in the truth of what he had heard.   But the
juror may have received impressions upon his mind by
means much less authentic than those that have been
just alluded to.   He may not have been informed or

made up his opinion upon the whole case, but upon a statement of what might be entitled to be regarded by him as a material part of it. He may be ignorant of other parts not yet disclosed to him. His mind may not have been exercised, or may not have had the opportunity of being exercised, either as to the case in full, or the credibility of those whence his information may have been derived. There is in every bosom an irrepressible casuistry, ever ready to exercise the judgment upon every representation of criminality; more especially in crimes of a deep atrocity, such as homicide, which seems instinctively to rouse all the faculties of the mind and the sensitiveness of the soul. Upon such occasions the minds and the feelings of none are more apt to be roused into the formation of opinions upon what they may have heard that is material in the case than those who are the most intelligent and discreet and upright, and, at the same time, the most discriminating; such as are, of all the community, the most fit to sit in trial upon the criminal. They may, upon the intelligence which they have received, have formed opinions on the case, and even strong ones; but they were formed upon the hypothesis of the case as it was presented to them. If they are disqualified as jurors, then those best qualified will be excluded from passing between the Commonwealth and the prisoner in cases where vindication of guilt or innocence will be most vital. Courts should be careful in laying down rules as to the qualification of jurors which will throw jury trials and the administration of criminal justice into the hands of the most senseless and ignorant and least competent to pronounce a just and legal verdict. A hypothetical opinion, though it may be a strong one, and upon whatever information formed, unless it be such as overpowers the mind with conviction, has never been considered as a disqualification. I say, unless it overpowers the mind with conviction, because there may be cases, as where the opinion has been formed upon listening to the evidence in the case upon another occasion; and there it would be vain to treat it as hypothetical. But when it is ascertained, either by the express declaration of the juror or by palpable implication from his examination, that the opinion is only hypothetical upon the truth of the matters which he has heard, (less authentic than such as has just been referred to,) then the juror is to be deemed not unfitted for the rendering a fair and impartial verdict. When the juror swears himself free from prejudice or partiality, and that he can give the prisoner a fair and impartial trial, is it an unreasonable presumption that the opinion he has formed, to whatever extent or in whatever degree, is no more than a hypothetical opinion?

We would not, at all events, be warranted in presuming more in this case, when it is stated in the examination of the juror, "but from the rumour of the neighbours he had formed an opinion." In *Armistead's Case*, 11 Leigh 657, it was held that "generally opinions founded on hearsay or common reports in the country ought to be regarded as hypothetical, or so slight as not to disqualify the person entertaining them; unless, upon further examination, it should appear that this was not the true state of the juror's mind, but that he had been so inconsiderate and unjust as, upon insufficient evidence or no evidence at all, to have prejudged the prisoner's cause: and then he is doubly unfit to be trusted with it!" This principle was afterwards unanimously acted upon by this court in the case of *McCune & others*, 2 Rob. R. 771.

Nor can we find anything in the further examination of the juror to shew that the above was not the true state of the juror's mind. The presumption that the opinion, founded on hearsay or common report of the neighbourhood, was merely a hypothetical opinion, is not repelled by the disclosure that the opinion was still exist-

ing upon his mind. An opinion " regarded as hypothetical or slight " does not become less so because it may
be existing in the mind for six or seven months, or a
year, or for any period.    The continued existence of
impressions upon the mind, which do not in themselves
amount to disqualification, cannot become such by reason of their continuance on the mind.

Nor is it repelled because the juror, in speaking of the
opinion so formed, and such as it was so far upon the
matters above noticed to be considered, said, " which
he should stick to, unless the evidence should turn out
to be different from what rumour had reported it to be."
The mind that has formed an opinion, though hypothetical or slight, cannot be expected to relinquish that
opinion, if upon a revision of the case, with better lights
to guide the judgment, the facts and circumstances
should exactly or materially correspond with those which
made the first impression.    The judgment is not on
that account less impartial or more prejudiced, because
the same opinion recurs when the same elements are
presented for the formation of an opinion at the trial
as had given birth to the first opinion.    The hypothesis or slight impression resting on the mind may have
rested there without any prejudice or partiality, without
any prejudication of the weight and credibility of the
testimony or the inferences to be deduced from the facts
and circumstances in all their combination and the variety of views of which they might be susceptible in
the proceedings at the trial.    Several cases have occurred where the jurors, entertaining hypothetical opinions,
have stated that, if the evidence should correspond
with what they had previously heard, their opinions
would remain :    Nevertheless they have not been held
to be thereby disqualified on the ground that they would
adhere or stick to their former opinion.    But it is supposed that a stronger obstinacy of opinion is expressed
when the juror says in this case that he will stick to

his previous opinion, unless the evidence should turn out to be different from what it had been reported to be. But still the remark, even in this shape, must be reasonably understood to imply that the juror's mind was not made up. For, in the form in which the declaration of the juror is stated, it is fair to imply that if, *e contra*, the evidence should be different, he would adopt an opinion conformable with the testimony. We are, however, saved the necessity of considering critically the similar import of the two forms of expression. For in the case of *McCune & others* and also in *Moran's Case*, the statements made by the jurors as to their preconceived opinions was in a form of expression the same or similar to that in the examination of the juror in that respect in the present case. It is therefore considered that there was no error in admitting this juror.

The 6th error assigned in the petition is the overruling the application to set aside the verdict rendered by the jury.

On what ground this application was made the bill of exceptions does not state, nor was any particular ground stated in the argument of the counsel in error. Indeed none, as all the facts appear in the bill of exceptions, can justly be stated as a ground for such application. The jury have found the homicide to be murder in the first degree, and the court ought not but upon the strongest objections to disturb their finding. Every fact stated by the judge sustains the propriety of that finding; the previous grudge, the previous threatenings, the express malice, the deliberation and premeditation with which the deadly means of killing were provided by the prisoner, his coming with these deadly means to the house of the deceased, and his insults offered to him at his own door, as if to exasperate the deceased to an attack upon him, to justify or mitigate the killing upon which he had deliberated and premeditated; these all shew a murder which, upon the finding of

this jury, this court would have no warrant for pronouncing to be less than murder in the first degree; no, not
even if the acts of the deceased as shewn in this case,
under that resentment which was provoked by the prisoner, could be regarded as an assault upon the prisoner.
Upon the whole record the court can discover no error
whatever committed by the court below; and the
judges are unanimous in refusing the writ of error.

ESTILL, *J.* concurred in the opinion, except on the
first ground of error stated in the petition. He was of
opinion that the rejection of the special pleas in abatement was error, on account of which the writ of error
should be awarded.

WRIT OF ERROR REFUSED.

------

ERSKINE *v.* THE COMMONWEALTH.

COMMONWEALTH *v.* ERSKINE.

**December 13th.**

1. The malicious burning, by the owner, of a house on his own
   land, the house being then in the legal occupancy of
   another, is a violation of the act of 1847–8, ch. 4, § 7, p. 99.*
2. The malicious burning of wheat threshed from the straw is not
   a violation of the 6th section of the same act.

The case is sufficiently stated in the opinion of the
court delivered by *Field*, J.

The defendant was indicted in the Circuit court of
Ohio county, at its May term 1850, for felony. The in-

------

* The provisions of the 6th and 7th sections of the act are given
in the opinion of the court.

dictment contains seven counts. Upon that indictment
he was tried and acquitted upon the 3d count. He
was found guilty upon the other six counts, as to
which the finding of the jury was special; and it is upon
that finding that the questions we are called upon to
decide arise. The verdict of the jury is in these
words: " We, the jury, find the defendant guilty under
the first and fourth counts of the indictment, provided
the court shall be of opinion that he can rightfully be
so found guilty on both or either of the said counts,
under evidence proving that the out-house, or old out-
house, mentioned or described in the said counts, was
not adjoining any dwelling house, nor under the roof
of any, nor in the curtilage of any, but was in the
field, isolated, separate and apart from any dwelling
house; there being no dwelling house on the farm at
all. We find him guilty also under the second and
seventh counts of the indictment, provided the court
shall be of opinion that the said counts, or either of
them, are good and sufficient in law, and not to be disregarded by the jury. We further find, if the prisoner
can be convicted and judgment given against him as
aforesaid, on all or any of the said counts, that he be
fined five hundred dollars, and imprisoned three months
in the county jail. But if he cannot be so rightfully
convicted, and judgment be given against him on all or
any of the said counts, then we find him not guilty on
the same. We further find the prisoner guilty of the
fifth and sixth counts, if he can be lawfully convicted
under the said fifth and sixth counts of a misdemeanor,
and assess his fine at one hundred and twenty-five dollars. And we find the prisoner at the bar not guilty
upon the third count of the said indictment." Upon the
verdict as to the 1st, 2d, 4th and 7th counts of the indictment, the court rendered judgment against the pris
oner for the fine and imprisonment so ascertained by
the jury. Upon the verdict of the jury as to the fifth

VOL. VIII.—40

and sixth counts the Circuit court adjourned these questions to this court for decision :

" 1st. Whether the court ought to give judgment for the Commonwealth as for a misdemeanor upon the said finding of the jury upon the said fifth and sixth counts of the indictment, or shall arrest the same.

" 2d. What judgment ought to be given on the said finding upon the said fifth and sixth counts."

To the judgment rendered by the Circuit court upon the verdict upon the 1st, 2d, 4th and 7th counts, a writ of error has been awarded by a judge of this court; and thus the whole case comes before us. Upon looking into this record we are clearly of opinion that the 7th count is good; and this relieves us from the necessity of taking any notice of the 1st, 2d and 4th; for whether they are good or bad is rendered wholly immaterial by the finding of the jury, provided the 7th is good. The 7th count of the indictment charges that the said John Erskine, on the 30th day of February in the year of our Lord eighteen hundred and fifty, between the hours of ten o'clock in the night of the same day, with force and arms, at the county aforesaid, one building, on a farm of the said John Erskine situated in Ohio county aforesaid, and which was then and there in the occupation and possession of one Ely Prettyman, and of the value of sixty dollars, feloniously and maliciously did set fire to, and the said building, then and there situate, by such firing as aforesaid, feloniously and maliciously did burn and consume, against the statute in such case made and provided, and against the peace and dignity of the Commonwealth.

The statute under which this indictment was made is the 7th section of the 4th chapter of the Criminal Code, in the Session Acts of 1847–8, p. 99. After specifying, in previous sections, dwelling houses, jails, prisons, churches, town houses, colleges, academies and other buildings erected for public use, banking houses,

1851.
December
Term.

Erskine's
Case.

ware houses, store houses, manufactories and mills, barns, stables, corn houses and tobacco houses, the 7th section provides that any free person who shall maliciously burn any building whatsoever, not mentioned in this act, if the value thereof be one hundred dollars or more, shall be punished by confinement in the penitentiary for not less than three nor more than ten years ; and if the value be less than one hundred dollars, by confinement in the penitentiary for not less than one nor more than three years, or, in the discretion of the jury, by confinement in the jail not exceeding twelve months and by fine not exceeding five hundred dollars.   The house in question appears to have been situated upon the farm of the prisoner.   But it was at the time of being burnt in the occupancy and possession of another man, who had a qualified ownership therein ; and therefore the burning of that house maliciously by the prisoner was a violation of the said 7th section, and renders him liable to prosecution and punishment under that law.   We are therefore of opinion that there is no error in the record, and the judgment is to be affirmed.

The two adjourned questions arise upon the special finding of the jury upon the 5th and 6th counts of the indictment.   The 5th count charges a felonious, wilful and malicious burning at night of a large quantity of hay and wheat, threshed and cleansed, of the value of 165 dollars, in a barn situated on a tract of land belonging to the said John Erskine, but then in the occupancy and possession of Ely Prettyman.   The 6th count charges a burning at night, feloniously, wilfully and maliciously, 165 bushels of wheat, threshed and cleansed, of the value of 160 dollars, of the goods and chattels of Ely Prettyman, in a building situated on a tract of land belonging to the said Erskine, in the occupancy and possession of Prettyman.   These two counts were based upon the 6th section of the same law, which makes the mali-

cious burning of a stack of wheat, barley, oats, corn, or
other grain, or any stack of fodder, straw, or hay, felony.
But as the wheat and hay charged in these counts to have
been burnt were not in *stacks*, the burning was not a
felony under the 6th section. The jury convicted the
prisoner not of the felony, but of a misdemeanor, in burning the wheat and straw. This conviction upon an indictment under the statute for punishing wilful trespasses might have been proper; but the counts above referred to are not good under that statute. We are
therefore of opinion, and respond in answer to the questions adjourned, that judgment should not be entered
for the Commonwealth upon the finding of the jury
upon the 5th and 6th counts of the indictment; but
should be arrested, and judgment entered thereon for
the prisoner. Which is ordered to be certified, &c.

---

### COMMONWEALTH *v.* PICKERING.

#### December 15th.

An indictment for perjury must shew that the evidence which
the defendant gave was material. And therefore, if the evidence which the defendant gave before the grand jury is
not shewn clearly on the face of the indictment to relate
to an offence committed within the county, the indictment
is defective.

This was an indictment for perjury in the Circuit court
of Wirt county against Nelson A. Pickering. The defendant demurred to the indictment, and the Circuit court
with his consent adjourned to this court eight questions.
Of these the sixth was, Does the materiality of the defendant's evidence given before the grand jury sufficiently appear in the indictment?

And the eighth .was, What judgment ought to be rendered in this case upon the demurrer to the indictment?

1851.
December
Term.

Picker-
ing's
.Case.

The indictment is stated in the opinion of the court.

*The Attorney General*, for the Commonwealth.
*Fisher*, for the defendant.

LEIGH, *J.* delivered the opinion of the court.

The defendant was indicted in the Circuit court of Wirt for perjury in giving evidence to the grand jury empanneled in that court. The defendant demurred to the indictment, and, upon the argument of the demurrer, the court adjourned eight questions to this court.

The indictment alleges that on the        day of        1850, a grand jury was summoned and empanneled for the county of Wirt, and whilst they were examining and investigating the violations of the laws of the Commonwealth committed within the county, the defendant appeared in open court, and at his own instance was sworn by the court that the evidence he should give to the grand jury should be the truth, the whole truth, and nothing but the truth, the court having then and there competent authority to administer the said oath; and that whilst the defendant was being examined by the grand jury it then and there became material to enquire whether Alfred Fought, Esq.,(a justice of the peace for the Commonwealth of Virginia in and for the county of Wirt,) was present and was called upon to suppress a fight between the defendant and one John Hickman; and the defendant, being sworn as aforesaid, did then and there, in the said county, before the grand jury, falsely, wilfully and corruptly depose, swear and testify that Alfred Fought, Esq., (a Commonwealth's justice of peace for the county aforesaid,) was present and was called to suppress a fight between

1851.
December
Term.

Picker-
ing's
Case.

the defendant and John Hickman, and that Fought did then and there refuse to assist in quelling the said fight: Whereas the said Alfred Fought was not present at the time and place the said fight took place, and was not called upon to suppress the fight.

We shall first consider the question which submits to us whether the materiality of the defendant's evidence given before the grand jury sufficiently appears in the indictment. The criminal jurisdiction of the Circuit court of Wirt was limited to offences committed in the county; and the court had no authority to swear a witness to give evidence before the grand jury of the said court of an offence committed out of the county. It was therefore necessary to shew on the face of the indictment that the offence of which the defendant gave evidence was committed within the county: otherwise it would not appear that the court had jurisdiction of the offence, and the evidence could not be material, as no evidence given in a court having no jurisdiction to determine the case can be material. This indictment does not allege that the offence of which the defendant gave evidence was committed within the county of Wirt. It alleges that this offence was committed at the time and place at which the fight took place, but where the fight took place is no where stated. It might possibly have taken place in Wirt; but if the indictment shews on its face only that the evidence might have been material, it is not sufficient: it must shew that it was material. For this reason we are of opinion that the materiality of the evidence given by the defendant does not sufficiently appear in the indictment.

There are other objections to this indictment. It does not appear what was the question the grand jury was examining into, or for what purpose the examination was made. We may conjecture that it was made to ascertain whether Fought, either as a justice or

1851.
December
Term.

Picker-
ing's
Case.

individual, had been guilty of a neglect of duty; but whether as magistrate or individual we cannot with any certainty say. He is in the indictment called a justice of the peace, and it may be that the enquiry was whether he, as a justice, had been guilty of neglect of duty; but the allegation that he was a justice of the peace is made in such a manner that it does not certainly appear that he was a justice at the time the fight took place. If he was proceeded against as an individual, the indictment is defective for not shewing that he had been called on by any person who had authority to call upon him. For this uncertainty as to the question before the jury, the indictment may be bad, but we have not deemed it necessary to examine this question with much care, as the judgment must be entered for the defendant for other defects. One of the judges, however, is decidedly of opinion that the particular enquiry before the jury, and the object of it, ought to have been set out in the indictment, in order that the court might see whether or not the evidence of the defendant was material.

In answer to the sixth and eighth questions adjourned, this court is of opinion, and doth decide, that the materiality of the evidence given by the defendant to the grand jury does not sufficiently appear in the indictment; and that judgment on the demurrer ought to be entered for the defendant. And this court does not deem it necessary to decide any other of the questions adjourned. Which is ordered to be certified to the Circuit court.

1851.
December
Term.

## COMMONWEALTH *v.* KELLY.

### December 17th.

1. The mere user of a road by the public, for however long a time, will not constitute it a public road.
2. A mere permission to the public, by the owner of land, to pass over a road upon it, is, without more, to be regarded as a license, and revocable at the pleasure of the owner.
3. A road dedicated to the public must be accepted by the County court upon its records, before it can be a public road.
4. If a County court lays off a road, before used, into precincts, or appoints an overseer or surveyor for it, thereby claiming the road as a public road; and if, after notice of such claim, the owner of the soil permits the road to be passed over for any long time, the road may be well inferred to be a public road.

The case is sufficiently stated in the opinion of the court, which was delivered by *Leigh,* J.

At the Circuit court of law and chancery held for the county of Culpeper, on the 4th of June 1849, John P. Kelly was indicted for erecting and placing a gate and gate posts across a public road and highway in the county of Culpeper. The defendant pleaded not guilty; and the jury rendered a verdict against him.

The facts proved on the trial were, that there was no record establishing the road as a public road and highway, nor was there any record that the County court regarded the road as a public one, either by laying it off into precincts, by appointing surveyors of it, or otherwise: on the contrary, there was parol evidence which proved that no surveyor of the road had ever been appointed, and that the road had never been worked upon by any hands, public or private, but on one occasion, when a certain Staunton Slaughter, on the part of the road which run through his land, with his own hands worked on the road at a steep hill near his mill, and placed some saw-mill slabs in a wet place in the road. That the road had existed for forty or fifty years, but that the owners of the soil through which it was con- ducted, down to a period of about twenty-five years before the obstruction mentioned in the indictment, at their will and pleasure, changed the road; but that there had been no such change for between twenty and twenty-five years before the obstruction by the defen- dant. And it was proved that there was no reason to believe that any of the records of the County court of Culpeper had been lost or destroyed. This being the evidence, the defendant asked the court to instruct the jury, first, that they ought to find for the defendant on account of the absence of record evidence that the road had been accepted by the County court or by the county; 2dly, that they ought to find for the defen- dant, unless there was something in the evidence, be- sides the mere use of the road by individuals, no matter how general, to satisfy them that it had been accepted by the County court or by the county as a public road; and 3dly, that they ought to find for the defendant, un- less they were satisfied by the evidence that the road had been dedicated by the owners of the soil to the public use as a highway, and had been accepted as a highway by the general public of the county, and not by the local public only of a small neighbourhood around it. The court refused to give these instruc- tions; but instructed the jury that a road, to become a highway by dedication and long use, must have been accepted by competent authority; of which dedication and acceptance they were to judge from all the circum- stances before them. The defendant excepted to the opinion of the court for refusing to give the instructions asked for, and for the instruction given to the jury.

At first the court rendered a judgment against the defendant for the fine assessed against him, but subse- quently, on the motion of the defendant to award him

1831.
December
Term.

Kelly's
Case.

a new trial, set aside the judgment and adjourned the motion to this court.

The question adjourned is an important one, since to decide it it may be necessary to consider whether from user alone both a dedication and acceptance may be inferred. This question does not seem to have been directly submitted to this court; nor have we met with a case in which the question has been before the Court of appeals. In *Brander* v. *The Justices of Chesterfield*, 5 Call 548, Judges Tucker and Roane expressed opinions that as public roads are established by matter of record, matter of record only could be admitted to prove a road a public road; and in *Clarke* v. *Mayo*, 4 Call 374, Lyons, J. said there could be no public road unless it appeared of record. As in this State the County courts are alone authorized to establish public roads, we would have considered these opinions as settling the law, but for the cases decided in England by which roads have been established from long use.

By the cases to which we have alluded, a road may become a public one by reason of a dedication of a right of passage to the public by the owner of the soil and an acceptance by the public. But a dedication without an acceptance will not establish a public road. Best on Pres., 47 Law Libr. 133, side paging. We have no objection to this proposition: it is indeed sustained by the case of *Clarke* v. *Mayo*, 4 Call 374. But the cases in England go farther, and seem to decide that from mere user both the dedication and acceptance may be inferred; as if a man open his land so that the public pass over it continually, after a very few years the public will acquire a right of way, unless some act be done to shew that he intended only to give a license to the public to pass over the land and not to dedicate a right of way to the public. Best on Pres., 47 Law Libr. 133. To this proposition we cannot give our assent, and, from the wide difference in the state of the

1851.
December
Term.

Kelly's
Case.

two countries, we do not think that the decisions of
the English courts ought to have much weight with
the courts of this State on questions upon the establishment of highways.  In England the price of land is
high, and owners prohibit with great care all trespasses
upon it.  And in that country it may be that it rarely
happens that an owner permits a free passage over his
land, without intending to dedicate it as a road to the
public; and indeed, if a man, with a knowledge of the
decisions of the courts, should permit a free passage
over his land, the fair inference would be that he intended to dedicate it as a public road.  In this country
the price of land is not high, nor do owners of it
guard against trespasses on it with the same care; and
it is known to all who have lived in the country that,
until a recent period, owners frequently permitted roads
to be opened through their forests and other lands not
in cultivation without the least intention of dedicating
these roads to the public.  Many roads so opened remain for long periods, and indeed they are not often
closed until the owners have occasion to cultivate the
land through which they run.  Even in England there
must be an intention to dedicate the road, there must
be the *animus dedicandi*, of which the use is the evidence and nothing more.  Best on Pres., 47 Law Libr.
135.  And there the use may furnish evidence, for
aught we know, of an intention to dedicate.  A permission to pass over land may prove an intention to
dedicate or a mere license revocable at the will of the
owner; and we think that the mere permission to pass
over land ought in this State to be regarded as a license.
For why shall we infer that an individual makes a
gift of his property to the public from an equivocal
act, which equally proves an intention to grant a mere
revocable license?  The public is not injured by
this view of the subject.  It has the accommodation
of the road as long as the license continues, and after

the license is revoked the road may be made public, if the public convenience requires it, by making compensation to the owner.

It is clear that there must be not only a dedication, but an acceptance of the road. What is an acceptance? Is the mere passing over the road by individuals an acceptance? If so, what number of persons passing over it will amount to an acceptance—ten, fifteen, twenty, or what number? It is obvious, if the acceptance depends upon the number of persons passing over the road, there will be often great uncertainty whether the road be public or not, which may give rise to much troublesome litigation. To guard against this uncertainty and litigation, the right of acceptance ought to be vested in some public body. And we think that by the laws of this State this right is vested in the County courts. They alone are authorized to establish public roads, and they are to see that they are kept in repair. If we are right in this opinion, the acceptance of a public road must be by record; for the County courts can speak only by record. We do not mean that there must be a formal acceptance entered on the records of the court. Any entry shewing that the court regards the road as a highway will be sufficient, as laying it off into precincts and appointing surveyors or overseers over it and the like.

We do not wish to be understood as deciding that a road may not become a public road in any other manner than by the formal proceeding required by our laws. On the contrary, we are of opinion that if the County court lays off a road, before used, into precincts, or appoints an overseer or surveyor, thereby claiming the road as a public one, and if, after notice of such claim, the owner of the soil permits the road to be passed over for any long continuance, the road may be well inferred to be a public one. All that we mean to say is, that a mere permission to pass over a road is,

without more, to be regarded as a license, and that the
acceptance of a road must be by the County court and
proved by record.

We desire it to be understood that this opinion applies to roads in the country only, and not to streets and
alleys in towns.  As to them the acts of the corporation officers may have the same effect as the acts of the
County courts.  Nor is this opinion to apply to roads
laid off by the owner of the soil previous to a sale of
the lands in parcels, and with the view of enhancing
the sale.  Such roads, though not public roads, cannot
be closed by the owner of the soil.

The judgment of the court is: This court is of
opinion, and doth decide, that a new trial ought to be
awarded.  Which is ordered to be certified to the Circuit court.

<hr>

## THOMPSON v. THE COMMONWEALTH.

December 17th.

1. After-discovered evidence, in order to afford a proper ground
    for a new trial, must be such as reasonable diligence on
    the part of the party offering it could not have secured at
    the former trial; must be material in its object, and not
    merely cumulative and corroborative or collateral; and
    must be such as ought to be decisive, and productive, on
    another trial, of an opposite result on the merits.
2. Where the sole object and purpose of the new evidence is to
    discredit a witness on the opposite side, the general rule
    is, subject to rare exceptions, to refuse a new trial.
3. An objection to a venireman, that he is not qualified accord-
    ing to law, comes too late after he is sworn to try the
    issue.
4. A juror, called by the prisoner as a witness, states that on a
    certain morning during the progress of the trial, before
    the rest of the jury had risen, he rose, dressed himself, and
    went down stairs to the pavement before the door of the
    hotel where the jury were lodged for the night, for the
    purpose of meeting with a passer-by to send a message
    to his family; and after remaining there about five min-

1851.
December
Term.

Thomp-
son's
Case.

utes, and seeing no one passing, he returned to the rest of the jury. HELD: That the only proof of separation of the jury being that of the juror, the prisoner's witness, who negatives all abuse, tampering, or improper influence, the act of the juror is not sufficient grounds for setting aside the verdict and granting a new trial.

5. In the progress of a trial which lasts several days, upon the adjournment of the court at night, the jury are committed to the sheriff to be kept until next day. The most convenient and suitable accommodation which can be provided for the jury is in the third story of a large hotel, where they are placed in five different rooms, opening upon a common passage, which communicates with the street below by flights of stairs, the doors of their chambers being unlocked during the night, the jurors being unwilling to have them locked from apprehension of fire during the night, and there being no doors or other fastenings at either end of the passage. HELD: This is not a separation of the jury for which the prisoner is entitled to a new trial.

6. In the morning, before the court meets, the jury are walking out, accompanied by the sheriff, for relaxation and exercise, and pass the boundary line separating the county in which the trial is progressing from an adjoining county, and remain in the adjoining county a few minutes; but there is no separation, conversation, or communication with any one by any of the jurors. HELD: This is not a separation of the jury for which the prisoner is entitled to a new trial.

7. A jury in a criminal trial concur in opinion as to the guilt of the prisoner, but differ as to the length of time for which he should be sentenced to the penitentiary; and they agree that each one shall state the time for which he will send him to the penitentiary, and that the aggregate of these periods divided by twelve shall be the verdict. After it is done, they strike off the odd months, and all agree to the verdict, understanding what it is. HELD: This is not misbehaviour in the jury for which the verdict will be set aside and a new trial awarded.

8. It is not misbehaviour in a juror, between the adjournment of the court in the evening and its meeting next morning, to drink spirituous liquors in moderation.

9. A medical witness for the Commonwealth, being accidentally present at the hotel when the jury are brought there by the sheriff to be lodged for the night, invites the jury, in the presence of the sheriff, to drink with him, and some of them accept the invitation. The act was inadvertent, but

1851.
December
Term.

Thomp-
son's
Case.

intended only as an act of courtesy, and it was all in the presence of the sheriff. This is not sufficient to set aside the verdict and award a new trial.

At the April term for 1851 of the Circuit court of Henrico county Nicholas O. Thompson was indicted for the murder of his wife, Lucy Ann Thompson. He was tried for this offence at the same term of the court, and was found guilty of murder in the second degree; and the period of his confinement in the penitentiary was fixed by the jury at six years.

After the verdict was rendered the prisoner moved the court for a new trial, upon various grounds founded on the conduct of the jury during the trial. These, and the facts on which they are based, are all stated by the judge in delivering the opinion of the court. The court below refused to grant the new trial, and rendered a judgment upon the verdict. And thereupon the prisoner applied to this court for a writ of error, which was awarded.

*Cannon*, for the prisoner.
*The Attorney General*, for the Commonwealth.

THOMPSON, *J*. delivered the opinion of the court.

The prisoner was indicted for the murder of his wife, in the Circuit court of law for the county of Henrico, on the 17th of April 1851. The jury empanneled and sworn for his trial found him guilty of murder in the second degree, and by their verdict assessed the term of his imprisonment in the public jail and penitentiary at six years. He thereupon moved the court to set aside the verdict and grant him a new trial. His motion was overruled, and judgment rendered on the verdict; and he took a bill of exceptions to the opinion and judgment of the court overruling his motion. The bill of exceptions sealed by the judge sets forth the evidence offered in support of the motion, consisting of *ex parte*

1851.
December
Term.

Thomp-
son's
Case.

affidavits and examinations in open court of five of the jurors who tried the cause, the two deputy sheriffs who had charge of the jury, and of other witnesses, together with a certificate by the judge of all the facts proved on the trial pertinent to the question of guilt or innocence, as well as all collateral facts supposed to have a bearing on the motion for a new trial. At the last term of the court a writ of error was awarded on the petition of the prisoner, which has been elaborately argued at this; and the questions presented for adjudication carefully and maturely considered: And the result is a unanimous opinion of this court that there is no error in the judgment of the Circuit court. We proceed to state the grounds of that opinion as concisely as the number and importance of the points involved in our decision will permit.

The error assigned is, the refusal of the Circuit court to award a new trial. It does not appear from the record upon what grounds the new trial was asked in the court below. The grounds and reasons stated in the prisoner's petition and assignment of errors are: " 1st. That additional evidence had been discovered since the trial, which tended to shew that the witness for the Commonwealth upon whose testimony the prosecution rested was unworthy of credit or belief. 2d. Upon the ground that the *venire facias* which issued in this case was improperly returned and executed, two or more of the said *venire* not being qualified as the law requires. 3d. That there was irregularity in the conduct of the jury who tried the case, in this, that they separated after retiring from the bar and before the rendition of their verdict, and escaped from the custody of the sheriffs who had them in charge, and conversed with bystanders and persons not members of said jury. 4th. That there was misconduct of the said jury in this, that after retiring from the bar to consider of their verdict they, the said jury, founded their

1851.
December
Term.

Thomp-
son's
Case

verdict, not upon any principles known to or recognized by the law, but upon an arbitrary arith-
metical calculation or process which was equivalent to the casting of lots, and to the result of which
the said jury first bound themselves by a precedent
agreement." To these the prisoner's counsel suggested, *ore tenus* at the bar, additional specifications of
irregularity and misconduct in the jury, that is to say:
1st, misbehaviour or misconduct in partaking of ardent
spirits at all during the time they were enclosed and
charged with the case of the prisoner; and the more
especially in partaking of spirits furnished as a treat by
Doctor L. R. Waring, a professional witness of the
Commonwealth; and 2dly, that the visit of the jury
on the morning of the 19th April, in company with the
deputy sheriffs, their keepers, to the county of Chesterfield, amounted, in contemplation of law, to a discharge
or escape of the whole jury, or if not, that going out of
their county with the jury, if it did not put an end to
the duties, powers and functions of the deputies in relation to the care and custody of the jury, at least suspended them for the time being; so that for the period
of time during which the jurors remained in the county
of Chesterfield they were under the care and in the
keeping of unsworn officers.

Upon the first and second grounds stated as sufficient
causes for setting aside the verdict but little need be
said. As to the first, it is well settled, upon reason and
authority, both in civil and criminal cases, that after-discovered evidence, in order to afford proper ground for a
new trial, must be such as reasonable diligence on the
part of the party offering it could not have secured at
the former trial; must be material in its object, and not
merely cumulative and corroborative or collateral; and
must be such as ought to be decisive, and productive,
on another trial, of an opposite result on the merits.
And furthermore, when the sole object and purpose of

1851
December
Term.

Thomp-
son's
Case.

the new evidence is to discredit a witness on the opposite side, the general rule is, subject to rare exceptions, to refuse a new trial. These rules are, for obvious reasons, applied with even more stringency to criminal than civil cases. This case is wanting in most if not all of these pre-requisites of a new trial, and is certainly not entitled to any exemption from the general rule which interdicts it where the sole object is to impeach or discredit a witness on the opposite side. See Wharton's American Criminal Law at page 663, and the numerous authorities there cited.

As to the second ground, suffice it to remark there is no evidence of the existence of the fact, the disqualification of the veniremen, upon which it is predicated. It is not very obvious from the terms of the sentence, " that the *venire facias* was improperly returned and executed, two or more of the said *venire* not being qualified as the law requires," whether the objection is to the twenty-four first summoned, or the second *venire* which issued after exhausting the first, or the *venire* of twelve who were elected, tried and sworn ; but whether to the one or the other, even though the disqualification appeared in the record, the objection comes too late when taken for the first time after the jury is sworn to try the issue. Code of Virginia 1849, p. 628, ch. 162, § 4.

Third. *Separation of the jury.* The only evidence of actual separation is that of the juror Stubbs, who swore that on the morning of the 19th of April, before the rest of the jury had risen, he rose, dressed himself, and went down stairs to the pavement before the door of the hotel, for the purpose of meeting with a passer-by to send a message to his family ; and after remaining there about five minutes, and seeing no one passing, he returned to the rest of the jury. To hold that such a separation as this, proved only by the evidence of the absenting juror, and who at the same time

1854.
December
Term.

Thomp-
son's
Case.

proves that he saw and conversed with no one, and by
his oath positively negatives all abuse, tampering, or improper influence, leaving no room for presumptions, probabilities, or possibilities even, would be to establish it
as the law that a separation *per se* and irrespective of
circumstances, however temporary, innocent, or inadvertent, and however exempt from any presumption or
probability of tampering, abuse, or undue influence, is
sufficient to vitiate a verdict. In support of that proposition the counsel for the prisoner cited *McCaul's
Case*, 1 Va. Cas. 271; *Kennedy's Case*, 2 Va. Cas.
510; *Thomas's Case*, Ibid. 479; *Overbee's Case*, 1
Rob. R. 756; *Howle's adm'r v. Dunn & Co.*, 1
Leigh 455; and *McCann, jr. v. The State of Mississippi*, 9 Smead & Marsh. 465. In opposition to it, the
attorney general has cited and relied upon *Martin's
Case*, 2 Leigh 745; *McCarter's Case*, 11 Leigh
633; *Tooel's Case*, Idem 714; and the cases of
*Thomas* and *Kennedy*, cited by the prisoner's counsel.
*McCaul's Case* and *Overbee's* are the only Virginia cases cited for the prisoner that go to the
length of sustaining the proposition, or approximate
it, (if indeed even they do so,) whilst the cases of
*Martin*, *McCarter* and *Tooel* have countenanced a less
rigid and, in our opinion, more reasonable rule. The
truth is, since criminal trials have become so much
more protracted than formerly, and consequently the
juries, by reason of their frequent adjournments and
long confinements, so much the more frequently and
longer withdrawn from the supervision of the court,
and so much the more exposed to such irregularities as
this, some relaxation of such a rule as is contended for,
if clearly established by authority, would seem to be
called for: otherwise frequent miscarriages or mistrials
must inevitably occur, when there is not the lightest
presumption or probability or even possibility of injury
or injustice to the prisoner. But this case is distin-

1861.
December
Term.

Thomp-
son's
Case.

guishable from *McCaul's* and *Overbee's* in the character and circumstances of the separation and absence of
the jurors; and in a more important point still, in this,
that whilst in those cases the separation was proved by
other witnesses, in this it is proved by the juror alone,
*as a witness of the prisoner*, who, in the same breath,
negatives communication or conversation with any one,
and by consequence not only negatives the presumption
or probability, but even possibility, of tampering or
abuse of any kind. It is not necessary, therefore, to
overrule those cases in order to sustain this verdict. It
will be time enough to decide whether or not they
shall stand when a case similar in all respects shall
arise. When it does, if those cases shall be interpreted
to have decided that a separation *per se* will vitiate a
verdict, there will be against them and in the one scale
reason, an unwavering current of English authority,
ancient and modern, the overwhelming weight of American authority from our sister States, with the Virginia
adjudications before referred to; and in the other, only
the argument of the *stare decisis.*

In the next place it has been argued, if Stubbs's temporary absence from the jury be not a separation fatal to the verdict, that the jury were not kept together
and enclosed as required by law; that lodging them
apart, distributed in five different rooms in the third
story of the hotel, opening upon a common passage,
which communicated with the street below by flights
of stairs, the doors of their chambers being unlocked
during the night, and there being no doors or other
fastenings at either end of the passage or at both ends,
(as in *Kennedy's Case,*) amounts to or is equivalent to
a separation in contemplation of law: not that the jurors
did in fact leave their lodgings and separate by going
elsewhere out of the hotel, but that they might have
done so if they had been so minded, in disregard of
their duty and the injunctions of their keepers and of the

1851.
December
Term.

Thompson's
Case.

court. If by keeping together and enclosing, it be meant that jurors must be so kept and enclosed as to render separation and improper communication and conversation *impossible*, in many, if not in all cases, it would scarcely be within the compass of possibility, without resorting to the securities afforded by the four walls and the locks and bars of a prison, and a prison guard in addition. Such rigour as this, or any thing approximating it, would no more be tolerated now than the practice which prevailed in the olden time of keeping juries together " without meat or drink, fire or candle," or holding them in duress and carting them around the circuit, until they should agree in a verdict. They are now, instead of being dealt with and treated as anciently very like prisoners and culprits, entitled by law, whilst engaged in the performance of their necessary and important, but at the same time gratuitous and onerous duties, to needful and reasonable refreshments, and to have their comforts and convenience provided for and consulted, so far as is compatible with those salutary precautions, safeguards and restraints deemed conducive to the pure and impartial administration of justice. One of these is that in criminal cases they shall be kept together and enclosed in the custody or under the guardianship of the sheriff or his deputies. In *Kennedy's Case* it was held a sufficient compliance with this requirement when they were kept in the same number of rooms and similarly situated in all respects as in this case, save only that in *Kennedy's Case* there were at both ends of the passage doors which were constantly kept closed and fastened; whereas in this there were no doors or other fastening at either end of the passage whereby it could be made secure from intrusion. Now we readily concede, when it is practicable, it is preferable to have the jury lodged together in the same room, and on the circuit it is the practice of some of us always so to direct, if it be practicable; and it must be con-

1851.
December
Term.

Thomp-
son's
Case.

ceded that in *Kennedy's Case* there was a very near approximation to it, if it was not tantamount to keeping them in the same room. But shall we therefore hold that it was indispensably and absolutely necessary in a case wherein we are certified by the oath of the deputy sheriffs that such accommodations could not be procured at any hotel in the city of Richmond? We think not. The officer swears he procured the most convenient and suitable accommodation for the purpose the city afforded. He did all that was practicable; and we think that satisfied the requirements of the law; and in consideration of the circumstance that the jury were lodged in the third story of a large hotel, in the heart of a populous city, and the consequent peril from fire from being so situated, it was but reasonable so far to respect their fears and apprehensions as to leave the doors of their chambers unlocked during the hours of the night. Our opinion is, therefore, that the jury in this case was substantially kept and enclosed as required by law.

The last ground or allegation of separation is predicated upon the visit of the jury, accompanied by the sheriffs, across the river to the county of Chesterfield, on the morning of the 19th of April, before the meeting of the court. It is not denied but that the object of this excursion was innocent and legitimate, relaxation and exercise; and it is not pretended that it was attended with any irregularity such as actual separation, conversation, or communication with any one. Doubtless neither jurors nor the deputies dreamed of any impropriety or violation of law and duty in crossing over the boundary line between the two counties, any more than if for a like object they had been travelling in any other direction in the county of Henrico. But it is argued, the moment the deputies crossed into Chesterfield, by going beyond their territorial jurisdiction, their powers, duties and functions of sheriff *ipso*

1851.
December
Term.

Thomp-
son's
Case.

*facto* ceased, their oath to keep the jury was cancelled, and, by consequence, there was a constructive dissolution, discharge, or escape of the jury; or if not, that they were, for the time during which they remained in Chesterfield, in the custody or charge of unsworn officers; which is equivalent to a separation, or amounts to a constructive separation of the jury. It was not assumed as a proposition in the argument that the jury, by passing the limits of their county, was *ipso facto* discharged or dissolved: That such could not be the consequence of such an act might be safely affirmed, because of the total absence of a reason for such a rule of law. But if authority and precedent were necessary on such a point, it is furnished by the ancient practice of the English judges, of carting disagreeing juries around the circuit, from county to county, to coerce a verdict. Nor can we very well comprehend how it would determine the powers, functions and duties of the sheriff *quoad hoc;* or how it could absolve him from or cancel his oath to keep them. The most that could be urged, with any degree of plausibility, is that if the jury had chosen to separate or escape, the officers might not have had the power, whilst out of their own county, to prevent it; but the answer to such an argument is they did not so choose. Neither the jurors nor the officers could have dreamed there was any the least interruption or suspension of their respective functions and duties occasioned by an innocent promenade; nor was there in our opinion any. Nor can we very well comprehend the idea of a constructive discharge of the jury, effected by a constructive abrogation of the sheriff's powers and constructive cancellation of his oath. But we can understand what is meant by the constructive escape of a prisoner arrested under a *ca. sa.* by the sheriff's carrying him out of his county or jurisdiction, and the reason upon which the doctrine is founded: and it is to be presumed it was a fanciful or

1851.
December
Term.

Thomp-
son's
Case.

forced analogy between the two cases which suggested
this point to the prisoner's counsel; and he has laboured
for the purpose, if successful in maintaining it, of
bringing this case within the influence of the decision
of *McCann, jr.* v. *The State of Mississippi*, 9 Smead
& Marsh. 465, wherein it was ruled " that where a
jury, on a trial for murder, were, during a portion of the
trial, in the charge of an unsworn officer, and after the
retirement of the jury were for a long time wholly under his charge, and *nothing whatever appeared as to
his conduct towards the jury nor as to their demeanor,*
and the jury afterwards found the prisoner guilty of
murder, the verdict must be set aside." This case has
no bearing on ours; certainly none favourable to
the prisoner's cause, if the analogy fails, as in our opinion it manifestly does, but, on the contrary, it sustains
the opinion of the court. It appears from it that in
Mississippi the sheriff is authorized to employ bailiffs
to take charge of juries in criminal cases, but before he
is qualified to act he must either take an oath to keep
the jury in each particular case, or a general oath to
keep all juries that may be committed to him during
the term; whilst with us the sheriff or his deputies are
*ex officio* the lawful keepers, charged, under the sanctions of their official oath, to the performance of that
duty, and though it is our practice, and one to be com-
mended, out of abundant caution, and because it re-
minds the jury and the officer of his and their duty, at
each adjournment of the jury to repeat the oath, it has
been held by this court not to be indispensably necessary. In the case of *McCann, jr.,* before cited, the bai-
liff, (as proved by himself, and his was the only affidavit, and this the only fact proved on the record,) supposing the warrant of his appointment by the sheriff
sufficient authority for him, failed to take any oath,
either general or special: and the consequence of that
failure was to vitiate the verdict as before mentioned,

1851.
December
Term.

Thomp-
son's
Case.

and the operative reasons for this decision, it is manifest from the opinion of the court, were that nothing whatever appeared as to the conduct of the officer towards the jury and as to their demeanour, leaving the adverse presumption of sinister influence to arise, spoken of in another part of the opinion, where it is laid down that if " a jury in a criminal case, or any portion of it, have been exposed to undue influence, either by the whole jury being under the charge of an unsworn officer, and any of the jury have separated from the rest, and had intercourse or opportunity of intercourse with third persons, and it does not affirmatively appear that no consequences were effected upon the jury by such exposure, and the possibility of undue influence be not wholly negatived, the verdict of such jury will be set aside. It seems, however, said the court, to be otherwise if the record shewed that no undue influence had been exerted or attempted." If we are right in assuming that no separation but Stubbs's temporary absence is proved in this case, and that he, as the prisoner's own witness, has wholly negatived all undue influence either attempted or exerted, this may be well claimed as authority to sustain the opinion of the court, but not the cause of the prisoner.

Having disposed of the question of the separation, let us proceed to the consideration of another species of irregularity upon which, in the prisoner's petition and assignment of errors, he predicates his fourth ground of objection to or cause for setting aside the verdict, viz.:

*Misbehaviour or misconduct of the jury.* This objection is of a threefold character. 1st. To the mode adopted for taking the sense of the jury and arriving at or making up their verdict. 2d. Because on the night of the 18th and morning of the 19th of April some of the jurors partook of ardent spirits. 3d. Because the ardent spirits of which they partook on the night of the 18th was furnished at the cost of Dr.

1851.
December
Term.

Thomp-
son's
Case.

Waring, who had been examined by the Commonwealth as an expert or professional witness in the
cause.

1st. As to the mode by which the jury arrived at
a verdict. The evidence on this point consists of
the depositions of five of the jurors. We waive the
consideration and decision of the preliminary question
discussed at the bar, as to the competency of the evidence of jurors to impeach or invalidate their own verdict : and we purposely abstain, (it not being necessary
in our view of this case to decide it,) because of the
gravity and importance of the question ; and because it
has never yet been so maturely considered and solemn-
ly adjudged in Virginia, in any case brought to our attention, as to render it a settled question in causes either
civil or criminal.  The question is now well settled in
England against the competency, and the great preponderance of American authority is the same way:
And Chief Justice Hosmer, 5 Conn. R. 348, said, " The
opinion of almost the whole legal world is adverse to
the reception of such testimony, and in my opinion on
invincible foundations."  But proceeding upon the hypothesis of its competency, let us see if the evidence of
the jurors be sufficient to establish misbehaviour or misconduct, and not only so, but such misbehaviour as will
vitiate their verdict : for it must be borne in mind, in
considering every branch of this enquiry as to irregularity or misbehaviour, that many irregularities or species of misconduct may intervene in the progress of a
trial, which may expose juries or others to the penalties of a misdemeanor or contempt, and yet be insufficient *per se* to disturb the verdict.  By far the greater
part of irregularities and misbehaviours are of this character, where it appears they could have had no sinister
influence upon the verdict, affecting its integrity, purity
and impartiality.

1851.
December
Term.

Thomp-
son's
Case.

Unquestionably every verdict, whether in a civil or criminal case, but more especially in a criminal case, should be the result of reason, deliberation and honest conviction, and not the offspring of chance or accident. If a jury, therefore, should so far forget a sense of duty and the obligations of their oath as to determine their verdict by casting of lots, whether for whom to find, or the measure of damage, or degree of guilt and *quantum* of punishment, as the case may be, there is no doubt, upon reason or authority, as to the right and *duty* of the court to set aside the verdict, and award a new trial, if the fact be established to its satisfaction by competent testimony. But on the other hand, when a jury has deliberated and made up and returned their unanimous verdict, a verdict neither in conflict with the law or the evidence, it is due alike to public and private interests, and to the sanctity of and a becoming respect for the jury trial, that courts should not upon trivial grounds interfere or meddle with that verdict. The power to award new trials should be exercised with caution and circumspection, and only for good and sufficient cause. It is certainly a desideratum both to the parties and to the public that juries should agree upon their verdicts if possible, and as speedily as practicable. "*Expedit reipublicæ ut sit finis litium*" is as applicable to a protracted continuing as to the renewal or repetition of it when once determined, differing, if differing at all, not in the principle, but the degree. So expedient was it deemed in the early periods of English jurisprudence, that consent in a verdict was even extorted from the jury under the pains and penalties of hunger and thirst and other privations, and of being carted around the circuit with the judge, and held in a sort of duress, until they agreed. If it be sound policy to end litigation by the rendition of a verdict as soon as practicable, consistently with the purity, impartiality and integrity of the jury trial, though we may very properly nullify a ver-

1851.
December
Term.

Thomp-
son's
Case.

dict which was the result of a lottery, we should certainly be running counter to that policy to place a verdict like this in the same category. There is no real
analogy between the two cases; or if any, but seeming
and remote. One thing is certain, as the experience of
every one conversant with trials will attest, in some
cases, and these not a few, we have to choose between
the alternatives of tolerating the practice resorted to by
the jury in this case, and the indefinite postponement of
a verdict. If every juryman is to adhere pertinaciously
to his own judgment, regardless of the opinions of his
fellows, especially upon the question of measure of damage or degree of guilt or *quantum* of punishment; if
jurors are denied the privilege of harmonizing discor-
ding and reconciling extreme opinions by concession
and compromise, and meeting on middle ground, a
failure of justice, or what is tantamount, indefinite delay, is the inevitable consequence. What more, we would
ask, have the jury done in this case, than what we know
is of every day occurrence in trials in courts of equity,
where, when a question of damage or value or compensation arises before the master, and when witnesses
of equal credibility, or integrity and intelligence, differ
in their estimates, the master adopts as his assessment
an average of the estimates of such witnesses; and
this practice is sanctioned by a court of equity, which
is a court of conscience, as it is by law and justice.
Indeed in some cases it may be considered a rule of necessity as well as convenience. Would it not be an
anomaly, an inconsistency in our jurisprudence, amounting almost to an absurdity, to hold that a commissioner
in chancery may thus perform a duty in its nature judicial, with the approval of the chancellor, whilst for
so doing the same duty in the same way the verdict of
a jury is to be set aside by the court of law. Why
may not the jury deal with the estimates of each other,
which must be presumed to be honest and *bona fide*,

1851.
December
Term.

Thomp-
son's
Case.

until the contrary is proved, as does the master in chancery with the differing estimates of witnesses equally entitled to credence. We do not mean to say it is the bounden duty of the jurors in all or any cases to adopt such a rule: that is a question to be settled by their own consciences. It is for each to determine for himself, according to the intensity of his own convictions, the greater or less confidence he may entertain in the absolute correctness of his own standard of right, or in the infallibility of his own judgment, how far he can conscientiously yield and surrender up his own in deference to the conflicting opinions and judgments of his fellow jurors. That the jury have done nothing more in this case than, after first deciding the question of guilt, to adopt as their verdict as to the *quantum* of punishment the average of their assessments, we consider substantially proved by the two dissentient jurors, (we mean dissentient upon the question of guilt when the jury first retired,) Peay and Stubbs, upon whom the prisoner's counsel mainly, if not exclusively, relied to prove misconduct. Stubbs, it seems, gave one deposition and Peay three, the first an *ex parte* affidavit out of court, the second and third upon examinations in open court. We have deemed it unnecessary to analyse critically their statements, or to advert particularly or in detail to the confusion which pervades them, and the discrepancies between the several statements of Peay, especially between the third and the two first, because if there were any doubt upon their evidence as to what transpired in the jury room, the depositions of three other jurors, Blair, James and Ball, called and examined at the instance of the court, and who, if not more honest, appear from their examinations to be certainly more intelligent than the two first named, relieve the question of fact of all doubt and difficulty. From these concurring statements it appears when the jury first retired the question of guilt or innocence was formally taken.

1851.
December
Term.

Thomp-
son's
Case.

There is a diversity of recollection as to the number for acquittal; it was either two, three, or four; the probability is in favour of two. Of those for conviction, one was for murder in the first degree, the rest for a lower grade of homicide, murder in the second degree, and it may be some for manslaughter; though that does not clearly appear. After conference and discussion among the jurors upon the main question of guilt or innocence, according to the explicit and concurring evidence of these three jurors, all the jurors consented to find the prisoner guilty; and then arose the question of the degree of guilt and the *quantum* of punishment. It seems that no formal question was taken as to the degree of homicide; but it being understood that the juror who was for *hanging* was willing to come to those in favour of a lower grade of offence, and below a capital felony, they proceeded at once to the enquiry as to the term of imprisonment. It was proposed that it should be ascertained by each juror setting down the number of years he thought the offence merited, adding these numbers, dividing the aggregate by twelve, and adopting the quotient for their verdict. If in this process each and every juror fairly and *bona fide* set down a number of years within the *minimum* and *maximum* prescribed by law to the degree of guilt in his judgment commensurate to the offence, the same process would ascertain as well the degree of guilt as the measure of punishment, and render unnecessary the formal decision of the preliminary question as to the degree of homicide; for it was substantially decided by the length of the term of imprisonment; being over five years, the *maximum* of manslaughter, it was murder in the second degree, and so they all understood it, as all who have been examined expressly state. We are told by James that the proposition to set down, add up and divide by twelve was not a pre-cedent agreement binding the jury to acquiesce in the result of the experiment. That two calculations were

1851.
December
Term.

Thomp-
son's
Case.

in fact made; the first by way of mere experiment, to see how near the result would come to satisfying all. That when the last was made he added up the estimates of the other eleven before setting down his own, in order to ascertain what number he should set down to produce the result, or the nearest practicable approximation to it, his conscience approved. He thought six years the proper term of imprisonment, but he set down one year to reduce the average to six years, or thereabouts. If by adding up the eleven numbers before setting down his own he thus acquired an advantage over his fellows, the prisoner surely has no cause to complain, since it was used not to his injury, but in his favour. When the second and last estimate was made, which resulted in six years and some months, Peay and Stubbs expressed some dissatisfaction with the result. The odd months were then stricken off, and they acquiesced in the verdict for six years. They both say they consented to it in the jury room, and afterwards in open court, with a perfect knowledge of the character and effect of the verdict; that it was murder in the second degree, and for six years imprisonment; and this freely and voluntarily, without any undue influence from any quarter. It has been well remarked by a learned judge that the law requires jurors to unite in their verdict, but not in their reasons or motives. Establish it as the law that the jury room may be invaded, an inquisition held over the consciences of jurors, an enquiry instituted into their deliberations in order to find matter of impeachment in the mental processes by which they arrived at their conclusions and results, and the mutual concessions and compromises or other means by which they were enabled to reconcile conflicting opinions and meet on middle ground, and then hold that the mode adopted by this jury in arriving at their verdict was illegal and sufficient to vitiate it, and few verdicts will henceforth stand the test of such a scrutiny. In sup-

1851.
December
Term.

Thomp-
son's
Case.

port of our opinion on this point we cite *Shobe* v. *Bell*,
1 Rand. 39; *Price* v. *Warren*, 1 Hen. & Munf. 385;
*Cowperthwaite* v. *Jones*, 2 Dall. R. 56; and *Grinnell*
v. *Phillips*, 1 Mass. R. 542. The two last are persua-
sive authorities. The reasons of the judges who delivered the opinions in these cases are so pertinent to
the question under consideration, we conclude this part
of our opinion with a quotation from both. In the
case in Dallas, Shippen, President, said: " The first
objection, as to the manner of the jury collecting the
sense of its members with regard to the *quantum* of damages, does not appear to us to be well founded, or at
all similar to casting of lots for a verdict. In *torts* and
other cases where there is no ascertained demand it can
seldom happen that jurymen will at once agree upon a
precise sum to be given in damages: There will necessarily arise a variety of opinions, and mutual concessions
must be expected. A middle sum may in many cases
be a good rule, and though it is possible this mode may
sometimes be abused by a designing juryman fixing
upon an extravagantly high or low sum, yet, unless
such abuse appears, the fraudulent design will not be
presumed." And in that from 1 Mass. R. 542, Sewell,
Justice, said: " The record of a verdict implies an
unanimous consent of the jury, and is conclusive and
incontrovertible evidence of the fact. Besides, the secret intention and mental act of a juror can never be a
subject of legal enquiry, and from the necessity of the
case his conduct before the court is the best and only
evidence that can be admitted of his assent to a verdict
delivered in his presence. The members of a jury, before they agree, must argue the questions of the case
committed to them, and each may be supposed to express his opinion as to the general question for which
party the verdict shall be found, and if for the plaintiff,
for what amount of damages. It is not important, as it
seems to me, by what method a sum for damages shall

1851.
December
Term.

Thomp-
son's
Case.

be proposed, if finally there is unanimous assent of the
jury in the sum declared by their verdict." It is true
these were civil cases and ours is a criminal one; but we
can perceive no reason why that difference should
weaken the analogy or detract from their influence or
bearing in the least.

We will now briefly consider together the second
and third specifications of misconduct or misbehaviour
in the jury, for partaking of ardent spirits at all, and for
partaking of the treat furnished by Dr. Waring. In
support of these objections the prisoner's counsel cited
the Code 629, ch. 163, § 12; *People* v. *Douglass*, 4
Cow. R. 26; *Oliver* v. *Trustees of Springfield*, 5
Cow. R. 283; *Bryant* v. *Forster*, 7 Conn. R. 562;
and *Coleman* v. *Moody*, 4 Hen. & Munf. 1. And the
attorney general relied on 21 Viner Abr. 447–8, title
Trial, letter g; 2 Hale P. C. 306; *Commonwealth* v. *Ro-
by*, 12 Pick. R. 496; *Everett* v. *Youells*, 24 Eng. C. L.
R. 142; and 3 Rob. Pr. 247-8. According to the English
authorities, the only question ever made on the subject
of refreshments in eating and drinking has been, by
whom furnished? and not as to the kind: and they
have holden that if furnished by a party, or the *prevailing* party in the cause, it is sufficient ground for setting aside the verdict; but if furnished at the cost of
the jury or a third party, a stranger in interest to the
cause, whilst it might constitute misbehaviour and subject him to fine and imprisonment for the irregularity,
it would not affect the validity of the verdict; unless,
in addition to the mere irregularity, it was attended with
such circumstances of excess, abuse, or otherwise as to
create a reasonable presumption that it injuriously influenced the impartiality and purity of the verdict.
And there is no Virginia authority that lays down a
different rule and countenances the proposition that the
fact of ardent spirits entering into and forming part of
the refreshments, if used with moderation and tempe-

1851.
December
Term.

Thomp-
son's
Case.

rance, constituted misconduct in a jury; and if misconduct for which the jury might be fined, such an
irregularity as to vitiate the verdict.    The case of
*Coleman* v. *Moody,* cited for that purpose, is not only
not authority for such a proposition, but if not expressly, by strong implication, decides the contrary.   Nor do
we consider the New York adjudications referred to as
clearly establishing such a rule; though it must be confessed that some of the *dicta* of the judges in those
cases go to that extreme.    In the case of *The People*
v. *Douglass* the decision was "when the jury separate contrary to the instruction of the court, make use
of strong drink, and converse upon the matter they are
empanneled to try"; and this it appears was whilst
they were *sitting as a jury* and *during the progress of
the trial.*    But even in that case the rule is laid down
that the mere *separation* of a jury, without farther
abuse, is not sufficient ground of new trial, and that it
is not every irregularity that will render a verdict void.
*Bryant* v. *Forster* was a case where a juryman, while
engaged in the course of a cause, was permitted to leave
the court in charge of an officer, and who improperly
separated himself from that officer and drank about one
third of a gill of brandy.    The court said, " We cannot allow jurors thus of their own head to drink spirituous liquors while engaged in the course of a cause."

But grant that the New York cases cited from Cowen
have firmly settled the law in that State as contended ;
whilst it is admitted they are entitled to the most re-
spectful consideration on account of the high character
of the tribunal and the learning and ability of the
judges whose reasoned opinions they contain, and always proper to be consulted as lights to inform and
guide our deliberations, and weighed, adopted and followed so far as they persuade and convince, they cannot bind this court as authority.    And not being so
bound, we must say, with all due respect, they have

1851.
December
Term.

Thomp-
son's
Case.

not convinced our judgment and cannot receive our approval. We find the law laid down on this subject far more to our satisfaction in a case in 6 Greenleaf 37, in the following terms: "If ardent spirits constitute part of the refreshments, and appear to have operated upon any juror so far as to impair his reasoning powers, inflame his passions, or have any improper influence upon his opinions, the verdict would probably be set aside"; and in choosing between the New York and Massachusetts decisions on this point, we have no hesitation in preferring the latter as the most reasonable. In times past, when criminal trials were more summary, when they were generally decided in a day or at a sitting, when all refreshments were withheld until a verdict was rendered, it might have been a very wise and proper precaution, and one productive of but little if any hardship or inconvenience, certainly no more than the deprivation of other refreshments, to deny even the moderate and temperate use of ardent spirits whilst they were engaged in court sitting as a jury, or retired to their jury room to deliberate and consult of their verdict; but now, when trials are protracted and spun out for successive days and sometimes weeks, and since the law has provided that reasonable refreshments shall be furnished at the public expense, we do not know where this court will find its authority for imposing upon jurors the interdict of total abstinence during their confinement. It has the undoubted right, and it is its bounden duty, to require of those who are not given to total abstinence the strictest moderation and temperance in the use of ardent spirits, and to hold them, their keepers, and those who supply them, responsible *criminaliter*, as for a contempt, for any abuse or excess of indulgence; but in our judgment, however much we may approve and commend total abstinence in all, and on all occasions, and more especially on such an occasion as that of being engaged in performing the

1851.
December
Term.

Thomp-
son's
Case.

grave duty of a juror, deliberating upon an issue involving the life or liberty of a fellow being, we neither can nor ought, if we could, go farther. It is the right of jurors to be permitted to exercise the discretion and free will on the subject which belong to them out of the jury box; and ours both the right and the duty of holding them responsible to strict accountability for any abuse or excess, and, when there is reason to suspect that such excess or abuse has exerted a sinister influence, of annulling their verdict and awarding a new trial.

The only remaining question is, whether the well-intended but thoughtless and ill-timed act of civility and hospitality on the part of the Commonwealth's witness, Dr. Waring, in treating the jury on the night of the 18th of April, (in the presence of the officers who had them in charge, be it remembered,) shall vitiate this verdict. That the act was mere inadvertence, and the intent innocent, cannot be questioned, from aught that appears in this record to the contrary. His being there was purely accidental, as appears from the deposition of the deputy sheriff: He went upon his invitation. He had no interest in the cause, and no connection with it, except as a professional witness for the Commonwealth. It does not appear that he was hostile to the prisoner, or even knew him, or desired his conviction; it does not appear that there was the least question as to his credibility; but the contrary is fairly inferrible from the record. That it was an irregularity is not denied, in the witness, the jurors, and the officers permitting it; but one which, though brought to the attention of the court who presided over the trial, so far as appears from the record, passed without its animadversion, doubtless because of the absence of intention on the part of all concerned to commit any breach of duty or propriety. It cannot reasonably be presumed or suspected that any injury to the prisoner has resulted from the inadver-

1851.
December
Term.

Thomp-
son's
Case.

tence.   The jury, as we are certified by the judge and
the deputy sheriffs, were strictly temperate, a large proportion of them said to be Sons of Temperance; they
demeaned themselves with the most exemplary propriety during the whole trial, and have rendered a verdict
unimpeached and unimpeachable upon the merits, according to the law and the evidence, and of which,
if any error could be predicated, it would be an error
on the side of humanity and mercy.   To set aside such
a verdict for such an irregularity would, in our judgments, establish a precedent in our criminal jurisprudence much to be deprecated, because calculated to
multiply miscarriages in criminal trials, and impedi-
ments in the way of the conviction and punishment
of offenders, already sufficiently numerous and embarrassing.

JUDGMENT AFFIRMED.

COMMONWEALTH *v.* ADCOCK.

December 17th

1. A prisoner is remanded by the examining court to be tried for
   embezzling the goods of W. He may thereupon be indicted
   for embezzling the goods of A; the embezzlement being of
   the same goods for which he was tried by the examining
   court.
2. A prisoner is indicted for embezzling the goods of W, and at
   the fifth term after he was examined for the offence he is
   tried and convicted; but the verdict is set aside for a variance between the allegation and the proof, as to the
   ownership of the goods; and the case is continued. At
   the next term of the court the attorney for the Commonwealth enters a *nolle prosequi* upon the indictment; and
   the prisoner is indicted again for the same offence, the
   indictment in the first count being the same as in the former indictment, and another count charging the goods em-

bezzled to be the goods of A. Upon his arraignment he moves the court to discharge him from the offence, on the ground that three regular terms of the court had been held since he was examined and remanded for trial without his being indicted. The attorney for the Commonwealth opposes the motion, and offers the record of the proceedings of the Circuit court upon the first indictment, to shew that he had been indicted, tried and convicted; which was objected to by the prisoner. HELD:

> 1st. The record is competent, and the only competent evidence upon the question.

> 2d. The second indictment being for the same act of embezzling as the first, and the prisoner having been indicted, tried and convicted in time, and the verdict set aside for the variance, the second indictment was proper and in time; and the prisoner is not entitled to be discharged.

3. The exceptions or excuses for failure to try the prisoner, enumerated in the statute, are not intended to exclude others of a similar nature, or *in pari ratione;* but only that if the Commonwealth was in default for three terms without any of the excuses for the failure enumerated in the statute, of such like excuses fairly implicable by the courts from the reason and spirit of the law, the prisoner should be entitled to his discharge.

4. Though an offence committed before the Code of 1849 went into operation must, so far as the question of guilt, degree of crime, *quantum* of punishment and rules of evidence are concerned, be governed by the law in force at the time the offence was committed, yet, upon the question of the prisoner's right to be discharged from the failure to try him, arising after the Code went into operation, it must be governed by the law in the Code.*

---

*The various acts of assembly bearing upon this question are here given, on the suggestion of the judge who delivered the opinion of the court:

1 Rev. Code of 1819, p. 607, ch. 169, § 28. "Every person charged with such crime, (treason or felony,) who shall not be indicted before, or at, the second term after he shall have been committed, unless the attendance of the witnesses against him appears to have been prevented by himself, shall be discharged from his imprisonment, if he be detained for that cause only; and if he be not tried at or before the third term after his examination before the justices, he shall be forever discharged of the crime, unless such failure proceed from any continuance granted on the motion of the prisoner, or from the inability of the jury to agree on their verdict."

Sessions Acts of 1847–8, p. 144, ch. 20, § 12. "Any person held in prison on any charge of having committed a crime, shall be discharged from his imprisonment if he be not indicted before the end of the second term of the court at which he is held to answer, unless it shall appear to the satisfaction of the court that the witnesses on the part of the Commonwealth have been enticed or kept away, or are detained or prevented from attending the court by sickness or some inevitable accident, and except in the case provided for in the following section." The case provided for in the next section is the insanity of the prisoner.

P. 152, ch. 21, § 45. "Every person charged with felony, and remanded by the examining court to a Circuit Superior court for trial, shall be forever discharged from the crime whenever there shall have been three terms after his examination at which the failure to try the case was not caused by his insanity, or the witnesses for the Commonwealth having been enticed or kept away, or detained or prevented from attending court by sickness or some inevitable accident, or did not proceed from a continuance granted on his own motion, or from inability of the jury to agree in their verdict."

P. 122, ch. 11, § 10. "No person shall be held to answer on a second indictment, or other accusation, for any offence of which he has been acquitted by the jury, upon the facts and merits, on a former trial; but such acquittal may be pleaded by him in bar of any prosecution for the same offence, notwithstanding any defect in the form or in the substance of the indictment or other accusation on which he is acquitted."

§ 11. "Any person indicted or otherwise accused of an offence, who on his trial shall be acquitted upon the ground of a variance between the allegations and the proof, or upon any exception to the form or the substance of the indictment or other accusation, may be arraigned again on a new indictment or other proper accusation, and tried and convicted for the same offence, notwithstanding such former acquittal."

Code of 1849, p. 770, ch. 207, § 13. "A person in jail, on a criminal charge, shall be discharged from imprisonment if he be not indicted before the end of the second term of the court at which he is held to answer, unless it appear to the court that material witnesses for the Commonwealth have been enticed or kept away, or are prevented from attending by sickness or inevitable accident, and except also in the case provided in the following section." The case provided for in the next section is the insanity of the prisoner.

P. 778, ch. 208, § 36. "Every person charged with felony, and remanded to a Superior court for trial, shall be forever discharged from prosecution for the offence, if there be three regular terms of such court, after his examination, without a trial, unless the failure to try him was caused by his insanity, or by the witnesses for the Commonwealth being enticed or kept away, or prevented from attending by sickness or inevitable accident, or by a continuance granted on motion of the accused, or by reason of his escaping from jail or failing to appear according to his recognizance, or of the inability of the jury to agree in their verdict."

P. 751, ch. 199, § 15. "A person acquitted by the jury, upon the facts and merits, on a former trial, may plead such acquittal in bar of a second prosecution for the same offence, notwithstanding any defect in the form or substance of the indictment or accusation on which he was acquitted."

§ 16. "A person acquitted of an offence, on the ground of a variance between the allegations and the proof of the indictment or other accusation, or upon an exception to the form or substance thereof, may be arraigned again on a new indictment or other proper accusation, and tried and convicted for the same offence, notwithstanding such former acquittal."

The case is fully stated in the opinion of the court delivered by Judge *Thompson.*

*The Attorney General* and *Young,* for the Commonwealth.

*Robert G. Scott* and *Irving,* for the prisoner.

THOMPSON, *J.* delivered the opinion of the court.

The accused, the captain of a canal boat and carrier for hire on the James river canal, was, on the 7th of December 1848, committed by the mayor of the city of Richmond, upon a charge of feloniously embezzling and fraudulently converting to his own use a box of merchandise, delivered to him for transportation to Buchanan, the property of Word, Ferguson & Barksdale, merchants of the city of Richmond. He was examined and remanded for further trial by the Hustings court on the 18th of January 1849, and being admitted to bail, he entered into a recognizance with approved security to appear at the next term of the Circuit Superior court for the county of Henrico and city of Richmond. The witnesses for the Commonwealth were recognized to appear at the same term to give evidence in behalf of the Commonwealth. The accused failed

1851.
December
Term.

Adcock's
Case.

to appear at the first of the term, his default was recorded, his recognizance estreated, and a *scire facias*
awarded against him and his bail. At a' subsequent
day of the term he made his appearance; whereupon
on his motion the orders of default and award of *scire
facias* were set aside, and he was released from the
breach of his recognizance. In the meantime, however,
the witnesses for the Commonwealth, the two recognized, Ferguson and Blair, had appeared and been recognized to the next term, and the cause virtually continued: and then the prisoner was again let to bail and
recognized to appear at the next term. Neither at this
term nor at the first was any indictment found by the
grand jury. Whether the failure to send the indictment to the grand jury at the first term was owing to
the failure of the accused to appear before the Commonwealth's witnesses had been adjourned over and recognized to appear at the next term and the cause virtually continued, or whether the failure to indict at
both the first and second terms was owing to the absence of the witness Roberts, (the other two, Ferguson
and Blair, upon whose evidence the bill was even-
tually found, being present on both occasions,) the record
does not inform us, and therefore we can only conjecture. If the non-appearance of the accused at the first
term was the cause of the failure then, either in whole
or in part, the presumption is that the cause of the second failure was the absence of the witness Roberts. At
the third term, April 1850, the indictment was found;
and then and at the fourth term, November 1850, the
cause was continued on motion of the prisoner. At
the fifth term, April 1851, the indictment, which contained but one count, and laid the goods charged to
be embezzled as the property of Word, Ferguson &
Barksdale, came on for trial, was tried, and the jury
who tried it returned a verdict of guilty, and assessed
the term of imprisonment in the penitentiary at one

year.  The prisoner moved for a new trial, which was granted by the court upon the ground of a variance between the *allegata et probata* relative to the ownership or property in the goods which were the subject of the embezzlement.  The case then necessarily stood over to the November term 1851, for the new trial.  At that term the attorney for the Commonwealth, as it was his duty to do, to avoid a second failure upon the ground of variance in the event of the same evidence being adduced on the new trial, and the opinion of the court remaining the same upon the question of ownership, to wit, that the property of the goods was in the consignees, the Messrs. Ayres, of Buchanan, and not the consignors, Word, Ferguson & Barksdale, asked and obtained leave of the court to enter a *nolle prosequi* as to the first indictment, and to send up a new bill; which was found by the grand jury then in session; the prisoner, upon the motion of the attorney for the Commonwealth, being detained in custody to answer the new indictment based upon his examination by the Hustings court for the same offence, varying in nothing but in the incident of ownership or property in the goods.  This new indictment contains three counts, all charging the same *corpus delicti*.  The first embraces the old indictment in *totidem verbis*, laying the property of the goods in Word, Ferguson & Barksdale; the second alleges their ownership in R. M. & Francis Ayres; and the third alleges delivery by Word, Ferguson & Co. of the goods of R. M. & Francis Ayres to the accused, to be carried and delivered to them at Buchanan:  In short, the new indictment is the old one with two additional or superadded counts.  Upon his arraignment upon this new indictment the prisoner tendered a plea in abatement, setting forth that he had not been regularly and legally examined for the offence therein charged.  To his plea the attorney for the Commonwealth replied that he had been regularly and legally examined, and remanded by the Hustings court, for the offence whereof he was indicted; and vouched the record and proceedings of the examining court. To this replication the prisoner demurred *ore tenus ;* the attorney for the Commonwealth in like manner joined in the demurrer; and the court overruled the demurrer, being of opinion that the prisoner had been regularly and legally examined for the offence charged. Whereupon he moved the court to discharge him from the offence aforesaid, on the ground that three regular criminal terms of the court had been held since he was examined and remanded for trial before the same, for the said offence, without being indicted for the same; and in support of his motion he vouched the record of the examining court, shewing that he was examined and remanded for the offence on the 18th of January 1849, and shewing by the record of the Circuit Superior court that more than three regular criminal terms had been held since his examination, to wit, on the 3d day of May 1849, 13th of November 1849, 29th of April 1850, 8th day of November 1850, and 28th of April 1851; and alleging that at neither of these terms had he been indicted for the offence aforesaid. The attorney for the Commonwealth opposed the prisoner's motion for his discharge: and for the purpose of answering and negativing his allegation of a failure to indict in three terms, offered to introduce the record of the proceedings of the Circuit court upon the first indictment, shewing, or purporting to shew, that the prisoner had not only been indicted, but tried upon the indictment in due time, and found guilty by the verdict of a jury, and applied for and obtained a new trial of the court upon the ground of variance between the allegations and the proofs. To the introduction of this evidence the prisoner objected; but his objection was overruled, the evidence received and considered, and the prisoner's motion for his discharge overruled. Afterwards, however, the court, upon the motion of the prisoner, and by his consent and with the consent of the attorney for the Commonwealth, waived its decision upon the motion for a discharge, and the prisoner's objection to the evidence introduced by the attorney for the Commonwealth, and adjourned to the General court for its decision thereupon, because of their novelty and difficulty, the following questions:

First. "Ought the court, on the said motion of the prisoner to be discharged, to receive and consider the record and proceedings offered by the attorney for the Commonwealth?"

Second. "Ought the prisoner, on the motion made by him, as aforesaid, to be discharged from the crime with which he now here stands indicted, or from further prosecution for the same?"

The first question is free of all doubt and difficulty, admitting of a prompt and easy solution. We are all agreed that the evidence objected to ought to be received and considered; indeed, it is the only evidence admissible or competent on such an issue. The prisoner had alleged a failure to indict within the period of three regular terms; and to sustain the allegation had introduced the records of the examining court and of the Circuit court, shewing the date of his examination and the holding of more than three actual regular terms, and denied that he had been indicted at any of them. To such an objection or allegation, if untrue, but one answer could be given by the attorney for the Commonwealth—to traverse the failure, and allege the finding of an indictment or a trial, as the case may be, and vouch the record to prove it. Of the indispensable necessity of adducing record evidence to prove the fact of indictment or trial, there surely cannot be a doubt. The real question was as to the sufficiency of the evidence to support the issue on the part of the Commonwealth. That, in truth, is the issue involved

1851.
December
Term.

Adcock's
Case.

in the second question adjourned, and the only one worthy of serious consideration by this court. It would have been the only one adjourned, but for the informal and summary manner, *ore tenus*, in which the questions were presented in the court below. Had the prisoner, instead of his summary motion, pleaded specially his ground or matter of discharge, the attorney for the Commonwealth would have replied and vouched the record relied on by him; the prisoner would have demurred to the replication, and, upon joinder in demurrer, the issue would have been formally and regularly developed, which the second question adjourned presents for our decision—that is to say, whether he be entitled to his discharge in consequence of the alleged failure to indict or try within the term prescribed by law; or, on the other hand, whether the record adduced by the Commonwealth be sufficient to establish her pretension that he was indicted or tried in proper time to render him still liable to further prosecution for the offence.

This question has been elaborately and ably argued by the counsel for the prisoner, and by the attorney general and his associate, the attorney for the Commonwealth in the Circuit court for the county of Henrico and city of Richmond. But it is worthy of remark, whilst the counsel of the prisoner have on this occasion displayed their accustomed ability and ingenuity, and have by their arguments been conducted to the same goal, the right of the prisoner to his discharge, they have arrived at one and the same favourable conclusion from very diverse and conflicting premises, and by a very dissimilar, if not adverse, course of ratiocination. The first counsel argued that the accused had not been legally examined for the offence for which he was re-indicted, upon the ground that the offences charged in the first and last indictments were essentially different, and that therefore he was entitled to his discharge. But if precluded from raising that question, as it had been decided by the Circuit court, and was not adjourned to us, and upon the hypothesis that he had been properly examined, he contended that the *nolle prosequi* put an end to the prosecution, sweeping off, nullifying and rendering *functus officio*, not only the first indictment, but the examination of the called court, commitment and all; and that therefore the prisoner was illegally detained in custody, and was entitled to his discharge at the time he moved for it in the court below. On the other hand, the last counsel not only admits, but insists on, as concessums in the cause, not to be controverted by the prisoner or the Commonwealth, that the offence charged in the last is identical with that alleged in the first indictment, and that the prisoner was regularly and legally examined and remanded, and could not be again examined therefor; and he predicates his argument exclusively upon the Commonwealth's failure to indict in due time after the examination.

If the first counsel had been right in his premises, in assuming that the offences were not the same, that the party had not been legally examined, or that the *nolle prosequi* was productive of the consequences he supposed, the conclusion he drew from these premises did not follow, but the very reverse. The legitimate conclusion would be, that whilst the prisoner could not be arraigned and tried on this indictment, he was not to be discharged, but detained in custody until proceedings *de novo* could be instituted against him. But that the counsel is totally mistaken in his premises as to the non identity of the offence, the insufficiency of the examination, and the effects and consequences of a *nolle prosequi*, is as abundantly established by authority as it is manifest in reason. See *Halkem's Case*, 2 Va. Cas. 4; *Derieux's Case*, Ib. 379; *Mabry's Case*, Ib. 396; *Huffman's Case*, 6 Rand. 685; *Thomas's Case*,

2 Leigh 741; *Lindsay's Case*, 2 Va. Cas. 345; and
*Wortham's Case*, 5 Rand. 669.

The arguments of the two counsel are direct antago-
nisms of each other, and both cannot be sound.  One at
least must be repudiated, if either can stand the test of
analysis and criticism.  We have shewn that the first
stands condemned by reason and authority, and now let
us see whether the last (which is certainly more plausi-
ble) is any more tenable or sound, when examined and
tried by the same tests.  The objection taken by the
prisoner was for a failure to indict within three terms
after the examination.  It would have been more accurate and strictly technical to have objected for a failure
to try, since the penalty or sanction for a failure to indict is only discharge from imprisonment, whether with
or without bail we will not stop to enquire.  But as
there could be no trial without an indictment, we may
consider the objection for a failure to indict for three
terms as inclusive of and tantamount to charging a failure to try; and so considering it, we come to the consideration of the ground taken by the last counsel.  This
ground is, that a failure to indict for three terms after
the prisoner has been remanded entitles him to be discharged from the crime, unless the Commonwealth can
bring herself within some of the exceptions expressed
in the statute.  And that although for this offence the
accused was both indicted and tried in due time at the
fifth term upon the first indictment, according to the
provisions and within the exceptions or savings of the
statute, and was liable to be again tried at the sixth
term, when a *nolle prosequi* was entered and a new indictment found; yet the Commonwealth, by abandoning
the first and re-indicting him, has placed herself in the
same predicament as if no indictment had been ever
found or trial had or demanded until the sixth term, the
time of finding the second indictment and of his arraignment thereupon, and that consequently more than three

regular terms passed after his examination without indictment or trial; and the prisoner is therefore entitled
to his discharge under the statute. Whilst it is admitted
on all hands, and was so adjudged in *Vance's Case*, 2
Va. Cas. 132, 162, that the prisoner was triable again
upon the first indictment, it is insisted, nevertheless,
that he is not so liable, or to the same extent, upon the
new and more perfect one.

A construction of the law that would require us to
concur in such a conclusion as this would certainly be
productive of very inconvenient consequences, if it did
not convict the law itself of the grossest defect and
most palpable absurdity; besides bringing its provisions
in direct repugnancy and irreconcilable conflict with
each other. We should need no better illustration of
such effects and consequences than this case would furnish. The prisoner was charged with a high crime,
for which he was prosecuted with due diligence; because a diligence that satisfied the requirements of the
law. He was indicted at the third term, tried and convicted at the fifth, and verdict set aside because of a
variance. Three out of four of the failures to indict
and try between the examination and trial were owing
to his own default. He was confessedly liable to be
tried again on the same indictment, for nothing had occurred to discharge him from the offence: as liable to
trial on the same indictment as if he had been indicted,
tried, convicted, and the verdict set aside at the first
term instead of the fifth. Had he been acquitted for
the variance or by reason of a defect of form or substance in the indictment, he was, by the express provisions and injunctions of the law, liable to be again tried.
If so when acquitted for a variance or for a defect in
the indictment, *a fortiori* must he be when convicted
and the verdict is set aside by the court for such defect
or variance. In either case a new indictment would
generally be necessary, either to make the charge qua-

1851.
December
Term.

Adcock's
Case.

drate with the nature of the offence, or to adapt it to
the evidence disclosed by the first trial to avoid a re-
currence of the variance and a second failure to procure
an effectual and final conviction. To this indictment
a plea of *auterfois acquit* or *auterfois convict* would be
of no avail; and yet it is said, whilst the party still
continues liable to be tried upon the defective indictment or the one obnoxious to the objection of variance,
upon which he cannot be convicted, and notwithstanding the law repudiates his plea of former acquittal or
former recovery, and makes it the duty of its officers
to prefer against him an indictment adapted to the
offence and the evidence to sustain the charge, when
the new indictment is preferred he may plead to it a
failure to indict and try within three terms, and that it
is no good answer to the plea for the Commonwealth to
shew that, from the period of the examination down to
the date of the plea, she has been in hot pursuit and
diligently prosecuting, and the prisoner all the while
staving off and continuing and delaying a trial upon the
defective indictment; and not only so, but that she indicted, tried and convicted him upon that defective indictment. To justify such a construction of the law
as this, we should have to interpolate the 13th sec. of ch.
207, and the 36th sec. of ch. 208, at pages 770, 778, of
the Code of 1849, and read them as provisoes to sec.
16, ch. 199, page 751, of same Code, so as to authorize the trial and conviction of a party upon a new
indictment or proper accusation who has been acquitted
on the ground of variance, or upon an exception to the
form or substance of the indictment: *provided this new
indictment be found and trial had within three terms
of the examination*—a requirement or condition in
many cases even now an impossibility to comply with
or perform; and if we were to sanction the construction contended for, it would be so in most or all; because of the temptation it would hold out to culprits to

stave off a trial, so that, in the event of a defective indictment having been found or variance appearing on the trial, they could avail themselves of this statutory discharge. It would not only allow the accused to take advantage of his own wrong, if he has been successful in keeping the Commonwealth at bay for more than three terms on the defective indictment, but it rewards him with an acquittal for it. It makes it then his interest and his policy in all cases in the first place to stave off the trial by continuances and other subterfuges as long as possible; and then, after having exhausted all the delays of the law, he goes to trial upon an indictment defective in form or substance or obnoxious to the objection of variance, knowing that as the law *now is*, whilst upon such an indictment he cannot be effectually convicted if tried even on the merits, he can be finally and forever acquitted if so tried. He takes, then, the double chance of acquittal by the jury, and if he fail in that, a new trial from the court on account of the defect or variance; and is then secure by lapse of time from further prosecution for the offence upon a new indictment. And this would be the result no matter how the delays on the first indictment were occasioned; whether by inevitable accident, continuances for the prisoner, failures of juries to agree, setting aside of their verdicts, appeals to the General court by writ of error on the part of the prisoner, or otherwise. It would make the law grossly inconsistent with itself in providing that a party should be tried upon a new accusation or indictment, a party not discharged from prosecution for the offence upon the old and defective indictment, and yet to couple with it an implied proviso that would disable its officers by the use of any diligence from complying with its injunctions. It would be obnoxious to a still more glaring inconsistency. If the old indictment were so variant in its charges from the record of the examining court as to be abatable on that account, or so grossly defective in form or in substance as to require another examination to justify the finding of the true indictment, it is conceded that the party is not entitled to this statutory discharge, but is liable to be proceeded against *de novo* by commitment, examination and indictment, to trial and conviction; and yet for a minor defect, requiring no new examination, but only a new indictment to guard against a variance upon a second trial, the prisoner is entitled to his discharge. So that the construction contended for leads to the strange result that a prisoner's situation is better for being convicted, though abortively, upon a defective indictment, or one objectionable upon the score of variance upon the merits, than if acquitted by the jury for the variance or for the defect in form or substance; and the Commonwealth's condition is worse when the indictment is good on its face, both in form and substance, and only obnoxious to the objection of a variance, than when it is totally and incurably defective both in form and substance. The answer of the prisoner's counsel to all these incongruities and absurd consequences is, *ita lex scripta est*—it is so written and must be so interpreted—otherwise the provisions of the law entitling the accused to a discharge upon failure to try within the time prescribed might be evaded by means of defective indictments preferred against him, whereby he might be imprisoned or harassed for an indefinite time. And to guard against so remote and visionary a danger, so improbable if not impossible an evil as abuse and evasion on the part of the Commonwealth through her prosecutors, by such means and instrumentalities, we are invoked to adhere to the strict letter of this law, regardless of its reason and spirit, and of the effects and consequences of our construction, and of the controlling influence of another part of the same statute; whereby the law is rendered not only grossly defective and palpably absurd, but productive of the *practical mischief* of operating the acquittal and discharge from prosecution of atrocious offenders against the laws.

By adopting the construction contended for we should in truth be adhering to the letter and sticking in the bark; we should violate the just rules of construction as much as would he who should decide that the law mentioned by Puffendorf, which forbade a layman to lay hands on a priest, not only applied to him who hurts a priest with a weapon, but to him who laid hands on him for the purpose of doing him some office of kindness, or rendering him aid and assistance; or that the Bolognian law mentioned by the same author, which enacted that " whoever drew blood in the streets should be punished with the greatest severity," extended to the surgeon who opened the vein of a person that fell down in the street with a fit; or that, in the case put by Cicero, or whoever was the author of the treatise inscribed to Herenius, cited by Blackstone as illustrative of a construction of law by its reason and spirit, the sick man was entitled to the benefit of the law, (upon the vessel's coming safely into port, though his remaining was the result of inability from sickness to escape,) which law provided that those who in a storm forsook the ship should forfeit all property therein, and the ship and lading should belong entirely to those who staid in it.   1 Black. Com. 61.

If we trace our legislation on this subject from the revolution down to the present day, it will be apparent, as was well observed by the attorney general, that its whole purpose was and is to carry into practical operation the 8th section of the Bill of Rights, which guaranties to every one accused of crime a speedy trial, and thereby secures him against protracted imprisonment. And this provision of the Bill of Rights announced or enacted no new principle or safeguard of freedom.   It was but the re-affirmance of a principle declared and consecrated by the famous *habeas corpus* act, 31

Charles 2, ch. 2, that second *Magna Carta* of English liberty. By that act it is provided that every person committed for treason or felony shall, if he requires it, the first week of the next term or the first day of the next session of *oyer* and *terminer*, be indicted in that term or session or else admitted to bail; unless the King's witnesses cannot be procured at the time; and if acquitted, or if not indicted or tried in the second term or session, he shall be discharged from his imprisonment for such imputed offence. The object of this provision was to prevent the accused from being detained in prison an unlimited time before he is brought to trial. And the principal ground for bailing upon this act, and indeed the evil the act was chiefly intended to remedy, is the neglect of the accuser to prosecute in time. Even in case of high treason, where the party has been committed upon the warrant of the secretary of state, after a year has elapsed without prosecution, the court will discharge him upon adequate security being given for his appearance. And so also after any unusual delay in case of felony or any inferior offences. 1 Chitty Cr. Law 131, 159. Here, then, we have the prototype of the 8th section of our Bill of Rights, and our subsequent legislation on the subject. The acts of 1786, 12 Stat. at Large 340, and 1792, 1 Stat. at Large, N. S., ch. 13, § 10, p. 22, are but transcripts of the *habeas corpus* act, so far as they entitle the party to be bailed or discharged from imprisonment upon failure to indict at the first or second term or session, with a new and additional provision for a discharge from the crime upon failure to try at the third. The revised act in the Code of 1819, ch. 169, § 28, p. 607, is but a transcript of the preceding enactments, with the addition of the exceptions or savings of the failure to try proceeding from a continuance granted on the motion of the prisoner, or from the inability of the jury to agree. And the acts of 1847-8, sections 12 and 45, pages 144, 152, and the Code of

Virginia of 1849, p. 770, § 13, p. 778, § 36, omitting
the provision as to right to bail upon failure to indict at
the first term, substantially re-enact the other provisions
of the Code of 1819, as to the failure to indict at the
second and try at the third, with additional exceptions
or savings of the prisoner's escaping from jail or failing
to appear according to his recognizance.   No Virginia
case in point has been cited on either side of this question; and it is believed none can be found.   The prisoner's counsel relied on *Cawood's Case*, 2 Va. Cas. 527,
as a conclusive authority.   But it wants one important,
we might say indispensable feature, to render it at all
parallel with or analogous to this.   Cawood had not
been indicted at all; an indictment the finding of which
is not matter of record being tantamount to no indictment.   The great question in that case was whether the
accused had been indicted in legal contemplation.   The
court held, as there was no record of the finding, he
was not; that it requires not only the foreman's endorsement of " true bill," signed by himself, but a record
in court of the fact of finding, to make the bill a legal
bill of indictment:  And the residue of their decision followed as a necessary consequence, that if the prisoner
had been legally examined, and three terms had elapsed
without a legal indictment, he was entitled to be discharged from the crime.

　We have been referred by the attorney general and
his associate to *Barker's Case*, 2 Va. Cas. 122; *Vance's
Case*, Ibid. 132, 162; and *Levi Gibson's Case*, Ibid.
70, 111; not as direct authorities, but to shew a trial
after three terms, and a successful re-indictment and
conviction after the first had been abandoned, or after
errors in arrest of judgment had been sustained.   In
*Vance's Case*, though three terms had passed, the new
trial was upon the same indictment; and in *Barker's*
and *Gibson's Cases*, where the trial was upon new indictments, it does not appear that three terms had

passed, or that the question was raised if they had. So that, after all, we are left to decide this case without express authority to govern us, according to our views of the true construction of the law.

We are not left, however, without the lights of analogy to guide us, furnished by the construction put upon the old law by the General court in *Thompson's Case*, 1 Va. Cas. 319; *Lovett's Case*, 2 Va. Cas. 74; *Santee's Case*, Ibid. 363; and *Vance's Case*, before cited. They decided that the old law was not to be literally construed; that the word term used in the statute did not mean a special, but a regular stated term; and a regular or stated term actually holden, and not the expiration or lapse of the period for holding it fixed by law; and that a failure of the jury to agree was one of the exceptions or savings fairly and necessarily implicable, though not enumerated in the statute. And in *Vance's Case*, where three terms had passed, the court said, *it was not proper to let the prisoner have the benefit of the reversal of a sentence pronounced at one of these terms, and then put him in a better condition, in consequence of his having been convicted, than he would have been if the jury had been unable to agree upon a verdict against him.* The exceptions implied by the courts in the old law, and subsequently incorporated with additional ones in the Code of 1819, the criminal statute of 1847–8, and the Code of 1849, so far from favouring the conclusion contended for, that, upon the maxim of *expressio unius exclusio alterius*, they operated as a limitation upon or denial of the power and authority of the court to imply other exceptions than those enumerated, in our judgment rather favour the opposite conclusions: They shew a legislative approval of the interpretation of the courts by engrafting them in the Code and incorporating them into the written text from time to time as the decisions were made; not that they thereby intended to enact that they were the only exceptions that might occur or should be allowed, but that they were inserted out of abundant caution, and as declaratory provisions of what the law had been decided to be, and by fair and necessary implication would have been decided by the courts to be without these provisions or express exceptions.

It is a very immaterial question whether this case is to be considered as coming under the operation of the act of 1847–8 or the Code of 1849, for whether considered under the laws of 1819, 1847–8, or 1849, the decision would be precisely the same; but we deem it proper, since the question has been raised and discussed, to express the opinion we have formed, that although the offence was committed under the law of 1847–8, and, so far as the question of guilt, degree of crime, *quantum* of punishment, and rules of evidence are concerned, would be triable under that statute; yet upon the question of discharge, arising after the repeal of that statute, when the Code of 1849 was in operation, it must be governed by the Code.

The sole object and purpose of all the laws, from first to last, was to ensure a speedy trial to the accused, and to guard against a protracted imprisonment or harassment by a criminal prosecution, an object but little if any less interesting to the public than to him, and the means, sanctions, or penalties it employed for stimulating prosecutors and officers of the law to diligence in the prosecution was by declaring that the consequence of a failure to indict or try in three terms should operate a discharge from the crime or acquittal, unless it appear that the failure proceeded from no default or delinquency on the part of the Commonwealth, but from causes such as insanity of the prisoner, or the witnesses of the Commonwealth being enticed or kept away, or prevented from attending by sickness or inevitable accident, or by a continuance granted on the motion of the accused, or by reason of his escaping from jail or failing to appear in discharge of his recognizance, or the inability of the jury to agree on their verdict. Now if the law is to be construed literally, and we are to hold that the legislature has enumerated all the exceptions or savings that will excuse delay, by what authority was Vance tried after the lapse of three terms; by what authority could persons be tried a second term or oftener after much longer delay, occasioned by abortive trials, setting aside of verdicts, or arrests of judgments upon writs of error in the General court, as it is admitted on all hands they may be on the same indictment? It might be enquired what would be done in a case where the prisoner was too sick to be tried within the three terms, or were to ask for a continuance, or did not choose to do so if he could. The statute has in terms provided for the mental malady of insanity, but not for sickness or corporeal infirmity or disability. And finally, it might be asked how the absurdity could be reconciled of making the inability of a jury to agree upon a verdict a sufficient excuse, and at the same time holding a trial and conviction, and setting aside of the verdict by the court upon the motion of the prisoner, placing the law, to say the least, in as favourable a position to the Commonwealth in regard to diligence as the disagreement of the jury, to be no excuse. If a failure of the jury constitute a good excuse, *a fortiori* should a trial and conviction, as was held in *Vance's Case*, as to reversal of the sentence upon errors in arrest of judgment. The truth is the statute never meant, by its enumeration of exceptions, or excuses for failure to try, to exclude others of a similar nature or *in pari ratione;* but only to enact, if the Commonwealth was in default for three terms without any of the excuses for the failure enumerated in the statute, or such like excuses, fairly implicable by the courts from the reason and spirit of the law, the prisoner should be entitled to his discharge.

When it is admitted that the Commonwealth had the right to have tried the prisoner again upon the old and defective indictment, that he was not discharged from but still triable for the offence, we cannot understand how it is she has lost that right by resorting to a new and more perfect indictment. There was not the least necessity for the attorney for the Commonwealth to dismiss or quash, or enter a *nolle prosequi*, before he sent to the grand jury the new one. The pendency of the old would have formed no ground of objection to the new; and the counsel for the prisoner is wholly mistaken in supposing that a plea in abatement would have lain to the new. No such plea for such a cause is known to the criminal law. 1 Chitty Cr. Law 446–7 in margin, 304 top paging; Foster's Discourses on Cr. Law 104–5–6. Instead of the single indictment now found, the attorney for the Commonwealth, had he so elected, might have had a separate indictment for each count; might have had all found at one and the same term, or at three successive terms; might, the instant the court set aside the verdict on the first, have elected, without dismissing, quashing, or entering a *nolle prosequi*, to have him arraigned and tried on the second or third, instead of proceeding, as he now more properly claims to do, upon a single indictment with three counts. All these indictments for the same offence, no matter when found, if found before the party has become entitled to his discharge by reason of the Commonwealth's delay or failure to try, constitute, like so many counts in a single indictment, part and parcel of the same prosecution for the same identical offence; and, like a new or amended declaration filed upon leave to amend, avail to the same extent in protecting the Commonwealth against the bar of this statute as the new or amended declaration avails to protect the cause of action in a civil case from the bar of the statute of limitations, if the suit were instituted in time. Indict-

GENERAL COURT OF VIRGINIA.                683

1851.
December
Term.

Adcock's
Case.

ments, it is true, being the act of the inquest, are not
amendable like declarations in a civil suit, which are
the work of the suitor or his counsel; but new indictments found for the same offence are substituted in the
place of the old, and *quoad hoc* operate like the new or
amended declaration. So that when a prisoner pleads
to a new or second indictment, that he has not been indicted or tried in time, the new indictment having been
found and he being arraigned thereon when still liable
to be tried for the offence, it is an all-sufficient answer to reply, and shew by the record, an indictment
found in time, though a defective one, or to reply
and shew by the record, as in this case, a trial, though
an abortive one, and rendered so by the action of the
court in setting aside the verdict and awarding a new
trial, upon the prisoner's motion. Whatever objections
he could have made to being again tried upon the old
indictment, upon the score of failure to indict or try in
due time, he can make to the new, and none other.

We do not agree with the prisoner's counsel that he
has any cause to complain because the old indictment
forms one of the counts of the new. It was but a proper measure of precaution on the part of the attorney
for the Commonwealth to insert it. The prisoner was
not acquitted, but had been convicted on that indictment, and the verdict set aside for variance. Peradventure upon the second trial the evidence might vary
from the first, and render a conviction proper on that
count. It was therefore not only admissible, but altogether proper and regular so to frame the indictment
that the prisoner, if guilty, might be convicted upon
whichever of the three counts the evidence should sustain.

Although we have chosen to base our opinion and
rest our construction upon the reason and spirit of the
law rather than the letter, we are far from admitting
that it does violence to the letter; for it is questionable,

to say the least, whether it is not as well if not better
warranted by the words of the statute, taking its provisions in connection and construing them together
in order to avoid conflict or repugnance, as that contended for by the prisoner's counsel.  It requires a trial
to be had within three terms unless for some of the
savings or grounds of exception mentioned: a trial has
been had within the time required.   The statute
neither expressly says, nor can it be fairly interpreted
to mean by implication, that it must be an effectual or
final trial; because the same statute contemplated that
another sort of trial, an abortive one, might take place,
improperly convicting or acquitting, upon an indictment
defective in form or substance, or in consequence of a
variance; and, to meet that emergency, proceeds to require that the accused shall be liable to be again tried
upon a new or more perfect indictment, without any
proviso or condition that this shall be within three
terms from the examination: And to imply such a proviso or condition would in most cases operate a repeal
of the enactment requiring the new trial.  It would
certainly be as legitimate and fair to imply, that after
the trial had upon the first and defective count, the provision about discharge was exhausted and *functus officio*, and the Commonwealth, in all cases, remitted to
proceedings *de novo*, as to hold that you must imply
a requirement in many cases impossible to be complied
with, that the new trial upon the new indictment must
be had within three terms after the examination.  If a
*proviso* or condition must be implied, and we admit one
is fairly inferrible, it is this, and it is a proper medium
between the extremes, that where the party is not entitled to a discharge from the crime by any default, failure, or delay on the first indictment, he shall be tried
on the new one, with the same diligence, and the same
diligence only, as would have been required of the
Commonwealth upon the old one, had she continued to

prosecute upon that indictment. That when the charge in the new count is so variant from the old, or from the record of the examining court, as to require the interposition of the examining court by new examination, there the Commonwealth is not only entitled to, but bound to resort to proceedings *de novo;* but when the charge is so identically the same as to render a new examination neither necessary nor proper, then the new indictment is to be based upon the examination had, and to be proceeded on to trial and conviction or acquittal, as the case may be, subject to precisely the same objections for default or failure to try, and no other, that would have been applicable to the old indictment.

A question of considerable practical importance, arising upon the construction of this statute, but not in this case, was mooted or incidentally discussed at the bar, applicable alike to a prosecution whether upon the old or a new indictment: and that is whether there must be three successive failures to try or defaults at three consecutive terms, on the part of the Commonwealth, to entitle a prisoner to his discharge; or whether any three, occurring dispersedly or sparsedly in a series of alternate continuances or defaults, as well on the part of the prisoner as the Commonwealth, will suffice; as, for instance, suppose a case where ten terms have passed without trial or indictment, the Commonwealth continued the cause at the first term, the prisoner the 2d, 3d and 4th, the Commonwealth the 5th, the prisoner the 6th, 7th, 8th and 9th, and the Commonwealth the 10th, is the prisoner discharged by these three continuances, to wit, 1st, 5th and 10th? The judgment of this court in *Green's Case,* 1 Rob. R. 731, would seem to favour the construction which holds three consecutive terms or failures to be necessary, because in that case five terms had passed without trial. It was continued at the first term for the Commonwealth, at the 2d for the prisoner, and at the 3d, 4th and 5th for the Commonwealth; and the court said, " His right (the prisoner's) to his discharge upon the adjournment of the Circuit court, at its last term, (which was the 5th,) became complete and was consummated ": and, " That court, however, upon its adjournment ceased to have a capacity to pronounce by its order the discharge to which the prisoner was entitled by law "; and therefore it discharged him upon *habeas corpus;* whereas, if three *consecutive* failures were not necessary, he would have been entitled to his discharge at the end of the fourth term, instead of the fifth.   But it does not appear from the report of the case that this very question was directly raised, discussed, or considered by the court: and may be said, if adjudged or intended to be adjudged, to have passed *sub silentio;* or the court may have deemed it supererogatory to consider whether or not he was discharged after the 4th term, when the 5th had passed, which entitled him to it *a fortiori* and upon either construction.   If this case does not rule the point, it must be confessed it is a question of novelty and difficulty, upon both sides of which much may be urged; and that its decision either way is beset with doubts difficult of solution and objections not a little embarrassing.   We have come to no settled conclusion in our own minds either way; and as any opinion we might now pronounce, had one been formed, would be *obiter,* we purposely abstain from the intimation even of our present impressions or inclinations of opinion upon the subject.   It will be time enough to decide it when it shall directly arise, and we shall be called on to pronounce an authoritative decision, when it can be more thoroughly investigated and discussed by counsel, and more maturely and deliberately considered by the court than it behooves us or is now practicable for us to consider it.

For the reasons set forth and assigned in the foregoing opinion, we have come to the conclusion: *First.* That the Circuit court ought, on the motion of the prisoner to be discharged, to receive and consider the record and proceedings offered by the attorney for the Commonwealth. *Second.* That the prisoner's motion for a discharge from the crime with which he stood indicted, or from further prosecution for the same, ought to be overruled. And we respond to the questions adjourned accordingly. We are unanimous on the first, and Judge *Field* is the only dissentient on the second question.

FIELD, *J.* The only question which I deem it material to consider in this case is, whether the prisoner is entitled to be forever discharged from prosecution for the offence with which he now stands indicted, under the 36th section of the Criminal Code, chap. 208, Code of 1849, p. 778. For if he be entitled to such discharge, it is, as I shall presently shew, to be done under the provisions of that section; although the offence is charged to have been committed at a time when the Criminal Code of 1847-8 was in operation, and under which this prosecution commenced. The act of 1847-8 will be found in the Sessions Acts of that session, page 102, section 28. The present law in relation to the like offence will be found in the Code of 1849, page 730, section 21. The provisions of both are substantially the same, though there is some slight change in the words of the law, but such as does not change the effect of those sections. I will also remark that the act of 1847-8, above referred to, has been repealed, except as to offences committed whilst it was in operation; prosecutions for which, however, must be conducted under the present law for regulating criminal proceedings.

On the 13th of December 1848 the first court was
held for the examination of the prisoner upon the
charge of embezzling merchandise of the goods and
chattels of Word, Ferguson & Barksdale.   The examination was put off until January court 1849, when the
prisoner was examined and remanded to be tried for *the
felony with which he stood charged* before the Circuit
Superior court of law and chancery for the county of
Henrico and city of Richmond.

After this examination had taken place and the prisoner remanded for further trial, it was competent for the
attorney for the Commonwealth in the Circuit Superior
court of law and chancery of the county of Henrico
to prefer an indictment against the prisoner containing
one or more counts, or several separate and distinct indictments for the same felony, provided that the same
*fact*—*i. e.*, the same embezzlement—be set forth in each
count of the one indictment, or in all the several indictments: and none other but that same fact of embezzlement for which the prisoner had been so examined.   He might in each count or in each indictment
have charged the merchandise so embezzled as the
goods and chattels of different persons other than Word,
Ferguson & Barksdale. *Mabry's Case*, 2 Va. Cas.
396.   But in whatever form he might think proper to
present the case to the grand jury, it was certainly his
duty to make his election and prefer his indictment
within some period of time; and not to detain the
prisoner in custody for an indefinite period to await his
pleasure or convenience.   Nor could he prolong the
period by eking out his form of prosecution in driblets;
as would be the case if he could be allowed to prefer
an indictment at one term charging the merchandise as
the property of Word, Ferguson & Barksdale, at another
term as the property of Robert M. & Francis Ayres,
at another term as the property of some other person,
and so on, from term to term, presenting a new indict-

ment, varying only from those previously found in the ownership of the property. By such means the prisoner would be harassed until the end of time, and would be without redress; because, and this is allowable, as is said, the prisoner was not discharged of the crime at the time of presenting these several indictments, in consequence of the finding and the pendency of a previous indictment for the same fact. That these monstrous consequences may result from such an interpretation of the law are, in my opinion, sufficient to shew that such is not its true construction. Let us now enquire and see within what time is it that the indictment should be preferred; and from the failing to do which the prisoner is entitled to be discharged from further prosecution for the offence.

The 36th section of the act above referred to is in these words: " Every person charged with felony, and remanded to a Superior court for trial, shall be forever discharged from prosecution for the offence, if there be three regular terms of such court after his examination without a trial; unless the failure to try him was caused by his insanity, or by the witnesses for the Commonwealth being enticed or kept away, or prevented from attending by sickness or inevitable accident, or by a continuance granted on the motion of the accused, or by reason of his escaping from jail, or failing to appear according to his recognizance, or the inability of the jury to agree in their verdict." This section does not prescribe, in terms, the time within which the indictment is to be found; but as the finding of the indictment necessarily precedes the trial, it follows as a corollary that the law requires that he shall be indicted before the expiration of the third term after his examination, unless the failure to do so is to be excused upon some ground specified in the law. What are they? One is for the failure of the prisoner to appear according to his recognizance. I think the meaning of

VOL. VIII.—44

this is a failure to appear at a trial or at a time when a trial should be had upon the indictment.   But let it be conceded that it means his failure to appear when the grand jury could have taken cognizance of the indictment.   This was at April term 1849, which was the first term that was held after the date of the examination.   At that term the prisoner forfeited his recognizance by failing to appear.   Then, therefore, let us pass by this term as one at which the attorney was excusable for not preferring his indictment against the prisoner.

This brings us to the October term 1849.   At this term the witnesses for the Commonwealth failed to appear: and although it does not appear for what cause they failed to appear, yet the record in that respect, in the absence of proof to the contrary, shews a sufficient reason for excusing the attorney from presenting the indictment at October term 1849.   The next term was in April 1850.   The witnesses then attended on behalf of the Commonwealth, and an indictment was found by the grand jury, upon which the prisoner was arraigned and plead not guilty; and on his motion the trial was continued until the next term.   In this indictment the merchandise is charged as the property of Word, Ferguson & Barksdale, conforming in that respect to the description of the offence for which the prisoner had been examined in the County court.   But, as before remarked, the attorney could nevertheless have varied the charge as it respected the ownership of the property, and, if he had thought proper to do so, might have charged the merchandise as the property of twenty or more different individuals, in twenty or more different counts in the same indictment, or in twenty or more different indictments; all of which, whether different counts or different indictments, would have been separate, distinct and wholly foreign from and independent of each other; so much so that no defect, omission, or error in one could be supplied or corrected by a reference to any other of the said counts or indictments—a principle in pleading which should not be lost sight of in considering this case; indeed it should be decisive of it. The attorney adopted this course. He presented his indictment, charging the merchandise as the property of Word, Ferguson & Barksdale, at April term 1850; and as there was no excuse for his not then presenting the very same indictment which was afterwards found at October term 1851, (the fourth term thereafter,) the time from the lapse of which the prisoner claims immunity from prosecution then began to run. That was, in my estimation, the first term to be counted in favour of the prisoner.

At October term 1850, also, the last mentioned indictment might have been presented. There is no reason assigned for its not being then done. It is true that at that time the trial was postponed at the instance of the prisoner; but this continuance was a continuance of the *trial* upon the indictment which had already been found at April term 1850, and had no reference whatever to any other or future indictment, not at that time even in contemplation of the prosecuting attorney or any other person. The prosecutor was then satisfied with the form of his prosecution, and was full-handed with his testimony, as we must infer from his throwing upon the prisoner the necessity of getting a continuance of the cause, and which the prisoner obtained by his own affidavit shewing good cause for the continuance. Being full-handed as to evidence, there appears to be nothing to excuse him from then preferring the second indictment. This, then, I count as the lapse of the second term in estimating the delay, and the prisoner's claim to exemption from further prosecution. The next term was held in April 1851, when the attorney had all his witnesses before the court, and had no sort of excuse for not then preferring before the grand jury the second indictment; for it was at this term that the prisoner was tried and convicted upon the first indictment, and at this term that the verdict of conviction was set aside, because it had been found out upon the trial of the prisoner that the merchandise which had been embezzled by him was not the property of Word, Ferguson & Barksdale. And thus it appeared that the previous proceedings against the prisoner in the Superior court were wholly ineffectual for the purposes intended, and that the indictment was useless and unavailing, because of the mistake in the indictment as to the ownership of the merchandise. This was the third term, or the last link in the prisoner's title to be discharged from the crime by reason of the failure to try him at or before the third term after his examination. At this date the Code of 1849 was in force, under the 36th section of which, before recited, the prisoner has a right to claim his discharge.

But much reliance has been placed on the 16th section of chapter 199, Code of 1849, page 751. That section is in these words: " A person acquitted of an offence on the ground of a variance between the allegations and the proof of the indictment or other accusation, or upon an exception to the form or substance thereof, may be arraigned again upon a new indictment, or other proper accusation, and tried and convicted for the same offence, notwithstanding such former acquittal." Now this is no new law; it is an *old* principle clothed in a *new* dress. At first it appeared in the form of decisions by this court, and relates to a defence upon the plea of *auterfois acquit*. 1 Va. Cas. 164, 232; 2 Va. Cas. 89, 111, 273, 345; and 5 Rand. 669. The principle of these cases now assumes the form of a statute law. But, nevertheless, that statute should receive the same construction which the decided cases intended to establish. That statute was not designed to have the effect of repealing that law, which I will call the three term law, a law intended to protect a prisoner from unreasonable delay, by ensuring him a trial at or before the end of the third term of the court which should be held after his examination. Under the eighth article of the Bill of Rights of Virginia, a prisoner is entitled to a *speedy* trial; and this law was intended to secure to him the benefit of this principle. Can it for a moment be supposed that this great and humane article in the fundamental law of the land is to be disregarded and repudiated in all cases in which, from the mistake, (as is the case here,) the error, whim, conceit, or ignorance of an attorney, the prisoner would be enabled to escape from punishment, if allowed to enjoy the benefit of this benevolent principle of the Bill of Rights.

Benjamin W. Green was indicted for felony. His trial was not had within the three terms, because there was not time to try him at either of the three terms. Here was no default on the part of the court, or its officers. The delay resulted not from the want of diligence on the part of the attorney for the Commonwealth, nor from any other cause within the control of man, but altogether from the fact that for want of time the prisoner could not be tried. Yet upon an application to the General court, made on behalf of the prisoner, that court discharged him from all further prosecution for the crime. 1 Rob. R. 731. This decision accords with the spirit of the Bill of Rights and the laws in relation to criminal prosecutions, and serves to shew that prosecution, conviction and punishment, when brought against the truths set forth and declared in the venerated instrument before referred to, are but as dust in the balance. The intention of the legislature was to deprive the prisoner of the right of pleading in bar of a new prosecution any of the matters specified in the said 16th section; but not to deprive him of any other matter of defence which should arise upon other and independent considerations, such as a failure to indict within the three terms. It was neither more nor less than a legislative recognition of what has been laid down in *Vance's Case, Barker's Case, Gibson's Case*, and others to be found in our books of reports, in none of which had the three terms been held subsequent to the court of examination. And I defy a reference to a single case in which a new indictment had been allowed after the three regular terms at which the indictment could be found had passed by. *Cawood's Case* is, I think, a good authority to shew that it could not be done.

I am, for these reasons, in favour of discharging the prisoner from further prosecution.

# JUNE TERM 1852.

JUDGES PRESENT.

*Field,*      *Leigh,*
*Lomax,*      *Thompson.*

MULL's *Case.*

1852.
June
Term.

June 24th.

1. A motion for the continuance of a cause, on the ground of the absence of a material witness, properly overruled under the circumstances, though the prisoner swears to the materiality of the witness.
2. Under the circumstances the prisoner required to state who is the witness absent and what he is expected to prove.

William Mull was indicted in the Circuit court of Henrico county for grand larceny in stealing a gold watch and cloak, the property of George B. Goddin. When his case was called for trial he moved the court for a continuance until the next term, on the ground of the absence of James Mull, deemed by him a material witness. This motion for a continuance was made on the 27th of April 1852; and it appears that the cause had been called on the 17th of April, that being the first

day of the term, and the Commonwealth was then ready
for a trial, but the prisoner asked for delay upon the
ground that James Mull, his witness, for whom process
had not been issued until the 16th of April, had gone
to New York in the steamer City of Norfolk on that
day, and would return in her on Monday the 26th of
April. Whereupon the court, although the process had
not been executed, and although it appeared the witness
was a brother of the prisoner and lived in his neighbourhood in the city of Richmond, and had been here
for the preceding three months continuously, and had
not been summoned or examined either before the mayor
who committed the prisoner, or the examining court,
consented to delay the case until the 27th of April.
And now the prisoner being in court and the Commonwealth ready for trial, and it appearing to the court that
the steamer City of Norfolk, on which James Mull went
away, being employed, as it is reported, as a hand on
said steamer, returned to the city on the 26th, but that
said James Mull did not return in her, the court required
the prisoner to be sworn, and upon his examination he
stated that he thought he had other witnesses, some two
or three present, who would prove the same facts he
expected to establish by James Mull. That he expected to prove by said Mull that the articles charged in
the indictment to have been stolen from Goddin, he
(said James) had often heard prisoner say, but never in
the presence of Goddin, were not the prisoner's property, but were Goddin's; and had been pawned by Goddin to the prisoner. And the prisoner further said that
he then had a witness in court, who would prove (having
been then and there present) that Goddin had pawned
the articles alleged in the indictment to have been stolen.

The court overruled the motion and the prisoner excepted. And upon his trial he was convicted and sen-

tenced to three years imprisonment in the penitentiary. Whereupon he applied to this court for a writ of error.

*Scott*, for the petitioner.

BY THE COURT: The writ of error is refused.

---

## COMMONWEALTH *v.* TAGGART.

### June 24th.

An indictment for unlawfully selling ardent spirits to W will not authorize the proof of selling to C.

At the March term 1848 of the Circuit court of Wood county Edward M. Taggart was indicted for unlawfully selling to Edward Welling ardent spirits, without a license, to be drank where sold. On the trial the jury found a special verdict as follows: " We, the jury, find the defendant guilty, provided proof of the selling of ardent spirits to Robert Campbell will sustain the indictment: And if it does not sustain the indictment, then we find him not guilty."

With the consent of the defendant the Circuit court adjourned to this court the question: What judgment ought this court to give upon the verdict of the jury?

BY THE COURT: Judgment should be entered for the defendant.

COMMONWEALTH *v.* HAMOR *& wife.*

**June 24th.**

1. Husband and wife may be jointly indicted for a single act of
   retailing ardent spirits.
2. In such a case, if they are convicted, a fine must be assessed
   and a judgment rendered against each separately.

Seth Hamor and Tasa, his wife, were jointly indicted
in the Circuit court of Wood county for unlawfully retailing ardent spirits. The indictment contained but
one count, and a general charge that Seth Hamor and
Tasa Hamor, his wife, had unlawfully, without having a
license therefor, at their dwelling house, &c., sold by retail ardent spirits.

The defendants appeared and demurred to the indictment; and the Circuit court, with their consent, adjourned to this court the following questions:

1st. Can a husband and wife be jointly indicted for
a single act of retailing ardent spirits?

2d. Can the fine be jointly assessed, and a joint judgment rendered against both the defendants for the same
act of retailing?

3d. What judgment ought the court to give on the
demurrer to the indictment?

By the Court: In answer to the questions adjourned,
the court is of opinion and decides:

As to the first question, that a husband and wife may
be jointly indicted for a single act of retailing spirituous
liquors.

As to the second question, that the fine cannot be assessed jointly, and a joint judgment rendered against
both defendants for the same act of retailing; but the
fine should be assessed separately, and judgment ren-

dered against each defendant. See *Commonwealth* v.
*Roy*, 1 Va. Cas. 262.

As to the third question, the demurrer to the indictment should be overruled and judgment rendered against each of the defendants for 30 dollars; unless they plead.

But the court deems it proper to say that whether the wife should be convicted upon the indictment must depend upon the facts proved upon the trial, if defence shall be made.

1852.
June
Term.

Hamor
& wife's
Case.

---

## COMMONWEALTH *v*. NUTTER.

**June 26th.**

1. What a sufficient entry on the record of the finding an indictment for a misdemeanor by a grand jury.
2. What a good indictment for attempting to commit a felony.

At the April term 1851 of the Circuit court of Ritchie the record states that the grand jury " returned into court, and, among other things, presented an indictment against Thomas Nutter for felonious assault and battery." "A true bill."

The indictment contained five counts:

The first charged that Thomas Nutter, on the 22d day of February 1851, in the county aforesaid, with malice aforethought, in and upon one David Kuner, then and there being, feloniously, unlawfully and wilfully did make an assault, and with a certain knife which he, the said Thomas Nutter, in his hand then and there held, and had drawn and open, feloniously, wilfully and unlawfully did attempt to stab, strike at and cut with said knife, with intent in so doing, wilfully and of his malice aforethought, to kill and murder the said David Kuner, contrary to the form of the statute, &c.

The second count charged an assault with a knife with intent, feloniously, wilfully and unlawfully and of his malice aforethought, to kill and murder the said Ku_ ner.

The third count charged the assault with a club as in the first count; and the fourth count charged the assault with a club as in the second count.

The fifth count charged that the said Thomas Nutter, with malice aforethought, in and upon David Kuner, then and there being, feloniously, wilfully and unlawfully did make an assault, and with a certain knife which he, the said Thomas Nutter, in his left hand then and there had and held, being drawn and open, feloniously, wilfully and unlawfully did attempt to stab, strike at and cut with said knife, with intent then and there feloniously and unlawfully to commit the crime of murder upon the body of the said David Kuner, had he not been prevented and arrested from so doing, contrary to the form of the statute, &c.

The prisoner, upon being arraigned, moved the court to quash the indictment; but the court overruled the motion, with liberty to the prisoner to renew it at the next term of the court. The prisoner thereupon pleaded "not guilty"; and the case was continued.

At the next term of the court the prisoner moved for leave to withdraw his plea of "not guilty," which was granted. And thereupon he moved the court to strike the cause from the docket, because the finding of the indictment was not recorded. The ground of this motion was that in the order book of the court the four words, "presented an indictment against," had been erased. It appears from the statement of the clerk that after he had written the words he had erased them by drawing his pen repeatedly across each of the said words, and had then rubbed his finger over them, causing a blot for their whole length; he intending to have interlined them, but the interlineation had never been made by

him or any other person. The four words were, however, legible, and the erasing marks of the pen over them
were plain, and a large black mark or blot extended over
the words, apparently made by drawing a finger over
them whilst the ink of the erasing marks, or the words,
or perhaps both, was undried. The prisoner further insisted that the law knew no such offence as a felonious
assault and battery, and that the indictment produced
was not such as was described in the order book.

The court waived the decision of the question for
the time ; and thereupon the prisoner demurred generally to the indictment and to each count thereof; and
the attorney for the Commonwealth joined in the demurrer. Wherefore, as in the opinion of the court some
of the questions arising on the demurrer were new and
difficult, and involved the true meaning and interpretation of § 10 of ch. 199 of the Code of Va., p. 750–51,
the court, with the consent of the prisoner, adjourned to
this court the following questions :

1st. What judgment ought the court to give upon
the prisoner's motion to strike the case from the docket
in consequence of the non-recording of the finding of
the indictment as alleged by the prisoner under the circumstances aforesaid ?

2d. Do the first and fifth counts, or either of them,
set forth such an attempt to murder as to make the attempt to murder set forth in either of them a felony ?

3d. If either of them does set forth such an attempt
to murder as to make the attempt a felony, are the matters therein contained set forth in such legal and orderly
manner as that the demurrer to the first and fifth counts
ought to be overruled ?

4th. What judgment ought to be rendered on the demurrer to each count of the indictment, and on the demurrer to the whole indictment ?

*Fisher*, for the prisoner.

FIELD, *J.* delivered the resolution of the court.

The court is of opinion and doth decide, in relation to the first question adjourned, that the court ought to overrule the motion to strike the case from the docket.

In relation to the fourth question adjourned, that the demurrer to each count and to the whole indictment ought to be overruled.

And in relation to the other two questions adjourned, the court declines to express any opinion ; as these questions are, in the opinion of the court, prematurely adjourned.

---

## COMMONWEALTH *v.* WEBSTER.

### June 29th.

1. The common law writ of *capias pro fine* is unrepealed, and may be used by the Commonwealth.
2. Where there is a judgment in favour of the Commonwealth for a fine and costs of prosecution, the writ may issue for the fine and the costs ; but where the judgment is for costs without a fine, the writ is not a proper process to enforce the judgment.
3. Where a party is imprisoned upon a *capias pro fine* for a fine and costs, he can only obtain his discharge from imprisonment by paying the fine and costs. But the term of his imprisonment under such *capias* is limited by the provision in the Code of 1849. ch. 209. § 17. p. 781*.

At a special term of the Circuit court of Jackson county, held in January 1852, Samuel S. Webster ap-

---

*This act provides. " If a person who is sentenced to be confined in jail a certain term, and afterwards, until he pay a fine and the costs of prosecution, fail to pay such fine and costs before the end of said term, he shall continue in confinement until the same be paid or his discharge be ordered by the court. But the additional confinement shall in no case exceed six months from the end of said term."

plied to the court for a writ of *habeas corpus ad subjiciendum*, to be delivered from imprisonment in the jail of the county. The writ was issued; and the sheriff made a return thereon that Webster was in his custody by virtue of a commitment on four several writs of *capias ad satisfaciendum* issued from the clerk's office of the Circuit court of Jackson for fines and costs in cases of the Commonwealth against him: And he made the writs and the returns thereon a part of his return to the writ of *habeas corpus*. Two of these writs were for fines imposed upon Webster in prosecutions for misdemeanor, and the costs of the prosecutions; the other two writs were for the costs of other like prosecutions where no fine had been imposed.

Upon the return to the writ the court, with the consent of the parties, adjourned to this court the following questions:

1st. Whether a *capias ad satisfaciendum* can issue in behalf of the Commonwealth against a person convicted of a misdemeanor, on a judgment against him for a fine and costs.

2d. If such *capias* can issue, is there any means by which he may discharge himself without paying the fine and costs.

LOMAX, *J.* delivered the opinion of the court.

At common law the crown, for the recovery of its *debts*, could issue executions against the persons, and the goods and profits of the lands, and the goods and chattels, and the lands, of its debtors. That is, it might issue an execution of *capias ad satisfaciendum*, or of *levari facias*, or of *fieri facias*, or of *extendi facias*: And it might in one combine all these writs. In the case of a subject, whilst the writs of *fieri facias* and *levari facias* were the process of execution by which in all cases the judgments might be enforced, yet the subject also might have the execution of *capias ad satis-*

1852.
June
Term.

Webster's
Case.

*faciendum* in all recoveries for wrongs committed with
force; and the *extendi facias* for recoveries against an
heir for the debt of his ancestor.   These executions, all
of them, existed at common law; and however the statute may have enlarged the number of cases to which
some of them were made applicable, they were common law, not statutory, process.   The writ of *elegit*
was purely statutory.   For the recovery of *fines* to the
king, the usual process was against the person of the
offender by *capias pro fine*, if he did not pay the fine
which had been assessed, and against the goods and
profits of the lands by *levari facias*.   2 Gab. 606; 1
Chit. Cr. L. 660.   It is stated in the latter of these authorities that the imprisonment under the *capias pro
fine* was, in respect of such fine, not as a debt, but a
punishment for the crime, until the fine was paid.   It is
true that a *capias pro fine* is an execution to compel
the payment of the fine, as the *capias ad satisfaciendum*
is to compel the payment of the debt.   Notwithstanding
that point of resemblance, these two species of process
were never confounded in practice; and were kept sig-
nally distinct in the views of the legislature, in many
provisions made relating to the operation and the inci-
dents of a *capias ad satisfaciendum*.   In the original
structure of the two writs the levy of the *ca. sa.* was
made a direct satisfaction of the debt; but in the frame
of the writ of *capias pro fine* the imprisonment did not
purport to be a satisfaction of the fine; it was a part of
the punishment; and the fine still remained in full
force, and could only be redeemed by satisfaction of the
fine whenever it might be made.   The frame of the
writs of *ca. sa.* in its *teste* and return and the interval
between them was also distinguished from the other
writ.   The levy of the *ca. sa.* was attended with consequences that do not seem ever to have attended the
imprisonment under the *capias pro fine*—such as the
effect of a voluntary enlargement of the prisoner to dis-

1852.
June
Term.

Webster's
Case

charge the debt; the effect and the liabilities arising out of an escape; the provisions enacted for the maintenance of the prisoner whilst in custody; the privilege of the prisoner to avail himself of the proceedings of insolvency under a *ca. sa.*, which he did not have under the *capias pro fine,* (*Chapman's Case,* 1 Va. Cas. 138,) and which required an express statute to entitle him to these proceedings (Acts 1803, ch. 21, § 1; 1 Rev. Code 1819, p. 541); and the privilege of the prisoner in Virginia to discharge his person from custody under the *ca. sa.* by making a surrender of property, thereby in effect converting the *ca. sa.* into a *fi. fa.* In all of these particulars a distinction is observable between the *capias ad satisfaciendum* and the *capias pro fine;* and which never were wholly obliterated.

In some instances it will be seen in the books that a *capias pro fine* is a part of the judicial sentence pronounced by the court; as in the old precedents of judgments in trespass, or wherever the action was properly commenced by *capias ad respondendum.* In this and in other instances the judgment, in addition to the damages adjudged to the plaintiff, awarded a *capias pro fine* to the king. In none of the authorities does it seem to be stated that there is any difference whether the award of the writ is expressly a part of the judgment, or is silently a consequence of the judgment—whether it be judicially awarded or ministerially issued.

The Commonwealth has always occupied the place of the crown, with its prerogatives as to all the legal remedies, not expressly taken away by statute. The co-existence of both these species of process was distinctly recognized and established by the case of Chapman, above referred to, and by the act of 1803, which was the consequence of that decision. The remedy by *capias pro fine* was not abolished by that act because it destroyed one feature of distinction which existed between the two remedies. There is, therefore, no

ground for pronouncing that the two remedies did not
exist in full force and all their distinctness when the
Code of 1849 took effect.    In that Code the mere omission, from whatever cause, to re-enact the provision
contained in the act of 1803, continuing to the prisoner
the privilege of insolvency, cannot upon any principle
of statutory construction, take away the remedy to
which that privilege had been made an incident.    Nor
does it seem to be taken away merely because the severity of that process, as it existed at common law, may
not seem entirely reconcilable with the spirit of many
provisions of the Code which relieve the persons of our
citizens from process of imprisonment.    This remedy
cannot be considered as abolished because the legislature has enacted that on a judgment for money there
may be issued a writ of *fieri facias* or *elegit*, and that
certain other process of execution, not including the
*capias*, shall not issue.    Code, p. 711.    Nor will it, if
existing before in full force, as has been shewn, any
more be considered as abolished because the other distinct process of *capias ad satisfaciendum* shall not,
as enacted, p. 716, be issued or executed after that
Code took effect.    In none of these provisions of the
new Code, therefore, does there seem a sufficient warrant for the court to pronounce that the *capias pro fine*
has ceased to exist, with all the effects which attended
the levy of that process.

In the present case, two of the writs of *capias* under
which the petitioner was charged in custody were
merely for certain costs in prosecutions; how, or when,
or under what circumstances, does not appear.    They
are distinct from any prosecution in which there was a
fine assessed and remained unpaid; and the writs com-
mand that he shall be taken, &c., until he pay those
costs.    A *capias pro fine* in such a case clearly cannot
be proper process.    In the other two writs which were
issued, it was commanded that he be taken, &c., until

he pay the fines and the costs awarded in the prosecutions respectively against the petitioner. If originally any question could be raised, whether, upon a judgment for fine and costs, the costs could be included in the *capias pro fine*, that question seems to be settled by the provision in the Code, p. 783, which authorizes the clerk to include the costs in the execution which may be issued for the fine.

1852.
June
Term.

Webster's
Case.

The court is therefore of opinion, and doth decide, in answer to the question adjourned, 1st. That a *capias ad satisfaciendum* on behalf of the Commonwealth against a person convicted of a misdemeanor, upon a judgment against him for a fine and costs, cannot be issued ; but that for such fine and costs, though not for costs alone without the fine, there may be issued a *capias pro fine*, which, and not the *capias ad satisfaciendum*, appears by the record to have been the species of process that was issued in two of the cases. 2dly. That where a *capias pro fine* is issued for the fine and costs adjudged against the accused, and he is taken under that process, there is no means by which he can discharge himself without paying such fine and costs. Nevertheless, the term of his imprisonment under such *capias* is limited by the provision in the Code of 1849, chapter 209, sect. 17, p. 781.

Which is ordered to be certified to the Circuit court of Jackson county.

LEIGH, *J.* dissented.

1852.
June
Term.

## HENDERSON *v.* THE COMMONWEALTH.

### June 29th.

1. Though the mere breaking and entering the close of another
   is not a misdemeanor, yet if that entry is attended by circumstances constituting a breach of the peace, it will become a misdemeanor for which an indictment will lie.
2. The going upon the porch of another man's house armed, and
   from thence shooting and killing a dog of the owner of the
   house, lying in the yard, in the absence of the male members of the family, and to the terror and alarm of females
   in the house, is a misdemeanor, for which an indictment
   will lie.

At the April term 1850 of the Circuit court of
Wood county the grand jury found an indictment
against George W. Henderson, for that he did break
and enter the close of one Enos Pugh, situate in the
county aforesaid, and at the house of said Enos Pugh
did then and there, wickedly, mischievously and maliciously, and to the terror and dismay of one Nancy Pugh,
wife of said Enos Pugh, fire a gun in the porch of said
house, and then and there did shoot and kill a dog belonging to said house, without any legal authority, contrary to the form of the statute in such cases made and
provided, and against the peace and dignity of the Commonwealth.   On the trial the jury found the defendant
guilty, and assessed his fine at one hundred dollars:
whereupon he moved the court for a new trial, which
motion was overruled; and he excepted.

The facts proved upon the trial were as follows:
That some time about the 1st of March 1850, in the
county of Wood, the defendant came to the house of
Enos Pugh about eight or nine o'clock in the morning,
and then and there went upon the porch of the dwelling house, having his gun on his shoulder and his shot-
pouch about his neck.   A part of the family of Enos
Pugh was then in the house.   The defendant told

1852.
June
Term.

Hender-
son's
Case.

Nancy Pugh, wife of Enos, that he suspected her dogs for worrying and killing his sheep, and he had come to kill the said dogs. She told him that she did not believe the said dogs were guilty, and refused to have them killed, and forbade his doing so; but he, disregarding what she said, took his gun from his shoulder, still standing on the porch, and shot and killed one of the dogs; and then and there loaded his gun and shot another of said dogs and wounded him; the said dogs then lying in the yard near the said porch: One of the dogs being a large one and the other a small one, the large one being killed. That the smoke of the gun when fired passed into the dwelling house by the door. Nancy Pugh was much alarmed by the firing of the gun in the manner in which it was done; and two of her daughters, members of the family, were also greatly alarmed, and one of them, who was dyspeptic, so much so that she became sick in consequence of it, and had to call in medical assistance. At the time the above transaction took place there was none of the male portion of said Pugh's family at home; they being confined in the jail of Wood county, having been convicted upon accusations made against them by the defendant.

The other facts proved related to the question whether the dogs shot by the defendant were the same that had worried his sheep. They were not seen by any one to do it, or to be near the place where it was done; and the facts relied upon to shew their guilt were certainly not very conclusive against them; but it is not a question of much importance in this case.

After the court had overruled the motion for a new trial the defendant filed errors in arrest of judgment.

1st. That the facts stated in the indictment did not constitute a penal offence under any statute in force at the time the act was done.

1852.
June
Term.

Hender-
son's
Case.

2d. That they did not constitute an offence at common law.

But the court overruled the motion to arrest the judgment; and rendered a judgment upon the verdict for the Commonwealth. Whereupon the defendant applied to this court for a writ of error, which was allowed.

LOMAX, *J.* delivered the opinion of the court.

It is abundantly clear that the mere breaking and entering the close of another, though in contemplation of law a trespass committed *vi et armis*, is only a civil injury, to be redressed by action; and cannot be treated as a misdemeanor, to be vindicated by indictment or public prosecution. But when it is attended by circumstances constituting a breach of the peace, such as entering the dwelling house with offensive weapons, in a manner to cause terror and alarm to the family and inmates of the house, the trespass is heightened into a public offence, and becomes the subject of a criminal prosecution. The case of *Rex* v. *Storr*, 3 Burr. R. 1698, and *Rex* v. *Bathurst*, which was cited in that case, establish and illustrate both of these principles. Three of the indictments in that case were quashed, because they amounted merely to trespass *vi et armis*. But as to the fourth indictment, which was for entering a *dwelling house vi et armis*, and with *strong hand*, the objection to that indictment was given up by the counsel for the defendant, and the prosecution for that offence was sustained, whilst the three first indictments were ordered by the court to be quashed. From what was said in those cases, the circumstance that the place where the entry is made is a dwelling house, as reason would suggest, and the peace of those abiding under the sanctity of their home and the security of their castle would strongly require, is a most important circumstance to be taken into consideration in the aggravation

1852.
June
Term.

Hender-
son's
Case.

of trespass *quare clausum fregit* into a misdemeanor;
as is also the circumstance that the entry was made
with fire arms or other offensive or dangerous weapons.
The facts, as disclosed in this record for the purpose of
sustaining the motion for a new trial, shew a trespass
most aggravated in both of these circumstances; as
also in the destruction of animals within the personal
and domestic protection of the owners of the dwelling
house, and the alarm and dismay and other evils which
the violence occasioned to the unprotected females of
the family. No trespass could be aggravated beyond
the wrongs of a private injury and swell into the magnitude of a crime against the public peace, if the facts
stated in the record do not amount to a misdemeanor.
Therefore the motion for a new trial was properly overruled. It is hardly less clear that the frame of the indictment, in its charges of the circumstances accompanying the trespass, is sufficient to maintain the prosecution. Wherefore the errors in arrest of judgment
were also properly overruled. The judgment of the
Circuit court should be affirmed.

1852.
June
Term.

COMMONWEALTH *v.* WORMLEY.

(Absent *Lomax*, J.)

**June 30th.**

A sheriff, to whom a jury is committed in the progress of a criminal trial, walks with them to a neighbouring house, and
whilst there withdraws from the room where they are,
leaving them in the company of three other persons.
Although these other persons swear that there was no
allusion by them to the trial during such absence of the
sheriff, yet the verdict of the jury against the prisoner is to
be set aside, and a new trial directed.

At the October term 1851 of the Circuit court of
Chesterfield county John S. Wormley was indicted for
the murder of Anthony T. Robiou. He was tried at
the March term 1852, and was found guilty of murder
in the first degree. Whereupon he moved the court
for a new trial; first, upon the ground that the verdict
was contrary to the evidence; and second, on the
ground of misbehaviour on the part of the deputy sheriff and the jury. The motion on the first ground was
overruled. On the second ground, it appeared that the
jury, after several days delay in completing the panel,
were sworn on Saturday, and the witnesses for the
Commonwealth and the prisoner were also sworn; but
before any evidence was given in the court adjourned.
That the jury were committed to the charge of George
W. Snellings, one of the deputy sheriffs of the county;
and on the evening of the next day, Sunday the 28th
of March, by the invitation of Silas Cheatam, Esq., the
clerk of the County court of Chesterfield, who resided
about a half mile from the courthouse, the deputy
sheriff, accompanied by all of the jury, visited Mr.
Cheatam at his residence. On getting there, the deputy sheriff and jury went into the parlour, and Mr.
Cheatam, Wm. Amber, the son-in-law of Cheatam, and

1852.
June
Term.

Wormley's
Case.

Augustus L. Winfree, who was employed in guarding the jail, were all in the parlour with the sheriff and jury. Shortly after getting to Cheatam's the sheriff went out of the parlour, and into another room, between which and the parlour there was no connecting door; and when in the room to which he went, the jury were out of his sight. The sheriff remained about five minutes absent from the jury; and during that time the jury remained in the parlour, and the three gentlemen mentioned remained with them, except that Mr. Amber went out for a minute or two, and brought back with him a decanter of spirits, of which most of the jurors drank once, and some of them twice, though no one of them drank to any excess. The sheriff left the jury in the same way more than once, going into the same room, and leaving the same persons with them; but he was never absent at one time more than from five to ten minutes. When the sheriff left the jury he left no one in charge of them, nor did he admonish them or the other persons present to abstain from having any conversation upon the subject of the trial. He was the son-in-law of Cheatam, and his wife was there at the time. The jury staid at Cheatam's about an hour. The above was the statement, substantially, of the deputy sheriff. The three persons stated by him to have been with the jury in the parlour were also examined. They concur in their statements with the deputy sheriff; and they all say that whilst the deputy sheriff was absent there was no conversation between either of them and any of the jurors in relation to the trial. They and the jury conversed freely together in the absence of the deputy sheriff, passing jokes and telling anecdotes, but there was no allusion to the trial.

The deputy sheriff further stated that on the next Sunday he again had charge of the jury, and then permitted several of the jury to drink ardent spirits, without any permission or authority from the court. But on both these Sundays neither of the jurors drank enough to affect him.

The court, with the assent of the prisoner, adjourned to this court the following questions:

1st. Was there such misbehaviour on the part of either the jury or the sheriff as to vitiate the verdict, and entitle the prisoner to a new trial?

2d. What judgment ought the court to render on the prisoner's motion?

*The Attorney General*, for the Commonwealth.
*Robert G. Scott*, for the prisoner.

FIELD, *J.* delivered the opinion of the court.

The court is of opinion, in answer to the first and second questions adjourned, that the conduct of the sheriff in withdrawing from the jury at the house of Mr. Cheatam, and leaving them in the parlour in company with three other gentlemen, as is set forth in the record, was sufficient to vitiate the verdict of the jury; and that upon *that* ground a new trial should be awarded to the prisoner.

The court deems it proper to add that the conduct of the sheriff in conducting the jury to the house of Mr. Cheatam and withdrawing from them, under the circumstances disclosed by the evidence, was such misbehaviour on the part of that officer as to deserve the animadversion and censure of the court. The act should be condemned, because its tendency is to impair the purity of the trial by jury in criminal cases.

# INDEX.

---

## APPELLATE JURISDICTION.

1. Where an appeal or *supersedeas* is applied for since the Code of 1849 went into operation, the application must be governed by the act in the Code, ch. 182, § 2, p. 683.
*Clark* v. *Brown*, 549

2. In an action on the case for injury done to the plaintiff's land by the mill dam of the defendant, though the freehold and franchise was drawn in question, yet if the damages assessed by the jury are less than $200, the Court of appeals has no jurisdiction.    *Idem*, 549

## ARDENT SPIRITS.

1. When drinking ardent spirits by a juror, sitting in a criminal trial, is no ground for a new trial to the prisoner. See *New Trials*, No. 6, 7, and    *Thompson's Case*, 637

2. A license to one man to keep a tavern at his house in a village will not authorize another, who formed a partnership with the first in the sale of the spirituous liquors, which the first was authorized to sell under his license, to sell at a house on the same lot and within the same enclosure with the tavern.
*Hall's Case*, 588

3. An indictment for unlawfully selling ardent spirits to W will not be sustained by proof of selling to C.    *Taggart's Case*, 697

4. Husband and wife may be jointly indicted for a single act of retailing ardent spirits.
*Hamor & wife's Case*, 698

5. In such case, if they are convicted, a fine must be assessed and a judgment rendered against each separately.    *Idem*, 698

## ARSON.

1. The malicious burning, by the owner, of a house on his own land, the house being then in the legal occupancy of another, is a violation of the act of 1847–'8, ch. 4, § 7, p. 99.
*Erskine's Case*, 624

2. The malicious burning of wheat threshed from the straw is not a violation of the 6th section of the same act.    *Idem*, 624

## ASSIGNOR AND ASSIGNEE.

1. Eleven bonds are given for the purchase money of two thirds of a tract of land, payable at successive periods, and a deed of trust is given to secure them; and the obligee assigns the 5th, 6th and 7th of these bonds. The assignee is entitled to the benefit of the deed of trust.
*Schofield* v. *Cox & als.*, 533

2. There having been a prior incumbrance on the whole tract, the assignee is entitled, both against the obligee and an attaching creditor subsequent to the assignment, to have the one third not covered by the last deed of trust applied to pay the first incumbrance.    *Idem*, 533

3. The obligors having paid off the two first bonds, and having paid on account, both before and after the assignment, but without notice of it, more than enough to discharge the 3d and 4th bonds, though they might be entitled to insist that the amount over-paying these should be applied to the 5th bond, yet neither the obligee nor his attaching creditor is so entitled: And in the first case the assignee would be entitled, on the principle of marshalling assets, to be substituted on the other bonds not assigned, as against the obligee and attaching creditor.    *Idem*, 533

4. All the land being sold together, the one third and so much of the two thirds of the purchase money as is necessary, will be applied to discharge the first incumbrance, and the balance will be applied to pay the assignee.    *Idem*, 533

## ASSUMPSIT.

See *Executors and Administrators*, No. 3, 4, and
*Minor* v. *Minor's adm'r*, 1

## ATTACHMENTS—*Foreign.*

1. A creditor of a deceased debtor may proceed, by foreign attachment against the heirs residing out of the State, to subject land or its proceeds, in the State, descended to them from the debtor.
*Carrington & als.* v. *Didier, Norrell & Co.*, 260

2. If the land has been sold under a decree at the suit of the heirs, and is in the hands of a commissioner, he should be made a party as such, and

should be restrained by endorsement on the process from disposing of the proceeds. *Idem, 260*

3. A wife's interest as legatee in her father's estate, in the hands of the executor, may be subjected by the creditor of the husband, by a proceeding by foreign attachment, when the husband resides out of the State.
*Vance v. McLaughlin's adm'r, 289.*

4. Though service of the process upon the executor creates a lien upon the wife's interest in favour of the creditor, yet if the husband dies pending the proceedings, leaving the wife surviving him, the lien of the creditor is defeated, and the property belongs to the wife. *Idem, 289*

5. When the rights of an assignee will be preferred to the lien of an attaching creditor. See *Assignor and Assignee*, No. 2, 3, 4, and
*Schofield v. Cox & als., 533.*

6. An attaching creditor proving his debt, is entitled to a personal decree against his absent debtor, though the property attached may be adjudged to another claimant.
*Idem, 533.*

7. Though a home defendant claims the land in his possession as a purchaser, and shews a receipt for the purchase money, yet, as he does not pretend that he paid in money, and as his account against the absent debtor is not proved to the satisfaction of the court, the land will be held liable. *Kelly v. Linkenhoger, 104.*

8. In such case, upon an appeal from an interlocutory decree for the sale of the land, the appellate court will not reverse the decree because the court did not decree against the absent debtor, or direct the giving security as provided by law in behalf of absent defendants. That may be done in the final decree. *Idem, 104*

9. In a foreign attachment the absent defendant who does not appear in the court below cannot appeal.
*Lenows v. Lenow, 349*

10. But there being two absent defendants, who are sued for a joint debt, one of whom appears and answers, and there being a joint decree against both, upon the appeal of the one who did appear the decree will be reversed as to both. *Idem, 349*

## ATTEMPT TO COMMIT CRIME.

What a good indictment for an attempt to commit a felony.
*Nutter's Case, 699*

## ATTORNEY IN FACT.

A deed executed under a power of attorney commences in the name of the grantor by the attorney, and is signed in the name of the attorney for the grantor. It is a valid deed.
*Bryan v. Stump, &c., 241*

## AWARDS.

1. In an action on an award, if upon the face of the submission it does not clearly appear that the award does not cover the whole matter submitted, a demurrer to the declaration will not be sustained; but the defendant will be left to his plea of "no award"; to which the plaintiff may reply and shew that the award does cover the whole matter submitted. *Price v. Via's heirs, 79*

2. So if the parties may have waived a decision on one branch of the matter submitted, and requested the arbitrators to decide the other matters, though this is not stated in the declaration, a demurrer will not be sustained; but the plaintiff will be allowed to reply the facts to the plea of "no award." *Idem, 79*

## B

## BASTARD CHILDREN.

The father of a bastard child, whose mother was a married woman deserted by her husband, required to pay to the overseers of the poor a certain sum annually for six years, commencing from the birth of the child, if it should live so long.
*Lyle v. Overseers of the Poor of Ohio county,* 20

## BILL OF PARTICULARS.

1. The count in *assumpsit* by an administrator is for money had and received, and the bill of particulars merely states an account in which defendant is debtor to the administrator for money received, stating a sum certain. This will not admit

proof of admissions by the defendant that he had received from a third person a certain sum belonging to the intestate's estate

*Minor v. Minor's adm'r, 1*

2. Where a defendant relies on a specific payment or set-off by way of discount against a debt, an account stating distinctly the nature of such payment or set-off, and the several items thereof, must be filed with the plea; though the defendant may rely upon the parol admissions of the plaintiff to prove such payment. But this is not necessary where no specific payment is relied on, but the defendant offers proof of the admissions of the plaintiff that but a part of the debt is due.

*Rice's ex'or v. Annatt's adm'r, 557*

3. A set-off relied on is a note, which is filed with the papers: No other bill of particulars is necessary.

*Bell v. Crawford, 110*

## BONDS.

1. A bond with condition to convey land of which the obligor had neither title or possession passes nothing.

*Cales v. Miller & als., 6*

2. A committee of a lunatic is required on the record to give a bond for counter security, and the record says he gave it; but the bond taken was a new bond. The bond, acknowledged and certified as this was, became a part of the record, and is to be construed with the record as shewing what was required by the court; and therefore it must be taken that the court required a new bond.

*Berry v. Homan's committee, 48*

3. A bond is executed with the names of some of the obligors in the penalty, but it is signed by one whose name is not there: It is his bond.

*Idem, 48*

*Luster v. Middlecoff & als., 54*

4. As to liens of forthcoming bonds. See *Forthcoming Bonds*, No. 1, 2, 3, and

*Jones, &c. v. Myrick's ex'ors, 179*

*Myrick's ex'ors v. Epes & als., 179*

5. A forthcoming bond is signed by the debtor, a third person, and the creditor in the execution. The bond is valid to bind the debtor and the first surety; but the first surety is only a co-surety with the creditor, and entitled to contribution from him.

*Beale v. King, 78*

6. If debtor proves insolvent, the surety may be relieved to the extent of one moiety of the debt, either by bill in equity or by motion under the statute for the relief of sureties.

*Idem, 560*

7. A bond binding the heirs, given to an endorser to protect him from loss on account of his endorsements, will, on the death of the obligor, be an available security for simple contract creditors of the obligor to the extent that the notes endorsed by said endorser is paid out of the personal assets.

*Cralle & als. v. Meem & als., 496*

## C

### CAPIAS PRO FINE.

See *Executions*, No. 1, 2, 3, and *Webster's Case, 702*

### CASE.

1. Case is a proper remedy for the breach of an express warranty of soundness of a slave or other personal property.

*Trice v. Cockran, 442*

2. In case for a breach of a warranty of soundness of a personal chattel, it is not necessary to allege the defendant's knowledge of the unsoundness: And if it is alleged, it is not necessary to prove it.

*Idem, 442*

### CO-DEFENDANTS.

In a bill by a creditor against an administrator and his sureties, charging a *devastavit* by the administrator, and the liability of the sureties for it, though some of the sureties insist in their answer that under the circumstances one of the sureties is liable to the others, if they are liable to the plaintiff, though there is a decree for the plaintiff, and though it appear from the proofs that the *devastavit* was occasioned by the payment of a debt of inferior dignity to the surety sought to be charged, yet it is not a proper case for a decree between co-defendants.

*Allen & Errine v. Morgan's adm'r & als., 60*

### COMMISSIONER.

Under a decree for the sale of

lands, in a suit by heirs, the administrator of their ancestor's estate is appointed a commissioner to collect the proceeds of the sale. In a suit by a creditor of the administrator's intestate, to subject the proceeds of the land, the commissioner should be made a party as such; and if he is only a party as administrator, and without actual notice of the object of the suit he pays over the money to the heirs, he will not be liable to the creditor.
*Carrington & als.* v. *Didier, Norvell & Co.,* 260

## CONDITIONS.

For the construction of the condition of a bond of indemnity. See *Marshalling Assets*, No. 4, and
*Crulle & als.* v. *Meem & als.,* 496

## CONTINUANCE.

1. A motion for a continuance of a criminal trial, on the ground of the absence of a material witness, properly overruled under the circumstances, though the prisoner swears to the materiality of the witness.
*Mull's Case,* 695
2. Under the circumstances the prisoner required to state who is the witness absent and what he is expected to prove. *Idem,* 695

## CONVEYANCES—*Fraudulent.*

1. A deed executed *bona fide* to secure a loan of money, not to be enforced for ten years, is a valid deed as against creditors of the grantor. *Lewis & als.* v. *Caperton's ex'or & als.,* 148
2. A deed which conveys, without a schedule, household furniture, the various kinds of stock upon a farm, bacon and lard, to secure a *bona fide* debt, but not to be enforced for eighteen months after its execution, is valid against creditors, though made without the knowledge of the creditor, and the grantor was indebted to insolvency at the time.—By two judges. *Idem,* 148
3. A deed which conveys land to secure a *bona fide* debt, which is not to be enforced for two years, and only then or afterwards upon a notice of the sale for one hundred and twenty days, is valid against creditors. *Idem,* 148

4. Such a deed is valid though the execution of the deed is postponed for five years from the date of the conveyance; and the rents and profits of the property in the meantime are reserved to the grantor. *Idem,* 148
5. A deed which conveys future rents and profits of property conveyed in other deeds, which were reserved to the grantor in the previous deeds, for the purpose of paying a *bona fide* debt, is valid against creditors of the grantor. *Idem,* 148
6. A post-nuptial settlement made by a husband on his wife, of her personal property derived from her father's estate, but of which he retains possession, not having been properly recorded, is void as against the creditors of the husband. *Idem,* 148
7. A deed made by a husband embarrassed at the time, by which he conveys the proceeds of his wife's land, which had been sold, and the note for the purchase-money made to him, in trust for himself and wife for their lives and the life of the survivor, and during his life to be under his control and management, is voluntary and fraudulent as to creditors. *Idem,* 148
8. A deed which conveys land to secure a *bona fide* debt due to the grantee, and also a debt to the grantor's wife, which is voluntary and fraudulent as to his creditors, and the nature of which debt is known to the grantee, is null and void as a security for the first as well as the last mentioned debt, as against subsequent incumbrancers and creditors of the grantor.—By two judges. *Idem,* 148
9. A deed which conveys all the property of the grantor in trust for the payment of his debts, is valid, though it contains a provision that no creditor shall take any benefit under the deed who does not, within thirty days from its date, signify his acceptance of its terms and conditions; and further agree to release and acquit the grantor from all further claim for the debt acknowledged therein.
*Phippen* v. *Durham & als.,* 457

## COVENANTS.

1. There is a devise to J, with a

limitation over, upon his dying without issue at his death, to his brother R if he should survive him, or his representatives, and R dies in the lifetime of J. J sells and conveys the land to A; and R, though he does not convey the land, is a party to the deed, and J and R covenant as follows: That the said J, for himself and his heirs, and the said R as contingent devisee under the will of Col. J, by whom the said land was devised to J, do hereby covenant and agree to and with the said A, that they will warrant and defend the fee simple estate to said land, to him and his heirs forever, against the claim of themselves and their heirs, and the claim of any person claiming under them by virtue of the will aforesaid, and do relinquish and fully confirm to said A all the right they or their heirs now have or may hereafter have to said land, or any part thereof, to him and his heirs, free from the claim of the said J and R and their heirs, and of all other persons in the whole world. HELD: 1. That this covenant of R extends to the claim of his children to the land, though they claim not as his heirs, but as devisees under the will of Col. J. 2. That the covenant of R is a covenant running with the land, and a purchaser claiming under A, a part thereof, by a regular chain of conveyances, is entitled to the benefit of said covenant for his indemnity against the said claim of the heirs of R.
*Dickinson v. Hoomes's adm'r & als.,* 353

2. In an action of covenant for the failure to deliver to the plaintiff possession of a mill which he had rented of the defendant, the plaintiff not having sustained any special damage, he is only entitled to recover the difference between the rent which he contracted to pay and a fair rent for the property at the time when it should have been delivered. A conjectural estimate of the profits which might have been made is no legitimate basis on which to fix the damages. *Newbrough v. Walker,* 16

## CREDITORS.

See *Assignor and Assignee, Attachments, Marshalling Assets,* and *Trusts and Trustees.*

## CRIMINAL JURISDICTION AND PROCEEDINGS.

1. An indictment for a wilful trespass was against J. It was endorsed by the grand jury an indictment against T, "a true bill," and so it was noted on the record of the court. A writ having issued on the indictment against J, it should, on his motion, be quashed.
*McKinney's Case,* 589

2. In such case the court cannot amend the record so as to conform to the indictment. *Idem,* 589

3. What a sufficient entry on the record of the finding an indictment for a misdemeanor by the grand jury. *Nutter's Case,* 699

4. If a prisoner has been tried by an examining court and sent on for further trial before the Circuit court, and an indictment has been found against him, it is too late to plead in abatement that, or to move to quash the indictment because, there were irregularities in his examination before the committing magistrate. *Clore's Case,* 606

5. If it may be fairly understood from the record of the examining court, that the crime for which the prisoner is indicted is the offence for which he was examined, that is sufficient. *Idem,* 606

6. QUÆRE: If the setting aside a person called upon the *venire*, on the motion of the Commonwealth, is a ground of exception by the prisoner. *Idem,* 606

7. A prisoner being sent on for further trial by an examining court, which sat during the session of the Circuit court to which he is sent for further trial, that term of the Circuit court is not one of the two at which the statute directs that he shall be indicted, or that he shall be discharged from imprisonment. *Bell's Case,* 600

8. A prisoner is sent on by the examining court to be tried for embezzling the goods of W. He may thereupon be indicted for embezzling the goods of A; the embezzlement being of the same goods for which he was tried by the examining court. *Adcock's Case,* 661

9. A prisoner is indicted for embezzling the goods of W, and is tried

and convicted at the fifth term of the court after his trial before the examining court; but the verdict is set aside for a variance as to the ownership of the goods. There is then a *nolle prosequi* entered and a new indictment to suit the proofs. The prisoner is not entitled to be discharged from the crime because three terms had elapsed between his examination and the last indictment. *Idem, 661*

10. The excuses for failure to try the prisoner, enumerated in the statute, are not intended to exclude others of a similar nature; but only that if the Commonwealth was in default for three terms, without any of the excuses fairly implicable by the courts from the reason and spirit of the law, the prisoner shall be entitled to his discharge. *Idem, 661*

11. Though an offence committed before the Code of 1849 went into operation must, so far as the question of guilt, degree of crime, *quantum* of punishment, and rules of evidence are concerned, be governed by the law in force at the time the offence was committed, yet, upon the question of the prisoner's right to be discharged from the failure to try him, arising after the Code went into operation, it must be governed by the law in the Code. *Idem, 661*

12. In such case, upon the prisoner's motion for a discharge, the record of the Circuit court is competent, and the only competent evidence, for the Commonwealth, to prove that he had been indicted, tried and convicted within the time prescribed by law. *Idem, 661*

13. In prosecutions for felonies and other serious offences, the court will not, on motion of the prisoner, quash the indictment, unless where the court has no jurisdiction, where no indictable offence is charged, or where there is some other substantial or material defect. In other cases he will be left to his demurrer, motion in arrest of judgment, or writ of error. *Bell's Case, 600*

14. What is not a sufficient ground for a new trial. See *New Trials*, No. 2, 3, 4, 5, 6, 7, and
*Thompson's Case, 637*

15. What is a ground for a new trial. See *New Trials*, No. 8, and
*Wormley's Case, 712*

## D

### DAMAGES.

1. In an action of covenant for the failure to deliver to the plaintiff possession of a mill which he had rented from the defendant, the plaintiff not having sustained any special damage, he is entitled to recover only the difference between the rent contracted to be paid and a fair rent for the property at the time when it should have been delivered. A conjectural estimate of the profits which might have been made is no legitimate basis on which to fix the damages. *Newbrough v. Walker, 16*

2. See *Mills*, No. 1, 3, 5, and
*Calhoun v. Palmer, 88*

### DEBT.

1. An instrument, binding the parties thereto to pay a sum of money, purports to be under their hands and seals; but it is signed by one of the parties without a seal, and by the other parties with seals to their names. One action of debt may be brought against all the parties.
*Rankin v. Roler & als., 63*

2. In an action of debt, under the plea of payment, without a bill of particulars, the defendant may give in evidence the parol admissions of the plaintiff that but a certain part of the debt is due.
*Rice's ex'or v. Annatt's adm'r, 557*

3. When and what bill of particulars necessary. See *Bill of Particulars*, No. 2, and *Idem, 557*

### DECREES.

1. When there should not be a decree between co-defendants. See *Co-Defendants*, No. 1, and
*Allen & Ervine v. Morgan's adm'r & als., 60*

2. When a decree concludes a judgment creditor. See *Judgments*, No. 6, and
*Jones, &c. v. Myrick's ex'ors, 179*
*Myrick's ex'ors v. Epes & als., 179*

3. A decree which passes upon the whole subject in issue, so as to be final in its nature, is not converted into an interlocutory decree by the addition thereto of an order suspending the decree as to the amount of one item of the account involved in the cause, until the decision of another suit brought by another party, against both plaintiffs and defendants in the first suit, in which the amount of this item is claimed by the plaintiff.
*Fleming & als. v. Bolling & als., 292*

4. Upon an appeal by one party from a joint decree, the appellate court will reverse the decree as to both.          *Lenows v. Lenow, 349*

## DEEDS.

1. A party offering in evidence a deed purporting to be executed by a commissioner under the decree of a court, and conveying land, must offer with the deed so much of the record of the cause in which the decree was made as will shew the authority of the commissioner to convey the land described in the deed.
*Cales v. Miller & als., 6*

2. A deed by a commissioner under a decree directing a conveyance of land to or of which none of the parties to the suit had either title or possession passes nothing.   *Idem, 6*

3. A deed executed in 1799, which shews upon its face that the parties to it resided out of Virginia, was properly admitted to record upon the certificate of acknowledgment by the mayor of a city in another State, describing himself as such, and purporting to be under the seal of the city.             *Idem, 6*

4. The certificate is sufficient evidence that the grantor for the time resided in the said city, though the deed described him as being a citizen of another State.        *Idem, 6*

5. It seems that a residence, however temporary, is sufficient to authorize the acknowledgment of a deed there, by a non-resident of Virginia, under the act of 1792, ch. 90, § 5.            *Idem, 6*

6. A deed executed under a power of attorney commences in the name of the grantor by the attorney, and

is signed in the name of the attorney for the grantor.  It is valid.
*Bryan v. Stump, &c., 241*

7. See  *Conveyances—Fraudulent, passim,* and
*Lewis & als. v. Caperton's ex'or & als.,*                              *148*

## DEMURRER.

When a demurrer to a declaration upon an award will not be sustained. See *Awards,* No. 1, 2, and
*Price v. Via's heirs, 79*

## DEPOSITIONS.

1. The caption of a deposition describing it as taken in a proceeding of forcible entry and detainer, is sufficiently accurate to authorize the reading of the deposition, though the proceeding is for an unlawful detainer.   *Cales v. Miller & als., 6*

2. In a case of probat the deposition of an aged witness, taken *de bene esse,* allowed to be read, upon proof, either by witnesses or his own affidavit, of his inability to attend the court.   *Nuckols's adm'r v. Jones, 267*

## DETINUE.

1. Where a defendant in detinue dies, and the action is revived against his administrator with the will annexed, the plaintiff is entitled to demand from the administrator, not only the property sued for, but damages for its detention, and the costs incurred in prosecuting the action against the testator in his lifetime.
*Hunt's adm'r v. Martin's adm'r, 578*

2. The *scire facias* to revive the action of detinue against an administrator should suggest the coming of the property into the possession of the administrator since the death of his intestate. And the *scire facias* not being in the record, nor in the clerk's office of the court below, and no objection appearing to have been taken to it in that court, the Court of appeals will presume that it was in all respects regular.    *Idem, 578*

3. Where an action of detinue is revived against an administrator, and a judgment is recovered, the judgment for the damages for de-

tention of the property and the costs should not be against the administrator personally, but against him as administrator, to be levied of the goods, &c., of his intestate in his hands to be administered. *Idem, 578*

## DOWER.

1. Husband during the coverture sells and conveys land with general warranty, but his wife does not join in the conveyance. By his will he gives his whole estate, real and personal, to his wife for her life, remainder to her children. She is entitled to take under the will, and also to have her dower in the land sold. *Higginbotham* v. *Cornwell, 83*

2. That a provision for a wife in the will of her husband shall be held to be in lieu of dower, the will must so declare in terms: or the conclusion from the provisions of the will ought to be as clear and satisfactory as if it was expressed. *Idem, 83*

## E

### EMBEZZLEMENT.

A prisoner sent on by the examining court to be tried for embezzling the goods of W, may thereupon be indicted for embezzling the goods of A; the embezzlement being of the same goods for which he was tried by the examining court. *Adcock's Case, 661*

### ENDORSERS.

Several accommodation endorsers of negotiable paper are responsible in the order of their endorsements, unless there has been an agreement among them to be jointly and equally bound. And the burden of proving such an agreement is upon the prior endorser who seeks the benefit of it. *Hogue* v. *Davis & als., 4*

### ESTOPPEL.

### ESTATES.

## EQUITABLE JURISDICTION AND RELIEF.

1. A court of equity in Virginia may subject heirs living here, upon the covenants of the ancestor binding the heirs, to the extent of the value of land descended to them in another State.
*Dickinson* v. *Hoomes's adm'r & als., 353*

2. Under the circumstances of the case, the heirs held bound to account for only so much of the lands out of the State as they have actually gotten or may get possession of, with the rents and profits derived therefrom, after deducting the costs and expense of recovering the lands. *Idem, 353*

3. When a court of equity will not entertain a creditor seeking to enforce a deed of trust in which he has fraudulently obtained an advantage over other creditors. See *Fraud*, No. 3, and
*Phippen* v. *Durham & als., 457*

4. A principal executes a bond binding his heirs to his surety as endorser, with condition that he will, when required by the bank or the surety, pay off the notes, and so indemnify and save the surety harmless; and he dies leaving the notes not yet due, and they are protested, and afterwards paid by his administrator. The surety being entitled to resort to both the real and personal estate, and the notes having been paid out of the latter, the simple contract creditors are entitled to have the assets marshalled to the extent of the notes so paid, if they do not exceed the penalty of the bond.
*Cralle & als.* v. *Meem & als., 496*

5. Upon a bill by simple contract creditors to marshal assets, it is competent for the court, in its discretion, to decree a sale of the real estate in the hands of the heirs, some of whom are infants, for the payment of the debts: But it is premature to decree a sale before adjudicating the claims of the creditors, and so ascertaining the amount of indebtedness chargeable upon the lands of the decedent. *Idem, 496*

6. Though such a decree for a sale of land has been prematurely made,

yet if the sale is made and confirmed, the court will not set aside the sale on the petition of the purchasers, if upon the hearing it appears that the sale is beneficial to the infants.                    *Idem, 496*

7. The court having made a decree for a sale of real estate, on the petition of the adult heirs, and with the assent of the creditors, it is erroneous to proceed to sequestrate the rents of the other real estate in the hands of the heirs, for the payment of the debts, before deciding upon the claim of the purchasers to have the sale set aside.            *Idem, 496*

8. What relief will be given in equity upon an usurious contract. See *Usury*, No. 2, and
*Bell & als.* v. *Calhoun, 22*

### EVIDENCE.

1. A party offering in evidence a deed purporting to be executed by a commissioner under the decree of a court, and conveying land, must offer with it so much of the record of the cause in which the decree was made as will shew the authority of the commissioner to convey the land described in the deed.
*Coles* v. *Miller & als., 6*

2. What a sufficiently accurate description of the cause in the caption of a deposition to authorize it to be read. See *Deposition*, No. 1, and
*Idem, 6*

3. A record to which neither the demandants or tenants were parties is not even *prima facie* evidence against the tenant that the grantor in the deed to the demandants was heir at law of the grantee in the patent under which the demandants claim title.
*Duncan* v. *Helms & others, 68*

4. Upon a writ of unlawful detainer, defendant sets up title in himself. Plaintiff may prove that defendant entered on the premises under a parol lease from himself; though the lease proved was to continue more than a year.
*Adams* v. *Martin, 107*

5. A witness called to prove the hand writing of a paper offered for probat may be impeached by proof of what she has said about that paper at another time: But neither her capacity to judge of the hand writing

or her credit is to be impeached by what she may have said about some other paper.
*Nuckols's adm'r* v. *Jones, 267*

6. In an action of debt, under the plea of payment, without a bill of particulars, the defendant may give in evidence the parol admissions of the plaintiff that but a certain part of the debt is due.
*Rice's ex'or* v. *Annatt's adm'r, 557*

7. Upon a motion by a prisoner to be discharged, for the failure to try him within three terms, the Commonwealth relies on the fact that he was tried and convicted, and the verdict set aside for a variance. The record of the court is competent, and the only competent, evidence of these facts.            *Adcock's Case, 661*

8. See *Wills*, No. 4, and
*Nuckols's adm'r* v. *Jones, 267*

### EXCEPTIONS—*Bill of.*

1. In an action by an executor upon a refunding bond, after offering in evidence the record of the decree against him, he offers the execution which issued upon it and the return thereon, which is objected to, but admitted. The defendant excepts, and does not insert the execution in the exception. The relevancy of the evidence being obvious without an inspection of the execution, it is not essential that it should have been inserted in the bill of exceptions.
*Archer* v. *Archer's adm'r, 539*

2. QUÆRE: If the setting aside a person called upon the *venire*, on the motion of the Commonwealth, is a ground of exception by the prisoner.
*Clore's Case, 606*

### EXECUTIONS.

1. The common law writ of *capias pro fine* is unrepealed, and may be used by the Commonwealth.
*Webster's Case, 702*

2. Where there is a judgment in favour of the Commonwealth for a fine and costs of prosecution, the writ may issue for the fine and costs; but where the judgment is for costs only, the writ is not a proper process to enforce the judgment.      *Idem, 702*

3. Where a party is imprisoned upon a *capias pro fine*, for a fine and

costs, he can only obtain his discharge from imprisonment by paying the fine and costs. But the term of imprisonment under such *capias* is limited by the provisions of the Code, ch. 209, § 17, p. 781. *Idem, 702*

## EXECUTORS AND ADMINISTRATORS.

1. The official bond of an executor contains in the penal part the names of the executor and several sureties, and there is no blank for the name of another; but it is signed and sealed by all those whose names are in the penal part, and also by another person. It is the bond of all, including the last mentioned person.
*Luster* v. *Middlecoff & als., 54*

2. The official bond of an executrix only binding the obligors for the due administration of the personal assets, the sureties are to no extent responsible for the rents and profits of the real estate.
*Hutcherson, &c.* v. *Pigg, 220*

3. In *assumpsit* by an administrator for a debt due his intestate in his lifetime, the defendant cannot set off a debt due him for money paid as the surety of the intestate since his death. *Minor* v. *Minor's adm'r, 1*

4. The count in *assumpsit* by the administrator is for money had and received, and the bill of particulars merely states an account in which the defendant is debtor for money received, stating a sum certain. This will not admit proof of an admission by the defendant that he had received from a third person a certain sum belonging to the intestate's estate. *Idem, 1*

5. All the sureties of an executrix should be parties to a suit by legatees for distribution, or a sufficient reason should be shewn for failing to make them parties, before a decree is made against one of them.
*Hutcherson, &c.* v. *Pigg, 220*

6. A personal representative of a deceased insolvent co-obligor in a bond is not a necessary party to a suit in equity by the executrix of the obligee against the administratrix of one of the obligors.
*Montague's ex'x* v. *Turpin's adm'x & als., 453*

7. Where a defendant in detinue dies, and the action is revived against his administrator, the plaintiff is entitled to demand from the administrator, not only the property sued for, but damages for its detention by the intestate, and the costs incurred in prosecuting the action against his intestate.
*Hunt's adm'r* v. *Martin's adm'r, 578*

8. Where an action of detinue is revived against an administrator, and a judgment is recovered, the judgment for the damages for detention of the property and the costs should not be against the administrator personally, but against him as administrator, to be levied of the goods of his intestate in his hands to be administered. *Idem, 578*

8. Judgment against an administratrix upon the bond of her intestate is conclusive of the validity of the debt against the administratrix.
*Montague's ex'x* v. *Turpin's adm'x, 453*

9. A sale of bonds of the estate by an executor, at a discount of eighteen per cent., when the circumstances of the estate does not require it, is a *devastavit*.
*Pinckard* v. *Woods, &c., 140*

10. Land in which a widow is entitled to dower being sold by the executor under a charge for payment of debts, he should be credited in his account of the proceeds for the amount he has paid the widow for her dower interest.
*Meeks' adm'r, &c.* v. *Thompson & als., 134*

## EX POST FACTO LAWS.

See *Criminal Jurisdiction and Proceedings,* No. 11, and
*Adcock's Case, 661*

# F

## FELONY.

1. The malicious burning, by the owner, of a house on his own land, the house being in the legal occupancy of another, is a violation of the act of 1847–8, ch. 4, § 7, p. 99.
*Erskine's Case, 624*

2. The malicious burning of wheat threshed from the straw is not a vio-

lation of the 6th section of the same
act. *Idem, 624*

## FINES.

1. How judgments for fines on prosecutions by the Commonwealth may be enforced. See *Executions*, No. 1, 2, 3, and *Webster's Case, 702*

2. Upon a joint indictment against husband and wife for selling ardent spirits, if they are convicted, there must be a separate fine against each.
*Hamor & wife's Case, 698*

## FORCIBLE ENTRY AND UNLAW-FUL DETAINER.

1. In a proceeding of forcible entry and detainer, the court failing to meet on the day to which it is adjourned, the cause is not discontinued, but stands adjourned, by operation of law, to the next County court. *Mann v. Gwinn & als., 58*

2. Upon a writ of unlawful detainer, the defendant sets up title in himself. The plaintiff may prove that the defendant entered on the premises under a parol lease from himself; though the lease proved was to continue more than a year.
*Adams v. Martin, 107*

3. In a writ of unlawful detainer, the defendant claiming title under a deed to himself and another, as joint tenants, that other person is not a competent witness for him to sustain his right of possession.
*Idem, 107*

4. The caption of a deposition describing it as taken in a proceeding of forcible entry and detainer, is sufficiently accurate to authorize the reading of the deposition, though the proceeding is for an unlawful detainer. *Cales v. Miller & als., 6*

## FORTHCOMING BONDS.

1. A forthcoming bond has the force of a judgment, so as to create a lien upon the lands of the obligor, *only* from the time the bond is returned to the clerk's office.
*Jones, &c. v. Myrick's ex'ors, 179*
*Myrick's ex'ors v. Epes & als., 179*

2. There being no evidence that the bond was returned to the clerk's office before the day on which there was an award of execution thereon by the court, it will be regarded as having been returned to the office on that day. *Idem, 179*

3. A forfeited forthcoming bond not returned to the clerk's office until some day in the term after the first, when there is an award of execution thereon, does not relate back to the first day of the term.
*Idem, 179*

4. Though a forthcoming bond is forfeited, and not quashed, yet in equity the lien of the original judgment still exists; and if the obligors in the bond prove insolvent, so that the debt is not paid, a court of law will quash the bond, and thus revive the lien of the original judgment. And a court of equity, having jurisdiction of the subject, will treat the bond as a nullity, and proceed to give such relief as the creditor is entitled to under his original judgment. *Idem, 179*

5. A forthcoming bond is signed by the debtor, a third person, and the creditor in the execution. The bond is valid to bind the debtor and the first surety; but the first surety is only a co-surety with the creditor, and entitled to contribution from him. *Booth v. Kinsey, 560*

6. If debtor proves insolvent, the surety may be relieved to the extent of one moiety of the debt, either by bill in equity or by motion under the statute for relief of sureties.
*Idem, 560*

7. In such case the notice on the forthcoming bond is not defective for failing to name the obligee as a co-obligor. *Idem, 560*

## FRAUD.

1. A purchase of bonds from an executor at a discount of eighteen per cent., with knowledge that the condition of the estate does not require the sale, is a fraud in the purchaser, though he may know that they do not amount to more than the executor's interest in the estate; and the executor not having paid to the other legatees their portion of the estate, the purchaser will be compelled to repay the money to them.
*Pinckard v. Woods, &c., 140*

2. If the sureties of the executor have been compelled to pay the

amount to the legatees, they may recover from the purchaser.

*Idem, 140*

3. A deed of trust to secure creditors requires them to signify their acceptance of it by signing it within thirty days, and to release the debtor. The creditors being dissatisfied with its provisions, it is agreed between them and the debtor that they will not sign it; but two of them, who had entered into this agreement, sign the deed the day before the thirty days expire, with the avowed purpose that it is for the benefit of all. Afterwards one of these comes into equity to enforce the deed for the benefit of himself and the other who signed. A court of equity will not entertain him.

*Phippen v. Durham & als., 457*

# G

## GAMBLING.

1. Betting on a horse race is not gaming within the meaning of the 5th section of the 10th chapter of the act of the 14th of March 1848, concerning crimes and punishments, and proceedings in criminal cases.

*Shelton's Case, 592*

2. A storehouse in a village, late at night, after persons cease to come to the store to purchase goods, and the door is locked, is not a public place, within the meaning of the statute against gaming. *Feazle's Case, 585*

## GUARANTOR AND GUARANTEE.

1. A letter of credit addressed to W & W may be proved to have been intended for W, W & Co., so as to hold the writer bound to the latter upon it.

*Wadsworth & als. v. Allen, &c., 174*

2. A guarantor may specify in the letter of credit which he gives the terms on which he will be bound; and if the terms are complied with, he is bound, though the law, in the absence of all prescription of terms in the letter of credit, would have prescribed the performance of other acts by the party seeking to subject him upon his guarantee.

*Idem, 174*

3. A guarantor undertaking to pay upon receiving reasonable notice of

the failure of the principal debtor to pay the debt when due, dispenses with notice of the acceptance of the guarantee by the party to whom it is addressed, even if the law would have required such notice.

*Idem, 174*

4. What is reasonable notice of the failure of the principal debtor to pay, is a question for the jury.

*Idem, 174*

5. The fact that the principal debtor gave his bond for the goods he purchased did not release the guarantor. *Idem, 174*

# H

## HEIRS.

1. Heirs will be held liable in Virginia, upon the debts and covenants of their ancestor binding the heirs, to the extent of real assets descended in another State, if by the laws of that State they would be liable on such debts and covenants: And a court of equity in Virginia may enforce the liability.

*Dickinson v. Hoomes's adm'r & als., 353*

2. Under the circumstances of this case, the heirs held bound to account for only so much of the lands out of the State as they have actually gotten or may get possession of, with the rents and profits derived therefrom, deducting the costs and expenses of recovering the lands.

*Idem, 353*

3. A creditor of a deceased debtor may proceed, by foreign attachment against the heirs residing abroad, to subject land or its proceeds, in the State, descended to them from the debtor.

*Carrington & als. v. Didier, Norvell & Co., 260*

4. So he may proceed against them as absent defendants in equity to marshal the assets, and thus subject the land descended to them.

*Idem, 260*

5. See *Practice in Chancery. No. 4,* and *Idem, 260*

## HUSBAND AND WIFE.

1. When wife entitled to dower though claiming under the will of her husband. See *Dower, No. 1, 2, and Higginbotham v. Cornwell, 83*

# I

## INDICTMENTS.

found, is not surplusage. If it is not surplusage it is useless.

*Bell's Case, 600*

2. Where the indictment in the caption names one county, and in the body speaks of the prisoner as of another county, the charging the offence to have been committed in the county aforesaid is error, it not being alleged with sufficient certainty that the offence was committed in the county in which the indictment was found. *Idem, 600*

3. An indictment for perjury must shew that the evidence which the defendant gave was material. And therefore, if the evidence which the defendant gave before the grand jury is not shewn clearly on the face of the indictment to relate to an offence committed within the county, the indictment is defective.

*Pickering's Case, 628*

4. What a good indictment for an attempt to commit a felony.

*Nutter's Case, 699*

## ISSUE OUT OF CHANCERY.

Where the subject matter in controversy is of the nature of unliquidated damages, and the accuracy and credit of the witnesses is impeached, an issue should be directed.

*Isler & wife v. Grove & wife, 257*

## J

## JUDGMENTS.

1. When a forthcoming bond has the force of a judgment. See *Forthcoming Bonds*. No. 1, 2, 3, and

*Jones, &c. v. Myrick's ex'ors, 179*
*Myrick's ex'ors v. Epes & als., 179*

2. A judgment confessed in court in a pending suit, and the oath of insolvency taken thereon by the debtor upon his surrender by his bail, has relation to the first moment of the first day of the term; and therefore the assignment by operation of law has preference to the lien of a forthcoming bond returned to the clerk's office after the first day of the term. *Idem, 179*

3. Though a forthcoming bond is forfeited, and not quashed, the lien of the original judgment continues. *Idem, 179*

4. Lands subject to a judgment lien, which have been sold or encumbered by the debtor, are to be subjected to the satisfaction of the judgment in the inverse order in point of time of the alienations and incumbrances; the land last sold or incumbered being first subjected.

*Idem, 179*

5. A judgment creditor, having by his conduct waived or lost his right to subject the land first liable to satisfy his judgment, is not entitled to subject the lands next liable for the whole amount of his judgment, but only for the balance after crediting thereon the value of the land first liable. *Idem, 179*

6. A judgment creditor concluded by a decree in a cause in which he is a defendant, though he has at the same time a suit depending against the same parties to enforce his prior lien. *Idem, 179*

7. A judgment against an administratrix upon the bond of her intestate is conclusive of the validity of the debt against the administratrix.

*Montague's ex'x v. Turpin's adm'x & als., 453*

## JURORS.

1. On a trial for murder it is a ground of challenge to a juror for cause, by the Commonwealth, that he says he has conscientious scruples about the propriety of capital punishment, and is opposed to it, and if the proofs shew the prisoner guilty of murder in the first degree, he does not know that he will convict him.

*Clore's Case, 606*

2. An opinion formed alone from rumour, but existing on the mind at the time, and to which opinion he will stick unless the evidence turns out different from what rumour had reported it to be, is not good cause of challenge by the prisoner, where the juror says he has no prejudice or partiality for or against the prisoner, and he believes he can give him a fair and impartial trial according to the evidence. *Idem, 606*

3. An objection to a venireman, that he is not qualified according to law, comes too late after he is sworn to try the issue.

*Thompson's Case, 637*

4. What is not misbehaviour in a juror for which a new trial will be granted to a prisoner. See *New Trials*, No. 6, 8, and　　*Idem, 637*

## L

### LANDLORD AND TENANT.

Upon a writ of unlawful detainer, the defendant sets up title in himself. The plaintiff may prove that the defendant entered on the premises under a parol lease from himself; though the lease was to continue more than a year.
*Adams* v. *Martin, 107*

### LEGATEES.

1. A legatee being dead, a decree for the distribution of the estate should be in favour of his personal representative, and not of his distributee.
*Luster* v. *Middlecoff & als., 54*

2. Testator devises a tract of land for payment of a particular debt, and the land is sold; but the creditor receives only the first payment of the purchase money, and the balance is applied to the payment of other debts of the testator. Whether or not the land was the primary fund for payment of the particular debt, the debt was in fact the debt of the testator's estate, for which a legatee is responsible on his refunding bond.
*Archer* v. *Archer's adm'r. 589*

3. In a bill by persons claiming as legatees or assignees of legatees, against defendants as legatees or assignees of legatees, under the same will, for distribution of the slaves bequeathed to the legatees jointly, the presumption is, in the absence of all pleadings and proofs to the contrary, that the persons made parties to the suit as legatees are not fictitious persons or mere pretenders to the characters assumed in the proceedings.
*Ball & als.* v. *Johnson's ex'or & als., 281*

### LIENS.

1. A vendor of lands retains the title in accordance with the contract. He has a lien on the land for the purchase money, as against creditors and incumbrancers of the vendee;

and this though the vendee has subsequently executed a deed by which he conveys other property to secure the purchase money.
*Lewis & als.* v. *Caperton's ex'or & als., 148*

2. What is a valid lien by deed of trust. See *Conveyances—Fraudulent, passim*, and　　*Idem, 148*

3. There being several deeds, conveying in succession the same property, and not merely the equity of redemption therein, every successive incumbrance binds all the property not absorbed in satisfaction of previous valid incumbrances. And if some of the incumbrances are declared void at the suit of a creditor of the grantor, such creditor is not entitled to have his debt substituted in the place of such void incumbrance to the extent thereof; but the subsequent valid incumbrances have preference.　　*Idem, 148*

4. Where there are several deeds of trust on the same property, how the trust fund shall be appropriated. See *Trusts and Trustees*, No. 2, and　　*Idem, 148*

5. From what time a forthcoming bond forfeited is a lien. See *Forthcoming Bonds*, No. 1, and
*Jones, &c.* v. *Myrick's ex'ors, 179*
*Myrick's ex'ors* v. *Epes & als.. 179*

6. The lien of a forfeited forthcoming bond, returned to the clerk's office during the term, and on which execution is awarded, does not relate to the first day of the term.
*Idem, 179*

7. Though a forthcoming bond is forfeited, and not quashed, yet the lien of the original judgment continues.　　*Idem, 179*

8. In what order and to what extent lands are subject to satisfy a judgment lien. See *Judgments*, No. 4, and　　*Idem, 179*

9. A debtor contracts to give a lien on two adjoining tenements, to secure a debt, and the creditor is in possession of one of the tenements under an agreement by which the rent of the tenement is to be taken in satisfaction of the interest of the debt. Afterwards the debtor, becoming embarrassed, conveys all his property in trust to pay his debts. The creditor is entitled to enforce his equita-

ble lien not only against the debtor, but his creditors.

*Ott's ex'r* v. *King & als., 224*

10. The lien of an attachment levied upon the interest of a wife in her father's estate, in the hands of the executor, is terminated by the death of the husband pending the proceedings, his wife surviving him.

*Vance* v. *McLaughlin's adm'r, 289*

## LIMITATION OF ESTATES.

1. Prior to 1819 a testator devises to his three daughters, by name, his estate, both real and personal, "to them and their heirs lawfully begotten of their bodies. And in case either of my daughters should die without heir or heirs as above mentioned, the surviving ones to enjoy their equal part." This is an estate tail, which by the statute is converted into a fee. And the limitation over is after an indefinite failure of issue, and void.

*Nowlin & wife* v. *Winfree, 346*

## LIMITATIONS—*Statute of.*

1. A promise which will remove the bar of the statute of limitations must be a promise to pay a particular debt: A promise to settle with the claimant is not enough.

*Bell* v. *Crawford, 110*

2. If a part payment will take a case out of the statute, it must be a payment upon the specific debt, and not a payment upon account.

*Idem, 110*

3. The statute of limitations does not commence to run against the owners of the remainder in slaves, in favour of a purchaser of the life estate, until the death of the life tenant.

*Ball & als.* v. *Johnson's ex'or & als., 281*

## LIS PENDENS.

A creditor of a deceased debtor sues heirs residing abroad, to marshal the assets, and subject lands or their proceeds in the State descended to them. The land has been sold under a decree at the suit of the heirs, and is in the hands of a commissioner of the court, who is also administrator of the deceased debtor. Though this person is a party, as ad-

ministrator, to the creditor's suit, yet not being a party as commissioner, if he has no knowledge of the object of the suit, and pays over the money to the heirs under the order of the court whose commissioner he is, he will not be affected by the *lis pendens* of the creditor's suit, so as to be held liable to pay it over again to the creditor.

*Carrington & als.* v. *Didier, Norrell & Co., 260*

# M

## MALICIOUS BURNING.

See *Arson*, No. 1, 2, and

*Erskine's Case, 624*

## MARSHALLING ASSETS.

1. The creditor of a deceased debtor may proceed in equity against his heirs residing abroad, as absent defendants, to marshal the assets, and thus subject the land or its proceeds, in the State, descended to them from the debtor.

*Carrington & als.* v. *Didier, Norrell & Co., 260*

2. If the land has been sold under a decree in a suit by the heirs, and the proceeds are in the hands of a commissioner of the court, he should be a party as such, and be restrained by injunction from paying away the money in his hands. *Idem, 260*

3. Though the commissioner is a party, as administrator of the deceased debtor, if he has in fact no knowledge of the object of the suit, and pays over the money to the heirs under an order of the court whose commissioner he is, he will not be liable to pay it again to the creditor. *Idem, 260*

4. A principal executes a bond binding his heirs to his surety as endorser, with condition that he will, when requested by the bank or the surety, pay off the notes, and so indemnify and save the surety harmless; and he dies leaving the notes not yet due, which are protested as they fall due, and are afterwards paid by his administrator. The surety being entitled to resort to both the real and personal estate, and the notes having been paid out of the latter, the simple contract creditors

are entitled to have the assets marshalled to the extent of the notes so paid, if they do not exceed the penalty of the bond.

*Cralle & als. v. Meem & als.*, 496

5. Upon a bill by simple contract creditors to marshal the assets, it is competent for the court, in its discretion, to decree a sale of real estate in the hands of the heirs, though some of them are infants, for the payment of the debts: But it is premature to decree a sale before adjudicating the claims of the creditors, and so ascertaining the amount of the debts chargeable upon the lands of the decedent. *Idem, 496*

## MILLS.

1. A jury of inquest in a mill case are induced, by the opinions expressed and facts stated by the father of the applicant, to report that no person will sustain damage from the dam allowed to be built; and the inquisition is confirmed by the court. This inquest and judgment is no bar to an action for damages sustained by the father against a vendee of the mill, which were not actually foreseen and estimated by the inquest.

*Calhoun v. Palmer, 88*

2. The defendant relies on the inquisition and judgment authorizing the dam as the grounds of his defence; he cannot therefore deny the ownership of the land by the applicant for the mill. *Idem, 88*

3. The conduct of the father does not defeat his right to recover damages for the injury he has sustained. *Idem, 88*

4. Where a mill owner does not raise his dam at first as high as he is authorized to do, that will not preclude him from raising it to the full height authorized by the inquest, provided he does not thereby occasion injury to others. *Idem, 88*

5. The father having united in the conveyance of the mill to the vendee, he cannot recover damages for any injury done to him by the erection of the dam, to the extent the injury existed at the time of the conveyance. *Idem, 88*

## MISBEHAVIOUR.

See *New Trials*, No. 5, 6, 7, 8, 9, and
*Thompson's Case*, 637
*Wormley's Case*, 712

## MISDEMEANOR.

1. Though the mere breaking and entering the close of another is not a misdemeanor, yet if that entry is attended by circumstances constituting a breach of the peace, it will become a misdemeanor for which an indictment will lie.

*Henderson's Case*, 708

2. The going upon the porch of another man's house armed, and from thence shooting and killing a dog of the owner of the house, lying in the yard, in the absence of the male members of the family, and to the terror and alarm of females in the house, is a misdemeanor for which an indictment will lie. *Idem, 708*

## MISTAKE.

When a court of equity will restrict the assignment of a security to the purpose of fully satisfying the assignee for the purposes of the assignment; the assignment having been made by the assignor under a misapprehension of the amount of the security. *Jennings v. Palmer, 70*

## N

## NEW TRIALS.

1. A new trial will not be granted on the ground of after-discovered evidence, upon the affidavit of a party that he has been informed and believes that certain witnesses will give important testimony, without proof, by affidavit of the persons or others who have heard them, of what they will state; and especially if their evidence is merely cumulative, and the cause has been pending for a length of time, and these newly discovered witnesses live in the county and within a few miles of the party who makes the application.

*Nuckols's adm'r v. Jones, 267*

2. After-discovered evidence, in order to afford a proper ground for a new trial, must be such as reasonable diligence on the part of the party of-

fering it could not have secured at the former trial; must be material in its object, and not merely cumulative and corroborative or collateral; and must be such as ought to be decisive, and productive, on another trial, of an opposite result on the merits. *Thompson's Case, 637*

3. Where the sole object and purpose of the new evidence is to discredit a witness on the opposite side, the general rule is, subject to few exceptions, to refuse a new trial. *Idem, 637*

4. What separation of a jury on a trial for felony is not sufficient to entitle the prisoner to a new trial. *Idem, 637*

5. Jurors concurring in the guilt of the prisoner, each sets down the time for which he thinks he should be confined in the penitentiary, and the aggregate is divided by twelve; and after the result is ascertained they all concur in it as their verdict. This is not misbehaviour in the jury which will entitle the prisoner to a new trial. *Idem, 637*

6. It is not misbehaviour in a juror, between the adjournment of the court in the evening and its meeting next morning, to drink spirituous liquors in moderation. *Idem, 637*

7. And it is not misbehaviour, for which a new trial will be granted, though they drink upon the invitation of a witness for the Commonwealth, if it is done in the presence of the sheriff, and obviously where the invitation to do so is merely intended as an act of courtesy. *Idem, 637*

8. In walking out for exercise the jury, with the sheriff, pass beyond the limits of the county in which the prosecution is pending. This is no ground for a new trial. *Idem, 637*

9. A sheriff, to whom a jury is committed in the progress of a criminal trial, walks out with them to a neighbouring house, and whilst there withdraws from the room where they are, leaving them in the company of three other persons. Although these other persons swear that there was no allusion by them to the trial during such absence of the sheriff, yet the verdict of the jury is to be set aside and a new trial awarded. *Wormley's Case, 712*

## NON DAMNIFICATUS.

1. The plea of *non damnificatus* is a good plea only where the condition is to indemnify and save harmless. The plea should go to the right of action, and not to the question of damages. *Archer v. Archer's adm'r, 539*

2. Wherever the plea of *non damnificatus* is a good plea, it is equivalent to the plea of "conditions performed." And if this last plea has been pleaded, it is no error to refuse to admit the other at a subsequent term. *Idem, 539*

## NOTICE.

1. A notice on a forthcoming bond is not defective because it only mentions those obligors in the bond to whom the notice is intended to be given. *Booth v. Kinsey, 560*

2. What notice to guarantor necessary. See *Guarantor and Guarantee*, No. 2, 3, and *Wadsworth & als. v. Allen, &c., 174*

3. Whether the notice to a guarantor is sufficient, is a question for the jury. *Idem, 174*

## P

## PARTIES.

1. In a creditor's suit, either by foreign attachment or to marshal assets, against heirs residing abroad, the lands descended having been sold under a decree at the suit of the heirs, and the proceeds being in the hands of a commissioner, he should be a party as such; and his being a party as administrator of the deceased debtor is not enough. *Carrington & als. v. Didier, Norvell & Co., 260*

2. In a bill by persons claiming to be legatees or assignees of legatees, against defendants as legatees or assignees of legatees, under the same will, for distribution of the slaves bequeathed to the legatees jointly, the presumption is, in the absence of all pleadings and proofs to the contrary, that the persons made par-

ties to the suit as legatees are not
fictitious persons or mere pretenders
to the characters assumed in the proceedings.
*Ball & als.* v. *Johnson's ex'or & als.,* 281

3. In such case, the case being a
proper one upon its merits for distribution of the subject amongst those
entitled thereto, the bill should not
be dismissed for want of parties, or
of proof that the parties were what
they professed to be; but the court
should direct the plaintiffs to amend
their bill and make the proper parties. *Idem,* 281

4. A personal representative of a
deceased insolvent co-obligor is not
a necessary party to a suit in equity
by the executrix of the obligee
against the administratrix of one of
the obligors, to enforce payment of
the bond, so as to require the plaintiff to have one appointed and make
him a party.
*Montague's ex'x* v. *Turpin's
adm'x & als.,* 453

5. All the sureties of an executrix should be parties to a suit by
legatees for distribution, or a sufficient excuse should be shewn for
failing to make them parties, before
a decree is made against one of them.
*Hutcherson, &c.* v. *Pigg,* 220

## PARTITION.

A brother and sister, both of whom
are married, own a tract of land
jointly. In 1802 the brother and his
wife and the sister and her husband
unite in a deed of partition of the
land, and from thence to the present
time the land is held in severalty by
the parties respectively and those
claiming under them. The partition
is valid and binding on the parties,
though no certificate of the privy
examination of the wives is annexed
to the deed.
*Bryan* v. *Stump, &c.,* 241

## PARTNERS.

A partnership for the manufacture
of iron is composed of four persons,
the names of two of whom do not
appear; and they live at a distance.
The acting partners buy land in
their own name for the purpose of
obtaining from it wood to be used in

the manufacture of iron, and so far
as it is paid for it is paid for out of
the partnership effects. The land is
partnership property, and the partnership having failed, the two dormant partners are liable to the vendor for the balance of the purchase
money. *Brooke* v. *Washington,* 248

## PAYMENTS.

How payments are to be applied
as between an assignee and attaching creditor of the obligee. See *Assignor and Assignee,* No. 2, 3, 4, and
*Schofield* v. *Cox & als.,* 533

## PERJURY.

An indictment for perjury must
shew that the evidence which the
defendant gave was material. And
therefore, if the evidence which the
defendant gave before the grand jury
is not shewn clearly on the face of
the indictment to relate to an offence committed within the county,
the indictment is defective.
*Pickering's Case,* 628

## PLEADINGS.

1. An instrument, binding the parties thereto to pay a sum of money,
purports to be under their hands
and seals, but it is signed by one of
the parties without a seal, and by the
other parties with seals to their
names. It may be sued upon against
all the parties in one action, as on a
joint promise.
*Rankin* v. *Roler & als.,* 63

2. The plea of *non damnificatus* is a
good plea only where the condition
is to indemnify and save harmless.
The plea should go to the right of
the action, and not to the question
of damages.
*Archer* v. *Archer's adm'r,* 539

3. Wherever the plea of *non damnificatus* is a good plea, it is equivalent to the plea of "conditions performed." And if this last plea has
been pleaded, it is not error to refuse
to admit the first at a subsequent
term. *Idem,* 539

4. A plea which professes to go to
the whole action, but answers only a

part of it, is defective and demurrable.

*Hunt's adm'r* v. *Martin's adm'r, 578*

5. In case for the breach of an express warranty of soundness of a personal chattel, it is not necessary to allege the defendant's knowledge of the unsoundness: And if it is alleged, it is not necessary to prove it.

*Trice* v. *Cockran, 442*

## PRACTICE AT COMMON LAW.

1. In a proceeding of forcible entry and detainer, the court is constituted and then adjourns to a day certain. The court failing to meet on the day to which it is adjourned, the cause is not discontinued, but stands adjourned, by operation of law, to the next term of the County court. *Mann* v. *Gwinn & als., 58*

2. When a demurrer to a declaration upon an award will be overruled, and the defendant put to his plea of " no award." See *Awards*, No. 1, 2, and *Price* v. *Via's heirs, 79*

3. In *assumpsit* defendant pleads " *non assumpsit*," and with it files an affidavit of set-off, and the set-off, which is a note. Though there is no plea of set-off or bill of particulars, the evidence in relation to the set-off is properly admitted.

*Bell* v. *Crawford, 110*

4. Where the plea of " conditions performed " has been pleaded, it is not error for the court to refuse at a subsequent term to admit the equivalent plea of " *non damnificatus*."

*Archer* v. *Archer's adm'r, 539*

5. When a bill of particulars is, and when it is not, necessary to be filed with the plea of payment to let in the evidence. See *Bill of Particulars*, No. 2, and *Rice's ex'or* v. *Annatt's adm'r, 557*

## PRACTICE IN CRIMINAL CASES.

See *Criminal Jurisdiction and Proceedings*.

## PRACTICE IN CHANCERY.

1. A legatee being dead, a decree for the distribution of the estate of his testator should be in favour of the personal representative of the legatee, and not of his distributee.

*Luster* v. *Middlecoff & als., 54*

2. The obligors in a forfeited forthcoming bond being insolvent, a court of equity, having jurisdiction of the subject, will treat the bond as a nullity, though it has not been quashed, and proceed to give the proper relief.

*Jones, &c.* v. *Myrick's ex'ors, 179*
*Myrick's ex'ors* v. *Epes & als., 179*

3. Where the matter in controversy is of the nature of unliquidated damages, and the accuracy and credit of the witnesses is impeached, an issue should be directed.

*Isler & wife* v. *Grore & wife, 257*

4. Heirs residing out of the State having instituted a suit for the sale of land descended to them, and the same having been sold, and the proceeds being in the hands of a commissioner directed by the court to collect them, a creditor of the ancestor, seeking to subject these proceeds to the payment of his debt, should apply by petition to the court to be made a party in the cause, and to have the fund applied by proceedings in that cause to the payment of his debt.

Or if he proceeds by foreign attachment, the commissioner should be a party, and be restrained by endorsement on the process from disposing of the proceeds.

Or if the creditor proceeds against the heirs to marshal the assets, there should be an injunction to restrain the commissioner from paying away the money in his hands. And the commissioner, though a party, as administrator of the debtor, to the creditor's suit, but having in fact no knowledge of the object of it, paying over the money to the heirs under the order of the court whose commissioner he is, will not be affected by the *lis pendens* of the creditor's suit so as to be liable to pay it over again to the creditor.

*Carrington & als.* v. *Didier, Norrell & Co., 260*

5. When parties will be presumed to be what they profess to be. See *Parties*, No. 2, and *Ball & als.* v. *Johnson's ex'or & als., 281*

6. When there is a proper case upon the merits for relief, the bill should not be dismissed for want of parties, or of proof that the parties

are what they profess to be; but the court should direct the plaintiffs to amend their bill and make the proper parties, and direct a commissioner to ascertain and report the persons entitled to the property.  *Idem, 281*

7. Creditors, at whose suit the debtor has taken the insolvent debtor's oath, come into equity to set aside a deed for fraud on its face, and because the beneficiary in the deed had committed a fraud on them in professing to sign it for the benefit of all, and yet claiming the exclusive benefit of it.  Though the court thinks the deed valid, yet, being satisfied that the signing creditor signed for all, the court will give all the benefit of the deed, and distribute the fund in the creditors' suit.
*Phippen v. Durham & als., 457*

8. In a suit to marshal assets, the court may, in its discretion, decree a sale of lands in the hands of the heirs, though some of them are infants: But it is premature to decree a sale before adjudicating the claims of the creditors, and so ascertaining the amount of indebtedness chargeable upon the lands of the decedent.
*Cralle & als. v. Meem & als., 496*

9. Though such a decree for a sale of land has been prematurely made, yet if the sale has been made and confirmed, the court will not set it aside on the application of the purchasers, if upon the hearing it appears that the sale is beneficial to the infants.  *Idem, 496*

10. The application of the purchasers, in such a case, to have the sale set aside, should be by petition in the cause.  And if they proceed by bill to enjoin the collection of the purchase money, and have the sale set aside, the bill should be treated as a petition in the cause and be brought to a hearing with it.
*Idem, 496*

11. The court having made a decree for a sale of real estate, on the petition of the adult heirs, and with the assent of the creditors, it is erroneous to proceed to sequestrate the rents of the other real estate in the hands of the heirs for the payment of the debts, before deciding upon the claim of the purchasers to have the sale set aside.  *Idem, 496*

## PRIVY EXAMINATION.

QUÆRE: If the certificate of the privy examination of a *feme covert*, made under the act of 1792, which purports in the body of the certificate to be under the seals of the justices, but in fact no seals or scrolls are affixed to their names, is valid to bar the *feme*.
*Bryan v. Stump, &c., 241*

## PUBLIC PLACE.

A storehouse in a village, late at night, after persons cease to come to the store to purchase goods, and the door is locked, is not a public place, within the meaning of the statute against gaming.  *Feazle's Case, 585*

# R

## RECORDS.

1. The official bond of a committee of a lunatic, given in obedience to the order of the court, and its execution certified on the record, is a part of the record, and may be looked to to ascertain what kind of bond the court required to be executed.
*Beery v. Homan's committee, 48*

2. When a record is evidence.  See *Criminal Jurisdiction and Proceedings*, No. 12, and  *Adcock's Case, 661*

3. When a record is not evidence. See *Evidence*, No. 3, and
*Duncan v. Helms & others, 68*

## REGISTRY OF DEEDS.

1. A deed executed in 1799, which shews upon its face that the parties to it resided out of Virginia, was properly admitted to record upon the certificate of acknowledgment by the mayor of a city in another State, describing himself as such, and purporting to be under the seal of the city.  *Cales v. Miller & als., 6*

2. The certificate is sufficient evidence that the grantor for the time resided in said city, though the deed described him as being a citizen of another State.  *Idem, 6*

3. It seems that a residence, however temporary, is sufficient to authorize the acknowledgment of a deed there by a non-resident of Vir-

ginia, under the act of 1792, chap. 90, § 5. *Idem, 6*

## RELATION.

1. To what time a judgment confessed in a cause relates. See *Judgments*, No. 2, and

Jones, &c. v. *Myrick's ex'ors*, 179
*Myrick's ex'ors* v. *Epes & als.*, 179

2. A forfeited forthcoming bond being deposited in the clerk's office during the term of a court, and execution awarded upon it, does not relate back to the first day of the term. *Idem, 179*

## REMAINDERMEN.

The statute of limitations does not commence to run against the owners of a remainder in slaves, in favour of a purchaser of the life estate, until the death of the life tenant.
*Ball & als.* v. *Johnson's ex'or & als.*, 281

## ROADS.

1. The mere user of a road by the public, for whatever length of time, will not constitute it a public road.
*Kelly's Case*, 632

2. A mere permission to the public, by the owner of land, to pass over a road upon it, is, without more, to be regarded as a license, and revocable at the pleasure of the owner. *Idem, 632*

3. A road dedicated to the public must be accepted by the County court upon its records, before it can be a public road. *Idem, 632*

4. If a County court lays off a road, before used, into precincts, and appoints an overseer or surveyor for it, thereby claiming the road as a public road; and if, after notice of such claim, the owner of the soil permits the road to be passed over for a long time, the road may be well inferred to be a public road.
*Idem, 632*

## S

## SECURITIES.

1. A debtor assigns certain securities to his creditor, in satisfaction of his debt, being at the time under a

misapprehension as to their amount; and they prove to be largely more than is necessary to discharge the debt. A court of equity will restrict the effect of the assignment to the full satisfaction of the debt.
*Jennings* v. *Palmer*, 70

2. What will be binding as a guarantee. See *Guarantor and Guarantee* No. 1, 2, 3, and

*Wadsworth & als.* v. *Allen, &c.*, 174

3. A deed of trust is given to secure several bonds, some of which are afterwards assigned. The benefit of the deed of trust will pass with the assignment.
*Schofield* v. *Cox & als.*, 533

## SET OFF.

1. In *assumpsit*, by an administrator, for a debt due to his intestate in his lifetime, the defendant cannot set off a debt due to him for money paid as the surety of his intestate since his death.
*Minor* v. *Minor's adm'r*, 1

2. In *assumpsit* defendant pleads *non assumpsit*, and with it files an affidavit of set-off, and the set-off, which is a note. Though there is no plea of set-off or bill of particulars, the evidence in relation to the set-off is properly admitted.
*Bell* v. *Crawford*, 110

3. A joint interest in husband and wife cannot be set off by a debt due from the husband.
*Glazebrook's adm'r* v. *Ragland's adm'r*, 332

## SETTLEMENTS.

1. An unrecorded post-nuptial settlement by a husband on his wife, of personal property derived from her father's estate, of which he retains possession, is void as to his creditors.
*Lewis & als.* v. *Caperton's ex'or & als.*, 148

2. Property conveyed in trust by a husband for himself and wife, by deed not duly recorded, is sold under a decree at their suit against the trustee, and conveyed by deed duly recorded. It is valid against a subsequent creditor of the husband.
*Glazebrook's adm'r* v. *Ragland's adm'r*, 332

3. Where, by express contract be-

fore marriage, the husband releases all his marital rights to the wife's property, both during marriage and if he survives her, the wife is to be regarded to all intents as a *feme sole* as to such property; and there is no necessity that the marriage contract or settlement should limit the property to her next of kin upon her failure to appoint, but it will pass as if the wife died *sole* and intestate. *Charles* v. *Charles, 486*

## SLANDER.

1. It is no defence in an action of slander, even in mitigation of damages, that previous to the speaking of the slanderous words charged in the declaration, the plaintiff had used equally offensive and insulting words towards the defendant.
*Bourland* v. *Eidson, 27*
2. In an action of slander, under the plea of not guilty, the defendant may, in mitigation of damages, prove any facts as to the conduct of the plaintiff in relation to the transaction which was the occasion of the slanderous language complained of, which tend to excuse him for uttering the words, provided the facts do not prove or tend to prove the truth of the charge complained of, but in fact to relieve the plaintiff from the imputation involved in it. *Idem, 27*

## STATUTES.

1. The act of 1792, ch. 90, § 5, 1 Stat. at Large, N. S., p. 85, regulating conveyances, construed in
*Cales* v. *Miller & als., 6*
2. The act of 1847-8, ch. 4, § 7, p. 99, in relation to the malicious burning of a house, construed in
*Erskine's Case, 624*
3. The same statute, § 6, in relation to the malicious burning of stacks of wheat, &c., construed in   *Idem, 624*
4. The act, Code of 1849, ch. 207, § 13, p. 770, as to a prisoner's right to be discharged if not indicted within two terms after his examination, construed in        *Adcock's Case, 661*
5. The act, Code of 1849, ch. 208, § 36, p. 778, as to a prisoner's right to be discharged from the prosecution if not tried within three terms, construed in              *Idem, 661*

6. The act, Code of 1849, ch. 199, § 16, p. 751, as to proceedings if a prisoner is acquitted for a variance, construed in            *Idem, 661*
7. The act, Code of 1849, ch. 209, § 17, p. 781, limiting imprisonment in cases of fines, construed in
*Webster's Case, 702*
8. The act, Code of 1849, ch. 182, § 2, p. 683, regulating the jurisdiction of the Court of appeals, construed in
*Clark* v. *Brown, 549*

## SUBSTITUTION.

1. When sureties of an executor entitled to be substituted to the rights of legatees to recover money from purchaser of bonds from the executor. See *Fraud*, No. 1, 2, and
*Pinckard* v. *Woods, &c., 140*
2. When an assignee of a bond entitled to be substituted to the rights of the assignor to a security for that and other bonds. See *Assignor and Assignee*, No. 3, and
*Schofield* v. *Cox & als., 533*
3. When simple contract creditors entitled to be substituted to the rights of the obligee in a bond of indemnity. See *Marshalling Assets*, No. 3, and
*Cralle & als.* v. *Meem & als., 496*

## SURETIES.

1. When sureties of an executor are entitled to recover from the purchaser of bonds from the executor the amount of the bonds. See *Fraud*, No. 1, 2, and
*Pinckard* v. *Woods, &c., 140*
2. When a guarantor is bound on his guarantee. See *Guarantor and Guarantee*, No. 1, 2, 3, 4, 5, and
*Wadsworth & als.* v. *Allen, &c., 174*
3. The official bond of an executrix only binding the obligors for the due administration of the personal estate, the sureties are to no extent responsible for the rents and profits of the real estate.
*Hutcherson, &c.* v. *Pigg, 220*
4. All the sureties of an executrix should be parties to a suit by legatees for the distribution of the estate, or a sufficient excuse shown for not making them parties, before a decree is made against one of them.              *Idem, 220*